# Communing with the Gods

Consciousness, Culture and the Dreaming Brain

*by*

*Charles D. Laughlin, Ph.D.*

Daily Grail Publishing

**Communing with the Gods: Consciousness, Culture and the Dreaming Brain**
Copyright © Charles D. Laughlin 2011.

Cover image: "Supernatural", by Adam Scott Miller (www.adamscottmiller.com)

All rights reserved. No part of this book may be reproduced, stored, or transmitted in any form without permission in writing from the publisher, except by a reviewer who may quote brief passages for review purposes.

ISBN: 978-0-9807111-6-5

Daily Grail Publishing
Brisbane, Australia
publications@dailygrail.com
www.dailygrail.com

# CONTENTS

| | |
|---|---|
| Dedication | 7 |
| Acknowledgements | 9 |
| Chapter 1: Introduction | 13 |

### Part One: Background

| | |
|---|---|
| Chapter 2: The Anthropology of Dreaming | 35 |
| Chapter 3: Modern Anthropological Theories of Dreaming | 69 |
| Chapter 4: Experience and the Dreaming Brain | 95 |
| Chapter 5: Lucid Dreaming | 133 |

### Part Two: Dreams and Cultures

| | |
|---|---|
| Chapter 6: Phenomenology of Dreaming | 165 |
| Chapter 7: Cultural Theories of Dreaming | 197 |
| Chapter 8: Sociocultural Aspects of Dreaming | 235 |
| Chapter 9: Dreaming in Religion, Shamanism and Healing | 269 |
| Chapter 10: Archetypal Dreaming | 305 |
| Chapter 11: Dreaming and the Self | 331 |
| Chapter 12: Transpersonal Dreaming | 359 |
| Chapter 13: Dream Yogas | 393 |

PART THREE: A NEUROANTHROPOLOGY OF DREAMING

Chapter 14: A Neuroanthropology of Dreaming     427
Chapter 15: Dreaming in the Modern Age     465
Chapter 16: Conclusion     499

Bibliography     509
Index     561

# Dedication

I dedicate this book to my late friend and colleague, Eugene G. D'Aquili (1940-1998), with whom I had the great pleasure and privilege to work for many productive years. He helped me learn that the reality behind societies and cultures is people with brains in their heads.

## Acknowledgements

I wish to thank the following individuals for their help during the writing of this book. They should not be held accountable for any of the author's views, mistakes or excesses. Many thanks to Paul Devereux, Charla Devereux, Dr. Michael Winkelman, Dr. C. Jason Throop, Dr. Susan Parman, Dr. Klaus-Peter Koepping, Dr. Deborah Hillman, Jeremy Harte, Kristi Thompson, Rodney Malham, Margaret Stephens, Dr. Vincenza Tiberia, Dr. Stanley Krippner, Raymond Robertson and Dr. Marianne "Mimi" George. Many thanks to my copy editors, Arlene Osborne and Greg Taylor, without whom this book would border on gibberish

*Our religion is the traditions of our ancestors – the dreams of our old men, given them in the solemn hours of the night by the Great Spirit; and the visions of our sacred medicine men, and is written in the hearts of our people.*

From a speech attributed to Chief Seattle of the Duwamish

# Chapter 1

## Introduction:
## Toward a Neuroanthropology of Dreaming

> When my dream was near the moon,
> The white folds of its gown
> Filled with yellow light.
> The soles of its feet
> Grew red.
> Its hair filled
> With certain blue crystallizations
> From stars,
> Not far off.
>
> Wallace Stevens, "Six Significant Landscapes"

> We all dream; we do not understand our dreams,
> yet we act as if nothing strange goes on in our sleep
> minds, strange at least by comparison with the logical,
> purposeful doings of our minds when we are awake.
>
> Erick Fromm

The most common alternative state of consciousness among human beings is dreaming. All normal humans sleep, and during sleep they dream, whether or not they remember their dreams when they awaken. We actually spend a quarter to a third of our lives sleeping and dreaming. Yet as common as dreaming is among our species, it is still a phenomenon of mystery and confusion, and of fascination to scientists wishing to understand how the brain, the mind and consciousness work. How often do we awaken and are puzzled by scraps of dreams? I recently woke remembering having curly black hair like that of a young Vincent D'Onofrio, one of my favorite character actors (not my real straight grey hair), and two ears on the right side of my head. I even felt the two ears with my fingers. One of them had a hole into my head and the other didn't. I brushed some hair down over the two ears hoping no one would notice, and wondered if a plastic surgeon might be able to make me normal again. What on earth does all that mean? And why do people dream about such strange, even bizarre events while asleep? Do all people on the planet share this kind of experience? If so, why? And what significance do various peoples attribute to such experiences? And what use are they? These and numerous other questions about our dreaming arise quite naturally in anyone even the slightest bit self-aware, and they are the subject of this book.

Small wonder that many scientific disciplines have a keen interest in dreaming. Neurophysiologists study what is happening in the brain when we sleep and neuropsychologists wish to find the parts of the brain that mediate the experience of dreaming. Neuroscientists generally believe, and with good evidence, that dreaming is a function of neurophysiological processes that are not only universal to human beings, but to all animals with cortical brains (Hobson 2002:19, 73). Infants in the womb — and as newborns — spend much of their time dreaming, most of it in *rapid eye movement* sleep (or REM; ibid:76; Laughlin 1991; Feinberg 1969), and people continue to dream until they die. Sleep and dreaming are obviously critical to the healthy development and adaptation of humans and animals of any age; for sleep disorders are often associated with diseases of various sorts, and systematic sleep deprivation can produce serious reduction of cognitive functions and result in something very like psychosis (Kushida 2005). It is fair to say, then, that dreaming has important biological functions helping the organism to adapt and thrive (Moffitt, Kramer and Hoffman 1993).

Since the late 19th century, psychology and psychoanalysis have studied dreaming for what it can tell us about the human psyche and its many abnormalities. William James considered dreaming consciousness just as interesting as waking consciousness, and had a tremendous influence upon modern psychological thinking about dreaming (Bulkeley 1997; Van de Castle 1994). Dream analysis has been fundamental to psychoanalysis ever since the great healer, Sigmund Freud, published his book, *The Interpretation of Dreams*, in 1900 and suggested that dreams express unfulfilled desires and sexual conflicts. Carl G. Jung, Alfred Adler and others followed and expanded Freud's ideas and have led to a number of different approaches to the use of dreaming in therapy and self-discovery (Green, Ullman and Tauber 1995).

The field of sociology is rather a late-comer to the serious study of dreaming. As Roger Bastide noted, "For sociology, interested only in man awake, the sleeper might as well be dead" (1966:199). Sociologists at the present time take the view that dreams are a product of social activity, and that dreams are influenced by, and in turn influence social interaction. As Fine and Leighton write, "Sociologists routinely assert that culture develops through interaction. How, then, might we explain private, hidden dreams? Not only does the content of dreams include interaction, but dreams draw on previously experienced interaction and are often presented in social situations" (1993:96). Much of the material upon which sociologists draw for data on dreaming in non-Western societies comes from ethnography, but so far as I know, sociology has yet to develop any interest in how the brain produces dreaming, or how dreaming is used in smaller scale, more traditional societies.

All normal humans dream, and all cultures acknowledge the fact of dreaming to one extent or another. And yet what people dream about, the physical conditions in which they sleep and dream, whether they pay any attention to dream content in their waking lives, whether they share their dreams, how they interpret and integrate dream material into their daily lives, how groups put dreaming to pragmatic uses – all of these factors vary enormously among individuals, and especially across cultures. This broadest of perspectives on dreaming is the specific domain of anthropology, a discipline with over a century and a half's interest in the topic, and which has recorded aspects of the culture of dreaming among societies all over the planet.

With all this general interest in dreaming on the part of various scientific disciplines, it is curious that there is so little cross-fertilization between the disciplines in individual research reports, either those coming out of clinical or laboratory research, or out of ethnographic field reports and theoretical work. This is really obvious in the paucity of exchanges between neuroscience and anthropology. Most neuroscience research occurs in a Western setting and draws its subjects and patients from Western societies. Neuroscientists pay very little attention to research on dreaming from non-Western peoples. On the other hand, anthropologists virtually ignore the neurosciences, and have done so for over a century. In light of the advances in neuroscientific research on the biological processes that mediate consciousness and experience, this lack of interdisciplinary coordination is not only indefensible, it is just plain silly.

It is the intent of this book to remedy this situation as much as possible. The book is multi-disciplinary. While primarily centered upon the anthropology of dreaming, I will bring to bear as well the research and explanations available in all the other concerned disciplines, and especially research findings and theories in neuropsychology and other neurosciences. I will present the evidence available from the standpoint of being both a neurologically trained anthropologist (a *neuroanthropologist*) and a dream ethnographer who has extensive experience with Tibetan Tantric Buddhist dream yoga (see Chapter 13).[1]

After years of research on dreaming and other *alternative states of consciousness* (hereafter simply *ASC*), I have concluded that an anthropologically informed *neurophenomenology* turns out to be of the greatest value in developing introspective, qualitative and esoteric cultural data, and in building explanations of phenomena within a neuroanthropological frame of reference (see Laughlin, McManus and d'Aquili 1990:12-18; Laughlin and Throop 2001, 2006, 2008, 2009; Lutz, Dunne and Davidson 2007). What this means is that *Communing with the Gods* will be grounded, where appropriate, in my own direct experience, both at home and during fieldwork in other societies, and at the same time will show how both the neurobiology of consciousness and the cross-cultural variation in meaning are integral to a full

---

[1] During the 1973-74 academic year, the author studied neuropsychology as a Senior Fellow of the Institute of Neurological Sciences, University of Pennsylvania, under a NSF postdoctoral fellowship. From 1978 - 1985, the author studied Tibetan Tantric Buddhism as a monk, making numerous trips to the monasteries of his preceptor, Chogye Trichen Rinpoche (1920-2006), in Nepal to study. He studied dream yoga as well with the Venerable Karma Tenzin Dorje Namgyal Rinpoche (1931-2003).

understanding of the role played by dreaming in cultural experience (Jackson 1989; Laughlin and McManus 1995).

There is nothing new about this approach to studying and explaining cultural phenomena. From the moment my late friend and colleague, Eugene G. d'Aquili (1972; d'Aquili and Newberg 1999; Newberg, d'Aquili and Rause 2002), and I met at a conference entitled *Theory on the Fringe: New Directions in Anthropological Theory* held at the State University of New York in Oswego, New York in 1972, we planned and wrote a number of works designed to show the importance of neuroscience for anthropology – a synthesis we called *biogenetic structuralism* (see Laughlin and d'Aquili 1974; see also Haule 2010:187-195). This was a rather cumbersome title, I freely admit, and made sense only in the context of the structuralist writings of Claude Lévi-Strauss which were all the rage in 1970s anthropology. Our argument at the time was that if Lévi-Strauss' "structures" were real, then they must refer to circuits of brain cells. In those early days we suggested a methodology that would require that all scientific perspectives onto a cultural phenomenon be considered when developing explanations (Rubinstein and Laughlin 1977). We later put together a team of ethologists, neuroscientists, psychologists and anthropologists to develop an evolutionary and biocultural account of ritual – ritual behavior being a cultural universal, thus pointing to a fundamental set of biological processes (d'Aquili, Laughlin and McManus 1979).

As much as the label biogenetic structuralism made sense during the brief structuralist era, our approach is more appropriately termed *neuroanthropology*, a tradition in anthropology that had its recent origins in the works of Eliot D. Chapple (1909-2000; see Chapple 1970; Chapple and Coon 1942) and of Earl W. Count (1899-1996) in the middle of the last century. Count, in his magnum opus, *Being and Becoming Human* (1973), argued that each and every species inherits the generalized pattern of adaptation of its "anlage;" that is, its precursor species. The total package of species-typical adaptation patterns Count termed that species' "biogram." The heritable *architectonics* (structures) of the nervous system and the brain provide the structure of every species' biogram. Found within each species biogram are the limits of possible organizations of consciousness and action, which then develop relative to the adaptational circumstances of the individual and the group – that is, develop as cultural variations. Thus for Count it was appropriate to speak in terms of the human "brainmind" as an inextricably component of the human biogram, and as the one and only organ of consciousness. Indeed, he argued that only when anthropology reached the point where the brainmind became its central object of study could the discipline be considered a mature science (1958, 1990).

Professor Count's views about the future of anthropology as a science were as sound then as they are today, but my expectations are far more guarded than they once were. I have learned that as with any discipline, many anthropologists are unable to see beyond the bounds of their Western cultural and graduate school conditioning. Western conditioning with respect to dreaming is, as we shall see, aberrant when compared with dreaming among non-Western traditional peoples. Anthropology draws students who are primarily of Western cultural backgrounds. Moreover, anthropology – American anthropology in particular – has a great stake in "cultural constructivism" (or "cultural relativism") — that being the notion that cultures vary freely in their belief systems and institutions, and that the individual is a product of the culture in which he or she is reared. This is a doctrine associated historically with Franz Boas (1858-1942) and his battle against the prevailing racism of his day. In its extreme versions, cultural constructivism denies even the possibility of cultural universals – our human species somehow passed over an evolutionary Rubicon where behavior, thought, emotions and other things human no longer depended upon our biology. Hence, developing a point of view that allows for both the universality and the variation of cultural features has been a serious challenge for anthropology, despite the existence of a strain of structuralist reasoning going back to the very beginning of the discipline – but more on this in the next chapter. So anthropologists are often encumbered in their study of dreams by both negative cultural conditioning, and a constructivist point of view toward dreaming culture.

This outmoded situation needs fixing – badly! Once again I will develop a neuroanthropological account of a human universal – in this case dreaming – that also exhibits considerable cultural variation in its experience, its contents and its sociocultural applications. I will show why such variation occurs, and the neurobiological processes that mediate the variance. I will take full advantage of the strength of anthropology with its cross-cultural perspective and its methodology of "participant observation" – that is, learning about alien cultures by actually living with the people and participating in their way of life for lengthy periods of time. In this way we will be situated in the broadest possible naturalistic and empirical field of data possible. You may also notice that I will usually refer to "dreaming" rather than "a dream" wherever possible. This is because I will be accounting for a process, not merely a thing. As Price-Williams and Degarrod (1996:16) have written, "It has become commonplace to assert that our root Indo-European language tends to reify events which are essentially processual in nature. The term 'dream' could be considered just such an example. In English we tend to say that 'I had a dream' in the same way as we might say 'I had a sore thumb'." But dreams unfold as a stream of consciousness, not as a physical appendage – a dynamic interplay among myriad neurophysiological systems in the brain.

## An Important Caveat – The Rule of Minimal Inclusion

I have routinely applied a methodological dictum when dealing with the complex interactions between brain, consciousness and culture — that being *the rule of minimal inclusion*: that is, "…any explanation of behavior must take into account any and all levels of systemic organization efficiently present in the interaction between the system operating and the environment of that system" (Rubinstein and Laughlin 1977:462). With respect to explaining dreaming, this rule requires that any account of dreaming include within its purview each and every level of causation — including neurophysiology, consciousness, development, environment and sociocultural influences — influencing the scope of inquiry. Therefore, any approach that focuses upon a single level of process to the exclusion of other levels may be considered *ipso facto* either incomplete or downright wrong. The approach taken in this book has followed the rule of minimal exclusion wherever the evidence allows it, and has incorporated all levels of causation pertaining to dreaming. I will continue to do so in modeling the self in relation to dreaming.

## Consciousness and States of Consciousness

Dreaming consists of one or more *state of consciousness* (*SOC*), so in a sense this book is about consciousness with a focus upon those states that arise during sleep. So let me make it clear from the outset just what I mean by consciousness and states of consciousness. As d'Aquili, McManus and I defined the term in our book *Brain, Symbol and Experience* (Laughlin, McManus and d'Aquili 1990:90), consciousness refers "...to the ongoing stream of experience that is mediated by a functional neural complex." Experience here includes awareness of what is going on. The important implication of this definition is that consciousness is mediated by dynamic, ever changing brain circuits and networks. There is no such thing as a state of consciousness that is not produced by a discrete neural system (see Chapter 4 for a more detailed account of neural systems). I am not merely conscious, I am a physical body that is conscious. Psychiatrist and neuroscientist, J. Allan Hobson (1999, 2001, 2007) comes close to our definition by modeling consciousness as a phase space created by the intersection of three variables, "...activation level (A), input-output gating (I), and neuromodulation ratio (M)..." (2007).[2] This is what he calls the *AIM model* of states of consciousness. All three variables are dynamic, and in interaction with each other they produce the flux in states of consciousness which tend to recur in a cyclical pattern. Obviously this is a simplistic model, for the neural ingredients mediating SOC are also hierarchically organized (Dietrich 2007:242-244). I would consider the AIM model and others like it as refinements of Charles Tart's (1975) original account.

Adam Rock and Stanley Krippner have raised an interesting point that all useful definitions of consciousness make the distinction between consciousness and the contents of consciousness (Rock and Krippner 2007a, 2007b). They argue – quite rightly in my estimation – that "states" of consciousness are often conflated with "contents" of consciousness. But I do not think that the problem is solved merely

---

[2] Activation is the energy level of the state, input-output gating is whether sensory input or behavioral output are switched on or off, and neuromodulation ratio has to do with the relationship between aminergic and cholinergic neuron activity, the latter being correlated with REM sleep and the former with being awake.

by chucking out the notion of states, but rather in making it clear that traditional peoples appear to usually categorize dreams by their content – a witchcraft dream, a dream where I met my familiar, a scary dream, etc. But the metaprocesses that distinguish states may also be recognized and categorized by peoples; e.g., they know when they are dreaming, in trance, drunk, wide awake, sleepy, etc. As we shall see later on, natural categories usually have fuzzy boundaries – not nice crisp and exclusive categories that scientists and philosophers like to use in their work.

I tend to imagine consciousness using a theater metaphor. Conscious is an ongoing meta-movie, states of consciousness are scenes or individual films tailing one another in that movie. I am both aware that I am watching a movie and that I am absorbed in the contents of the movie. I may be aware that the movie I am watching now is *Casablanca* and not *Terminator III*. I am aware that my brain is both the cine projector and the theater, and that the ego – the "me," or the I with the eye – is the more or less aware point of view upon the movie. Some scenes in the movie relate to the outside world (the waking scenes) and some to the inside world (the dreamscapes) – and, of course, the projector switches off from time to time and there is an intermission during which there is no consciousness at all. With no projector or theater (no brain activity), there is no movie (no sensorium). Without the I with the eye, there is no awareness of the movie, and hence also no consciousness. But hey! Don't carry the metaphor too far. There is no real "me" *in* the theater, because I *am* the theater, the projector, the screen, the movie, even the popcorn. And the movie runs on and on, ranging in content from fantasies and dreamscapes to documentaries about the world outside the theater, and the self within the theater. Depending upon how phenomenologically astute I am, I can watch the movie being produced, the contents of the movie as they arise and pass away, the properties of each scene or film (color or b&w, emotional or non-emotional, exciting or boring, awareness that is minimal, dull, vivid or lucid), or the properties of the I with the eye – the witness witnessing the witness witnessing. All right already, enough!

I will not be getting into the many controversies in cognitive science and neuroscience about the definitions and nature of consciousness, for that would take us off in the wrong direction. Suffice to say here that only approaches to consciousness that are grounded in evolutionary biology and neuropsychology, and that are amenable to ethnological application will be of any value to us in our study of dreaming. For example, changes in and development of dreaming and other SOC over time clearly involve changes in synaptic connections in neural circuits – that is, the development of consciousness reflects the development of the brain (LeDoux 2002). What it also means is that humans are not the only animals on the planet that are conscious. Furthermore babies in the womb and in their pre-and perinatal life are conscious. As far as this book is concerned, you can take it as an empirical given that animals and babies dream (see Chapters 4 and 14).

## Intent and Outline of the Book

*Communing with the Gods* is not just another compendium of all the weird and wonderful ways that humans differ in their dreaming. One of the great anthropologists of dreaming, Jackson Steward Lincoln, wrote such a work three quarters of a century ago (1935) and it is still in print and well worth the read. Rather, my intent in writing this book is to present the reader with a full account of dreaming, grounded both in the range of dreaming experiences and dream cultures around the planet, and in the biological processes that explain this range. In order to lay an effective groundwork for examining the neuroanthropology of dreaming, I have to first introduce the reader to the history of anthropological interest in dreaming, as well as the neurobiology and neuropsychology upon which my explanations will depend.

In Part One of the book, I will present this background information that is more than likely absent from most discussions of individual cases of dreaming cultures. In Chapter 2, I will summarize the history of anthropological interest in dreaming and show how approaches to dreaming have changed with different theoretical orientations. Chapter 3 will take a look at the state of the art in contemporary anthropology, and will summarize some of the more interesting contemporary ethnological theories of dreaming. We will turn to neuroscience in Chapter 4 by summarizing what we know about the dreaming brain, and where contemporary psychophysiological and neuropsychological research has taken us in our understanding of the neural structures mediating dreaming and other SOC. Chapter 5 will extend the discussion of neuroscience to cover the fascinating research being done on the phenomenon of lucid dreaming. I will show how our brain mediates lucidity in dreaming and what adjustments must be made in our concept of lucidity to make the notion applicable across cultures. Only after these preliminaries will we all be on the same page when we turn to the phenomenology and ethnology of dreaming.

The ethnographic literature on dreaming is both enormous and largely unsystematized. Part Two of the book will examine the great wealth of ethnographic evidence about *dream cultures*[3] around the world collected by many fieldworkers over the past century. In Chapter 6, I will begin our ethnographic coverage where all good dream research *should* begin; namely, with the experience of dreaming – as the great phenomenologist, Edmund Husserl, often said, we will begin by "returning to the things themselves." Although the dream-as-dreamt is fundamental to understanding dream culture, I will show why it is difficult for one to carry out research on the subjectivity of the Other without taking the trouble of exploring one's own subjectivity. Relying upon the reports of other people about private experiences creates an impediment I have elsewhere called the "problem of the phenomenological typewriter" (Laughlin 1989). There are ways around this problem, but they all require some degree of phenomenological sophistication – a prerequisite skill set that is as often as not absent in the ethnographer upon whom we depend to bring us the evidence we need to evaluate dreaming in an alien culture.

Chapter 7 begins our sociocultural picture of dreaming among non-Western peoples. All societies have dream cultures, and these are examined using the model I call the "cycle of meaning" – that is, that dreaming is bound up in the society's worldview and myth/ritual system in such a way that dream experiences become significant and useful to people within their total frame of reference. Dream cultures guide the individual's understanding and categorization of dreams.

---

[3] The concept of "dream cultures" – meaning societies in which people consider dreams to be very important in their lives – is attributed to ethnologist Alfred Kroeber by Devereux (1937:417n).

They also determine how dreaming is used in a practical way to attain socially valued ends. Some groups go so far as to incubate dreams in order to attain information from the spiritual world. Chapter 8 reminds us that we are a species of social primate. For most peoples the interpretation of dreams is a social act. Groups develop systems of meaning pertaining to dreaming – systems that guide individuals and groups to the appropriate interpretation of dream symbolism. Sharing of dreams varies across cultures – some people share openly, some only with close kin or friends, and others do not share at all. Still, the meaning attributed to dreams and the uses to which dreams are put are essentially social. Dreams also fill a role in expressing and resolving conflict, as well as in producing social and cultural change, a very important function that allows cultures to revitalize themselves and adjust to a dynamic environment. Witchcraft attacks and cures often play out in dreams, and are one way conflicts are manifested. Dreams are commonly the inspiration for performances and traditional art.

In Chapter 9, we turn our attention to the religious, spiritual and ethnomedical significance of dreaming. Religion is defined as institutional responses to "matters of ultimate concern" which may be revealed and perhaps even solved in dreams. We focus on shamans and the shamanic process, and show how shamans and other healers become recruited through dreaming. Dreaming and shamanism has been linked for thousands of years, and continues so to the present day among many traditional peoples. We take on the issue of magical causation and how this is evidenced in dream relations and in waking attributions. The role of dreaming in the cause and cure of disease is commonplace among societies where symbols are used to diagnose and heal.

Virtually all societies recognize certain dreams as being more important than the normal run of dreams. These are the "big" dreams, the archetypal dreams we examine in Chapter 10. We describe the work of C. G. Jung and what constitutes an archetype in some detail, because this is one aspect of dreaming that is often misunderstood. We show that the archetypes are biologically inherited circuits and networks of neural cells, and that how they develop and express themselves very much depends upon cultural conditioning – especially conditioning of the dream life. Archetypes are encountered during dreaming and are associated with great meaning and numinosity. Examples of archetypal dream material are given from societies around the world. Contemporary anthropologists have become quite interested in the idea of the "self," what it is, how it develops and what role culture plays in constructing a social self. Chapter 11 contributes to this issue as we get into the nature of the self and how dreams may be an experiential window on the self. We parse out the different approaches to the self and suggest that an experiential orientation is the most productive, especially when relating dreaming to self-awareness. This leads to a discussion of the self as essentially archetypal. Some dreams may thus be understood to be "selfscape" dreams in which one may watch the internal communication among parts of the self as they reorganize and interact.

Chapter 12 takes us into the weird and at times bizarre world of transpersonal dreaming. By transpersonal dreams, I mean dreams that have an impact upon the individual or the group much as any other type of transpersonal experience, an experience that transcends ego consciousness and may result in change or growth in the psyche of the dreamer. Some transpersonal dreams may also be paranormal in that they involve "spooky" magical causation, as in precognitive dreams, telepathic dreams, co-dreams, remote viewing dreams, etc. Transpersonal dreaming may introduce us to "other than human beings" – to spiritual entities (like witches, angels, demons, dead relatives, etc.) that play a part in our understanding of our self and our reality. Some societies have developed systematic methods and disciplines for seeking spiritual development via dreaming. Chapter 13 focuses upon societies with dream yogas. These practices are defined and some of the methods used cross-culturally to incubate dreams are described. Much of the chapter is taken up with the description of my own explorations while a Buddhist monk and practicing Tibetan Tantric dream yoga. I discuss the results of Tantric practices and discuss the importance of being clear about one's interpretive frame when doing this kind of work.

Part 3 of *Communing with the Gods* ties together the many threads presented from the ethnographic record and from neuroscience into a single theoretical account of dreaming. Chapter 14 presents a neuroanthropological theory of dreams. We begin with the evolution of sleep and dream, covering the functions of dreaming in non-human animals and other primates. We show that the evolutionary forces resulting in a complex prefrontal cortex and its executive functions also led to the evolution of true language. This combination allowed for the first time in phylogenesis the social sharing of subjective experience, and particularly dreams. With this innovation, the functions of dreaming became more complex, now playing additional adaptational roles in the construction of worldview, motivating social activities and attaining self-knowledge. Chapter 15 applies this theory of dreaming to an analysis of dreaming in the modern world. It has been suggested that humanity has outgrown dreaming. Nothing is further from the case. I suggest that not only is dreaming still important, it might be crucial in ameliorating the pernicious effects of materialism upon what is arguably an un-sane post-industrial society. We explore different avenues of modern dreamwork, including the dreamwork movement and the variety of groups available as support structures for individuals wishing to seek healing through dreaming.

I have written *Communing with the Gods* for serious students of dreaming in mind. But it is also accessible to the intelligent layperson, because I do not assume any specialized knowledge on the reader's part and present all the ingredients necessary to develop a broad understanding of dreaming across cultures and in one's own life. But I have an abhorrence of simple models of complex reality, for they rarely take one very far in science. And there is no reality more complex than our own brain, dreaming or otherwise. The book can be read from a variety of perspectives. There will be readers who come to the book motivated solely by a personal interest in dreaming. We all dream, and I am assuming most readers will have some experience of their own dream life. The book will broaden the reader's perspective on their own dreaming, for contrasting one's experiences with those of peoples around the world might suggest ways that we may understand and use our dreaming in new ways. Perhaps for instance one did not realize the potential for direct involvement in one's spiritual nature through awareness and incubation of dreams. The reader who is a student of dreaming, and has accrued sufficient experience as a dreamworker, may already know the possibility of using dreaming in one's own healing and self-understanding, or if one is a therapist, one may come to realize that dream healing is very common and natural across cultures. Western psychotherapeutic theories aside, the involvement in dreaming can increase the range of tools one has in virtually any style of therapy.

Students of anthropology with a serious interest in psychological anthropology (concerned with how culture influences the personality, the self, the senses, or emotions) will find the book educational and a challenge to some of the more orthodox perspectives in the field. The book is also written with the possibility of it being used as a text. I would hope the student would derive an appreciation for how enriching adding neuropsychology and psychophysiology to their studies might prove. In my opinion, any approach to psychological anthropology that does not include the study of dreams is poorly conceived. The professional dream researcher may never have considered the natural range of dreaming in non-Western societies around the globe. One may have just assumed that "normal" dreaming among Western subjects is representative of people everywhere. As the reader will discover quickly in these pages, nothing could be further from the case. One is left with the impression that dreaming in many societies is far more lucid on average than among Western dreamers.

Neuroscientists will find there is much to ponder in the book. A reader may have had little exposure to either the ethnography of dreaming or a neuroanthropological account of dreaming or other psychological phenomenon. Perhaps certain views on the nature of dreaming have been taken for granted. This book should broaden the scope of any neuroscientist interested in dreaming among the human species. The bibliography for this book is comprehensive and up-to-date as of this writing.

## A Quiet Word to Anthropologists

Many readers drawn to this book will be professional anthropologists with various specialities that may be interested in dreaming and other SOC. These readers will be familiar to some extent with the ethnographic literature on dreaming, the senses, the self and consciousness generally, and many will be aware of the history of, and the debates about theoretical explanations of dreaming – especially as regards the role played by culture in the formation and interpretation of dreams. What most anthropologists reading this book will *not* be familiar with is neuroscience, and the extent to which neuroscience is solving problems with increasing anthropological relevance. This is a shame, for everything that anthropologists study – every aspect of culture, of symbolism, of social action, of interpretation and knowledge – are the processes, products and artifacts of brain states. One of the major reasons why anthropology has failed to become a normal science is because of its strong aversion to viewing humanity as a biological species of primate and thus studying what we know about the evolution, structure and functioning of the human brain.

The approach I use in this book (and have done for the past four decades; see Laughlin and d'Aquili 1974; Laughlin, McManus and d'Aquili 1990) depends upon the merger of ethnology and neuroscience to explain dreaming and dream culture. Anthropology is the study of humanity and neuroscience is (in part) the study of humanity's brain – makes sense, doesn't it? But I approached the task of writing this book with a decided handicap, for my understanding of dreaming – and consciousness generally – is derived from this merger, and yet my fellow anthropologists, with the exception of a few remarkable individuals like Victor Turner (1983) and Michael Winkelman (2010), are ill-prepared to use this material. Anthropological interest in the brain is, with the exception of physical anthropology, all but non-existent. For example, the glaring absence of anthropology within the new multi-disciplinary field of *social neuroscience* is not only unfortunate, it is absurd. Do you think I am exaggerating here? Not a bit – check out Cacioppo, Berntson, Taylor and Schacter (2002) and Cacioppo, Visser and Pickett (2005), two leading texts in social neuroscience. There's not an anthropologist in the lot, and this is just plain embarrassing!

But the anthropological reader need not remain ignorant of the neuroscientific side of my presentation in the following pages. One thing a more eclectic anthropologist might want to do is pick up a copy of Joseph LeDoux's wonderful book, *Synaptic Self: How Our Brains Become Who We Are* (2003) and read it in tandem with the present work. The first thing I did after finishing my Ph.D. work in anthropology at the University of Oregon forty years ago was obtain a postdoctoral fellowship for a year's study at the Institute of Neurological Sciences at the University of Pennsylvania. That set me up beautifully to follow the exciting developments in the neurosciences and apply them where I could to issues of relevance to ethnology and linguistics. But why bother, you might ask? Because it opens up channels of research and potentially powerful explanatory models that are otherwise beyond the mainstream anthropological purview. Take, for example, the problem of interpreting and explaining abstract symbolism in Paleolithic rock art. What was the inspiration for early abstract imagery in this amazing art? Well, J.D. Lewis-Williams and T.A. Dowson (1988) delved into the neuropsychology of entoptic imagery for a possible answer, and developed a theory based in part upon neuroscience research. "Entoptic" images are geometrical patterns (lines, dots, squiggly lines, lacey fields of intersecting lines, etc.) discerned by consciousness and that are due to events within the eye itself, or between the eye and the cortex of the brain – phenomena like floaters, phosphenes, capillary fields before the retinae, etc. This very plausible and powerful explanatory account would not be possible had anthropologists not looked to the neurosciences for insights.

Time moves on, and the longer anthropology veers away from establishing itself as a normal science, interdisciplinary neuroscience will catch up and pass us, leaving it to others to explain the evolution of consciousness and culture, and developing robust theories that can in the same stroke account for the universal properties of human language, social relations and culture and its myriad variations (see e.g., Edelman and Tononi 2000; Cummins and Allen 1998; Koch 2004; Dietrich 2007; Donald 2003). My concern here is to continue to foster a scientific anthropology (see also Kuznar 2008 on this issue). It is my hope that, as our group did with our approach to the evolution and functions of ritual in *The Spectrum of Ritual* (d'Aquili, Laughlin and McManus 1979), I will again be able to show how the incorporation of biology and especially neuroscience into an anthropological analysis of dreaming can produce a more robust perspective than can be generated out of an outmoded constructivist approach alone. You be the judge as to whether or not I succeed.

## Summary and Segue

*Communing with the Gods* is a book about dreaming, dream cultures, the spiritual dimensions of dreaming and the evolution of dreaming. The explanatory frame of reference comes from modern neuroscience as applied to the myriad dream cultures across the globe. Much of the book will be taken up with a close examination of dreaming among non-Western societies that pay attention to their dreams. As we shall see, there is a qualitative difference between the majority of societies that do value their dreaming and the minority that do not. This distinction will be crucial in putting together a comprehensive account of dreaming. But first we have to examine the long history of the anthropology of dreaming. This may prove to be as novel to students of anthropology as it is to the lay reader. It has certainly been a fascinating journey for me.

PART ONE

# Background

# Chapter 2

# The Anthropology of Dreaming

> The majority of human beings from all ages and all areas of the world share a curiosity about one of the most common and yet probably most fascinating of human experiences, the dream. What sort of personal experience the dream is, what it may mean for the dreamer and his group – these are among the most tantalizing questions that have occupied man from the distant past into the continuing present. Belief systems, mythologies, religions, and even sciences have been outgrowths of attempts to answer these questions.
>
> Carl W. O'Nell, *Dreams, Culture, and the Individual*

Human experience seems to alternate across a range of states of consciousness (SOC) – the scenes in our ongoing experiential movie — from those concerned primarily with adaptation to external *extramental reality*[1] to those oriented toward internal relations within our internal extramental reality, or being. The most common alternation of SOC is between what we call "waking" and "dreaming" states. This waking-dreaming alternation is universal to people everywhere – and as we shall see, to other animals as well. As the epigraph above implies, all peoples recognize the necessity of sleep and the (usually) daytime preoccupation with social interaction and subsistence activities. Thus one may find within any culture information, beliefs, stories or rituals pertaining to dreaming, whether

---

[1] I am very much a realist (Devitt 1991). By "extramental reality" I mean the world as it is apart from any knowledge or experience we may have of it. This contrasts with "cognized" or "experienced" reality which is the way our brains construe reality for our own consumption. External extramental reality is the real world external to our being, and internal extramental reality is the real nature of our being.

or not dreams in and of themselves are considered important in any particular society. Information about dreams and dreaming are as common as, say, information about eating or sex. All people eat, all people have sex and all people dream. And just as the typical cuisine, or techniques and proscriptions pertaining to sex are universal to culture, so are beliefs about dreaming.

These questions are the very stuff of anthropology, and have been for generations. For readers unfamiliar with the discipline, anthropology in the United States consists of four sub-disciplines: *sociocultural anthropology* (the study of living peoples), *physical anthropology* (the study of the physical remains and biological nature of people), *archaeology* (the study of ancient peoples by way of their artifacts), and *linguistics* (the study of human communication) – sometimes referred to as the "four square" approach to the study of humanity. Some introductory texts will add a fifth sub-discipline called *applied* or *action anthropology* (the study of how best to help people based upon scientific knowledge). Pick up any recent textbook in American anthropology and you will find most if not all of these sub-disciplines described in detail (the one I used when teaching introductory anthropology was Kottak 2008 because of its grounding in ecology).

For the purposes of this book, however, we are mainly interested in sociocultural anthropology, which is after all what the vast majority of professional anthropologists do. Most anthropologists pick a research "field" – like a group of people or an institution somewhere in the world, travel there and live with the people and then report on what they find out. I, myself, spent a year living with an East African tribe called the So (Tepes, Tepeth,) in Northeastern Uganda. They were experiencing a killer drought at the time and my research had to do with how the people adapted to those conditions. Later on, I became more interested in spiritual practices and religion, and made lengthy field trips to Nepal to live in monasteries and study Tibetan Tantric Buddhist practices with various meditation masters (see Chapter 13), and then among the Navajo people of the American southwest to study healing practices, states of consciousness and cosmology. While a few anthropologists have gotten into experimental research, most ethnographers are naturalists – they take the people as they find them, participate as much as they can in their daily life, and record what they observe. This is what we ethnographers call the method of *participant observation* (DeWalt 2010).

No one can observe the dreams of another (unless they are telepathic). Dreams are private experiences and the best one can do is either approximate the dreaming of the Other (see Chapter 6), or elicit dream reports from people and then find out what people think about the dream story – the distinction here is between the *dream-as-dreamt* and the *dream-as-told*. Most of the dream research done by ethnographers is the collection of dreams-as-told – which are in effect *dreams-as-remembered* filtered through language, cultural symbolism and social practice — as well as how the people interpret their dreams, and what they do with the information made public by the interpreted dream. There has been very little scope in the past for participant observation in dream ethnography, partly because of lack of dreaming skill on the part of the fieldworker, and partly depending upon a situation in which the ethnographer's own dreams-as-told may be legitimately involved in the research. For example, Barbara Tedlock describes how her husband, Dennis, had dreamed "…of receiving an ear of corn from an unknown person at a party; when he opened the husk the corn was already roasted, with butter, salt, lime juice, and chili powder on it" (1992c:105). He reported his dream to the Quiché shaman with whom he was apprenticing and obtained the dream interpretation that made sense to those Guatemalan people. But as straightforward as Dennis Tedlock's participant observation would seem, it is actually quite rare in the ethnographic literature (but see also Santos-Granero 2003:182 for a similar example). Much more common has been the practice of collecting dream reports and then submitting them to psychoanalytic analysis, or some other Western procedure. The reasons for this paucity of participant observation in dream anthropology will become apparent later on. Right now I want to trace the history of thinking about dream ethnography from its inception.

## HISTORY OF ANTHROPOLOGICAL THOUGHT ON DREAMING

The history of thinking about dreaming in anthropology is every bit as lengthy and rich as in neuroscience and psychology (see e.g., Lang

1897; Lincoln 1935; O'Nell 1976; von Grunebaum and Caillois 1966; Tedlock 1992a; Laughlin, McManus and d'Aquili 1990:4; Mageo 2003a; Schulman and Stroumsa 1999a; Lohmann 2003a, 2007; Stewart 2004a; Heijnen and Edgar 2010). A number of writers have examined relevant theories of dreaming (see O'Nell 1976, Mageo 2003b:4-7; Stewart 2004b; d'Andrade 1961; Kennedy and Langness 1981; Goulet and Young 1994; Lohmann 2003b). Needless to say, theories purporting to explain dreaming took on the coloring of whatever theoretical school was in vogue at any particular time in the discipline.

## Adolf Bastian and Dreaming

It is all too common to begin the story of the anthropology of dreaming with the work of Edward B. Tylor (1832-1917) for whom dreaming was a central issue in his account of the origins of religion (see e.g., Lohmann 2003b:2; Kennedy and Langness 1981:250; Tedlock 1992b:2, to name but a few). While it is true that from the earliest days of anthropology, *ethnology*[2] has had an interest in the cross-cultural study of dreaming, the story actually begins earlier than Tylor. The story begins in earnest in the mid-19th century with the writings of the German anthropologist, Adolf Bastian (1826-1905), who laid out the first systematic ethnographic project, the intent of which was to leave the comfy walls of the academy and go out into the field among living societies and collect information about their ways of life before they died out or were tainted by contact with Western imperialist societies (Fischer *et al.* 2007; Shamdasani 2003; Koepping, 1983; Lowie, 1937).

Bastian was an inveterate fieldworker and carried out more extensive ethnographic fieldwork than almost any other ethnographer has done in the history of ethnology to the present day, visiting cultures around the world over the course of 25 years of constant traveling. During those visits to far-away societies, he collected and published an astounding amount of ethnographic material information on dream beliefs and practices (e.g., his 1894 record of his researches among the peoples of New Guinea and Togo, *Zur Mythologie Und Psychologie Der Nigritier in*

---

[2] The term "ethnology" was coined by Adam F. Kollár (1718–1783) of Vienna in 1783.

*Guinea (Einschliesslich Des Colonial- Gebietes Togo) Mit Bezugnahme Auf Socialistische Elementargedanken.* In that one volume alone, he recorded the belief that the soul leaves the body and may morph into animal forms, soul-loss in dreams, and dream visits at night by ancestors – these being motifs in dream cultures documented later in the ethnographic record. Alas, Bastian's emphasis upon doing lots of fieldwork fizzled out later on in the 19th century with ethnologists preferring to rely upon reports from abroad by missionaries and military correspondents, and taking only short trips, if any, "into the field" themselves.

It is curious that North American anthropology has paid so little attention to Bastian. It may be that he was German, not an Anglo, and that few of his writings have made it into English (see Koepping 1983 for a sample of Bastian's writing in English). But I suspect that the problem lies deeper than this – in a kind of systematic ignoring of a strain of structuralist thinking that predominated in Bastian's thinking, and passed on through him to Tylor and Émile Durkheim (1858-1917), then through Lucien Lévy-Bruhl (1857-1939) and to some extent Franz Boas (1858-1942), the founder of American anthropology, to Claude Lévi-Strauss (1908-2009; see Koepping 2007), and in due course to our own theoretical work (Laughlin and d'Aquili 1974; Laughlin, McManus and d'Aquili 1990). In other words, anthropology has been concerned with both the structural underpinnings and content variation in consciousness since at least the time of Bastian, and despite some rather biased accounts of the history of anthropology, that concern has continued to the present day. And, of course, the same strain exists in the history of psychology as well – a strain that will also become relevant in chapters to come — again starting with Bastian and passing eventually to Carl G. Jung (1875-1961) and thence to Mircea Eliade (1907-1986) and James Hillman (1926-).

## Bastian and the Psychic Unity of Mankind

The linchpin idea that permeated much of 19th century thinking about the origins of human ethnicity and consciousness was the "cultural idealist" notion of the *psychic unity of mankind.* "Idealism" derives from the Latin word *idealis,* meaning "idea;" referring in this context to a belief that knowledge and experience about the world derives from certain innate structures of mind that, among other things, manifest themselves in dreams. The presumption was that there exists a single, overarching human nature that permeates all peoples in all places on the planet, regardless of the particularities of their sociocultural organization and their environment. All people everywhere (including so called "civilized" folks) are born with the same mental and physical potentialities which will cause them, when presented with similar problems, to create similar solutions. However, because peoples are faced with quite unique circumstances by their geographical locality and their history, their societies and cultures will diverge in time and appear, at least on the surface, to be quite different from one another.

Johann Wolfgang von Goethe (1749-1832) had earlier developed the notion of structure in biology he called "ur-phenomenon" (Ger: *Urphänomen*),[3] but Bastian was really the first serious proponent of the psychic unity view in ethnology during the 19th century. This was a period when Germany was a major player in science, and Bastian was Germany's leading social anthropologist (Koepping, 1983; see also Lowie, 1937:Chapter 4). He believed that the mental acts of all people are the products of physiological mechanisms characteristic of the human species (what today we might term the genetic loading on the organization and functioning of the nervous system). Every human mind inherits a complement of species-specific "elementary ideas" (*Elementargedanken*), and hence the minds of all people, regardless of their race or culture, operate in much the same way, structurally speaking. It is the contingencies of geographic location and historical background that we have to thank for the different variations in how these elementary ideas manifest themselves within different sociocultural traditions, and the various levels of sociocultural complexity. According to Bastian, there also exists a lawful "genetic principle" by which societies develop over the course of their history from exhibiting simple sociocultural institutions to becoming increasingly complex in their organization.

These elementary, inherited psychological processes can be studied in a systematic, objective and comparative way, Bastian taught, and

---

[3] The prefix "ur-" meaning "primitive" or "archetypal, and "phenomenon" meaning the appearances of things – hence the structure underlying biological appearances (Seamon and Zajonc 1998:4, 25-27).

the more one studies various peoples – including their dream cultures – the more one sees that the historical influences on the culture are of secondary importance compared with the elementary psychological structures that mediate experience and cultural categories. Through the accumulation of ethnographic data, we can study the psychological laws of mental development as they reveal themselves in diverse regions and under differing local conditions. Although one is speaking with individual informants, Bastian held that the object of research is *not* the study of the individual *per se*, but rather the "collective mind" of a people as iterated in the experience, thought and actions of individuals. In other words, the ethnographer is after the "folk ideas" (*Volkergedanken*) of a particular society – folk ideas like various beliefs about and interpretations of dream experiences. The individual is like the cell in an organism, a social animal whose mind is influenced by its social background. The "elementary ideas" (*Elementargedanken*) are the structures from which the "folk ideas" develop. From this perspective, the social group has a kind of group mind, a social "soul" (*Gesellschaftsseele*), if you will, in which the individual mind is embedded and influenced.

Bastian believed that the elementary ideas are to be scientifically extracted from folk ideas (such as the belief that ancestors may visit one during a dream and communicate important information) as varying forms of collective representations (*Gesellschaftsgedanken*). An example of a collective representation might be the facility of the human brain to animate the image of a dead relative (or any other image for that matter) during dreaming, thus making it possible to interact with the "ancestor" in a very life-like way. Because one cannot observe the collective representations *per se*, Bastian felt that the ethnographic project had to proceed through an analytical process by which one deduces the elementary ideas (e.g., ability of the brain to store and animate images of long-dead relatives) from the data on folk ideas (e.g., belief in ancestor visitations while dreaming).

Let me offer a personal example, so that we share a common understanding of the distinction between folk ideas and elementary ideas. In one of the most important lucid dreams of my life, I was parked in a car in a forest. As I looked left out of my window over my forearm, I noticed a huge brown bear on its hind legs plucking and eating berries. The bear was very close, perhaps ten feet from me, and upon subsequent reflection, it was a very human-like bear with very intelligent human-like eyes. I was afraid and looked in the other direction and saw a chrome revolver laying upon the passenger seat. I grasped the gun and turned to look back at the bear. The bear turned its eyes toward me and slowly shook its head in a negative gesture. I looked back at the gun in my hand and laid it back on the car seat. My fear disappeared. Looking back at the bear, it nodded and went back to eating berries. In that instant I knew, in the dream, that I had found my personal totem or familiar, and so it has turned out to be. Now, here is what I took from it. Besides the obvious lesson that this is how some people get the notion of a totem or spiritual familiar, it taught me that my brain can present images that are an amalgam of features from human and animal sources stored in memory – in this case part human, part bear. This facility is the "elementary idea" behind the "folk idea" that I interpreted as my totemic animal. The bear was a "folk idea" and the neurocognitive processes by means of which my unconscious speaks to me by amalgamating imagery is the "elementary idea." Incidentally, when I described this dream to some of my Navajo friends, they agreed that Bear had visited me and established a protective relationship with me. I have worn a bear claw belt buckle ever since, and still have the medicine bag that was given to me with little bears sewn on it.

Now both Native Americans and Anglo-Americans share an environment in which there are or have been brown bears. So it is quite natural, Bastian might have said, that both I and, say, one of my Navajo friends might have had a dream like mine. But it is very unlikely that a traditional Australian Aborigine would dream of a brown bear. He or she could easily have a dream like mine, but instead of a bear it might be a wallaby or a wombat, animals that live in the Australian Outback. Perhaps different folk ideas from two different cultures and environments, but I would venture to argue, the same elementary idea. Why? Because I doubt there is more than one neurocognitive system in the human brain that amalgamates human and animal forms to form a single symbol that incorporates qualities of both species. Think about it. We routinely see anthropomorphized animals all the time in the entertainment media – Bugs Bunny, the

"Beast" in the Beauty and the Beast, duck mascots cheering on fans at a game. One might argue the same elementary idea produces all these amalgams. We will see as the book moves along that this relationship between the various transformations of imagery in dreams may be linked to neurocognitive possesses that mediate, and even create them.

What Bastian argued for was nothing less than what today we might call a "cross-cultural social psychobiology." The key to developing this solidly empirical study of human consciousness was to collect as much ethnographic data as possible from all over the world. Through ethnographic research, he argued, we can study the psychological laws of mental development as they reveal themselves in diverse geographical settings. Thus, in modern day parlance, our different sociocultural forms are due both to transculturally shared (i.e., what C. G. Jung called "archetypal;" see Chapter 10) processes inherent in our human psychophysiology, and to our development (or enculturation) within a particular social and physical environment. The method was sound – actually the only method available during an age when neuroscience was in its infancy. Today, of course, there are scientific methods that allow us to independently observe and measure the activity of the brain processes mediating such phenomena. An example is Michael A. Persinger's (1987; 2001; see also d'Aquili and Newberg 1999) neuropsychological research on temporal lobe mediation of paranormal and spiritual experiences – but that is getting ahead of our story, so more on that later.

It is true that Bastian was an evolutionist through and through. He firmly believed that the folk ideas of the "savage" people he visited and researched were simplified versions of collective representations that become developmentally complexified in those found in modern civilizations (Koepping 1983:47). But it is a mistake of the first water to lump Bastian in with the 19th century "unilineal" evolutionists, for unlike many of them, Bastian held that environmental and cultural-historical forces mold the unique evolutionary track taken by each specific society. He advocated a kind of "multilineal" evolutionism of the sort later espoused by Julian Steward (1902-1972) and his "cultural ecology" approach that influenced so many ethnologists in the 20th century.

## The Unilineal Evolutionists

The evolutionary take on the psychic unity of mankind was extremely pervasive in 19th century philosophy and social science, and included among many ethnologists. And as it happens, many of the ethnologists of the time were also interested in dream cultures. For example, Andrew Lang (1844-1912) was a literary man – a prolific poet, novelist, historian and collector of weird and wonderful stories – who was interested in the ethnography of folklore and fairy tales. He was also quite interested in psychical research – what we would call today paranormal psychology – and was one of the founding members of the Society for Psychical Research, an organization that also included C. G. Jung and William James as members. He wrote a book in 1897 entitled *The Book of Dreams and Ghosts* that examined the relations between dreaming and paranormal phenomena.

The pre-eminent evolutionist, at least from the Anglo-American perspective, as well as the penultimate whipping-boy for 20th century anti-evolutionist and anti-structuralist critics, was Edward B. Tylor. Tylor took a brief trip to the United States and into Mexico in 1856 and returned to England to write about it. He never ventured out into the field again, but his interest in the evolution of culture (a concept he was the first to clearly define; see Tylor 1871:1) and religion set the pace for Anglo anthropology for some time. He derived many of his ideas about evolution from geologist, Sir Charles Lyell (1797-1875), who was an avid Darwinist. But Tylor's central influence was his friendship with, and the writings of Adolf Bastian. He had read them all, a fact that he acknowledged in his obituary of Bastian: "In the meantime a fellow anthropologist, like myself a student of Bastian's voluminous writings, placed in my hands a summary account of what he had drawn up of the great anthropologist's travels and of his published writings, which, I may remark, occupy between two and three feet on my bookshelves, and run toward 10,000 pages, not counting his articles in the *Zeitschrift für Ethnologie*" (Tylor 1905:138). Tylor likewise remarks upon the paucity of English translations of Bastian's works.

Edward Tylor was the first ethnologist to specialize and systematize the anthropological study of religion. As Paul Radin wrote in his introduction to Tylor's *Religion in Primitive Culture*, "Tylor's most signal contribution to anthropology lies, it is generally agreed, in his discussion of religion. Many people, anthropologists as well as laymen, seem to think that this aspect of thought begins and ends with his doctrine of animism. But that is hardly the case. Tylor's achievement is much greater than that. It may be said that he was the first to give us a well-thought-out history of religions from the beginnings up to the time of the great Egyptian and Sumerian-Babylonian civilizations" (Radin 1958:ix). Tylor painted the picture of religious beliefs, grounded in *animistic* experiences, evolving from Paleolithic times through to the present in a unilineal trajectory from simple to highly complex. This is spelled out in his magnum opus, *Primitive Culture*, volume one of which, *Origins of Culture*, discusses the evolution of religion and culture generally, while volume two, *Religion in Primitive Culture*, discusses the origins of religion in the experience of, and belief in animism.

Animism for Tylor is the belief in spiritual beings and souls, and permeates all religious cultures from the most primitive hunter-gatherers to the most advanced industrial civilizations. An animistic society holds the belief that all animate (animals, birds, trees, crops) and inanimate (rivers, mountains, air) forms have an inner spiritual essence or "soul," and that these souls may be directly experienced by people as animated spirits in their dreams, visions and other ASC. The nature of animism is easiest to research among "low" or primitive societies (shades of Bastian here), and that is precisely what he did for us in volume two. He emphasizes that in some societies, the belief in the spiritual soul is derived from dream experiences in which the soul (read dream-ego) "quits the body" and wanders around – again, as we know today, a common theme of dreaming cultures worldwide (1871:Vol. 2:24). As we shall see later on, many peoples believe that their dreams are real – that they are the experiences had by their dream-selves wandering about in another dimension of reality. It is while dreaming that we can encounter and interact with the otherwise hidden spiritual dimensions of anything, organic or inorganic.

I have neither the space nor the inclination to track all of the various criticisms of Tylor's evolutionism, or those of his contemporaries, Lewis Henry Morgan (1818-1881) and Karl Marx (1818-1883), for that is not the purpose of this book. However, I will say that in rejecting whole clothe the work of Tylor, critics have thrown out the baby with some admittedly questionable and obsolete bath water. Where many anthropologists have gone wrong is in failing to understand that religions are commonly founded in *direct personal experience*, sometimes in the dream state, sometimes in other ASC-like visions, drug trips, fantasies or "waking dreams," and so forth. That is why the issue of animism will not go away, because under whatever appellation, the experience of one's spiritual self separating from one's physical body happens all the time in dreams, as does the experience of animated mountains, constellations, rock formations, as well as anthropomorphic animals and shape shifting beings. Such experiences, shared by people everywhere, call out for comprehension within the context of their general worldview.

## Functionalism and the Rise of Freudian Psychoanalysis

It took a Polish ethnographer, Bronislaw Malinowski (1884-1942), to kick-start Bastian's ethnographic project when the young scientist found himself stranded in the Trobriand Islands for the duration of the First World War. The quality of his ethnographic reporting from the Trobriands, especially his now-classic 1922 ethnography, *Argonauts of the Western Pacific*, made it embarrassingly clear to everyone that a lengthy period of fieldwork was a prerequisite to good ethnography. Prior to his period of fieldwork, Sigmund Freud (1856-1939) developed a method for treating neurotic patients by application of dream analysis, as well as free association (one expresses anything that comes to mind freely and without suppression) and transference (the patient redirects repressed childhood feelings to the therapist). He called this method *psychoanalysis*. When he published his book, *The Interpretation of Dreams* (2010 [1899]), his thinking immediately filled a void in anthropology that was being created by the rejection of 19th century evolutionism. Malinowski received a copy while still in the field and became quite interested in Trobriand dreaming, as reported in his volumes *Sex and Repression in Savage Society* (1927) and *The Sexual Life of Savages* (1929). Trobriand Islanders appeared not to be all that interested in their normal everyday dreams – at least not in revealing them publicly. However, they do make a distinction that is quite common cross-culturally between normal (Malinowski calls these "free" dreams) and important dreams had by powerful people and having to do with magic and spirits (Malinowski's "official" dreams; 1927:93). Under the influence of Freud's theory that dreams are motivated by the unconscious, libidinous desire for "wish-fulfillment," Malinowski reported material on the erotic dreams he collected.

According to Freud, the dream-as-dreamt and the memory and expression of the dream-as-told is called the *manifest content*. From the manifest content of a dream, the psychoanalyst is able to deduce the hidden, unconscious *latent content* lying below and motivating the dreaming experience. From the collection of many such dreams over time, patterns of latent content can be analyzed and lead the analyst and patient to a better understanding of the patient's previously unconscious drives. It is interesting here to contrast Freud's method with Bastian's. Freud held that the orientation of dream interpretation was the individual, while for Bastian the gathering of dreams and other folk ideas was done in order to understand society-wide collective representations. Bastian would ideally collect as many dreams as he could from individuals within a society and derive patterns generalized to the entire culture. For Freud, the individual's dream may contain elements derived from the patient's daily social life, but the latent content applied only to the motivation of the patient. One can see the influence of Freud on ethnographic fieldwork in, for example, the approach of George Devereux (1908-1985), an ethnologist and psychoanalyst who did extensive fieldwork among the Mohave Indians. He developed a method that included the psychoanalysis of individual informants/patients *in situ* – within their everyday cultural context (Devereux 1969).

The approach to studying native dreaming based upon the Freudian presumption that there is a "manifest" level of a dream that may be interpreted and understood by the dreamer or a native dream interpreter (see Chapters 7 and 8), and a "latent" level that is both somehow more "real" and that is understandable only to the Western psychoanalyst, had an enormous influence upon how dream ethnography was carried out (e.g., Eggan 1966; Roheim 1949; Tuzin 1975). Freud's influence was greatest out on the more psychological wing of the "functionalist" school in Europe. Functionalism arose from the ashes of 19th century unilineal evolutionism. The focus became the society as it is naturally found within a particular time and environment, the view being that societies are like organisms, they are a totality that is made up of parts that all interact to maintain the whole. Each institution, belief, practice, story, etc. was said to "function" in such a way as to keep the organic society intact and adaptive – just as the pancreas, kidneys, and lungs operate to keep the whole body intact and adaptive. Without getting into the tautological logic marring the typical functionalist explanation of cultural institutions (see Hempel 1968; McCauley and Lawson 1984), the study of dreaming shifted to show how dream reports, institutionalized dream interpretation and especially the "latent" content of dreams served to maintain the intact, adaptive social fabric. Gone from consideration was any concern about underlying universal elementary ideas or collective representations. Dreams take on a distinctly, and often overtly Freudian overtone in the hands of functionalist ethnographers.

Let us return to the great Bronislaw Malinowski as a prime example of how functionalism and psychoanalysis coalesced. Malinowski was the first to point up the cultural flexibility that must be built into Freud's Oedipus complex. Malinowski noted that in Trobriand, being a matrilineal society, the central figures in repressed Oedipal dreams must be the mother's brother, rather than one's biological father, and one's sister rather than one's mother:

> In the Trobriands there is no friction between father and son, and all the infantile craving of the child for its mother is allowed gradually to spend itself in a natural, spontaneous manner. The ambivalent attitude of veneration and dislike is felt between a man and his mother's brother, while the repressed sexual attitude of incestuous temptation can be formed only towards his sister. Applying to each society a terse, though somewhat crude formula, we might say that in the Oedipus complex there is the repressed desire to kill the father and marry the mother, while in the matrilineal society of the Trobriands the wish is to marry the sister and to kill the maternal uncle. ...It is actually well known that 'other people' have such dreams — "a man is sometimes sad, ashamed, and ill-tempered. Why? Because he has dreamt that he had connection with his sister." "This made me feel ashamed,"

such a man would say. I found that this is, in fact, one of the typical dreams known to exist, occurring frequently, and one which haunts and disturbs the dreamer (1927:80, 95).

Sex itself is quite free-wheeling in the Trobriands, and there is far less repression than among Westerners. Malinowski pondered this fact and wondered whether the reason why the natives seemed not to dream a lot, or pay much attention to their dreams might be because Freud's thesis is correct (1927:93). In any event, Malinowski took the Freudian position that the principle function of brother-sister incest dreams was as a psychological defense mechanism to alleviate otherwise destructive emotions within a matrilineal social structure.

## Franz Boas, the American School and Dreams as Culture

Freudian theory also permeated much of the thinking about dreaming among American anthropologists. Anthropology as a professional discipline was founded by the German immigrant, Franz Boas (1858-1942), who spent a formative period researching the Inuit of Baffin Island, before returning home to study with Bastian during 1886-87 at the Royal Ethnographic Museum in Berlin. Because of the pressures of antisemitism, and his growing interest in North American native peoples, Boas migrated to the United States and eventually ended up Professor of Anthropology at Columbia University where he put together the first department of anthropology and offered the first doctorate in the field.

Franz Boas is generally considered the "father of cultural anthropology." This is not true of course, considering Edward Tylor defined the term in English, and Bastian used its German equivalent. But it is quite true that the school he founded in the New World emphasized the study of culture more than other schools of anthropology had done previously. Moreover, Boas' name and the methods he espoused are commonly associated with relativist (or constructivist) notions of human nature – that is, the idea that in some way our species transcended biological conditioning when it became fully cultural in its patterns of adaptation – a kind of Rubicon event that occurred way back in the late Paleolithic somewhere. The naive assumption here is that there was some kind of leap from "nature" to "nurture" during the evolution of humanity. But Boas himself was neither so naive, nor was he completely comfortable with an extreme relativist view of human culture. One need only consider Boas' discussion of psychic unity in his book *The Mind of Primitive Man* (1910) in which he wrestled with the tension between his conviction that all people everywhere are born with the same mind, and yet some cultures appear to be more "advanced" in terms of technological and social adaptation than others. His overwhelming concern methodologically was with recording the narratives of traditional peoples verbatim, and in using these texts as data upon which to eventually ground a solid science of human nature and consciousness – a research strategy he, in fact, derived from and shared with Bastian's project.

Boas however was very critical of the "comparative method" as formulated by Bastian and others in the 19th century (Boas 1896). The method assumed that similar folk ideas from different places on the planet had to be produced by the same elementary idea – the same structure — whereas Boas realized that the same folk idea – the same cultural trait to use a more up-to-date American term – from different places could actually be produced from different structures, different causes. So he struck the comparative method from his methodology and argued that much of the apparent resemblance among cultures within the same geographical area was most likely due to *diffusion* of traits over time. Ethnographers, he taught, should focus on collecting verbatim records of the language and culture of specific peoples and place them within their appropriate culture area. The American approach toward the study of dreams was to be limited to recording the dreams of informants, along with their interpretations and associated stories, rituals, dramas and other activities. This became known as the "historical method."

It is important though to keep Boas' criticisms of his European forebears in perspective. Boas was trained in psychophysiology and was an authority on the "anthropology of the senses," as it is now called (Boas 1889). He knew the body and he knew a great deal about the neurophysiology of his day. But he was hampered in the same way that all the 19th century social scientists were by the lack of a useful neuroscience. There simply was no way to independently confirm that the same elementary idea (read "neurocognitive system") produced similar folk ideas or culture traits in disparate parts of the globe. So Boas was playing it cautious while at the same time forwarding the project Bastian so passionately espoused, the intense collection of cross-cultural data.

Boas' apparent anti-theory stance[4] left a vacuum in what became on the ground a more naturalistic enterprise likened to collecting butterflies and tacking them up on a cork board. This did not stop fieldworkers, however, from asking "why" and "how" questions — the sorts of questions that lead to theorizing. This was very much the case for the study of dreaming. For the more psychologically oriented ethnographers, Freudian psychoanalysis filled that void. Thus was born the "culture and personality" school of Margaret Mead (1901-1978), Ruth Benedict (1887-1948), Abram Kardiner (1891-1981), Anthony F.C. Wallace (1923-) and other American anthropologists – leading later to what we now call "psychological anthropology." Based upon Freudian principles, culture was seen as having a formative role in the development of the personality of society's members. They focused especially on a person's early years and on the child rearing practices of the society.

The culture and personality folks were quite naturally interested in the role of dreaming in this process. Wallace espoused the Freudian notion that dreams express, as he said in the title to one of his papers, "the wishes of the soul" (Wallace 1958). Margaret Mead (1952) wrote an elegant article tracing the myriad similarities between the field ethnographer and the psychiatrist. Both learn by entering the alien world of the Other, both note how the Other "handles" him or herself in the world, both are interested in the Other's attitudes, values and actions. Both are concerned about how the Other's social relations condition them to express or repress their emotions. And of course, both are very interested in the Other's dreams. Mead held that anthropologists wasted

---

[4] I say "apparent" anti-theory stance because, of course, Boas never gave up theorizing. Note the theoretical assumption underlying his cultural area focus that historical diffusion of traits is more likely the cause of cross-cultural similarities than ecological or neurological causes (see Jorgensen 1983 for empirical confirmation of this hypothesis).

a lot of time studying the differences of meaning of dream symbols cross-culturally. Only with the advent of the psychoanalytical method of latent content analysis could the study of dreaming reach "a high enough level of abstraction" (ibid:429).

Not every dream ethnographer agreed with Mead's giddy embracing of Freudian methods. One of the most avid dream ethnographers during the mid-20th century was Dorothy Eggan (1901-1965). In an article in 1949, she took her fellow ethnographers to task for shirking their responsibility to collect dreams from societies in which dreaming is held to be important. She noted that it was the prospect of having to psychoanalyze dream material that fieldworkers found daunting, for it required (1) one to consider Freudian methods valid for non-Western peoples, and (2) special training that most anthropologists do not have (1949:177-178). Still, she argued, research on dreaming and dream-related traits was necessary for a full accounting of personality within a particular cultural context. "The issue for social scientists then is whether dream material *as a form of personal document* can provide useful information without considerable additional investment for the student in training and field hours" (ibid:178, Eggan's emphasis).

In true Boasian tradition, Eggan collected hundreds of dreams from her Hopi informants over a number of years. The Hopi pay a lot of attention to their dreams and have very clear consensus interpretations of elements arising in dreams. For instance, to dream of yucca root means death, because the Hopi, Navajo and other peoples in the American southwest use the suds from the root to cleanse the body of the deceased. Also, specific kinds of dreams require actions due to beliefs associated with dream symbolism. "Of great importance in the recording of their dreams is a Hopi belief that they are significant, and that in order to negate the effects of a bad dream it must be told immediately on awakening, even though a reluctant listener must be aroused in the middle of the night; after this recital the dreamer must go outside and spit four times" (ibid:179). There was thus an interest among American anthropologists of the culture and personality era to fully integrate dream experiences within the overall view of culture – culture being made up of traits that are historically transmitted down the generations and diffused from one society to another. Eggan went further and showed how dreaming and myth may interact in a manner that can relieve anxiety in the dreamer (Eggan 1955:447), thus adding a functionalist overcast to what was essentially a Boasian method.

## The Return of Structuralism

The structuralist strain that, as I have said, runs through anthropology from its very inception popped up again in the '50s and '60s in Europe in the person of the French anthropologist Claude Lévi-Strauss (1908-2009). Influenced by sociologist Émile Durkheim (1858-1917), the linguists Ferdinand de Saussure (1857-1913) and Roman Jakobson (1896-1982), and of course Sigmund Freud (wasn't everyone?), Lévi-Strauss developed a method by which one deduces the underlying, unconscious structures of mind producing the apparent variety of cultural forms; forms such as descent systems and myth. He spent much of his later energies in analyzing the structure of myths which he considered a kind of language embedded in a story. Myths are often strange and surreal with fantastic characters and seemingly arbitrary and unpredictable outcomes. But this is just myth at its most superficial level. What struck Lévi-Strauss as significant was that these weird stories recur over and over across cultures. This must be because, he argued, there is a universal "deep structure" underlying myths, the same as there is an underlying structure of the novel, à la Roland Barthes' (1915-1980) analysis of the structure of literary forms, or a symphony, à la Heinrich Schenker's (1868-1935) analysis of the structure of classical music. His method is based upon the axiom that a myth sets up a problem. The elements are established in a series of *binary oppositions*[5] which produce a tension leading eventually through mediation to a solution. The structure is a-temporal in the sense that the symphony is a-temporal – it is a single timeless structure that simultaneously contains both problem and solution, but that requires time to unfold in the telling or the playing. Incidentally, Lévi-Strauss, like Bastian and

---

[5] Lévi-Strauss was not always up-front in acknowledging the work of others that influenced him. He was undoubtedly aware of Schenkerian analysis of the symphonic form (Littlefield and Neumeyer 1992) and was clearly influenced by the writings of C. G. Jung, particularly with respect to binary oppositions and the psyche (see d'Aquili 1975 on Lévi-Strauss' debt to Jung).

Durkheim before him, was quite aware that there must be some kind of physiological basis for the "deep structures" he claimed to adduce from mythic narratives, but it is only in 1971 at the end of *L'Homme nu*, the last of the four volumes of his magnum opus, *Mythologiques*, that he actually admits that his structures must have something to do with how the brain works.

As far as I know, Lévi-Strauss never took up the study of dreams in any serious way. However, others that followed his methods have done so. Premier among them is the work of the British social anthropologist, Adam Kuper (1941-), who, in a series of important articles, has sketched out a structuralist method for analyzing dreams (Kuper 1979, 1983, 1986; Kuper and Stone 1982). Taking his lead from Lévi-Strauss' analysis of myth, Kuper (1979:645) notes that in many societies, myth and dreaming interpenetrate – that is, as ethnographer Kenelm Burridge put it for the Tangu people of New Guinea, "…much of the content of dreams tends to become articulate in myths, and myths, or parts of myths, are retold in dream" (Burridge 1972:129; see also Eggan 1955; Kracke 1992; Brown 1992). Kuper summarizes his approach in the following way:

> …the initial premiss or situation of the dream is developed to yield new situations, which in turn eventually produce a final resolution of the issue with which the dream is engaged. In principle it should be possible to state the rules by which the transformation from one situation to another is effected. I shall argue that these rules can indeed be stated, and that they are the same as the rules which have been found to generate the transformations which occur in and between myths. To sum up, dreams are viewed here as modes of argument, in which the dreamer moves from one proposition to another through the application of general transformation rules until a resolution of the dream problem is achieved. (1979:647-648)

Myths are thus stories that communicate a problem and its solution in the outer social world, while dreams are stories that communicate internally within the mind of the individual – perhaps between the individual's dream ego and his or her unconscious. In any event, the analysis of the internal structure of the dream is the same as for a myth.

Just as for myths, there exist mental structures mediating dreaming that are both universal to humanity and that operate to organize dreams according to a finite number of rules, including making semantic distinctions by way of binary oppositions (flying birds as opposed to walking birds), and then by transformations involving the inversion (dreamed man dies, actual man lives and prospers), negation (dreamed non-man, actual man), reversal (dreamed Y causes X, actual X causes Y) and substitution (dreamed bull stands for an actual man) of dream elements. What he is getting at is that the human mind is structured cognitively to process problems arising in dreams in the same way as they are in mythological thought.

Of course Kuper is aware that when he is applying the structural analysis to a dream it is to the dream-as-told by the dreamer, and not the dream-as-dreamt. This is, as always, a phenomenological "remove" from the experience of the dream which has been rendered a text through the filter of language. A structural analysis of a dream using Kuper's approach has an added advantage, because other than accepting the existence of the unconscious, it is devoid of many of the ethnocentric assumptions of the Freudian approach. It also recognizes the possibility that elements of a dream may be borrowed from myth, and vice versa, an important factor we will return to later in the book.

## HOLOCULTURAL AND STATISTICAL STUDIES OF DREAMING

Another kind of research began to emerge during the second half of the 20th century – the *holocultural* study; that is, a study in which a hypothesis is tested by correlating various traits using a worldwide sample of cultures. Developing a worldwide sample became easy after the creation of what is called the Human Relations Area Files (HRAF). The HRAF (referred to by those in the know simply as the "her-aff") consists of a vast database of ethnographic materials based upon a global sample of cultures, organized by a complex system of codes. The brainchild of George Peter Murdock (1897-1985), the HRAF was made available to many universities and other institutions in 1948, and almost immediately used to test various theories pertaining to the world's cultures.

Probably the most important holocultural study of dreaming done to date was that of Roy d'Andrade (1961) and published in a now hard-to-find collection of articles in Francis L.K. Hsu's first edition of *Psychological Anthropology*. Although this work was completed a half-century ago, it stands as totally unique, and as a brilliant example of how the HRAF can and should be used. D'Andrade begins with the fact that, although dreaming is a species universal, not all societies emphasize the importance of dreaming, or do so in exactly the same way. It has been suggested since Freud entered the picture that chronic feelings of anxiety produced by certain cultural practices like the incest taboo may increase the importance of dreaming in such societies. D'Andrade reasoned that subsistence patterns range from those societies that emphasize adherence to social norms, sanctions, and procedures (agricultural and animal husbandry) to those that emphasize individualism, isolation and self-reliance (hunting and fishing). Peoples of the latter kind tend to place individuals in anxiety producing situations more often than those of the former kind – hence the emphasis upon dreaming as a means of seeking and controlling supernatural powers via dreaming. D'Andrade looked for the presence or absence of several traits indicative of "control of the supernatural" dreams (hereafter, COSD) in the dream reports from a worldwide sample of 64 societies drawn from the Human Relations Area Files. His analysis showed a significant correlation between hunting and fishing subsistence patterns and COSD. Of the 20 societies with agriculture and animal husbandry, 25% showed evidence of COSD. Of the 19 societies having agriculture without animal husbandry, 58% emphasized COSD, and of the 25 societies that practiced hunting/fishing (with or without animal husbandry), 76% emphasized COSD. If one excludes the six hunting/fishing societies that also practiced animal husbandry, of the remaining 19 societies that practiced hunting/fishing only, 78% sought COSD. These findings seem to confirm that those societies that put their members in situations that produce greater anxiety, also attempt to minimize risk, in part by seeking control over supernatural forces encountered during dreaming.

Expanding on this confirmation, D'Andrade also reasoned that the farther away a male has to move from his parents, the more likely he would tend to feel "on his own" and anxious, and thus seek to control supernatural beings through the medium of dreaming. In a similar way he showed a significant correlation between post-nuptial ("after we're married") residence patterns and COSD among males. In a sample of 57 societies worldwide for which there was sufficient information, of the 11 societies in which the married son lives in their parents' household, 27% emphasize COSD, of the 25 societies in which the married son lives in the same village or local group as their parents, 40% emphasize COSD, and of the 21 societies in which the married son lives in a different village or local group, 81% exhibit COSD. Again, confirmation of the hypothesis, leading to the suggestion that those folks who face systematic anxiety also seek control of their situation in part at least through dreaming.

Erika Bourguignon (1972) carried D'Andrade's work further by reasoning that "hallucinogenic trance" states are closely allied with COSD; so closely in fact that it is hard to tell where trance leaves off and dreaming begins (see Voss et al. 2009 for neuropsychological confirmation; see also my discussion of dream yoga in Chapter 13). She combined her holocultural research on trance states with D'Andrade's work, and examined the correlation between trance and dreaming using a sample of societies that overlapped with D'Andrade's sample. She was able to confirm that the use of dreams to control supernatural powers does indeed correlate with the institutionalized practice of entering trance states.[6] This would seem to add support to the notion that peoples that face uncertainty, individualism and conditions that demand self-reliance do take measures to gain some measure of control over their situation by way of trance states and dreaming.

Calvin S. Hall (considered by many psychologists to be the "father" of modern dream research; see Hall 1953) and Bill Domhoff tested various ideas about the manifest content of dreams among men and women. In Hall and Domhoff (1963a), the authors note that expression of aggression in dreams is both frequent and undisguised. They examined "1,490 aggressive interactions which occurred in 3,049

---

[6] Bourguignon showed that of the 54 societies in D'Andrade's sample, 37 (69%) have trance present and 17 (31%) have no trance present. Of the 37 societies with trance present, 23 (62% of total with trance present) also have COSD, while 14 (38%) have trance present without COSD. Of the 17 societies without trance, 5 (29% of total without trance) have COSD and 12 (71%) are without COSD.

dream narratives collected from 1,940 males and females ranging in age from 2 to 80" from among the dreams collected by Hall from American university students (ibid:259). They found a number of interesting things, including that children of both sexes experience the most aggression in dreams – with no proclivity for males to experience more than females – and that the overall incidence of aggression drops away after the age of 30. After the age of 12 however, a marked sex difference emerges with females experiencing increasingly fewer aggressive incidents compared with males. "In male dreams, aggression with other males stays high throughout life. Much of the aggression with males is with male strangers. The male stranger is a red thread which runs through the maze of our data. A male stranger is a party to 56 per cent of the aggressions with male characters." Females tend to dream of aggression between a male and a female, whereas males tend to dream of aggression between males.

The same two authors published another study (1964) in which they refer to this database and ask, "...we found that dreams are filled with anger, hostility, hatred, physical assault, and murder... . What is the situation with respect to friendliness, affection, and love? Is the other of the two great forces, 'eternal Eros,' equally represented in dreams" (ibid:309)? Sadly, the answer was "no," for the 3049 dreams contained 1490 incidents of aggression and only 711 incidents of friendliness. "A majority of the 711 friendly acts consists of mild expressions of friendliness, such as a greeting, waving, shaking hands, kissing, complimenting a person, or doing a small favor. Major acts of friendliness like saving a life, protecting someone from danger, or rendering a major service are rare. Love, altruism, humanitarianism, benevolence, generosity, and unselfishness, on any large scale, are not characteristic of the dream world. Hate and violence are" (ibid:309).

Hall and Domhoff (1963b) published yet another study in which they combine the data from a number of studies completed on American college students, and found that the 3874 dreams collected from 1399 males featured 5811 characters, exclusive of the dreamer, and that 3695 of these characters were male and 2116 were females. The percentage of male characters for male dreamers was 64. Meanwhile, the 3065 dreams collected from 1418 females featured 5342 characters, exclusive of the dreamer, and of these 2782 were males and 2560 were females. The percentage of male characters for female dreamers was 52, or roughly half. The fact that males dream of male characters more often than female characters, and that females dream of both sexes more or less equally may be a universal property of dreaming cross-culturally. This hypothesis "is suggested by evidence from the dreams of two widely separated ethnic groups, the Hopi of southwest United States and the Yir Yoront of Cape York, Australia. The Hopi dreams were collected by Dorothy Eggan during the years 1939-1942, and the Yir Yoront dreams by R. [Lauriston] Sharp during 1933-1935" (ibid:279). Robbins and Kilbride (1971) tested these findings using a small collection of dreams from some Bantu speaking peoples in Uganda and found the same pattern. If this is a universal pattern in the dreams of males and females, how does one account for the difference? Hall and Domhoff suggest that it may be because we dream about that which concerns us most during our waking life, and that males confront different problems than do females, and that "the unresolved problems of males center more around their relationships with men than with women, and those of females are focused upon their relationships with both sexes about equally" (1964:280). There are other possible explanations, but we will get to those later in the book.[7]

## Ethnography, Culture and Dreaming

I have thus far traced in broad strokes the history of anthropological interest in dreaming up to the latter part of the 20th century. I will stop there for the moment and make a few points before we take up more contemporary anthropological theories of dreaming in the next chapter. Suffice to say it is obvious that how an ethnologist approaches

---

[7] It should be noted that Kenneth Colby (1963) examined content differences in the reported dreams of men and women cross-culturally. He analyzed 549 dreams reported by 366 men and 183 women from 75 traditional societies worldwide and looked for sex differences in the occurrence of 19 "qualities" or themes. Themes that were particularly distinct were men dreaming of "wife" (his or someone else's) and women dreaming of "husband" (hers or someone else's). Men also tended to dream of weapons, coitus, death and animals more often than women, and women dream of mother, clothes and female figures more often than men.

the study of dreams has a lot to do with their theoretical orientation. Bastian collected dreams as evidence of a society's "folk ideas" which could then be used to deduce the elementary ideas generating them. Evolutionists collected dreams and dream beliefs as evidence of how the "savage" or "primitive" mind of humans worked. Dream beliefs and the social use of dreams were for the functionalists part of the warp and weave in the social fabric which allow people to adapt, and for the Boasians another set of traits that derive from a people's enculturation and acculturation. And finally, for structuralists the dream is, like a myth or a descent system, the manifestation of a deep structure within the unconscious mind of each member of the group. Over the decades, anthropologists have used different approaches to collecting dreams and dream culture, and different theories about what dreaming is all about and how it works. Throughout the history of anthropology, however, ethnographers have been collecting data on dream reports, dream beliefs and dream related activities, despite their theoretical orientations, and this is the very best that anthropology has to offer to the scientific study of dreaming. That naturalistic project has produced roughly speaking a century and a half of data pertaining to hundreds of dream cultures across the planet. This is why a good chunk of this book is given over to a summary of those data, organized around some of the more common uses to which groups have put to dreaming.

Most sociocultural anthropologists today consider themselves to be students of *culture*. Exactly what is meant by the term "culture" varies enormously (see Kroeber and Kluckhohn 1952 for a comprehensive review of meanings of the term "culture"). Which definition of "culture" we wish to use here is far from a trivial matter because the discipline has long debated the relative importance of nature and nurture in human affairs. By and large anthropologists to the present day have opted for what might be called the *naive culturological perspective* – that being, as I mentioned above, when our species developed culture, it left its biological, "instinctual" nature behind. The discipline has for over a century emphasized the significance of socially shared and learned patterns of mentation, social interaction and behavior, and the "oddities and quiddities" of cultural variation became the stock-in-trade of professional anthropologists for generations – do a people include spiked wheel traps in their tool kit or not, do they organize inheritance along the matriline or the patriline, do they use a form of money in their exchange or not, do women stretch their necks with neck rings or not, how many words do they have for snow or fish or moonbeams? As we have seen, except for brief flirtations with various structuralist approaches, the principal stream of North American, English speaking ethnology has been oriented toward these culturological preoccupations, and away from concerns about universal elements of psychocultural and sociocultural life. The primary influence in this regard was that of Boas who, being a German Jew and having suffered antisemitism firsthand, was understandably against racism in any form (Stocking 1974). He thus stood opposed to what Graham Richards (1998:137) calls the late Victorian "scientific racism" of the evolutionists.

## What Does "Culture" Mean?

What we want to do here is embrace a definition of culture that does not reify the mind-body dualism inherent in the naive culturological perspective. We also want a definition that is applicable to an understanding of what we have come to understand as the organ of culture – the human nervous system. Because humans are social primates, the influences of social factors upon the dream experiences of individuals is considerable and crucial, as we shall see. In this respect, I find it sensible to view culture as a *system of information* (e.g. Roberts 1964; D'Andrade 1984; Shore 1996). Perhaps the first to recognize the power of this perspective was Ward Goodenough (1954, 1971) who developed his model of culture by analogy from genetics. As a species consists of a gene pool, so too do societies create a "culture pool" – or *information pool* – for its members (Goodenough 1971). People learn their culture (i.e., they become *enculturated*) as individuals from the time they are born, and perhaps even before birth. Indeed, as Anthony F.C. Wallace (1970:109-120) argued, social adaptation for all peoples requires an organization of cognitive diversity such that the information within each person's mind becomes functionally integrated with the information located in the minds of other group members. Not everyone has to learn to be a plumber – one needs only know what a plumber is and how they are useful in the scheme of things. Members of a society can learn from others whatever they need to know to be recognized as a functioning member of the society, but that does not mean that any one member knows all the information in his or her society's information pool. As Goodenough wrote, "As I see it, a society's culture consists of whatever it is one has to know or believe in order to operate in a manner acceptable to its members, and to do so in any role that they accept for any one of themselves. Culture, being what people have to learn as distinct from their biological heritage, must consist of the end product of learning: knowledge, in a most general, if relative, sense of the term" (1954:36).

It is the brain-mediated mind that enables learning and as such the learning of culture takes place in the neurophysiological structures of the individual brain – in a real sense, the only existence "culture" has, other than as an abstraction in the minds of anthropologists, is information contained in the brains of group members, their actions and interactions, and their artifacts (texts, tools, landscapes, buildings, fire pits, so forth). Nonetheless, we may still speak of "culture" as an information pool with considerable utility, for it allows us to integrate socially influenced and shared learning into our understanding of dreaming and dreaming related symbolism and action. Again, we are using the term information in the broad traditional sense that includes imagery, emotions, patterned behaviors and responses, and thought – we do not mean to imply an overly cognitive view of culture, but rather the full range of styles of knowing (see Howes 1991).

## Monophasic and Polyphasic Cultures

There is a distinction that is very important for us to make at this early juncture, and to keep in mind throughout the rest of this book – the difference between monophasic and polyphasic cultures. In modern materialist Western cultures, children are typically taught to disattend their dream states and to focus on adaptational interactions with the external physical world (see Mageo 2003b; Wax 2004). Children are taught from infancy that dreams are not real ("It's just a dream, dear, go back to sleep"), and thus they just happen and can be ignored. Elementary schools typically do not address one's dream life, and information obtained in dreams, if any, bears little or no relevance to the waking world. Dreams, therefore, tend not to inform culture all that much, especially with respect to spiritual issues (see Blainey 2010 on "entheophilic" vs "entheophobic" worldviews; see also Walsh 2007:Chap. 24). These Western societies exhibit what we call *monophasic cultures* (Laughlin, McManus and d'Aquili 1990:293; Laughlin and Throop 2001; McManus, Laughlin and Shearer 1993; LaHood 2007; Saniotis 2010; Rodd 2006) which tend to skew the development of consciousness away from ASC and toward perceptual and cognitive processes oriented outward to the external world.[8]

Tara Lumpkin (2001) has argued that monophasic societies operate to limit "perceptual diversity" among its members:

> In the same way, I see monophasic consciousness as one part of perceptual diversity—the part based on waking rational thought and the scientific method. But the entire system of consciousness is far more complex and, in breaking it down and valuing only one of its parts, waking rational consciousness, one loses the value of the whole. I propose that in disavowing polyphasic consciousness (perceptual diversity), we may be losing the emergent properties of polyphasic consciousness. Coming from developed Western cultures, which highly value monophasic consciousness and the scientific method, we may not even be aware of what we are losing. And it is altered states of consciousness, which speak through symbols and intuition such as dreaming, imagining, and meditating, that often allow us to grasp the whole in a way that the scientific method can never provide.

The implication here is that by developing a monophasic culture, society is in effect reducing its adaptational viability. I will return to this issue, and to Lumpkin's insights in Chapter 15.

Monophasic orientation towards dreaming leaves its mark on the research and accounts of Western anthropologists for whom dreams must often be demythologized in order for them to become meaningful – that is, the dream must make sense to rational thought in the

---

[8] We were unaware of psychologist, J.S. Szymanski's use of the terms monophasic and polyphasic sleep when we coined the terms in the '80s.

waking state to make any sense at all (Tedlock 1992b:4; Bourguignon 2003:137).⁹ I think this fact in part explains much of the attraction of Freudian dream analysis, because one need not pay serious attention to the manifest content of dreams, or to the sociocultural repercussion of dreams. Yet so extreme is the disattention to ASC in our Western European societies that complementary spiritual movements have arisen over time to assuage the sense of spiritual poverty felt by many – movements that include those focused on dreaming (see Chapter 15).

The state of affairs among modern, industrial, Western European societies stands in sharp contrast to both our own pre-industrial history and the pre-industrial histories of other modern, industrial societies such as Japan, China and Brazil during which dreaming and dream interpretation were highly valued. "People in the medieval and early modern period often saw dreams as communications from God – or from the Devil. For the ancients, dreams were perhaps more like visitations. Dreams might predict the future or carry messages" (Pick and Roper 2004:3; see also Parman 1991:Chap. 2 and 3; Kruger 2005). Aside from Western European societies, there are in excess of 4000 cultures on the planet today, and roughly 90% of them seek out and value experiences had in ASC, and especially in dreams (Bourguignon 1973; Bourguignon and Evascu 1977).

---

⁹ Demythologization is a tip-off to the monophasic conditioning of the researcher who feels the necessity to impose an "etic" analysis to tease out the dream's significance. Typical of such analyses is the distinction between the "manifest" content of the dream (the dream as experienced by the dreamer) and the "latent" content of the dream (the supposed unconscious motivation underlying the dream). Monophasic dream analysis generally requires the imposition of a Western theory of dreaming, identity and self for the meaning to become clear. This is not to say that there may not be unconscious processes going on in the dream – indeed there probably are such processes operating in every dream – but the methods used by ethnologists have frequently masked the native's own dream theory. Moreover, if the people are routinely lucid in their dreaming, the experiences will be inherently meaningful because working memory and thought are incorporated in the process. My own bias is a more transpersonal one that embraces the fact that in many societies one's identity is essentially polyphasic – that one's identity transcends the limits of the waking ego structure (Laughlin 1989, 1994a; Laughlin, McManus and Shearer 1983, 1993; Walsh and Vaughan 1980), and that the native's understanding of dreaming may be couched in transpersonal terms (see Obeyesekere 1990:65-68; Ewing 1994 on this issue).

We call these *polyphasic cultures*, meaning that they value experiences had in the dream-life, as well as those had in trance states, meditation states, drug- and ordeal-driven visions, etc. (see Locke and Kelly 1985). I am not imposing a logical-type distinction between monophasic and polyphasic cultures here – I wish to imply rather that there are also societies whose dream cultures are intermediate between extreme monophasic and polyphasic systems, and that societies do, in fact, range from no interest in dreaming to intense interest in dreaming with every combination in between. What I do wish to show is that there exists a kind of watershed between the two extremes where disattention to ASC altogether will produce an extremely monophasic standpoint, identity and culture conjoined to an extremely materialistic political economy.

I also recognize that there are individuals, indeed groups and professions, within Western society that are "into their dreams" to some extent. After all, as the reader will see in Chapter 13, I am one such maverick. But polyphasic cultures are quite different from the one to which most of us Westerners are familiar. These are societies in which dream experiences are often conceived by most people as different aspects of reality, not unreality (indeed, most people on the planet, even those in monophasic cultures, rarely if ever make a distinction between experienced reality and extramental reality). Their sense of identity incorporates memories of experiences had in dreams and other ASC, as well as had in waking life. Indeed, the people may not have a word in their native tongue that exactly glosses "dream" in the precise Indo-European sense (Basso 1992; Merrill 1992:199). What we call a "dream" may be considered by others to be the *polyphasic ego* (soul, spirit, shadow, etc.) of a person experiencing another domain of reality (e.g., Herr 1981:334 on fuzzy boundaries among Fijians between what we call dream, hallucination and vision; Merrill 1992 on this issue among the Ramámiru of Mexico). Dream experiences, just as waking experiences, inform the society's general system of knowledge about the self and the world, as well as the development of a person's identity (see Ridington and Ridington 1970). One can thus understand why ethnographer Jean-Guy Goulet's Guajiro (a South American people) hosts would not allow him to live with them unless he "knew how to dream" (1994:22). One may also understand why the anthropology of dreaming has for generations focused upon polyphasic cultures, perhaps because they are so at-odds with our Western everyday and materialist expectations (see Lang 1897; Kennedy and Langness 1981; Lincoln 1935; O'Nell 1976; Shulman and Stroumsa 1999b; Tedlock 1992a, 2003; von Grunebaum 1966; Lohmann 2003a; Mageo 2003a; Stewart 2004a, 2004b; Woods and Greenhouse 1974).

## Summary and Segue

Anthropology has a long and fascinating history of interest in dreaming and dream cultures. For Adolph Bastian, dreams held the key to some of the universal structures of the human mind, a strain of structuralist thinking that has threaded its way through the discipline to the present day. The history of the discipline wended through various theoretical and methodological orientations, each gaining purchase on the field by harshly criticizing the previous orientation. It is fair to say though that most of the attention paid to dreaming by ethnographers during the 20th century was on the variety of cultural difference. We have defined culture as an information pool, access to which defines members of the culture. And the crucial distinction has been made between monophasic and polyphasic societies, the latter characterizing the vast majority of the world's 4000-plus cultures. As we turn to the contemporary era, we will see that many of these strains in orientation continue, but some really interesting developments occur that will perhaps bring about other shifts in orientation.

# Chapter 3

# Modern Anthropological Theories of Dreaming

> It is a matter of common agreement among persons engaged in psychological investigation, whether of the Freudian school or another, as well as a matter of common experience to those who for any reason have made a definite and consistent effort to remember their own dreams, that dreams are neither an irrelevant nor an isolated mental activity, but rather a characteristic arrangement of such activity; and that, as such, they are almost certainly universal. In this connection students must recognize a widely noted primitive preoccupation with dreams, as well as the frequently recorded fact that fantasy has for nonliterate peoples varying degrees of reality. It would seem, therefore, a truism to say that any item which appears important to a group investigated cannot reasonably be ignored in an examination either of culture or of individual behavior.
>
> Dorothy Eggan (1949)

Ethnographic studies of dreaming cultures have documented how social expectations, symbolic attributions and environmental conditions may impact dreaming and the interpretation of dreams (Parman 1991; Obeyesekere 1990:54; Shulman and Stroumsa 1999b:3; Graham 2003:5). For instance, it was said by traditional Eastern Cree hunters of Labrador that, "If a man could no longer remember his dreams upon awakening, he could no longer hunt" (Flannery and Chambers 1985:4). Cree hunters, beginning in their teens, sought to have special spirit visitors appear to them in their dreams and establish a relationship with them. These visitors would then mediate between the hunter and the animals being hunted. So attention to dreaming was very important to the Cree, and they considered the loss of dream recall as aberrant.

Dreaming is a fact of life for everyone on the planet, and as we have seen, every society deals with this fact in its own way. Some societies, like we Western folk, typically ignore our dreams, unless they become relevant in therapy or in one or another spiritual practice. We know from psychological research that all it takes for us to get in touch with and involved in our dream life is merely to develop a wholehearted intention to do so – perhaps augmented by writing down one's dreams in a dream journal (that's how I began my dreamwork years ago). What do anthropologists today make of dreaming, dream reports and dream cultures cross-culturally? In the last chapter, we saw how some of our forefathers and mothers in the discipline made sense of dreaming and drew data about dream cultures into their understanding of culture as a whole. But theorizing about dreaming did not stop with Lévi-Strauss or Margaret Mead. Indeed, there are a myriad of theories about dreaming among anthropologists today that are at least as interesting as those of our ethnological forebears.

I want to consider a number of these theories in the present chapter before we move on to discussing how our brain produces the mind-movies we call dreams. I want to do this in part because anthropological descriptions tend to counter the more ethnocentric views of some neuropsychologists and other dream researchers who more often than not ignore both the phenomenological and the sociocultural aspects of dreaming. These newer theories also seem to transcend adherence to the more global theoretical fads that, as we have shown in the last chapter, characterized anthropology since its inception (e.g., evolutionism, culturology, psychoanalysis, so forth). Indeed, in contemplating cognitive neuroscience accounts of dreaming in relation to his experience as an ethnographer, Murray Wax (2004:86) suggests that it is in fact dreaming that makes possible "the intense conjoint relationships of group living." He suggests that without dreaming people go "insane" and are no longer able to operate "as sensitive, responsible social beings." In short, sleep and dreaming are requisite to society. As we shall see in the next chapter, people really do not "go bonkers" in any dramatic way with sleep loss, but this more recent finding (e.g., see Webb 1992) does not disconfirm the crux of Wax's reasoning (see Chapter 15).

So let us peruse a few of the more interesting contemporary anthropological theories of dreaming for what further light they may shed on this most mysterious and interesting part of our daily lives.

## DREAMING, IDENTITY AND THE SELF

A number of contemporary theorists have become interested in the role of dreaming in the construction of a sense of self and social identity. As the great ethnologist, Irving Hallowell (1892 – 1974) taught, self-awareness is a cultural universal, but the extent to which dream experiences are incorporated into one's self-concept will vary from person to person and culture to culture – the key variable being access to self-related memory of past dream experiences (1955:96). The immediate question is, what does "self" mean? Perhaps one's response to this is, "I know what my self is, it's *me*." This naturally takes us right back to the writings of George Herbert Mead (1863-1931) who helped found social psychology and whose writings eventually led to *symbolic interactionism* in sociology. He was focused on the social self and distinguished between the "me" – all of the socially conditioned bits and pieces of my being – and the "I" – the active center of my being that engages the world in a creative way. Taken together, the "I" and the "me" constitute the self – an entity that develops in interaction with the outside world, especially within a network of social relations and the communication with other persons (Silva 2007).

At the other extreme, the picture of the self as painted by C. G. Jung is already present in nascent form in the neuropsychological nature of the child, and does *not* depend upon culture for its existence. The nascent forms, "or archetypes" (see Chapter 10), develop during early life to form the more adult versions of the self. The self is the sum total of all that is conscious and unconscious, including the collective unconscious (i.e., the neural structures we inherit as members of our species; Jung 1931; Shamdasani 2003; Laughlin 1996). The self is the repository of all the archetypes, both nascent and developed, and archetypal imagery such as that found in dreams may be considered symbolic expressions of parts of the self emerging into consciousness. In other words, dreams may be considered communications between different parts of the self with the conscious self. This *intra-psyche communication* is required in order to keep the self from fragmenting into its constituent "complexes" – what we have elsewhere called the *holistic imperative* (Laughlin, McManus and d'Aquili 1990:150; see also Krippner and Combs 2002:79). As we shall see later on in the book, for Jung, dream symbols are the language of the complexes, and through direct phenomenological participation in one's dream life, one may take part in the organic re-organization of the self (Jung 1960; see Chapter 11).

Jeannette Marie Mageo (2003b, 2004, 2006) has brought these versions of the self together in her account of dreaming cross-culturally. She notes that for many ethnologists, the notion of the self as a unitary whole is fiction (ibid:9; see also Ewing 1990). She uses C. G. Jung's concept of the self as an example of the unitary view that she presumably rejects. In my opinion, however, this is a serious misreading, oversimplification and distortion of Jung's ideas. One need only consult his discussions of psychopathology (e.g., Jung 1960) to see that the fragmenting of the self is quite common, and at times severely maladaptive. What Jung does say in various places is that the self[1] will seek unity where possible, a very dynamic process that is ongoing and never complete, even in the healthiest of people. After all, the psyche[2] is an organic process, indeed a neurophysiological one, and just like the other organs of the body, will seek intra- and inter-organic wholeness. Jung, of course, was not the first to see the self as made of organic components seeking unity. The holistic view of self goes back in ethnology through Bastian (again) who wrote: "Since our consciousness searches for the completeness of the organism and the fullness of the individual, each malfunctioning of the thought process must necessarily lead to somatic disturbances which after a while will effect the whole of the organism" (quoted in Koepping 2005:196).

---

[1] What I mean by the word "self" in this book follows Jung's meaning – which is to say the unitary property of the psyche. For Jung, the self is an archetype – often the archetype of the holistic property of the body and brain, and may appear in dreams as mandalas, which symbolize all possible unity of opposites in the psyche (Jung 1969f).

[2] Whenever I use the word "psyche" it will be in the explicitly Jungian all-inclusive sense: "By psyche, I understand the totality of all psychic processes, conscious as well as unconscious" (Jung, 1971: Def. 48 par. 797).

But Mageo's point is very well taken, ignoring for the moment her unfortunate selection of Jung as a straw man for her argument. Social conditions can and do cause both acute and chronic fragmentation of the self to one extent or another. That is what repression and projection are all about after all, keeping hidden from consciousness aspects of the greater self that may cause problems for the ego given the person's social and environmental circumstances, and perhaps projecting them onto others. In any event, Mageo hypothesizes that in dreaming we confront the various parts of ourselves that take the guise of "figures that are condensations of several people we have known in life or in fiction" (ibid:9). As she puts it, "...dreams engage us nightly in what might be called a phenomenological descent into the self" (2003c:23). This is quite evident to anyone who has done serious Jungian dream (or active imagination) work. A movie actress or a girlfriend might pop up in dreams representing the male dreamer's *anima* – the unconscious feminine parts he has repressed over a lifetime in order to face the social world as a male, and that one may project outwards onto the people.[3] Through interaction within the dream-world — an inner *theater of mind* (Laughlin, McManus and d'Aquili 1990: Chap. 8) in which the various complexes interact as characters in a saga of the depths – one may come to read the internal state of the self-system at that time. For example, one may note which figures from one's waking life are associated with fear, revulsion, hatred, anger, aversion, lust, affection, etc., and thus come to understand what parts of one's self are being projected out upon the world. And through the twin processes of condensation and projection, our dream characters impact both the self and the Other, or as Mageo (2003b:10) writes:

> The self, then, is much larger than its conscious identifications; dreaming provides insight into the congeries of identities that it encompasses. ...[O]ne might view the self as involving a continuing process of incorporating others to make an identity. In dreams this identity is then splintered into part selves who derive from these others and who carry our emotional reactions

---

[3] I know this process well, but obviously cannot speak of the process from the female point of view, especially as the female confrontation with her *animus* is not just a mirror image of the male's.

to them. Upon waking, the part selves we meet in dreams are projected back onto others, who later enter our dreams representing our own feelings for us – and so-on ad infinitum.

For Mageo (2004:151), there is an essential incompleteness to the elements and symbols of a dream. This "quasi-opacity of dream memories" (ibid:152) calls out for interpretation. We are impelled to seek meaning in the dream memory – assuming we are not more lucid and the meaning is already present in the dream – even if we are a typical member of a monophasic culture and we label the dream as inconsequential, as "just a dream" and not relevant to us in our waking life. This refers to what my colleague, Eugene d'Aquili, liked to call the *cognitive imperative*: the wired-in function of the neurocognitive system to "assimilate and order" novel stimuli into one's more or less coherent cognized world (1972:8; d'Aquili, Laughlin and McManus 1979:167; Laughlin, McManus and d'Aquili 1990:166). Dream symbols are like holograms, Mageo suggests: "The images of dreams, I propose, are projections of patterns left by life inadequately mediated by schemas, which are aptly rendered as incomplete figures" (ibid:153). This is in keeping with the fact that our neurocognitive system operates on a *symbolic principle* (Laughlin, McManus and d'Aquili 1990:163) by which anything we perceive, in dream, vision or ordinary waking consciousness operates as a symbol that penetrates into our neural networks to complete their meaning. The difference between most dreamers in a monophasic culture and those in polyphasic cultures is the extent to which this penetration *occurs within the dream.*

Mageo (2001, 2004) has developed an interesting technique for fleshing out the meaning of dreams among her Samoan students. Being a type of projective technique, she calls her role-playing method "dream play" in which a student picks a favorite character out of a dream and acts it out. The student carries on conversations in the dream persona and is addressed by others in that persona. Mageo's intent was to flesh out what she called the "hole" in the student, which made sense to them because apparently Samoans conceive of the self as being many faceted. The results of this method are just fascinating. I would like to quote Mageo's (2004:155) report at length so as to give an accurate portrayal of the method:

Let us turn to the first dream. I call the young woman who dreamed it Lau.

> I am in a party at the Utulei beach. There are many people having fun, drinking and enjoying themselves. I am sitting under a tree and watching what people do. I'm sitting by myself. I then turn to my left side, and there is a child, a little girl. She is so pretty. She walks by herself toward the beach. When she reaches the waves, then she stops and looks all around. . . . I get up and start walking to her and she keeps on looking while I am walking. I ask her, but she doesn't answer.

The little girl's speech is the missing part in this dream. Without prompting from me, Lau first chose to role-play her.

> *Girl:* I'm White, blond hair, blue eyes, 3 years old and I can't speak English or Samoan. I speak Spanish.

Here an absence of speech, a pure negative, is replaced by linguistic inability. Next, Lau chose to role-play the blond hair.

> *Lau:* You are so nice. Can I have yourself?
> *Hair:* Thank you, how come you like me?
> *Lau:* Because you look great and I want you to be mine.
> *Hair:* Well, it's okay, but you can't have myself.
> *Lau:* Why? Please, I really like you.
> *Hair:* Well, even though you like me, just forget it.
> *Lau:* Please, it's better for me to have you or else someone comes and destroys you.
> *Hair:* It's okay. I don't care.

Lau concluded, "The part of me the image hair represents is . . . I'm good for looking for a good husband." One might not see why a pretty child would represent a young woman's attractiveness, but in practice looking is what this girl does. In the dream report, Lau says the dream girl "looks all around . . . and she keeps on looking." In old Samoa, hypergamy [seeking a spouse of equal

> or higher status], "looking for a good husband," meant pursuing a man whose offspring would forward family status; this was a key practice associated with the girl's role... . One method through which girls sought to attract high-status husbands was through bodily display. Hair decoration was a part of this display. Typically, girls shaved their heads but left tufts and tails hanging down, which were often bleached to a light reddish shade... .

Not only does the method work wonders in a therapeutic and pedagogical sense, but also as a way of integrating cross-state meanings – that is developing a system of meanings that are integrated with respect to symbols encountered in more than one SOC. In a very real sense, Mageo's approach to dream analysis is analogous to the relations that may exist between myth and ritual drama in some societies (see Turner 1982; Schechner and Turner 1985). Moreover, it presents a laboratory for exploring the psychodynamic effects of ritual performance of dreams which does occur among some peoples (e.g., see Chapter 8 for dream performance among the Xavante people of Central Brazil).

## Selfscape Dreams

Likewise focusing upon the relations between the individual's self and his or her society, Douglas Hollan (2003b, 2004, 2009) has isolated for analysis what he calls *selfscape dreams* – memorable dreams that "reflect back to the dreamer how his or her current organization of self relates various parts of itself to itself, its body, and other people and objects in the world" (2004:172). Selfscape dreams leave a distinct emotional and imaginal memory, and operate to mediate the dynamics of the self with the dynamics of both the internal and external cognized world (see Chapter 11). These dreams are found universally because, although they may vary in detail from place to place, they perform the same psychological function, that being an expression of the self and its transformations to the dream ego (2009:320). Quite naturally then, the selfscape dream may perform in this way in the aftermath of trauma. "Whether or not disturbing dreams or nightmares reported in the aftermath of traumatic events give us an undistorted re-presentation of those events, they tell us something very important about the dreamer's state of self, perhaps at the moment the trauma occurred, but certainly in the present, as the person copes with memories or reminders of past experiences" (Hollan 2009:319).

Trauma sustained in childhood can have a profound influence on the development of the self over a lifetime, and expressions of self-organization in dreams (Barrett 1996; Kalsched 1996; Nader 1996). A dreamworker, or a healer working through the dreams of a patient can come into contact with a virtually encysted complex, sealed off from the rest of the self and often working at cross-purposes with the adult ego – very much Mageo's fragmented self. I will offer a personal example of this process in Chapter 13. Working with, or through the medium of the selfscape dream may well be one of the most potent methods of psyche re-integration available. We will return to this topic in Chapter 11 when we discuss selfscape dreams as a form of intra-psyche communication.

## Self and the Function of Dreaming

My mentor in graduate school at the University of Oregon was ethnologist Joseph G. Jorgensen, an ethnologist and methodologist of the first water. I remember one class in which he was lambasting structural-functionalist explanations because of the logical fallacies upon which their arguments were so often based. Then he said, "But you know, everybody is a functionalist when you get right down to it" – or words to that effect. I later understood what he meant after I had done some ethnographic fieldwork of my own and could easily see how this ritual or that exchange had the effect of keeping things flowing and together. If one looks carefully enough, one can discern a functionalist element in all the various schools of anthropological theory we discussed in the last chapter. And functional accounts still arise today with respect to dreaming and society.

Murray L. Wax has been reflecting upon the functions of dreaming for a long time, but what is particularly interesting to me is that he thinks about dreaming in both its neurobiological and its sociocultural contexts (1998, 2004). Modern neuroscience removes the experience of dreaming from the natural context of intimate social relations and ethos of the dreamer and re-frames dreaming as a cognitive process: "Current neuropsychological research addresses *behavior* and mental processes attributed to *the brain* regarded as a *wet computer*... . Research attention is deflected from the relationships and responsibilities of social interaction and toward cognitive process. Yet viewed historically, the facts are that human beings at all times and places have required sleep and engaged in dreaming. From an evolutionary perspective, this is striking. What functions are thereby being served" (2004:86)?

I am reminded of the story told by Emil W. Menzel, a renowned comparative psychologist who worked on primate intelligence, curiosity and creativity. He tells of spending a lot of lab time early in his career testing the intelligence of olive baboons and reaching the conclusion that they were pretty stupid animals (1967). Later on, circumstances took him to Kenya for a conference and while there he took the opportunity to take a look at his beloved baboons in the wild. Well, to make a short story even shorter, he stood among the baboon troops aghast at how intelligent they appeared to be on their own home ground. He learned there and then an important lesson which he urged upon his fellow researchers – namely, make sure your laboratory questions make sense relative to the real environment of the animal in the wild. So too with neuroscience and dreaming. We need not ignore what neuroscience has to tell us about the dreaming brain, but it is up to us as anthropologists to put their findings in the proper context. And that is what Wax does by pointing out the fact that dreaming is universal and that it is always situated in a sociocultural context. What then can be the function of dreaming in that evolutionary context?

> I hypothesize that it is *dreaming* that enables the intense conjoint relationships of group living. The data have long been evident. Without REM [rapid eye movement] sleep – without dreaming – people become "insane": Not only do they deteriorate in mechanical and cognitive abilities, but they lose the very capacity to comport themselves as sensitive, responsible social beings.

Wax's insight is, I think, quite sound, even pivotal (see Chapter 15). He urges us to consider the universal biological factors producing sleep and dreaming before we raise questions about the meaning of dreams – something we will do in the next chapter. He argues that both sleep/dreaming and group adaptation have been with us as long as we have been social primates. Dreaming, in other words, is a necessary condition for social life. Standing Freud's wish fulfillment on its head, Wax suggests that dreams "deal with the problematics of living and growing" (2004:86). Sharing one's dreams with others of the group, a quite common practice cross-culturally (see Chapter 8), has the effect of increasing the psychological adjustments necessary for social life by, among other things, letting others in on one's real feelings about things.

## Dreaming and the Adjustment of the Self

A special issue of the journal *History and Anthropology* (21(3)) is full of papers in which dreaming is seen to function as a mechanism for making adjustments to the self in relation to dynamic circumstances in the society and environment of the individual. In the introductory article to that volume, Adriënne Heijnen and Iain Edgar note that all too often anthropologists have presumed that while the waking life of a person is embedded in social interaction and communication, the dream life is a very idiosyncratic domain in which society has little influence. On the contrary, they write (2010:220-221):

> Our argument is that dreams are evoked not only by childhood memory or basic emotions, but also by experiences of the dreamer, cosmologies and embodied knowledge on the nature of social relationships and shared cultural knowledge – among others, dream theories. Evidence for this can be provided by the experience of anthropologists who have conducted fieldwork on dreams in societies other than their own... . With time, as understanding of local dream theories deepens and the knowledge learned in the new context becomes embodied, anthropologists have noticed that some of the images appearing in their own dreams began to resemble the images which are considered to be

important in the local context. Dreams ... are not the evidence of a withdrawal from the world but emerge from and in their turn influence social life.

In other words, culturally patterned events, interactions and experiences had in waking life can and do have a profound influence in how the individual mind constructs its dreams. Hiejnen (2010) offers the simple example of pregnant women in Iceland who dreamed that an ancestor was passing their name on to their unborn child, and this was acted upon. This is a case where the dreamer and the dream are but a conduit between a past generation and the future generation, thus being influenced by and influencing social relations.

## ANIMISM AND DREAMING REDUX

Among many societies, people will say that everything in their environment consists of an external perceptual aspect, and an inner, living spiritual aspect. Common objects — from our Western viewpoint both "organic" (birds, trees, grass, people, fish, etc.) and "inorganic" (rocks, mountains, whirlwinds, rain, etc.) – are alive. For example, among the more traditional Navajo people (or *Diné* as they call themselves) who live in the American southwest, and among whom I lived and worked off and on during the 1990s, the world is essentially a spiritual cosmology addressing most of the "matters of ultimate concern" that define any of the world's major religions. What makes Navajo religion so very interesting is its emphasis upon the central concept of *hózhó* – a term that is hard to gloss in English, but which is usually translated as "beauty," or "harmony." The term, however, also carries the connotations of "proper order," "health," "good" (including its moral sense), etc. *Hózhó* is a spiritual path, a way of life, an ideal and dynamic process of living, and is a quality that one wants to realize in one's being to match its natural counterpart in nature (Witherspoon 1977:151).

The Navajo — like so many other peoples around the globe — have noticed that we cannot actually see the air that surrounds us and that we breathe. We only know air by its movement and its effects (rustling of leaves, whirling dust, the sensation of the breeze on our skin, etc.). Not surprising then, that in Navajo cosmology the hidden, vital, motivating dimension of things is called *nilch'i*, or "wind" (McNeley, 1981). Physical reality — indeed, all things in the perceptual world, including people — are motivated by this one, vast, cosmic Holy Wind that flows in and out of all things (*bii'asti*, the "animating energy within"), and that underlies and vitalizes the normally hidden totality of the universe. Wind underlies the vitality, dynamics and movement of nature, from the contemplation of which people may attain their intuitions about the purpose of existence. And it is an imbalance or disruption of that portion of the "wind that stands within" (*nilch'i hwii'siziinii*; McNeley, 1981) each person that leads to disease and misfortune.

Small wonder then, that dreaming is of prime importance to the Navajo (Morgan 1932; Dadosky 1999; Krippner and Thompson 1996; Lincoln 1935:207-240 *passim*). Navajo interest in dreams centers primarily on maintaining the individual's and the group's state of *hózhó* – in this case meaning wellness (Reichard 1990:550; Sandner 1991). Dreams may indicate a number of things that may influence health, including the possibility of a "skinwalker" (werewolf) attack, childhood dog or snake bite, future drought, and so forth (see Chapter 9 on Navajo healing). As with many peoples, the temporal orientation of dreams is more generally upon the future – divining problems before they arise. Dreams are the experience of the "wind that stands within" one — or more simply put, their spirit. In dreams one may seek guidance, uncover one's spiritual path, diagnose problems, and communicate with the spirits of other beings and things, all being aspects of the one Holy Wind. Dreams of particular spirits, like that of a bear, skinwalker or ghost may require a healing ceremony, depending upon the views of a diagnostician (Morgan 1932; Sandner 1991:30-33). Thus, the Navajo present us with a classic animistic cosmology. The whole universe and everything in it is alive, animated by the inner essence of the all encompassing Holy Wind. Moreover, the Navajo understand, as do all peoples on the planet, that most of the causality operating in everyday life is, like the wind, invisible to waking consciousness, but can be perceived in the dream state. This is the situation that leads in many societies to the presumption of a universal spiritual force imbuing motivation and meaning to otherwise inexplicable events.

Nurit Bird-David (1999; see also Nielsen 1991) has offered us a beautifully reasoned re-evaluation of Tylor's concept of animism, controlling as she does for both modernist and materialist attitudes biasing the views of many anthropological critics. She makes the point that for many peoples, the absolute body-spirit (body-mind) duality inherent in Western thinking will not do as an ethnological standpoint. For many peoples, dreaming is a portal into a parallel reality (see also MacDonald et al. 1988 on portalling), one in which one may experience the inner essence of beings and things, including one's self. People who have dream cultures do not merely *believe* the dream world *to be* real, they *experience* the dream world *as* real – just as we Westerners are conditioned to experience our waking states as reality, despite ample phenomenological and neuropsychological evidence that everyday reality too is but a construct of our brain.

Bird-David notes that early critics of Tylor asserted that animism referred to a "childish" error of logic by which the "primitive" mind projected his/her own psychological nature onto everything around them. They generally fail to understand that people with polyphasic dream cultures *experience other beings and things around them as being animate*, having consciousness and capable of communication. Indeed, the Navajo speak of the inner essence of all beings and things as "people," as in all the various Holy People (*Diyin Diné'e*): Blue Corn Boy, Big Fly, Water Sprinkler, Child of the Water, etc. As a consequence of realizing all this, Bird-David stands the typical critique of Tylor and animism on its head — namely, "Can it be that a Tylorian kind of 'dream thesis' helps explain not the emergence of primitive animism but, to the contrary, the modernist break from it" (ibid:S79)? Instead of the so-called "primitive" mind having made a drastic logical error, might the error not be on the part of monophasic Western thinking? Might not the distortion of understanding of traditional polyphasic peoples by modern ethnologists derive from their inability to enter the domain of dream life so commonplace among many other peoples? And might not dream reality constitute a special experiential domain in which the principle of *entelechy*[4] operates to make the normally invisible forces in the world visible, alive and interactive – a visible reality so palpably

---

[4] The vital force motivating beings and things.

real that it is projected directly upon the world without any necessary reference to "waking" rationality? Consider how fluidly people in a dream culture may shift from one SOC to another, with each SOC interacting with the others. Ruth Underhill (1936:42) quotes a Papago Indian woman who, becoming tired of working in her field, lay down on the ground to rest:

> In front of me was a hole in the earth made by the rains, and there hung a gray spider, going up and down, up and down, on its long thread. I began to go to sleep and I said to it: "Won't you fall?" Then the spider sang to me:
>
> > Gray spider
> > Magic making
> > At the cave entrance hanging
> > Do not think I shall fall
> > Twice I go up and down
> > And I return again
> > Therefore I am hanging, hanging here.

It is true to say that among the Papago people of the American southwest that dreaming is a very interactive process. A Papago may wander by a particularly intriguing rock formation and make a note to return there at night (read: in their dream) and listen to the story of the rock (Underhill 1946). They may then share the story with others and that rock becomes a part of the sacred landscape.

## Animism, Simulacra and Anthropomorphism

As we shall see in the next chapter, our experiential world in any SOC is a movie projected onto reality. For example, everyone knows the experience of looking into the clouds and seeing faces, or looking at mountains and seeing reclining figures, breasts, wings, sailing ships, so forth. Everybody on the planet has experienced this at one time or another. The figure is called a *simulacrum* (pl. *simulacra*), and among many peoples the phenomenon is associated with both dreaming and animism within their dream cultures. Paul Devereux (1992, 1997, 2000, 2010) has thought long and hard about simulacra and the origins of religion. According to Devereux, a simulacrum is, "the illusory image of a face, castle, animal, human figure or other shape or form seen in the chance configurations of clouds, the coals of fire, the bark of a tree, reflections in water, the cracks, crevices and projections of a rock face, or other surface" (2000, p.157; see also Michell 1979 for a cross-cultural compendium of simulacra). Cultures all over the planet recognize sacred places that are named for these chance resemblances; for instance, Sleeping Ute Mountain in Colorado, the Paps ("breasts" in Gaelic) of Jura in the Hebrides, or the Grandfather and Grandmother rocks on Samui Island off Thailand (Devereux 2010:24-37).

The neuropsychology of this phenomenon is clear enough (Laughlin and Loubser 2010). The human brain is designed to apperceive whole events and objects from partial sensory information (see Chapter 5). The mind abstracts patterns of sensory information and makes sense of them. We never have all the possible information about anything we perceive. A flash of yellow in the grass becomes a lion on the prowl, and everyone heads for the trees. Whether or not an actual lion is present, the reaction is adaptive, for the brain does not have to take the time for the full presence of the lion before it makes a judgement and takes action. The implications of these humble beginnings of symbolic cognition are quite significant, for it seems highly likely that the evolution of iconography ran something like this: The natural facility of the brain to apperceive whole objects from partial sensory data – a proclivity that among other things allows the evolution of various kinds of imitative defense adaptations among animals (e.g., moths whose wing patterns look like owls) – eventually led to the recognition in simulacra of forms considered vital to individual development and to an adaptive worldview for the group. Perhaps individuals began to recognize – literally *re*-cognize or apperceive — natural objects as symbols linked to salient and emotionally charged images encountered in their dreams and visions. They recognized in natural formations the images of group leaders, ancestors, archetypal dream figures, mythological characters encountered in stories and dramas, or figures and geometrical patterns encountered after consuming psychoactive herbs. Because these images were considered powerful, numinous and sacred (i.e., related to mythic lore), so too were the evocative natural features in the environment. The landscape itself became deeply endowed with symbolic-cosmic meaning, rich with the suggestive power of spiritual significance (Devereux 1992, 2010).

Through the evocative power of simulacra, features in the local environment could have operated as a mnemonic device to bring both external and internal reality into accord by way of shared symbolism, and perhaps even as ritual drivers producing dreams and other ASC. By way of ASC, or symbolism associated with extraordinary experiences, such simulacra could accrue the power to actually evoke elements of the cosmology by themselves. For instance, these simulacra might have evoked experiences which brought to mind the existence of divine beings, normally invisible power grids and lines, and attributes of multiple realities encountered in dreams and visions; for, in recognizing symbolic images in what would otherwise be considered inanimate natural objects, individuals might have come to perceive the mysterious workings of hidden forces and divine beings. Moreover, perception of naturally occurring features could possibly index extra-sensory realms of causality and have given rise not only to the idea that there was more than one reality, but, that there was also some significant (perhaps even causal) connection between multiple realities. This may well have lead to the first pilgrimages in which natural features became associated with powerful entities and events that occurred in mythic times, and re-enacted in ritual dramas and in incubated dreams. Thus, the landscape became "sacred" and movement in and around simulacra could operate to remind participants of the timeless relation between contemporary and mythic eras.

As humans became technically more proficient, they became capable of altering and elaborating simulacra and the landscape to enhance the evocative power of symbolically rich natural features. Perhaps they built in additional features – e.g., altered the acoustics of caves and other chambers to enhance the effects of singing and chanting (Devereux 2010:125-137; Jahn, Devereux & Ibison, 1996) and projected entoptic images as ornamentation (Lewis-Williams and Dowson 1988). Perhaps they also added impressionistic imagery to cave walls and sacred landmarks for the purposes of initiation, pilgrimage, dream incubation, so forth. Thus the facility of the simulacra and landscape for evoking

ASC, and as reminders of such experiences, became elaborated and more effective at renewing the associations between individual dream and trance experiences and the people's numinous cosmology. Eventually, humans became so technically proficient that they could produce wholly artificial icons from raw materials – perhaps the historical origin of sacred art – and thus free themselves entirely from dependence upon naturally occurring simulacra. Architecture and iconography came to prevail in human symbolism – in some cultures tied in with notions of a sacred landscape (e.g., Australian Aboriginal Dream Time, Chinese *fung sui*), and in other cultures with little, if any reference to landscape or other natural simulacra.

## Psychoanalysis and Dream Culture

Lest I leave the reader with the impression that Freudian thinking is a thing of the past and no longer playing a role in contemporary theory, rest assured that it is alive and well in the anthropological study of dreaming (Dombeck 1991:14-22; see also Van de Castle 1994). Mind you, I may well give the psychoanalytic approach short shrift, for I remain very skeptical of the projection of Freudian notions by Western analysts upon the presumed "latent" content of the dreams of traditional peoples (e.g., a number of the authors in Mageo 2003a; see also Kilborne 1981:180, 1992; Foulkes 1985).[5] Aside from being fallaciously *post hoc* and unfalsifiable, such analyses fail in my opinion to respect the native's own explanations and local theories of dreaming (Irwin 1994:11; Wax 2004; Harris 2009:9). I am not saying there may not be latent content to native dreams – there almost certainly is — but the imposition of strict Freudian attributions is no way to discover such content. Even in our own Western context, the same dream may inspire different interpretations, even among psychoanalysts (Wax 1999:2) – naturally raising the question which interpretation is the "real" one? No, we must learn to come at the issue of latent content from a better angle. We may,

---

[5] Such methods are examples of what anthropologists call "etic" analysis, as opposed to "emic" analysis which begins with the way the natives understand their experiences (see Headland, Pike, and Harris 1990).

for instance, carry out a closer study of the peoples' own dream typologies and local theories of interpretation. To remain empirically authentic, all dream research among traditional peoples should begin with the *dream experience* itself (see Tedlock 1981; Irwin 1994:5; Stephen 1995; also see Chapter 4 on the necessity for a "radical empiricism" in dream research), which after all is intrinsically coherent and meaningful (Irwin 1994:15), and then proceed to elicit the native dream report, dream sharing, local dream theories and uses – a methodology that implies that the ethnographer enter the field with the expectation of *learning about native dreaming by dreaming themselves and sharing their dreams with their hosts where appropriate* (see Chapter 6).

But in more recent times, many of the obvious criticisms of the Freudian approach found in *The Interpretation of Dreams* have been dealt with. One glaring failing was the view that the manifest content of dreams reported by native informants was irrelevant – it was only the latent content that counted. This approach was so pervasive in psychological anthropology during the mid-20th century that it led Dorothy Eggan to write, "Freudian dream theory and interpretative techniques had so firm a grip on the minds of most researchers that it was virtually impossible to think in terms of manifest content only" (1961:555). Also, the practice of ignoring the influence of native cosmology and dream culture upon the meaning of dreams has slackened a lot since the early "culture and personality" days.

Melford Spiro (b. 1920) is one of the most influential figures in this tradition and his most recent formulation of this approach is based on the assumption that one must take into account the interleaving of psychodynamic and cultural processes (e.g., the relationship between defense mechanisms and replication of anxiety-provoking cultural ideologies), if one is going to adequately understand both the impact of culture on consciousness and the impact of consciousness on culture (1994, 1997). Spiro contends that theories of cultural reproduction that do not address the interrelationship between culture and consciousness in the context of psychological pre-adaptation are at a significant disadvantage in explaining why it is that empirically false and anxiety-provoking cultural propositions are often still internalized by cultural participants – there to manifest themselves in dreams. For example, Spiro interprets the "Ideology of the Superior Male" and the "Ideology of the Dangerous Female" in Burma as cultural resources that may be utilized by social actors in the construction of "culturally constituted defense mechanisms" that pop up in dreams and fantasies. As he notes, while these two ideologies are empirically false and anxiety-provoking, they are still readily internalized by Burmese men. According to Spiro, these ideologies are perpetuated in Burma, as well as in other cultures, because they are ultimately beneficial both to the individuals who internalize them and to the culture that constitutes them. Individuals who internalize these belief systems are able to partially fulfill in dreams what would otherwise be frustrated unconscious wishes and desires. At the same time, the culture of these individuals facilitate the reproduction of cultural forms by recruiting intra-psychic conflict in the service of cultural propositions, and in the process motivate the enactment of socially sanctioned roles.

## Jovenil's Dream

Ethnographer and psychoanalyst Waud Kracke has developed the use of Freudian methods in clinical interviews with informants among the Kagwahiv people of Amazonia (1981, 1992, 2003). In these interviews, often many discussions with the same informant over a lengthy period of time, Kracke was able to elicit dreams within the context of a thorough background in the local cosmology and dream culture. Although I cannot do justice to the complexity of his analysis of the dream, I will give the reader a taste of the kind of work this involves. One of his most articulate informants, Jovenil, reported this dream during the sixth of a lengthy series of interviews (Kracke 1981:265):

> José Bahut [an older man, of the opposite moiety] was having intercourse with his wife [Camelia]. Everyone saw it. Suddenly his dick was very big. Patricio [Camelia's younger half-brother] grabbed his dick and pulled it, and it snapped. "Why did you break my dick?" "Because you were screwing my sister!" Patricio was fixing José's dick with a vine thong, and it got real thin. – It's funny, my dream! – Aí, they said, "Did your dick snap?" Aí, a lot of blood came out, his dick got rotten. Patricio fixed his dick,

it got real thin. Homero [Patricio and Camelia's father] scolded Patricio. "Why did you snap his dick? He'll die!" "No, he won't die," he said.

In order to understand this curious dream, one must first understand that Jovenil, the dreamer, was in mourning for his dead children. One must also understand that the Kagwahiv are organized patrilineally[6] with totemic patrimoieties,[7] and that they live in small groups and take a great interest in their dreams, often sharing them, especially with their healers. By associating the dream elements with other information volunteered by Jovenil, Kracke was able to get the informant to relate the dream to childhood events, like having once seen José Bahut's penis when Jovenil was still a boy, and having received a scolding from his mother. Moreover, dreaming of a vagina is equated in local dream culture with dreaming of one's self being cut, and hence, considered a dangerous portent.

The role taken by Kracke was apparently to draw attention to different elements encountered in the interviews so that the informant himself could see the associations, and thus hopefully relieve his underlying anxiety, anguish and guilt. What ties the dream in with Jovenil's mourning for his children is the fact, also elicited in the series of interviews, that José Bahut's young wife Camelia was Jovenil's parallel cousin[8] (his "sister") with whom he had an incestuous relationship as an adolescent. Kracke suggests that if Jovenil be substituted for José in the dream, it might make clearer an underlying sense of guilt and anxiety over the consequences of his illicit affair - consequences that might have included the death of his children.

As I say, the process by which Kracke unravels the latent content of Jovenil's dreams is both interesting and complex, but this is sufficient,

---

[6] Descent through the male line: me, my father, my father's father, etc.

[7] Society divided into two halves with respect to marriage eligibility, and associated with a totemic symbol like wombat, wallaby, kangaroo, etc.

[8] In a patrilineal society, my father's brother's children are my parallel cousins, and normally they will be called by the same term as my brothers and sisters. My "brother" may be my biological brother or my father's brother's son. My parallel cousin "sister" would be as taboo as my own biological sister.

I think, to give a flavor of the method — and to point out why I feel uncomfortable with Freudian dream analysis in non-Western settings. Consider if you will, to what extent is Kracke "discovering" the latent guilt behind the dream, and to what extent is he projecting it upon the manifest narrative. His story is compelling – I would even bank on him being right – but ultimately one cannot know, for there is no independent method for confirming the analysis. As Heijnen and Edgar (2010:219) note, "…when anthropologists are confronted with dream theories whereby dreams are interpreted as gateways to other temporal and spatial realms, hermeneutics still often arise from a psychological and/or psychoanalytical paradigm, evoking an analysis whereby local interpretations are deconstructed and substituted by universal meanings, such as feelings of fear, which in their turn are thought to become transformed into cultural messages in the process of communicating these feelings by culturally accepted means."

## Poststructuralism and Postmodernism

Every generation or so anthropology seems to undergo a paroxysm of self-doubt and reformation. These are episodes of self-criticism motivated out of moral or political concerns having very little to do with the actual collection of ethnographic data or a paradigm shift in theory, and everything to do with philosophical and historical events happening at the time. One of these episodes occurred, as mentioned in the last chapter, under the influence of Boas' intense desire to rid anthropology of any vestige of racism. Another arose in the 1970s as a response to the so-called "second wave" of feminist politics that began in the 1960s. And another also occurred in the 1970s when the profession discovered that ethnography had been used during the Vietnam War as a cover for espionage by the CIA (see Jorgensen and Wolf 1970). Still another episode occurred in reaction against structuralism with the so-called "poststructuralism" and "postmodernism" movements initiated by the philosophical ruminations of a number of mainly French writers, among them Michel Foucault, Jacques Derrida, Pierre Bourdieu, Roland Barthes and Gilles Deleuze. There are fine distinctions to be made between poststructuralism and postmodernism, but overall they amount to the same thing with respect to our present topic, and would not be worth mentioning except for the influence these philosophers have had on anthropology in general, and the ethnographic study of dreaming in particular.

*Postmodernism* is a philosophical view that is essentially anti-science, anti-theory-building and anti-objectivism, and holds that any intellectual activity that de-humanizes people, or makes their communication, interaction, or selves an object of scientific scrutiny is wrong-headed, insensitive and destructive. The whole business of postmodernism is very vague when you get right into it – there are as many postmodernisms as there are postmodernists, and the actual effect on the doing of ethnography has been virtually nil (see Pool 1991) – except as we saw above to redirect the focus of questions more toward "personhood," the self and interactions between selves — in itself, a very useful outcome. However, other effects have been less benign. The movement has virtually paralyzed some ethnographers from writing straightforward accounts of their data. The writing of ethnography itself has become hugely problematical for some researchers (Clifford and Marcus 1986; Spencer 2001). As a result some really tangential writing customs got changed – for instance, folks we used to call "informants" or "subjects" become "co-investigators" or "co-researchers." Jargon changed to become more politically correct, but the way we collect data has remained pretty much the same as advocated by Boas in the early 20$^{th}$ century.

The over-politicized movement of the 1980s and 1990s has also had a much more important and unfortunate effect in quelling hypothesis-testing and theory-building – a process that is at the very heart of science. This has left many young anthropologists in confusion about their project (Lather 2001). My take on it all is that postmodern anthropology may be considered just one more cultural reaction against Adolf Bastian's project (see Chapter 2) which, by its very nature, requires the eventual development of a science of universal structures and properties capable of explaining the apparent diversity of cultural forms. For whatever historical and cultural reasons, anthropology continues to resist becoming a nomological, "normal" science, and continues on as a naturalistic enterprise analogous to biology before Darwin and chemistry before Dmitri Mendeleev and the periodic table (see Kuznar 2008 and Lett 1997 on this issue).

As I say, I would not take the time for this issue, were it not for the fact that postmodernist rhetoric has had a pernicious effect upon both anthropological theory-construction and comparative ethnology, and has even seeped into the anthropology of dreaming (see Barbara Tedlock's 1991 diatribe against the kind of dream research done by comparativists like Hall and Domhoff 1963a, 1963b, 1964, Domhoff 1996 and Hall and Van de Castle 1966.). Science, however, is on about causation, and, as virtually all epistemologies among the world's cultures will attest, most causation is invisible – hidden from direct perception. This fact also looms large in the study of dream-related epistemology, as we shall see. Seeking, discovering and modeling causation is the *sine qua non* of science, and science accomplishes this endeavor through theory-building – the construction of statements about the world that both make causation visible, and that are tied very closely to observation (experimentation and fieldwork). Yet postmodernists appear to find this process demeaning to humans when we study ourselves as the scope of inquiry. Unfortunately for their position, the only way that a science of human society and culture can proceed is by way of theory-building, and the construction of theories requires the application of a comparative method (Fred Eggan 1954). I, for one, never felt demeaned when I volunteered as a subject in sleep studies in the Carleton University sleep lab, and have never considered what I was doing as an ethnographer among various peoples as demeaning to my hosts and informants.

## SUMMARY AND SEGUE

Contemporary anthropology continues to be interested in dreaming and in dream cultures around the world, and good solid ethnographic data continue to be produced from the field. The orientation of dream ethnographers has shifted, as it always has, influenced by the fads and theories that are so much a part of the anthropological scene. Many have focused on the role of dreaming in the development or construction of the social self. Also, there has been some resistance to wholesale acceptance of Freudian analysis used in non-Western settings. Some structuralist thinking has surfaced to enrich ethnological explanations of the functions of dreaming. And Tylor's suggestion that religion first arose from dream encounters with spirits has had a resurgence. But the influence of anti-scientific dogmas ("postmodernism") has had a dampening effect upon theory-building and comparative research in ethnology generally, and ethnographic dream research in particular.

Meanwhile, dream research in the neurosciences has burgeoned to the point where the exclusion of neurobiological data and theories from the anthropological purview is not only counterproductive, it is just silly. We now know a good deal more about how the brain mediates dreaming and other ASC than was available to Boas, Lincoln or Mead. We will begin to introduce some of these data and insights in the next chapter so that, as we move forward into the fascinating range of ethnographic data on dreaming, we do not leave our bodies behind. Keeping the brainmind in mind will maintain the right balance, I think, so that we will come out the other side with the ingredients necessary to build a general neuroanthropological account of dreaming and dream culture.

# Chapter 4

# Experience and the Dreaming Brain

> ...[T]he self is not a seamless, unfractionated whole, but rather the end product of a complicated series of feedforward and feedback loops within a broad and open system of information exchange. This self system encompasses the synaptic structure of the brain, intrapersonal processes of memory and symbolic formation, and interpersonal, self-other configurations as organized and shaped through familial, social, and historical processes.
>
> Douglas Hollan (2003)

When we "dream," what we are really doing is experiencing while we are asleep. It is a curious fact about anthropology that while the discipline has evinced great interest in dreaming and dream cultures over the century and a half of its existence, it has shown little interest in sleeping. True, one will find lots of information in the ethnographic literature about the cultural accouterments of sleep; who one sleeps with, when and where one sleeps, what one wears while sleeping, varieties of sleeping surfaces, beliefs about sleep, etc. (see Super *et al.* 1996). But little can be found pertaining to sleep itself. Yet it is obvious to anyone that dreaming is somehow connected with sleeping. Think about it. Anthropologists on the whole embrace Darwinian evolution which incorporates the notion that species evolve adaptive ways of behaving in order to live long enough to propagate their kind. Yet here we are, a "nearly-hairless ape" who, along with other animals with brains, sleep a good third of our lives, virtually comatose and vulnerable to predation, attack, fire, falling trees, flash floods and other dangers. As sleep involves massive paralysis of our perceptual systems and skeletal muscles, as well as virtual unconsciousness with respect to our physical environment, we spend a third of our lives in a condition in which our ability to respond to real-world contingencies is seriously diminished. Why then does everybody need to sleep? What do we get out of it? That we *do* need sleep is beyond question. So it seems obvious that sleeping and its associated dream states must have biological functions that in some way "beef-up" the fitness of our species (not to mention the fitness of dolphins who have to sleep with only one side of their brains at a time so they won't drown).

## Why Do We Sleep?

As we noted in the last chapter, if we are systematically deprived of sleep, we do experience some cognitive and behavioral deficits, although not from the loss of REM sleep as Murray Wax suggested (see Webb 1992). Loss of REM sleep, wrongly associated early in sleep research with total loss of dreaming, does not appear to drive people crazy (Siegel 2003:96). Dreaming we now know also occurs during non-REM (NREM) periods and in sleep onset (see below; see also Hobson 2002:80; Foulkes 1985; Nielsen 1999). We can experience a little bit of what sleep deprivation feels like when we wake up out of a sound slumber, or are awakened abruptly by an alarm clock, and feel disoriented, sluggish and poorly coordinated. We are not at our cognitive or social best until we have time to wake up. This is called "sleep inertia" (Dinges 1990) and is a minor problem compared with the effects of systematic sleep deprivation due to insomnia, sleep apnea or experimental sleep loss. Even moderate sleep loss can produce cognitive and motor effects similar to alcohol intoxication (Williamson and Feyer 2000), and total sleep deprivation over a lengthy period of time can prove cognitively detrimental and occasionally fatal (Anch *et al.* 1988:8-14; Horne 1985; Van Dongen *et al.* 2003; Everson, Bergmann and Rechtschaffen 1989).

Sleep deprivation affects the brain more than it does the rest of the body (Horne 1985). Sleep does not appear to be required merely by body fatigue, which can be eliminated by relaxing down-time. That means that the selection for a sleeping brain has been a steady refrain in evolution for millions of years, possibly a function that arose with the evolution of the earliest brains (see Chapter 14 for a full discussion of this issue). So what is it that sleep provides that is so necessary to the well being of the brain that it over-rides other considerations like increased vulnerability to predation? In my opinion, the twin keys to understanding why our nervous system needs sleep are to be found in the facts that:

1. **Our brain, and those of mammals and birds as well, is a trophic system** – from the Greek *trophē*, meaning "food." As Dale Purves (1988) has shown, it is common enough to think of the brain as having dominion over the body. But the brain is made up of cells that need to be fed, and the body controls the availability of food. Consider how hard it is to seriously think about anything just after finishing a huge meal. All one wants to do is lie down and rest. That is because much of the blood that would be required to think has gone to process digestion. It is significant that NREM sleep is associated with a global decrease in cerebral blood flow, while REM is associated with increased blood flow to specific areas of the brain (Palagini and Rosenlicht 2011:183).

2. **Our brain is an organic, self-regulating system**; that is, our brain is a complex system of cells that is constantly involved in a dynamic process of growth, development, interaction and change. We have elsewhere described the brain as a "community of cells" (Laughlin, McManus and d'Aquili 1990:34), by which we meant that our brain is like a vast human community in which the neurons and "support" cells are living organisms that organize themselves socially at both the local and global levels, and that communicate among themselves. Cells and communities of cells have to change, grow, re-organize and adjust to each other as the internal conditions and feedback loops within the system change. Keep in mind that our brain is the most complex system in the known universe. And the most complex part of our brain is what is called the *neocortex* – the sheet of neural tissue that is layered over evolutionarily older systems like a pancake covering a sausage in a pig-in-a-blanket (Fuster 2003; see Figure 4.1). The cortex is all crinkled up, forming ridges (one ridge called a *gyrus*) and valleys (one valley called a *sulcus*) giving the surface of our brain the look of a really big walnut. Under one square millimeter (or less than $2/100^{th}$ of a square inch) of cortex that is perhaps 4-6 millimeters (or 0.16 - 0.24 inches) thick, there will be approximately 100,000 neurons, and many times that

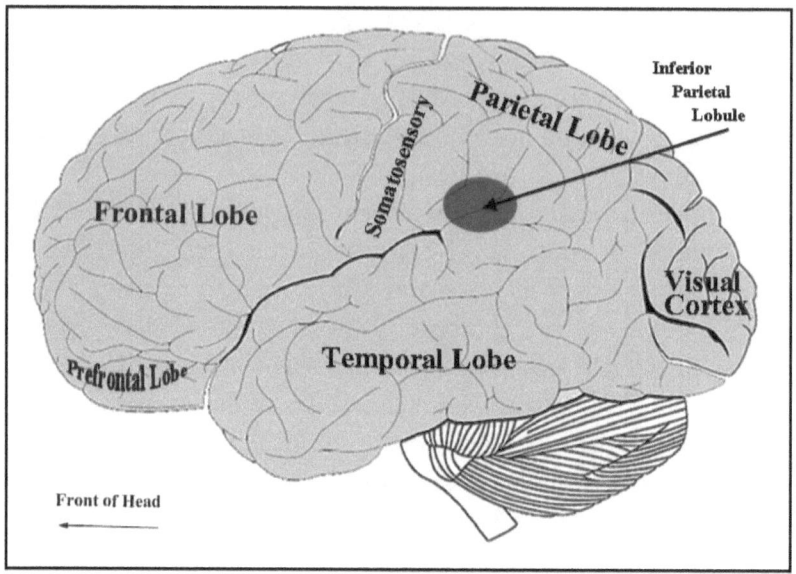

**Figure 4.1. Left Hemisphere of the Human Brain.** Illustration shows various cortical features including the temporal, frontal and prefrontal lobes and the primary visual cortex.

many "support" cells (Koch 2003:71). And all those cells are exquisitely organized, communicate with each other, consume energy and require sleep — and as we shall see further on, dreaming.

Neuroscientist Joel H. Bennington and his colleagues (Benington 2000; Benington and Heller 1995; Benington and Frank 2003; Frank and Benington 2006) have carried us a long way toward understanding the functions of sleep. The Benington group (2000; Benington and Heller 1995) has shown that sleep is "homeostatically" regulated from within the brain. The need for sleep increases during our waking states and decreases while we sleep. More specifically, the amount of energy (in the form of glycogen) available to our brain cells decreases during the day, and increases during NREM sleep during the night (NREM comprises around 80% of our adult nightly sleep). I repeat, our brain is a trophic system. It requires and uses up energy to "do its thing," and it has a very limited ability to store either energy or other metabolites, such as oxygen. That is why we are in danger of passing out or even dying if the blood flow to our brain is cut-off for just a few seconds. Another way to look at it is that our brain accounts for perhaps 1/50th of our total body weight, and yet consumes 1/5th or more of the energy we take on-board as food. Just think about how fatigued one can get just sitting around studying. Our brain turns food into experiences.

The Benington group has also amassed considerable evidence in support of the idea that sleep facilitates the consolidation of memory, and does so by increasing "synaptic plasticity" – that is the ability of the global system of synapses involved in memory storage to change and grow. Once again, to make sure we are all on the same page – a *synapse* is a point of connection between nerve cells (or *neurons*). Figure 4.2 shows a simplified synapse between the *axon* (an appendage reaching off the body of a nerve cell like the tentacle of a squid) and a *dendrite* (a smaller appendage like hair growing out of the body of the nerve cell). The axon communicates with the dendrite by releasing tiny bubbles of a chemical messenger (called a *neurotransmitter*) across a tiny gap (*synaptic junction*) between the transmitting cell and the receiving cell. Synaptic plasticity is the ability of the cell to change the quality and properties of this biochemical communication. It might help a bit to realize that there exist more synapses in your brain than there are stars in all the galaxies in the known universe! Within the dynamic, ever-changing structure of all these synapses are stored the records of all our memories (both personal and inherited), and sleep plays a major role in potentiating, storing, associating, changing and developing the structures that mediate those memories (Katz and Shatz 1996; LeDoux 2003: Chap. 5).

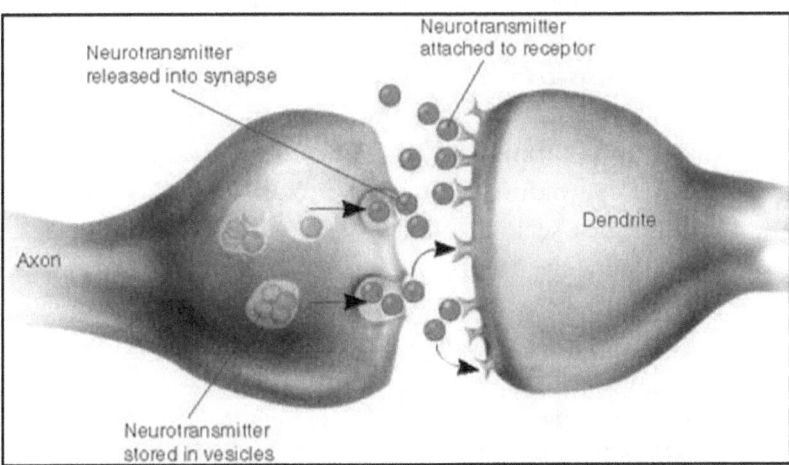

**Figure 4.2. The Synapse.** Artist's depiction of the synapse between two neural cells, on the left the "presynaptic" area and on the right the "postsynaptic" area. The transmitter substances travel across the gap to communicate one cell with another.

Michael Anch *et al.* (1988:18) have also presented evidence that critical growth hormones are produced during slow wave sleep (NREM) which facilitates the growth of new synaptic connections between nerve cells. Anabolic activity is greater during sleep, including a greater rate of tissue construction facilitated by a greater secretion of growth hormone. All of which supports the notion that a principal function of sleeping is the facilitation of cognitive and cortical development (McManus, Laughlin and Shearer 1993). Sleep is a major venue for apprehension of intuitive knowledge.[1] It is a common experience, usually reported anecdotally, to fall asleep with a problem and wake up with a solution. Keith Richards, the guitarist and inspired song writer for the Rolling Stones reports in his memoir, *Life* (Richards and Fox 2010), that he went to bed one evening as he usually does with his guitar at hand and a tape recorder on his bedside table. He woke up the next morning and noticed the tape recorder was on and the tape had finished recording. He played it back and discovered that at some point during the night he had recorded a riff and some lyrics and then 45 minutes of himself snoring. That recorded riff eventually became the famous song, "I Can't Get No Satisfaction," recorded by the Stones and others. He had no memory of having literally "dreamed-up" that tune.

Deirdre Barrett (2001) has compiled a lot of the more famous anecdotes and research pertaining to creativity and problem-solving during sleep in her book *The Committee of Sleep*, the title having been taken from a comment made by John Steinbeck.[2] The experiences of scientists, poets, artists and musicians are described, as well as the results of experimental research into the properties and processes that constitute the "committee." The most common descriptions are by various artists – painters, poets, writers, actors, so forth – who find and sometimes seek inspiration from dream imagery. I know this process intimately, for I have painted pictures encountered in or inspired by dreams, usually during hypnagogic or hypnopompic

---

[1] The word "intuition" is a fairly fuzzy term that refers to a range of types of knowing. The root of the English word derives from the Latin *intuitus* meaning roughly "the act of achieving knowledge from direct perception or contemplation."

[2] "It is a common experience that a problem difficult at night is resolved in the morning after the committee of sleep has worked on it" (John Steinbeck as quoted in Barrett 2001:ix).

**Figure 4.3. "In the Temple."** Acrylic painting by the author of an image encountered in a hypnagogic state.

states. Figure 4.3 is one such piece, a black and white photo of one of my own acrylic paintings entitled "In the Temple." The great modern artist, Jasper Johns was first inspired to develop his unique style when he painted an American flag after having dreamed of himself doing that (ibid:1; see Figure 4.4). Interest in the artistic brain has swelled to the point that it has led to a new field of interdisciplinary neuroscience called *neuroaesthetics* (Skov and Vartanian 2009).[3] Other scholars have linked ancient cave art with dreaming (Lewis-Williams 2002).

As David Foulkes (1999) has also shown with his research on children, sleep and dreaming produce the conditions for creative development: "We've seen how, from the very outset, dreaming *is* creative, that it produces novel organizations of experience. Almost always, even for the youngest child who can dream, the dream creates situations or events that never before have been encountered in just that form" (ibid:123, emphasis by Foulkes). Foulkes is referring to dream creation, but there is evidence that creative solutions to problems encountered while awake may be worked-out or facilitated during sleep, whether or not a dream is involved. Wagner *et al.* (2004)

---

[3] The term "neuroaesthetics" has been attributed to psychologist, Semir Zeki.

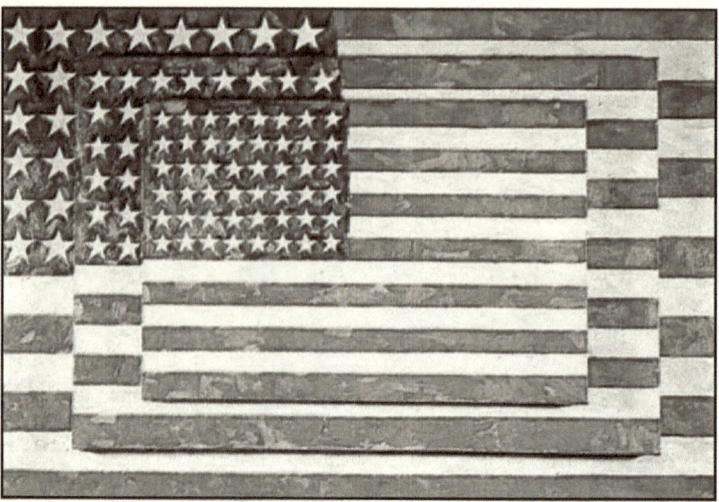

**Figure 4.4. "Three Flags."** Painting by Jasper Johns (1958), inspired by a dream.

have reported on a series of ingenious experiments in which subjects given tasks with hidden rules and allowed to sleep before they have to solve the problem, reach solutions faster than subjects not given the opportunity to sleep. They conclude in this way:

> The task representations associated with sleep-dependent gain of insight may be restructured by activity of the hippocampus and related medial temporal lobe structures, which, in connection with prefrontal cortical areas, are considered to play an essential role for generating awareness in memory... . Reactivation of hippocampal cell assemblies during sleep... is regarded as a mechanism by which recently encoded materials stored temporarily in autoassociative hippocampal networks are played back to the neocortex where they are gradually incorporated into preexisting knowledge representations. This process of incorporation underlying long-term storage of previously acquired memories then forms the basis for a remodeling and qualitative restructuring of memory representations. Thus, our data support the concept that sleep, by hippocampal-neocortical replay, not only strengthens memory traces quantitatively, but can also "catalyze" mental restructuring, thereby setting the stage for the emergence of insight.

It is now clear that sleep is "wired-in" to our body. It is an evolutionarily old process required by the metabolic and developmental nature of the organism (see Chapter 14). We cannot live without sleep, despite the fact that under natural circumstances sleep might increase our vulnerability to attack, predation and other dangers, much as it does for other mammals. But the next obvious question is: I get it that I have to sleep to live, grow and be healthy, but why do I have to dream? What is the connection between sleeping and dreaming?

## The Neuropsychology of Dreaming

Questions about the biological functions of dreaming are far harder to answer than are the functions of sleep, mainly because we are talking about experience, not just about metabolism, neural rejuvenation and somatic down-time (Fiss 1986). It is obvious that there must be such functions, for as far as we know, all mammals and birds that sleep also dream (see Vaughan 1964 for evidence of dreaming among Rhesus monkeys). And, as we have said, dreaming is a human universal. Moreover, dreaming happens when we sleep, so there has to be a connection between sleep and dreaming. But first, in order to account for dreaming from an evolutionary point of view, we have to understand how the brain actually makes experiences happen – and I mean all kinds of experiences, for the brain produces all experiences (all SOC) in much the same way, dreaming included. Viewed from this standpoint, if one can account for how the brain produces experience generally, one *ipso facto* has accounted to some extent for the experience of dreaming – although the question would still remain, why waste energy producing experience in the midst of sleep?

Complex SOC are relatively stable and recurrent over time and, as we said, are recognizable by the individual, and within a culture, as distinct from other states (James 1904a, 1904b, 1976 [1912]; Laughlin and McManus 1995; Laughlin, McManus and d'Aquili 1990:11; Tart 1975; Hobson 1988, 1999:23; Pribram 1980:49; Throop 2002, 2003). The neural processes that mediate consciousness, that mediate a specific SOC, indeed that mediate each and every moment of experience are *componential* in their structure (Hebb 1949; Purves

1988; Hobson 2007; Hollan 2003; Damasio 2010:Chap. 8; Kahn 2007; Sporns 2010; McGilchrist 2009:220, Changeux 1985; Donald 2001:101; Revonsuo 2006:10-14); that is, they are the product of many neurophysiological structures that combine in a distinct, recurring and hierarchical organization of circuits, making each state they mediate familiar and subjectively identifiable. When I am "dreaming," "drunk," "high," "depressed," "feeling sick," "angry," so forth, I am identifying with a discrete SOC the internal organization of which has specific, identifiable qualities or "tells" – such as flying while "dreaming," stupid doziness and awkwardness when "drunk" and psychedelic light shows when "tripping" on magic mushrooms. Yet most of the neural structures that combine to produce a one familiar SOC are common to other SOC (Pagel 2008:63). For instance, common to all experiences in whatever SOC is what Antonio Damasio has called *core consciousness* that "provides the organism with a sense of self about one moment – now – and about one place – here" (1999:16). Core consciousness is mediated in part by a number of evolutionarily older neural centers, including areas in the brain stem and areas in the somatosensory and cingulate cortex (Figures 4.1 and 4.5) – these at the minimum mediate

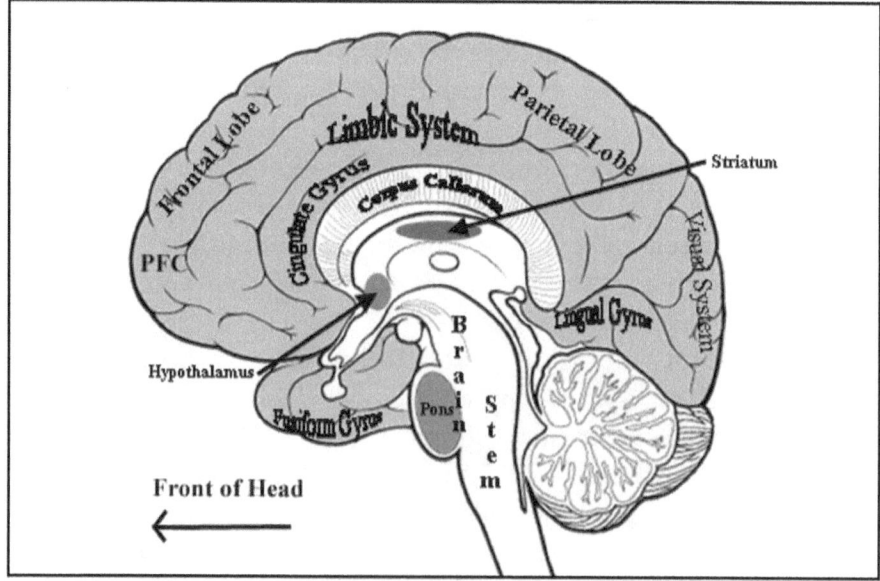

**Figure 4.5. Sagittal View of the Brain.** The human brain sliced in half down the middle and featuring the brain stem, limbic system, parietal lobe and hypothalamus.

arousal, sense of the body in space, and emotion within consciousness. Damasio makes the point that damage to other and newer cortical areas may lead to impairment of function, but not to core consciousness itself (Damasio 1999:270-272).

Likewise, there is a certain part of the temporal lobe in the region of the fusiform and lingual gyri where there is an area that processes our sense of color (Figure 4.5). If this area is destroyed, color disappears from perception in waking life, from dreams during sleep, and even from memory (Edelman and Tononi 2000:53; Damasio 1999:268). In other words, the same area of the brain mediates the appearance of color in all experiences. On the other hand, certain components of distinct experiences will differ. For instance, there is a particular neuro-chemical that is present and associated with memory during waking states that is absent during "normal" dreaming (Hobson 1999:21). In sleep states, sensory input and motor output are massively inhibited, while they are relatively uninhibited in waking states. Changing or adding components to core consciousness will change experience, and may change the more global SOC, perhaps in novel ways, as in first experiencing lucidity in dreams or first encountering spirit beings in visions.

## The Standard Neuropsychology of Dreaming

So that we are all on the same page with respect to the neuropsychology of dreaming, let me summarize, without too much technical detail, what we know about dreaming from the Western neuropsychological point of view. We all dream on and off all night long (whether we remember our dreams or not) in both "rapid eye movement" (REM) and "non-rapid eye movement" (NREM) periods of sleep (Moffitt *et al.* 1982). REM and NREM are driven by evolutionarily older nuclei in the *brain stem* (especially nuclei in the *pons* and areas of the *basal ganglia* such as the *striatum*, as well as the *hypothalamus*, collectively called the *reticular activating system*; see Figure 4.5), and alternate in a lawful manner all night long, with REM sleep states increasing in duration from a few minutes at the beginning of sleep to 30 minutes or so toward the end of sleep (Braun *et al.* 1997; Moorcroft 2003:24). Up to the time of this writing, sleep stages are defined upon *electroencephalographic*

(*EEG*) measures – that is, the measure of electrical field activity over the surface of the cortex.

It has become clear that REM/NREM states are *not* synonymous with dreaming, nor are sleep stages and dreams driven by the same neural mechanisms. As Stoerig (2007:709) notes, so far there exists no clear physiological indication that a person is dreaming within the usual laboratory research situation. There is an exception, and that is when a lucid dreamer is able to signal they are dreaming from within the dream to researchers in the sleep lab (next chapter). Furthermore, there is considerable evidence now that it is not REM mechanisms *per se*, but frontal lobe (dopamine) systems that drive dreams (Solms 2003). Thus REM and the components requisite to mediating dreams are biologically somewhat distinct, but obviously interconnected. The biological functions of both REM/NREM alternation and dreaming are not yet completely understood, but it seems to me obvious that REM at least is especially involved in facilitating neural adaptation to a dynamic waking world, and the construction of neural models and episodic memory (Hu, Stylos-Allan and Walker 2006; see also regional blood flow above). For instance, there is a curious type of research during which subjects wear prismatic glasses that have the effect of reversing the visual field. Eventually the subjects habituate to this condition. During the period of adaptation, however, the percent of time they spend in REM goes way up (Zimmerman, Stoyva and Metcalf 1971).

Dream recall – that is, remembering dream experiences after being awakened in a sleep lab — is very roughly 80% during REM sleep and 45% during NREM (Nielsen 1999:106-107).[4] Normal dreaming among Western subjects usually takes the form of hallucinatory perceptual events that are mediated by secondary sensory association areas of the cortex and high-level visual neurons in the fusiform gyrus and other temporal cortical areas that control imagery (Koch 2004:109), and emotion mediated by various nuclei in the limbic system (Pace-Schott

---

[4] One needs to be cautious here, for almost all the sleep lab research has been carried out using university students as subjects, most of whom are products of Western cultural conditioning. Hence the role of ethnocentrism in both the experience of dreaming and the data collection needs to be emphasized (also see Wax 2004:91 on this issue).

2011; Stoerig 2007; see Figure 4.5). At the same time, the primary visual area (often referred to as "V1"; see Figure 4.1) is suppressed – hence our dreaming brain, however vivid, is largely "blind" to the outside world.

It is also critical to understanding how the brain mediates dreaming to distinguish between "perception" and "imaging." Perception normally involves both sensory stimuli and attention-shifting. Indeed, one of the major functions of behavior is the control of perception (Powers 2005; see also Geary 2005). Moreover, the processing of percepts is fundamentally different than the processing of imagery. It is true that images in one's dream, especially in a lucid dream, can "grab" one's attention, but this grabbing does not require motor based attention-shifting – no moving of the eyes, head and body to bring the stimulus into central focus (Kosslyn 1996:102-104).

There are two further phases of sleep and dreaming that bear mention for phenomenological and ethnographic reasons, those being the *hypnagogic* imagery that may arise during sleep onset and the *hypnopompic* imagery that may arise during sleep offset. The hypnagogic and hypnopompic states have very short durations (something like 5 seconds) in typical Western subjects (see Dinges 1990). As we fall asleep we may experience a blending of both external stimuli and internal imagery as the body relaxes and slips into Stage 2 sleep. The same occurs as we leave sleep and enter the waking state (see e.g. my own hypnopompic mandala experiences in Chapter 13). Most of us Westerners tend to ignore such images and hence tend not to remember them later on, but they do become memorable, salient and interpretable among dreamers in other societies, most notably those that use various ritualized forms of *dream incubation*. Dream incubation (from the Latin for "sitting on eggs") means that special ritual techniques are used to evoke and direct dreaming toward the solution of a particular problem, fulfillment of a specific intention, etc. (Tholey 1983; see also Laughlin et al. 1986 on the ritual control of experience; see Meier 2009 on incubation rites among the ancient Greeks); e.g., the practice of *dharnā* among Bengali Hindu pilgrims (Morinis 1982), and in meditative practices involving dreaming such as those used in Tibetan Tantric dream yoga (Chapter 13).

The individual stimuli used in waking life to incubate, evoke and intensify dreaming (or other ASC) are called *ritual drivers* (Laughlin,

McManus and d'Aquili 1990:146; Lex 1979; Locke and Kelly 1985:30; Jilek 1982).[5] Any number of things can penetrate into and influence the dream life from waking life (Schredl 2003), and these may be orchestrated for particular effects, usually in religious rituals with the intent of evoking significant dreams and visions (Winkelman 2010:79-88). Here is an example from the ethnographic literature – Frank Speck's description of the practice of driving dreams among the Naskapi Indians of Labrador (1963 [1935]:188):

> We have seen how, when the soul-spirit of man is strong and active, he believes that he may expect from it continual direction and guidance in all affairs. Accordingly, frequency of dreams is a blessing. Anything that will induce dreaming is a religious advantage: fasting, dancing, singing, drumming, rattling, the sweat bath, seclusion, meditation, eating certain foods, as well as drinking animal grease..., various kinds of medicine, both alcoholic drinks and drugs, when such things... can be gotten.

Note that many drivers are repetitive, rhythmic, even percussive (Neher 1962). Such stimuli also include flickering lights, repeating chants and mantras, all of which are known experimentally to effect the "tuning" of the autonomic nervous system and synchronize various other functions of the nervous system (Gellhorn 1967; Gellhorn and Kiely 1972).

## The Prefrontal Cortex and Dreaming

There is usually a corresponding decrease in the participation of *prefrontal cortical* (PFC) areas, as well as the *inferior parietal lobule*, the latter mediating aspects of conceptual thought, during what we in the West consider "normal" dreaming (Soerig 2007:709; Braun *et al.* 1997). The PFC is the anterior part of the frontal lobes (Figures 4.1 and 4.5), which is the part of the brain from about the middle of the cortex forward and that is given over to the mediation of actions of all sorts (expression of emotion, movement of the eyes, speech,

---

[5] The term "driver" was coined by Ernst Gellhorn in his work with autonomic system tuning (see Gelhorn and Kiely 1972).

movement of the limbs, so forth; Fuster 2008:2).[6] The PFC is perhaps the most important part of our frontal cortex from the perspective of the anthropology of dreaming, for as we shall see: (1) the extent of PFC involvement as a component in the structure mediating our dreams makes an enormous difference in the intentionality, quality, lucidity, continuity and plot-line of our dreams (Pace-Schott 2007), (2) the extent of involvement of the medial prefrontal cortex determines the social quality of dreams (Amodio and Frith 2006), and (3) the evolution of the PFC among *hominins*[7] is the single most important reason why we developed the higher cortical functions we humans enjoy today. The PFC is the evolutionarily youngest part of our brain (Jerison 1973, 1985; Rilling and Insel 1999), and has expanded in proportion to the overall neocortex in relation to the apes, while the motor areas of the frontal lobes have shrunk (Geary 2005:230; Schoenemann, Sheehan and Glotzer 2005; Corballis 2011:204; Deacon 1997). In addition, the human PFC exhibits more interconnections when compared with ape brains, both within the lobe and between the lobe and other areas of the brain. This is the area of neocortex that makes our foreheads bulge out above our eyes more than, say, a chimpanzee's or the family dog's, and that makes our species of nearly hairless apes so very clever.

The PFC is the seat of our brain's executive functions and intelligence (Miller, Galanter and Pribram 1960; Pribram 1971; Changeux 1985; Fuster 2003, 2008; Hobson 2002:140; Geary 2007:237, 277) – by which I mean the part of the cortex that integrates and temporally orders lower action centers, contributes along with other cortical areas to general intelligence and problem-solving, that moderates and suppresses emotion, that binds time in spatiotemporal bundles and makes *plans* for the future (i.e., we can do something today that will only come to intended fruition tomorrow, or next week; see Miller, Galanter and Pribram 1960; Amodio and Frith 2006), that generates ideal simulations of the world, and that mediates *working memory* (i.e., "the temporary retention of information – sensory or other – for the performance of a

---

[6] If you could look 90 degrees upward and inside your skull, you would be staring at your PFC (Figure 4.1).

[7] The hominins consist of modern humans and all of their direct ancestor species.

prospective act to solve a problem or to attain a goal;" Fuster 2008:138). If we wish to carry out a complex, purposeful activity over a duration of time, simulate an ideal solution to a problem, delay motor responses until the situation is sussed-out, the involvement of the PFC as a component of our neural activity is essential, as it is for all other primates.

Lack of PFC involvement in "normal" dreaming is the reason why there is a relative poverty of recall, continuity, temporal plot-line and reflexive awareness, as well as enhanced affect, in dream recall (Pace-Schott 2011). It was long thought that dreaming was basically "deficient" in cognitive functioning and intentionality (Purcell, Moffitt and Hoffman 1993). The implication here is that only by recall of dream content and the application of waking interpretive functions could order and meaning be brought into dream material – an implication fairly common in psychoanalytic treatments of dreams (see Chapter 3). However, as we shall see in the next chapter, the "discovery" (by science, but long known to many non-Western traditional peoples) of lucid dreaming brought this view into question. In lucid dreaming, a "transience" of PFC activation during the dream state will operate to alter the components of the neural network mediating the dream (Dietrich 2007:243), entraining not only some or all of the executive functions of the brain, but also the level of arousal, of involvement of midbrain vestibular system mediation of spatial orientation (Snyder and Gackenbach 1991), emotion and autonomic system tuning (LaBerge, Levitan and Dement 1986).

**Processing Imagery**

Dreaming is primarily made up of images – images (in all sensory systems, but primarily visual and auditory) that may or may not derive from percepts. We may experience a Shetland pony whose image is stored in memory from a real experience, or a dragon that we have only seen in pictures and movies and that are stored in memory, or objects that are archetypal in origin and totally novel to our experience. All such imaginary objects are freed from control of both sensory perception and motor-based attention-shifting, and thus may appear in bizarre situations and surreal forms.

Visual imagery, being the most predominant in dreaming, seems to involve many of the same systems that are involved in perception. The primary visual cortex, or area V1 (Kosslyn 1994:19-20) is involved in producing images while awake with the eyes closed, but not when the images are dreamed. Also, it was once thought that the right hemisphere of the brain mediated dream imagery, but this is no longer such a simple matter. Experiments with patients having undergone right hemispherectomies have shown that they dream in the same way as people with intact brains (McCormick *et al.* 1997). McNamara, Clark and Hartmann (1998) have shown some differences in dream content among right and left-handed dreamers. Kosslyn (1994:312-319) has reviewed the data on cerebral lateralization and has concluded that under specific circumstances, both the right and left hemispheres participate in the generation of images. However, Piller (2009) has reported task related evidence of right hemisphere dominance in lucid dreaming (next chapter).

## NEUROPHENOMENOLOGY AND THE DREAMING BRAIN

I suspect that very few people on the planet are actually aware of themselves as an experiencing brain. Indeed, in a very Heideggeran[8] manner, the neural mechanisms underlying our mental activity just vanish from awareness, if the mechanisms ever *were* an object of our scrutiny to start with. It is very tempting to focus upon ourselves as minds, as most anthropologists do, and forget we are bodies that are doing the "mind-thing" – that "mind" is one of the things our body does. Actually, the problem is an existential one. We have trouble translating ideas about what is happening in our brains into the qualities and elements of our on-going direct experience. Most folks reading this book know how to drive, but few know sod-all about how a modern high-tech automobile works – nor, strictly speaking, is that knowledge

---

[8] Martin Heidegger (1977) showed that when we get in the habit of using a technology (stone tool, laptop, refrigerator, etc.), the technology itself becomes largely invisible and is just incorporated into our bodily acts (hammering, surfing the internet, getting a cold beer, etc.). In the same way our hand becomes invisible in the act of grasping, our brain is invisible in the act of thinking, so forth.

necessary for us to have all sorts of adventures on the road. But in the present anthropological context, being ignorant of how the brain mediates our experiences will not do, for our problem is to explain dreaming, not just enjoy the ride.

It will help us to build a bridge between brain and experience to cultivate a *neurophenomenological* strategy – to move backwards as it were from experience to the neurophysiological structures that mediate experience. A long time ago while I was a fellow at the Institute of Neurological Sciences at the University of Pennsylvania, I had to give a talk before all the Institute's neuroscientists. So, instead of wisely chatting with them about how traditional peoples conceive of the brain and its functions, I naively addressed them about the great need for anthropology to become more conversant with the neurosciences so that we could bridge from body to mind, and stop reifying the ages old mind-body dualism that so pervades the discipline. Well, the talk went over like a lead balloon. Why? Because they already knew they were experiencing brains, and were wondering what the big deal was all about, and why I was boring them silly with my rant. So let me define some terms and shift our orientation so that we can conceptually bridge from our experience to our brain processes. Then it will make sense for us, as it was for my long-suffering Institute audience, to speak of dreaming and the brain in the same breath.

## Experience, Radical Empiricism and Pure Consciousness

First of all, what do I mean by experience? My understanding of the term harks back to the 19th century and Wilhelm Dilthey's (1833-1911) discussion of how sociology and anthropology need to be grounded in a "descriptive psychology" of human consciousness, and a deep study of "lived experience" (German: *Erlebnis*; see Dilthey 1977, Throop 2002). Sounds a bit like Adolph Bastian again, doesn't it? Well, in fact Dilthey had read and approved of Bastian's work (Koepping 2005). As my friend and colleague Jason Throop writes of Dilthey, "In contrast to Kant's view that experience arises only with the conceptual patterning of sensation, Dilthey asserts that lived experience… should be understood as a primordial "given" to human consciousness… . From Dilthey's perspective, experience is granted a certain primordial structure, coherence or selfgivenness that exists prior to the active conceptual patterning of sensation seen as central to Kantian formulations of synthesis... . Put differently, for Dilthey the coherence of experience is given directly in experience itself and is not solely a product that is actively constructed by acts of consciousness" (Throop 2002:4). In more modern neuropsychological terms, *experience* for our purposes is the movie the brain produces for itself – a movie that is presented to our consciousness as a field of sensory particles comprising what neuropsychologists call the *sensorium* – the normally unitary sphere of all sensory experience (Laughlin 1992; Laughlin, McManus and d'Aquili 1990). Everything we see, imagine, smell, hear, taste, touch, think in words and say sublingually in our heads is realized within the sensorial field. As Dilthey might have stressed, just as a movie projected before us is already organized, so to is the movie within our theater of mind already ordered and, to some extent at least, meaningful.

Second of all, I follow in the tradition of William James' *radical empiricism* with respect to the study of consciousness and experience. James presented the core of his ideas about radical empiricism in two key articles entitled "Does 'Consciousness' Exist?" and "A World of Pure Experience," both published in the same year and in the same journal (James 1904a, 1904b). These articles and supporting papers and documents were collected in the volume entitled *Essays in Radical Empiricism* (James 1976 [1912]; see also Taylor 1994:353-354). James' radical empiricism is a method of doing science that requires: (1) that all of the ideas and theories in science be grounded in lived experience, and (2) that no experience be excluded from the scientific purview (Taylor 1994:353-354). James was, as I am, an anti-dualist and a monist. Both the knower and the known, subject and object, perceiver and perceived are founded upon *pure experience* (James1976:4-5). By pure experience James (and Dilthey) meant a level or stage in the constitution of experience that exists prior to cognitive acts. Pure experience is the unsullied field of subjective, sensory immediacy upon which is built a more and more extensive picture of the world as the hierarchy of cognitive acts mold objects, relations and meaning within the field. This is a process of formation that takes only a split second in normal states of consciousness — so fast does it occur that we are relatively unaware of the process of construction. The sensorium at its most primitive level of initial processing is James' "instant field" of pure experience. Are the sensorium and James' "instant field" merely theoretical concepts? By no means, for the sensorium and its constituent sensory particles are strictly empirical – actually radically empirical – for they are empirically present every moment of consciousness, although they normally require the skills of a trained contemplative[9] or phenomenologist to apperceive them *as such* (see Laughlin, McManus and d'Aquili 1990:24-33; Laughlin and Throop 2009; see also Harding 1986 for a delightful Zen approach to discovering the sensorium). When we speak of a dream-as-dreamt, we are referring to a fully embodied understanding of dream experience (Thompson and Varela 2001; Varela, Thompson and Rosch 1991; Csordas 1990, 1993, 1994), and that James' pure experience is a description of an initial stage in the nervous system's processing of sensory experience.

## Neurophenomenology at the Micro Level

Now, let us use a more powerful lens for a moment and examine what is happening in the sensorium at a microscopic level – examine the moment-by-moment flow of the sensorium the way a skilled contemplative might. Our lens reveals that sensory perception unfolds in a continuous iteration of "now moments," or pulses of sensation (Dainton, 2006: Chap. 5; Damasio, 1999:126; Wallace, 2007:137). I will call these pulses *experiential epochs* (Laughlin and Throop 2008).[10] Each momentary epoch is the real "now" of experience – a neuropsychological version of James' "instant field." Only a skilled contemplative who is able to slow, center and clear their mind of all

---

[9] We have argued elsewhere for the importance of *mature contemplation* (the trained, skilled and experienced application of contemplation) in the study of the essential structures of experience and consciousness (Laughlin, McManus and d'Aquili, 1990: Chap. 11; Laughlin and Throop, 2008). I will not waste space arguing for its relevance and efficacy here.

[10] We have earlier called these pulses of experience "perceptual epochs" because we were specifically dealing with perception and consciousness, but the internal dynamics of perception and those of dreaming are the same for the most part. It is merely a convention to call experience of the external world "perception" and of the inner world "interoception," etc.

distraction can discern each epoch as it flickers in awareness. Normal, common sense experience is really a perceptual operation of binding the present epoch with memory of those that have gone just before the "now" moment and those that are anticipated to arise just after the "now" moment.[11]

The *experiential epoch* is the fundamental, molecular unit of temporal processing of sensory information (e.g., Koch, 2004: 256), whether that information comes from perception by way of sensory organs, or from imaging generated from inside as in dreams, fantasies or visions. All other processes are cognitive acts that are layered over experiential epochs. The essential function of perception is the detection and comprehension of patterns within a series of perceptual epochs (i.e., experiential epochs stimulated from sensory receptors). Sensory patterns are detected and matched with knowledge stored in memory, both short-term recall of recently past epochs and longer-term percepts and concepts from past cognitive acts. The same occurs internally with imaging. When we become aware of an image before our mind's-eye, that image flickers in the same way that the perceptual field does. The percept and the image are arising in the same sensorium, mediated by many of the same neural processes.

Dream imagery is stimulated primarily from within the body, with each experiential epoch arising and passing as an ordered field of sensory particles (something like computer monitor pixels). The sensorium is not located in one area of the brain. Quite the contrary, because the neural substrate for experience is componential, it will be distributed over wide areas of the cortical and sub-cortical areas of the brain (Edelman and Tononi 2000:Chap. 5). These many components "do their thing" in parallel, and then combine in a unitary field of consciousness (McClelland and Rumelhart 1986). We should note that there are occasions when a stimulus from outside the body may penetrate imaging processes and encroach upon a dream. I once was having a dream in which a light got brighter and brighter until it was an intense cold white light pervading the whole sensorium. I awoke to find that a full moon was shining upon the back of my head through

---

[11] This is a very Husserlian view of time-consciousness (Husserl, 1964; Brough and Embree, 2000; Kortooms, 2002; Laughlin and Throop 2008); i.e., our basic phenomenological view of time-consciousness is little different than Edmund Husserl's.

my bedroom window. Many of us have dreamed of a phone ringing in their dream only to awaken to the sound of their alarm clock.

## Dreaming and the Quantum Brain

There is another ingredient to add before we end our summary of the neurophysiology of sleep and dreaming. It is one that is generally not included in texts on the subject, and may strike the reader as perhaps too "way-out" for consideration. Nonetheless, that ingredient is the relationship between the dreaming brain and the quantum universe – in other words, the *quantum brain* dreaming. This remains a very controversial topic because the world of quantum physics is itself so non-commonsensical at times (Globus 1998). Yet the possibilities in this field have been researched by very serious scientists and it seems like an essential consideration to me in order to account for some of the more extraordinary types of dreaming we will encounter later in the book (see Chapter 12) – types including precognitive dreams, co-dreaming and telepathic dreaming, as well as some of the more transpersonal and creative aspects of dreaming. It is entirely possible that some of these phenomena might well be the products of *quantum dreaming* – that is, dreaming caused by quantum memory, quantum computation and quantum communication (Nunez 2010).

The cosmos is vast, perhaps infinite, and most of the space in the cosmos is a vacuum. Yet some physicists tell us that the vacuum of space is a "plenum void" – a space that is full of energy. Some speak of the "vacuum fluctuations," "zero point energy," and even use the old term "ether," and argue that everything is part of everything else by way of this all-pervasive sea of energy. Atomic physicist David Bohm (1917-1972) for instance argued that reality has two orders, the "explicate order" of matter and space and time, and an "implicate order" of energy in which everything is entangled (everything is "implicated" in everything else) and there is no spatial distance or time (Bohm 1980, 1990). As Bohm and Hiley (1995:381-382) wrote:

> Our proposal in this regard is that the basic relationship of quantum theory and consciousness is that they have the implicate

order in common. ...The essential features of the implicate order are... that the whole universe is in some way enfolded in everything and that each thing is enfolded in the whole. However, under typical conditions of ordinary experience, there is a great deal of relative independence of things, so that they may be abstracted as separately existent, outside of each other, and only externally related. However, more fundamentally the enfoldment relationship is active and essential to what each thing is, so that it is internally related to the whole and therefore to everything else.

If you think about this for a moment and then go back to the description of the Navajo theory of the Holy Wind and the discussion of animism in the last chapter, you may see that the same intuition is being addressed in both traditional cosmology and modern physics. It might also suggest to you that we may well interact with the "whole" (the Holy Wind), as well as other things at a distance in time and space in our dreams. Bohm's thinking, as well as this whole issue, will become very important in Part 2 of this book (see especially Chapter 12) when we come to address paranormal aspects of dreaming.

German biophysicist Fritz-Albert Popp has found that living cells spontaneously emit weak biophotons in the visual to ultraviolet range and those cells living in communities, like carrots, cockroaches or brains, are literally bathed in electromagnetic fields by means of which the cells communicate their states, and coordinate their activities with each other (e.g., Popp, Gu and Li 1994; Chang, Fisch and Popp 2010). Popp and his colleagues have even built machines that can measure the freshness of foods by monitoring biophoton emissions; for as the cells die out, so too do their light emissions. This is not the place to argue for or against the existence of zero point energy or the ether. I will simply state that there is enough evidence from many quarters that such energies exist and that our brains are bathed and enfolded in such fields. For our present purposes, I am going to call this field of energy in the universe the *quantum sea.*

An interest has existed for many years in the possible relationship between the brain and the quantum sea (e.g., Bohm 1990; Beck and Eccles 1992; Deutsch 1985; Lockwood 1989; Penrose 1989; Stapp

2003, 2007; Jibu and Yasue 1995, 2004). The question has repeatedly been raised as to how the neurocognitive processes that mediate consciousness may also influence and be influenced by events at the quantum level. I myself have argued that neural circuits may be "prepared" to operate as transducers of patterned quantum activity (Laughlin 1996). Transformations of neural activity may produce transformations in the structure of the sea, and vice versa. Thus local causation based upon biochemical interaction among neural cells may be transformed into non-local causation based upon biophysical activity between cells, brains and other structures or entities in the sea.

This suggestion still remains a hypothesis at this time, for it is one that is the very devil to confirm. To my knowledge, no one has unequivocally demonstrated quantum effects of cellular activity, except for the evidence of non-thermal, weak biophoton activity mentioned above. However, there are several promising avenues of research into possible mechanisms — avenues that are sufficiently interesting that they have led a number of serious scholars to consider processes that mediate brain-quantum interaction. For example, Evan Harris Walker (1977; 2000:217-218) has suggested that the quantum phenomenon known as "tunneling" may occur at the synapse, an idea taken up in more detail in Beck (1994) and in Beck and Eccles (1992). "Tunneling" occurs when an electron penetrates a barrier that in classical terms should be impenetrable. Also, a number of scientists have produced interesting research regarding the possible role of quantum entanglement in the navigation of birds using weak magnetic fields (see Ritz *et al*. 2009; Cai, Guerresch Briegel 2010). This phenomenon would involve entangled particles in certain chemicals in the cells of the bird's retinae.

Herbert Frohlich (1968, 1980, 1986; Frohlich and Kremer 1983) and others (Bond and Huth 1986) have attempted to demonstrate "coherent" effects in cell membranes related to weak external electromagnetic fields that cannot be merely attributed to heating the system. "Coherence" is a central concept in quantum physics and refers to events correlated over time or space. This means that in a coherent system, activity at one place in the system is directly connected to activity in another place in the system (Frohlich 1986:243). All objects from simple atomic particles to complex biological organisms are by definition made up of coherent energies. But what is being suggested here is that events in the quantum sea may produce coherence, say, in membrane activity across the entire expanse of a neural network (involving thousands, perhaps hundreds of thousands of cells, and millions of synapses), or vice versa – that the activity across a neural network may produce coherence in the essentially a-temporal and non-local quantum sea.

There is now evidence pointing to the importance of electromagnetic oscillations at the cellular level that are not merely caused by changes in the ambient temperature.[12] Frohlich (1986) has hypothesized that coherent oscillations (similar to the so-called "Bose-Einstein condensation") in certain protein structures may be triggered by a common, low energy electromagnetic field, and thus may provide a mechanism for information storage and retrieval over a wide expanse of organic tissue — an inherently quantum process. Such electromagnetic fields may function in many types of cells, including neural cells, to control physiological processes (e.g., membrane potential, release of neurotransmitters at presynaptic sites, etc.; Bond and Huth 1986:293; Popp, Li and Gu 1992). Frohlich (1980) has also suggested that highly polarized membrane components may be deformed by external electromagnetic fields. It is now known that natural and man-made electromagnetic fields have effects upon biological processes (Persinger 1974, 1980; Grundler, Kaiser, Keilmann and Walleczek 1992).

Another plausible biophysical mechanism of direct consciousness-quantum sea interpenetration is to be found in the coherent properties of microtubules (Hameroff 1994, 1998; Jibu et al. 1994; Mershin, Nanopoulos and Skoulakis 1999). Microtubules form a protein latticework of cylindrical pathways in the cell that are known to be involved in regulating and organizing the activity of the cell, transporting neurochemicals to the synapse, etc. (see Figure 4.6). Jibu et al. (1994) have suggested that the ordered water molecules within the hollow core of these microtubules may manifest a property of "super-radiance" and much like a laser, transform incoherent electromagnetic energy into coherent, non-linear photon pulses within the tubule. Such a pulse would also be a kind of "soliton wave" in that it might propagate without much energy loss and with little energy requirement.

---

[12] See Kaiser 1978 for a review of non-thermal, electromagnetic oscillations in biological systems and Bischof 1994 for an excellent history of bioelectromagnetism; see also Eichwald and Kaiser 1993.

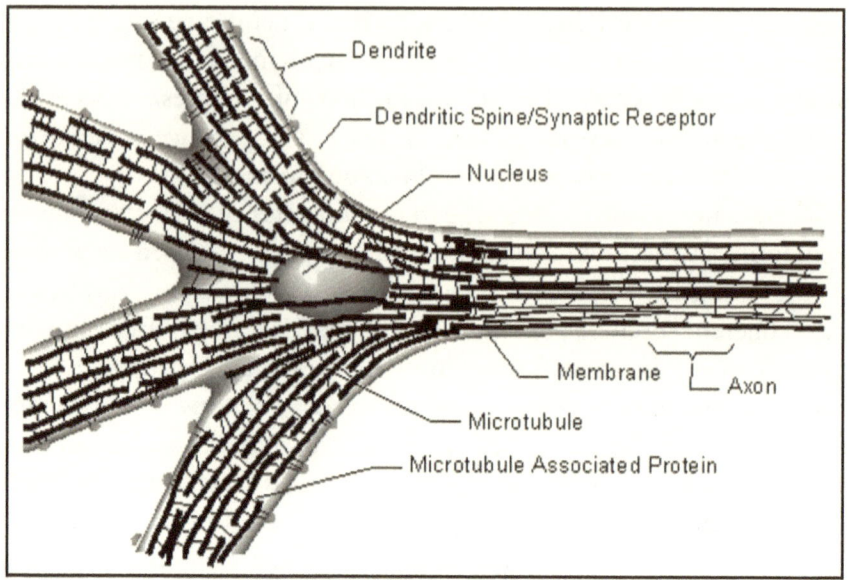

**Figure 4.6. Neurons with Microtubules.** Artist's depiction of the huge number of microtubules to be found inside the body, axon and dendrites of a nerve cell.

This picture of electromagnetic activity in the structure of the cell is consonant with the suggestion by Fritz Popp and his colleagues (Popp et al. 1984; Gu and Popp 1993; Popp, Li and Gu 1992; Ho, Popp and Warnke 1994) that the regulation of cellular organization in biological systems may be accomplished by a coherent pattern of weak biophoton emission, as mentioned above.

Although there has not yet been a definitive demonstration of direct neural-quantum sea interaction, the evidence is suggestive enough to prompt some researchers to hypothesize that brain-quantum sea interpenetration may operate something like a "quantum computer" (Hameroff 1998; Deutsch 1985; Wallace 1993a, 1993b). That is, information and "computations" may be organized within the pattern of coherent quantum activities. These "computations" may be detectable by neural networks and used in higher order processing – may indeed facilitate insight, problem solving and memory storage, as well as other more parapsychological phenomena such as precognition and co-dreaming. While I do agree with Penrose's (1989) arguments against narrow AI-type computational models of consciousness, it does seem possible on the strength of parapsychological and ethnographic evidence that information exchange of a broader kind may be occurring between the conscious brain and the quantum sea, and between brains via the sea (see Radin 1997; Puthoff, Targ and May 1981; Walker 1970, 1973, 1975 who relate quantum physical and parapsychological phenomena). The implications of dreaming brain<–>quantum sea interactions are profound and far reaching, *if they turn out to be true*. The role of dreaming may turn out to involve adjustments of neural networks to information gleaned from the sea, and thus sometimes be the expression in imagery of neural transduction. In other words, some dreams might depict brain-quantum energy interactions that might involve "spooky" phenomena like remote viewing, precognition and so on. We will just have to wait and see.

### Evolution, Neurognosis and the Dreaming Brain

A few neuroscience dream researchers have begun to lodge their thinking within evolutionary theory, which makes them a lot more interesting to anthropologists and archaeologists. For instance, Antti Revonsuo (2000, 2006; Valli and Revonsuo 2007) has argued that dreaming is well-organized and coherent, and operates as a simulation of the perceptual world, especially the simulation of threatening events. But these threats make more sense for people living in an ancient world than they do for people living today. He lodges this explanation within the context of *evolutionary psychology* as formulated by Barkow, Cosmides and Tooby (1992), Cosmides and Tooby (1995), Tooby and Cosmides (1995), and Buss (2004). Evolutionary psychologists argue that many of the adaptive processes of the human brain were developed and more or less hardwired during the lengthy period of the Pleistocene (from 1.8 million years ago to around 12,000 years ago) and that adaptations that do not make much sense in today's environment do make sense when examined within the social contexts and physical environments typical of Paleolithic peoples.

Anthropologist Susan Parman (1979) has likewise floated an interesting theory linking dreaming and play, and as far as I know is the only scholar to have done so. She bases her reasoning upon the common view of dreaming among mammals as being a symbolically rich experience in which problem-solving in waking life is rehearsed. Dreaming has thus a long evolutionary history, as does play, during which the symbolic content of dreams no doubt increased along with the evolution of the neocortex. A complex brain is designed to operate upon interesting stimuli, while the total organism requires substantial down-time to conserve energy and carry out necessary developmental and metabolic activities. A complex brain does not do well under conditions of sensory deprivation, hence a major function of dreaming may be to keep an optimal amount of psychological activity going while somatic down-time is accomplished. Parman suggests that, "It is logical to extend this argument from the realm of sleep to the world of waking, and to suggest that play is analogous, if not homologous, to dreaming because it arises from the same neurophysiological need. The need for the disruption of synchrony, provided internally during sleep, is met during waking by institutionalized or noninstitutionalized forms of play" (ibid:23-24). Just as play increased in complexity up to and including games (i.e., ritual play; see Laughlin and McManus 1982) during phylogenesis, it seems likely that dreams also did so. It also seems likely that dreaming and behavior only become fully integrated with the emergence of the hominin line. That is, only humans seem to exhibit the often elaborate behavioral consequences of dreams, including the acting-out of dreams, the ritual consequences of dreams and the performance of dreams (see Chapter 8 for a further discussion of this issue).

One of the most intriguing explanations for why we dream while we sleep was floated by the great English anthropologist, William H.R. Rivers – a participant in the famous Torres Straits Expedition in 1898 – who wrote a good deal about dreaming (see e.g., Rivers 1917, 1923). He reasoned, as have many since, that the physiological requirement of sleep places animals at a competitive disadvantage. And as we know that environmental stimuli can and do penetrate into the awareness of animals, as they do humans, dreams will allow the most sensitive member of a herd to perceive and emotionally respond to dreamed dangers, reacting to them and waking the rest of the herd in the process (Rivers 1923:183). Not bad reasoning I should say, considering the period in which he was writing. We will return to Rivers' seminal thinking about the functions of dreams in Chapter 8.

## Mental models, Neurognosis and Dreaming

Brains build *mental models* of reality, and the mental models constructed by human brains are heavily influenced by both inheritance and culture (Laughlin and d'Aquili 1974; Laughlin, McManus and d'Aquili 1990; d'Andrade 1995; Shore 1996; Donald 1991, 2001). Roy d'Andrade defines a mental model in this way, "A model consists of an interrelated set of elements which fit together to represent something. Typically one uses a model to reason with or calculate from by mentally manipulating the parts of the model in order to solve some problem. Every schema serves as a simple model in the sense that it is a representation of some object or event" (d'Andrade 1995:151). We are using "model" as a metaphor for how the mind works. It's curious, isn't it, that we humans invent technologies and then use them as models for how the mind that made the technology works – the mind is "like a clock," "like a switchboard," and most recently "like a computer?"

Think about a model for a moment. We usually use the term to label a simplified technical construction of some more complex construction. We build model airplanes that really fly like "real" airplanes. In a sense, the model airplane (car, boat, train, so forth) *represents* the "real" airplane in that it has some elements in common – wings, a motor, landing gear, control surfaces – and if we wish we can study the properties or behavior of the "real" airplane by studying the model. We might build a model of a car or plane and put the model in a wind tunnel to study its aerodynamics. An architect will build a model of a proposed shopping mall out of balsa and plastic in order to give the client a sense of what his project will end up looking like. Yet in many, many ways the model is not at all like the "real" thing it represents. The model plane is made of balsa or styrofoam and not aluminum or titanium, can't carry heavy payloads or passengers, has no toilets or seats or hydraulic systems, no black boxes or transmitter. The model is thus a simplification of the real thing. Mental models are likewise simplifications. Anything in the real world modeled by the brain is always *transcendental* relative to the mental model, which is to say that there is always more to reality than is, or ever can be modeled by the brain.

In my work the term "model" has a much more specific meaning. A mental model is an organization of nerve cells and support cells, and that organization mediates our experience of the thing, process, event, thought, relationship, etc. being modeled, whether imaginary or "real." In other words, all mental models are and must be neural models. There is no such thing as a mental model that is not mediated by a neural model. What difference does this make? All the difference in the world, for when it comes to anthropologists, authors may write whole books about mental models without any reference either to the brain at all, or the constraints that neurobiology imposes on the nature of mental models. More specifically, anthropologists often treat the brain as though it is a "blank slate" during infancy and cultural models are just sort of poured into the nascent mind from outside adult society. The trouble with this view is that the brain is never at any point in its development a "blank slate" (see Pinker 1997, 2003 on this issue). The brain is organized from its first appearance in gestation, and just increases its vastly complex organization of neural networks as the fetus, infant and child develop. Yes, there is *plasticity* (flexibility, ability to change) in all neural structures, but plasticity is always limited and varies in its pliancy depending upon how dedicated is the function of the model (see LeDoux 2003:8-9) and the neurons that compose it (Ebbesson 1984). For instance, neural networks in primary sensory association areas are less plastic than, say, networks in secondary sensory association cortex.

I will go further than this. Virtually all cognitive neural models begin to operate as models as soon as they are organized – remember, they are living cells that organize themselves into circuits, not microchips. Neural models begin as nascent structures that function in a rudimentary way as models, and those models that are involved with knowing reality begin life as *neurognosis* – as species-specific, primitive knowledge about the world and self that are "already there" in a very human way before learning begins and enculturation starts (Pinker 1997; Gazzaniga 1998:9; Carey 2001:67). As neuroscientist Dale Purves (2010:233) notes,

> ...the circuitry of nervous systems such as ours has evolved to contend with one fundamental challenge: How to generate useful perceptions and behaviors in response to a world that is unknowable directly by means of sensory stimuli. The strategy that has emerged to deal with this problem is governed by history, not logical principles or algorithms. Based on feedback from the

empirical consequences of behavior, accumulated information about operational success is realized over evolutionary time in inherited neural circuitry whose organization is then modified to a limited extent by individual experience.

This neural circuitry forms models that have been passed down through DNA and are formed during neurogenesis under the direction of genetic inheritance (Laughlin and d'Aquili 1974:Chap. 5; Laughlin, McManus and d'Aquili 1990:43; Laughlin and Loubser 2010; Pinker 1997; LeDoux 2003:84; Ebbesson 1984; Carey 2009:Chap. 3). *Neurognostic models* mediate our nascent cognitive-perceptual stance to the world, and from that neurognostic stance we begin our active exploration of self and world, modifying, growing and developing our models in response to feedback from the world (Miller, Galanter and Pribram 1960). Neurognostic models are what C. G. Jung referred to as "archetypes" and emerge and begin to develop well into our 20s, particularly the evolutionarily youngest areas of frontal and prefrontal cortex.

Depending upon our physical and cultural environment, some neurognostic models will develop and other models remain relatively undeveloped, and may even die (Changeux 1985; LeDoux 2003:80-82; Katz and Shatz 1996). Some models mediate thought while others mediate images, feelings, perceptions, etc., and their respective development is highly influenced by culture. In a neurobiological sense, "enculturation" is actually the social influence upon neurognostic development. For instance, a baby is born perceiving faces, because there are areas of the cortex that are neurognostically structured to process faces. Enculturation molds the development of these models so that recognition of specific faces and meanings associated with various faces become literally "in-formed" (Varela 1979) – associated by way of neural growth and new synaptic connections with other cells mediating memory (see Figure 4.2).[13] Donald Hebb (1949) showed years ago that

---

[13] The reader should be aware that nerve cells can connect with each other in other ways than an axon synapsing on a dendrite. They can connect axon to axon, axon to cell body and dendrite to dendrite as well. Synapses may be excitatory (urging the recipient cell to fire) and inhibitory (urging the recipient not to fire). In addition, nerve cells may communicate through electrochemical means from cell body to cell body, and by way of the myriad glial cells that surround them and provide them trophic sustenance (see Pagel 2008:62).

the more often a pathway (through a series of cells, nerve tracts and synaptic connections) is activated, the stronger it becomes and the more likely it will be the pathway used in the future – again, by the way, a trophic process. Moreover, the connections that cell A have with cell B will influence other cells connections with cell B (Purves 2010:64). The elaboration of neural networks is a very systematic process, nothing like a random assortment of cells and contacts among cells.

What does any of this have to do with dreaming?

1. **Babies dream archetypal dreams.** Well, for one thing, there are neuroscientists, cognitive scientists, anthropologists and other dream researchers who have claimed that fetuses in the womb and infants don't dream, even thought they exhibit REM activity galore during sleep. Why? Well, they don't dream because they have nothing to dream about. My answer to that claim is that babies dream "archetypal" dreams because they have fully functioning brains at and before birth (Rakic 1995; Gazzaniga 1998:2) and have a lot to dream about as their neural structures grow, "do their thing" during sleep and express themselves in dream imagery and feelings. They have a rich internal dream and waking world that just happens to be less conditioned by external environment than it will increasingly become (see Chapter 10). Babies have an internal world full of faces and hands, nascent landscapes, geometric figures and other archetypal motifs, mediated by neurognostic models that are active and expressing themselves within the baby's sensorium as they develop. I would wager that a fetus' dream life is more rich and interesting than its waking life, but there is no way as yet to know for sure.

2. **Dreaming has many functions.** Understanding that human consciousness and dreaming are organized and active from early fetal days points us toward a better understanding of the biological and developmental functions of dreaming. There really is no single function of dreaming – the functions of dreaming are manifold and depend upon the state of the brain at the time of the dreaming (Kuiken and Sikora1993; Hartmann 2011:Chap. 11). Dreaming is the expression within the sensorium of neural models that may be developing, readjusting and establishing connections among themselves or with other models, may be simulating or rehearsing waking experiences (Donald 1995), may be working to solve problems and seek information, may be consolidating

memories (Stickgold and Wamsley 2011), may be expressing links between emotions and images (Hartmann 2011), may be working through "day residue" issues, may be expressing repressed desires and emotions, may be dominated by traumatized imagery-emotion structures that remain thwarted in their development (see Barrett 1996; Kalsched 1996; Hartmann 2011 on trauma and dreams), and so forth. Dreams are, in other words, the symbolic expression in consciousness of whatever the cognitive/emotional/imaginal parts of the brain are on-about at the moment. Dream imagery may be a synesthetic experience of activities going on unconsciously elsewhere in the nervous system and the body (see Hunt 1989 on this issue; Ramachandran 2004:Chap. 4). For instance, acid reflux in the digestive system might manifest itself as dreams of conflict and pain not logically associated with the ailment. If neurognostic models are being potentiated in development, corresponding dream imagery may be distinctly archetypal. An active and advanced Jungian dreamworker can easily track the development of their psyche by recording dreams and carrying out "active imagination" in the waking state. The dream therefore is a stage upon which the brain portrays its ongoing activities (developmental, problem-solving, expression of repressed material, consolidation of memories, etc.) in often surrealistic plays.

3. **Dream symbols may be pregnant with meaning.** Dream symbols may be, like those in myths and fairy tales, "pregnant with meaning" (Cassirer 1957:202; see also Laughlin, McManus and Stephens 1981; Kunzendorf 2007; Hall 1953). Images and other elements making up the manifest content of dreams are often *polysemic* – they have multiple meanings associated with them, but hidden from view. Symbols are like a kid's toy magnet that is put under a piece of paper with iron filings sprinkled atop the paper, and then as the magnet is moved around under the paper, the pattern of iron filings is moved around as well. Only in this case the paper is turned over so all one may see is the magnet and the pattern of iron filings is hidden. The magnet is the symbol and the iron filings are the meanings attracted to and organized upon the symbol. As Ernest Hartmann (2011) notes, the amount of "condensation" found in polysemic dream symbols may be greater than symbols in the waking state. Dreams are the manifestation of the active and creative seeking of associations that may produce what

he calls central images – images such as being caught-up and swept away by a gigantic tidal wave in the wake of trauma and associated "tidal" emotions (ibid:12; see also Kunzendorf 2007). Thus cultural symbols as images realized in the individual brain are what might be called *innervated metaphors* (see Chapter 11), by which I mean a pattern of neuro-perceptual activity mediating the experience of an image becomes entangled with other, hidden associations in memory, emotion and behavioral networks. If you are like me, all I have to do to evoke an aversive response from my body is imagine I have cut my finger. The image is an innervated metaphor, and the meaning for me is the emotional and other somatic responses to which the metaphor is wired.

Let me offer a personal example of a pregnant dream image. When I started researching this book in earnest, I had a dream in which I was one of President Obama's team. I was in a room with Mr. Obama, who was sitting off to my left and slightly behind me. My role was as his advisor to evaluate a report being given by another man in front of me to my right (he was white). The report went on and on and it had to do with technical stuff that I do not remember. The overall tone of the dream was positive excitement. When I awoke and thought about the dream, several ideas suggested themselves to me. In my dreams black people (usually strange females) almost always signal a message from the unconscious. They are often walking up a spiral staircase from below and are walking or standing to my left, my feminine side. But Mr. Obama is a male, is the current President of the United States and is a known figure whom I associate with "high intellect," moral resolve and positive power – in other words, the unconscious is now "in charge." At the same time, the speaker was on my right, is also male and represents the masculine, conscious and rational-intellectual side of my being. So for me, the dream is a reflection of the state of my self at the time – my "selfscape" (see the last chapter and Chapter 11) – during a period when I have turned away from my normally more balanced, retired way of life to a state of intense activity in researching and writing this book. I (my waking ego) was essentially standing as mediator between unconscious intuitive processes which are "in charge" at the moment and the vast amount of material I am sifting through from the technical literature on dreaming and dream cultures. Mr. Obama appears as a single symbol condensing many meanings, including the King archetype, an active unconscious, being "in charge" of what is happening (I have more than once had the sense that the book is "writing itself"), an active engagement of the unconscious intuitive functions with the rational, and so forth.

4. **Inter-SOC library of symbols.** When one takes an interest in one's dream life over a lengthy period of time – as is often the case with people in polyphasic cultures — that dream life becomes more than a "selfscape," a relatively passive reflection of what the brain and body are doing at the time, and morphs into an interactive medium of communication between normally unconscious processes and a conscious dream ego. Indeed, as one becomes more and more involved in interpreting one's dream symbolism, a "library" of symbols and meanings develops (Chapter 12; see also Hall 1953). In dreamwork, the brain's library of eidetic images becomes a shared language for both the conscious ego in different SOC and the unconscious parts of the self. It is by means of this library of shared knowing that integration of the self, including consciousness, becomes possible. Achieving this intra-psychic integration is frequently *de rigueur* in polyphasic cultures; e.g., Dorothy Eggan (1966) on Hopi dreaming and childhood emersion in religious symbolism, and Chidester (2003) on dream interpretation in Zulu religion.

Thus, the neurobiological functions of dreaming can vary depending upon the sophistication of conscious involvement in dream experiences, and the extent of development of the component neural structures mediating the dream content. The extent of the development of neural components mediating the dream will determine the content, complexity, qualities and significance of the dream. As we have shown, the more involved the prefrontal cortex is in the structures mediating the dream, the more organized, coherent and complex the material, and the more salient the meaning to the dreaming ego. The role of culture in developing or thwarting a sophisticated approach to dream phenomenology is paramount. It is probably true to say that cultural influence upon neural development leads to a patchwork of neurognostic models across cognitive domains that are highly developed, partially developed and under-developed, especially in situations where their development has been thwarted in waking life. Active dreamwork may operate to maximize development of neurognostic models, particularly those that are excluded from the montage of models that are recurrently active in waking life. In the same way that the neural systems mediating the movements of our fingers may vary in their development from learning to grasp tools and coffee cups to learning to play a Bach sonata, so too may the sophistication of the content of our dream experiences range from simple to complex. And for the same reason – in one case the development of the neural facility has remained minimally developed and in the other case development has been optimized. Always remember, the brain is a trophic system, and will expend its available energy doing what is necessary for adaptation. But adaptation has two poles: adaptation of the organism to the external environment (getting food without becoming food), and adaptation of neural subsystems to each other within the nervous system. One may to some extent influence the direction and extent of development in the latter sense by bringing conscious intention into the dreaming process. We will return to this issue in Chapter 14.

## Summary and Segue

Our brain is a self-organizing, trophic system of cells that requires sleep in order to channel metabolic energies and processes into growth and development of neural circuits, many of which mediate experience in different SOC. Sleep probably is as ancient as are brains, and if deprived of sleep, animals, including humans, face serious and even dire consequences. Dreaming and sleep are driven by different systems and dreaming has a number of functions, including the expression within consciousness of unconscious neural development, intra-psychic communication, problem-solving and creative intuition, working-through issues arising in waking life, the consolidation of memories, expression of repressed desires, etc. The brain may operate as a quantum computer, and dreams may be influenced by cellular interaction such that other brains and events distant in spacetime may influence the imagery in dreams.

Of particular importance is the extent to which the prefrontal cortex is involved in the neural system mediating dreams (Dietrich 2007).

The typical situation among Western dreamers is for the PFC to be "turned off," resulting in the absence of higher cognitive and executive functions within the dream. But with increased PFC activity, the nature of dreaming is significantly changed to greater vividness, lucidity and complexity of plot-line. Next, we will take up the interesting topic of lucid dreaming and its relation to the planet's dream cultures.

# Chapter 5

## Lucid Dreaming

Our truest life is when we are in dreams awake.

Henry David Thoreau

There have been three major breakthroughs in the scientific study of sleep and dreaming over the past century: (1) *The discovery of the reticular activating system (RAS)* in 1949 by Giuseppe Moruzzi and Horace Magoun (Magoun 1953). The RAS regulates arousal and the sleep-wake cycle, as we mentioned in the last chapter. (2) *The discovery of the rapid eye movement (REM) sleep stage* by Eugene Aserinsky and Nathaniel Kleitman (1953). Rapid eye movements are correlated with fast wave electrical activity across the cortex, as we also mentioned in the last chapter. Finally, (3) *the "discovery" of lucid dreaming*, the experience of coming awake in a dream. I want to devote this chapter to a discussion of the third "discovery," lucid dreaming, for it impacts directly upon our understanding of the experience and significance of dreaming cross-culturally.

### Lucid Dreaming

I have put "discovery" in quotes when speaking of lucid dreaming, because I wish to emphasize that the only discovery involved was on the part of dream researchers, not dreamers in polyphasic dream cultures who simply take lucidity for granted, or for that matter not dreamers who have explored their dreaming and written about their findings over the decades. Lucid dreaming was first labeled as such and considered clinically significant by a Dutch psychiatrist named Frederik Willems van Eeden (1860-1932; van Eeden 1913) and first considered scientifically by Celia Green in her 1968 book, *Lucid Dreams* (Green

1968). Others in the 19th and early 20th centuries described lucidity in reporting their dreams; e.g., Mary Arnold-Forster (1921) in her book *Studies in Dreams* which recounts experiments in autosuggestion leading to incubation and lucidity, and the Marquis d'Hervey de Saint Denys in his 1867 book *Les rêves et les moyens de les diriger; observations pratiques* (now published as *Dreams and the Means of Directing Them*; de Saint Denys 1982; see also Hobson 1988:34) which describes the results of dream incubation and lucidity.

What then is lucid dreaming – or at least as far as science is concerned? A dream is lucid if *we are aware within the dream that we are dreaming and that we are not awake* (Green 1968; Gackenbach 1991a; Gackenbach and LeBerge 1988; Snyder and Gackenback 1991:55; LaBerge 1985:2; Tedlock 1999:94). Usually something causes us to wake up in a dream, almost always during the REM state (Ogilvie *et al.* 1978, 1982; LaBerge 1990; LaBerge *et al.* 1981), and we become aware that we are awake and that we are dreaming. There is a lot wrong with this definition of lucidity from an anthropological point of view, not the least being its inherent ethnocentricity. It assumes a culture in which waking states and dreaming states are distinct, one being associated with active awareness and the other not. We would hardly expect that kind of distinction to be made by folks brought up in a fully polyphasic culture. Moreover, it assumes that one "wakes up" in what passes for "normal" dreaming in Western society, and that this is a rare event. And, perhaps most importantly, a dream can include intervals of lucidity without "finding your hands" or other methods researchers use to increase awareness in dreams (see Price and Cohen 1988). But we will get into this later after we look at the state of lucid dream research a bit more closely.

There is currently a great interest in lucid dreaming among researchers. Certainly the premier lucid dream researcher today is Stephen LaBerge (b. 1947) who took his Ph.D. at Stanford University in 1980 on the topic of lucid dreaming. He has shown that lucid dreaming can be a learned skill (1980), has led the way in developing techniques for eliciting lucidity in dreamers for research purposes (1985, 2009), and has demonstrated that lucid dreamers can communicate with researchers while still dreaming, thus enabling confirmation of lucidity states with measures of psychophysiology underlying sleep stages (LaBerge 1990, 2010; LaBerge *et al.* 1981).

Moreover, for the purposes of this book, LaBerge has developed a theory of dreaming in keeping with the thesis I am trying to build – namely that dreaming is another domain of experiences had by the brain that produces and consumes them, and that hard and fast distinctions between waking and dreaming are not phenomenologically accurate (LaBerge 1994). "In our view, the distinction between lucid and nonlucid dreams is not as clear-cut as the definition suggests and fails to do justice to the subtlety of the actual experience. We feel the contemporary distinction has misplaced focus away from what we consider the essential variations in dream cognition underlying dream lucidity" (LaBerge and DeGracia 2000). As icing on the cake, LaBerge manifests a healthy scepticism similar to my own of the "Rube-Goldberg contraption" that is Freudian dream theory (LaBerge 1994:28).

## Lucid Dream Experiences – A Sampling of Motifs

But before we get further into the theoretical stuff, let me give you a sample of lucid dream reports out of the literature and my own experiences so that we have a common ground for thinking about the topic. Hugh George Callaway (1885-1949) was an English writer and occultist who was also an avid lucid dreamer from an early age. Under the pseudonym, Oliver Fox, he published many of his experiences with *out-of-body-experiences* (OBEs) in articles that were later republished after his death in a book with the unfortunate title, *Astral Projection* (1962). Here is his report of his first lucid dream, had when he was sixteen (c. 1901; ibid:32-33):

> I dreamed that I was standing on the pavement outside my home. The sun was rising behind the Roman wall, and the waters of Bletchingden Bay (sic) were sparkling in the morning light. I could see the tall trees at the corner of the road and the top of the old grey tower beyond the Forty Steps [in Southampton, England]. In the magic of the early sunshine the scene was beautiful enough even then. Now the pavement was not of the ordinary type, but consisted of small, bluish-grey rectangular stones, with their long sides at right-angles to the white kerb.

I was about to enter the house when, on glancing casually at these stones, my attention became riveted by a passing strange phenomenon, so extraordinary that I could not believe my eyes – they had seemingly all changed their position in the night, and the long sides were now parallel to the kerb! Then the solution flashed upon me: though this glorious summer morning seemed real to me, I was *dreaming*! (emphasis by Fox)

Note that it is a discrepancy between an expectation appropriate to the waking life and what he was experiencing that awakened his critical faculties to the extent that he realized he was dreaming. LaBerge (1985:30) quotes a dream had by van Eeden that illustrates this classic feature of lucid dreams:

…I dreamt that I stood at a table before a window. On the table were different objects. I was perfectly well aware that I was dreaming and I considered what sorts of experiments I could make. I began by trying to break glass, by beating it with a stone. I put a small goblet of glass on two stones and struck it with another stone. Yet it would not break. Then I took a fine claret-glass from the table and struck it with my fist, with all my might, at the same time reflecting how dangerous it would be to do this in waking life; yet the glass remained whole. But lo! When I looked at it again after some time, it was broken.

Notice that van Eeden twigs that he is dreaming and exercises his will within the dream, but notice also that there is an obdurate quality to the dream production – the systems mediating the dream resist his will, at least for a time. In both Buddhist and Jungian dreamwork, the over-zealous exercise of will may actually interfere with symbolic communications from the depths (i.e., the unconscious).

Flying and sexual arousal are two common features in dreams of all sorts, and particularly in lucid dreams. LaBerge (1985:83) shares a dream had by Miranda, one of his laboratory dreamers who had been instructed to signal when she was in a lucid state, and then again when she had a sexual experience with a male:

Miranda had a three-minute lucid dream in which she successfully carried out the experimental task – exactly as agreed upon. In her report, she said that she seemed to be lying in bed still awake, with someone's hands rubbing her neck. Recognizing the improbability of someone being in her room, she suspected she was dreaming, and tested her state by trying to float into the air. As soon as she found herself floating, she was convinced she was dreaming and made the agreed-upon signal as she floated through her bedroom wall. Finding no one in the polygraph room, she proceeded through an unopened window outside. Continuing to fly, she found herself over a campus resembling Oxford and Stanford.

The dream continued with Miranda finding a random male and signaling her intention to begin a sexual adventure, had an orgasm, signaled again to the researchers, and woke up. Of course, Freud did link flying and sexuality, and this may well be the case for many Western dreamers. But flying is also a common motif in the dreams of non-Westerners and quite likely has no sexual over- (or under-) tones. Notice also that the dream body is able to pass through apparently physical barriers at will.

Flying into "outer" (some like myself would interpret "inner") space is an adventure I have had many times over the years, especially when I was involved in doing what is sometimes called "star group" meditations.[1] Here is one such dream reported by Robert Waggoner (2009:36):

> There are many people around, like a family dinner or picnic. Somehow I become lucid and find that my flying control is excellent. I effortlessly fly from room to room with grace, precision, and awareness. I play around with moving objects in the rooms. One woman notices me and acts seductively. I choose to ignore her. I think about what to do and decide to try to fly out into the stars. I begin to fly and keep flying and flying. I'm

---

[1] There are, no doubt, many names for this kind of meditation. A group of people sit around holding hands and meditating upon a real or imagined (seems to make little difference which) blue light above and in the center of the group. Experiences often involve flying and trips into outer space.

astounded! I can't believe how far I'm going and everything stays the same. ...I continue flying into outer space. I begin to fly past planets. This is incredible! Finally, I decide to stop. I look down about forty degrees and there's a large planet with rings and four moons. I notice that two of the moons seem to have ghostly rings around them while others don't. The main planet's ring is kind of orangish gold. Two of the moons are to the right, with a third almost halfway behind the planet. The fourth moon is on the left side of the planet. I marvel at the profound sight of seeing an entire planet hanging in space. It's so incredibly silent and still. I decide to keep going, and do, but don't find anything new, so I turn back with the intent of flying through the outlying rings of the planet. I head toward the rings and, as I do so, I begin to feel energy hitting me as I move through the ring. (Here, I believe I momentarily lose my lucidity or have a total scene shift.) I am back on Earth, still flying. It occurs to me that this has been quite a long lucid dream.

Notice that in his dream, he exercises control, a major factor for those exploring lucidity for its own sake. In doing so he chooses not to embrace other opportunities, such as the woman who notices him and acts seductively – which in, say, Jungian dreamwork might be considered an invitation to engage his anima (see Chapter 10). This exercise of control for control's sake is distinctly Western, and may in fact interfere with the flow of the dream (Hunt 1989:120), something that is less likely to occur in non-laboratory, non-Western circumstances.

During the period of my life when I was engaged in intensive meditation in the Tibetan Tantric Buddhist tradition (see Chapter 13), I spent a lengthy retreat completing a basic "foundation" practice called the "mandala offering" (Tib. *kyil khor*; see MacDonald *et al.* 1988 on the use of mirrors in shamanic traditions generally). I made a contraption out of the glass from a round shaving mirror glued to the bottom of a small bowl. Gripping the upside down bowl with the mirror-side up in my left hand, I built a mandala from saffron-dyed rice held under the mirror in a plastic tub. I would build the sacred landscape of Mount Meru and other features while reciting a mantra, and then wipe the mirror clean (rice falling back into the tub) and start building the mandala all over again. Over and over, 100,000 times I repeated this ritual for an average of 12 hours a day until it was completed.

You will not be surprised to learn that the mirror and saffron rice imagery penetrated into my dream life where I had repeated experiences in which I was aware I was dreaming and was watching my mind build all sorts of figures out of saffron-colored particles – like Lego blocks — often emerging out of bodies of water (pool, lake, sea) and I (dream-ego indistinguishable from waking-ego) was sometimes aboard a boat. I recall sailing through a placid sea with gigantic "icebergs" made of saffron bits floating by. I was often aware within the dream that the intent of the practice was to see that my mind built things out of particles, and that the mirror itself was the mind of "pure" potential out of which the particle forms emerged and then dissolved. Some of the experiences were emotionally positive, others negative. Moreover, the images constructed before my dreaming eye were often communications from the "inner teacher" using shared meanings and motifs. The Buddhist practice in this dream context is just to watch what arises with as much awareness as possible and with the least interference from the dream-ego.

Without, I hope, sounding patronizing, if one has not experienced a lucid dream, then one will have little idea of just how "real" a dream experience can be. This is no different than saying that if one has not been on a magic mushroom trip, one cannot know what it is like – or a high altitude gas balloon flight, or scuba diving, so forth. In lucid dreaming one often has the sense of being *more* awake and aware in the dream than in waking life – something I also have experienced while scuba diving. With respect to dreaming, I suspect this is due in part to the simplified neural systems that mediate the dream "movie." Everything in a stage play is significant and part of the plot line – as Chekhov once put it, "One must not put a loaded rifle on the stage if no one is thinking of firing it." There is far less available in the dream upon which to focus awareness. But the sense of heightened awareness can be numinous. LaBerge (1997:30) quotes a dream report from the mathematician J. H. M. Whiteman (1961:57):

> After [attending a concert by a celebrated string quartet]... I remember going to bed with mind peacefully composed and full of a quiet joy. The dream, during the night that followed, was

at the beginning quite irrational, though perhaps more keenly followed than usual. I seemed to move smoothly through a region of space where, presently, a vivid sense of cold flowed in on me and held my attention with a strange interest. I believe that at that moment the dream became lucid. Then suddenly,... all that up to now had been wrapped in confusion instantly passed away, and a new space burst forth in vivid presence and utter reality, with perception free and pin-pointed as never before; the darkness itself seemed alive. *The thought that was then borne in upon me with inescapable conviction was this: "I have never been awake before"* (emphasis mine).

## Ritual Control of Experience and Incubating Lucid Dreaming

As anyone knows who has taken interest in their dream life, all it takes to increase dream recall is the intention to do so. The mind and its consciousness tend to follow intention. The more interesting a thing becomes, the more awareness and knowledge, and even neurocognitive development accrues in that domain. It is true to say that literally anything one turns one's interest towards can become a portal into a vast domain of experience and realization. Become interested in postage stamps and pretty soon you are haunting stamp shops, stamp shows, reading stamp magazines, etc. The same is true of dreaming.

There are many techniques available for increasing dream recall (see e.g., Fox 1962; Garfield 1974; Gackenbach and Bosveld 1989; Waggoner 2009:265-268). All one needs to do is Google "dream recall" to find all kinds of on-line approaches to dreaming. Methods include laying a tablet and pen beside the bed at night and concentrating upon remembering one's dreams just before drifting off – in other words, *autosuggestion*. An expert can hypnotize a person and lay in appropriate post-hypnotic suggestions. One can drink a half glass of water while telling oneself to recall a dream and then finish the water first thing upon waking. The techniques are many and some are very old, for what one is doing in a sense is rediscovering ancient ritual techniques used to incubate dreaming (see Chapters 4 and 7 on dream incubation). The point to underscore here for ethnologists is that cultural symbols and expectations, ritual practices, personal intentions, events happening during the day, emotional turmoil, all of these things can penetrate into and influence what happens in the dream life (LaBerge and Rheingold 1990). The permeability and interpenetration of SOC is the most important factor in understanding ancient oracles and other methods used to stimulate visions and dreams during initiation ceremonies.

Many techniques for stimulating engagement in and recall of dreams operate by decreasing the abruptness of the *warp* between SOC (Laughlin, McManus and d'Aquili 1990:142). Every transition from one SOC to another involves a relatively rapid reorganization (or warp) of the neural systems mediating consciousness. We can say that one SOC "warps" into another SOC. Sleep onset and its associated hypnagogic are an example of a warp. It normally happens in just a few seconds. The problem in increasing awareness in dreams is a problem in transferring information across the warps between sleep stages. Nothing really "moves," of course, from one SOC to another. The neural system mediating the dream state must retain enough of the structure of the preceding state so that it is available during the dreaming. For instance, one has to keep the intention to wake up in the dream, or communicate with researchers during the dream, as part of the new organization of the neural system mediating the dream. The challenge is to literally *re*-member the intention. Advanced methods of ritual control over dreaming operate to minimize the reorganization of SOC on each side of the sleep onset warp (see Chapters 7 and 13 for examples).

Very few people in our culture experience spontaneous intervals of lucidity in their dreams (LaBerge 1985). We have already discussed why this happens – in a word, it is because we are culturally conditioned to disengage our prefrontal cortex from the neural organization mediating dreams (see Chapter 4). Henceforth when I speak of "lucidity" in dreaming, or "going lucid," or "being lucid," or having a "lucid dream," I am implying an increased involvement of the PFC. My claim is that there is no lucidity without PFC involvement (see Hobson, Pace-Schott and Stickgold 2003:45). So, the trick in producing lucidity is to reverse this lifelong habit and increase PFC involvement. We take our first steps when we increase our interest in the process – that by definition activates PFC processes, at least in the waking state. Thus, the games we have to play in order to increase lucidity may be fairly strenuous for some. To learn to become lucid in our dreams is valuable enough, but for ethnologists the experiences gained will enable one to better empathize with and understand our informants in polyphasic cultures where some degree of lucidity is the norm. Ethnologists capable of lucid dreaming, like Barbara Tedlock (1999) and Fernando Santos-Guereros (2003), are worth many times their weight in Boases and Tylors, at least to the ethnographic study of dreaming.

Within the literature on lucid dream research are to be found a number of techniques for incubating lucidity (LaBerge 1985, 2009:Chap. 3; LaBerge and Rheingold 1990; Waggoner 2009; Green 1968; Tholey 1983). These techniques are extensions of those designed to increase dream recall, but the challenge for Westerners is, as I have mentioned before, daunting. Yet the challenge can be met and surpassed. The methods used are generally variations on the *ritual control of experience* (Laughlin *et al.* 1986).

What do I mean by "ritualizing" and "ritual?" And what do I mean by "control?" *Ritualization* refers to the universal tendency of animals to routinize a sequence of behavior for the purpose of completing a task or communicating information. Ritualization may or may not be conscious to the animal – it probably is not. It is just a sequence of behavior that they either inherit or develop that gets something done or communicated. Examples are threat displays among gorillas, pre-copulatory displays among birds, shaking hands among some nearly-hairless apes, "sings" among coyotes, etc. We take the same route to school or office, we tie our tie in the same way every time we are unfortunate enough to have to wear one. *Ritual* is a more complex form of ritualization and is more likely to be conscious to the animal, as for example in a "rain dance" among chimpanzees, or group hunting strategy among arctic wolves, or morning bathroom rituals among nearly-hairless apes. *Ceremonies* are very formalized, often complex rituals carried out only by nearly-hairless apes with a great deal of awareness and cultural significance; e.g., the Catholic Mass, a wedding ceremony or funeral. Ceremonies are cognized as a special event, generally are named ("we're going to Mass," "we're sitting shiva"), and are distinct from other events and behaviors. "One may trace the evolutionary progression of ritual behavior [among animals] from the emergence of formalization through the coordination of formalized communicative behavior and sequences of ritual behavior to the conceptualization of such sequences and the assignment of symbols to them by man" (d'Aquili, Laughlin and McManus 1979:37).

*Control* means that ritual is used to exert influence over neural processes to intentionally produce a desired experience. Ritual action in the waking state can produce experiences had in ASC, and in particular, dreaming. Ethnographically speaking, rituals of this kind, as well as more elaborate ceremonies, are a cultural universal. All human societies perform ceremonial rituals and most of these are integrated within a cosmological system involving myth and spiritual practices (see Chapter 8 on the "cycle of meaning"). When societies consider it important for a person or group to have a specific experience – usually for spiritual or initiatory purposes – they position a ritual before the experience in order to incubate the desired qualities and content of the experience. The ritual may incorporate drivers such as psychotropic substances, repetitive activities like dancing, chanting, drumming, praying, flickering lights, etc., dramatic enactments such as mystery plays, masked dancers, etc., or ordeals like long distance running, physical pain (wearing a shirt into which angry hornets have been sewn, putting hooks in the breast and hanging from a tree limb), or doing scary things like jumping out of a 70 foot tree with a 60 foot rope tied to the ankles (Laughlin *et al.* 1986; Winkelman 2010). Ritual preparation for an experience may be understood psychophysiologically as a means of warp control – setting things up for the proper transformation of neural systems mediating a "peak" experience valued by the people.

The ritual incubation of lucid dreams rarely requires such radical and arduous activities, although participation in such rituals will not leave the dream life unaffected. But the principles are much the same, as we shall see in Chapter 13 when we discuss meditating one's way into the dream states. Stephen LaBerge uses a method of lucid dream incubation he calls *mnemonic induction of lucid dreams* (*MILD*). The method simply applies ritualized mnemonic devices like many of us use to remember people's names. One visualizes the thing you will be later doing in the dream when you wish to become lucid, or remember to do some task. "The visualization that I use to organize my intended effort is: 'Next time I am dreaming, I want to remember to recognize I am dreaming.' The 'when' and 'what' of the intended action must be clearly specified" (LaBerge 1985:140). LaBerge goes on to break his method down into several steps (ibid:141):

1. During the early morning, when you awaken spontaneously from a dream, go over the dream several times until you have memorized it.
2. Then, while lying in bed and returning to sleep, say to yourself, "Next time I'm dreaming, I want to remember to recognize I'm dreaming."
3. Visualize yourself as being back in the dream just rehearsed; only this time, see yourself realizing that you are, in fact, dreaming.
4. Repeat steps two and three until you feel your intention is clearly fixed or you fall asleep.

MILD is a straightforward way of ritualizing the control over the sleep onset warp, pairing a rehearsal of dreaming with an intentional task. Visualization practices in incubation are common cross-culturally, and may or may not be evoked by ritual drama or some other external stimulus.

Psychologist and dream researcher Paul Tholey (1937 - 1998) developed a set of methods for incubating and manipulating lucid dreams. One of these is called the *reflection technique* (Tholey 1983a) which was tailored to both increase awareness during dreaming, and also to maintain awareness while entering sleep onset – the latter being important to such practices as Tibetan dream yoga (see Chapter 13). This "…technique rests on the following basic assumption. If a subject develops while awake a critical-reflective attitude toward his momentary state of consciousness by asking himself if he is dreaming or not, then this attitude can be transferred to the dream state" (ibid:80). Again we have cross-warp transference of information. One should ask this question – am I dreaming? – as often as possible, especially near the time of falling to sleep, and during any waking experience that resembles a dream. Associating the "critical" question with a potential dream scenario helps to incubate one's first lucid dreaming experience, while repetition of the question proximal to sleeping increases the incidence of lucidity that night.

Another of Tholey's methods is called the *intention technique* in which one "should try as intensely as possible to imagine that he is in dream situations which would typically cause him to recognize that he is dreaming. Even better would be an attempt to carry out a simple action in the dream simultaneously" (ibid:80). This is a rehearsal technique that ritualizes an association between an act, like looking for one's hands in the dream, with dream-typical situations in the waking state. Yet another method mentioned by Tholey is a very common one that he calls the *autosuggestion technique*. Referring back to Heinrich Juergens' first use of the term autosuggestion in his 1953 work, *Traum-Exerzitien* [Dream Exercises], Tholey notes that "the subject suggests to himself, if possible immediately before falling asleep and while in a relaxed state, that he is going to experience a lucid dream. A conscious effort of will must be avoided. ...The effectiveness of suggestive formulas can be improved by employing special relaxation techniques" (ibid:81).

Psychologist Robert Waggoner, himself a lucid dreamer of no mean ability, used LaBerge's MILD technique to good effect, and reports on Tholey's and other techniques as well (2009:268-281). Among other things, Waggoner notes that the following methods and tips seem to help some dreamers reach lucidity (ibid:73-74): Sleep in a different location; vacations, holidays and other changes in daily routine; taking up yogic practices; being in a positive mood; excessive physical and mental activity during the day; making certain dietary changes; taking certain vitamins; changes in the weather; and sleeping in particular locations like sacred sites.

## Psychological Theories of Dreaming and Lucidity

Lucid dream research has given rise to a raft of theories of dreaming and lucidity. Let us touch on several of these by those psychologists who (1) are themselves lucid dreamers, (2) have a deep interest in lucid dreaming and (3) have spent years researching dreams and dreaming in sleep labs or work with children. These are the psychologists who are likely to be of the greatest interest to us as we move on to considering dreaming cross-culturally. There are other psychological theories that do not take neuroscience, development and the role of awareness into consideration in their thinking about dreaming, and those are theories of little interest to us here.

**1. Stephen LaBerge: Dreaming and Perceiving.** Our premier lucid dream researcher has developed a theory consonant with our own as to the function of dreaming. "I propose that dreams result from brain activities using internal information to create a simulation of the world, much like the process of waking perception, minus sensory input. According to this assumption, human dreaming is the result of the same perceptual and mental processes that we use to comprehend the world when awake. In order to understand dreaming, we need to understand perception, and vice versa: from this perspective, to perceive is to dream. More precisely, perception is dreaming constrained by sensory information; dreaming is perception independent of sensory input, and thus without external constraints" (LaBerge 1994:28).

**2. Awareness and Self-Reflection in Dreams.** Allan Moffitt, Robert Hoffman and Roger Wells developed a sleep lab back in the 1970s in the psychology department at Carleton University in Ottawa, Canada, where I taught anthropology. A lot of good research was done in that lab, and a number of excellent students emerged from their program, including the late Jon Shearer with whom I wrote my earliest papers on ASC (Laughlin, McManus and Shearer 1983, 1993; Laughlin *et al.* 1986). Another student in that lab, Sheila Purcell, carried out research on the role of self-reflection in dreams (Purcell *et al.* 1986; Purcell, Moffitt and Hoffman 1993). She and her colleagues have shown that the degree of self-awareness or self-reflection in dreams ranges on a continuum (punctuated by 9 steps) from absence of a dream ego through the presence of a passive dream-ego to full lucidity where the dreamer exerts some degree of control over the content, events or emotions within the dream (Purcell, Moffitt and Hoffman 1993:219). They found that self-reflection during dreaming is a learned cognitive skill, and that the development of this skill has spill-over effects upon waking consciousness. As we also wrote, "The extent of awareness within dream [states] varies enormously, and it is the single most important variable in determining both (1) understanding in and of the dream, and (2) the locus of control of dream content" (McManus, Laughlin and Shearer 1993:38).

**3. The Developmental Dimension of Dreaming.** A number of lucid dream researchers have recognized that when awareness becomes an ongoing part of any SOC, the SOC will develop cognitively along Piagetian lines (e.g., Piaget 1962; Foulkes 1985). Our own work led us inescapably to this conclusion with respect to dreaming (McManus, Laughlin and Shearer 1993:38): "We are not saying that dream [states] function as a dialogue between, and reorganization of, internal systems only in polyphasic individuals and cultures. Rather, dream [states] operate to reorganize internal systems whether or not the ego is polyphasic. The question is to what extent there is participation by higher cortical processes in all [states] of consciousness" (ibid:40). It is important to mention that lucid dreaming *per se* is not inevitable in any particular individual, or for that matter in any particular social group.

David Foulkes has done remarkable dream research with children, and from this perspective he reasons that "dreaming is simply the operation of consciousness during sleep (and some other states), and I observed that dreaming develops more slowly and later than is generally believed" (1999:146). He hypothesizes that as consciousness develops via Piagetian stages, the complexity of consciousness will influence the complexity in all SOC, including dreaming. It is not clear to me, however, to what extent Foulkes appreciates Piaget's notion of *horizontal decalages*. Jean Piaget held that development across experiential domains or tasks is usually uneven with cognitive processing being relatively advanced in one domain and relatively primitive in another domain (Piaget 1941; Kreitler and Kreitler 1989). It is my contention that the neural organization mediating any specific SOC will undergo development, whether it be experiences under the influence of psychotropic substances like the lifelong use of *ayahuasca* by Brazilian shamans, or experiences had while lucid dreaming. To enter apprenticeship to an *ayahuasca* shaman, or to begin a career as a lucid dreamer is tantamount to an invitation to cognitive development in that respective domain.

Following on from the work of Foulkes with children and the Carleton University group, Jayne Gackenbach (1991b:287) argues "that lucidity is only the beginning and that consciousness in sleep, when it arises as part of the natural growth cycle, is both psychologically and biologically a developmentally advanced form of dreaming." Drawing from the descriptions by experienced meditators, she has hypothesized a five stage model of the development of lucidity in dreaming, all of them being essentially "post-formal operational" stages[2] in the Piagetian sense. I would add to this that culture has an enormous role to play in when and to what extent the importance of dreaming is felt by the individual. Life-long polyphasic peoples will likely manifest far less in the way of severe horizontal *decalages* between waking and dreaming states.

**4. Harry T. Hunt and Expanding the Types of Dreams.** One of the most refreshing analyses of dreaming is that of cognitive psychologist, Harry T. Hunt, whose book *The Multiplicity of Dreams* (1989) is one of the few treatments of dreaming that considers both lucid dreaming and archetypal structures. This is because Hunt insists that any account of dreaming must take into consideration all types of dreams. In developing a typology, he is also one of the few psychologists or neuroscientists to cover the anthropological literature:

> There do seem to be relatively distinct types of dreaming, each with its own line of development and potentially one-sided exaggeration – as permitted or perhaps demanded by the subjective clouding or single-mindedness of dreaming. There are (1) relatively mundane dreams that seem to be based on mnemonic consolidations and reorganizations; (2) Freud-type relatively fantastic, pressure-discharge dreams, often based on complex rebus-like wordplay; (3) dreams based on somatic states and illness; (4) dreams based on aesthetically rich metaphor; (5) dreams based on problem-solving and deep intuition (perhaps extrasensory?); (6) lucid-control dreams; (7) the variety of nightmare; and (8) a Jung-type archetypal-mythological form of dreaming (Hunt 1989:76; numbering added by author).

These are not exclusive types, but rather natural types with fuzzy boundaries that overlap and intermix. They are in keeping with the position I have taken (Chapter 4) that there is no one

---

[2] This is a Piagetian way of saying that someone is dreaming quite abstractly.

psychophysiological or evolutionary function for dreaming, but rather multiple functions that come into play depending upon the extent of personal development, the culture of the group and the environmental conditions faced by the person and the group. We will return to Hunt's findings in Part Two of the book when we consider archetypal dreaming (see Chapter 10).

**5. Gordon Globus and the Importance of Phenomenology and Creativity.** Various authorities over the years have questioned whether true creativity, inspiration or spiritual guidance arises during dreaming. It was Freud's contention that dreams were made up of day residues blended with wish fulfillment. Psychiatrist and philosopher Gordon Globus presents a wonderful critique of the essentially anti-creative views of Freud in his book *Dream Life, Wake Life* (1987). He then goes on to show that dreams are the product of intentionality, thought and abstraction. What populates our dreams are *not* concrete objects from waking life haphazardly arranged, but abstract images that represent the intentional meanings of – sometimes surreal – unconscious thought. As Globus (ibid:61) puts it:

> I have argued against Freud that the creativity of dreaming consciousness is first-hand, "de novo." The role of memory of concrete waking experiences is to provide something abstract (e.g., not a particular horse but the meaning of "horse," not a particular three-phrase movement but the meaning of "three-phase movement"). Other operative meanings are related to both unconscious wishes and unconscious defenses against those wishes which were also active during waking. The life-world of dreams is generated by these active intentional meanings. Lucid dreams demonstrate the creative power of intentionality in remarkable fashion.

As we shall see in the next chapter, Globus argues for grounding our theories of dreaming in phenomenology, and in particular the phenomenology of Edmund Husserl (1859-1938). There must be a "return to the things" in Husserl's sense — in this case a return to the direct experiences of the dreaming life-world, rather than merely to dream reports. It is only through the common ground of the dreaming *life-world*³ – the patterns, elements and processes all humans have in common as dreamers – that we can come to understand the significance of dreaming for our species. The abstract nature of dream images is one such common and universal property of dreams.

Robert D. Bruce (1975:43) reports a dream he had while working among the Lacandon Maya: "I dreamed of a large howler monkey (or perhaps a small ape – *actually it looked more like an artist's conception of Zinjanthropus*), a young one clinging to its dead mother, lying in shallow water." Note that the "howler monkey doesn't look like a howler (which abounds in the area where he was living), but more like an ancient hominin. Is this some kind of random mistake? A mere pastiche of ape-like elements? Hardly. Globus would, no doubt, point to this as an abstract image in the sense that it is the representation in the dream of a condensation of meanings in the unconscious. (As my late friend and colleague, John McManus, liked to say, "There are no errors in the unconscious.") I will return to Globus' views in the next chapter.

## Summary of the Science of Lucid Dreaming

It seems clear that the involvement of consciousness in dreaming manifests as a continuum of awareness from virtually absent, through degrees of vividness to the occurrence of lucidity, thence to full involvement of the highest cognitive capabilities of the individual. It is also clear that the neuropsychological structures mediating dreams undergo development over time. It is not clear to me that lucid dreamers "control" their dreams entirely – I certainly have never been able to do so — but the self-aware dream ego is certainly capable of guiding events by directing attention to this, rather than that aspect of the unfolding dream (e.g., go down this tunnel and not that one). With respect to the cross-cultural data, one does not run into the exercise of control over dreams very often. I suspect that this emphasis in lucid dreamwork is an

---

³ Life-world is English for the German *Lebenswelt*, a concept Edmund Husserl introduced into his phenomenology in his *The Crisis in European Sciences and Transcendental Phenomenology* (1937). The life-world is the ground of direct experience that we all hold in common, which is as close to "objectivity" as is possible, given the inherent subjectivity of human experience.

artifact of Western ethnocentricity. Autosuggestion is another matter, for "flying" shamans will commonly go to sleep intending to travel to a specific place or engage a specific spirit.

I am in agreement with LaBerge (2010) that no hard and fast distinction can be made between "normal" dreaming and lucid dreaming. Rather, one kind of dreaming phases into the other kind of dreaming by degrees, especially outside the sleep lab environment. It is well for anthropologists to remember that most of the subjects of lucid dreaming experiments have been Western university students, presumably conditioned by their upbringing to disattend their dreams. Despite this cultural trend, many do recall their dreams, but they tend on average to be low down on the Purcell *et al.* (1992) continuum. I will go further than this and suggest that in most polyphasic cultures, no such abrupt distinction is made or culturally labeled. That is not to say that other distinctions are not made — traditional cultures frequently do make distinctions and apply their own local dream typologies.

Another thing that we must keep in mind when applying the kind of sleep lab data we have been examining above to the ethnographic situation is that dream reports are at least two removes from the dream. There is the *dream-as-dreamt*, the *dream-as-recalled* and the *dream-as-told* in a natural social setting.

**1. The dream-as-dreamt.** The dream-as-dreamt is a more or less vivid experience arising in the individual brain, and is mediated by a distinct organization of neural systems. Whether, and to what extent, ego awareness is present in the experience is determined by the organization of the mediating neural systems, in particular the extent to which PFC processes are entrained to the system (see Chapter 4). Involvement of the PFC will bring with it an increase in working memory and a resulting continuity in the "plot line" of the dream. An analogous condition would be that I watch a *Star Wars* movie on the big screen.

**2. The dream-as-recalled.** The dream-as-recalled is an act of memory in which the content of the dream is literally *re*-called, brought back into the sensorium from short or long term memory storage. The sooner the remembering occurs (such as just after being awakened from the dream in a sleep lab), presumably the more accurate will be the recall. But recall will always be selective, and will tend to highlight dramatic imagery, significance and emotion. Another analogous condition might be that I play the *Star Wars* movie over and over in my mind as I leave the theater, recalling all the good bits.

**3. The dream-as-told.** The dream-as-told is the dream report I write in my dream journal, recite to the ethnographer, recount to my family and friends, report to the lab person that just woke me up. The dream memory has been converted into a narrative, a text. Unless I am an artist and draw or paint my remembered dream imagery, my dream report is now inextricably filtered both through the structures of memory and the structures of language. Another analogous condition might be that my friend asks me what the *Star Wars* movie was about and I give him a blow-by-blow description of what I remember about the movie.

Even during the duration of the dream, assuming there is any dream-ego presence at all, it is little different than perception (LaBerge 1985) in that the "searchlight" of awareness will focus here and not there, pick out salient features and disattend others. There is no way we can be aware of everything in the dream any more than we can be aware of everything during waking perception, nor can we recall every nuance of the dream. Our attention and recall are selective, and the set of personal and cultural expectations we bring into the dream will influence the experience, and hence the recall and the telling (LaBerge and Rheingold 1990). LaBerge (1994:30; Kahan, LaBerge and Levitan 1997) has shown experimentally that in effect recall and telling of a lucid dream is little different than recall and telling of the *Star Wars* movie. There is a loss of information at every stage until the telling of the dream is but a shadow of the original experience.

## The Anthropology of Lucid Dreaming

The inevitable loss of information between the dreaming and the telling is extremely important for ethnographers to understand, for it may not be possible for a non-dream-recalling, or a non-lucid dreaming fieldworker to discern at which level of the continuum of dream awareness the informant is operating. Put in another way, it is often difficult to determine on the basis of dream reports alone whether the informants were lucid during their dreams. In addition, it is our

Western custom when telling someone about a dream we had to preface our story by labeling it as a dream – we might say something like, "Hey, I had this neat dream last night. I was in my grandmother's apartment and... ." We would never just start out telling someone, "Hey, I was in my grandmother's apartment last night and... ." On the other hand, we feel no such necessity to label a story about something we experienced while awake – we just start off telling the story, like "Hey, I went over to my grandmother's place last night, and... ." Other cultures may or may not signal such a distinction. In many polyphasic cultures making such a clear-cut distinction between dreaming and waking experiences may well not be used, for dreaming and other ASC are considered to be extensions of reality, especially if the dreaming is highly lucid (see Nielsen 1991 on the reality sense in dreaming).

Let us turn our attention to what anthropology has to say about lucid dreaming. What I will endeavor to do is tease out indicators of lucidity in ethnographic dream reports. This is not an easy challenge, for it is unlikely that any ethnographer writing before the mid- to late-1980s had heard of lucid dreaming because the concept had not yet reached a wide audience. And many ethnographers since then have ignored the issue. Thus the distinctions imposed upon dream reports in the ethnographic literature are most often either Freudian – e.g., "manifest" vs. "latent" content, "conflict" or "wish fulfillment" dreams, etc. – or local cultural dream typologies.

To make matters worse, there is a systemic problem of ethnocentrism in how Western psychologists have experienced and defined lucid dreaming. As you can see from the summary of the psychophysiological research above, the emphasis is upon an ego suddenly coming awake in the dream – I am lucid when I become aware that I am dreaming. "I," "I," "I" – a very Western focus on the ego, on the individual having the experience, and especially on *taking control* over dream elements, events, and even plot line rather than upon watching whatever experience unfolds (Hunt 1989:120). Lucid dreams in which there is no emphasis upon the dream ego "doing its control thing" have been called "quasi-lucid dreams" (Purcell *et al.* 1985) or "pre-lucid dreams" (Green 1968:23; Metzinger 2009:143). Walters and Dentan (1985b:86) define "quasi-lucid dreams" as those in which "dreamers are aware of dreaming but do not control the content of their dreams." Barbara

Tedlock picks up on this distinction, but it makes little difference in her discussion of lucid dreaming cross-culturally.

My feeling is that one would be hard-pressed to find records of lucid dreams among traditional peoples of the strict Western sleep lab sort, whereas lucid dreams of the "quasi" kind are very likely universal (Walters and Dentan 1985a), if by that we refer to a continuum of awareness in the sense postulated by Purcell, Moffitt and Hoffman (1993) above. So, I am going to dispense with the distinction between lucidity and quasi-lucidity, because it is an ethnocentric and experimental distinction of minimal use when it comes to the ethnographic evidence. While it is true that some traditional people have reported being awake to the fact they are dreaming (Tedlock 1999:94-98 *passim*), it is usually incidental to the dream experience which is usually already vivid and significant. Henceforth, when I speak of lucid dreams and lucidity, I am talking about dreaming in which I am inferring that PFC involvement is enhanced, the brain's executive functions are apparently operating in the dream and some degree of awareness of the dream *qua* dream may or may not be present. My suspicion is that the latter characteristic is often present, but not reported.

## Lucid Dreaming Cross-Culturally

Let us examine a number of lucid dreams from the ethnographic literature so that we can get a flavor for the phenomenology behind what we are talking about. This dream was collected by Myrna Walters and Robert Dentan (1985b) while they were teaching Han Chinese students in Beijing, China. The student is male and is writing in English for a class. Keep in mind that because of Marxist-Leninist indoctrination, modern materialist Chinese normally exhibit little interest in their dreaming:

> A few days ago, I had a very, very strange dream. The dream was *just like a play showing on a stage*. I dreamed that there were two heroes fighting against [each other]. The two were the best fighters in the world, like Beowolf (perhaps it was because that I read the epic Beowolf that I could have such a dream). One of

the heroes was just [by] himself whereas the other had a lot of fighters with him. The group of fighters caught the hero several time[s] but he fled away every time. Once the hero lost one of his shoes, so he had to stay in a room, and the group of fighter[s] knew this. The other hero came silently and all of a sudden, he locked the door and locked the hero in the room. The hero of the group laughed loudly and went away. The fighter in the room was very angry and tried to seek a way of going out. At this time, one of the "second class" fighter[s] in the group came. The [hero pleaded with] him to unlock the door. The fighter agreed without any hesitation but he [had] a condition. That is, the hero should fight with him, because the "second class" fighter thought he could win over the hero. The hero was confident that he could win over him and agreed. The fight[er] unlocked the door and the hero came out, saying "I have no time to waste on you" and ran away. The fighter was angry: "I thought you were a whole man, but you are not." The hero, hearing this sentence, [ran] back again, and both of them got ready to fight. At this time I woke up. (emphasis mine)

Notice that the student reflects upon how the dream appears like a stage play, implying that he was watching from the audience. Walters and Dentan (1985b) suggest this represents a psychological distancing of the dream ego from the "play." Notice also that there is back and forth dialogue among the protagonists and that there is a continuity of plot, resulting in something of a story line, however surreal.

Here is another dream recorded by Walters and Dentan (1985b) from a male Chinese student:

People were playing on the skating rink joyously. Miracle appeared suddenly. Someone were riding bicycles on the surface of melted ice water and didn't sink! They were moving forward in an incredibly fast speed. One by one, the bicycle driving seemed to be ridiculous. Under the cliff there was the ice surface and on the top of the cliff there was a closet. I was changing my clothes with a man I know well but did [not?] know his name in the closet. With a great sound, a bomb exploded in the middle of the cliff. I was just about to look what was happening, another explosion frightened me. *I was trying to make myself to believe I was dreaming. It was so horrible. Wake up! It didn't work.* A bomb exploded inside the closet. Fortunately enough, the bomb was one for teaching, and was not very destructive. No one was hurt. Several bombs just traveled in a curved trace to reach us and explode while we were withdrawing. My acquaintance had been wounded. Someone were shouting cheerfully that they had done an excellent experiment. "You must be terrified, mightn't you?" one of my former classmates asked me. I didn't know where he came from. "No," I replied, "but my elder brother did."

This dream features the very common surreal elements we find in dreams in all societies – bicyclists speeding across water without sinking, a changing room up on a cliff high above the water. With fright and concern there is the attempt to waken and perhaps manipulate the dream, to avoid the anxiety by leaving the scene. Again, there is comprehensible dialogue, this time between the dream ego and a classmate.

In a very remarkable article, Fernando Santos-Granero (2003) describes the scary dreams of a twelve year old Yanesha boy named Pedro Casanto who lived in eastern Peru and who had recently lost his father. He offers these examples to show how the Yanesha, like many other traditional peoples, pay attention to their dreams and use what we would call "lucid dreaming techniques" to manipulate events in nightmares. After Santos-Granero shared one of his own dreams with the boy, the boy opened up to him and confessed he had been tormented by dreams of his father chasing him and trying to kill him. When he finally asked his mother how to handle these dreams, she drew upon Yanesha shamanic knowledge and told him what to do (ibid:182):

> She told her son that the first step to hinder his father's attacks was to become aware in his dreams that his father was dead, and that the one who was attacking him was not his live father, but his father's "shadow soul"... .Pedro Casanto followed her advice. In his first dreams, his father looked vital and had a healthy countenance. But when Pedro Casanto forced himself to become aware in dreams that his father was dead, the latter, he told me,

appeared to him with the pale skin of the gravely ill and the contorted face of the dead.

The nightmares continued for months, but in the process Pedro learned to wake up in his dream and to fly away so as to avoid his father's assaults. He became very adept at flying in his dreams, practicing over the course of many dreams, but alas, his father learned to fly also and continued to haunt him. Approximately eight months after the nightmares began, Pedro garnered enough courage to confront his father's soul and attempt to kill him. In a final dream, Pedro finds his father, and then flies away with the intention of tiring his father out and then deceiving him and set him up to be killed. He leads his father here and there, hiding and then appearing, playing like he is tired and then flying away. Finally (ibid:184):

> His father was already tired. Then Pedro Casanto hid behind a mountain. He flew around it and approached his father from behind. Pedro Casanto was carrying an old and blunt machete his mother had given him some time ago [in waking life]. He continued flying and approached his father from behind without being seen. When he was slightly above his father, he slashed him with his machete, opening a large wound on his father's back. His father started falling to the ground. He fell like a rag from high above.

Since having that dream, Pedro was never again haunted by his father's soul. The lucid dreaming technique, really a form of incubation, was, just as occurs in the Western sleep lab, imposed from the waking life into the dream life. Pedro woke up enough to learn to fly and escape his father, but more importantly for our purposes, the dreams, especially the dénouement in the last dream, sees Pedro carrying out an intention developed in waking life and carried out in the dream. He successfully carries out a strategy to its conclusion.

Ethnographer Robert D. Bruce spent a lot of time working with the Lacandon Maya in Chiapas, Mexico. The Lacandon pay a great deal of attention to their dreams, and often carry out ritual retreats in which dreaming plays a large role. Here is a dream Bruce himself had during his time among the Lacandon:

I dreamed I was walking with a slender Occidental woman (dressed in traditional Lacandon clothes) on the trail around Lake Najá to the air strip. As we crossed a sandy stream at the edge of a clearing (neither of which exist, except in my dream), she commented that she was afraid of meeting a jaguar or puma, as I had neither a gun nor a machete. I laughed at the idea of seeing a jaguar so close to Najá, and explained to her that they are now nearly extinct. At that moment I heard the almost whistling sigh of a large animal, and saw a very large puma, bright and tawny colored, and as robust as an African lioness. (The sex of the animal in the dream was not distinguishable.) The woman lifted her huipil [dress] and drew a short-barreled, small .38 caliber revolver. (It could have been either a S&W Chief's Featherweight or a Colt Cobra, though in the dream, I was not certain whether it held 5 or 6 shots.) She handed it to me, and the puma approached us on diagonal course, slowly, casually, with no air of menace... except that it was simply too close. I aimed at the thorax, trying for an angle slightly behind the shoulder, but still crossing the thorax. The angle was wrong, and I wondered if the load of the cartridge was sufficient to pass through the shoulder. I fired anyway, through the shoulder. It charged and I fired several times, rapid fire, until it disappeared behind a small shed (like a milpa granary) which was right beside me, but which I hadn't noticed previously. I waited for it to show again, but only then realized that I hadn't counted my shots, so I didn't know if I had any left or not. Then I heard a voice (not the woman's, as she had simply disappeared from the dream) call "Be careful. It is dying, but still alive!" Then I awoke.

Notice that Bruce's dream was in color, there was dialogue between the dream-ego and the woman, there was rational information about the rarity of the jaguar, and there is considerable cogitation about the most effective shot and concern over not counting his shots. All this indicates considerable thought involved in the dream.

Robin Ridington (1988b:Chap. 9) did extensive fieldwork among the Dunne-za (Dene Tha, or "Beaver") Indians of the Doig River area of British Columbia. He recorded many hours of singing and teaching by elder *Naachin*, or Dreamers. They are considered to be prophets and are specialists in journeying on the Trail to Heaven, the pathway that all people follow to the afterlife. As one of the Dreamers, Charlie Vahey, told Ridington, "A person who is a Prophet doesn't just dream for himself, he dreams for everybody" (ibid:77). The Dreamer is able to traverse the Trail to Heaven at will in their dreams. He (ibid:99),

> ...is able to leave his body on earth and fly like a swan along a trail of song that is *Yagatunne*, the Trail to Heaven. Even here at Doig I had seen him go into one of the old houses while people sat quietly on the grass in a circle keeping watch. For several hours we waited quietly and kept the space around where he was dreaming clear of disturbing noises of kids and dogs and people on horseback. When he came out of the house the old man began to sing and speak to the people. It might have seemed to an outsider, that he was just an old Indian taking an afternoon nap, but to the people keeping watch, the hours he slept were actually weeks or months of travel within sight of heaven. Dreamers are people who can fly through to heaven and return to their bodies on earth. The people kept watch over him because they wanted to give him a center to which he could return.

The journey on the Trail to Heaven is an intentional one. It indicates lucidity and considerable control over events, and remarkably keen memory for songs and other information retrieved from the dead ancestors.

## Indicators of Lucidity Cross-Culturally

I could offer many other examples of lucidity in the dreams of peoples around the globe – see, for example, the dreaming of shaman Ruby Modesto in Chapter 13. But these are sufficient to give a flavor of the kind of dreams that are quite common among polyphasic folk, especially among shamans and healers. What we want to do now is present a list of indicators of probable lucidity that is of use with dream reports from traditional peoples. There are, of course, lucid dream questionnaires used by Western dream researchers, probably the best known being Jayne

Gackenbach's and its refinements (LaBerge and Gackenbach 1987). The significant indicators of lucidity in Gackenbach's questionnaire are the ability to fly, to "almost magically" control events, to intentionally heal oneself, and to intentionally problem-solve. These are not requisite experiences or definitive of lucidity in the ethnographic sense. As we said before, one should seek indicators that help one place dreams on something like Purcell's 9 point scale. Here are some of the indicators I have found useful in evaluating the degree of vividness and lucidity in ethnographic dream reports:

- Aware one is dreaming while dreaming (rarely paired with exercise of control)
- Ritual drivers are used in incubating the dream
- A dream yoga is being used to produce dreaming
- Carrying out intentional exercises or commands
- If ethnographer is a lucid dreamer and asks the right questions: "like being awake"
- "Phenomenologically speaking, lucid dreaming tends toward sensory clarity, bodily presence, and an expansive emotional thrill or numinous religious feeling" (Tedlock 1999:94)
- Vivid and brilliant colors
- Wanting a scary dream experience to "be a dream"
- Exercise of control: change scene, make it stop, fly away, go somewhere else
- *Déjà vu* – dreamer knows they have dreamed this before – memory of past dreams within the present dream
- A plot line of significant duration (indicating working memory)
- Recursivity: dreams within dreams within dreams, etc.
- Meditation or trance within the dream
- Meaningful dialogue, especially when important information is exchanged or delivered, songs sung
- Carrying out an intention formulated in waking life in the dream – going on intended journey
- Awareness of the physical body and out-of-body experiences
- Self-interpreting dream — the dream is meaningful within the dream

## SUMMARY AND SEGUE

Dreaming ranges along a continuum of lucidity from being hardly aware of the dream as it is unfolding to extreme lucidity where one knows one is dreaming in the dream and can carry out missions, exercises, experiments and even communicate from within the dream. Lucidity is determined by the extent to which the executive functions of the prefrontal cortex of the brain are involved in mediating dream happenings. Culture has an enormous influence on lucidity and how lucidity is used by the dreamer. Lucidity is a characteristic of the "big," important, "culture pattern" dreams had by peoples around the world. It is particularly a quality of shamanic dream journeys.

We have taken the position that dreaming is actually experience had while sleeping, and that the neuropsychology of dreaming is much the same as waking consciousness. We will now turn to dreaming in the non-Western, cross-cultural arena in Part 2 of the book. We will begin by emphasizing the importance of grounding dream research in the direct experience of dreaming.

PART TWO

# Dreams and Cultures

# Chapter 6

# Phenomenology of Dreaming

> I have argued at length against those who would deny a life-world to dreaming, and we have concluded that their position is without merit. Having admitted a dreaming life-world, we now can examine more closely the claim that dreaming and waking life-worlds are essentially indiscernible.
>
> Gordon Globus, *Dream Life, Wake Life*

Dreaming is first and foremost a life-world, a domain of experience (Rycroft 1979:2). The more discerning reader may notice that I give little time to arguing against those theorists that don't "get that." Anyone into their dream life knows the truth of things that others who have not studied their dream lives cannot know. This is not a statement of privilege or elitism, it is rather a statement of empirical fact, implied as such by the application of Jamesian radical empiricism (Jackson 1989). Dreaming is a domain of experience universal to everybody on the planet, whether or not they recall dreams in their waking life or not. All such experiences are grist for the scientific mill, and no dream experience can be considered outside of the scientific purview. And yet for many ethnographers – including myself when doing my first fieldwork among the So of Northeastern Uganda (Laughlin and Allgeier 1979) – little to nothing is said about dreaming in their reports. Dreaming is either considered irrelevant to their project (my case), or they may well not appreciate the importance of dreaming to their hosts, unless they stumble across its significance in a society that openly share dreaming. As my mentor, Joseph Jorgensen, used to say, you cannot control for the questions the ethnographer fails to ask. This is especially true when using ethnographic reports in a cross-cultural comparative study such as is done in holocultural research.

As I have said before, a scientific anthropological account of dreaming must begin with and never lose track of a phenomenology of dreaming. To those who work with their dreams, this might seem like a statement of the obvious. But alas, ethnographers, most of whom are raised in Western cultures, find it methodologically more convenient to relegate dreams to the status of cultural objects that can then be explained away by processes of sociocultural construction. As Charles Stewart (1997:878) notes, "While acknowledging the personal, psychological dimension of dreams, the anthropological tendency has been to treat dreams as social facts and cultural texts, thereby sensibly placing them inside the recognized framework of anthropological expertise. The only danger here is that we may become so comfortable with the idea of dreams as cultural constructions that... we disregard dreams as experiences; as a result, the semiotic dimension (representation) so subordinates the phenomenological as to displace it... ."

An adequate anthropology of dreaming must ground itself in experience, and that requires a phenomenological approach of some kind. We need ethnographic dream researchers like George Gillespie (1985, 1988b, 1997) who have immersed themselves in their own dream phenomenology before tackling dreaming among polyphasic peoples. But wait a minute – what do I mean by "phenomenology?" Well, just as there are as many post-modernisms as there are post-modernists, so too are there many phenomenologies (Kockelmans 1967). The term derives from the Greek *phainómenon* ("that which appears") plus *lógos* ("study of"), and is the term that Edmund Husserl used to label his approach to the study of subjectivity. Phenomenology is fundamentally a method for studying one's own consciousness. It is a method, for instance, that Husserl used to examine his own temporal subjectivity in his book *The Phenomenology of Internal Time-Consciousness* (1964 [1928]), and which we used to develop a neurophenomenology of time consciousness (see Laughlin 1992; Laughlin and Throop 2008). So when I speak of phenomenology here, it is specifically the Husserlian version – an approach that has proved quite useful in anthropology (see Laughlin and Throop 2009; Jackson 1996).

## Husserl, Globus and the Epoché

The main obstacle to the study of one's own experience is that we have a lot of personal and cultural baggage to sort out. We have feelings and views, beliefs and concepts about things, and we think we know a lot about ourselves. After all, it is "me" I am studying – who should know "me" better than... well, me? Think about it a moment. When we look up in the sky at night, we do not see points of light, we see "stars" and "constellations." We already know what we are looking at. By the same token, when we look inward at our mind, we do not see mere sensations, we see "anger," "love," the face of our mother. We enter the study of our mind already knowing stuff, for there is really little novelty left in our experiences – not like there was when we were children. This stuff we know is derived from a lifetime of learning, developing and enculturation. Edmund Husserl called the sum total of all this knowing our *natural attitude* and teaches us to hold all of it in abeyance so that we can scrutinize experience as it actually arises. We want to be able to examine the properties of experience as they present within our sensorium. Husserl called this holding of prior knowledge in abeyance *bracketing*.

The term bracketing is a metaphor, of course. Just as we might [bracket] a word in a sentence in order to single it out, so too do we "bracket" a belief or attitude about an experience and metaphorically "set it aside" as irrelevant to our empirical task. By bracketing all our preconceptions we enter what Husserl called the phenomenological *epoché* (another Greek term, this time meaning "suspension;" pronounced *E-po-shay*, not *E-pock*). What is suspended are all judgements, identifications, conceptions, attitudes, beliefs, and anything else that might interfere with our direct study of experience. What Husserl was *not* advocating was a philosophy of un-knowing. He was developing a method for studying the productions of one's own brain from the inside-out, and in the process of developing this method, he discovered what was for him a unique and distinct SOC he called "the epoché," a SOC not unlike the Zen notion of "beginner's mind" (Suzuki 1970). The phenomenological epoché is not an intellectual point of view, it is an ASC during which one's phenomenal mind stands before one's mind's eye in stark, raw, unfolding purity, refreshed in every moment by the neurophysiological systems that mediate our sensory experiences. It thus takes an effort to develop the skill to enter that ASC and use it empirically. This is a rare skill among social scientists, even for those interested in waking experiences. It is so much harder for most of us Westerners to accomplish this skill in the dream life.

We can now return to Gordon Globus' book, *Dream Life, Wake Life* (1987) mentioned in the last chapter. What Globus would have us do is develop the epoché and apply it to the study of dreaming (1987:64). More specifically, if we bracket our preconceptions and judgments in both the waking life and the dreaming life – what he calls a "double epoché"[1] – we can ask and answer some fundamental questions (ibid:65). If we set aside our belief in the reality of waking life and our belief in the unreality of our dream life, we find that the two life-worlds are "indiscernible" (see also Kirtsoglou 2010:323). That is, both life-worlds are pure experience and merely on that basis, one cannot tell them apart. Thus waking and dreaming experiences are legitimately life-worlds – they are equally *lived* — and must be studied as such (again, this is pure Jamesian radical empiricism at work). Now, this conclusion makes a lot of sense ethnologically because so many of the peoples we anthropologists have studied consider dreaming to be just as real as waking, or, as in the case of Buddhist and some other psychologies, both states are equally illusory.

Can we tell dreaming and waking apart on other grounds? Sure. "The answer here is that the differences [our] reflection notes are not fundamental but related to sensory functions, which are highly restricted in sleep and open during waking. The dream life is like the wake life, except that there is no flowing array of sensory stimulation available to modulate it. *As lived*, the dream life is an authentic life, but reflection reveals that it is a peculiar unmodulated life because of the sensory restriction" (ibid:65; author's emphasis). By applying the epoché to the elements of our experience in dream and waking lives, we actually perceive images of "people" and "plants" and "animals" and "clouds" as real. They are right there before the mind's eye. In the dream we react and interact with these images because they are real to us in that life-

---

[1] This is not literally true, for it is the application of the same phenomenological epoché in two different domains of experience.

world (Craig 1987). What else can we discern about our dreams relative to our waking experiences? Globus reports that there is a distinct "single-mindedness" about dreams. Dreams tend to proceed along a single train of thought, as opposed to waking life where there are many more distractions and alternative possibilities. Also, dreams seem to be vague, "hazy," and "less vivid" compared to waking life.[2] They are more bizarre and symbolic than waking life (ibid:84). Maintaining reflection within the dream life seems harder than in waking life. Globus goes on to use this phenomenological approach to argue for a cognitive theory of dreaming, but that is beyond our present concern. The point I want to emphasize is that a phenomenological approach to dreaming opens a way to bridge the gap between our own dream experiences and those of our informants in other societies.

## The Problem of the Phenomenological Typewriter

A common assumption on the part of ethnographers is that "we cannot get into the native's head" – we cannot know first-hand what our informants are experiencing at any given time (Dentan 1986:318; Hollan 2004:171; Kirtsoglou 2010:322-324). Trouble is, this seems obviously true to commonsense, but is actually untrue in an important methodological sense. Yes, I cannot get into your head as if I have a video camera behind your mind's eye monitoring what you are seeing and hearing, etc. But that is not what is required when studying the Other's experiences. All that is required (issues of rapport aside) is that I train myself to approximate in my own experience what my informants are describing to me. This is "participant observation" in the deepest sense of the term, or what Tedlock calls "observation of participation" (1991b) in which the ethnographer not only observes his/her hosts doing their thing, but also observes him/herself participating in the lives of the hosts. But more than this, I am suggesting that the ethnographer observe his/her participation in what are essentially transpersonal

---

[2] I suspect that Globus is not referring to lucid dreams, for the emphasis upon "haziness" and lack of "vividness" do not describe the experience quite commonly had in a lucid dream.

experiences (see Chapter 12). It is not sufficient to do ethnography among a Brazilian people whose cosmology is heavily informed by experiences had under the influence of *ayahuasca* without attempting to follow one's hosts into the experience – the *ayahuasca* life-world. It is simply impossible to comprehend experiences one has not had oneself. So it is with dreaming. Recounting his work with the Dene Tha Indians of Alberta, Canada, Jean-Guy Goulet notes that, "Dene informants are firm in their conviction that individuals, including ethnographers, who have not directly experienced the reality of revelation or instruction through dreams and visions do not and cannot understand a crucial dimension of the Dene knowledge system" (1998:xxix).

Again, the problem is the loss of information that occurs between the dream-as-dreamt and the dream-as-told (see Faber, Saayman and Touyz 1978; Edgar 1999; Charsley 1973:244 on this distinction and difficulty of studying the former) – what I once called the "problem of the phenomenological typewriter" (Laughlin 1989). If one is a monophasic ethnographer, one is seriously hampered in comprehending the dream life of the Other, especially if one is doing work in a polyphasic culture. I say hampered, but I do not mean the problem is insurmountable at all, not if one is willing to retrain oneself phenomenologically. One may prepare oneself by applying a phenomenological stance in which one evaluates his or her own waking and dream lives. To what extent does one measure up to the skill of the Other in entering the dream world? By applying the indicators we discussed in the last chapter, is it apparent that one's hosts are lucid dreamers? Where on Purcell *et al.*'s continuum of awareness do they appear to lay based on their shared dreams? If they do appear to be fairly lucid in some of their dreams, and you, the ethnographer, have trouble even recalling one dream per week, then perhaps the demands of the fieldwork dictate that you beef-up your dreaming skills. This is simply applying the methodology of transpersonal anthropology that is based upon the presumption that, if you haven't been there, you don't know what you are talking about. Put more positively, if you wish to know what the native is experiencing, you have to enter his/her state of mind by following in your host's footsteps (see Chapter 12).

This is *not* "going native" – that old taboo and very silly bugaboo in ethnology (see Ewing 1994; Turner 1993). Archibald Belaney, a.k.a

Grey Owl, to the contrary, no one can actually go native in any total sense. Rather, this is an exercise in transpersonal research – in the present case, accruing skill as a dreamer – and using the skill to engage one's hosts at their own level. Over the course of the previous pages I have mentioned anthropologists who have engaged their informants by recounting their own dreams. Dennis Tedlock used his own dream to enter into discussions with his Quiché informant who said his dream was a positive one, but had he given the same dream account to one of his previous Zuni informants, the interpretation would have been negative (in Barbara Tedlock 1992c:105). Robert Bruce (1975:38-65) included his own dreams in with Lacandon dreams and evoked native interpretations of the entire corpus.

What makes this injunction-driven, dream-approximation approach different from "going native" is that one is applying a *perspectivist* method, rather than merely taking a relativist's position of accepting the native explanation of things at face value. From the view of perspectivism, one carries out, say, Ken Wilber's injunction (see p. 388) and then talks to one's informants about whatever experiences arise and sees what they say, but *one is under no obligation to agree with or believe the informants' account of one's experience.* An informant might interpret your dream as being a visitation from an "ancestor," while your own interpretation is that the dream was centered on an "archetype." "Ancestor" and "archetype" label points of view about the dream forms, not the forms themselves. Obviously, you are not in the field to record your own interpretation of dreams, but to elicit your hosts' experiences and view of things (see La Barre 1980:39). You may discover that it is appropriate for you to keep your own views to yourself, or as a matter shared with your co-workers or your journal, while at the same time remaining open to any and all experiential opportunities.

## PHENOMENOLOGICAL INGREDIENTS OF DREAMING

In Chapter 4 we saw that the experience of dreaming depends upon the particular organization of neural systems mediating the dream. Many of the components of dreaming are the same components operating during waking life. Color, form, speech, activities, relations among forms, feelings, olfactory components – all are present in both dreaming and waking of experience. Also the degree of awareness, self-awareness, working memory, recursive imagery and plot line, modulation of emotion, etc., mediated by the PFC range from minimal to maximal in both kinds of experience.

Now I wish to look at a few different phenomenological categories of dreaming – i.e., sensory and other elements – that are universal to all peoples on the planet and look for the indicators that uniquely mark and define natural dream categories. By "categories," I am not talking about logical types with crisp boundaries, but of natural categories which have fuzzy boundaries, that often overlap, but that have distinct exemplars that best represent to the individual the category to which their experience belongs (see Rosch 1977; Rosch *et al.* 1976; Laughlin 1993). This is the same kind of categorical system that all cultures have with respect to plants and animals – an ethnobiological system of nomenclature that group according what Atran and Medin (2008:19-20) call *generic species* designations, like "spruce," "chickadee," "pike," etc.

I am in effect updating C.G. Seligman's (1873-1940) view that ethnology can isolate universal *type dreams* that are mediated by the same or similar neurophysiological components. As Seligman wrote (1932:219):

> The anthropologist, when he has gathered a series of dreams from a number of representative peoples of sufficiently varied race and culture, should, by comparing these, be able to decide whether the mental content and functions which are active in dreams are psychologically inherent in the nature of the human organism [i.e., "type dreams"] or culturally determined. Indeed, the implications are even wider; if it is found that savage dreams conform in constitution and function to the theoretical explanations offered by psychologists working on the dreams of folk of Western race and culture, we may well be prepared to accept as actually demonstrated the claim that the savage mind and the mind of Western civilized man are essentially alike; for what holds of one mental function may be taken to hold of any other, since no mental function can be isolated from the organic whole which we call the mind.

If one can get past Seligman's rather 19th century language and silly views about "savages" having minds like "children," one can find the recognition of the importance of dreaming as furthering Adolf Bastian's ethnological project (see Chapter 2). In this respect at least Seligman was way ahead of most ethnologists today. Thus far we have covered the phenomenology and neuroscience involved in lucidity and the disconnection of dreams from sensory input. Now we will look at a few other natural categories of dreams and reflect where possible on their universality and neurophysiological structures. In this way, I hope to dispel the notion that one cannot "get into the head" of our informant in a scientifically useful way, and also to show how a neurophenomenological analysis of experiences of all kinds can be accomplished, and how it may shed light on local dream theories and the uses to which dreams are put.

## Knowing and Believing

Ethnologists often speak of a people's "beliefs" with respect to local knowledge. When dealing cross-culturally with the different ways of knowing this way of referring to local knowledge makes some sense, for it allows the fieldworker to dodge any question of the truth-value of the hosts' ethnoepistemology. Yet it also distorts the phenomenology of knowing, for the way we Western English-speakers use the word "belief" tends to imply a hedge on certainty of knowledge – as in, "well, I *believe* so," or "that was what she believed anyways." What is lost in using the term for the local knowledge of folk is the sense of *apodicticity*[3] in the act of knowing. For many peoples, there is no suggestion that dreaming is fantasy. "Rather, they take them to be literal experiences of the dreamer's soul – as Tylor first proposed – the gripping reality of a dream while it is being experienced is certainly a powerful reinforcement of the idea in the waking afterthought" (Tuzin 1975:563).

Jean-Guy Goulet (1987) takes up the distinction between belief and knowledge with regard to Dene Tha ways of knowing. "Among

---

[3] From the Greek for "capable of being demonstrated" or "absolutely certain;" see Laughlin 1994c.

the Dene Tha, as among other Northern Athapaskans," writes Goulet, "'knowledge that has been mediated is regarded with doubt. True knowledge is considered to be that which is derived from experience' (Scollon and Scollon 1979:185). This view has profound implications for what Dene consider the proper way to teach or inform not only their children and each other, but also the inquisitive ethnographer approaching them to learn about their ways and their religion" (1987:115-116). In other words, the Dene Tha value knowledge from direct experience, regardless of the SOC during which the knowledge is derived. Only through direct experience can one achieve that sense of the apodicticity of knowledge. In Dene terms, if I know something, I know it because I experienced it, and an ingredient of the experience is the immediate sense of apodicticity – the certainty that "this is the case," or "this is not the case." This is not a logical, but an existential certainty. This creates a conundrum for the Western ethnographer, for if I "know" with absolute certainty that the radiant being I experienced in my dream was an archetype, but my host knows that the radiant being in her dream was a ghost, then I am more or less forced by the expectations of my role as ethnographer to write up her knowledge as a "belief" – "the Tiddle-di-dum believe in ghosts" — while my personal knowledge remains apodictically sound. One runs into this flavor of ethnographic skepticism in virtually all Freudian analyses of "latent" dream content. Getting at the supposedly more real, "latent" meaning of the dream easily sidesteps the issue of apodicticity altogether, for the informant's reported "manifest" knowledge may be methodologically ignored (see Price-Williams and Degarrod 1996).

The Dene Tha handle this issue quite forthrightly – namely, they choose not to share knowledge with anyone unprepared to understand it. "Dene tend to exclude those who are not perceived as knowing from those among whom they discuss experiences of dreams, visions, and power. Such discussion occurs only between those who are 'in the know.' To one who 'knows' and understands, Dene offer a degree of explanation according to their estimation of his or her understanding. This estimation of the ethnographer's 'knowledge,' more than the investigator's own research agenda, determines the flow of information between the two, information that most often takes the form of stories, the significance of which at first simply escapes the ethnographer" (ibid:114). As Goulet puts it, "true knowledge is personal knowledge" and the only access to knowledge gleaned from dreaming is by way of learning the skill of dreaming, in the way I suggested above (see also Ridington 1988a:103).

This seems to me ample motive for us ethnologists to bracket our attitudes about the unreality of dreams. The monophasic ethnographer is most likely predisposed to be skeptical of the notion of true knowledge derived from dreaming. As William James wrote in *The Principles of Psychology*, "The world of dreams is our real world whilst we are sleeping, because our attention then lapses from the sensible world. Conversely when we wake, the attention usually lapses from the dream-world and that becomes unreal. But if a dream haunts us and compels our attention during the day, it is very apt to remain figuring in our consciousness as a sort of sub-universe alongside of the waking world. Most people have probably had dreams which it is hard to imagine not to have been glimpses into an actually existing region of being… " (1890:923n).

One crucial outcome of the bracketing of our Western belief in the unreality of our dreams is that we can better appreciate one very significant pattern in the phenomenology of dreams cross-culturally – that in dreams, entities and forces that are normally invisible (not present in consciousness except as concepts or icons) during a person's waking life may become visible, tangible and palpable during dreaming (see Sumegi 2008:31). This particular distinction between waking and dreaming phenomenology is a near-universal across traditional cultures. For example, Meggitt (1962) notes that among the Mae Enga of New Guinea, ghosts are invisible while one is awake, but visible in dreams. There are innumerable examples of societies in which dead relatives and ancestors, mere shades or shadows during the waking state, become significant characters and causal agents in dreams. Irving Hallowell (2002), in reflecting upon the worldview of the Ojibwa Indians, speaks of "other-than-human persons" encountered within dreams. He notes, "While in all cultures 'persons' comprise one of the major classes of objects to which the self must become oriented, this category of being is by no means limited to *human* beings. In Western culture, as in others, 'supernatural' beings are recognized as 'persons,' although belonging, at the same time, to the other than human category" (ibid:20).

We may find that in our hosts' world, they do not merely "believe" in "other-than-human persons," but actually know them. They know them because they encounter them – interact with them – in their dream life. It is this crucial distinction that Jean-Guy Goulet (1998:254) is getting at when he writes:

> I agree with Geertz that we can neither live other people's lives nor magically intrude on their consciousness, whether members of our own culture or of another. But to see the task of the ethnographer as Geertz defines it precludes some of what we can do and learn in the field, not only about others but also about ourselves in our interaction with them. Ethnographic work can – but does not need to – go hand in hand with the anthropologist's experience of dreams and visions. These often become part of interactions with others.... More than merely listen to what others say about their lives, then, anthropologists pay attention to their own lives, including their inner lives. They observe and listen to other people's responses to their accounts of their own dreams and/or visions experienced while living among these others. To do so is to become an experiential ethnographer.

## Emotional Dreaming

There is a perennial debate among anthropologists whether emotions are universal or culturally constructed, depending upon which side of the universalist/constructivist watershed the theorist falls on. My view, being a neuroanthropologist, has been that emotions are both universal to the species and vary somewhat from society to society depending upon individual development, enculturation and interpretive discrimination (Laughlin and Throop 1999). In other words, the neural systems that mediate emotion develop just as do all other neural systems. More specifically (see Figures 4.1 and 4.5), emotionality in humans and other big-brained mammals is mediated by a complex interaction among PFC, sensory and association cortex, and subcortical tissues, the latter including the limbic system (which mediates certain effects like anger, fear, depression, etc.), the thalamus (which accomplishes the gating of information between cortical and subcortical areas), the hypothalamus (involved in arousal, regulation of endocrine and autonomic nervous system activities and information about internal states) and, via the inferior temporal lobe, the hippocampus (involved in perceptual recognition and memory; see Gray 1982, Fuster 2008, Stuss and Benson 1986).

As the reader by now understands, the higher the involvement of the PFC in mediating emotion, the more culturally influenced modulation of emotion can and will occur in the dream – i.e., there may be more modulation of emotion in a lucid dream than in a dream that is basically images and emotions. Dreams had on the lower end of the continuum of PFC mediation often present as *emotional dreams* – that is, where the predominant state is a link between images and emotions. They are often bizarre in nature and may be intense in effect. Just the other night I had one of these dreams. I was amongst a group of men and they were circling me and I felt threatened and very anxious. I struck out with my foot at the man closest to me and the impulse was so strong my real leg struck out and stubbed my toe on a very real chair by my bed. What is significant and so common with this dream is that the group of men exhibited not the slightest gesture of threat in either their faces or their body language – they were totally devoid of intent or effect. Their mere presence was menacing to my dream ego. When I have such dreams, my impression is that it was the anxiety calling forth the imagery, not the imagery evoking the effect. But these are low level, "normal" dreams with insufficient PFC involvement to ask that question whilst still in the dream (see Herr 1981:339).

It is clear from neuropsychological research that emotion may be induced unconsciously (Damasio 1999:47). The emotions we feel in dreams may originate in day residue memories (I was worried all day about my daughter's plans) or from chronic feelings (anxiety about possibly losing my job), or in some cross-cultural situations, general anxiety about having any dream experiences whatsoever because that's when the soul is vulnerable to witches and other nasty things that go bump in the night (see Reay 1962). It is possible for intense emotion to arise during sleep in the apparent absence of any imagery. This can occur during NREM sleep, and when this happens in children it is called *night terrors* (or *pavor nocturnus*; see Barrett 1996:11; Hobson 2002:89; Hunt 1989:24).[4]

This brings us to the question of nightmares (Jones 1951; Lincoln 1935:122; Belicki and Cuddy 1991; McNamara 2008; Hufford 1982). A *nightmare* is our Western label for a really scary dream that happens almost always in REM sleep (but cf. Belicki and Cuddy 1991:100), although in some societies the closest label for such dreams is simply having a "bad dream" (Tonkinson 2003:101n4) My dream above of being menaced by a group of men borders on a nightmare, but the degree of anxiety and dread I felt was minor compared with the terror that may accompany a full-blown nightmare. The terror felt in a nightmare is not merely a simulation of emotion by any means. The feeling may be accompanied by intense parasympathetic reactivity, increased heart rate and other physiological symptoms, sometimes severe enough to cause injury and (fortunately rarely) death (McNamara 2008:5). Most nightmares had by Westerners seem to entail being chased. Here is a good example of an "ordinary" nightmare from Deirdre Barrett's book, *Trauma and Dreams* (1996:102):

> I was out on the street. I had just come out of a party. This gang of men started chasing me. I didn't know quite who they were. They got closer and closer. I felt someone put his hand on me and then I woke up terrified. I've had dreams something like this for many years. In my childhood it was usually monsters chasing me. There was almost always something after me. I couldn't get away. I usually woke up just before I was hurt or killed.

Most accounts I have read of nightmares in the clinical literature imply that the imagery in the dream produces the intense negative emotion. As I mentioned above, working phenomenologically with my own negative-effect dreams has led me to suspect that either the emotions

---

[4] I am purposely not getting into dreaming associated with psychopathologies in this book, but I should point out that serious trauma may create the conditions for very disturbing and recurring emotional dreams (Kalsched 1996:Chap. 1) – for example, post-traumatic stress disorder (PTSD) may result in chronic dreams of being overwhelmed by a tidal wave or some other gigantic and unstoppable menace, accompanied by panic, fear or terror (see Barrett 1996:100; Hartmann 2007, 2011).

and the imagery are co-occurring, or more likely the negative emotion evokes imagery that would make symbolic sense of the otherwise objectless feelings – as seems to be the situation in night terrors and imageless NREM nightmares.

There are societies in which the incidence of nightmares is very high. These are often groups who are enculturated to associate dreams with danger, emotional and social conflict, visitations from scary beings, etc. In Fiji, for example, where people live on many small islands and where a great deal of tension exists between the sexes, and repression of divisive feelings is necessary to keep local harmony intact, the incidence of negative dreaming and nightmares is pervasive (Herr 1981). Although Fijians have nightmares of the kind with which we would identify, not all their scary dreams have apparent menacing plots and characters (ibid:338). As Herr notes, "…many of the examples of nightmare reported have no such obvious expression of conflict and anxiety. Rather, the response by the dreamer is one of great fear to a dream experience which in description contains no such obvious 'classic' source of trauma. They are nightmares, rather, because they involve dream encounters with other persons, animals, or spirit-entities, encounters that are by their nature potentially dangerous" (ibid:139). Again, there is at least the suggestion of intense emotion evoking the dream perceptions, not the other way around. Fijians appear to be conditioned to fear dreaming altogether. The imagery arising in any particular dream may make little difference to the scary experience of the dream. Not surprisingly, Fijians show a great interest in dreams, although it is generally negative, and will greet each other in the morning with the question: "You did not dream last night?" – meaning, did you sleep well without being disturbed by any nasty dreams (ibid:333).

George Foster characterizes the Tzintzuntzan people of Mexico as living fairly happy lives in which they gain satisfaction from their work, festivals, craft work and contact with people at various ceremonies. "At the same time, and particularly in contrast to the character and worldview of middle class Americans, Tzintzuntzeños exhibit a high degree of fear, apprehension, mistrust of others, and lack of self-confidence. They see, and verbalize, life as a 'struggle' in which a man's goal is to 'defend' himself and his family against the world 'without obligations' to others, that is, without making himself more vulnerable by being dependent on people whose actions he cannot control…" (1973:107-108). The Tzintzuntzan recognize two types of dreams, one being the *sueño* or normal dream, and the other the *pesadilla*, or nightmare. It is very interesting that the Tzintzuntzan do not consider the *pesadilla* to be a dream, for it, "…always occurs when ego is falling asleep, still half awake and not fully unconscious. Although the content of *pesadillas* is specific and limited, *it is the bodily state* that is critical to the definition. A *pesadilla* is always, and without exception, a terrifying experience, which robs ego of the power of movement and speech, and which leaves him in a cold sweat, awake" (ibid:109).

Negative feelings about dreaming and nightmares may be associated with witchcraft and other scary entities. According to Marie Reay, the Kuma people of New Guinea manifest a great deal of tension in their social lives. A lot of their anxiety finds its way into their dreams, which they call *wur kum banz*: "*Wur* is 'sleep,' *kum* is 'witchcraft,' and *banz* is 'honey.' We can translate the phrase freely as 'sweet witchcraft while you sleep,'" (Reay 1962:460) meaning that what at first blush may look attractive may well be evil in disguise. The "sugar-coating" falls away and the underlying conflict and anxiety become manifest to the dreamer, and he or she is unable to resolve the situation. Reay offers us a typical description of such a dream, not unlike my own dream above (ibid:460):

> The dreamer is alone fighting a vast crowd of men whose faces he can see but dimly. They are nearly overpowering him when he manages, with colossal effort, to brush them all aside with a single gesture and knock them down. But they spring up and rush at him again. In order to escape them, he spreads his arms like the wings of a bird and tries to fly away. He is not always successful; in one man's experience, the attackers grabbed the dreamer's legs and prevent him from flying.

Reay emphasizes that the faces of the men are dimly perceived and unrecognizable. In my dream above, the faces were more clearly seen, but devoid of expression and unrecognized. Again, the suggestion that anxiety and fear predominate, and perhaps evoke the imagery.

The Dobuans of Melanesia are beset by witchcraft and the spirits of the dead at every turn. Witches and ancestors often haunt the dreams of people (Fortune (1963:152):

> On other occasions a woman would wake from a nightmare convinced that the flying witches were chasing her spirit and were just outside baulked by her spirit's luck in getting home before them. Then the night would be hideous with a ghastly yelling or alternate high and low shrieking, expressing such fear in its very sound as to be contagious enough to myself who knew its origin.

Among Haitian people the dead are known to walk at night in the form of such horrors as zombies and werewolves. The dead come alive in the dreams of children (Bourguignon 1954:263), and the gods and the dead may visit the dreamer in order to offer messages. Talking in one's sleep is understood to be a message from the dead or the gods, often in a language that only the gods and the priests can understand. If disturbing dreams and nightmares are confusing to the dreamer, he or she may consult a *vodun* priest who is considered to be an oneirocritic. As is typical in traditional societies, the dream will be interpreted within the *vodun* worldview. The message may be read as a demand from the gods for certain ritual procedures to be carried out.

Another interesting motif in Kuma dreaming is the morphing of figures that at first appear benign or attractive into something evil and menacing (ibid:462): "The dreamer makes love to a strange girl before he discovers that she is really a *masalai* or evil bush spirit masquerading as a human. He is horror-stricken and desperately afraid, but it is too late to avert the consequences of his action." Reay's informants told her that all men have such dreams from time to time. The shape-shifting motif is one that I know well, and will discuss again in Chapter 13. It is a universal experience in dreaming and in mythology. For example, in the many versions of the vampire myth derived from eastern Europe, the vampire usually presents as a charming, attractive and engaging form, only to morph into a scary and dangerous man-beast (werewolf, vampire) or other carnivore (wolf, bat, owl; see Jones 1951; Beresford 2008).

There is a special type of nightmare we can call the *incubus dream* (Jones 1951: Chap. 3).[5] This is an experience of oppressive dread and terror, accompanied by feelings of suffocation, motor and speech paralysis, and a heavy weight bearing down on one's chest (see Hufford 1982 on the "Old Hag" experience; see also Jones 1951:20; McNamara 2008; Mack 1970).[6] Incubus dreams come in many forms:

> Sometimes the sufferer is buried beneath overwhelming rocks, which crush him on all sides, but still leave him with a miserable consciousness of his situation. Sometimes he is involved in the coils of a horrid, slimy monster, whose eyes have a phosphorescent glare of the sepulcher, and whose breath is poisonous as the marches of Lerna. …A mighty stone is laid upon his breast, and crushes him to the ground in helpless agony…. . (MacNish 1830, quoted in Woods and Greenhouse 1974:261)

Pamela Stewart and Andrew Strathern (2003:50) report an incubus dream had by a school girl among the Hagan of Papua New Guinea. The girl had been sent to school a distance from her home. She didn't like being there and failed to take her exams so she could go home. "She attributed her failure to the actions taken by one of her father's co-wives (who had died earlier and was, therefore, jealous of the living) in a dream sequence the night before she was to be tested. In this dream, the father's co-wife came to her and pressed her body down on top of [the girl's] body in a suffocating manner, making her severely ill and unable to take her tests the next day."

The folklorist Maximo Raqmos (in Hufford 1982:237) reports this incubus attack upon a Filipino male named Aguas:

> At about one o'clock, Aguas felt that someone was staring at him. He opened his eyes and looked around. At the window he saw an

---

[5] The term "incubus" is from the Latin *incubare*, "to lie down on," while the term "succubus" — the female version – comes from *succubare*, "to lie under."

[6] The incubus experience may have a sexual component in which case the *succubus* is a female demon that is seducing or having sex with the male dreamer (if the dreamer is female, then the demon will be male and called an *incubus*).

old woman, the lower part of her body missing, staring at him, her greying hair standing up and with her lips open in a devilish grin. Her eyes were bloodshot and big. He was so frightened that he tried to scream but nothing came out of his mouth. He tried to wake his companion up but he could not move. He tried to close his eyes but couldn't. After a couple of minutes, the *aswang* [demon] flew away.

The experiential elements of incubus dreams are generally extreme, mind-numbing terror and an explicit or inexplicit object of the terror. Once again, one wonders if many such attacks are due to a panic attack going in search of both an appropriate sensory experience and an object.

## Out-of-Body Experience Dreams

One experience that is often associated with flying cross-culturally (see Chapter 5) – especially when the dreamer is fairly lucid – is separation from the physical body (Shields 1978; Alvarado 2000; Blackmore 1992). This is the classic *out-of-body experience* (OBE), *soul flight*, or *astral projection* occurring during dreaming. "In the majority of spontaneous out-of-the-body experiences the subject seems to be observing his physical body from some point outside it…" (Green 1968:20). Such experiences appear to be mediated by structures lying in the area of the temporo-parietal junction (TPJ) on both sides of the cortex (Blanke *et al.* 2004, 2005; see the area just below the inferior parietal lobule in Figure 4.1). Subjects electrically stimulated in that area often report having spontaneous OBEs. The suggestion is that a spontaneous OBE in trance or dream may be due to a change in the normal waking interaction between the frontal lobes and the TPJ (Winkelman 2010:122).

Although Celia Green (ibid) made a phenomenological distinction between OBEs and lucid dreams, later research by Levitan *et al.* (1999) shows that both types of experience involve higher central nervous system (in my opinion, especially PFC) mediation. In any event, this distinction is really academic when applied to much of the non-Western ethnographic data. Discovering one is either out of one's body, or in one's body and aware of the fact, in the dream seems far less salient in polyphasic dream cultures where the focus within the dream is wandering and seeking distinct and edifying experiences. But Green is quite right to point out the phenomenological markers of the OBE, for it has been argued that this experience is commonly interpreted by people as evidence for the existence of a "soul," an inner spirit, or a spiritual essence that in some way transcends the physical body, and perhaps survives after death. This was precisely the argument Andrew Lang (see Chapter 2) made in his 1909 book *The Making of Religion*:

> It was not only on the dreams of sleep, so easily forgotten as they are, that the savage pondered, in his early speculations about life and the soul. ...Reflecting on these things, the earliest savage reasoners would decide (1) that man has a "life" (which leaves him temporarily in sleep, finally in death); (2) that man also possesses a "phantom" (which appears to other people in their visions and dreams). The savage philosopher would then "combine his information," like a celebrated writer on Chinese metaphysics. He would merely "combine the life and the phantom," as "manifestations of one and the same soul." The result would be "an apparitional soul," or "ghost soul." ...This ghost soul would be a highly accomplished creature, "a vapour, film, or shadow," yet conscious, capable of leaving the body, mostly invisible and impalpable, "yet also manifesting physical power," existing and appearing after the death of the body, able to act on the bodies of other men, beasts, and things. ...When the earliest reasoners, in an age and in mental conditions of which we know nothing historically, had evolved the hypothesis of this conscious, powerful, separable soul, capable of surviving the death of the body, it was not difficult for them to develop the rest of Religion.... .

This simple and phenomenologically appealing theory was dismissed by anthropology with the rejection of all things 19th century – a case perhaps of throwing the phenomenology of the soul baby out with the evolutionist's bath water.

Suffice to say that in my opinion, despite Lang's antiquated prose, his reasoning, like E.B. Tylor's, was sound enough. Consider the fact that we discussed above, that many polyphasic cultures interpret dreaming as reality, in this case a domain of reality in which the normally invisible soul becomes visible – "palpably" real in Lang's sense – and is able to leave the physical body behind and wander. It is hardly absurd to conclude that somehow this experientially real soul can escape and survive death, and may have done so many times in dreams. Moreover, consider also that when you ask the mainstream Westerner how he knows he has a soul, he rarely points to direct experiences, but rather has recourse to scripture and other received knowledge. But there was a time in our cultural history when we would have pointed to the ability of the soul to leave our bodies in dreams and other ASC (see Parman 1991:22-26 on Classical Greece). Here is an example of a typical OBE dream from Western culture (Whiteman 1961:60):

> While in bed and apparently awake, I perceived a visual opening with circular boundary, within which there was presented a scene in bright sunlight and vivid colours. It appeared to be a park, with many people walking peacefully about. At the same time I was aware of the physical body lying on its back in bed, but not altogether as if I were in that body. It was as if I were apart and watching the physical body watching. Again, appearing to think in the physical body, I conceived a wish to transfer consciousness to a free personal form. Immediately I rose and walked forward towards the opening. The opening appeared to enlarge itself gradually, but before entering wholly within it I had to pass over a patch of sandy-coloured ground, as if bared for excavation. It seemed to represent a gulf between two spheres of existence. Passing through, however, I reach the park and mix with the people. There is difficulty in distinguishing details, as if the eyes are out of focus and cannot be brought under steady control; but a general brightness of the light around is very noticeable.

Common to such dreams are awareness of the physical body and a separation of consciousness from it, and sometimes a return to it (see my own experiences in Chapter 13; also Alvarado 2000:186). Also common are experiences of falling, passing through portals (MacDonald *et al.* 1988) and tunnels, and of course flying. Wandering aimlessly may occur, or a journey to a specific location where information may be obtained (very common cross-culturally).

Once again, when considering these elements and motifs in OBE dreams, it is absolutely crucial for Western researchers to bracket both our belief in the unreality of dreaming and in the reality of waking, for the common sense Western view is that the body I experience while waking is my "real" body and the body I may experience in a dream is "unreal." In fact the "real" body I experience while awake is just as much of a neuroperceptual construct as my dream body, save, as Globus noted above, the input from my exteroceptive and interoceptive senses in the waking state which are disconnected during sleep (Laughlin 1997b). So if I experience my consciousness as outside of, and away from my body in a dream or trance state (I have; see Chapter 13), the "body" I am outside of is as much a neural construct as the dream ego (embodied or unembodied) in the dream – or for that matter in waking OBEs (see Merleau-Ponty 1962). My impression from OBE reports of dreamers and meditators is that the realness of the waking, "physical" body is part of the taken-for-granted natural attitude typical of Westerners prior to accomplishing the epoché. To some extent at least, non-Western dream cultures also reveal this conceptual bias, for all peoples carry around their culturally influenced natural attitude toward experience.

Numerous examples of OBE dreams pepper the ethnographic literature. Robert Laughlin reports several in his marvelous compendium of Zinacantán (southern Mexico) dreams, *Of Wonders Wild and New* (1976). Here is one:

> Well, it seemed that I was at Ak'ol Ravol. I was with some Chamulans [Catholics] there – there at the church. "Go, Romin," a Chamulan said to me, "Go, bring me this!" he said, but it wasn't clear what I was to bring – just, "Go, go and bring it, because it is needed very badly right now," he told me. And he gave me a black cow. I mounted it. I went to bring whatever it was that was needed. Quickly I mounted it. I went off to bring it. [I was] there at the white house, just inside the meadow, but the black cow was flying terribly high, it seemed. It jumped over the fences, the tall trees, everything. Then on the return trip, the cow gored me. My leg was pierced, but lots of blood flowed from my leg. But the

cow spoke to me. "I will cure your leg," she said. "But will it get well?" I asked. "It will get well. It won't take long to cure," she said. And she began to lick my leg. It got well immediately. And I woke up. (ibid:34)

The dreamer is aware of himself standing in the church from his point of view on the back of the black cow.

In keeping with Western OBE dream phenomenology, soul flight plays a significant role in non-Western shamanistic religions. As ethnologist Michael Winkelman (2010:48) writes: "The shaman's ecstatic state was characterized as a soul flight.... The shaman's classic flight may take a variety of forms involving some aspect of the practitioner – called the soul, spirit, or animal familiar – that separates from the physical body, entering into an experiential world and interacting with spirit entities." The best explanation for the universal incidence of what is called by Western philosophers the problem of "mind-body dualism" (see Crane and Patterson 2000) is that our nervous systems are designed to produce a variety of experiences that may be interpreted as subjective evidence that the physical body and elements of consciousness are distinct entities (Laughlin and Throop 2009).

## Bliss in Dreams

Another important ingredient of dreams are experiences of flow — sensations of bliss within the body that are commonly interpreted as *psychic energy* transformations (i.e., spirit, astral body, energy body, *piti, chi, qi, prana, dumo, kundalini*, etc.). I am not speaking here of the rational concepts and terms found in various religious and philosophical systems, but rather the raw, direct experience of the flow of body energy during the dream. These energy flows can range from being quite subtle, as in pleasure (frisson, tingle, flush of delight), to full-on, mind-blowing ecstasy (rapture, rush, orgasmic bliss, ecstatic bliss) with every gradation in between (happiness, joy, elation, exhilaration, euphoria). The term used in reporting these feelings will generally depend upon their intensity, the context in which they arise, and the imagery associated with the feelings. The hallmark in every case is the *flow* (Csikszentmihalyi 2008), however local or global the feelings, and in whatever part of the dream body they are felt. Bliss often accompanies lucidity and flying, which is possibly why Freud and others have mistakenly reduced all manifest flying content to repressed sexuality. Bliss may become so intense as to be transpersonally ecstatic – that is, the consciousness is transformed beyond the boundaries of normal ego awareness.

An excellent example of an "ecstatic" dream was shared by lucid dreamer, Daryl Hewitt (1988):

> I suddenly become lucid in the dream as I am walking in the hallway of my high school. I am very glad to be lucid, and to be virtually as aware as in waking life. As usual, I want to get outside, into the light. Walking down the hallway I come to the exit, but my attempt to open the door is thwarted by the hulk of a wrecked truck. Realizing it is only a dream, I manage to get through the door enough to grasp the vehicle with both hands and heave it up and to the side almost without effort. Outside, the air is clean, the sky blue, the scene pastoral and brilliantly green. I run through the grass and leap into the air joyously. Soaring through the treetops, I become entangled in branches, and have to hover while extricating myself. Finally above the limbs, I continue my flight to a few hundred feet high. While flying, I think, "I've flown so many times before, maybe I'll try a floating meditation in the sky." Having decided on the attempt, I ask for help from the "Higher," saying aloud, "Highest Father-Mother, help me to get the most out of this experience!" I then roll over backwards and cease attempting to control my flight, without fear of falling. Immediately I begin to float through the sky, upside down with eyes closed, the sun beaming brilliantly down upon me, filling my head with light. I feel like a feather floating lazily through the air. During about five minutes of floating, I gently but firmly push thoughts that arise out of my mind, as in my waking meditation practice. *The less distracted I am by thoughts, the more intensely aware and genuinely joyous the experience becomes - what I can only describe as ecstasy.* Gradually I become aware of my body in bed, and as I awaken there is

a feeling of lightness and well-being which is hard to describe. (emphasis mine)

I agree with Davidson (1976: 359) that there exists only one theoretical formulation in the neurosciences that may account for psychic energy experiences. That perspective is Ernst Gellhorn's theory of autonomic-somatic integration (Gellhorn 1967, Gellhorn and Loofbourrow 1963; see Lex 1979 for a summary). According to Gellhorn's model, the somatic system that controls the distribution and utilization of metabolic energy in the body is comprised of two complementary (sometimes antagonistic) systems, each of which entrains functions located in cortex, core brain and lower autonomic and somatic structures. One system contains the sympathetic nervous system and the other the parasympathetic nervous system. The active change in relations between these two systems is called *tuning*, or *retuning*, and the feelings associated with retuning the two systems are of the psychic energy sort (Gellhorn and Kiely 1972; see Laughlin 1994b for a summary of Gellhorn's model). Orgasm is the most common, dramatic experience of bliss due to a tuning of the two systems.

Bliss states have been reported in the context of non-dream related, religious and spiritual practices world-wide. The dancing of the Bushmen adept which brings about the arising and ascension of enhanced psychic energy (*n/um*) may be interpreted as an example of bliss activity leading to an ASC the Bushmen call *Kia* (Katz 1982). Carol Lederman (1988) reports such an experience during her investigation of a Malay shamanic ritual. She found Malays reluctant to talk about their experiences of the 'Inner Winds' had during trance states. "They told me that the only way I could know would be to experience it myself" (ibid:805). Eventually, her shaman/teacher sat her down and began a ritual that led to her entering a trance state. "At the height of my trance, I felt the Wind blowing inside my chest with the strength of a hurricane" (ibid:806). When she described her feelings to her informants, they responded, "Why did you think we call them Winds?" (ibid: 806; see also Lederman 1991).

Bliss experiences are associated in one way or another with dreaming as well. Indeed, they may be quite important culturally, as in the case of the Quiché Maya who recognize official dream interpreters. These interpreters are considered to have an inner "lightning" soul. The lightning travels around in the bloodstream of the interpreters who "describe the sensation of body lightning as feeling as though air were rapidly moving through their flesh in a flickering or undulating manner, similar to the pattern of exterior sheet lightning as it moves at night over lakes" (Tedlock 1981:315). Trained interpreters are able to discern information from the precise pattern of movement of the lightning in their bodies. Ecstasy is common to the initiation of shamans among Siberian peoples (Eliade 1964, 1966), although the bliss aspect of "ecstasy" as used by Eliade is secondary to the primary connotation of "soul flight," OBEs and other elements of a transpersonal experience (Walsh 2007:14).

## Numinous, Culture Pattern and Archetypal-Titanic Dreaming

As our last example of a natural dream type, I would like to take up what Harry Hunt calls *archetypal-titanic* dreams (1989: Chap. 9). As he notes, this is a kind of dream quite similar to Lincoln's *culture pattern dream* (Lincoln 1935:22), and what others refer to variously as special, "big," significant or memorable dreams. "These dreams may be rare in the dream lives of most people, yet they surely occur to many as memorable exceptions. Some, like Jung and tribal shamans, seem to dream in an archetypal style characteristically. The major defining feature of these dreams, part and parcel of their uncanny-numinous quality and aesthetically rich structure, is the powerful sense of felt meaning and portent conveyed directly within the dream" (ibid:129). These are the kind of dream that polyphasic cultures value as sources of information, communication with the spirit world, so forth. They are generally very lucid and heavy with portent, feature radiant, mythological and other numinous characters (hence "archetypal") and may be accompanied by intense bliss and other notable bodily or "kinesthetic" sensations (hence "titanic"). Right now, I do not want to get into what constitutes an archetype in the strict Jungian sense, for that will be a topic I take up in Chapter 10. It is sufficient here to note that the distinction between everyday dreams and archetypal dreams is fundamental to Jungian dreamwork: ". . . 'little' dreams are the nightly fragments of fantasy coming from the subjective and personal sphere, and their meaning is limited to the affairs of everyday. That is why such dreams are easily forgotten, just because their validity is restricted to the day-to-day fluctuations of the psychic balance. Significant dreams, on the other hand, are often remembered for a lifetime...." (Jung 1969e:290).

What I do want to do here is point up the phenomenological ingredients of the archetypal-titanic dream that make it so memorable, and recognized as special in different dream cultures. Let me begin with one of my own dreams as an example, for I am in touch with the subtle nuances of the memory of the dream-as-dreamt which are often lost in third person dream reports. I call this my *Read Ezekiel dream*:

> I had a uniquely profound dream after spending what was perhaps the most intense, months long, and transformative meditation retreats of my life. I dreamed that I was standing hand in hand with my child self under a fiery arch that had morphed from two enormous serpents that had arisen on each side of us and touched their heads above us. I was lucid and watching the scene from a position behind the fiery portal and my dream selves, so I could see they were located on a vast plain upon which stood the ruins of a city. I knew in the dream that I was looking at the transformation of my self after the realizations of the past retreat. I was beginning to awaken from the dream and was in a hypnopompic state when a fiery golden chariot being drawn by huge golden horses appeared out of an intense, almost blinding golden light, and a deep, booming voice called out, "Read Ezekiel!" This image could not have lasted more than a few seconds, but I awoke knowing that I had not (and indeed have never since) experienced a dream like that.

Being a Buddhist I did not own a Bible and did not recall ever reading the book of Ezekiel before, though the fiery chariot motif could well have been presented in my childhood Methodist bible classes. I obtained a copy of the Old Testament later that same day and was astonished when I read of God appearing before the prophet in the form of a fiery chariot pulled by *Chayot* (mystical angels), and that much of the book was about the destruction of the old Jerusalem and the construction of the City of God upon its ashes. I also noted that the creatures pulling the chariot in my dream were definitely horses, and not the mythical angels of the Biblical imagery – a good example of cultural impact upon the experience of archetypes.

This dream happened nearly thirty years ago, and it is still as clear and meaningful to me today as it was then. This was not the only spiritual guidance dream I have had by any means (see Chapter 13), but it was certainly unique and memorable, particularly because of its numinosity. It is an example of what William Harris (2009:23) calls an "epiphany" dream wherein "…an authority figure visited the sleeper and made a significant pronouncement, and that was the dream." This kind of dream was apparently much more common during antiquity than it is today.

What makes a dream – or any other "epiphany" experience – numinous? *Numinosity* is a feeling of the presence of divinity. The word derives from the Latin *numen*, "spirit," and was used as a theoretical concept by the German theologian Rudolf Otto (1869-1937) in his extremely influential book *Das Heilige* (1917), which was later translated into English with the title *The Idea of the Holy* (1958). Otto distinguished two aspects of numinosity: the *mysterium tremendum*, or the invocation of fear and trembling, and the *mysterium fascinans*, or the feeling of fascination, wonder and awe. People who have numinous experiences feel they are in the direct presence of the sublime – in communion with god(s), spirits, ancestors, and other supernatural entities and forces. This was the overwhelming sense I had within the Read Ezekiel Dream. My experience was wholly positive – more along the lines of the *mysterium fascinans* — the feelings were those of ecstatic bliss coupled with awe and a sense of profound mystery.

Numinosity is one of those feeling terms that is contextual in its meaning. The feeling elements are those we have already discussed above under emotion and bliss, and are mediated by the nervous system in the same way as in other types of experiences. It is the context of manifest spiritual content that makes a dream specifically numinous. We would not greet a friend and say, "I am feeling quite numinous today." Rather, it is the set of feelings we have when in the presence of something we perceive to be far greater than ourselves that makes the content seem numinous. For me, it was in part the intense bliss of the hypnopompic state plus the deep booming voice and the image of the huge fiery chariot that blended together to produce a memorable, meaningful and numinous experience.

Thus, numinosity is a phenomenological ingredient of culture pattern dreams world-wide, whether those dreams be positive or negative, blissfully or terrifyingly awesome. Almost all societies recognize the difference between everyday normal dreams and the very special dreams of spiritual salience and social importance (Casto, Krippner and Trartz 1999; Bulkeley 1995). Such dreams may be life-changing in their consequences, leading the individual to a specific career, or leading the group to collective action. Ethnologically, they are an example of how profoundly culture and the universal properties of neural processing blend to produce distinct phenomena that seem to vary across cultural boundaries.

## Summary and Segue

We have begun our discussion of dream cultures by returning "to the dreams themselves," to paraphrase Husserl. We looked at what a phenomenological approach to dreaming entails – mainly the cultivation of a phenomenological epoché in which we bracket our beliefs and cultural baggage about dreaming and examine the elements of dreaming directly within the confines of our own consciousness. We have done this for several reasons:

One, this exercise reminds us of the distinction between the dream-as-dreamt and the dream-as-told. Because telling a dream involves editing the memories of the dream, and filtering experience through conceptual and linguistic categories, information is inevitably lost in the mental act of transforming the former into the latter. Most of the data on dreaming from ethnography are dreams-as-told by informants, sometimes in response to questions by the ethnographer and sometimes during dream sharing. Two, it is possible for the ethnographer to "get into the native's head" to the extent that the fieldwork process includes learning to access dreaming in much the same way as one's hosts. Ken Wilber's injunction (see p. 388) – if you want to know this, do this – applies, and we have seen that there are societies in which people will consider their ethnographic guest strange if he or she does not know how to dream properly.

Three, when one examines the elements of dreaming using a phenomenological approach, and then seeks what is known about the neurophysiology and neuropsychology of those elements, then one enters the comparative study of dreams with a neurophenomenological appreciation of the relationship between universal biological processes and cultural variations based upon those processes. No matter where one goes in this world, it is always brains doing the dreaming, and brains operate on certain universal structural principles that developed during a lifetime and have been influenced in their growth by personal experience, the environment and culture. And four, it is clear from the phenomenology of dreaming and visions that at some point in the increase of lucidity, it is very difficult to tell from the ethnographic descriptions we have whether the adept is reporting a dream or a vision (Stephen 1979:5). Bourguignon (1972:427) notes that, "...dreams and visions are not always distinguished in the reporting or probably even phenomenologically in the experiencing... ." This has very much been my experience while doing Tibetan dream yoga, as I will describe in Chapter 13.

We must keep in mind that dreaming is experience, dream-telling is a social process. Most of what we know about people's dreaming we must infer from their dream reports along with consideration of the neuropsychology that may be behind the experience being narrated. All cultures recognize dreaming and have a more or less consensus theory about what dreams are, where they come from, what they mean and what to do about them. As Dentan (1986:321-322) remarks, "...it is possible to say that among any of the world's peoples, there is a body of lore about dreams (*oneirology*), usually a way of interpreting them (*oneirocriticism*), and often a way of using them (*oneiromancy*). At least some individuals or classes within any ongoing society will take dreams and dream lore seriously. Attending to dreams is what anthropologists call a 'cultural universal,' a custom found among all peoples, everywhere." The attention paid to dreams is universal precisely because *everyone is a dreaming brain*. When the ethnographer finally realizes this fact, he or she is then better positioned to play the role of participant observer in the broadest possible way (Nuttall 2007:348; Goulet 1994; Tedlock 1991). This should result in a more in-depth – "thicker" (Geertz 1983) – comprehension and description of local dream practices, dream cultures and the uses that dreams are put to.

# Chapter 7

# Cultural Theories of Dreaming

> Chucking Freud, I began, like any good *tabula rasa*, at the beginning, building up sensory impressions from the rudimentary experiments on sleep and dreams. But as Hume demonstrated, you can go only so far with mechanical associations guarded by skepticism and must begin to look for relationships, patterns, insights – an inductive-deductive process. And the most important step in getting a handle on dreams was to realize that they are not simply electrochemical explosions in an evolutionary context, but electrochemical explosions interpreted in a cultural context.
>
> Susan Parman, *Dream and Culture*

Every dream culture includes at its core a theory of dreaming. In this context I use the term "theory" loosely to mean a body of knowledge that accounts for, explains, helps one understand, evaluates, prescribes appropriate action about, and expresses a particular subject matter – in this case dreaming. A culture's theory of dreaming is generally expressible in language and thus may be communicated. It may also be expressed symbolically in art, poetry and performance (Rivers 1917). Unlike a strictly scientific theory, a *cultural theory of dreaming* usually has pragmatic consequences – implications for the waking life world of everyday people (Lohmann 2010:228). A cultural theory of dreaming will usually involve *praxis*, a built-in social process for transforming dreams into practical use. Very often the theory-praxis relationship is straightforward, on the order of "if you dream this, then you should do this, or not do that." According to Anthony F.C. Wallace's (1958) classic paper, "Dreams and Wishes of the Soul," the dream theory of the 17th century Iroquois people held that dreams were considered to be an expression of the desires of the soul, and hence such desires had to be either literally or symbolically fulfilled in waking life in order to avoid illness and other possible calamities.

Take, for instance, the cultural theory of dreaming of the Dobu Island people of eastern New Guinea – a view that seems quite common cross-culturally. The Dobu claim that each person has a body and a spirit or ghost, and that the ghost survives the death of the body and lives on Bwebweso, the Hill of the Dead (Fortune 1963 [1932]:180). The shadowy spirits of the dead may take palpable shape while dreaming (ibid:181):

> In sleep the spirit goes forth; the spirits of witches and sorcerers go on their evil errands, the spirits of the sleeper sometimes go to Bwebweso …and there hold conversations with the dead. There are magicians …who have power over their spirits to send them forth thus. Not only witchcraft is carried on by women who have incantations that charge their spirits with death-dealing errands, and [magicians] possess incantations that send their spirits to Bwebweso to meet the dead, but lovers also send their spirits forth to play upon the spirit of the loved one; and persons wake up shrieking and howling from nightmare cast in witchcraft terms.

Small wonder then that dream life is considered by Dobuans to be dangerous, fraught with perils from witchcraft, from sorcery and from the ghosts of the dead.

In societies like the Dobuans', the group's theory of dreaming will almost always be part of, and consistent with, the group's more global worldview. For instance, if a society understands the spirit world to be a dangerous place, inhabited by demons and witches and other supernatural beings, and with peril lying at every hand, one would not expect their theory of dreaming to be positive with respect to soul flights and other treacherous events arising during sleep. The social group holding a theory of dreaming may be a community, a tribe, a nation, or may be a club, a movement, a church, or an association of some sort. What matters is that the group is socially organized and all the members access the group's cultural or sub-cultural information pool.

I have mentioned before that in the West we tend to disattend dreaming and consider the experiences had in dreams to be unreal, irrelevant and ignored. But that was a gross over-statement on my part, for while it is true for most Westerners – and for that matter, most members of any extremely materialist society – it is not true for all (Collins 1984). For instance, here in the United States there are groups, movements and associations full of people who highly value dreaming for spiritual and therapeutic purposes (see Chapter 15). There are "New Age" groups (Heelas 1996), lucid dream groups, Freudian and Jungian dreamwork support groups and associations (see various in Ullman and Limmer 1999), meditation groups, and so on, that use dreaming in one way or another to further self-understanding, healing and spiritual growth (see Deborah Hillman 1999). Each of them will have a theory of dreaming that is more or less consistent with the group's worldview, or the psychological views of the respective school of psychotherapy.

However, in this section of the book I am interested primarily in dream cultures encountered among non-Western and traditional societies – the types of social groups that ethnographers have consistently focused upon ever since the days of Bastian in the 19th century. So when I speak of cultural theories of dreaming, it is with the planet's 4000-plus cultures that I have in mind.

## Dreaming and the Cycle of Meaning

How a person feels and thinks about dreaming depends in large measure upon their society's worldview. The worldview of intact traditional societies tends to be a *cosmology* – a body of knowledge that views all events and processes in the world as interacting in a more or less coherent and entangled way. A culture's cosmology is a complete explanatory system, often expressed in *mythopoeic*[1] forms – in stories, songs, iconography, art, drama and rituals. The cosmology influences social interactions, legal processes, diet, perceptions of sickness and

---

[1] The term "mythopoea" was coined in 1931 by J.R.R. Tolkien to label the process of making myths. I use it here to refer to anything that symbolically expresses the cosmology, be it in sacred stories, ritual symbolism, drama, performance, so forth.

death, astronomical events, interactions with the spirit world, and so forth. In other words, the society's cosmology tends to be all-pervasive. That does not mean that everybody's understanding or version of their group's cosmology are exactly the same, or that their experience is always consistent with the worldview. As Turner and Bruner (1986:33) write, "…meaning arises when we try to put what culture and language have crystallized from the past together with what we feel, wish, and think about our present point in life." As John Cove (1987:28), an anthropologist and student of Northwest Coast Indian mythology, notes: "…the relationship between mythological and lived-in realms is never completely isomorphic. Each is more or less than the other. If the first has particular significance, it is in giving a foundation for meaning in the second." Keeping in mind that a culture is a pool of information *more or less* available to individual members of the group, not everyone shares exactly the same information, or understands things in exactly the same way, or has the same experiences opinions or memories, or for that matter agree about the meaning of things (see Devereux 1957 for variance among the Mojave Indians; Broch 2000 for variation in notions of reality among the Timpaus Islanders of Indonesia; Hollan 1989 for different dream beliefs among the Toraja of Indonesia; Kracke 1979 for differences in dream interpretation among the Kagwahiv of Amazonia). In many societies there are recognized specialists who are considered to know more about the cosmology and its implications than everyone else.

In such societies, the cultural theory of dreaming is part and parcel of the cosmological worldview. As Jean-Guy Goulet (1998:105) emphasizes for Dene Tha cosmology, the individual elements of the worldview are *self-validating*; that is, they are (1) internally self-consistent, with each element interacting with other elements in a gestalt-like systemic way, and (2) they include views about appropriate evidence for the truth-value of theories. In order to fully understand how cultural theories of dreaming (or for that matter, cultural theories of anything) interact with the individual's experience of dreaming, it will help to model the various interactions before getting into specifics. We have found it useful to imagine that cultural information interrelates with individual experience in a *cycle of meaning* (Laughlin, McManus and d'Aquili 1990: 214-217; Laughlin 1997c; Laughlin

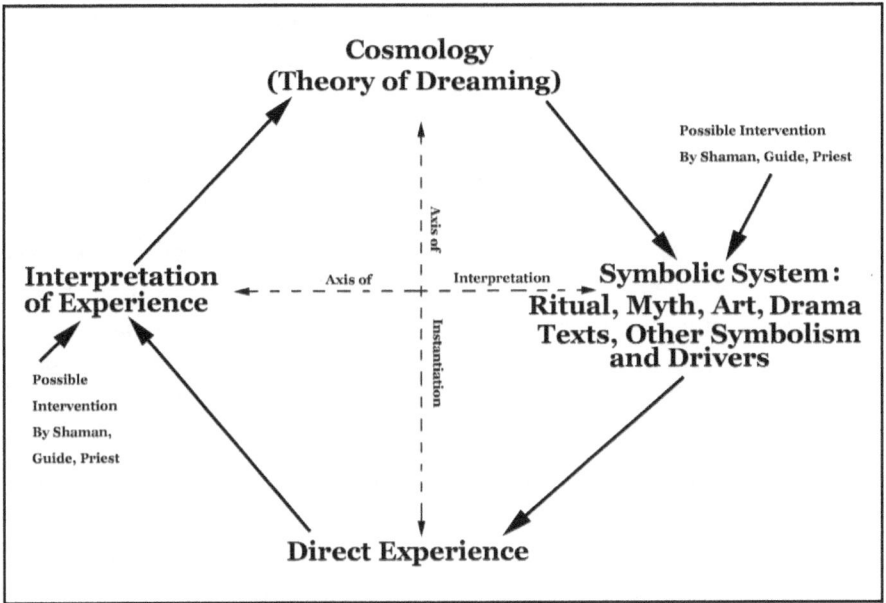

**Figure 7.1. The Cycle of Meaning.** The society's cosmology, including its cultural theory of dreaming, is expressed symbolically in various ways, including its myth-ritual complex. Symbolic expression and action leads to direct experiences that are interpreted in such a way that the cosmology is animated and self-validated. Shamans or priests in some societies may influence the process by controlling the symbolic expression and again by helping to interpret experience.

and Throop 2001). Traditional cosmologies are expressed through the societies' mythopoeic and symbolic system, which includes their mythology, ritual, mobiliary and parietal art, architectural constructions, drama, performance, sacred landscape and games (see e.g., Rivers 1917). All the different symbolic media comprising a traditional symbolic system are interconnected within the context of cosmological understanding. They are variant expressions of a single reality as understood by the people.

The cosmology as expressed symbolically is part of a living system of meaning for people born under the influence of an intact and relatively stable traditional culture. The cosmology and its symbolic representations are lived, and in the living, the cosmology is animated and self-validated within the crucible of each person's consciousness (see Figure 7.1).

The cosmology is mainly carried around in people's brains, aided by symbolically rich, mnemonic materials like myths and other stories.

Myths and stories are a living reality among people who have an intact cosmology (Laughlin and Throop 2001).[2] As Alfonso Ortiz (1972:135) noted, the associations, principles and assumptions upon which a traditional cosmology is founded are rarely, if ever, worked out by people. Rather, most people accept and participate in accordance with the worldview they inherit from their culture pool. This participation results in real life experiences that are in turn interpreted in terms of the cosmology, thus completing a semi-negative feedback loop which instantiates the cosmology, or the cultural theory of whatever, in individual experiences and which also self-validates the truth of the people's system of knowledge (Ricoeur 1962, 1968). Specialists are sometimes involved in the ritual and the interpretive phases of the cycle. Shamans and priests are often ritual specialists and keepers of the esoteric teachings pertaining to the spiritual domain of life.

The cycle of meaning is never static – it is never totally closed to input and change. Some positive feedback is essential, for direct experiences can, upon occasion, lead to alterations in interpretations, which in turn can change cosmological information, elements of a cultural theory, and the mythopoeic reflections of that cosmology found in myth, stories, songs, procedures, etc. As Kennedy and Langness (1981:249) aptly wrote:

> Of all forms of supernatural revelation and supernatural intervention, dreams are by far the most universal, and to the majority of people, surely the most interesting. They are experienced and remembered daily by many of the world's people, and all people remember dreams on occasion. All cultures of which we have any knowledge regard dreams as puzzles, cryptic sets of symbols, pregnant with important information related to the anxiety-producing questions in which human beings are always prone. The often enigmatic quality of dream images, coupled with cultural beliefs about their divine importance in human affairs, has given rise to countless systems of symbolic interpretation and to the widespread role of the dream interpreter.

---

[2] Lucien Levy-Bruhl (1923) called this intimate engagement with a people's symbolic system "mystical participation."

Gananath Obeyesekere, in fact, argues that a great deal of creative impetus in culture change stems from ritually-induced experiences in dreams and other ASC. He explains that these states are characterized by their great creative capacity and their ability to "generate subjective imagery and cultural meanings" (1981:169). Moreover, he argues that myth is itself directly produced from and influenced by ASC, thus requiring an integration of the creative and conventional sides of culture. The experiential byproducts of ASC can be "reworked by the conscious mind, and [as such] brought in line with the needs of the individual and the demands of culture" (ibid:181). In keeping with the cycle of meaning, Obeyesekere reasons that culture and myth therefore "feed back into the [ASC], influencing the thought structure of these states" (ibid:181). Laura Graham (1994) presents evidence along these lines when she shows how young males among the Xavante Indians of Brazil process dream-songs. During their initiation process, youths are encouraged to seek a new song-performance while dreaming. These song-performances are received from the ancestors. "Since dreams belong to the domain of individual subjectivity while their expression depends upon socialized forms of signification, dream re-presentation offers a particularly potent means of signaling the uniqueness of individual subjectivity as well as sociability between individuals. Xavante celebrate the complex dialogic processes between subjectivity or 'inner experience,' and 'outward expression' in the process of sharing songs, represented first as individually dreamed compositions then in collective performances in which the dream-song representing subjective experience becomes socially shared experience" (ibid:725). New material is created and then shared in recurring group performances, thus ensuring a flow of novel forms into the mythopoeic symbolism of the group.

This process of rendering creative subjectivity into socially shared mythopoeic symbolism and ritual action is actually quite common. As Broch (2000:15) has noted, "Studying idiosyncratic doubts and ambivalence can yield important information on cultural processes. Social and cultural creativity are often most dynamic where idiosyncratic ideas influence well-established constructions, or what is, by consensus, regarded as real." These two attributes of the cycle of meaning – creativity and conservatism – can be illustrated in terms of the following hypothetical example of a very common type of dream incubation. A culture might hold that while one is asleep, one's soul can depart from the body thus freeing it to obtain culturally valued information about events in the world. A member of such a culture who wishes to discover something important about the future might therefore be inclined to use a culturally specified ritual to incubate lucid dreams. Dream incubation then evokes dreaming in which an individual is able to experience themselves as a conscious soul flying free of the body, thus enabling them to visit, say, the home of the dead and there discover information about future events. The dream experience

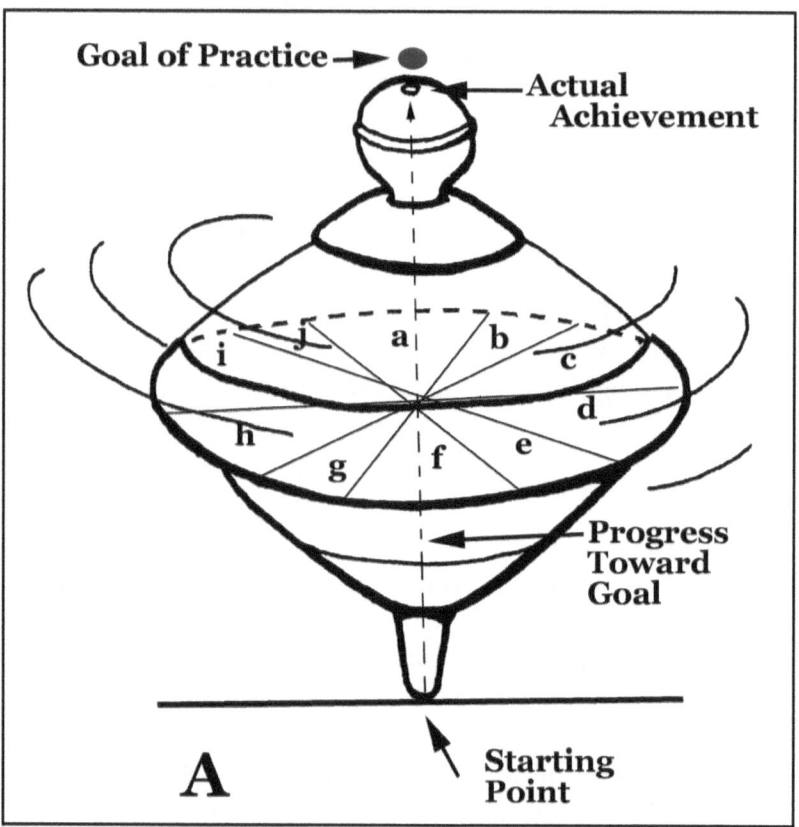

**Figure 7.2.** A child's top represents the relationship between different theories of dreaming (or other ASC) and direct experience. In image 'A' the top is spinning, representing an intact system in which rituals and other techniques and drivers evoke dream experiences that are directed at realizing the goal of practice. Achievement and goal are consistent. This is a living system in which every element of the cycle of meaning is operating well. The different slices of the middle "pie" plane (a, b, ... j) represent different mythopoeic aspects of the cosmology and conventional interpretations.

not only instantiates the cultural theory of dreaming, but it also confirms the veracity of the society's customary interpretation of such dreams. Conversely, in the process of incubating dreams a precocious dreamer may indeed have some novel experience in the land of the dead – say an interaction with a novel entity or spirit that falls outside of the interpretive framework provided by the cosmology. The dreamer may attempt to elaborate a new interpretive framework that can (given the proper circumstances) serve to modify the original cultural theory (see Devereux 1957 on this process).

This hypothetical example is of a fully intact cycle of meaning. But the connection between a society's cosmology (or theory of dreaming) and direct experience can be broken. This has happened historically when some political authority outlaws ritual practices for one reason or another – as happened to practitioners of the Sun Dance in the 19th century (Voget 1984). In contrasting an intact cycle with a disrupted cycle, I find it useful to use anthropologist Agehananda Bharati's (1975:32) metaphorical model of the child's top. The spinning top in image 'A' (Figure 7.2) represents a living cycle of meaning in which the practices and techniques evoke direct experience that instantiates the cosmology and its constituent theories and interpretive frames. The path of practice and experiences leads from the beginner's starting point and will eventually reach the goal of the mythopoeic system. Not everyone reaches full realization of such an esoteric path. Often it is the individual who does go further – rises "higher" — that becomes the shaman, prophet, "road chief," healer, oneirocritic, visionary, etc., and who acts as a guide to others on the path. Individual achievement, however great or small, is consistent with the stated goals of the system and its various interpretive frames.

The fallen top in image 'B' (Figure 7.3) represents a disrupted cycle of meaning in which the various practices and techniques no longer operate, and experiences are not evoked that are consistent with the various mythopoeic elements of the system. This is a dead system in which achievement cannot possibly lead to the realization of the stated goal. Shamans, if they still exist, will resemble priests in a dogma-dominated institution bereft of its esoteric inspiration. Direct experience no longer instantiates the cosmology or theory, and natural revitalization feedback into the cosmology no longer works. Such systems, under certain historical circumstances, may be revived, reestablished. This happened, for instance, later in the 20th century when various ordeals previously practiced in the Sun Dance were resurrected (Jilek 1982; Voget 1984). Or a new cycle of meaning may be created or borrowed from another society to fill the gap, as with modern dreamwork movements in our own society.

A society's cosmology and symbolic system are ultimately the product of the creative imagination of its people. I am not talking

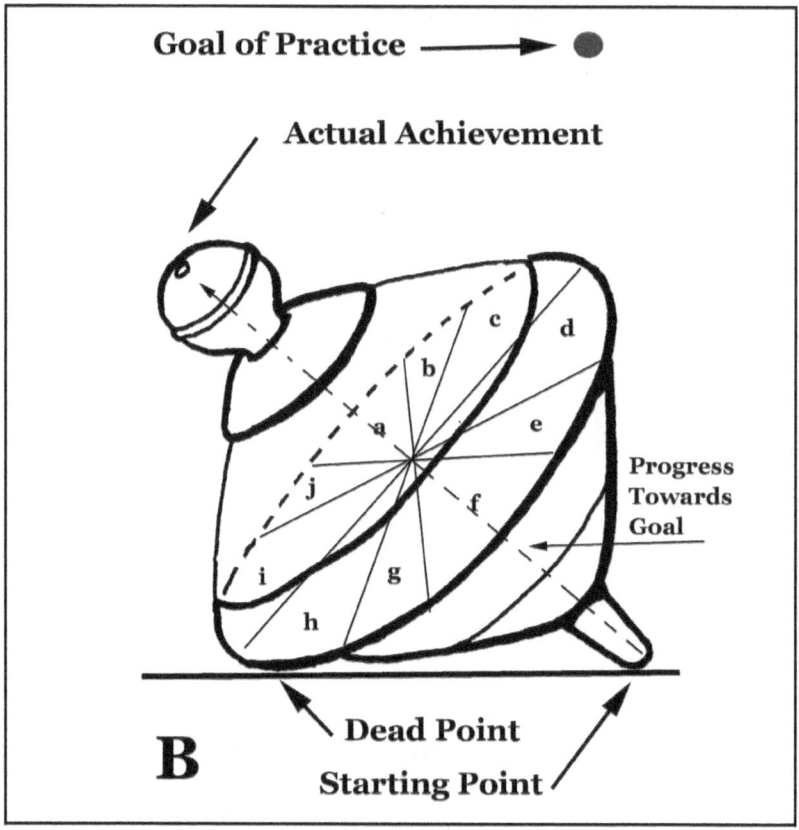

**Figure 7.3.** The child's top in image 'B' has stopped spinning, representing a disrupted cycle of meaning in which direct experience is no longer consistent with the society's cosmology or theory of dreaming. The ritual practices are no longer operating, and achievement cannot lead individuals to the goal of the mythopoeic system. Achievement no longer can realize the goal of the practice. The different mythopoeic frames (a, b, ... j) are rendered phenomenologically "dead" and lifeless when the system stops at its dead point.

about imagination in the mundane fantasy sense (i.e., imagined unreality), but rather the *Imaginatio* in Henry Corbin's (1969:179) sense – the exercise of the creative intuitive faculties associated with imagery by which the essentially invisible aspects of reality become envisioned. As Corbin noted, modern Western culture is marked by a vast chasm between its conception of "reality" as described by science and "reality" as imagined by people: "In short, there has ceased to be an intermediate level between empirically verifiable reality and unreality pure and simple" (ibid:181). In traditional societies this intermediate level by which reality is imagined is the spiritual domain, which seamlessly bridges the gap between knowledge about the world and direct experience.

Although dynamic and open to some change, traditional cosmologies do tend to be conservative of meaning. They resist change in knowledge, for the principle function of a society's worldview is to assure both a complementarity of experience for society's members, as well as reflect the authenticity of experience. The traditional cycle of meaning is the product of an inherent *effort after meaning* (Bartlett 1932) as opposed to an *effort after truth* (Earl Count, personal communication, 1990; see also Laughlin and Throop 1999, 2001; Garro 2007 for applications). That is, the cognitive processes of the human brain operate to associate what is arising moment by moment within the sensorium with information stored in memory – in Bartlett's (ibid:44) terms, "an effort to connect what is given with something else." The effort after meaning is the effort expended by the brain to interpret experience as redundant – as an instantiation of a pattern already stored in memory. The effort after truth, however, shifts the orientation from attributing meaning to the given toward discovering what is novel in the given and then evaluating the veracity of meaning by comparison with the experienced novelty. In other words, the effort after meaning is a quest for the correspondence between an experienced given and information in memory, while the effort after truth privileges anomaly over redundancy of a particular given.

As the cycle of meaning model implies, the information encoded in sacred stories and other symbolic media informs lived experience, and that is why myth is found to be so intimately associated with ritual activity. Émile Durkheim (1858-1917) long ago held that ritual is a mechanism through which individuals are able to harmonize their subjectivities with one another and with the cosmological system as expressed in a particular society's corpus of myths. His view of the close connection between ritual and mythology is evidenced in his assertion that "If myth is withdrawn from religion, ritual must also be withdrawn....Indeed the rite is often nothing other than the myth in action" (1995 [1912]:79). More recently, Victor Turner (1985, 1992, Turner and Bruner 1986) argued that embodied ritual, not disembodied myth, is the cornerstone of religion. As is implied in the cycle of meaning model, religion is an active process with ritual enactment at its very core (d'Aquili, Laughlin and McManus 1979, Laughlin 1989, Laughlin et al. 1986; see also Rappaport 1999). Dream incubation operates in the same way, to harmonize the cultural theory of dreaming with individual subjectivities so as to instantiate and confirm the society's worldview, or if necessary, alter it such that harmony is reestablished and the cycle of meaning is rejuvenated.

## CULTURAL CATEGORIES OF DREAMING

Most cultural theories of dreaming recognize two or more categories of dreams. We have already discussed those that distinguish everyday dreams from culture pattern dreams (Lincoln 1935:22). This is a distinction that appears to be universal, at least among polyphasic peoples. But different cultures also make distinctions that are of particular relevance to their way of life and their environment, and that are generated out of, and make sense relative to their particular culture theory of dreaming. With respect to an intact cycle of meaning, the mythopoeic system may inform people about specific categories of dreams. Moreover, rituals and other techniques may be oriented toward producing certain types of dreams, and may indicate the appropriate interpretation to be attached to dream reports. We Anglophone Westerners also have our dream types; e.g., "nightmare," "OBE dream," "wet dream," "co-dream," "day dream" (for fantasy), and of course "lucid dream." Our dream types are "natural" categories distinguished by distinct qualities (see Chapter 6): "nightmares" by intense fear, "wet dreams" by erotic content and nocturnal emission, so forth.

Anthropologists have not infrequently applied *etic*[3] dream typologies to non-Western cultures (e.g., Hall and Van de Castle 1966; see Lohmann 2007:36 on this issue) — that is, typologies that make sense, not to their hosts, but within the frame of reference of an ethnological or psychological theory of dreaming. As we have already seen, Freudians like to speak of "manifest" and "latent" content in dreams, "day-residue" dreams, "wish fulfillment" dreams, "nightmares" and "Old Hag dreams," etc. I am not very interested in etic typologies here for they may or may not make any sense relative to the native cultural theory. What I am interested in are the more *emic* systems – categories derived from the people themselves. In societies with intact cycles of meaning, such systems are generally consistent with and derive from the local cultural theory of dreaming. Also, they derive their explanatory, interpretive and phenomenological power from the local theory. The cultural theory of dreaming, as I have said, derives from the society's cosmology, which means that many of the social relations inherent in the cosmological worldview are repeated in the theory of dreaming. As Kilborne (1992) has shown, dream classification may be entangled with social hierarchy and status, both of dreamers themselves and in assessing the content of their dreams.

One distinction that we sometimes make in our own Western society, despite our monophasic proclivities, is between dreams that "come true" – we dream of some event that actually comes to pass in waking life — and those that are merely illusions or hallucinations. The distinction between "true" and "false" dreams is not uncommon in traditional societies, and usually has implications for dream theory praxis. For instance, Roger Lohmann has recounted the historical impact of "true" dreams among the Asabano people of Papua New Guinea. The Asabano have undergone a great deal of change since first contact with world cultures, and their worldview has changed as a consequence. But the role of dreaming within their cycle of meaning has for most folks remained intact (2010:228):

---

[3] The distinction between "emic" and "etic" originated with linguist Kenneth Pike who generalized from the terms "phonemic" and "phonetic" to all knowledge about a society's culture (Headland, Pike and Harris 1990).

> There is agreement... that certain dreams are true, while others are false or at least unworthy of action. The surest way for them to feel certain that a dream is true is for it to match current or future events in waking life. When asked to explain the mechanism behind such apparent matches, people refer to cultural dream theories. For the Asabano, a true dream might be a supernatural revelation, the perceptions of wandering souls, or both. Those dreams judged false are supposed to be either "just thoughts" or illusions shown to dreamers by supernatural beings.

The Asabano have always held that dreaming is the time of the day when one is free of one's body and can wander around in supernatural realms and have direct interactions with spirit entities. These entities – sprites, angels, etc. – show things to people and provide information, like where to hunt. If they dream of a supernatural entity, they consider that entity real, and the events shown to them may well come true. When asked why the people converted to Christianity after contact with missionaries, many responded they did so because they dreamed of Jesus and angels, and were in effect directed to change (Lohmann 2000, 2010).

Douglas Hollan (1989) describes three types of dreaming recognized by the Toraja of Indonesia:

- ***Tindo***: These dreams are about the previous day's happenings. They are not considered real dreams, "Rather, villagers seem to think of them as a form of nocturnal cogitation... ." (ibid:168). These dreams are low on effect, and are considered of little importance.
- ***Tauan***: These are scary, nightmarish dreams and are of two subtypes: those dreams that feature reliving some traumatic event in the dreamer's past, and those that are spirit attacks. These are accompanied by intense anxiety.
- **Real *Tindo***: These correspond to the "big" dreams of so many other peoples around the globe. They are infrequent, but easily recalled due to their vivid content. "Such dreams are of special interest to the Toraja because some of them are thought to be predictive of future events. Thus, there are two subtypes: Those that are prophetic and those that are not" (ibid:170).

Benjamin Kilborne (1992) has suggested that the degree of elaboration of dream classification in a society may be proportional to the importance of dreaming in that society. Although there are no holocultural data to support this correlation – indeed, such a study might be hard to design in such a way that measures of interest are independent of measures of elaboration of classificatory systems – it does make some sense, for that is the impression one has of the ethnographic literature of polyphasic peoples. In any event, modern Moroccans hold the distinction between true dreams that are divinely inspired, and false or deceitful dreams derived from other sources (ibid:185; see below on Islam generally). Dream categories vary with the informant, but many seem to consider dreams divisible into: (1) message dreams – divinatory dreams dreamt in holy places, (2) warning dreams – messages received from ancestors, etc. offering advice and cautions about the future, essentially divinatory dreams, (3) preoccupation dreams – dreams driven by internal positive or negative emotions, and (4) normal ("day residue") dreams – problem solving dreams, etc. Only the first category is considered true beyond question, for they derive from Allah and true dreams are associated with safety and harmony, while false dreams may derive from the *djinn* spirits who may be good or bad, and may be harmful and destructive.

Anthropologist Philippe Descola (1989:441) notes that for the Achuar folk of Ecuador, all dreams foretell events. Moreover, "The Achuar distinguish three broad categories of dreams according to their content and the rules of interpretation to which they can be submitted: the *kuntuknar* dream, the *mesekramprar* dream and the *karamprar* dream."

- ***Kuntuknar* dreams**: These "…are a positive precondition of hunting and, to a lesser extent, of fishing. They are not an exclusive male prerogative, for they can be dreamed by women and even by predatory animals (dogs, jaguars, anacondas). Although Achuar men are solitary hunters, they often bring along one of their wives to handle the pack of dogs; these belong to women and are trained and raised by them. Furthermore, since hunting (with blowguns and, more seldom, shotguns) also offers an opportunity for marital sexual relations, sometimes difficult to indulge in within a crowded polygynous household, the presence of women on hunting expeditions is deemed perfectly natural. In principle, no man can undertake a hunting expedition if he or his wives have not dreamed a kuntuknar the previous night, particularly if he hopes to encounter big game such as peccary. Failing an adequate dream, the hunter might meet some animal but will not manage to kill it" (ibid: 441). These dreams may be incubated, peopled with unknown persons who may be equated with certain animal species, feature inverted meanings, and should remain secret between the dreamer and spouse.

- *Mesekramprar* **dreams**: These "…foretell a negative or dangerous event for the dreamer or his close kin: a death, an accident, an attack by an animal, a combat with enemies or a disease sent by a shaman. These bad omens can be dreamed by anyone and they are commented on with concern by the household, since their outcome affects the well-being of the local community as a whole. Their manifest content exhibits more variety than the imagery of the *kuntuknar*: they feature aggressive animals, uncanny personal experiences, trifling but irritating incidents, or seductive human beings, the latter being generally anonymous as in *kuntuknar*. The rule of interpretation mainly consists, here also, in an inversion between the apparent content of the dream and the message it portends, in terms of the nature/culture axis: the attributes and behaviour of animals forebode specific human deeds, while human acts announce the actions of particular animals. For example, a dream of charging peccaries will be interpreted as the presage of a skirmish with enemy warriors, while a man dreaming of sexual intercourse with a woman is thus warned of a possible snakebite" (ibid:442).

- *Karamprar* **dreams**: These "…are dreams wherein a personal relationship is established with a being spatially remote or ontologically distant, but always known to the dreamer. These beings either enter in a dialogue or deliver a message: the meaning of the dream is thus homologous to its explicit content and it does not require a key of interpretation. The entities that appear in this category of dreams may be living persons temporarily estranged or absent, deceased relatives or acquaintances, a whole range of tutelary spirits, magical objects in human form, certain kinds of animals, or the embodiment of personal destiny" (ibid:442).

Dream classification generally follows the particular economic realities of a people. Hunting societies, like the Achuar above, will generally distinguish hunting dreams from other forms of dreaming. This has certainly been the case among Eastern Cree peoples so long as they were making their living as hunters (Flannery and Chambers 1985; Speck 1963; Ridington 1988a). As Speck (1963:187) notes: "To dream (*pwamu*) is a religious process of these people. The hunting dream is a major object of focus.... It is part of the process of revelation by which the individual acquires the knowledge of life." But in younger generations that no longer hunt for a living, the distinctions have no salience.

## CULTURAL THEORIES OF DREAMING IN ACTION

For monophasic peoples, dreams are synonymous with *un*-real, but for most peoples on the planet, dreaming is at least as real as waking experience, and sometimes *more* real. Why? Because dreams are often understood to make normally invisible forces visible, provide information about the otherwise hidden world of spirit, and give access to power – the same functions that myths perform (Meggitt 1962; Laughlin and Throop 2001). As Roger Lohmann writes, "Sleep is a doorway, and dreams are roads and destinations. In dreams, people visit other places, change the shape of reality, and gain insight into causes and connections secreted beneath the cosmos of waking life" (2003b:1). This is a very difficult notion for many Western observers to get their minds around, hence my emphasis in the last chapter upon developing the phenomenological epoché. Only when we bracket and suspend our own Western cycle of meaning, and take dreaming as it presents to us within our own consciousness can we begin to approximate the cycle of meaning that informs our hosts' dreaming. Among North American Native peoples generally, little distinction is made between the dream-as-dreamt and waking experience. One domain of reality phases into another in a natural flow (Irwin 1994:18). The dreaming reality shifts so that, as I say, forces invisible in waking life become visible and accessible in dreaming life. Thus, Native American dreaming "is given a strong ontological priority and is regarded as [a] primary source of knowledge and power" (ibid:19).

All of the world religions (von Grunebaum and Caillois 1966; Bulkeley 2008; Levtzion 1979), as well as those of smaller scale societies recognize certain motifs as spiritually salient in their dreams – those that feature death, gods and ancestors, totemic animals like snakes and bears, sexuality, healing and diagnosis, prophecy, demons and other creatures of nightmares, soul-flight, so forth (Bulkeley 1995). Spirits, ghosts, long dead ancestors, gods, heroes, etc., whose presence one may only sense, but not observe in the waking life, may take on form when they appear as characters in a dream (d'Andrade 1961:298). Dream characters may communicate in one way or another with the dreamer. As a consequence, people may understand dreaming as a means of communicating with the normally invisible forces that influence their daily lives, and perhaps obtaining valuable information.

Myths come alive during dreaming and in other ASC (Dennis Tedlock 1999). That is why I call the cosmology-direct experience relationship an *axis of instantiation* in the cycle of meaning model. This is how it works. A society's cosmology is depicted in their corpus of sacred stories. People have perhaps heard these stories repeatedly since they were small children, and seen them enacted in ritual dramas and other performances (e.g., Hopi *Kachina* ceremonies; see Eggan 1966) — the stories and their characters are stored in memory and become the basis for comprehension within the dream state. This is what Lincoln (1935) was getting at with his distinction between everyday personal dreams and culture pattern dreams. Over and above the numinous quality of the latter (see last chapter), culture pattern dreams gain their status because of their relationship with the sacred stories. Australian Aborigines recognize that dreams about the Dreamtime – the spiritual dimension of reality – are distinctly important (Hume 1999). Price-Williams and Gaines (1994), drawing from Françoise Dussert's unpublished doctoral dissertation on Warlpiri ceremonies, note that Dussert "…enumerated several categories of night dreams, and the fourth type included night dream experiences over a period of two to three months, which have as their theme a specific Dreaming (i.e., a story)" (ibid 376).

In an intact mythopoeic system, the characters encountered in culture pattern dreams often instantiate and thus enliven and confirm the existence of characters inhabiting the people's cosmology. As Waud Kracke (1991:205) put it, "...in some cultures, dreams constitute a kind of democratic mode of personal verification of mythical truth, in that dreams may be a mode of direct contact with supernatural beings, and means of visiting normally inaccessible cosmic realms, which are open to ordinary people without shamanic vocation or priestly initiation... ." This is why one cannot over-emphasize the reciprocal, and even causal relationship between myth and dreaming, especially in polyphasic societies (Eggan 1955; Kracke 1992; Laughlin and Throop 2001; Dennis Tedlock 1999). The cosmology as depicted in myth and enacted in ritual becomes palpably real during dreams, trance states and visions (Stephen 1995:107). Myth and dreams-as-dreamt (not necessarily dreams-as-told that are influenced from language) moreover appear to share the same structure in terms of rules, magical causation and mythopoeic relations (see Kuper 1979; Descola 1989 on this issue). Dreaming in turn may provide new material to be incorporated in sacred lore, as well as new practices (songs, techniques, relations among ritual elements) for enactment (Wallace 1958; Bulkeley 1994:11). Again, in the context of Native American dream theory, Irwin (1994:21-22) writes, "In the Native American context, dreaming is a form of knowledge. It reveals the activities of the mysterious powers – their engagement with or relationship to the dreamer. The dream is a medium of knowing, a way of experiencing the reality of the lived world, a faculty of perception; the religious vision might be regarded as an intensification and heightening of this knowledge." This is why among the Indian societies of the Great Plains, the quest for spiritual vision dreams was (and continues to be) as common as it was important (Benedict 1922). In the context of their cosmologies, dreaming is a state in which people experience both the known and the "mysterious." Dreams instantiate the mythic worldview and at the same time empower the dreamer with direct knowledge of the mysteries (Tedlock 2004a).

Dream theory for the Muria of India is straightforward, and like many other East Indian peoples, involves the adventures of the *jiwa* or soul which leaves the body. This is a folktale told about the *jiwa* and dreaming (Elwin 1991[1947]:475):

One day long ago two men went to a blacksmith's shop to rest. One fell asleep, the other sat by his side watching. Presently from the sleeper's mouth there came out his *jiwa* in the form of a lizard and went to feed. A dog saw it and chased it into an ant-hill. There it saw a pot full of rupees.

The other man covered the sleeper's face with coal-dust for a joke. When the *jiwa* returned it did not recognize its body with the blackened face, and went away seeking for it elsewhere. By and by the second man noticed the lizard going to and fro, and soon realized what had happened. He quickly cleaned the sleeper's face, and the lizard, recognizing the body, entered it, and became a *jiwa* again.

When the sleeper awoke he told his friend what he had seen in his dreams, and they went to the ant-hill and found the rupees. This is a true tale of what actually occurred.

Implicit in this story is not only the view that the soul may leave the body during sleep – a very common scenario cross-culturally – but also that useful information may be accrued during the wanderings and adventures of the soul.

Among many African peoples, cultural dream theory holds that it is quite common for ancestors to pass on to a higher plane of existence and that they then may mediate between divine (normally hidden) forces and the living (Parrinder 1962:61). They may communicate via dreams of a distinctive character, and may warn the living of impending dangers, and even suggest the cause of the dangerous events. The So (Tepes, Tepeth) people, among whom I did a year's fieldwork, are horticulturalists and cattle-keepers who live on the sides of mountains in Karamoja District, northeastern Uganda. They recognize the existence of a high god called *Belgin* who is a very vague and remote character who lives atop the mountains, but has little to do with people or affairs on Earth. Rather, it is by way of the ancestors – the ghosts of important people who are still remembered and propitiated in ceremonies – that a relationship is forged between the living and the spirit world. The ancestors are considered intermediaries between the living people and

*Belgin*. Dreams are an important vehicle for interacting with the ghosts of the ancestors, especially dreams had by important male elders who belong to a ghost cult called the *Kenisan* (Laughlin 1972).

Among Haitian people, the dead are known to walk at night in the form of such horrors as zombies and werewolves. The dead come alive in the nightmares of children (Bourguignon 1954:263). Moreover, the gods and the dead may visit the dreamer in order to pass on messages. Talking in one's sleep is understood to be a message from the dead or the gods, often in a language that only the gods and the priests can understand. If disturbing dreams and nightmares are confusing to the dreamer, he or she may consult a *vodun* priest who is considered to be an oneirocritic. As is typical in traditional societies, the dream will be interpreted within the *vodun* worldview. The message may be read as a demand from the gods for certain ritual procedures to be carried out.

Dreaming is, for some peoples, a direct source of learning, knowledge and power (Hallowell 1955). George Devereux (1957:1036) describes the Mojave Indian cultural theory of dreams in much the same way:

> All students of Mohave culture report that magical powers, and the knowledge of the myths, skills, and songs pertaining to them, are supposed to be acquired in dream.... Given the fundamental similarities between the beliefs and curing rites of various shamans, and between the songs sung by various singers who "learned" a given song cycle in dream, not only anthropologists but even some Mohave informants reached the conclusion that actual learning in a waking state is responsible for the acquisition of the knowledge and skills related to some specialty, but that this knowledge remains barren, i.e., ineffective, unless it is also "dreamed." Thus, after allowing me to record his ritual curing songs, a shaman explained that this would not enable me to cure people by singing these songs, because I had not "potentiated" them by learning them also in dream.

Bearing in mind that Devereux was a Freudian psychoanalyst as well as being an anthropologist, and that he had a theoretical stake in interpreting dreams as "day residue," this description still evidences the importance of dream experience to the fulfillment of Mojave theory of knowledge and empowerment.

This link in the chain of proper knowledge is mirrored by Robin Ridington (1988) who makes clear that "hunting dreams" among the subarctic Dunne-za enable the hunter to establish a relationship with the animals he hunts and with the normally invisible spirits that influence his success or failure. Moreover, one may be directly instructed and guided toward paths of knowing while dreaming. Denise Nuttall (2007:345) reports that during her lengthy apprenticeship with the great East Indian *tabla* player, Usted Zakir Hussain, she repeatedly had what she called "tabla dreams" in which Zakirji would visit and instruct her. The same experience was reported by Katherine Ewing (1994:574) who was visited by her teacher in dreams while researching Sufi practices in Pakistan. The Ese Eja of Peruvian Amazonia seek the names of their children from dreams (Peluso 2004). In their dreams, people interact with animals and receive the "true name" of their child. This process brings direct experience in dreaming, naming and notions of personhood into accord with the spiritual aspects of Ese Eja cosmology.

The classic example of the integration of dreaming and cosmology is that found among the Australian Aborigines (Tonkinson 1978:15-17, 2003:93; Poirier 2003; Price-Williams and Gaines 1994). The Aborigines tell us that in mythical times – or what they call the Dreaming, Dreamtime, the Law, or more recently Power (Hume 1999) — hero spirits created the world people later inhabited. People understand that the Dreamtime happened a long time ago, and yet is still present today. In other words, Dreamtime is essentially timeless (ibid:2). Dreamtime is "still and moving all at once - like days and seasons, in a regular sequence, a sequence (or a change) of sameness" (Williams 1986:16). Individual dreaming is an expression of the Dreamtime, the link between contemporary dreaming and the Dreaming being seamless. All the power accrued by shamans derives from the Dreamtime and is accessed by way of "night" dreaming (as Price-Williams and Gaines 1994:373 call dreams that are actually experienced by Aborigines). Interpretations of "night" dreams are always in terms of Dreamtime characters, landscape features, power sources and adventures. Every person has a dream spirit that can travel anywhere it wishes in the Dreamtime domain. Every landmark has its place in the sacred stories of the Dreamtime and these features are recognized during "night" dreaming. As Robert Tonkinson writes, "Their human forefathers who first peopled their territory must have sensed a need to ground metaphysical conceptions in the stones, sand, and streambeds of the physical world, to unite spirit and substance and in this way render much more immediate and meaningful the essential unity of the two realms" (1978:15). People seek and receive instructions and knowledge in "night" dreams, and conceive of such information as having been bestowed upon them by mythopoeic Dreamtime forces. New rituals may be derived from inspiration in individual "night" dreams, and then as time passes and the rituals spread from group to group, such rituals may be viewed as having derived collectively from the Dreaming (2003:94). Nancy Munn in reporting on a Walbiri Aborigine's "night" dreaming noted that "the dreamer felt himself to be both a kind of observer of the events of the dream and at the same time an actor in the dream, identified with the ancestors" (1973:114).

Ellen Basso (1992) has made the important point that, contrary to the Freudian orientation towards past events, developmental issues and traumas in dream interpretation, many cultural theories of dreaming are oriented toward events yet to come. The Kalapalo of central Brazil "are a people whose dreaming is interpreted quite clearly with reference to the future of the dreamer" (ibid:88). As with so many people, during dreaming the dreamer's *akũa* ("interactive self") leaves the body and wanders about having adventures. The soul may be visited by powerful spiritual beings that are able to cast "song spells" and are given the names of living forms from waking life. These are mythological beings that may also appear in human form while awake. These contacts with such beings are dangerous, but they also afford the dreamer the opportunity to derive knowledge about the beings, information about events and the ability to use that information in the future. People who accrue many contacts with these beings may become shamans. Interpretation of dreams pertains to the future constitution of the dreamer – "...for the Kalapalo interpreting a dream is a process of acquiring illusory (but not inaccurate or deluded) self-knowledge, which is imaginative understanding of one's unconscious motives and proclivities. It is, in other words, acquiring knowledge of the interactive self" (ibid:101). The process of dreaming and interpretation of dreams is very much one of self-revelation, and this process feeds back into the future realization of maturity.

## Ritual and Incubation

Myth and ritual go hand in hand; i.e., ritual is the most common expression of myth in action. Ritual refers to patterned, repetitive, structured, and sometimes rule-driven sets of behavior that may be as simple as brushing one's teeth to elaborate ceremonies like the Mass or sitting Shiva or doing a *puja*. Rituals, when they are conceptualized by people as such, are usually given a label – e.g., the Sun Dance, a church service, a football game, a parade, a funeral, a graduation ceremony, etc. Rituals may or may not be associated with a mythology, but no intact cosmological cycle of meaning will be without ritual expression to some extent. It is possible for a mythology to be lost over time and people continue to carry out rituals that were once pregnant with meaning, but are no longer so, bereft as they are of their role in an intact cycle of meaning.

A common misconception in our highly industrialized world is that ritual is something that goes on only in traditional societies, while we, being the product of scientific enlightenment, lead rational, non-ritualistic lives. But the facts are otherwise. All human cultures, including our own, use ritual as the physical and metaphysical means for dealing with everyday life, and the mystery and unpredictability of the natural, social, and cosmic realms. Indeed, humans are not alone in this, for ritual plays significant roles in the social lives of most animal species – its pervasiveness in human life reflects its origins in age-old biological and evolutionary processes (Laughlin *et al.* 1986; d'Aquili, Laughlin and McManus 1979; Laughlin, McManus and d'Aquili 1990:276; Winkelman 2010:232; Grimes 2010; Turner 1969, 1982).

When a society deems it important to control the experience of its members in some respect so that experience is coherent with, instantiates or realizes some aspect of the group's mythology or worldview, they will intervene in the axis of instantiation by putting a ritual in place so as to evoke the desired range of experiences. The classic example of this process is the "rite of passage" which operates to transform the individual from one status to another in a life crisis – for instance puberty rites (see Van Gennep 1960 [1909]). This myth-ritual-experience relationship is fundamental to all religious systems and may in some societies include dream incubation (refer back to Chapters 4 and 5 on incubation). Techniques of dream incubation will also vary in complexity from simple autosuggestion to more dramatic ceremonies and performances. Incubation rituals will be designed to evoke the range of experiences desired by the society during dreaming, and to influence the content of significant, culture pattern dreams (see Reed 1977 for an experimental approach to studying dream incubation; also see Paul Devereux 2005 on the results of the Dragon Project incubation experiments at Carn Ingli, or "Hill of Angels," in the Preseli hills of south-west Wales – which was the apparent source of the Stonehenge bluestones).

The classic example of incubation is that practiced by the ancient Greeks (Meier 1966, 1967, 2009; Bulkeley 2008; Walde 1999; Hamilton 1906; Van de Castle 1994). Like the Moroccans above, the Greeks distinguished between true dreams and false dreams. A "large proportion" of their dreams would seem to have been *theophanic* – that is, featured deities — and, "...as long as the god appears true to his attributes and to his cult-image, the dream is favorably interpreted. The slightest flaw in this respect, however, renders its meaning ominous" (Meier 1966:311). Dreams of this sort were of two types, real dreams and allegorical dreams. The former were straightforward in interpretation and were "lived out by the dreamer" quite soon after the dream, while the latter were enigmatic and may take a long time to come true, if at all (ibid:311; see Chapter 8). In any event, Greeks assessed dreams by whether they would come true and whether what ensued was good or bad.

Dream incubation was as widespread in ancient Greece as it was old. Meier (2009:77) suggests that the practice goes back to 3000 B.C. Hence dream incubation in Greek society is a vast topic. However, all we want to do here is get a flavor of the rituals and their effects upon dreaming, so I will take advantage of Carl Meier's excellent description of the practices at the oracle of Trophonius (a hero in Greek mythology) at Lebadea in Boeotia, central Greece.[4] Trophonius' incubatorium was a fairly inaccessible cave into which supplicants had to enter to consult the oracle after having spent some days purifying themselves and bathing in the river Hercyna. Animals were sacrificed and eaten, and priests read the entrails of the animals to determine the propitious time for the descent into the cave. When the time came, the incubant was bathed in the waters of the Hercyna, then made to drink out of two springs near the cave which were said to wipe past thoughts from mind. This step is crucial according to Meier, for, "…[a]mnesia is an essential condition if the patient is to give himself up completely to the experience of incubation" (ibid:83). The incubant was shown the statue of Trophonius, put on white linen and was swaddled in cloth bands like a child. He was then given a ladder to descend into the cave where he wiggled feet first (birth in reverse according to Meier; ibid:84) into a hole not much larger than his body. He carried honey cakes (associated with prophesy; ibid:91) to feed the serpents who lived in the cave (associated with healing in all temples dedicated to Asclepios, Trophonius and other gods and heroes of healing). The incubant then spent a day or more inside the cave (as a "prisoner" of the god; ibid:92) until he communicated with the oracle – i.e., had theophanic dreams and visions. He then left the cave, again feet first (death and rebirth symbolism; ibid:101), then would be seated on a throne where he described to the priests in great detail what he had experienced while the priests recorded everything he said. The priests would offer an interpretation of what he had encountered (Bulkeley 2008:159) and then he was turned over to his friends who took him away to a temple where he gradually recovered from his experience.

Another example of formal ritual preparation for dreaming is *dharnā*, or "dream incubation," practiced by contemporary Hindus when they take a pilgrimage to the retreat center and incubatorium at Tarakeswar in the state of West Bengali, India. As with the ancient Greeks, Hindu pilgrims are usually seeking cures for ill-health or for answers to vexing problems. E.A. Morinis (1982:257) describes the dream incubation in this way:

---

[4] For similar practices at the temple at Epidaurus and other centers of the Cult of Asclepios, see Mary Hamilton's fascinating 1906 book, *Incubation: Or, the Cures of Disease in Pagan Temples and Christian Churches*.

To get hold of Śiva, the *dharnā-jātri* (pilgrim) performs the following ritual. Having arrived in Tarakeswar, sometimes having observed austerities en route, the pilgrim contracts the services of an officiating priest of the temple (a Brahman), then begins the practice of austerities in the temple compound. He or she initiates the ritual by having the fingernail of the smallest finger chipped by a temple barber (right hand for a man, left for a woman), has a last ritual meal and bath in the temple tank, then takes a place under the portico before the deity's shrine room. There the *dharnā-jātri* will lie fasting until the deity appears in a dream to give instructions on how the pilgrim is to overcome his difficulty. If the dream is not received within a reasonable time, the pilgrim gives up in disappointment. Not infrequently, pilgrims die while giving *dharnā*, more likely from the seriousness of their illnesses than from starvation.

Hindu dream theory (derived from myths and other texts) holds that dreams may, under the appropriate circumstances, be a portal though which communion with a deity may occur, and through which cures, information and other boons may be received by the supplicant. One establishes the bond of obligation with the deity by one's austerity and sacrifice (a process described for cultures generally in Marcel Mauss' classic 1924 essay, *The Gift*). The appropriate conditions are facilitated by ritualizing the procedures the supplicant must follow – drivers including arduous pilgrimage, sacred space and iconography, special clothing, lying prostrate most of the day and night in an uncomfortable bed, fasting and body posture, even torture (see Benedict 1922 for ritually driving visions among Plains Indian cultures) – much of this overseen and controlled by the priest who offers prayers and other rituals in aid of the supplicant's goal.

The dreams had by supplicants are often rich in Hindu symbolism. Morinis (1982:159-160) offers several as examples, including this one: "One pilgrim, on the fourth night of his *dharnā* austerities, had a dream in which a huge *sannyāsi* (renunciant), looking like Śiva, with matted hair, a string of beads and a trident, stood before him. The *sannyāsi* said: 'In the morning you will find a black dog before the temple gate. He will be holding a *baiguni* (an aubergine slice fried in butter) in his mouth.

Eat what remains of the *baiguni* and you will be cured. The *sannyāsi* then disappeared." The interpretive phase of the *dharnā* process – i.e., the *dharnā* cycle of meaning – is again controlled by the priest in his role as oneirocritic. "It should be apparent as well that the priests have an influential role in interpreting the dreams and their instructions to the pilgrims. ...It is the priest who decides whether the dream that the pilgrim relates to him is indeed the gift from the deity, and it is the priest who tells the pilgrim how to go about following the dream instructions" (ibid:262). As with all such systems, interpretation offered for a dream will be couched in orthodox Hindu symbology. Thus, the Hindu cosmology and dream theory are put into practice in the *dharnā* rituals which, if they work, give rise to special culture pattern dreams that are then interpreted in a language and set of pre- and proscriptions that are consonant with Hindu doctrine.

Hebraic culture during the Greco-Roman period of history considered dreaming to be quite important to spiritual life (Lorand 1974:151):

> The sages of the Talmudic period, who understood their people well, knew how to use ... mystical material to shape Hebrew life. Dream interpretation was used by the sages and rabbis for that purpose; dreams were interpreted as having ethical and religious significance as well as prophesying the future, and thus were used to mold religious, social, and political behavior and thought. Dreams became a source of guidance for the heads of the colleges in making decisions on moral and spiritual matters, and were used quite frequently in this manner. Teachers were able to appeal to the popular imagination through dream interpretation.

Moreover, due to Greco-Roman influences during that period, Hebrews would visit the Temple of Asclepios seeking dream incubation for healing purposes (ibid:152).

Cultural dream theories and dream incubation have been integral to Islam since its founding (see above on Morocco specifically). "The scriptural tradition differentiates between three kinds of dream. First come true spiritual dreams, *ru'an*, inspired by God; second come dreams inspired by the devil; third come dreams from the *nafs*, or ego which are considered unimportant" (Edgar and Henig 2010:251).

Throughout the Islamic world, *Istikhara* or dream incubation is practiced to resolve uncertainty and cure sickness. In its simplest form, *Istikhara* involves the ritual reading of passages from the Koran, prayers to Allah and reflection upon the problem before the mind. Edgar and Henig give us the example of a man who was a consultant to an NGE using *Istikhara* to seek guidance on an investment he was contemplating with some unknown people. He dreamed about: "...a large white cake which was cut into pieces: as white is a good colour and had a happy feeling so he went ahead with the investment; half way through the investment people turned out to be too clever; he had invested a lot of money and they were wondering if it had been a good investment, but when the money was returned it was much more than was expected; there was a rocky period but it came out well eventually" (ibid:255).

In some Islamic cultures, a healing specialist may be approached to carry out the *Istikhara* prayers: "...the healers are often asked for praying Istikhara by Muslim women while they are considering their marriage choices. Similarly, among Muslim women in the mountains of Central Bosnia, ...an individual doing Istikhara is not an unknown practice and often precedes their marriage-concerned decisions. In their confirmatory dreams, Muslim women often dream about a house with a nice colourful garden and with many flowers around, or about a house with a small wild garden and with sheep and lambs in it. These often-mentioned dream images emerge in narratives to become culturally shared patterns and idioms of well-being as conceived by Muslims in the mountains" (ibid:256). Again, the orientation is frequently toward resolving uncertainty about future events, not accounting for past developmental and traumatic issues.

Dream incubation in one form or another is spread widely across traditional cultures. The large corpus of dreams collected by Robert Bruce (1975) while he was living with the Lacandones were mostly recorded during a two month "incense burner renewal ceremony" at the temple or "god house." During the course of this ceremony, "... all of the men participating in the ceremony ...were subjected to ritual seclusion which involved, among other things, sleeping in the temple. The nights were very cold in this wall-less structure... and especially so during the darkest hours just before dawn. Very often we rose to rebuild and sit around the fire, and to talk of any subject at hand as we watched the Morning Star rise over the steep mountains to the East of Najá. Perhaps the most frequent subjects were cosmology, traditions and dreams which we had just had" (ibid:39).

Certainly one of the most interesting and dramatic examples of dream incubation is the Sun Dance among the Plains Indian cultures of the United States and Canada. Fred Voget (1984) has written on the Sun Dance among the Crow peoples and notes that as with other Plains cultures, traditional Crow practiced individual fasting in order to evoke dreams that would give them power and knowledge about their future (ibid:13). In olden days, people received their Sun Dance bundle through dreaming, and were thereafter able to sponsor a Dance (ibid:105). These ceremonies were normally concerned with revenge and killing enemies. They practiced self-torture by hanging from the lodge poles by hooks piercing the chest, a painful ordeal that would drive visions (Lowie 1915:45). Today, any high status male can sponsor a Sun Dance, often after having a dream directing him to do so. Dancers participate in a Sun Dance either because they feel the need, or they have been told to participate by a spirit person in a dream. (Voget 1984:313). The dancer fasts, prays and offers the spirit person tobacco to "bind" him. After fasting and dancing for hours, even days, a dancer may have a vision or dream of one or more of the spirit persons that becomes a source of ecstatic power for the dancer and his group (Jorgensen 1972:213).

Vishvajit Pandya (2004) offers a particularly fascinating description of dream theory, incubation and social praxis among the Ongee people, one of the small groups of hunter-gatherers that inhabit Little Andaman Island in the Bay of Bengal, India. The Ongee say that the body is divided into two parts, the "inner" body or what I will call the soul and the "external" or physical body. During the day time, as people go about their daily tasks while inhabiting their physical bodies, they leave their distinct smells behind wherever they move. At night, when they fall asleep, their souls leave their bodies and must go back to all the places they have been the previous day and collect all their olfactory spore. A dream is like a spider web to the Ongee, made up of all the sundry connections between paths, places and objects encountered during the dream journey.

Dreaming for the Ongee is anything but an individual affair. The people sleep in a cluster of covered sleeping platforms that face each other across the campground – their incubatorium is really their home. When they lay down at night, there is a great deal of talking and singing, most of it having to do with what went on during the day and what people have dreamed and expect to dream that night. It is a time of collective dream interpretation, and as Pandya emphasizes, discussion of dreams around the group is intended to reach a consensus understanding of what is going on in their collective dreaming. They liken this process as bringing each small spider web (individual dream) into accord with everyone else's web, and forming one huge spider web that hopefully catches all that is to be caught (i.e., remembered). While this group exchange is going on, one member after the other falls asleep with the intention of dreaming about material of interest and relevance to the group, a lot having to do with hunting pig and turtle, and collecting jackfruit and other goodies. In the process, the people reach some consensus as to what actions need to be taken in the future. Pandya presents us with a marvelous transcript of the kind of interchanges that go on just before sleep (ibid:140):

Shelter 1 (man): I better find a small tree like the one I see in the dreams to cut down to make a new canoe for my nephew.

Shelters 4, 5, and 6 (women): We have been dreaming rains and the thatch is leaking, we need to get some new thatching made!

Shelter 3: We are running low on the supply of warm red clay. We need to get some. I have smelt the rains in my dreams and felt shivering cold, but I have not seen where we are going to get red clay!

Shelter 7 (belonging to a *torale* ["spirit communicator"]): I have had dreams of downpour—we must get the thatching work done—and I have seen that close to the tree trunk for the canoe is a stock of red clay!

Shelter 1 (man): Yes! Yes! There is lots of red clay near the tree we need to get for making the canoe. The spirit communicator is right, and I hear all of you seeing rain and feeling cold nights.

Shelters 2 and 8: We should go looking for the thatching material tomorrow and then start cutting down the tree trunk and on the way back we can start bringing back red clay lumps. We have been smelling rain on the hot ground, and we will need the thatching and the warming red clay.

Ongee dream theory emphasizes the crucial importance of individual dreams, and the social process of bringing dreams (like little spider webs) into a concerted interpretation and praxis. The dream incubation is not formal as in the case of the *dharnā* rituals described above. Dream incubation is as it were *in situ* within the at-home, everyday group dynamics of the people. Each person is being primed by a group-generated autosuggestion prior to sleep as to what they must do and find out in the dream. Yet the dreaming is open to new information during the dream adventure. When they recount their dreams the next day, the interpretive process is developed in the context of dream sharing and discussion. Collective dreaming may in turn determine what groups of people will spend their day doing. Two things are quite clear to me from the report of Ongee experience: One is that the Ongee routinely experience lucidity in their dreaming. And two, it is a wonderful example of interpenetration of information between waking and dreaming states – life seems to flow through the waking-dreaming cycle with a continuity we here in the West would find quite alien.

In addition, what I find so interesting is the Ongee emphasis upon olfactory phenomenology. I am one of those people who have no sense of smell, so olfaction is a foreign concept to me. In all the lucid dreaming I have done in my life, nothing like a smell has ever been part of one of my dreams, although I readily experience sounds, tastes and textures. My friends tell me I am apparently missing something, for as Alfred Gell (1977:29) has argued, "There is a profound connection between the olfactory dimension and the dimension of other-worldliness, which is only inadequately expressed in the phrase 'odour of sanctity.' The very words 'spirit' and 'essence' reveal the fact that the vehicle for an ideal or absolute truth which would be, at the same time, concretely within reach, would have to be something like a vapour, a distillate of more mundane reality." This is why smell is so fundamental to magic, Gell suggests, and why some peoples acknowledge the power of olfaction and associate it with dreaming.[5] Gell (ibid:29) goes on to describe "…the concept of smelling among the Umeda villagers of New Guinea, for whom smelling is intimately connected with dreaming, and for whom dreaming means having access to higher truth." It is characteristic of smells that they are both ephemeral and incomplete. They are the distilled essence of something real, yet at the same time they have the evanescence of spirit. So in order to magically attract wild pigs, the Umeda hunter makes up a sachet of specific plants the combined odor of which is considered pleasing to pigs. He will also sleep with that sachet either close to him or under his head so that the odor will evoke a dream "…which betokens good hunting according to the system of dream-augury followed by the Umedas" (ibid:32). Among other things, this is an excellent example of the simplicity and efficacy of olfactory dream incubation.

In some societies, the dream incubation process may begin in childhood. Paul Radin (1936) left us a poignant description of how the Ojibwa and Ottawa Indians reinforced the importance of dreaming for children in their puberty ceremonies prior to the 19th century, and how this practice came into disuse under the onslaught of rapid culture change. The change these peoples endured was sufficiently drastic that they ceased to evidence an intact dream theory cycle of meaning (ibid:233). Prior to this change, however, these people put their boys and girls through a ritual fast, perhaps left alone in the forest, and then discussed what their dreams revealed about the child's future role in society. Johann Georg Kohl, writing in the 19th century, described an Ojibwa male named Agabegijik's experience of fasting and dreaming (2009 [1860]:136):

> I remember that my grandfather, when I was a half-grown lad, frequently said to my father, in the course of the winter, "Next

---

[5] As an aside, this makes me wonder how important olfaction might be in canine dreaming, or audition in dolphin dreaming, or song in passerine bird dreaming (see also Sperber 1996 on olfactory symbolism).

spring it will be time for us to lead the lad into the forest and leave him to fast." But nothing came of it that spring, but when the next spring arrived, my grandfather took me on one side, and said to me, "It is now high time that I should lead thee to the forest, and that thou shouldst fast, that thy mind be confirmed, something be done for thy health, and that thou mayst learn thy future and thy calling." My grandfather then took me by the hand, and led me deep into the forest. Here he selected a lofty tree, a red pine, and prepared a bed for me of branches, on which I should lie down to fast. …Then my grandfather said to me that I must on no account take nourishment, neither eat nor drink, pluck no berries, nor even swallow the rain-water that might fall. Nor must I rise from my bed, but lie quite still day and night, keep myself strictly, and await patiently the things that would then happen.

Young Agabegijik abandoned his retreat that spring, but the next year in the spring he tried his fast again, and this time he had his dream after 8 days of fasting. In his dream a spirit in the form of a man visited him and invited him to attend a council. After flying there through the air, he found a wigwam, inside which sat four men around a white stone. When he sat upon the stone, he saw a multitude of people sitting around him. He was ordered to look down and saw the entire world laying below him. Then he was ordered to look up and saw the entire sky hovering close above him. He was then asked whether he wished to go up to the sky or go down to the earth. He chose the sky and was told to ascend, at which point the back of the white rock became a ladder-like pillar. He climbed up the ladder to a great height where he found four white-haired old men sitting in the air around the pillar (ibid:138-139):

> A dazzling cupola [dome] was arched above them. I felt so light that I wished to go higher, but the four old men shouted "Stop!" all at once. "Thou must not go higher. We have not permission to allow thee to pass. But enough that is good and great is already decreed for thee. Look around thee. Thou seest here around us all the good gifts of God – health, and strength, and long life, and all the creatures of nature. Look on our white hair: thine shall

become the same. And that thou mayst avoid illness, receive this box with medicine. Use it in case of need; and whenever thou art in difficulty, think of us, and all thou seest with us. When thou prayst to us, we will help thee, and intercede for thee with the Master of Life. Look around thee one more! Look and forget not! We give thee all the birds, and eagles, and wild beasts, and all the other animals thou seest fluttering and running in our wigwam. Thou shall become a famous hunter, and shoot them all!"

Agabegijik was ordered by the four old men to return to earth, so he climbed back down to his bed in the red pine tree where he found that three days had passed during his adventures. He eventually heard his grandfather calling him to return home where he lay for three days recovering from his ordeal (ibid:140).

## Summary and Segue

Every culture on the planet provides a worldview which includes a theory of dreaming, sometimes with an appropriate dream typology. Societies having more polyphasic cultures include a theory of dreaming that ensures that people pay attention to their dreams. This is accomplished through enculturation of the young who are encouraged to participate in their dream life and associated activities. The worldview of most traditional societies takes the form of a cosmology which is expressed in mythopoeic media such as myth, ritual, art and so forth. The culture as an information pool contains a rich corpus of symbolic forms that may come alive in dreams and other ASC. These forms, when encountered in the dream life condense a great deal of information – metaphorically speaking, like the child's magnet coalescing a large and organized collection of iron filings which it drags along with it when it moves. One of the most common patterns cross-culturally is the future orientation of dreams, dream incubation and interpretation – dream-as-omen is considered by some to be a virtual cultural universal (see Kracke 1991).

Dreaming is involved in the society's mythopoeic cycle of meaning in such a way that important culture pattern dreams are interpreted so as to be conceived by people as confirming and vivifying their worldview. This we have called the axis of instantiation. Because of the intimate connection between lived dream and other ASC experiences, and the worldview, change in the worldview may occur as novel experiences arise and are interpreted such that new information, new songs and ritual procedures may be added and other information and practices may be dropped. Thus, as long as the cycle of meaning remains intact, the worldview of a people may be revitalized over the generations to fit a changing world (see Dennis Tedlock 1999). If the link between experiences and worldview is broken, the latter may lag behind experience and eventually become irrelevant to people. One of the ways that many societies ensure that experiences remain on track with the worldview is by ritualizing the evocation of states of consciousness, be they dreams, visions, drug trips, meditations, etc. The cultural theory of dreams distinguishes types of dreams and mythopoeic means are laid-on to increase the likelihood that the desired experiences are incubated and do arise. There is always a process of interpretation to complete the cycle, and in polyphasic cultures that almost always involves a social process.

# Chapter 8

## Sociocultural Aspects of Dreaming

> ...I have pointed out that self-identification and culturally constituted notions of the nature of the self are essential to the operation of all human societies and that a functional corollary is the cognitive orientation of the self to a world of objects other than self. Since the nature of these objects is likewise culturally constituted, a unified phenomenal field of thought, values, and action which is integral with the kind of world view that characterizes a society is provided for its members. The behavioral environment of the self thus becomes structured in terms of a diversified world of objects other than self, discriminated, classified, and conceptualized with respect to attributes which are culturally constituted and symbolically mediated through language. Object orientation likewise provides the ground for an intelligible interpretation of events in the behavioral environment on the basis of traditional assumptions regarding the nature and attributes of the objects involved and implicit or explicit dogmas regarding the "causes" of events.
>
> A. Irving Hallowell (2002 [1960]:19)

We human beings are a species of social primate. Almost everything we do, think, say, feel and imagine is imbued with social significance. We are born into and are reared by a group of adults that influence every aspect of our mental development and our activities. Dreaming is no different than any other SOC in that respect. As anthropologist Irving Hallowell (1976) and others following after him have shown, dreaming and dream sharing are thoroughly social acts (Bourguignon 2003, Wax 2004; Kracke 1992;

Graham 2003; Edgar 1999; Price-Williams and Degarrod 1996; Dombeck 1991:Chap. 3). Whether or not dreams are socially shared, they are still social experiences (see e.g., Levine 1981, 1982 on the Gusii people of Kenya who do not share dreams). McNamara *et al.* (2005:130) researched social relations within the content of dreams among a small sample of men and women in the United States. They found that: "(a) social interactions were more likely to be depicted in dream than in wake reports, (b) aggressive social interactions were more characteristic of REM than NREM or wake reports, and (c) dreamer-initiated friendliness was more characteristic of NREM than REM reports." I know of no comparable research done cross-culturally, but my impression from the ethnographic record suggests that dreaming in all societies is a highly social experience. Whether or not the aggression-friendliness variable also characterizes REM-NREM states cross-culturally is something that would be very interesting to discover.

There are many uses to which dreaming is put by societies, and when specific uses are of social importance, be it for the purposes of relieving anxiety, healing, prediction of future events, finding of lost objects, battling witches and sorcerers, seeking of initiatory visions, prescription of appropriate ritual acts, etc., those uses are typically institutionalized. The dream-as-dreamt becomes a dream-as-told, and thus a dream-as-text in the telling. The dream-as-text is a blend of memory, of language, and of social context, and as such invites attention, reflection, discussion, interpretation, and, at times, responses by others (Obeyesekere 1990; Kracke 1992; Kilborne 1981; Groark 2009). As we saw in the last chapter, dreams may require ritual activity that may operate as a mediator between the individual's dream-as-text and the society's worldview (Graham 2003; Chidester 2008a). I have termed this relationship the *axis of interpretation* in the cycle of meaning model (see Figure 7.1), a set of cognitive and feedback relationships equally as important as those I called the axis of instantiation in the last chapter. This interpenetration of mythopoeic form and interpretation of lived experience may, depending upon the society, have consequences for economic, political, kinship, status and military relations and decision-making.

## Dream Interpretation

What does it mean to interpret a dream? The word "interpret" comes from the Latin *interpretari* meaning to "explain," "expound," or "understand." The implication is that the thing being interpreted is somehow associated with other information that broadens, clarifies or confirms the meaning of the thing. "Yes, I know it's a cigar, but what does it mean?" The cigar derives its additional meaning from associations with other objects, with context, with intent, or with convention. For Freud, the cigar may be associated with male genitalia — or not. It all depends on context. In Chapter 4, I showed that objects and relations in dreams are typically both "pregnant" with meaning and polysemic. Dream objects are commonly condensations in image form of multiple and overlapping associations. My father in a dream may be both the King archetype, my superego and my father, all at the same time – again, like the child's magnet, drawing multiple clusters of iron filings into a single pattern. This is why dream interpretation, or *oneirocriticism* to use the technical term, may be considered as both an art and a skill.

I also showed in Chapter 4 that the neural network mediating any experience in consciousness is componential. It is a system made up of component neural circuits that link up, however briefly or enduringly, to mediate our moment by moment flow of experience. When we recognize a face as a face, one set of neural structures is active. When we recognize that face as our father's, a more elaborate system of structures is at play. This is no trivial matter – it is the magic of neurocognitive association that we take so much for granted in anthropology. We take it for granted — until, that is, it begins to fail. Consider what happens to those who are unfortunate enough to contract Alzheimer's Disease. We begin to suspect someone has Alzheimer's when their ability to put those components together in the normal way is disrupted. Their memory begins to fail – by which I mean that the ability of the brain to link up various components of normal perception has become compromised due to the growth of neurofibrillary tangles (abnormal tangles of proteins inside neural cells), senile plaques (polypeptide aggregates), as well as loss of neurons and their synaptic processes (Pietrini, Salmon and Nichelli 2009:205; Damasio 2010:230). The Alzheimer's victim loses the ability to interpret what they are experiencing. Their father's face is still a face, but for them it is no longer familiar – an interruption of the interpretive process called *prosopagnosia*. Brain lesions can disconnect the association between various linguistic functions – an impairment called an *aphasia*. A person may be able to hear and understand speech, but can no longer produce meaningful speech. Or, a person may be able to see writing on the page, but no longer know what the symbols mean. I am mentioning all this in order to emphasize that interpretation requires an active, neurophysiological circuitry between different components of the brain, many of which involve the laying down and retrieval of memory. Interpretation therefore requires the meaning of the thing being interpreted to be already stored in memory.

In a society with an intact polyphasic cycle of meaning, the significance for a child of symbolic elements in sacred stories, performances and art may start out as fanciful images – like the cutesy, big head-little body animals from a Disney cartoon. But when their dream experiences, shared with others and discussed by parents, become associated with the society's mythopoeic symbols as they grow up, the symbols may come alive as it were and memories of direct experiences become a significant part of the meaning of those symbols. If I dream of Jesus praying at Golgotha (which did happen to me), the event is for me no longer "dead" text, but living experience. I cannot thereafter hear the story without visualizing the Jesus of my dream. This is the axis of interpretation in action. The symbolic stories, etc., evoke dreams and other ASC that are then interpreted in such a way as they vivify and augment the meaning of the symbolism in direct experience. This is a cognitive and reciprocal feedback relationship which is crucial to understanding how a people's worldview and cultural theory of dreaming remains open to change and revitalization. The mythopoeic expression of the cosmology gives rise to experiences (usually in the form of culture pattern dreams) that are interpreted such as to accrue, alter, elaborate, as well as reinforce meaning. This may in some cases be such a slow and subtle process that the people themselves are unaware of the change in significance.

In our society we are often on our own interpreting our dreams, assuming that we bother with them at all. Because most of us have not been raised to pay attention to our dreams, and have not been enculturated to expect important experiences during our dreaming, most of us have to come up with our own interpretations. Which is to say that we will likely make idiosyncratic associations based upon our individual memories, values and spiritual upbringing (if any). If one pays close attention to how we interpret our own dreams, we can see that the act of interpretation is often an intuitive process that makes associations among memories, typically without the filter of language. We remember our dream, and our mind leaps to associations – we do not tell ourselves our own dreams. Our interpretation occurs within the dream-as-remembered, not the dream-as-told. This is a distinction that many anthropologists fail to make, but one that is phenomenologically crucial. The meaning of my dream may arise within the dream itself, depending upon how lucid I am as dreamer. Further associations may pop up and become attached to my dream when I recall the dream later – all without resorting to language and rational thought.

However, if we share our dream with another person – a friend or family member perhaps, or a therapist, doctor, pastor or dreamwork colleague — our dream-as-remembered gets filtered through language processing and some degree of rationality (Groark 2009). If that person gets involved in a discussion with us about the meaning of the dream, they become an informal dream interpreter – an *oneirocritic* – and the interpretive process may combine information from their memory as well as our own, filtered through their language and rational processes (Stewart 1997: 885). In polyphasic societies, dreams are often discussed freely. Interpretation is typically standardized and the meanings attributed to dreams are usually couched in terms that are consonant with the prevailing worldview, and the symbolic imagery that expresses it in narrative, song, drama, art and other forms of mythopoeic representation. Group members typically have been enculturated as to the meaning of a system of object categories for which there exist appropriate meanings and significances when they pop up in dreams.

## Dream Sharing

As we have seen, dream experiences are of great interest to many peoples all over the planet. Moreover, they commonly put their dreaming and their dream cultures to use. Just as a hunter-gatherer might recreate with considerable drama the story of his or her daily adventures in the bush, so too may people in some societies relish hearing about the adventures had during the SOC we call "dreaming." Also as we have seen, the information derived from these dream accounts may have an important role to play in a people's self and social identity, decisions made in everyday life, planning future actions, and accruing spiritual understanding and power. Take for example the routine sharing of dreams among the Mehinaku people of the Xingu River headwaters in Brazil (Gregor 1981). People sleep in hammocks hung close together in a long house. During the night, they wake up to add fuel to the communal fire and reflect upon their dreams. In the morning they recall a number of dreams from the night and share them with others immediately after waking. Dreams are the adventures had by one's "eye soul" during sleep when it detaches from the physical body and wanders around. Another classic example is the Aborigines of the western desert lands of Australia (Tonkinson 2003:92; Price-Williams and Gaines 1994). Each individual has a dream spirit that can leave their body at night and wander to places, and see and do things – e.g., seek out and request the aid of rainmaking spirits. They later have conversations about what they dreamed and what their individual adventures mean for the commonweal.

As Murray Wax (2004) notes, in many small scale hunting and gathering societies – like the Mehinaku above — dream sharing is an everyday, immediate social practice. Among the 19th century Zulus of southern Africa, dreaming was a very practical affair in which communications from ancestors might necessitate ritual actions to keep them happy (Chidester 2008a) – in this case dreams not only invited social engagement, but social action as well. Waud Kracke (1992:32) notes for the Parintintin, a small, previously hunting-gathering group in Brazilian Amazonia: "Dreams like myths... are to be told. Waking at daybreak, or in the middle of the night at 2 or 3 a.m., one may often hear someone narrating a dream to a few others as they warm themselves by the fire. During the day over work, a person may interrupt gossip about current events to entertain work companions with a dream." Dreams complete their usefulness in their telling, in their sharing, and in their practical consequences (see Stephen 1979 for examples of socio-behavioral consequences of dreams in Oceania). Among many small societies, everybody seems to be an oneirocritic and the content of the dream becomes as it were public property as interpretation approaches group consensus. As we saw in the last chapter, the Ongee share their dreams around the fire at night and in the morning just after waking, and the group consensus as to the meaning of a person's dream will have an influence upon the activities of that person during the day (Pandya 2004; for other examples, see Goulet 1994 for the Guajiro of Columbia, and Flannery and Chambers 1985 for the Cree of Subarctic Canada).

S.R. Charsley (1973) found that dream sharing had become an integral part of an African church service in Uganda. This church was of the Pentecostal variety and the early part of the service consisted of singing, dancing, confessing, etc. common to this kind of Christianity. But the latter part of the service was given over to dream sharing (ibid:247):

> After collective and simultaneous confession, once all were again calmly seated, the Clerk would call for people to tell what they had seen while praying, i.e., visions, or what they might have seen during the night, i.e. dreams... . In a successful service this would set off a stream of visions, dreams, interpretations, confessions and forgivings, often mingled but tending to come in that order. Tellers would begin by specifying the date, time, and general circumstances of their dream, and would then tell it through without interruption or comment, whether it was a few brief sentences only or a long, involved narrative. ...Dreams would often result in confessions, and confession in forgiving.

This is an interesting situation in which the dream sharing takes place within a ceremonial ritual, and the process of dream telling is integrated into the overall intentions of the ritual, which involves emotional release, confession and forgiveness.

The social context of dream sharing is often important in influencing how the dream is told. Presumably how one tells one's dream in church will differ from how the same dream would be shared in the bosom of the family. Gilbert Herdt (1992) notes that for the Sambia, a hunting and horticultural society in Papua New Guinea, dream telling is dependent on what he calls "discourse frames." Sambians "...operate and behave in three types of social situations: public, secret, and private. Social action in these situations corresponds to three different types of discourse: public talk..., secret talk..., and private talk... . These discourses are, in turn, structured by cultural rules, premises, expectations – frames that organize behavior" (ibid:59). How one relates a dream within each of these frames will influence how the dream will be told. Dreams told when just waking up in the men's or women's house, or when sharing with a friend are private tellings. Dreams related in certain healing ceremonies are considered for public consumption. Those shared in rituals, however, are considered secret. Social status also influences the telling of dreams in Sambia. As Herdt notes, men share more dreams than women, elders more than younger folk, and children's dreams are considered trivial and often false (ibid:63). Sexual dreams are never shared publicly, only secretly or in private.

## Standardized Dream Interpretation

Where dream sharing is routine, the meaning of dream objects and events is fairly standardized and systematic. One may often discern principles underlying the meaning attributions used in these systems. One of the most common principles of interpretation is that of *reversal* — or the Jungian "law of opposites" – where the meaning attributed to the dream motif is its logical opposite. The 19$^{th}$ century Zulu understood this principle in which the real meaning of a motif was its antithesis; e.g., to dream of marriage means death, to dream of death means marriage, so forth (Chidester 2008a:31). Not all societies share dreams quite so freely. Among the Mekeo people of Papua New Guinea, dreams "...are regarded as dangerous knowledge, to be handled with the greatest discretion..." (Stephen 1995:139). When

Mekeo share dreams, it is usually with family members and other intimates, and messages derived from dreams almost always pertain to one or more of a short list of portents considered crucial to people (ibid:120). Mekeo shamans heal people by traveling in their dreams to power places in search of their patients' lost souls (ibid: 198). The shaman appears to be an adept at dreaming, more so than laypeople, and able to dream lucidly and organize their dream experience around a specific intention.

Barbara Tedlock (1992c:105-106) tells the interesting story about her husband, Dennis Tedlock, who had a dream while in the field among the Quiché Maya. He had a dream "of receiving an ear of corn from an unknown person at a party; when he opened the husk the corn was already roasted, with butter, salt, lime juice, and chili powder on it." He did not eat the corn, however. Tedlock realized that had her husband reported that dream to a Zuni interpreter where they had previously done research, it would have been viewed as a very bad omen; that he would die if not treated to avoid a drastic outcome. But instead of a Zuni interpreter, he reported his dream to a Quiché interpreter. He was told it was a good dream, but that the next time he dreamed of receiving a gift of food from an ancestor spirit, he should eat it immediately. One of the obvious lessons to be drawn from this story is that interpretations of the same material may vary widely across cultures, and perhaps even among different interpreters within a single society (e.g., LeVine 1981 on the Gusii). In other words, there is nothing "wired-in" or instinctual about meaning attributions at the cultural level – except where it comes to archetypal dreaming — which we will get back to in Chapter 10.

On the other hand, from a scientific point of view, the often exotic laundry lists of meaning attributions (so-called "dream books;" see O'Nell 1976:32; Kruger 2005:Chap. 1) that many societies use to guide dream interpretation is often less revealing than the cognitive and social processes involved in the societies' oneirology. As we have seen, in most societies the cycle of meaning operates to integrate dreaming and other SOC with waking states into a unitary flow of experience, while at the same time it operates to condition the meaning of all these experiences within a single frame of reference – that being society's worldview, social structure and social action – the "learned and shared" aspect of most definitions of culture.[1] To put it in Durkheimian terms, the society imposes a cycle of meaning in order to make sure that their "collective representations" (Durkheim 1995 [1912]; Throop and Laughlin 2002) inform all domains of experience. It seems to me far more interesting to focus on the social and cognitive processes involved in the cultural effort after meaning than the semantic differences among the weird and wonderful attributions being laid on dreams. Douglas Hollan, for instance, shows vividly how Toraja dreamers (Chapter 7) use and manipulate interpretive categories and symbols, and social processes to attain individual goals: "Among the Toraja, villagers may share knowledge of a wide range of cultural beliefs regarding such things as the etiology, typology, and interpretation of dreams, yet the individual *usage* of such beliefs in the construction and interpretation of dreams may vary widely" (1989:182).

For those who are not inundated with the ethnographic dreaming literature, it might be well to sample the kind of attributions made by folks in different societies in order to get the exotic (from our Western point of view) flavor of the process. The classic "dream book" approach to "canned" interpretations of dreams is that of the ancient Greeks (Meier 1966, 67, 2009; Walde 1999; Harris 2009). Take for example the famous *Oneirocritica* (The Interpretation of Dreams) by the 2nd century Greek philosopher and dream interpreter, Artemidorus of Daldis (White 1975). Artemidorus carried out research among all the written material on dreaming of his day, and something like ethnography among market place diviners (ibid:13). He developed a full-on theory of dreaming that recognized "day residue" content and somatic wish fulfillment – ingredients of Freud's theory. Artemidorus notes that "…it is natural for a lover to seem to be with his beloved in a dream and for a frightened man to see what he fears and, again, for a hungry man to eat and a thirsty man drink…" (ibid:22). He also emphasized that the dream interpreter know both the culture and

---

[1] This relates to what Gene d'Aquili and I were talking about in our early work under the cumbersome label, the "cognitive extension of prehension" (Laughlin and d'Aquili 1974: Chap. 4). Putting it simply, the human brain allows the experiences of individuals to diverge from a social consensus reality, and societies thus have to incorporate methods to standardize the meaning of diverse individual experiences in order to mount effective social action.

personal situation of the dreamer before interpreting his dreams. He further distinguishes dreams that are merely day residue experiences (*enhypnion*) from those that augur future events (*oneiros*), and thematic dreams (future outcome of augury is the same as in the dream) from allegorical dreams (those that "signify one thing by means of another;" ibid:22-24). These and other principles are used to develop a comprehensive dictionary of meanings for dream elements and events (see Table 8.1).

Similar systems of interpretation of specific dream motifs are quite common in the ethnographic literature. Bruce (1975:38-65 *passim*) notes such a system for the Lacandon people (see Table 8.2). The list could go on and on. The attributions are not arbitrary, for they make sense given the environment of the Lacandon and their cosmology. Dreams are interesting to the Lacandon because they are considered prophetic.

### Table 8.1

### Standardized Greek Dream Interpretations

| Dream Motif | Meaning |
|---|---|
| see one's own children, especially newborns | anxiety, cares, worries about one's children |
| dreamer in swaddling clothes and suckles | will have a long illness (unless his wife is pregnant) |
| having long hog's bristles | will face dangers like the hog itself |
| having more than two ears | will find someone (wife) who is compliant |
| having sex with an unknown woman | if pretty auspicious, if ugly the opposite |
| flying around tiled roofs, houses and blocks of houses | disturbances and confusion of the soul |
| half-finished works | total failure, or project will never get started |
| things in accord with "nature, law, custom profession, names, or time" | Auspicious, but dreaming the opposite is inauspicious |
| building a hearth in a foreign land | death for a man who does not intend to marry, or who does not live there |

## Table 8.2

### Standardized Lacandon Dream Interpretations

| Dream Motif | Meaning |
|---|---|
| needle | snake fangs |
| hurricane | foreigners will come |
| waves on the ocean | people are dying far away |
| rope with frayed end | snake with open mouth |
| being given sugar | someone coming who will make much pleasant conversation and joking |
| flood waters | coming of people or *ladinos* |
| copper coins | encounter with a snake |
| eating honey | a pleasant visitor with much joking |
| "god house" on fire | fever among the men |

Moreover, interpretations tend to be internally consistent within the logic of the mythopoeic symbol system shared by the people (see R.M. Laughlin 1976:7-9 for a Zinacantán Mayan dream book).

Gregor (1981) likewise offers us a lengthy list of meaning attributions for the Mehinaku of Brazil (see Table 8.3). As in most such "dream book" interpretive systems, there always appears to be an internal logic to the attribution system. For example, for the Mehinaku, things made by one's wife stand for the wife herself. Hence the bow cord, always made by one's wife stands for wife. Objects closely associated with the dreamer may stand for his or her children. Wounds and vaginas look alike, snakes and penises look alike, so the dreaming of the one will suggest the other. Dreaming of a particular red pigment worn by women as body ornament suggests menstrual blood. On and on it goes, attributions based upon cognitive principles such as reversal, metaphor-simile, metonymy, part to whole, synaesthesia, etc., all of which are involved in myth-making as well.

In another example, the Mae Enga of New Guinea exhibit the pattern of limited and standardized meanings for particular objects and events in the dream. M.J. Meggitt (1962:224-226) lists a number of such attributions (see Table 8.4). Again, these attributions may seem

### Table 8.3

**Standardized Mehinaku Dream Interpretations**

| Dream Motif | Meaning |
|---|---|
| vagina or labia | sign of a wound – shouldn't use ax or knife |
| fruits of any kind, esp. eating fruit | male and female sex organs |
| wasp stings | disease |
| fire | fever |
| flying ants | tears, may lose a kinsman |
| melting wax | dreamer will be weak, lazy or fatigued |
| a bow cord breaks | dreamer's wife will die |
| a pet | children |
| kinsman goes on long trip | a kinsman will die |

### Table 8.4

**Standardized Mae Enga Dream Interpretations**

| Dream Motif | Meaning |
|---|---|
| sees or touches gourds on vine | good fortune (unspecified) |
| male given woman's skirt | will receive a live pig |
| picks or breaks gourds on vine | bad fortune (unspecified) |
| sees or feels rain | clansmen will weep for dead member |
| sees worms or snails | will attend a funeral of someone he knows |
| sick man dreams of a dance | will die soon |
| sees fireflies in his house | someone will do sorcery against him |
| meets a snake or cassowary (large flightless bird) in the forest | visitation by a ghost |
| visited by a dead relative | the ancestor is angry with him |
| sees a rainbow | someone he knows will die |

arbitrary to us, but as with virtually all peoples, the Mae Enga use the lateral logic of like = like and part = whole to draw the associations. A sick man dreaming of a public dance is dreaming of the get-together his relatives will have after he dies. The Mae Enga loathe worms and lizards that they associate with the grave. And so on, exemplifying that although the attributions vary enormously across peoples, the cognitive processes by which these attributions are drawn are universal.

As a final example (see Table 8.5), the Muria people of India recognize dreams as the wanderings of the soul and some motifs in the soul's adventures are given standard interpretations (Elwin 1991[1947]:476-477). As arbitrary as some of these attributions may seem, they are taken very seriously by Muria, "…and often guide a man's conduct. The *chelik* [boys] may refuse to go on a Pus Kolong expedition if one of them has a dream of a tiger shortly before they set out. A *motiari* will be wise if she avoids visiting the *ghotul* [dormitory] the day after she has dreamt of a river in flood, for this suggests that her menstrual period is imminent" (ibid: 478).

## Table 8.5

### Standardized Muria Dream Interpretations

| Dream Motif | Meaning |
| --- | --- |
| one's dead parents | lucky – shows they still love dreamer |
| drowned in a river | very good – the Yer Kanyang [nixie] loves the dreamer and wants to marry |
| sinking under water | if male, wife is pregnant and will have a son |
| an elephant | symbol of prosperity |
| a kotri fish | dreamer will receive money |
| a motiari [maiden] | a Kanyang [nixie] will attack dreamer |
| fire | someone will die in the house |
| tiger | dreamer will be hungry, or a witch is planning an attack on the dreamer |
| flying in the air | certain death |
| raw meat | witchcraft |

## Specialized Dream Interpreters (Oneirocritics)

In some societies everyone is an oneirocritic and participates in dream sharing and interpreting, as we have seen above. In other societies however, oneirocritical specialists are recognized who may be consulted for a dream interpretation, especially for culture pattern dreams. They may be individuals with a reputation for prophetic dreams, and people will pay close attention to what they make of their own and others dreams. Meggitt (ibid:220) reports that one such Mae Enga man dreamed that he was standing on a hillside when men of the neighboring clan joined and followed him singing as well. He interpreted this as foretelling a renewed dispute over border issues, and took steps to bring the parties together to discuss how they might avoid the dispute. Meggitt makes the point that such a dream had by another man without that reputation might have been ignored.

The specialist may also be a healer, shaman or priest, as we saw in the case of Greek dream incubation. The shaman may in fact have found his or her vocation via dreams, and may be the individual considered to have the most experience in negotiating dreams and other ASC (see Chapter 9). Where specialists are consulted, the interpretation will usually be of the "dream book," standardized attribution type. Benjamin Kilborne (1981:296) makes the interesting point that in Morocco where dream symbols are standardized and there are dream books available to anyone who wishes to consult them, few people interpret their own dreams, but would rather rely upon the professional oneirocritic (often the Koranic schoolmaster) to help them reach the proper understanding of special dreams. In the process of interpretation, the interaction between dreamer and oneirocritic is important, and as Kilborne says, the dream-as-reported becomes a text upon which both the dreamer and the oneirocritic project meaning. The meaning reached during a session is always consistent with a Koranic belief system. Barbara Tedlock (1981) also notes the importance of the dream interpreter among the Quiché Maya. Many people become initiated as oneirocritics and they function as healers and diviners as well. Tedlock writes that the interpreter will apply a number of general rules in attributing meaning to symbols while at the same time taking into consideration the dreamer's everyday situation.

## Dreaming and Sociocultural Change

As our cycle of meaning model suggests, a people's intact system of dream interpretation is rarely a closed one. If that were the case, then the axis of instantiation would eventually fail as interpretations veered further and further from dynamic, everyday contingencies. Moreover, an over-conservative and static view of dream significance would violate what we know about how the brain works (see Chapter 4). Thinking, associating and consolidating of memories and data processing continues to occur in the brain during sleep even in the absence of consciousness (Walker 2000:203). We would assume that this processing would manifest in dream content. Hence, we need to acknowledge the creative aspect of dreaming across cultures (Krippner, Bogzaran and de Carvalho 2002:Chap. 3; Heijnen and Edgar 2010:223-224; Kirtsoglou 2010; Graham 1994). As Eggan (1955:447) mentioned with respect to Hopi dreaming, creativity and art, "Even in the realm of imagination then, including folklore and dreams, thinking processes are not only limited by one's language and perception, but are also stimulated by them. Therefore, culture and creativity cannot be examined separately for, as Herskovits [1950:403] expresses it, 'The creative life does not lie outside the influence of the enculturative experience.' On the contrary, 'in his experimentation' the artist is 'unwittingly' guided by it."

Once again I will mention that among Icelanders, creativity and problem solving in dreams is quite marked. According to Heijnen (2010:308), "Around 10% of the respondents to a survey, recently conducted by the Social Science Research Institute, University of Iceland, experienced the appearance of a deceased person in a dream expressing the wish to pass his or her name onto a — at the time of dreaming — unborn child, while 75% believed this to be possible... . This practice is generally designated in Icelandic as *aðvitja nafns* (to seek a namesake) and consists of the idea that through the naming of newborn children with the help of dreams, substance can flow from the dead to the living, who are often, but not necessarily, genetically related." Thus, dreaming of this sort both solves a problem of naming the newborn, and maintains a continuity of inter-generational relatedness.

Michelle Stephen (1979) amassed a great deal of evidence on cultural change in Melanesia and came to the conclusion that dreams and other ASC have played an important role in cultural innovation among societies encountering situational changes. Melanesians generally hold that ancestors appear to them in dreams and give advice, and in some cases the dreamer is admonished to make changes to adapt to novel situations:

> Altered states of consciousness – dreams, trance and possession – I have argued, play a highly significant role in traditional Melanesian societies, both as religious experiences and as sources of innovation. Religious change and flexibility was, therefore, the norm. When drastic change was necessitated by warfare, migration or natural disaster, innovative cults arose to meet the challenge, in which the possession of the whole community and not just the prophet or medium occurred, enabling a swift "conversion" to take place. With the intrusion of the white man, guidelines from the ancestors as to how to deal with the new and devastating force was sought through the usual channels, in some cases resulting in only minor modifications of existing rituals and social practice, and in others, the development of full-blown religious and social revolutions, depending on the circumstances of contact and the ideological adjustments made by different cultures. (ibid:20)

There is perhaps no more famous example of how problem solving in a dream can impact cultural change than that of the dream-inception of Mahatma Gandhi's non-violent resistance to the British *raj* in India. When the imperialist legislature passed the restrictive Rowlatt Acts after the First World War, Gandhi cast about for an adequate response. He records in his autobiography (Gandhi 1957:337) that: "The idea came to me last night in a dream that we should call upon the country to observe a general [hunger strike]." His idea was implemented leading to the non-violent independence movement that came to fruition in 1947.

## Dreams and Conflict

Quite obviously then, dreaming may be a factor in important social processes, whether they be involved in determining or assessing daily group activities, or whether they contribute to events of historical importance. We have already seen examples of this above and in earlier parts of the book. We have seen how dreams may influence and be influenced by myth and ritual, how dreaming may operate to alleviate group anxieties and result in culture change. When a society considers the experiences had while dreaming to be those in another reality, and one in which the normally hidden forces causing events become palpable, it is small wonder that dreaming and dream interpretation play a major role in collective decision making and social action. Indeed, the ethnographic literature is rife with examples of the various social processes in which dreaming plays its part, including as we have seen the use of dreams as auguries influencing political, warfare, status, economic and religious domains. Let us take a look at a few more social processes so as to better understand how dreaming can become such an integral part of the social life of peoples. We will skip for the moment the role of dreaming in religion and healing, for that relationship colors all other domains of social action in traditional societies. We will take up this issue in a later chapter.

One of the first anthropologists to criticize Freud's assumptions about wish-fulfillment and dreaming was the great English neurologist, psychiatrist and ethnographer William H.R. Rivers (1864-1922). In his lecture "Dreams and Primitive Culture" (1917) and his book *Conflict and Dream* (1923), Rivers argued that the content of dreams studied in military hospitals and cross-culturally indicate that conflicts occurring contemporaneously with the dream were more important than those derived from the early life of the dreamer (see Smith 1923). Moreover, there were other considerations about conflict than repressed sexual motives and meanings. Keep in mind here that Rivers was also a psychiatrist who worked with soldiers in the First World War who suffered from conflicts and neuroses stemming from their battlefield experiences – dreams associated with what later became recognized as *post-traumatic stress disorder* (see Barrett 1996; Kalsched 1996). "Dr. Rivers' chief argument is that dreams are attempts to solve in sleep conflicts which are disturbing the waking life. The character of the dream, at any rate in so far as its emotional aspect is concerned, depends upon the degree in which this attempted solution is successful" (Smith 1923:v). The conflicts arising during the waking life depend upon the cultural situation in which the dreamer finds him- or herself. Tacking dream content onto a single supposed motivation, as the Freudians would have us do, may cause us to miss the culture-specific and contemporaneous motivations underlying manifest content. As Rivers wrote, "[Freud's] interpretations seemed to me forced and arbitrary, and the method so unscientific a kind that it might be used to prove anything" (Rivers 1923:5). Rivers emphasizes the empirical aspect of dream studies, and how very often the process of working through of conflicts in dreams is often frustrated and unsuccessful, thus perpetuating the conflicts.

*Conflict and Dream* is essentially a compendium of dreams of this sort; dreams of either Rivers or his patients. What makes Rivers' approach especially compelling to me is that it stems quite explicitly from his own phenomenology. As he writes (ibid:7-8):

> For many years I have been the habitual subject of an experience in which, as soon as I become aware that I am awake [i.e., in the hypnopompic state], I find that I am thinking, and have for some time been thinking, over some problem, usually in connection with the scientific work upon which I am at the time engaged. Many of the scientific ideas which I value most, as well as the language in which they are expressed, have come to me in this half-sleeping, half-waking state directly continuous with definite sleep. When I began to analyze my dreams I frequently had a similar experience in which as soon as I was awake I found that I was already having, and had for some time been having, thoughts about a dream, the dream itself being still clearly in my mind. In some cases it was difficult to say where the dream ended and the unwitting analysis had begun, but a distinction was usually possible, owing to my lack of imagery when awake.

I emphasize Rivers' experience here for it mirrors my own. Indeed, something akin to this has happened repeatedly during the writing of this book. Thus, Rivers' account of dreaming takes into consideration, not only the manifest-latent content levels of analysis, but the creative problem-solving function of dreaming. Take for instance a dream from one of his patients he calls the "ichthyosaurus" [an ocean dwelling dinosaur] dream:

> In this dream the patient was being accused of the murder of two people in Paddington Station, while an ichthyosaurus was looking on. While being taken away by the police, the ichthyosaurus spat venom at him. The dreamer was taken to a Court of Justice where a letter was produced which incriminated him, but made no mention of his brother who had also been concerned in the murder. The dreamer awoke frightened and sweating.

Rivers interprets the dream as having been due to both the patient's experience as a soldier in the Great War and to some conflict arising the day before the dream. The dream reflected his knee-jerk suspicion of the motives of military quartermasters, or anyone like a quartermaster – represented by the ichthyosaurus. This dream was followed by others, all with the same motif of conflict between himself and quartermaster figures (e.g., the steward of the hospital in which he was being treated). The dream series illustrated for Rivers an unsuccessful conflict resolution in the patient. In just such a fashion, the highly dramatic and symbolic content of dreams in traditional societies may reflect this kind of inner conflict which may or may not be solved during dreaming (Rivers 1917).

Julia Levine (1991) carried out a cross-cultural study of conflict in the content of dreams of children from three groups of dreamers – Irish, Israeli and Bedouin. She used dream reports of children's dreams: "These dream reports were rated along stylistic dimensions…, that is, self-representation, representation and number of other dream characters, activity, and realistic quality of the dream, as well as by content – the nature of the conflict. Conflict was defined as the frustration of a motive, presence of a threat, or the result of two or more incompatible response tendencies. It was hypothesized that the representation of conflict in children's manifest dreams would vary with the sociocultural context of the dreamer" (ibid:473). She did indeed find cultural variation in the dreams of different groups. Not surprisingly the Irish and Israeli children were more alike than either were to Bedouin children. The Bedouin children were more likely to report conflict as very realistic, "occurring between a nonhuman, unfamiliar opponent and a group of highly related comrades..." (ibid:485). Also, Bedouin dreams tended to involve natural and realistic threats to actual survival. For instance: "I dreamt that a wolf came and took one of our sheep. My father came with his gun and he shot the wolf and broke its leg. My mother was in the tent and I was watching my father. I was very glad that he shot the wolf" (ibid:477). The Irish and Israeli children tended to report dreams in which conflicts were between people, and for the Israelis they were often conflicts over their personal independence.

For example: "I dreamt that I came to my father's house and we were planting a lawn. And there were lots of people there, young women and men, which I didn't know, and they wanted to enter the house. They were throwing this yellow fruit, that is growing now, at Mac, my dog. Mac was very frightened. I told the people to go away, and they said 'We didn't ask you.' They looked for the key to get inside my house, until my father came, and then he really drove them away" (ibid:477).

Sarah Levine (1981) has worked with women's dreams among the Gusii, a Bantu speaking people living in western Kenya. She has written an intriguing article exploring the dreams had by women about Levine herself. One of the women she worked with, Sabina, was newly pregnant and faced with an infidelity on the part of her husband, a migrant worker, who had taken up with another woman and was living with her in a distant place. Sabina was afraid that she had been abandoned and that she would not have enough resources to get by. She reported the following dream to Levine: "She was in labor. Getuka – the investigator, as the people called my husband [ethnographer Robert Levine] – took her to the hospital. The nurses asked 'Who will sign the register?' Sabina said, 'Getuka will sign,' and he did so. They put her into bed where she was covered with two blankets but was naked underneath. She told her eldest daughter to go home to fetch some clothes for her" (ibid:288). This is not a particularly sexual dream, for Gusii women give birth naked, though usually not in hospital. What it possibly does indicate is that she solved the problem of abandonment in her dream by replacing her husband with Levine's.

## Witchcraft and Dreaming

One of the more curious associations between dreaming and conflict has to do with witchcraft (see also Chapter 9 on dreams and healing). We have the great English social anthropologist, E. E. Evans-Pritchard (1902–1973), to thank for our more modern understanding of the psychological and social role played by witchcraft in society. In his famous study of the Azande people of the Sudan, *Witchcraft, Oracles and Magic Among the Azande* (1937), Evans-Pritchard showed how both witchcraft and magic play a part in social and political institutions, and are a daily factor in the lives of people – even people in our own Western societies (see Wintrob 1973 on witchcraft and illness in the United States). The use of witchcraft and sorcery by the Azande is linked to social status, for only males and the political elite were able to use oracles, divination and other magical means to uncover and identify evil doers. Moreover, he showed that most uses of magic had to do with protection from the use of magic by other people – thus signifying the presence of conflict in the community.

In many classic accounts of witchcraft, the belief in witches is directly connected with both conflict and dreams. Monica Wilson's account of witchcraft among the Nyakyusa of Tanzania is a case in point. The Nyakyusa, like many peoples in Africa and elsewhere, fear witch attacks. For them, a witch may take the form of a python curled in the belly of someone. If that person holds a grudge against another person (usually a relative or someone living close at hand) they will launch an attack. The attack is ostensibly a search for good food and drink, they say, but they choose as victims people with whom they have argued. "All this happens in dreams. Nightmares of being throttled, of being chased, of fighting, and of flying through the air are taken as evidence of an attack by witches; and, if a man wakes up suddenly at night in fear and sweating, he knows that 'they' – the witches – have come to throttle him. The witches are thought to fly by night on their pythons or 'on the wind;' they attack either singly or in covens; and they feast on human flesh" (Wilson 1951:308). Each village has one or more "defenders" who can perceive the witches while dreaming as they fly about doing their evil and can fight them off and protect the village.

A slightly different pattern of association between social conflict and witchcraft is found among the Tangu people of New Guinea. For the Tangu, dreams reveal truths about causation in social relations in the same way that myths do, though the former are personal and the latter public (Burridge 1969:164). One does not will a dream to occur, the dream has a life of its own and is thus independent of both the dreamer's ego and the community's values. Dreams may cause the dreamer to suffer or to prosper, depending on conditions. The most common culture pattern dreams are visitations from ghosts and ancestors who may admonish and advise the dreamer about issues current in social relations. But sometimes the dreamer will be visited by an evil person called *ranguma* who may exhibit a number of traits indicative of what we would call witch, sorcerer, assassin, etc. (ibid:133). If such a person comes into conflict with one of his neighbors, he may launch a magical attack on his victim and his target will become sick and perhaps eventually die. If the sick person is diagnosed with a *ranguma* attack, the sick person is urged to confess any and all conflicts he may have had with people – including any wrong he may have done to people. From this confession, various suspects who might have a motive to harm the sick person are uncovered. The word is sent out to the various communities about the confession in the hopes the *ranguma* will recall his attack.

If all this fails, then the family of the victim have recourse to a "dreamer-diviner" who is adept at seeking the truth of matters in dreams (ibid:141-142). Acting as a kind of detective, the dream-diviner will attempt to identify the *ranguma* from the available suspects through intuitive and dream insights. They will generally focus on people thought to be oddballs, and will attempt to coerce the suspect into confessing and paying a compensation to the sick person. If the sick person recovers and is able to return to work, he will return the compensation to the apparent *ranguma*, thus involving the latter in reciprocal exchange. "One case observed in the field took some seven months to play itself out. The victim, formerly an extremely robust young man, was unable to hold his food, and was eventually reduced to a scarcely breathing skeleton. At last the alleged *ranguma*, identified and coerced by dream-diviners, confessed. Within a week the victim was on his feet and out and about" (ibid:145n). Burridge (ibid:143) also mentions that if a man dreams of a *ranguma*, it will often be because he suspects that his wife is being adulterous, or that unwanted attentions are being paid to his daughter. Moreover, being a matrilineal society, there is some tension and ambiguity between a husband and his wife's brother with respect to his sons, and this may give rise to *ranguma* situations, both in dream and in actual *ranguma* attacks requiring the services of the dreamer-diviner.

## "Psycho-cultural Time-Lag" in Dreams

S.G. Lee (1958) carried out an interesting statistical analysis of manifest dream content among a sample of Zulu dreamers, both male (N = 139) and female (N = 414). His research turned out to be somewhat controversial. The reason for this is that he found:

> ...that dream content, for the particular sex, is derived almost exclusively from areas of social experience permitted by the culture *in the indigenous system of sanctions*, of some 50 to 100 years ago. Thus women, acting under a traditionally very strong cultural imperative, dreamt of babies and children, while cattle, the acquisition of which is their chief economic goal and source of prestige, appeared in the dreams of men. Zulu women, in the nineteenth century, were allowed no part in the handling of cattle. This was a very strong taboo, relaxed for only one day in the year. Nowadays, however, most of the women must perforce work with the cattle, as the majority of the men are away from home for some 10 months of the year as a result of the migrant labour situation. The women show no conscious guilt over this handling of cattle, so far as could be ascertained in personal interviews. (ibid:270; emphasis Lee's)

From these findings, Lee hypothesized that there exists a "psycho-cultural time-lag" between the realities of waking life and the "superego-driven" and highly stereotyped dream content. The values of the culture as it exists only in the collective memory of the people remain alive and well in the dream life. This is a theme taken up by

Robert A. Levine (1966:21-22) in his analysis of politico-economic development and personality change in African societies. He reasons that "Although the amount of time required is speculation, it seems highly likely that there will be a substantial – that is, easily perceptible – lag between the social change and the personality change it causes."

Other ethnographers have failed to find such a time lag in the content of dreams among the peoples they studied. For instance, Kenneth E. Johnson (1978) analyzed the content of a sample of 59 dreams from 60 men and women collected by Richard Thompson from students attending Makerere University, Kampala, Uganda in 1975. This was a period of tremendous sociocultural and political upheaval due to the brutality and ignorance of Idi Amin, a dictator who took over and ruled Uganda from 1971-1979.[2] Johnson found no difference in the content of dreams of men and women, and the content "...reflects the dreamer's culturally constituted experience, more particularly the current political and social reality in Uganda. The students in Uganda are in a very precarious situation, which can account for both the large number of unpleasant dreams and for the few dreams with achievement imagery. The fact that the majority for both objects and settings in the dreams are modern also argues against any type of time-lag in dream content" (ibid:220).

Philip Kilbride (1973) also failed to find any evidence for a "psycho-cultural time-lag" in dreams among various groups of Baganda, but keep in mind that his data also cover a period in which the Idi Amin tragedy was unfolding. He analyzed the manifest content of dreams from three groups of Baganda: rural dwellers, school students and urban dwellers. He found that the content of dreams was consistently modern and in keeping with everyday conditions being faced by Baganda in all three categories, except that while rural and school students tended to believe that their dreams would come true, the urban dwellers believed they would not. He offers a number of modern content dreams from these groups. Here is one from a female urban dweller employed as a secretary: "Last night I dreamt that the police were taking me in prison for emergency, but as soon as we got to prison people started fighting and many broke out. I also ran out with them.

---

[2] Incidentally, Amin took over Uganda a year after I left the field among the So people of northeastern Uganda.

The police looked all around the town for us. At last they caught some of us and took us back. They were going to beat us when I woke up suddenly" (ibid:32). By way of contrast, here is another from a female farmer: "One night I dreamt that my young sibling was very sick and he was in Rubaga Hospital, but the nurses did not pay any attention to him. Each of them was just passing by till at last I took him away; and one nurse helped me, and the other nurses were very angry and quarreled very much" (ibid:32).

It is hard to know what to make of the "time-lag" hypothesis floated by Lee and supported by LeVine. The studies supporting the notion are considerably different than those that find no evidence for it, and thus are not strictly comparable. One thing none of the scholars writing about the issue mention are the holocultural studies of sex and dreaming I covered back in Chapter 2 — to wit, there is evidence that male and female dreams tend to differ in content cross-culturally, and hence the lack of gender distinctiveness in the Makerere student dreams seems aberrant and may be due to the frightening conditions brewing during those troubled times. It may well be that extreme anxiety over personal safety and the unpredictability of events may have had a profoundly penetrating effect upon the dreaming life world of the Makerere students. Moreover, although the Zulu and Nigerian peoples researched by Lee and LeVine had undergone considerable change, their cultures' cycle of meaning remained largely intact, and the values embodied in narratives and other mythopoeic symbolism continued to influence dream content despite changes in daily activities. Remember, dreams are not always on about "day residue," especially with culture pattern dreams among peoples with an intact cycle of meaning.

## Dreaming and Performance

The reader may recall that I mentioned in Chapter 4 an intriguing theory put forth by Susan Parman (1979) linking dreaming and play as homologous processes in the evolution of the brain. She suggests that both function biologically to rehearse or simulate actions that may be both developmentally important and adaptive in the waking life of a hominin or other animal. This homology presumably emerged before human-like culture became a dominant factor in hominin adaptation. In order for this to be true, the neural structures mediating the simulation must be the same as those mediating the waking activity – a view that has been termed more recently the "virtual reality" hypothesis. That is, the tissues that develop as a consequence of "rehearsal" must be the same tissues that produce the more developed waking skill. Research has now shown this to be the case: "A question of direct relevance to the virtual reality hypothesis is whether the enactment of dream behaviors utilizes the same brain circuits as those which mediate those very behaviors in waking. A review of the lucid dreaming literature supports the identity hypothesis..." (Hobson 2009:43).

Daniel Erlacher and his associates (Schredl 2003; Erlacher and Schredl 2008, 2010; Erlacher and Chapin 2010; see also Hobson 2009) have developed a number of studies showing that the more important an activity or interest area is in the waking life, the more frequently that activity or interest will pop up in dreams. Schredl (2003) showed that the more time one spends doing something in waking life, the more dominant that activity will present in the dream life. Erlacher and Schredl (2010) went on to study dreams among athletes and demonstrated that the more time spent in athletic activities, the more frequent those activities will appear in dreams. In addition, Erlacher and Chapin (2010) have summarized the body of evidence supporting Hobson's "virtual reality" hypothesis. In my opinion Parman's evolutionary "rehearsal" theory implies something like Hobson's hypothesis and is given strong support by the research done by Erlacher *et al.*

Parman's account of dreaming and play makes sense when one considers the importance of dreams among polyphasic cultures. First of all, it would go far in explaining the commonality of incubation cross-culturally (Chapter 7). The more an individual ritualizes their sleep preparation and dream intentionality prior to dreaming – through pilgrimage, sleeping in sacred places, rituals rife with drivers like fasting, ceremonial activity and meditation – the more likely the neural circuitry mediating those pre-sleep activities will become involved in the actual dreaming itself. Second of all, as we know, time spent in social interaction and subsistence practices among traditional societies makes up a significant, and perhaps major, fraction of the day's activities.

Thus, one would expect those activities to predominate in the dreams of traditional people. Thirdly, the more dream material penetrates into daily activities – as in the case of peoples like the Ongee (Chapter 7) who act-out dream material in their everyday lives – the more one will find a continuity between dream activities and waking activities.[3]

By implication, this "rehearsal" function of human dreaming would be accentuated in the case of societies that act out dreams in ritual performances. Harking back to the cycle of meaning model in the last chapter, in a sense, ritual mythopoeic enactment of a peoples cosmology may be considered a "rehearsal" for the dream experience, and vice versa. Again, this would ensure a positive feedback loop into what might otherwise be a static and eventually obsolete ideological system. Songs and ritual enactments while awake may operate to "incubate" dreams, and dreams may operate creatively to "rehearse" and simulate waking song and enactment. Thus, dreaming and waking states become more integrated.

Laura Graham (2003) offers us a glimpse of just this kind of social process among the Xavante people of Brazil. Xavante dreaming and dream sharing epitomizes many of the aspects of dream-based sociocultural processes we have covered over the past several chapters, especially dream sharing, creativity within their cycle of meaning and reinforcement of social status relations within the community. As is so common in polyphasic cultures, dreaming is considered a type of experience of reality in which one may commune with the gods and acquire knowledge and information important to the community at large. Elders in particular may learn new dream songs (*da-ñoʔre*) while dreaming. Graham's book is centered upon one elder's – Warodi by name – dream song and how it came to be the center piece for a ritual performance.

An elder like Warodi may have a dream (obviously lucid considering the extent of focus, clarity of detail, thoroughness of learning and working memory involved) which he then re-tells around a campfire to other elders. The dream may involve a meeting with the gods of mythological lore in which new ritual instructions and new *da-ñoʔre* are revealed. The elder re-tells the dream and sings the songs to teach

---

[3] All things being equal, one would expect this to be the case for other traditionally important ASC.

the other elders. This leads later on to a ritual enactment of the dream by costumed dancers and singers. The ritual drama is conceived locally to be both a re-enactment of the history of their mythopoeic drama and the introduction of new and creative material that becomes part of the tradition of the people. As Graham notes, "A myth has a life that is born though its tellings. And each new telling has the potential to vary, even minutely, details of the previous tellings" (2003:8). This is especially true when the myth-telling is causally entangled with direct experience, as is the case with any intact cycle of meaning.

## Dreaming and Art

Dreams have presumably been a source of artistic inspiration for thousands of years – especially for art that is associated with the spirit world. In most of the societies anthropologists have studied, artistic production generally is associated with spiritual and mythopoeic elements of culture. Thus, in traditional societies, artistic expression may be yet another medium by which individual dream content enters the domain of social influence and action. We now know that aesthetics is inherent in the human brain (Skov and Vartanian 2009; Ramachandran 2004:Chap. 3), and therefore that all peoples experience an aesthetic sense (Dissanayake 1988; Maquet 1971, 1986). Indeed, it is Ellen Dissanayake's (1992) view that artistic elaboration of this kind operates to make an object "special" relative to the culture's cycle of meaning and constituent ritual practices.

We are all presumably aware of the core importance of dreaming to the history of artistic expression in our own Western cultures (Hobson and Wohl 2005) — most notably with the emergence of surrealism (Bradley 1997:Chap. 3). Those who have explored the phenomenology of their own dreaming will know that there are many occasions, especially during the hypnagogic/hypnopompic states when beautiful abstract imagery will spontaneously appear before the mind's eye. I, for one, have painted a number of such images over the years derived from my dreams (see Figure 4.3). The trouble is that the term "art" is a Western one, derived from the Latin for "skill" or "craft." Many traditional societies speak languages in which there really is no word meaning what we do by "art." Yet artistic skill and the recognition of quality in the making of things is a cultural universal (Gell 1998, Laughlin 2004a).

Among the Daribi people of Papua New Guinea, artistic patterns are routinely inspired from dreaming (Wagner 1972:74):

> The talents and skills involved in a number of craft specialties, including the decoration of arrow-shafts, the making and playing of bamboo flutes, and the weaving of belts, armbands, and string bags, are all thought to be acquired in dreams. Of course, anyone can try to learn these techniques, but real talent, like hunting luck, can only represent something additional to ordinary effort, and must be obtained through a dream. Thus, a Daribi who sees a badly decorated arrow-shaft will conclude that "this man did not have a dream."

Among the Tukolor people of Senegal, West Africa, dreaming, the spirit world and art are intimately connected in their dream culture (Dilley 1992). Like so many peoples we have discussed here, the Tukolor hold that dreams are the adventures had by their souls while wandering in the spirit world (ibid:74). They also make the distinction common to Islamic groups between normal everyday dreams and culture pattern dreams, the latter being far more important. Tukolor weavers understand that their craft originates in the spirit world, and there are sacred stories that link dreaming and their ancestors (ibid:77-78). It is through dreams that the weaver is connected with the mythopoeic sources of inspiration: "The type of dream inspiration they receive is either of a practical/artistic nature in that new cloth patterns or solutions to technical problems may be found, or it is of relevance to their body of weaving lore with the purpose of mystically improving a weaver's abilities or afflicting another weaver. In this latter category is included *cefi*, verses and incantations with mystical power to affect the physical world, and these verses are akin to poetry in that they employ metaphor, trope, analogy and allusion" (ibid:80).

All designs found in Aboriginal iconography are derived from dreams (Munn 1973:55). Price-Williams and Gaines (1994) carried out a series of interviews with 37 Australian Aboriginal artists that, among other things, asked them about the role played by dreaming in inspiring their imagery. Not surprisingly they found that dreams were integral to creativity. As one painter said, "If I had a dream: for example, women and men dancing, I would get up in the morning and start working. As I go along..., the dream comes back to my head, and I paint and design" (ibid:378). As with Aborigines generally, artists make the distinction between everyday dreams and culture pattern dreams – those that involve the sacred stories – and are inspired primarily by the latter (ibid:379). Their dreaming is frequently lucid: "Very real. See and hear and feel and touch. When *very* real, it is a special dream. Difficult to tell the difference between [what is happening] now ...and special dreams" (ibid:379).[4]

## SUMMARY AND SEGUE

For most peoples on the planet, dreaming is a thoroughly social process, and dream sharing is a social act. Both in content and in praxis, social relations predominate in dreams. For many peoples, dreams – especially important culture pattern dreams – are a matter of social concern. Interpretation of such dreams is often a group activity, and may lead immediately or eventually to social action. When the interpretation of such dreams is deemed to be important to the group, the interpretive process becomes institutionalized, thus incorporating the dream experience into the more global cycle of meaning – vivifying what I call the *axis of interpretation* of the cycle. Direct experience during dreaming or other ASC is involved in a positive feedback loop into the system of social meanings comprising the symbolic system of the group. The role of certain individuals within the group may become specialized as a recognized dream interpreter or oneirocritic. Such individuals are often also the people's healers, teachers and priests or shamans.

In many societies, especially small-scale hunting and gathering societies, dream sharing is an everyday occurrence. Sharing may be informal, as when waking up in the morning and telling the night's dreams to those around you, or more formal as in the case of pilgrimage

---

[4] For pictures of Aboriginal art depicting themes drawn from culture pattern dreams, see Sutton (1997).

or within a church service. In all these cases where dreaming, and especially getting at the meaning of dreams is important, interpretations will tend to be standardized. In some cases, the meaning of motifs and elements in a dream is established by consulting a dream-book type list of meanings. In these situations, the interpretation will always be in terms of the society's cosmology and mythopoeic textual and narrative traditions.

A number of social processes may be discerned in relation to dreaming. A common one is the resolution of conflict. When there exist social, political, economic and personal conflicts in the dreamer's daily environment, it is quite common for such conflicts to pop up in dream motifs. Indeed, the dream content may express a successful or unsuccessful process of resolution. Conflicts may be represented by witchcraft and sorcery attacks that may be successfully warded off by prompt action based on the dream experience. It would seem that much of dream life is something of a "rehearsal" or simulation of problem areas encountered in waking life, and in those cases in which dreaming is incubated and the results of dreaming enacted in performances, the waking and dreaming life worlds become more integrated.

Thus far I have been speaking about social and cultural processes in general. But there are areas of "ultimate concern" for people – matters like birth, disease, death and life after death, catastrophe, the uncertainty of future events, and the invisibility of real world causal relations. Consideration of dreaming in relation to these concerns takes us into the domain of what we in the West would normally call "religion" or "spirituality." That will be our focus in the next chapter as we attempt to place the universal experience of dreaming and social involvement in dreaming within its cross-cultural and phenomenological context.

# Chapter 9

# Dreaming in Religion, Shamanism and Healing

> The influence of dreams upon the lives of [traditional] peoples is a theme which has often attracted the interest of students of human culture. These phantom visitations of the night have done much to determine human beliefs concerning the nature of the soul and of its continued existence after death, and many peoples still trust greatly in the value of dreams as guides to the ordering of their daily conduct.
>
> W.H.R. Rivers (1918:5)

Probably no anthropologist who has studied dreams cross-culturally would deny the obvious importance of dreaming to people's spiritual life and religious institutions. As we have seen in past chapters, virtually all polyphasic cultures have developed a worldview that recognizes the reality of the dreaming life-world with its experiences of a spiritual dimension full of gods, spirits, ancestors, ghosts, mythical beings and magical causation. Moreover, an intact polyphasic system incorporates both a mythology (sacred lore) and ritual, as well as perhaps other mythopoeic elements like games, art, drama, dance and daily techniques and practices. And yet, many of these societies simply have no word in their language for what we call "religion." To make matters more interesting, anthropologists will differ in how they conceive of religion as a cross-culturally valid concept, and whether they think any particular element of religion is universal to cultures everywhere.

## Religion Defined

Let me sample a few definitions of religion by my colleagues to give the reader a sense of the variation in meaning:

- Robert N. Bellah (1964:358): "… a set of symbolic forms and acts which relate man to the ultimate conditions of his experience."
- Charles Glock and Rodney Stark (1965): "Religion, or what societies hold to be sacred, comprises an institutionalized system of symbols, beliefs, values and practices focused on questions of ultimate meaning."
- Clifford Geertz (1973:90): "A religion is a system of symbols which acts to establish powerful, pervasive, and long-lasting moods and motivations in men by formulating conceptions of a general order of existence and clothing these conceptions with such an aura of factuality that the moods and motivations seem uniquely realistic."

I could go on quoting anthropological definitions for the rest of the chapter, but to little purpose. The term "religion" is, as Benson Saler (1993:Chap. 4) has amply shown, rife with all sorts of Western cultural baggage. Yet most of them do seem to center upon several characteristics common to cultures everywhere, namely:

- Religions are about matters of "ultimate concern" (Tillich 1957:41-54; 1963) such as conception and birth, death, the afterlife, disease, catastrophe, ASCs (in particular, dreaming), hidden causation, the origins of things, the uncertainty of future events, the transcendental, the transpersonal and relations with cosmos.
- Religions make a distinction between those matters that are sacred (related somehow to the sacred stories) and those that are profane (unrelated to the sacred stories).
- Religions operate to resolve the tension between the individual's direct experience and society's system of cosmological, sacred and moral knowledge.
- Religions are expressed in a system of mythopoeic symbolism that integrates sacred lore, ritual practice, iconography and other symbolic media.

- Religions in polyphasic cultures are concerned with evoking, realizing and interpreting alternative states of consciousness, and in particular, culture pattern dreams.

Etymological dictionaries tell us that most likely "religion" comes from the Latin *religio*, "reverence for powers or forces," and *religare*, "to tie back or bind." Nowhere in the ancient meanings of the word is there any mention of churches, passing the plate, sermons, hymnals or priests – the kinds of things the layman in our society associates with religion. The root meaning of "religion" as far as I am concerned points to the sublime nature of being. The emphasis is upon unity and entanglement, hence "binding," the same root meaning as "yoga," which is from the Sanskrit root meaning to "yoke" together or "unite" with the spiritual, with the All. So, for our purposes, *religion* refers to the institutionalized knowledge, practice and collective experience of a people uniting individuals with the sublime, the spiritual, and the sacred dimension of being. The word "sacred" in turn tends to have two meanings in anthropology, one is hermeneutical and the other experiential. Something is sacred because it relates to a people's mythology, or it is sacred because it is *numinous* (see Chapter 6). An encounter with the numinous is by definition a transpersonal experience. As Jung liked to say, "… the experience of the self is always a defeat for the ego." We will return to Jungian notions of religion and dreaming in Chapter 10. In any event, either definition of "sacred" is fine with me, for they cover what ethnographers often find when doing research on religions among traditional peoples.

Every traditional, intact worldview includes a religious system that operates through a cycle of meaning – whether or not they call it something like "religion." As mentioned in the last chapter, every religious system has at its core a mythology – a set of sacred stories that often account for the origins (cosmogony) and sometimes the future (eschatology) of the people, their relation to their land, the intent of existence, the relationship of the people to the supernatural or spiritual domain. Often coming alive in ASC, the mythology prescribes the moral tone of the people and transmits adaptationally important information down the generations. The central importance of mythology to religion has been acknowledged by most anthropological scholars over the years.

Émile Durkheim, for instance, emphasized that the reality expressed in myth is not merely the figment of imagination, *but is reality itself imagined* (1995:12). Many ethnologists find that this reality base must be so, for the contingencies addressed in myth often indicate important elements and issues fundamental to the adaptational style of a people (Rappaport 1984, 1999). Some students of religion have acknowledged the adaptational significance of myth. Claude Lévi-Strauss (1964) has noted that myth is concerned with fundamental dilemmas of human existence – dilemmas that may have very serious adaptational consequences. Mircea Eliade (1963) understood myth as a comment on the human condition generally, and noted that traditional peoples code myth as a "true story" or a story about reality. Both neuroanthropologist Earl Count (1960) and theologian Paul Tillich (1957, 1963) saw a society's myth as a description of a people's understanding of "the world as problem" – an expression of the "ultimate concerns" of a society. Social phenomenologist Alfred Schutz (1964) goes further and suggests that myth refers to transcendental experience and the boundaries of a people's view of multiple realities.

How a religious system is organized socially will vary a great deal. Religions can range from simple to complex, from those with little or no social hierarchy to those evidencing elaborate social relations with differentiated roles and functions – they may even form bureaucracies. Anthony F.C. Wallace (1966) proposed four categories of religion, each subsequent category subsuming the previous category:

- **Individualistic:** most basic; simplest. Example: vision quest.
- **Shamanistic:** part-time religious practitioner, uses religion to heal, to divine, usually on the behalf of a client. The Tillamook have four categories of shaman. Examples of shamans: spiritualists, faith healers, palm readers. Religious authority acquired through one's own means.
- **Communal:** elaborate set of beliefs and practices; group of people arranged in clans by lineage, age group, or some religious societies; people take on roles based on knowledge, and ancestral worship.
- **Ecclesiastical:** dominant in agricultural societies and states; are centrally organized and hierarchical in structure, paralleling the organization of states. Typically deprecates competing individualistic and shamanistic cults.

There is a reasonable presumption here that the organization of a people's religion tends to mirror the complexity of the society, and is influenced by demographics, level of socio-political integration, technological advances and subsistence patterns. Polyphasic dream cultures may be found in all of these categories. With increasing hierarchy, however, the social importance of dreams may vary and reflect the social status of the dreamer, those he or she shares dreams with, and those being dreamed about.

## Shamanism Defined

Anthropologist Michael Winkelman (1990, 1992, 1996, 2004, 2010) has made a career of studying the neurobiology, evolution and phenomenology of shamanism. He would agree with Wallace, I think, that the form of religious practice of a people will mirror the organization of society in general:

> The relevant socioeconomic conditions underlying the evolution of shamanic healers involve: (1) the absence/presence of hunting and gathering versus agriculture as the major source of subsistence; (2) fixity of residence (nomadic versus sedentary lifestyle); (3) political integration beyond the level of the local community; and (4) social stratification (classes and castes/hereditary slavery). These relationships of socioeconomic conditions to forms of magico-religious practice were established as being independent of diffusion…" (2010:63).

I agree with Winkelman, as well as with Hultkrantz (1978) and Rock and Krippner (n.d.), that the global incidence of shamanism as a religious institution cannot be entirely accounted for by historical diffusion, but rather by:

> …the psychobiological bases of human consciousness and its adaptation to social and ecological conditions of hunter-gatherer societies. This is possible because the alterations of consciousness basic to selection, training, and professional activities occur

spontaneously under a wide variety of circumstances – injury, extreme fatigue, near starvation, and as a consequence of a wide variety of deliberate procedures... . Consequently, shamanism was reinvented or rediscovered in diverse cultures because these experiences provide important adaptive capabilities. These are derived from their usefulness in meeting challenges to survival, including healing through stress reduction and other physiological changes that enhance systemic integration of the information-processing strata of the brain... . (Winkelman 2010:64-65)

Naturally enough, my own emphasis has been upon the neuropsychological processes exhibited by those who seek insights, knowledge and power from direct encounters with the sublime (see also Winkelman 2004; Rock and Krippner n.d.). Gene d'Aquili, John McManus and I liked to speak of the *shamanic principle* that may be found operating at all levels of institutional complexity (Laughlin, McManus and d'Aquili 1990:149-150): "From the transpersonal perspective, the many discussions of shamanism, like those which focus on social status, initiatory rites, healing techniques, cosmological sources of power, historical change, and cross-cultural influences upon traits, frequently overlook a fundamental experiential and structural principle: there is an almost universal drive among humans to seek and explore alternative [states] of consciousness..., and those who become adept at attaining valued [states] are expected to help others attain such experiences... ." Winkelman does not commit this error, but many do and such discussions carry one away from the centrality of the shamanic principle to virtually all polyphasic cultures. It is true that shamans, in the strict sense of the term, are typical of simpler societies where the social organization and the polity are not structured beyond the local community (Czaplicka 1914:197-198).

The shamanic principle is operating in most polyphasic cultures, whether there exists an institutional religious hierarchy or not. The principle was working as much among classical Mayan states (Freidel, Schele and Parker 1995; see Tedlock 2004b on notion of "shaman-priest") as it was among the Siberian Chuckchee. Indeed, it is operating to some extent in the New Age "neoshamanism" movements in our own contemporary society (see Chapter 15; see also DuBois 2009:Chap. 14).

Thus "shaman" is the label that many anthropologists and students of religion use for traditional mystics, spiritual practitioners and healers, and as such shamans represent humanity's ancient encounter with, and interpretations of alternative waking and dreaming states, and their spiritual consequences (Bulkeley 1995:2; Krippner 1990a,1990b; Tedlock 1999; Winkelman 2010:2; Lewis-Williams 1987; DuBois 2009:6; Sumegi 2008:11).[1]

## THE DREAMING SHAMAN

Dreaming is often integral to the calling, selection and empowerment of shamans, and presumably has been since perhaps the beginning of the Upper Paleolithic some 40,000 years ago. As Paul Devereux (1993:136) wrote, "It is difficult for us, in our secularized culture, to appreciate the strong drive felt by most archaic and traditional peoples to access supernatural realms, to experience altered states of consciousness. So, bound by the perspectives of our peculiar Western lifeway, we have to make a special effort to try to understand the need for *trance*, particularly shamanic trance, in other kinds of societies, present and past."

Barbara Honegger (1979) has argued that the famous Bird Man glyph found in one of the shafts of Lascaux Cave in France, part of a mural that has been dated to more than 16,000 years ago, most reasonably depicts a dreaming shaman (Figure 9.1). Some authorities have interpreted the Bird Man as a shaman in trance, but Honegger suggests that, "Another plausible interpretation of the Bird Man at Lascaux, since he is alone and *prone*, is that he is *dreaming*. His most unusual physiological features – his bird-like head and 'hands' – have already been accounted for by the universal symbolism of his calling. His remaining striking physiological feature – an erect phallus – can be

---

[1] Eliade (1964) considered shamanism to be an early form of religious institution, but scholars since then have considered the term to be a catch-all concept referring to various techniques of healing, ritual practices and exploration of alternative states (Krippner 2002; Winkelman 2010; Rock and Krippner n.d.). Moreover, there is some question as to whether the visions experienced by some shamans occur during dreaming or waking states. Krippner (2002:967) notes that "shamanic traditions do not use terms that easily translate into *alterations* of consciousness."

**Figure 9.1. The Bird Man mural in Lascaux Cave.**

accounted for by the dream hypothesis" (ibid:9). In case the reader is not aware of the fact, penile erection is common among males in REM stage sleep.

To get a clearer feel for the relationship between dreaming and shamanism, let me offer some examples of dreaming shamans from simpler hunting-gathering and horticultural societies. But keep in mind that, as I mentioned in Chapter 6, when lucidity of dreaming and visions exceeds a certain point, it is hard to tell the difference between a dream report and a vision report (Bourguignon 1972). The classic origin of the concept of the shaman is from the part-time priestly institution among a number of Siberian groups (Czaplicka 1914: Chap. 8). These manifestations of shamanism range, it seems, from the very informal practices to formally recognized specialists. A shaman's calling may be inherited or not, depending upon the group. All shamans appear to be afflicted with psychological problems. For instance, among the Koryak, "...people about to become shamans have fits of wild paroxysms alternating with a condition of complete exhaustion. They will lie motionless for two or three days without partaking of food or drink. Finally they retire to the wilderness, where they spend their time enduring hunger and cold in order to prepare themselves for their calling" (Jochelson 1975 [1908]:47; keep in mind the effects of these privations upon dream incubation). Being a hysteric was interpreted as being afflicted by spirits, and the calling to become a shaman was a cure. The cure occurs because the budding shaman accepts the spirit(s) involved in producing the symptoms, and learns to control them. Sometimes the calling comes in a dream. For instance, among the Tungus "A dead shaman appears in a dream and summons the dreamer to become his successor. One who is to become a shaman appears shy, distrait, and is in a highly nervous condition" (Czaplicka 1914:177). Novice shamans among the Chukchee are commonly isolated, either going off into the forest for days at a time, or remaining alone in a room. They will often sleep and dream a lot (ibid:179). Among the Buryat, a child who is to become a shaman manifests these signs: "He is often absorbed in meditation, likes to be alone, has mysterious dreams, and sometimes has fits during which he is unconscious" (ibid:185).

Lewis-Williams (1987, 2002:218-221, 253-254) has emphasized the importance of dreaming to San Bushmen shamans, a rather neglected subject in both the ethnography of trance dancing and the archaeological study of shamanic rock art. As with the Bird Man glyph above, many just assume that what is being depicted are shamans in trance states, whereas there is ample evidence from ethnographic sources that San shamans are adept lucid dreamers as well. Drawing from the fieldwork of D.F. Bleek, Lewis-Willams (ibid:168) quotes a Bushmen informant as saying about a shaman that, "He lies asleep by us, his magic walks about while we sleep here." The shaman sleeps and dreams and exits his body to wander around and protect his community from evil doers. The same power (*//ke:n* or "magic") fuels both the trance dance and the lucid dream. "For the shamans, sleep was like the dance and therefore an active rather than a passive condition" (ibid:168).

Among the Dunne-za, a subarctic hunting people, the initiation of each man is by way of a vision quest (Ridington 1971; Ridington and Ridington 1970). The vision is sought through a series of dream experiences in which the would-be hunter encounters spiritual animals described in myth who initiate him and bind mythic time with the present. His relationship with the archetypal "boss" of each animal species he hunts depends upon these early encounters. His success as a hunter is determined by the knowledge and power bestowed by the respective animal "boss." Shamanic initiation is an extension of this series of dream encounters, but more explicitly through death, initiation by a community of shamans in heaven and then rebirth on the earthly plane. Through these dream-visions the shamanic initiant establishes a relationship with the "boss" of humans, and obtains his "god songs" that give him the power to guide the "shadows" of men along the path to heaven.

Shamans among the Paviotso, an American Plateau Shoshonean tribe living in Nevada, may be of either sex, and commonly obtain their calling and receive their powers through dreaming (Park 1934:99): "A man dreams that a deer, eagle, or bear comes after him. The animal tells him that he is to be a doctor. The first time a man dreams this way he does not believe it. Then he dreams that way some more and he gets the things the spirit [ancestor] told him to get... . Then he learns to be a doctor. He learns his songs when the spirit comes and sings to him." Societies all through Melanesia recognize that there are ritual-dream specialists who are able to access their power through dreaming and use it to heal, chat with ancestors, cause sometimes nasty things to happen through magic, and predict future events.

For the Bororo people of Brazil, dreaming is a phase of everyday life during which one's soul (*aroe*) experiences things. It is during dreaming that the nascent shaman (*bari*) gets the first clues to his life's career (Crocker 1985:201-202):

> The first and recurring shamanistic dream is one of soaring very high above the earth, "like a vulture," accompanied by the soul of some living relative who is often, but not always, a shaman. From his remote perspective, the dreamer perceives a curiously altered but perceptually vivid world, in which "things are very little and close to one another." (One nonshaman said he had been terrified by his first airplane flight: "It was just like the *bari's* dream.") Suddenly he sees a large cloud of smoke rolling across the savannah emitting flashes of light "as sparks flying from a fire."

The great, moving pall of smoke indicates that illness will happen in the community, and specifically to any individuals seen in the dream. The novice shaman will continue to dream about events that come true in waking life. Later he hears voices while alone and will offer the spirits tobacco smoke, and will discover game he would like to kill. If his hunting is successful, he knows he has established a special relationship with the spirits, which is confirmed by episodes of possession and disturbing dreams. There will follow dreams in which the apprentice shaman is tested by the spirits and which expand his experiences of the spirit world. Eventually the shaman becomes a conduit for information between the spirits and the community.

Gilbert Herdt (1977, 1992; see also Lohmann 2004) contributed one of the early, detailed descriptions of shamanism in New Guinea – that being among the Sambia, a horticultural people of Papua New Guinea. The *kwooluku* or shaman is a major figure in Sambia religion. It is a role that is bestowed upon an individual who has shown a "calling" for the job in their childhood. Dreaming, as well as other ASC, is at the core of this calling, for they presage a shaman's career. Parents pay great attention to their children's dreams, especially when the child has a nightmare. "If the child awakes from a frightening nightmare – especially if it is crying and shaking – a parent (or caretaker) may hold the child, inquiring what was dreamt. They may immediately interpret the dream. If one or both of the parents, or caretakers, are shamans, they may interpret the dream to 'show' …that ghosts have an exceptional interest in the child. Alternatively, non-threatening dreams with a recurring figure may be viewed as a manifestation of the shamanic familiar of the same-sex parent which is believed to have taken a 'liking' to the child" (ibid:155-156). These are indications that the child may later on be possessed by the familiar of the parent. It is by virtue of having this familiar that a shaman may enter trance and visit the spirit world, a world populated by malevolent beings that cause illness and destruction. A powerful female shaman named *Kwinjimaambi* told Herdt (ibid:156) of a significant dream she recalled from childhood:

> When I was a [premenstrual] girl…, I had no husband yet. I had a dream. I saw my deceased mother. She said to me: "If you want to *kwolya* (individual healing ceremony), you must gather these leaves… . It was at the time of my brother's… first stage initiation. I woke up. These leaves were adhering to my skin; I do not know how they got there. I knew then that I could become a *kwooluku*. My father… said to everyone: "My sons will not become a *kwooluku*; Kwinjimaambi will."

Her mother had been a shaman and the dream was a sign that her mother's familiar would eventually become hers. During her childhood she could expect to observe and absorb the behaviors of many adults entering trance states, encountering spiritual beings and carrying out rituals. The shaman eventually becomes an oneirocritic with the power to control spirits and to seek lost souls (Herdt 1992:67).

Among the Daribi people, also living in New Guinea, the *sogoyezibidi* ("tobacco-spirit") or shaman attains her (sometimes his) spiritual power from a close relationship with a ghost who aids the shaman in divining, diagnosing and curing. "The sogoyezibidi's relationship with a ghost, like that of an ordinary medium, is initiated by the ghost itself, and the novice must undergo the trials and discomforts common to all spirit-possession. Someone may tell a close relative or clanmate, 'When I die my ghost will come to you and make you a *sogoyezibidi*.' Afterward, when the person who made the promise dies, he will appear to the one he has 'marked' in a dream and present her with a bamboo tobacco pipe, signifying the fulfillment of his promise" (Wagner 1972:141).

The spiritual nature of dreaming and dreaming-specialists is commonplace in Amazonia as well. Some groups recognize healing shamans who begin their careers and hold their power through dreaming. Among them are the Asurini do Tocantins (Fausto 1994). A young novice shaman is trained by an older shaman, and then is put to a test where in the dream he must eat the food of the jaguar, some bloody meat, and wake without vomiting. Having passed the test he must then dream of the jaguar itself and suck a *karomara* (a "dream thing" that likes to eat raw flesh) from the jaguar and hold it in his mouth. This "object" gives the shaman the power to heal. He heals others by sucking the *karomara* that is eating away at the patient's innards and spitting it out – thus a kind of "sucking doctor."

Among the Zinacantan Indians of Chiapas, Mexico, shamans are of various types. The full-on shaman, whose practices in healing and other matters is very similar to the classic pattern of Siberian shamanism, is selected by the ancestral gods,

> ...who command him to become a *h'ilol* and instruct him in all the information requisite to curing. Informants describe various forms of this supernatural confrontation. The version that seems

> to be most commonly held is that over a period of several years the subject experiences a series of dreams in which he is summoned before the [ancestral gods] in their dwelling inside the mountain peak of *muk\*ta vic*. Here the individual is told that he has been chosen to become a *h'ilolo* and is given patients whom he must cure. (Fabrega and Silver 1970:474)

Once he becomes a shaman, he treats patients with various illnesses, as well as those suffering from stress, conflict and anxiety.

During his fieldwork in Nepal, Danish anthropologist Peter Skafte interviewed a shaman named Ashok (Ashok and Skafte 2001[1992]:235) who related a dream he had when he was sixteen:

> My village is on the crest of a big spur that extends down from the mountains. Below the village, on one side, there is a huge cliff, and below that cliff is a small temple dedicated to *Bajra* (the thunder god). One day, when I was sixteen years old, I was herding cattle near that temple. It was a hot afternoon, and I lay down behind the temple and fell asleep. I had a wonderful dream in which *Bajra* stood before me. He had a long beard streaked with gold, and he wore beautiful clothing. *Bajra* said, "It is time for you to learn to become a shaman. I will be your teacher." When I awoke, I was trembling in the area of my heart, but the trembling stopped as I drove the cattle home. Later that evening, I suddenly went into a trance – I began to shake and I could not utter a word. My brother-in-law, who is a shaman, was summoned. He tried to find out which spirit had possessed me, but it would not reveal itself. I remained in trance, without speaking, for a week.

Some time later, in another dream, *Bajra* appeared and taught the young man a mantra. He awoke and went over to his brother-in-law's altar and taking down his drum, began to drum and chant and shake. His brother-in-law requested the possessing spirit to reveal itself. "*Bajra* answered through me," said Ashok. "I am *Bajra* and I come with good intentions. Ashok must become a shaman and you must be his guide. Open his eyes so that he can see to travel the right way to the upper, middle, and lower worlds."

Shamans commonly derive specific powers by way of dreams and visions (Halifax 1979; Narby and Huxley 2001; Winkelman 2010; Narby and Huxley 2001). They may be given the gift of healing, of long life, of foretelling the future, of changing the weather, of killing in battle, seeking lost objects or souls, and so forth by contact with "other-than-human" beings that present themselves in dreams (Benedict 1922). For instance, according to Clark Whissler (1870-1947) who collected dreams among the Blackfoot Indians (reprinted in Lincoln 1935:259-260), a shaman went out on a fast and on the fourth day dreamed that: "Sun man and moon woman and their son, the morning star, appeared. The man gives him his body and says, 'You will live as long as I.' The woman gives power over rain. The son gives for a hat, a plume of eagle feathers and tail feathers of a magpie. Given power over the rain at the sun dance." He continues this series of dreams during his fast and further accrues the power to stop bleeding and to handle red hot stones.

But not only may a shaman accrue powers from spirit beings, but he may also require instructions and even commands he dare not ignore. Among the 19th century Iroquois, according to A.F.C. Wallace:

> ...a dream could thus reveal the wishes not only of the dreamer but also of the supernatural who appeared in his dream. Frustration of the wishes of a supernatural was dangerous, for he might not merely abandon or cause the death of the dreamer, but bring about disaster to the whole society or even cause the end of the world. Hence, dreams in which such powerful personages as *Tarachiawagon* (culture hero and a favorite dream-figure) appeared and announced that they wanted something done (frequently for the dreamer) were matters of national moment. Clairvoyants were called upon; the chiefs met, and discussed ways of satisfying the sometimes expensive or awkward demands of the dreamers (representing the powers above), or of averting the predicted catastrophe. Not infrequently this type of dream also bore elements of personality transformation for the dreamer, who in his identification with the gods assumed a new role as prophet, messiah, and public censor and adviser.

Among the Numic-speaking societies of the American Great Basin, shamans, dreaming and power were inextricably bound up with ritual enactments and healing. "Supernatural powers are obtained in dreams. A prospective shaman might involuntarily dream of power (in the form of spirit helpers), or seek out guardian spirits through dreams at sacred places (e.g., caves). Dreaming is a necessary prerequisite even for inheritance of shamanic ability through family members. Repeated unsolicited dreams are common to the novice shaman, but differ in form and content in different shamans. In general, auditory sensations predominate at first: The spirit helper instructs the novice about paraphernalia, songs to sing, the dances to be carried out while curing" (Myers 2004:292-293).

The great ethnographer, Ruth Bunzel (1898-1990), recorded transcripts of statements made by Quiché shamans in Mexico. Shamans are often recruited from among the ranks of the sick. Diviners will be consulted and if they conclude from reading their signs that the young patient is destined to be a shaman, the patient is asked to tell about any dreams they might have had bearing on the matter. One such report was of a father consulting diviners on behalf of his young son, and told his son, "...they also asked, son, whether you have not had signs in your dreams, that it is true what the diviners say? Think and try to remember, boy." The son replies, "It is true, my father. It happened some time ago that I dreamed that I was making divinations before a woman, and another time that I was burning incense in the door of the church" (Bunzel 1952:323). If the family decides to allow the boy to follow the path of the shaman, he will become an apprentice to a shaman and all through the process he will be asked to report any dreams that seem important.

Tarahumara (Mexico) shamans are not recruited using dreams, but rather pupils are selected by older experienced shamans, often from their own household. But dreaming is nonetheless important to the training of a shaman. A man becomes a shaman by apprenticeship. One shaman named Lorenzo gave Wendell Bennett the following partial description of his training: "He was first instructed by his uncle, Jesús, for a period of a year. He was taught to sleep at night with great care, in order to learn from his dreams what made people sick" (Bennett and Zingg 1976:256). Lorenzo went on to study the techniques of curing by helping the elder shaman until he was considered capable. Later on, Lorenzo carried out cures such as this one: "A child had thrown stones into one of the deep river whirlpools, where the water people live, although it realized that this was a bad thing to do. That night, the child dreamed that a large animal came out of the water hole and seized it. Thus the child became ill. Lorenzo was summoned, and he sent his soul out to arrange ransom" (ibid:259-260).

In South Africa, numerous churches have been founded on the basis of the dreams of Bantu prophets (Sundkler 1948:265):

> "Please, sir, one day I was asleep, I dreamt of this church. 24 September 1933, I was dreaming about this church." In these terms, the Rev. J.M_____ informs the Native Affairs Department in Pretoria of the beginning of a new religious organization under his leadership, the African Baptized Apostle Church. The place of dreams in independent Churches, especially those of Zionist type, is very considerable. In order to understand the religious life of leaders and followers in these organizations a study of their dream life is essential.

Indeed, dream cultures among Bantu speaking peoples – particularly the Zulu – is both elaborate and crucial to understanding their cosmology. The Zulu distinguish between three types of dreams, "those sent by ancestors, those sent by wizards, and ordinary spontaneous dreams" (ibid:265-266). It is the ancestors who dialogue with the living about matters of "crises, illness, or death in the family" (ibid:266), and it is from the ancestors that one receives a calling to be a healer or diviner:

> Ndlulangaye Ngcobo, a famous diviner in northern Zululand, told me about his call: He saw in a dream the spirits of his father and of an old diviner. They told him to go to Polela river [running east of Lesotho] where he would become initiated. He walked for two days, and arriving on the third day, he recognized the diviner who had been pointed out to him. There and then his initiation started. In the case of a diviner, dreams play a central role. Not only must his call be extended by the ancestors through a dream, but he has to go on dreaming in order to assert himself as a real

diviner. To receive clear dreams, he avoids certain food and he smears himself with white earth. It is characteristic of the diviner that, as in Ndlulangaye's case, rivers and pools and water seem to form an integral part of his dream. This is obviously related to his daily visits to a river where he performs purification rites (ibid:266-267).

Among some groups, notably the American Plains Indian societies of old who practiced the more extreme ordeals of the Sun Dance, the suffering involved in becoming a shaman was great. Ruth Benedict (1922:8) tells us this about shamans among the Dakota Indians:

> The final tortures of the sun dance, here as nowhere else, were reserved for those who desired to become shamans, and the ultimate purpose of the ordeal was the obtaining of the vision [dream or revelation] which was granted at any time before the dispersal of the next winter's camp. Or, a candidate might go to an individual shaman, who accompanied him to an isolated spot and tied him as in the sun dance; or he might himself cut off and offer bits of flesh in the presence of the shaman.

Why would someone torture themselves to attain a vision or to incubate a dream? What is the relationship between the gift of one's flesh to the gods and bestowal of power? What often goes unsaid in reports of these traditions is the magical causation implied in the relations between dreamer and the "other-than-human" agents he or she encounters, and in the bestowal of powers, especially when, as is almost always the case, the dream is seen as an augur or as a diagnosis of illness. So before we shift gears into a discussion of the use of dreaming in healing, I want to take a moment to address the issue of magic.

## Dreaming and Magic

Science has had a major impact on the world's cultures, both those of Westerners and for peoples in more traditional societies that have had intensive contact with modern industrial societies. Yet, as anthropologist

John Cove (1987) notes, an absolute distinction between science and traditional worldviews may be more apparent than real. The actual impact of science is perhaps most felt in the degree to which its views relate to everyday life. It is interesting that, whereas modern science is, like traditional worldviews, in the business of explaining phenomena by revealing or modeling hidden forces, science usually does not produce an integrated, meaningful life-world for most people influenced by the scientific worldview. The reason is straightforward. Science does not create a cycle of meaning for most people. Yes, we do operate on a germ theory of disease, but few of us actually experience germs – we don't see them, feel them or hear them. They are a concept. Of course, the conceptual and technological byproducts of science influence our life-worlds, and have done so for three centuries or more – "better living through chemistry," and so on. But science typically usurps the cultural position of traditional worldviews and thereby exacerbates a general sense of anomia or alienation from the kind of worldview that makes a totally integrated and meaningful life-world possible. When we examine this problem in a cross-culturally comparative way, we are led to ask the question of the *relationship between meaning and causation in experience*. What exactly is causation, as contrasted with meaning, and why is it possible for science to produce models of the former without enriching the life-world of most people with the latter in any deeply meaningful way? How do the fundamental assumptions about the nature of the world and how we come to know it differ in science compared with traditional worldviews?

There are four attributes of the scientific model of causation that are particularly worth noting: (1) cause and effect are usually conceived to be distinct events (A bumps into B), (2) cause and effect are conceived as occurring in time with the cause always preceding the effect (A bumps into B at time $t^1$ and B moves and bumps into C at time $t^2$), (3) cause and effect must either occur within the same location in space, or have a trajectory of interactions between elements in space (A bumps into B, B bumps into C, C bumps into… N), and (4) teleological, or purposeful causation in nature is often considered at best to be normatively suspect, and at worst to be blatantly "religious," "metaphysical," or *magic* (see Suppe 1989:284-285). Think about why Einstein called the causation described by quantum physics as "spooky." Here you have two particles that are connected at time $t^1$, they whiz off in different directions at the speed of light and at time $t^2$ they are still causally connected. Spooky indeed! But only from our modern mechanistic point of view.

The view of cause and effect as distinct events occurring at two points in time forms part of the natural attitude of science because it is the common sense view of causation held in Western cultures (Jaspars, Hewstone and Fincham 1983:4). Our notion of causation has become mechanical because we naturally assume there must exist some mechanism involved – a physical system with parts that operate on each other in time. Thus, for instance, ideas like that of "backward causation" (B causes A where B happens at time $t^2$ and A happens at time $t^1$) are considered absurd (Faye 1989:9). So too is the notion of "causation at a distance" (A causes B where A and B are in different locations and there is no mechanism between the two). Scientific causation may be considered, therefore, as one possible model of a much more extensive spectrum of causal events recognized by non-scientific peoples all over the planet. Take as an example the phenomenon of the "evil eye," which involves the sense of being stared at. Colin Ross (2010) has argued that this common experience may actually be caused by the brain of the recipient picking up what he calls "ocular extramissions" from the person doing the staring. He backs this hypothesis up with the fact that, "…brainwaves can be detected at short range in an electromagnetically insulated environment using a high-impedance electrode. The results of the recordings demonstrate that an electromagnetic signal emerges from the eyes, and that in some frequency ranges it has greater amplitude than the field emerging through the skull…" (ibid:52-53). These electromagnetic emissions can be remotely detected, "…using high-impedance electrodes that make no physical contact with the person…" (ibid:53). So a commonly reported ethnographic phenomenon that has tended to be pooh-poohed as so much superstition by experimental scientists might suddenly become a topic of legitimate field research, only because there is now a plausible mechanical explanation to replace the presumption of spooky magic.

Again, it was Professor Evans-Pritchard (1937) who set us anthropologists on the right path in his research into magical causation as experienced and conceived by the Azande (see Chapter 8). He showed us that the Azande operated on a quite different model of causation than we do, and it influenced their lives every day; that is, they used magic on an everyday basis. Magic, oracles and divination were used to confront the "reality" of witchcraft. Information was gleaned from oracles and divination about who was using witchcraft, and to thwart that use. Witches harmed others through directing mystical power at their target. Moreover, things happened in a magical way – like in the world of Harry Potter. After all, said Evans-Pritchard, people are not interested in what percentage of folks walking along this path will trip over that root, but rather why my son tripped over that root and yours did not — why him specifically and why at that time? Perhaps he was hexed? Or unlucky?

But what does "luck" mean if not another word for magic? Among the Mae Enga of New Guinea, as with so many peoples, there is no such thing as randomness in events. "The causal or sky beings [experienced in dreams] also dispense individual good and bad luck. Men attribute to actions in the celestial world the occurrence of the unpredictable in earthly affairs, the intrusion of circumstances that normally they can ignore as extraneous. Thus, it is bad luck when a skilled axeman cuts himself or a careful householder loses a pig; it is good luck when a man dodges an arrow fired point-blank in a skirmish" (Meggitt 1965:109). Again, among the Kyaka of New Guinea (Bulmer 1965:139): "A ghost [encountered in dreams] can help and harm his surviving near kin. He can protect them from danger, help them in war (by lending strength to a man's weapon arm), foster their fertility and that of his pigs. He can also inflict sickness upon them and kill them." Thus, happenstance is due to the fickle nature of the gods and various "other-than-human" beings that come to be known in dreams and visions.

People everywhere are quite empirical in a concrete way (Lohmann 2003b:5). If dreams are another domain of reality, then the information I derive from dreams may be real. And if the information is real, then causation involved in the information is real, even though the A that causes B may be at a distance with no mechanism between, or distant in time with no A bumping into B bumping into C, etc. The causation may be mythopoeic or symbolic – for instance, the bit of my flesh I offer the gods may "stand for" my whole being, or things done to a lock of my hair left carelessly on the ground after a haircut may happen to me (so-called "sympathetic magic").[2] If I fly to the island of the dead, I am able to fly because of mystical power. How is the spirit in my dream able to "see" into the future and foretell events? What kind of causation is involved? Truth is, most people are "people of action" and not philosophers (Radin 1927). They don't ask such questions. The information is there because the spirit or ancestor has mystical foresight. Those among my readers who believe in the efficacy of prayer have a perfect example of mystical causation. How else but through magic can "God know the desires of your heart" – or for that matter, your dreams – before you can voice them in prayer?

The concept of magic is thus fraught with all sorts of Western cultural baggage, a lot of it negative (see Greenwood 2009:Chap. 8). This fact tempts some anthropologists to avoid the term. As Stephen (1995:xii) mentions in her study of Mekeo religion, "Since a system of beliefs and rituals that can most easily be identified as magic forms the basis of Mekeo cosmology, it is 'magic' that is central to this study. At once our discussion is placed in danger of foundering against the reef of hoary and inappropriate connotations attached to the very idea of magic both in popular Western culture and within the specialized culture of anthropological and sociological discourse. Obviously my concern here is with the latter, but this removes few difficulties owing to the many negative associations the term *magic* carries – labels condescendingly applied to modes of thought deemed primitive, archaic, and childish."

Among the Lakalai people of New Britain, "Certain capabilities which are widely shared by spirit-beings are quite outside ordinary human potentialities. Many spirit forms [as experienced in dreams] can change their shape, make themselves invisible, move over great distances in a moment's time, fly through the air, enter the body of a living person, capture human souls, cause environmental upheavals and catastrophes, and survive bodily injuries, including dismemberment, which would kill a man. It is symptomatic of man's kinship with the spirit-beings that he can approach some of these feats through the independent action of living souls in sleep, the special powers conferred by magical procedures, or the presence or aid of a spirit" (Valentine 1965:167-168). There is no

---

[2] While I was doing fieldwork among the So of northeastern Uganda, I used to see mothers trim their children's hair and then carefully pick up every scrap of hair and burn it to keep those of ill will from using it against the mother or her child.

mechanical A bumping into B bumping into C here! Indeed, causation is "spooky" and magical. My intention, therefore, follows Stephen's, which is to use the concept of magic as developed by Evans-Pritchard and other anthropologists and leave it to you, my dear reader, to get with the program. Keep this magical causation in mind as we proceed to look at the role of dreaming in cultures of healing.

## Dreaming, Sickness and Healing

In an essay, "The Sorcerer and His Magic," Claude Lévi-Strauss (1963[1949]) tells the story of Quesalid, a reluctant shaman among the *Kwakiutl* of Vancouver Island, British Columbia. He took the story from the autobiography of the shaman published by Franz Boas (1930). The way the tale goes, Quesalid decided to learn how to shamanize because he was skeptical of the reality of shaman's power. He thought shamanic methods were based upon fraud. But, once he learned to heal people using the various theatrical methods of the trade, Quesalid discovered he was very good at it, and was considered by many to be a particularly powerful healer. During his apprenticeship, he learned among other things the skills of the "sucking doctor" – he placed a feather in his mouth and made his gums bleed and then spit out the bloody feather after apparently sucking the object causing the illness from his patients. He gradually came to realize that these tricks actually work. When he treated a sick youth, who had a dream in which Quesalid saved him by extracting something like a worm from his belly, the youth got better – "he believed strongly in his dream about me" wrote the shaman (Boas 1930:13).

The tale of Quesalid the shaman, as told by Lévi-Strauss, turns out to be part fact and part legend. Harry Whitehead (2000) has done a masterly job of deconstructing the myth of Quesalid and tracking down the real story behind Boas' account of the man, and the man's account of himself. It makes engrossing reading. As it turns out, Quesalid was a man named George Hunt who was Boas' main informant and often his co-author on matters having to do with the Kwakiutl, and the details of his life are far more complex than the legend. But all of that, fascinating as it is, is beside the point for our purposes. What it does reveal is what I like to call, "Boas' Puzzle" – namely that shamanistic healing practices all over the world are often based upon crude trickery and theatrical performance, and Boas really never came to grips with the fact that dramaturgy and "hocus-pocus" can actually work to heal. Boas (1966:121) himself notes, "...it is perfectly well known by all concerned that a great part of shamanistic procedure is based on fraud." To be fair, Boas was mulling over this apparent contradiction long before modern research into the "placebo effect" got under way (Moerman 2002a, 2002b; see Benedetti 2008 for the history of research on the topic).

## Symbolic Healing

Boas' Puzzle became a central theme in the development of theories of *symbolic healing* (Moerman 1979; Dow 1986a, 1986b). To see how this kind of healing works, and the role played by dreaming and symbolism in healing, let us look at healing from a broader perspective. *Healing* (from the same Old English root as whole, hale, health, holistic, etc.) means to make whole or sound, to be uninjured, to patch up, and so forth. Healing is a natural faculty of biological systems that have evolved to return their organism to a state of healthy equilibrium. With respect to advanced organisms, this is in part the function of their immune system.

When I used to teach courses in medical anthropology, I would begin with what I called a "stair step model" of healing (see Moerman 2002b for a similar view). Let us assume that when someone living in a traditional society gets sick, roughly 70% of them will get better if they do nothing about it at all – they just carry on with normal everyday activities. But if the sick person takes off work and rests, it will increase the likelihood they will get better, and better faster, because there are more metabolic resources available for the healing. Now, if in addition, they receive TLC from their family – given special foods, kept warm, hydrated and happy, and not allowed to do things for themselves – then the likelihood they will get better increases even more. In addition, let us suppose that in the community there is an acclaimed diagnostician who is called upon to remove the uncertainty about what is wrong with the patient. This again increases healing because people's anxieties are assuaged. Finally, let us also suppose that the diagnostician is also a knowledgeable herbalist and prescribes some appropriate medicines, then the likelihood of recovery gets still better.

So, the process of getting well within the traditional culture of healing involves these steps: rest, TLC, diagnosis and medicine. If this is all the society's culture of healing requires when someone gets sick, then one can see how the healing process may be augmented by the culture of healing, and all of this makes perfect sense to us from a biological and medical point of view. But the typical traditional culture of healing doesn't stop there. In a majority of societies, there is an additional step that completes the culture of healing, that being the addition of elements of symbolic healing. Medical anthropologist, James Dow (1986:56) has suggested that symbolic healing involves the following universal properties (repeated here in my own words):

- The experiences of both healers and healed become generalized through their integration with the mythopoeic symbolism of the culture's mythology – healing becomes not merely somatic, but sacred.
- A sick person seeks a healer who can diagnose the sickness within the group's cycle of meaning – diagnosis is in terms of the sacred stories.
- The healer links the patient's emotions to "transactional symbols" (mythological symbols associated with sickness and the healing process) drawn from the society's cycle of meaning.
- The healer manipulates the transactional symbols to readjust the patient's emotions and other inner states.

Harking back to our discussion in Chapter 4 of how "transactional" symbols work like a child's magnet, the manipulation of symbols in the experience of a patient may operate to transform not only the patient's mood and mental state, but also engage the neural and endocrine systems, and the various organs and processes of the immune system, which in turn may affect other somatic tissues. Research has shown that guided imagery (guided visualization) may be used effectively in the treatment of disease. The effects are not due merely to a general placebo effect, but can actually direct the immune system to act upon the site of disease and injury (see Trakhtenberg 2008 for a review of the science). It is clear that the use of imagery (through theatrical methods, suggestion or otherwise) has been part of the shaman's healing methods from time immemorial.

Dreams may indicate what is happening, for instance, in a pregnant woman's body, including the fact of pregnancy before confirmation by a test and the expression of the gender of the fetus among women who have chosen not to know the gender (Krippner, Bogzaran and de Carvalho 2002:Chap. 6). Moreover, the imagery in dreams may reflect somatic diseases (ibid:Chap. 7). Oliver Sacks (1996) wrote a paper in which he showed that dreams may presage actual physical illness before other symptoms of disease appear (see also Haskell 1985; Hollan 2004, Robert Smith 1990 for other references and discussions). He called these *neurological dreams*, and discussed patients having them who were afflicted with various maladies, including blindness, occipital angioma, seizures, sensory neuronopathy, Parkinson's and Tourette's syndromes.

A.P. Elkin (1891-1979) described the use of autosuggestion and imagery in healing rituals among Aboriginal shamans (Elkin 1994[1944]:41-43). Sick people will often have a notion of what has caused their condition – perhaps because of sorcery. They may have a dream that confirms this to them. They call for the shaman and if the healer recognizes that the patient is beyond help, he will tell the patient this and then use suggestion to ease his passing. Elkin notes that, "The patient, for his part, is in a condition of receptivity, of high suggestibility, and is ready to realize the idea suggested by the doctor's actions, by the objects he exhibits, and by his attitude of authority and certainty: the idea, namely, that the immediate cause of the illness has been removed, and that therefore he can recover. If, however, the doctor assures him and his people that he (the doctor) cannot extract the cause, or cannot bring back the wandering soul, then the patient likewise accepts the suggestion – the suggestion of death" (ibid:41).

If the shaman decides the patient is likely to survive, he will become very "vigorous" in his healing actions. The patient will be propped up and the shaman will gaze at him for a while, then move off some distance and, "…looking fiercely at him, bends slightly forward and repeatedly jerks his arm outward at full length, with the hand outstretched, to project magical stones into the patient's body. Then, going rapidly and with characteristic high knee action from one end of the cleared space to the other, he repeats the movements with dramatic action. Finally, he comes to the patient and by much mysterious searching finds the magical material cause of the illness, sucks it out, and displays it to all around" (ibid:43). What is happening here is classic "theater of mind" healing (Laughlin, McManus and d'Aquili 1990: 213-214). The crucial play is being enacted *within the patient's sensorium*, just as it is in a modern magician's show. Images are being manipulated within the "highly suggestible" sensory system of the patient and presumably the patient's neuro-endocrine and immune systems become engaged. That, plus the inevitable placebo effect, may account for any enhanced healing that might be the result of the shaman's performance.

When the process is reversed – that is, when a specific sickness produces specific dream imagery, the symbolic process may be used to diagnose illness by the shaman. Dreaming is involved in the Aboriginal shamanic principle in two ways. As we saw in Chapter 7, the shaman's calling involves dreaming. The diagnosis of the causes of sickness also involves dreaming, a very common practice cross-culturally. As Kuper (1979; see also Kilborne 1981:166) suggested, dreaming may operate as a medium of communication between the ego and the greater being, including between the dreamer and his or her own organs. Douglas Hollan (2004:177) underscores this kind of self-reflection when he writes: "Cultures that focus attention on dreams, categorize them, and label them, especially those that identify some types of dreams as prophetic, recognize that some dreams can be related, either directly or indirectly, to the fate and well being of the dreamer. For example, in Toraja [Papua New guinea], what I am calling selfscape dreams (and what the Toraja refer to as *tindo*) may motivate a person to initiate or terminate some type of behavior that significantly alters how he or she experiences the world or parts of him- or herself, such as making amends to family, neighbors, or ancestral spirits" (see Chapter 11 on "selfscape dreams").

## Dreams and Healing Cross-Culturally

The role of dreaming in causing, divining, diagnosing and healing sickness is widespread among the world's cultures. Always keeping in mind that in most cultures dreaming is considered to be another domain of reality, it is small wonder that events in dreams may operate in a "spooky" and magical way to produce sickness in our "waking" mind and body, and vice versa. Moreover, because of the special relationship that often obtains between the dreamer and ancestors and spirits, it is also no wonder that dream events may augur sickness, the options for avoiding sickness and the proper treatment of sickness.

> Conditions of illness or emotional stress are most frequently attributed, in the dream ethnography, to the actions of the sacred beings, either as a consequence of the infringement of social or religious prohibitions or as a directing of negative or harmful power through sorcery or other shamanic practices. Alternatively, an illness might be a sign of a particular psychic or shamanistic ability. Conditions of stress or emotional disturbance might evoke the pity of the dream-spirits to give aid, particularly if the individual addresses them in a humble manner. In every case, the state of being ill is commonly attributed to the mysterious actions of the many beings that pervade the lived world. (Irwin 1994:89)

When James Dow did his fieldwork among the Otomi Indians of Central Mexico, he decided to work intensively with one well known and respected healer, Don Antonio (Dow 1986b). He thus produced one of the most detailed and intriguing descriptions of healing shamanism in the literature. Accessing power and techniques to heal through his dream life was central to Don Antonio's career:

> When I became a shaman, I began to see how to cast out illness in my dreams. It was like looking at a printed page. The shaman receives knowledge, what sorts of illness one person has, what sort another has, in his dreams. This knowledge comes from God. Fortunately, God gave me this gift. ...Learning how to cure from dreams is like being taught to read as a child. You ask your teacher, "What is this or that called?" and your teacher tells you. You ask about the meaning of things and you receive answers as a child might receive answers about the meaning of a word. In this way you receive knowledge about illnesses. These things are revealed to you alone in your dreams. Make a promise well and righteously to the sacred Virgin, and she'll

tell you what you want to know. ...As you're curing the patient, your dreams tell you what the problem is and who the enemies are that have caused the illness. Your dreams tell you what is needed for the cure. If an air [an evil spirit] has attacked the patient, you'll be able to talk to it in your dreams, just as if it were a person. You have to deal with airs, because if an air is not paid, it'll not leave the patient alone. When it has been paid, it'll go. (ibid:51-52)

The Otomi distinguish two general types of illness, "good" and "bad" (ibid:53-54). Good illnesses are those that can be treated with medicines alone, and Don Antonio believes that modern physicians are best at curing those, although as a shaman he is adept at herbal medicines as well. Bad illnesses, on the other hand, are not cured with medicines, and so modern doctors cannot cure them. Bad illnesses are due to intentional magical harm done by people and spirits – attacks done by sorcery and airs. Don Antonio and his colleagues specialize in curing bad illnesses by diagnosing the being responsible and placating them in some way.

Shamans, dreaming and healing among the Navajo are quite dear to my heart (see Chapter 3 and Laughlin 2004b; see also Cooper 1984; McNeley 1981; Morgan 1932; Sandner 1991). Individuals may themselves realize that they have lost their *hózhó*, their "way of beauty," or have contracted a disease, and they may diagnose the cause and cure of their own illness for themselves.[3] Navajos pay a great deal of attention to dreams as omens of misfortune or disease, and will self-diagnose based upon symbolic elements in a dream (Sandner 1991:261-265). If they become aware of the cause of their malady, they may seek out an herbalist (*azee' neigeedii*, "one who digs medicines") for medical treatment, or a medicine man (*hataałi*, "singer") for a healing ceremony (Dadosky 1999).

There is a welter of ways one may become sick, including casual contact with non-Navajo people, proximity to lightning or whirlwind, contact with spiritually dangerous wild animals like bear, coyote, scorpion, snake, etc., inappropriate behavior at a ceremony, violating

---

[3] The best description I have ever read of this process is to be found in Tony Hillerman's novel, *The Blessing Way*.

a tabu (e.g., attending a ceremony while menstruating), and from proximity of the spirits of the dead. The greatly feared psychological disorder, known as the Moth Frenzy (*iicháa*; symptoms of nervousness and anxiety, convulsions, fits of rage and violence) is associated with incest. The most feared source of illness is from witchcraft. All of these sources of evil and destruction may result in diagnostically significant dreams, and something has to be done about their portent (Lincoln 1935:209). This spur to action even includes shamans – according to Morgan (1932:402):

> If a shaman during a ceremony dreams that his patient is going to die he must leave and another shaman must be called. A dream interpretation may sometimes either arise or be confirmed by observations of events in the external world. For example when a Navajo dreams that he is dead, he means that in his dream, he was in the next world with the spirits of the dead... . To be there and to come back is not necessarily a bad dream; but if the dead beckon to the dreamer or he shakes hands with the dead, it means that he is going to die.

Among the Maracopa Indians and other Yuman peoples of southern Arizona, virtually all sickness and healing involved dreaming. They recognized four causes of illness and death: (1) having bad dreams, (2) soul loss, (3) witchcraft and (4) old age and violence (Spier 1970[1933]:280). Nearly all illnesses were attributed to causes 1 and 2 – having bad dreams and ancestors stealing away the soul during dreaming. "The most common cause was bad dreaming: such disorders as bowel complaints, diarrhoea, colds, pains in the chest and side, were attributed to it. Loss of the soul was also common, but less so: this brought about fainting spells" (ibid:280). Healing, too, involved dreaming. The healing shaman was able to diagnose due to receiving a revelation in a dream. "During the course of the cure he was not possessed, nor did he so much as call on his familiar for aid. He blew, breathed, and sucked on the patient, and brushed with the hand, to allay the fever or pain and to draw the illness from him" (ibid:280).

Among the cultures of Oceania, it is quite common for a professional dream-healer to be consulted when someone falls ill. On the island of

Aurora in the New Hebrides, the friends of a sick person may send for a dreamer who is paid in tobacco to seek out the particular ghost causing the problem. The dreamer "...sleeps, and in his dream goes to the place where the sick man has been working; there he meets some one, like an old man it is likely, or small size, who really is a ghost, and he learns from him what is his name. The ghost tells him that the sick man as he was working has encroached upon his ground, the place he haunts as his own, and that to punish him he has taken away his soul and impounded it in a magic fence in the garden" (Codrington 2005 [1891]:208). The dreamer entreats the ghost to give back the sick person's soul, for the sick one meant no disrespect. The ghost removes the fence and frees the soul, and this hopefully heals the afflicted one. Likewise, healers among the Manus people of the Admiralty Islands use both dreams and possession trance to diagnose the causes of illness (Fortune 1969[1935]:36). In dreams the healer sends his soul wandering into the past to see what events might have led to the patient's travail. He returns and accuses the patient of some vaguely worded sin or another. This may hopefully result in a confession by the patient, and thus a cure for his malady. Nancy Munn (1990:6) tells us that among the people of Gawa Island, located near Papua New Guinea, dreaming is seen "as 'seeing' ... during sleep; seeing is the prototypical form of knowing... . Dreams in particular are regarded as crucial means of giving visibility to the invisible witch and witch activities..." that cause disease. Dreams of a sick person may be interpreted by a healer as indicating that the source of the illness is witchcraft, and perhaps as revealing the identity of the witch. Dream imagery and the actions of the sucking-doctor reveal the previously invisible causation between the evil intent of another and the somatic symptoms of sickness.

In her research among the Mekeo of Papua New Guinea, Michele Stephen recorded interviews with two *feuapi*, or dream-healers. The dream-healer sends her dream ego out into the spirit world and recovers lost or stolen souls. The dream-healer is one who is capable of intentional dreaming (see Chapter 5) and uses her skills on behalf of patients on a fee-for-hire basis. Her interview with Josephina, one of the two *feuapi*, gives us a very clear picture of what the dream-healer experiences (1995:198-199):

When people are sick, and when they bring money and riches and give them to us, we bespell them. When I bespell them, then I lie down to sleep that night, and I go in search of their dream-selves. I go to the *faifai* water spirits' place; I go down into the water. They make ladders that go down. Other people don't see them, they don't know. When I sleep... when it's night, I see them and I go there. I go down... and I go along until I see the house where the person has been put. I ask, "Has that one just come here?" "Yes, that person came and now is staying here," they reply. "Well, now give me that person, I want to take him away from here." But if the water spirits refuse, I do not take the person. He stays there and I come back. The next morning the relatives of the sick person come to me and I tell them, "His dream-self has gone and I saw it there. I saw it but I was not able to take it or bring it back. It is still there." Then they go and get money and bring it, saying, "Take this money and then bespell him." When they bring money to give me, I say the spells and that night I take the dream-self and I bring it back. Then I give it to the sick person saying, "Last night I went and took hold of your dream-self and brought it and put it down in your place, then I went home. Then I woke up." And the sick person replies, "Now all is well, now I have recovered."

This pattern of dream healing is not unique to Oceania. In her analysis of a Sudanese healing cult, Pamela Constantinides (1977) tells us that recruitment into the cult depends first and foremost on a person having an illness. The person will come to the cult leader with their physical or emotional complaint – perhaps accompanied by reports of disturbing dreams – and the leader will determine whether the complaint is caused by possession by a *zaar* spirit. Diagnosis may take one of two forms: "Either the patient herself may act as a medium for the spirits which express through her their demands, or the cult leader, after what are said to be spirit-inspired dreams, or meditation, will convey to the patient what the spirit requires to cease troubling her" (ibid:66). There will follow a ritual in which a negotiation with the *zaar* will occur and the patient is eventually released from the possession.

Death for the Mambila of Nigeria is caused by the ancestors (Rehfisch 1971:310). A person is offered a bit of cooked chicken in a dream, and may or may not accept it. If they do, they head off to the land of the dead. But a person who is the victim of witchcraft may have a compulsion to take the proffered chicken and is doomed. There are exceptions, and Farnum Rehfisch (ibid:308) describes one such case for us. A woman was bedridden with a serious illness. She was surrounded by people who tried to get her to confess to every sin she had ever committed, in order to placate the person bewitching her; all to no avail. Then she went on a dream journey after ancestors appeared to her and offered her a tasty piece of chicken:

> Having accepted the food, she died and was taken to the world of the shades. There she found a village very similar to the one that she had left. The Mambila believe that the shades live in villages much like those of the living. Farms surround the settlement as is the case here on earth. The sick woman, however, found some differences. The shades owned vast quantities of coloured cloth of European manufacture, a commodity which had only recently become desirable to the Mambila. There were many chickens seen, far more than would be found in a village of the living and they had one odd characteristic, namely that all were white. The houses were all in an excellent state of repair and the settlement looked extremely prosperous. She began to speak to some of the ancestors, who asked her about her life on earth. When she mentioned she had left two small children behind, one two years old and the other four, they became very angry. They scolded her very severely for abandoning her offspring and they said that it was a mistake to have let her die. The next thing she knew she awoke on her bed.

The woman was apparently healed, and her adventure in the land of the shades verified once again some of the pivotal beliefs within Mambila cosmology and dream culture – that the ancestors live in villages, are prosperous and trouble free, have unlimited wealth and lots and lots of white chickens.

One of the more bizarre healing cultures in which dreams play a role is among some of the Peruvian Arawak peoples of Amazonia who hold that sickness is caused by witchcraft. There is nothing unusual there, except in this case it may be one's own child that is the witch. We have already seen in Chapter 8 that witchcraft is normally associated with social and emotional conflict in society. Here it manifests in the belief that children are introduced to witchcraft in their dreams (Santos-Granero 2004:274-275):

> In their dreams, they are visited by any of a number of demonic teachers… who are under the orders of Korioshpiri, the "father" or "ruler" of all demons. These demonic teachers, which include birds (cuckoos, nocturnal swallows), insects (grasshoppers, crickets), and the souls of other live and dead human sorcerers, appear to the sleeping child under human guise… . The evil spirits of the dead… are also reported as possible teachers of witchcraft… . The visiting demons place animal or fish bones, palm-leaf slivers, or other small objects in the child's palm, and then knock them off so that they will get buried in the ground. Once buried, these objects cause somebody to fall ill.

The demon teachers continue visiting the child in their dreams and coax the child to try bewitching on their own. They are offered human flesh to eat, and eventually the child starts burying magic objects him or herself. Eventually the child ceases to be human and becomes a demon, unless diagnosed properly by a shaman and the evil sucked out of them. In some groups, "Bad-tempered, sulky children were primary targets for accusations of sorcery" (ibid:276). Shamans are called in when someone gets sick, and they will try various diagnoses and techniques to make the patient well. But if the illness fails to respond to early ministrations, the shamans will suspect human sorcery, which they confirm with the help of their familiars while dreaming. Once the child-sorcerer has been identified, he or she is forcibly brought to the patient's home and subjected to severe punishments – including rubbing hot peppers in their eyes, being hung over a smoking fire and being tied down on the smoking rack, forced to live in the attic over a smoking fire, taken out and beaten – to force the child to reveal where they secreted the magic objects, and to scare them so they forget about doing sorcery altogether (ibid:277-

278). "If the victim improves, the accused child is beaten, ritually cleansed, and released. If the victim dies, the child witch is invariably condemned to death..." (ibid:279).

This is not a unique situation, for divining future diseases can be a very serious business. Jon Christopher Crocker (1985) reports a chilling historical event among the Bororo of Brazil in which the failure to report a dream caused multiple killings. For the Bororo, dreams had during labor have enormous power to predict future afflictions and need to be reported to the shamans immediately (ibid:54):

> One of the most terrible episodes in Bororo history came from failure to obey this rule. Early in the century villages were being decimated by a smallpox epidemic. A shaman of the souls discovered in communicating with the *aroe* [souls] that this illness had been dreamed about by a father during his wife's labor, but he failed to tell the *i-maruga* ["name-giver"] anything about it. The only way to stop the terrible affliction, which was killing dozens of Bororo, was to kill the baby. But the difficulty was that the souls did not know which child was involved, only that it had been born between two and six years before the beginning of the epidemic. The Bororo of the region put to death every child born during this period (ibid:343, n.7).

## Summary and Segue

A society's religious system, whether or not they have a word for it, is that part of the people's cosmology that explains and controls matters of ultimate concern. More particularly, it includes that part of the cycle of meaning that integrates meaning and practice with direct experience in such a way that matters of ultimate concern are accounted for and, to whatever extent possible, controlled. Human beings have been dreaming as long as we have been a species. Furthermore, the existential fact of dreaming has surely been an ontological and epistemological problem for as long as we have been self-reflexive. We have no way of knowing just when dreaming became a metaphysical problem, but it is a fair bet that it has been throughout much of our Paleolithic past, perhaps since the time of *Homo habilis* over 2 million years ago. Dreaming has certainly been our oldest ASC, and all societies must have had to come to grips with events happening in dreams and their relation to events occurring in waking states. Once again, this is why virtually all polyphasic cultures are essentially animistic, for it is by way of dreams that the inner animating forces in things become revealed.

One may most commonly and dramatically find the exercise of control being played out in both the divining and adaptation to future contingencies, and in the diagnosis and treatment of disease. Many cultures recognize that there are some individuals that are better at divining, diagnosing and healing than others. This recognition may be personified in a single, very powerful individual that may more or less fit the criteria of the classic shaman. Or, different individuals may be recognized as specialists in different aspects of control. In any event, a people's religion will very likely manifest one or more aspects of the shamanic principle, regardless of the complexity of social integration, or type of subsistence, political structure and community structure. If the society holds an intact polyphasic culture, then certain aspects of the shamanic principle will always be present – most notably the use of dream material as information about the hidden forces behind apparent events, and the divination of future events.

Societies with polyphasic religions will have an enormous influence upon the neurocognitive development of a sense of self in its members. From the time of birth, and perhaps even before birth, an individual will be surrounded by cultural influences associating their innermost experiences with those of the community and with the cosmos. As they began their dream lives in the womb, and are encouraged to attend dreaming throughout their childhood, awareness of dreaming remains an integral part of their self-knowledge throughout life. Depending upon how they, or perhaps a shaman or other oneirocritic interprets their dreams, the course of their life, their social role and career, and even their health and longevity may be determined. It is thus high time we spend some effort in examining the role of dreaming for the development of the self.

# Chapter 10

# Archetypal Dreaming

> The dream is a little hidden door in the innermost and most secret recesses of the soul, opening into that cosmic night which was psyche long before there was any ego consciousness, and which will remain psyche no matter how far our ego-consciousness extends. For all ego-consciousness is isolated; because it separates and discriminates, it knows only particulars, and it sees only those that can be related to the ego. Its essence is limitation, even though it reaches to the farthest nebulae among the stars. All consciousness separates; but in dreams we put on the likeness of that more universal, truer, more eternal man dwelling in the darkness of primordial night. There he is still the whole, and the whole is in him, indistinguishable from nature and bare of all egohood. It is from these all-uniting depths that the dream arises, be it never so childish, grotesque, and immoral.
>
> C.G. Jung, "The Meaning of Psychology for Modern Man"

It has frequently been my experience when I speak to anthropological colleagues about the archetypes, archetypal structures, or the collective unconscious – all pivotal notions in Jungian dream theory – they often seem to have a very vague idea of what I am talking. There seems to be a phenomenological gap between talking about archetypes as a concept and realizing them in direct experience – for instance, recognizing archetypal elements in one's own dreams. The gap is akin to the difference between knowing that walking 20 minutes a day is good for you, and actually doing the walking and experiencing the difference. Compounding the problem, my colleagues are usually unaware of the technical aspects of Jung's thinking and application of the "archetype" concept to psychological issues like dreaming, visions, fantasies, mythology, etc. This is somewhat ironic (and frankly not a little embarrassing) considering the fact that Jung was totally engrossed in the ethnology of his day, and grounded many of his discussions on ethnographic findings (see e.g., Hunt-Meeks 1983). As the concept of the archetype is fundamental to the neuroanthropological account of dreaming I am building here, I feel I must spend some effort at least in developing Jung's thinking in relation to my own, before we pass on to a more direct examination of archetypal dreaming across cultures. Those familiar with Jung and archetypes can skip the first part of the chapter and move on to the more ethnologically satisfying bits.

## C.G. Jung and the Archetypes

What does it mean to refer to "archetypes" and "archetypal structures?" My take on archetypes comes mainly from C.G. Jung's (1875-1961) own prolific writings on the subject, for it was he who developed the most complete account of the notion.[1] As many readers will know, Carl Jung was struck by the importance of universal patterns in the ideation of his patients, in myth and literature, and especially in his own dreams and fantasies (Stevens 1982; see also Van de Castle 1994: Chap. 7; Haule 2010). He first came to the idea of dream symbolism as reflections of primordial material in the unconscious during a trip he took with Freud in 1909 (Jung 1965 [1961]:158-161), and he parted company with Freud largely because of his teacher's inability to drop his positivist/materialist conditioning when dealing with material from the unconscious (1970 [1955/56]:473; Dourley 1984:38; Hobson 1988 *passim*) and to transcend his involvement with the subjective aspects of dreams and other symbolic products of unconscious processes (1956 [1912]:xxiii-xxvi) – an issue we have already discussed in Chapter 3. For Jung, dream symbolism was transparently meaningful and

---

[1] Jung did not invent the idea of deep structure by any means, but rather inherited the idea from Goethe who developed the notion of "ur-phenomenon" (Ger: *Urphänomen*), as well as from the writings of Hegel and Bastian.

understanding dreams does not require a false distinction between manifest and latent content. Of relevance to the anthropology of dreaming is his view that dreams are as vivid, complex and interesting as the waking world – a view he held in common with peoples from polyphasic cultures (Cahen 1966; Marjasch 1966).

He argued that human and animal experience is produced by the development of instinctive structures that are archaic, transpersonal, and even transcultural (Jung 1956 [1912]:3-6; see also Edinger 1972, Neumann 1969:270). He borrowed his earliest term for these structures, "imago," from Freud, and transformed its meaning from that of a constellation of images, ideas and emotions formed in early childhood to that of an independent constellation of primordial material inherited from the distant evolutionary past (ibid:44n). He later termed these structures the *archetypes* (1968b [1936/37]:43), and the total collection of these structures the *collective unconscious* (Jung 1968b [1934]:3-4):

> [The] personal unconscious rests upon a deeper layer, which does not derive from personal experience and is not a personal acquisition but is inborn. This deeper layer I call the collective unconscious. I have chosen the term "collective" because this part of the unconscious is not individual but universal; in contrast to the personal psyche, it has contents and modes of behavior that are more or less the same everywhere and in all individuals. It is, in other words, identical in all men and thus constitutes a common psychic substrate of a suprapersonal nature which is present in every one of us.

Jung's conception of the archetypes underwent alteration over the course of the half century between the time of his trip with Freud in 1909 and his death in 1961. It is thus a mistake to take his definition of the archetypes from any one era as definitive. Rather, it is far more illuminating to track the development of his ideas as his own psychological and spiritual understanding unfolded, primarily through a phenomenological exploration of his dreams and visions. Yet certain attributes remained fairly consistent throughout his writings. For Jung, the archetypes are the result of the evolution of the structure of the human psyche. Over and over again Jung emphasized that the archetypes are part of human inheritance – right up there with livers and lungs. They are extraordinarily stable and enduring structures (Jung 1970 [1955/56]:463) that form the fundamental organization of the psyche, that arise anew in every human incarnation, and that are akin to the instincts.

The archetypes themselves undoubtedly have changed during our evolutionary past — there is really no way to know for sure (1953 [1943/45]:368) — but in their present form they encode the recurrent structures that have mediated the typical experiences of human beings over hundreds of millennia and across all cultural boundaries (1970 [1955/56]:390; Stevens 1982:17; Krippner, Bogzaran and Percia de Carvalho 2002:149). In some instances, they encode recurrent experiential material from our pre-hominin primate past (1953 [1943/45]:96). Archetypal structures underlie all recurrent, "typical" (pan-humanly typical, not culturally or personally typical) ideas, images, categories, situations, and events that arise in experience (Hillman 1985:12; Stevens 1982:23). They contain no inherent content, but exist "at first only as forms without content, representing merely the possibility of a certain type of perception and action" (Jung 968c [1936/37]:48). Archetypes may manifest as "a priori, inborn forms of 'intuition'" (1969d [1919]:133). As the instincts impel us to act in a distinctly human way, so do the archetypes impel us to perceive and understand the events to which we instinctively respond in a distinctly human way (1970 [1955/56]:87). For Jung instinct and archetype are two sides of the same unconscious functional coin (1969d [1919]:136-137):

> Just as we have been compelled to postulate the concept of an instinct determining or regulating our conscious actions, so, in order to account for the uniformity and regularity of our perceptions, we must have recourse to the correlated concept of a factor determining the mode of apprehension. It is this factor which I call the archetype or primordial image. The primordial image might suitably be described as the instinct's perception of itself, or as the self-portrait of the instinct, in exactly the same way as consciousness is an inward perception of the objective life-process. Just as conscious apprehension gives our actions

form and direction, so unconscious apprehension through the archetype determines the form and direction of instinct.

Thus the archetypes may be characterized as being instinctual, a priori "meaning" and the collective unconscious as containing both the instincts and the archetypes (1969d [1919]:133-134).

The ubiquitous activity of the archetypes in the functioning of the psyche is an important factor in understanding Jung's conception of the evolution of consciousness and the unconscious, for most discussions of the archetypes, including his own at times, tend to emphasize a handful of relatively "big," dramatic forms; e.g., the Wise Old Man, the Great Mother, "internal" marriage, the anima and animus, the Mandala, the Divine Child, the hero, the Kore or Divine Maiden, the Trickster (humorous figures like Mullah Nasruddin in Sufi stories, or Coyote in Navajo stories), and sundry spiritual journeys and initiations, etc. These few forms are those that are particularly salient in important dreams and myths, whereas most archetypes mediate the "little," very mundane functioning of perception, cognition and activity in everyday psychological life. "Little" archetypes such as the object, the face, the hand, water, air, etc., may rise to the level of "big" archetype if used metaphorically in myth (e.g., the air element, the face of god) or practice (e.g., baptism in flowing water).

## Archetypes and Their Transforms

Jung made a point of emphasizing that we cannot apprehend the archetypal structures directly. All that we can know are the manifest archetypal images and ideas that arise in the symbolism of our own experience, or that we deduce from the ideas and images found in texts and other symbolic forms (1968d [1936]:56-57, 1969a [1946]:213). Moreover, the archetypes are not material that was once conscious and somehow got lost either in early childhood, or in some archaic hominin age. Rather, the archetypes have never been conscious during the course of either ontogenesis or phylogenesis (1968c [1936/37]:42, 1969a [1946]:210). Unconscious archetypal structures lie behind and generate the symbolism that is so fundamental to all mythological and cosmological systems, and are responsible for the patterned similarities among these systems (1969a [1946]:206, Edinger 1973:4). The archetypes produce such distinctive and universal motifs as the incest taboo, the unity of opposites, the King, the Goddess, the Hero, shape-shifting spirits and so on. It is clear in Jung's treatment that actual engagement with the archetypes is a dynamic and developmental process, involving both the assimilation of archetypal contents into consciousness and, as a consequence, the transformation and development of the archetypes themselves (1968b [1934]:5).

Jung's experience was that the attributes of the archetypes are known through reflection upon their various transformations — upon their manifestations in dreams, fantasies, projections onto the world, myths, art, etc. — a methodology not unfamiliar to students of other schools that attempt to define structure, such as those of Claude Lévi-Strauss and Jean Piaget. For example, as Jung points out, "We must, however, constantly bear in mind that what we mean by 'archetype' is in itself irrepresentable, but has effects which make visualizations of it possible, namely, the archetypal images and ideas" (1969a [1946]:214), and again, "Man knows no more than his consciousness, and he knows himself only so far as this extends. Beyond that lies the unconscious sphere with no assignable limits, and it too belongs to the phenomenon Man" (1970 [1955/1956]:368), and yet again, "The archetype as such is a psychoid [deep structural] factor that belongs, as it were, to the invisible, ultraviolet end of the psychic spectrum. It does not appear, in itself, to be capable of reaching consciousness. I venture this hypothesis because everything archetypal which is perceived by consciousness seems to represent a set of variations on a ground theme" (1969a [1946]:213; see also 1969a [1946]:231, 1968 [1944]:218). In addition, we never come to the end either of the transformations of which any archetype is capable, or of our knowledge or explication of any archetype (1968e [1940]:160).

An archetype may present in dreams, visions, fantasies and other ASC and shift its eidetic form within the experience of the individual, among individuals in a group, and across cultures. A lovely example was used by Krippner, Bogzaran and Percia de Carvalho (2002:150) involving the archetype of "internal" marriage. According to Jung, to reach spiritual maturity in the self, the male and female parts of ourselves must unite into a single conscious melding of opposites. But when the marriage archetype arises in dreams cross-culturally, how it is represented is influenced by the type of marriage customarily practiced in each culture, whether that be monogamous, polygamous, polyandrous, or even group marriage. Marriage patterns range enormously among the societies of the world, and most of these are quite alien to Western ways of doing things (see Parkin and Stone 2004). To take an extreme example, Gough (1961) described a curious form of marriage among some matrilineal Nayar of India in which the bride and groom "marry" before puberty, rarely sleeping and never living together, the woman having the sole responsibility to eventually bury her "husband." Now, one would not expect "internal" marriage imagery in Nayar dreams to be the same as, for example, Western monogamous, or African polygynous dreamers. So too will all archetypes express themselves via local imagery. Dreaming of the water archetype for a Kalihari Bushmen would be different in form than dreaming of water among people living on a South Pacific atoll.

Why is this distinction between the archetypes and their personal, collective and cross-cultural manifestations so important that it needs to be emphasized? For the very simple reasons that some authorities (1) do not understand this distinction, (2) conflate archetypal structure with archetypal symbol, and (3) equate the variation of manifest content mediated by archetypes with non-existence of universal archetypes. A good example is the extent to which Kelly Bulkeley (1994:Chap. 15) goes to acknowledge the depth psychology of profound spiritual symbolism in dreams, while in the same breath rejecting the universality implied in the notion of archetype. Bulkeley calls these symbols *root metaphors*: "Dreams do have a dimension of religious meaning; this dimension emerges out of the root metaphors in dreams. To understand fully the root metaphors of dreams requires an interdisciplinary integration of the different fields of dream study with a theory of interpretation and a theory of religious metaphor" (ibid:134). Notice that while calling for an interdisciplinary approach, he nowhere adds the biological or neuroscientific fields to the team. Reading between the lines in his description of Jung's approach to dreams (ibid: Chap. 5), I suspect he neither grounds his thinking in embodied processes, nor does he understand the crucial distinction between structure and transformation – a failing of many students who have mangled the two when struggling with the works of structuralists like Jung, Piaget and Lévi-Strauss.

In this regard, it is also critical to understand that Jung's whole approach was *essentially phenomenological* (see Chapter 6; see also Dourley 1984:39, 1993:16; Brooke 1999). The archetypes are not merely theoretical deductive concepts, but are derivable from introspection of patterns in one's own direct experience (1968d [1936]:56). We know the archetypes, not by merely thinking about them, but by experiencing their myriad transformations in the arena of our own dreams and other ASC, and then reflecting on the patterns (1968b [1934]:30). Indeed, there is no other way of coming to know the archetypes in any personally meaningful way.

What makes the activity of the archetypes distinctive in human affairs is the sense of profundity and numinosity (see Chapter 6) that commonly accompanies their emergence into consciousness (1969a [1946]:205, 1970 [1955/56]:390, 524). Their numinosity is derived from the fact that they store up and are conduits for affective and libidinous energies from lower levels of the psyche (1956 [1912]:232) – from the "core consciousness" as described by Damasio (2010). So numinous and transpersonal may be the eruptions of archetypal manifestations that the experience of them may lead to fascination, conversion and faith (1956 [1912]:232), and even to states of possession and over-identification with the imagery (1968b [1934]:39, 1968a [1944]:36, Edinger 1972:7). At the very least such experiences are affectively gripping and tend to dominate one's attention for a time until an interpretation of them is assimilated into the conscious ego. We have encountered this numinosity cross-culturally in the distinction between culture pattern dreams and everyday normal dreams (see also Hunt 1989:128).

## Archetypes and Development

It is crucial to our understanding of dreaming and the development of the self – and incidentally of dreaming among babies and children — that the archetypes are not solely an adult phenomenon. They are present from the beginning of life and, indeed, are the only foundation of childhood psychic development (1954b [1928]:52, 1968e [1940]:160). Another way to say this is that the ego — "the complex factor to which all conscious contents are related" (1959 [1951]:3) — is the result of the archetypes coming to know themselves. As an archetype grows and develops, it takes on associations (again, like the child's magnet collects iron filings) and eventually takes on the role of a *complex* – a complex being an archetype plus all of its associations stored in memory. These complexes become autonomous and seek to develop memory associations, but are rarely associated with the ego – the ego being the regnant complex of waking life. It is the encounters with unconscious, autonomous complexes during dreams that are for Jung (1969h [1948]; Young 1994) the origins of the idea of spirits.

This is the *uroboros* motif that Erich Neumann (1969:10) placed at the center of the evolution and development of consciousness; the self-devouring archetypal ground of all experience. Although his views about child consciousness may be considered quaint by some readers in light of experimental findings in modern developmental psychology, Jung was aware that a child's experience is thoroughly archetypal: "The child's psyche, prior to the stage of ego-consciousness, is very far from being empty and devoid of content. Scarcely has speech developed when, in next to no time, consciousness is present; and this, with its momentary contents and its memories, exercises an intensive check upon the previous collective contents" (1954a [1931]:44).

Although he rarely concerned himself with the consciousness of children, Jung clearly had a developmental framework in mind when discussing the nature of the archetypes and their development into complexes — especially in his earlier formulations (see 1969b [1931]). It is the unfolding collective unconscious and its nascent archetypal structures that produces the highly mythological contents of children's dreams (1954a [1931]:45). Eventually this unfolding landscape of archetypal material participates in a developmental dialogue with the emerging conscious ego that becomes the *sine qua non* of the process of *individuation* (i.e., the life-long development and integration of the psyche; 1953 [1943/45]:172-173, Edinger 1973, Dourley 1984). "In this way the conscious rises out of the unconscious like an island newly risen from the sea" (1954b [1928]:52).

Neumann (1969) picked up on the developmental thread in Jung's thinking (Jung 1953 [1943/45]) and, with the latter's full approval (see Jung 1969c), constructed a thoroughly developmental account of the archetypal imagery in mythology. On the assumption that ontology recapitulates phylogeny, Neumann (1969:xvi) — in a somewhat Piagetian manner — examined the stages of development of consciousness as reflected in the world's various mythological systems for clues as to the stages in the evolution of consciousness. Neumann, like Jung before him, treated archetypes as at least analogous to physical organs (Jung 1968e [1940]:160-161, Neumann 1969:xvi), and spoke of them as such – which is not at all far-fetched if one considers archetypal structures as being systems of neural circuitry. The archetype is as much an organ to the psyche as the liver is to metabolism. And as organs, archetypes develop during the course of life.

Edward Edinger (1985:98-99) borrows the alchemical term "coagulation" (yet another organic metaphor) for the process by which archetypes become activated in childhood and subsequently distorted and limited in their functions due to the assimilation of their structure (or circuitry) by the developing ego. The archetypes express themselves in emerging consciousness as images and ideas, and these transformations are actively assimilated into the conscious ego in such a way as to produce negative feedback which constrains further transformations. The process by which the ego assimilates essentially transpersonal, pan-human material gradually lessens the mysterious and numinous qualities of pure archetypal eruptions. It is an active process of perception, much like that modeled by J. Gibson (1979).

Indeed, the process of assimilation may become so active that the ego over-identifies with and feels responsible for producing these materials. Those of us who have spent time in spiritual disciplines may recognize the common phenomenon of individuals who over-identify with and personalize essentially transpersonal experiences (see Neumann 1954:336-337 on "secondary personalization," and Edinger 1972:7-16 on "inflation" of the ego). For Jung, this over-identification of ego with transpersonal experience may also account for certain dynamics of psychosis.

## The Ontological Status of the Archetypes

As noted above, Jung appeared to be undecided in his own mind about the ontological status of the archetypes (see e.g., 1968d [1936]:58; see also Dourley 1993). This state of affairs has led to considerable controversy over the decades. But I believe that the ambiguity was necessitated by Jung's inability to scientifically reconcile his conviction that the archetypes are at once embodied structures that bear the imprint of the sublime; that is, the archetypes are both structures within the human body, and represent the domain of spirit. Jung's intention was clearly a unitary one, and yet his ontology seemed often to drift into dualism and ambiguity, and necessarily so because the neuropsychology of his day could not envision a non-dualistic conception of spirit and matter. Nonetheless, he did posit the existence of dream-producing strata in the nervous system and suggested a role for the sympathetic nervous system in the mediation of dreaming. He did this in an eerily prescient way, considering the psychophysiological research that began not long after he raised the issue in 1952 (Jung 1969i[1952]:510-511):

> Thus we are driven to the conclusion that a nervous substrate like the sympathetic system, which is absolutely different from the cerebrospinal system in point of origin and function, can evidently produce thoughts and perceptions just as easily as the latter. ...one must ask whether the normal state of unconsciousness in sleep, and the potentially conscious dreams it contains, can be regarded in the same light – whether, in other words, dreams are produced not so much by the activity of the sleeping cortex, as by the unsleeping sympathetic system, and are therefore of a transcerebral nature.

Jung's dualism is further apparent in his distinction between the archetypes and the instincts which required for him a polarization of the psyche into those products derived from matter and those derived from spirit. He imagined the psyche as the intersection at the apex of two cones, one of spirit and the other of matter (1969a [1946]:215). One passage is worth quoting at length because it signifies by his use of the metaphor of the light spectrum the essential ontological dualism with which he was encumbered:

> Just as the "psychic infra-red," the biological instinctual psyche, gradually passes over into the physiology of the organism and thus merges with its chemical and physical conditions, so the "psychic ultra-violet," the archetypes, describes a field which exhibits none of the peculiarities of the physiological and yet, in the last analysis, can no longer be regarded as psychic, although it manifests itself psychically. But physiological processes behave in the same way, without on that account being declared psychic. Although there is no form of existence that is not mediated to us psychically and only psychically, it would hardly do to say that everything is merely psychic. We must apply this argument logically to the archetypes as well. Since their essential being is unconscious to us, and still they are experienced as spontaneous agencies, there is probably no alternative now but to describe their nature, in accordance with their chiefest effect, as "spirit,"... . If so, the position of the archetype would be located beyond the psychic sphere, analogous to the position of physiological instinct, which is immediately rooted in the stuff of the organism and, with its psychoid nature, forms the bridge to matter in general. In archetypal conceptions and instinctual perceptions, spirit and matter confront one another on the psychic plane. (1969a [1946]:215-216)

Jung certainly did not intend to produce a dualism between psyche and the material world, for he held that these are but two aspects of the same reality – hence the spectrum metaphor, rather than exclusive categories. Indeed, he would make statements denying that archetypes were anything other than our experience of the instincts; e.g., "There is, therefore, no justification for visualizing the archetype as anything other than the image of instinct in man" (1959 [1951]). Yet he fervently wished to avoid the two snares of physiological reductionism, which was on the rise in psychology with the writings of Wundt and other behaviorists, and materialism, which had been on the increase in scientific thinking since the 19th century. He felt strongly that Freudian psychoanalysis had become mired in this kind of self-limiting and anti-empirical thinking – a conclusion with which I heartily agree.

By now my own bias should be clear enough to the reader. The archetypes are either inherent systems of neural circuitry, or they do not exist (see Chapter 4) – as Jung himself wrote, they had been "stamped on the human brain for aeons" (1953 [1943/45]:68-69; see also Stevens1982). Lodging the archetypes in the brain does not mean that there are no spiritual contents or experiences involving the archetypes, or that there is no sublime dimension to reality. Quite the contrary, as we shall see in Chapter 12, we are forced by the evidence to consider transpersonal, parapsychological, "spookily" causal, divine and other spiritual elements in dream experience. This is why I introduced in Chapter 4 the possibility of quantum interactions between neural systems – including archetypal neural systems – and the quantum universe. The archetypes are species-typical structures made up of living cells that may well communicate with each other and with the universe at the level of quantum interactions.

## Encountering Archetypes in Dreams

Carl Jung was extremely interested in dreaming as a phenomenological window into the unconscious (see Jung 1965 [1961], 1968b [1934, revised 1954]; 1969e [1948], 1969g [1948], 1974, also Moorcroft 2003:174-178, Hunt 1989: Chap. 10). For Jung, the ordinary (for Westerners) everyday dream is "a fragment of involuntary psychic activity, just conscious enough to be reproducible in the waking state" (Jung 1974:68).[2] Yet, "[d]reams are neither deliberate nor arbitrary fabrications; they are natural phenomena which are nothing other than what they pretend to be. They do not deceive, they do not lie, they do not distort or disguise, but naively announce what they are and what they mean. They are irritating and misleading only because we do not understand them. They employ no artifices in order to conceal something, but inform us of their content as plainly as possible in their own way. ...they are invariably seeking to express something that the ego does not know and does not understand" (Jung 1954c[1924]:103). Dreams have their own logic, are often irrational – even surreal and bizarre – and often fragmented, full of puzzling and disturbing events and images. For this

---

[2] Jung is clearly not talking about lucid dreaming here.

reason, Jung says, most Westerners choose to ignore their dreams as "stupid, meaningless and worthless" (1974:69). However, dreams are, in fact, the expressions of the "dark recesses" of the unconscious, and if studied in the right way, may deliver valuable information about not only our unconscious personal self, but about the primordial, archetypal nature of our species. Jung did acknowledge that dreams may express repressed desires, but unlike Freud he considered there much more to dreaming than wish-fulfillment (Jung 1933:11):

> The view that dreams are merely imaginary fulfillment of suppressed wishes has long ago been superseded. It is certainly true that there are dreams which embody suppressed wishes and fears, but what is there which the dream cannot on occasion embody? Dreams may give expression to ineluctable truths, to philosophical pronouncements, illusions, wild fantasies, memories, plans, anticipations, irrational experiences, even telepathic visions; and heaven knows what besides. One thing we ought never to forget: almost the half of our lives is passed in a more or less unconscious state. The dream is specifically the utterance of the unconscious.

Harry T. Hunt and his associates (Hunt *et al.* 1982; see also Hunt 1989:Chap. 9) collected dream reports from undergraduates and examined them for various forms of content. They found that most dreamers have archetypal content from time to time that match the contents described by Jung for his own dreams. Where Jung's dreams differed from those of their subjects was in descriptions of mythological figures, where Jung's accounts are more like those had by the traditional peoples we have examined in this book. Hunt (1989:129) makes the important point that, "Like lucid and telepathic/problem-solving dreams, archetypal (and titanic) dreams are curiously resistant to free association. Free associations to [everyday] dreams usually branch out into background personal memories, but associations to these dreams tend to become more impersonal and to circle around the more striking details of the dream – conveying and heightening its 'sense of reality' in a way common to amplificatory methods." Experimental evidence suggests that the frequency and elaboration of archetypal material in dreams among

Westerners tend to increase with personal involvement in meditation and other spiritual practices (ibid:131; see also Faber, Saayman and Touyz 1978), a result that confirms my impression that such dreams occur more commonly among polyphasic peoples. As I will describe in Chapter 12, this has certainly been the case in my own experiences practicing Tibetan dream yoga.

Dreams are frequently out of phase with our own beliefs about ourselves, expressing as they often do the desires, urges, attitudes and proclivities of our entire being, not just those of our conscious ego. This is why they are so often experienced as highly charged emotional encounters. There comes a time in life, usually during and after our mid-lives, when the application of sustained, conscious engagement in the process of our own individuation will result in a fundamentally different kind of ego than the ego of people who remain unengaged in their psychic maturation. The role of dreaming in engagement with the unconscious is paramount, for it is through dreaming that the ego becomes directly informed by our essentially archetypal nature (Moorcroft 2003:175).

Like many of the traditional dream cultures we have examined already, Jung distinguished between everyday dreams that are produced from the "personal" unconscious, and the special dreams that arise from the deeper "collective" unconscious:

> The "big" or "meaningful" dreams come from this deeper level. They reveal their significance – quite apart from the subjective impression they make – by their plastic form, which often has a poetic force and beauty. Such dreams occur mostly during the critical phases of life, in early youth, puberty, at the onset of middle age (thirty-six to forty), and within sight of death. Their interpretation often involves considerable difficulties, because the material which the dreamer is able to contribute is too meagre. For these archetypal products are no longer concerned with personal experiences but with general ideas, whose chief significance lies in their intrinsic meaning and not in any personal experience and its associations. For example, a young man dreamed of a *great snake that guarded a golden bowl in an underground vault.* To be sure, he had once seen a huge snake in a zoo, but otherwise he could suggest

nothing that might have prompted such a dream, except perhaps the reminiscence of fairytales (Jung 1974:77, emphasis Jung's).

Jung was describing archetypal encounters had by monophasic Westerners – himself included to some extent — not polyphasic traditional peoples that may be more in touch with the archetypal dimensions of dreaming, and that have recourse to a culture of dreaming that supports integrative interpretations of "big" dreams for group members. Jung himself had to go in search of a dream culture that would help him make sense of what he was experiencing. He famously discovered such a dream-culture in the symbolism of latter-day alchemy (see 1959 [1951]; 2009:360; especially his 1970 [1955/56] volume, *Mysterium Coniunctionis*).[3]

What does an archetypal dream look like? I have already given several examples in previous chapters – dreams that fit the culture pattern category. In my own case I offered the Read Ezekiel dream (Chapter 6) which you may recall featured gigantic serpents that morphed into a fiery arch, a barren landscape, a fiery chariot and a mysterious, booming voice. It is pointless for me to try to understand that dream and its imagery by free association – that is, by free and uncensored association with events in everyday life (day residue), childhood experiences, etc., which is the *conditio sine qua non* of Freudian dream analysis. Rather, the imagery must be understood relative to either the mythopoeic material surrounding me in my culture — or failing that, in the mythology borrowed from other peoples and other times – or the meditative process of amplification Jung called *active imagination* (see Chapter 15; see also Jung 1968f:194, 1997; Price-Williams 1992:247; Mattoon 1978:149; Watkins 1976:42-50; Mageo 2001).[4] Serpents, arches, fire, golden light, booming voices

---

[3] It is a common experience for people who have done the kind of dream and "active imagination" work that Jung carried out (see Chapter 15) to find these books transparent, but those who only have an intellectual grasp of depth psychology find them virtually impenetrable.

[4] Jung wrote very little about the method of active imagination, for it is an advanced type of practice that one must experience to understand, but that can be dangerous if misused. It is a method by which, among other things, a mature meditator may gain control over the exploration of the unconscious directly in the waking state, thus relieving the burden of ego-unconscious self interaction upon the dream state (see Jung 1997; see also Chapter 15).

from spirit beings, these are all archetypal images that are universal to the collective unconscious of humans, and that accrue meaning for the ego (i.e., the conscious "me") through mythopoeic associations that expand outward endlessly in a developmental frame. I am still, all these years later, expanding my understanding of that dream – a process of adaptation that began with a close reading of the Book of Ezekiel itself.

That archetypal dreams exist is no longer in dispute (see Taylor 2009). Since Jung's time there have been numerous experimental studies demonstrating the archetypal loading of certain types of dreams. H.Y. Kluger (1975) carried out a statistical study of Jungian archetypes in manifest dream content. "Dreams were gathered from 218 subjects. In the effort to tap archetypal dream material three types of dreams were requested: childhood dreams, vivid dreams, and recent dreams. ... Childhood and so-called 'vivid' dreams were found to include significantly ...more archetypal dreams than those recent dreams. The results indicated that archetypal dreams do exist as a differentiable category of dreams and that archetypal phenomena may be discerned on the basis of the criteria set forth by Jung..." (Tiberia 1981:35). Cann and Donderi (1986) replicated Kluger's methods and tested hypotheses concerning the relations among personality types and the recall of archetypal dreams. Dream reports were collected from subjects in two stages: "...first, recall of the most recent, most vivid, and earliest remembered dreams (N = 146), and then dream recall on awakening, over an average of 23 nights, from 30 of the first-sample subjects. A total of 697 dreams was recorded. ...The dream diary recall data showed that Jungian intuitives, as measured via Myers-Briggs continuous scores, recalled more archetypal dreams; introverts, as measured via Myers-Briggs continuous scores, recalled more everyday dreams; high EPI neuroticism scorers recalled fewer archetypal dreams. The results support several propositions of Jungian personality theory."

## Archetypal Dreams Cross-Culturally

Jung was not the only student of dreams and culture that came to think in archetypal ways. As we have seen, there has existed an essentially archetypal strain in anthropology that dates back to Bastian's notion of *Elementargedanken* (see Chapter 2), which influenced Durkheim's thought in formulating his notion of *the categories of understanding* in his magnum opus, *The Elementary Forms of Religious Life* (1912 [1995]). Of central importance for Durkheim is the idea that the same social activity that provides the foundation for religion is further understood to be the generative source for the formation of a limited number of fundamental categories of understanding which serve to reflect our knowledge of reality (Throop and Laughlin 2002, 2007). Like Aristotle, Kant and Goethe, Durkheim holds that all people everywhere come to know the world filtered through the same fundamental categories of time, space, number, cause, class, person and totality. Unlike Aristotle and Kant, however, Durkheim argues that the origins of these categories are given directly in our experienced interaction with cultural, social and physical worlds. It should also be noted that Durkheim was familiar with Jung's early thinking, as were Durkheim's followers, Robert Hertz, Marcel Mauss and Claude Lévi-Strauss.[5]

In the previous pages, I have referenced many examples of archetypal dreams from other cultures, often labeling these as culture pattern dreams – the special dreams associated with instruction of the ego, numinosity and mythopoeic significance within the dream culture and cycle of meaning of a particular people. Newberg and D'Aquili (1994) have presented an excellent analysis of the universal aspects of the *near death experiences* (*NDE*) – that is, as neurophysiological circuits that are "prepared" to erupt into consciousness under the right conditions. "We hypothesize that in the complete NDE, two sequential archetypes are activated. The first we would call the archetype of Dissolution. In its full form, it is comprised of images of torture, hacking apart, burning and other horrifying conditions symbolic of the immanent death, fragmentation and dissolution of the corporeal self. This is followed by an activation of what we term the archetype of Transcendent Integration. It is this archetype which terminates the classic otherworld journeys in both the east and west and which comprises almost the entire experience of most contemporary NDEs" (ibid:6). The experience tends to be truncated and the positive NDE predominates in societies where there is a dominant expectation of an afterlife – e.g., in Christian societies. These archetypes may occur in various SOC in less dramatic and partial images, but "…it is only in their full presentation in dream

---

[5] See D'Aquili 1975 on the influence of Jung on the thinking of Lévi-Strauss.

consciousness or in the hyperlucid consciousness of mystical visions that their 'divine' or semi-divine qualities are fully manifest. It is in this sense that the archetype of Dissolution and the archetype of Transcendent Integration may be classified as mystical visions" (ibid:12).

In addition, let me add a few more examples from the ethnographic literature so we have a better flavor of encounters with archetypes and how polyphasic cultures tend to understand and use them. The Naskapi of Labrador say that the essence of a person, what they call *Mista'peo*, or the "Great Man," lives in people's hearts (Speck 1963[1935]:34-35):

> The Great Man reveals itself in dreams. Every individual has one, and in consequence has dreams. Those who respond to their dreams by giving them serious attention, by thinking about them, by trying to interpret their meaning in secret and testing out their truth, can cultivate deeper communication with the Great Man. He then favors such a person with more dreams, and these better in quality. The next obligation is for the individual to follow instructions given him in dreams, and to memorialize them in representations of art.

These representations are often geometrical patterns that show up in beadwork and other crafts done by native craftsmen. The Great Man is an example of what might be called the Teacher or Guru archetype. For the Naskapi, the appearance of the Great Man is consonant with their social structure in which elder males are considered to become wise and benevolent instructors. Both in the waking and dream life worlds, the ego of the individual grows by engagement with the archetype, and in the case of dreaming, the archetype facilitates and guides individuation.

The question of archetypal dreams and their relations with the mythology and cycle of meaning of peoples cries out for a holocultural treatment (see Chapter 2). But to my knowledge only one such study has ever been done. In a unique cross-cultural study of Jungian archetypal motifs, psychoanalyst Vincenza Tiberia (1981:73) used the data from roughly 300 societies available in the Human Relations Area Files to collect some 62 archetypal dreams from 43 different cultures spread over seven world areas. Using an analytical methodology developed from Mattoon (1978), Kluger (1975) and Hall and Van de Castle

(1966), she isolated the wide-spread cultural saliency of five archetypes: "the Archetypal Feminine" (e.g., The Great Mother), "the Self," "the Marriage," "the Ancestor Archetype," and "Losing Teeth." The first three archetypes were as described by Jung himself, while the last two were discovered in analyzing the cross-cultural data.[6] In order to share a flavor for this kind of dream as it is found across cultures, let me include a few examples of each of the five archetypal motifs isolated by Tiberia. All of these examples are taken from her dissertation:

**1. The Archetypal Feminine:** Referred to under different circumstances as the Great Mother or the Anima, the archetypal feminine may present as either light or dark, benevolent or sinister, the Divine Mother or the Terrible Mother, etc. (Neumann 1974). The transformations are endless, including radiant feminine figures, goddesses, succubuses, mother figures, nixies and sirens, etc. (see Laughlin 2001). Kohler (1941:20) records the dream of a Zulu man who encountered a naked, black woman who was suckling snakes from her many breasts located over her body, for him a positive experience. In contrast, Elwin (1991[1947]:483) reports this Devouring Mother dream from a Muria man from central India:

> A beautiful woman came to my children and said to them, "I am going to devour you, because your parents give me nothing to eat." The next day my children fell ill, and the Siraha [medium] declared that their sickness was due to Lagar Deo [chief goddess], who was angry that the customary offering to her three years after the first child had not been made, and she therefore wanted to kill all my children. So I dedicated two pigs to Lagar Deo to be allowed to wander freely and killed three years later. Once I had done this my children recovered.

And, Batchelor (1927:100) tells of a dream by an Ainu man who encountered "…an old woman wearing a seal-skin coat and smoking a long pipe," and sitting on the hearth. He then imagined he heard somebody calling him, and began to get out of bed, but the old woman shoved him back down. He believed the old woman had been in fact

---

[6] Robert Knox Dentan (1986:325) also isolated a number of content "uniformities" in dreams cross-culturally, including morbidity, feces for money and falling teeth.

the Goddess of Fire and that she had come to save his life (see Neumann 1974:285 on the Goddess of the Hearth motif).

Lincoln (1935:227) recorded a dream by a Navajo man who recalled this dream some 18 years after it had happened:

> I was in the mountains in a sort of cañon. On the top of the mountain there was a plane. I found an old arrow sticking in a bush. While looking at the arrow I saw something flying towards me from the south. It landed ten yards from me. I thought it was an eagle, but the eagle changed into a white lady who started walking up to me. She was wearing a white gown. In her left arm she was carrying something that looked like veils. She walked up close to me and every time she came close to me, I tried to protect the arrow. Then the lady spoke to me. When I was a boy, I used to have an eagle pet and the lady said to me, "I am the eagle you used to have." She said she wanted one turquoise bead with a hole in it. When I looked for my beads, they weren't there. I started for home to get it, but I woke up before I got there.

**2. The Marriage:** In Jungian psychology, The Marriage expresses the merger of the ego with one's cross-gender opposite – the male ego with the anima, the female ego with the animus. The state of mind expressed by marriage is one of love. Interestingly, during the interval I was working on this section of the chapter, I had a dream in which I was being married to an old friend, twenty years my senior, and we were seated around a huge table at a banquet celebrating the union. I was behind and to the right of my friend, embracing her with my left arm. I felt the blissful warmth of union. Then she moved off to my left and I noticed a bit of cloth over to my right. When I picked it up, I discovered it was a hand puppet that looked like her. I slipped it on my right hand and began mimicking her for the amusement of the assembled guests. Upon waking, I was aware that I was dreaming about The Marriage, and that my bride was an anima figure. I was interested in the fact of the hand puppet. For me, things on the left refer to right lobe processing and to the feminine, while things on the right refer to left lobe processing and the masculine (as for Jung himself; see 1967:341). I understood the import of the dream as a caution that anything I say or write can only be a simple representation and distortion of reality.

Curiously enough, Tiberia (1981:102) notes that in all the cases she found across cultures, the marriage motif in dreams was associated with death. This makes sense in Jungian terms; for, "the marriage, or the union of opposites, is a state in the individuation process which involves a kind of psychic death for the ego in that it must integrate new perspectives that have formerly been totally unconscious" (ibid:105). Peoples of the Rif in the Middle east, the Zulu in southern Africa, the Kol, Gond and Bhils people of India, Bulgarians, Samoans, and Yacatee Maya all associate dreams of marriage and marriage ceremonials as being associated with negative things happening, including death (ibid:102).

**3. The Self:** For Jung the Archetypal Self is that of totality and wholeness of the psyche. It is the expression of the entire psychic being, not merely the ego. Self images in dreams may be abstract symbols, such as mandalas, or figurative symbols such as heroes, gods, squared circle landscapes, etc. Our entire next chapter is given over to dreaming and the self, so I will not go into detail here, but will wait to present Tiberia's ethnographic data on the self where appropriate.

**4. The Ancestor:** Tiberia discovered two archetypes in the cross-cultural data that Jung himself had not covered. The Ancestor was one of them, and is surely one of the most common motifs in dream cultures on the planet, as we have seen in the dreams we have described earlier (ibid:106):

> A total of 22 dreams from 19 separate cultures in six world areas had as their central symbolism the figure of the "ancestor." Such dreams are always interpreted according to the particular features of the dream itself in one of two ways: either as signifying imminent death or as bringing a message from the visiting spirit. That is, sometimes the ancestor proffers helpful information, makes a request or merely visits, and in other cases the ancestor attempts to entice the dreamer or a member of his/her family into the realm of the dead.

Among the ancestor dreams examined by Tiberia are the following. A woman from the Aymara of Bolivia reported that, "Last night I dreamed of my husband, just as he was before [he died]. To dream of souls is not a good thing. Sometimes they come to advise us of some misfortune. Sometimes they come to take us away so that we, too, will die" (Tschopik 1951:215). Blackwood (1935:578) describes the dream of a Buka woman from the Solomon Islands who traveled to the land of the dead and who encountered her mother. This was considered to be a positive experience and she was glad to see her mother again. Blackwood notes that, "…one man said to dream of the dead means that the dead man wants to speak to you, another that it is a sign that the dead wish you to join them." Among the Zulu, "…the spirits often warn people in dreams against unsuspected enemies, or against coming dangers, but they may also cause them to be ill and die. …Dreams sent by the ancestral spirits can always be recognized, for they mostly come with a message from the dead" (Krige 1965:286).

Many ancestor dreams seem to issue what Tiberia (1981:110) labeled "a call of the dead." A Havasupai Indian man occasionally dreamed of his dead parents and friends, and did not enjoy the experience: "When I wake at dawn, I find I am not dead, I am still alive, and I want to sleep again, but peacefully. I say to the dead, 'I am not dead, I only saw you dead people. I am still alive. I want to sleep well so I can get up in the morning refreshed'. It is bad to dream of the dead; I do not want to dream of them; so go away" (Spier 1928:334). A Gros Ventre Indian man from Montana dreamed about his dead nephew who came to him and said, "You are not enjoying your life here. Where I came from is a good place." He replied that he had business to complete, and three days after the dream he became sick. He reflected that, "I thought a lot about the dream I have just told you. I nearly concluded that it might mean my time to die would come in the winter season. I am not afraid. I am resigned. If I live through next winter, I feel I will go past the crisis and live longer" (Cooper 1956:413).

**5. Losing Teeth:** The most curious archetype discovered in Tiberia's research is dreaming of losing, breaking, or illness of the teeth — a motif given only passing attention by Jung (1969e [1948]:283). What makes the motif doubly curious is that it, too, is related to death. In Iran, dreaming of "…a tooth which bleeds means the death of a member of the family; a tooth which does not bleed means the death of a friend; an incisor or a canine means the death of a close relative; a molar means the death of a distant relative; loss of all one's teeth means that death is near at hand for the dreamer himself" (Massé 1938:252). In a reversal of my own and Jung's left-right attributions, the Kogi people of Columbia consider the dream of losing a right tooth mean's the dreamer's father will die, and losing a left tooth one's mother will die (Reichel-Dolmatoff 1949-1950:288). The interesting question is why should the loss of teeth be associated with death? Tiberia (ibid:117) floats the idea, taken from the Chukchee culture (Bogoras 1904-1909:491), that teeth may be associated with the soul – "…losing of one's teeth is psychologically equivalent to losing the power to defend oneself against death." An additional case comes from the Muria people of India. Elwin (1991[1947]:483) reported that, "At Palmar, the Suel once dreamt that he was climbing up a huge stone. Suddenly he saw a *chaprasi* [messenger], he was frightened and tried to run away. He fell down and broke his teeth. When he awoke he found he had fever and only recovered after he had sacrificed a pig and made other offerings."

Thus, we see that archetypal dreaming is quite distinctive compared with more common, day-residue dreaming. They are essentially transpersonal (expand the domain of information available to the ego), often numinous, and frequently related through the people's culture of dreaming with their mythology and mythopoeic symbolism and ritual. In studying the archetype in action, it is crucial not to take a simplistic, essentialist stance, for the archetypes themselves – the neurognostic structures of the brain – are not observable. Only the imagery which is influenced by both the brain structures and the dreamer's culture are on display. They are each and every one of them transformations of the archetype as experienced directly in the dream, and the memory of the dream is often permanent and may have a profound impact upon the dreamer's life (Tiberia 1981:94).

## SUMMARY AND SEGUE

Not all dreams are about "day residue." Far from it in fact, for there are many dreams that seem to have little or no connection with what we did the day before or intend to do in the near future. They are the "big" dreams that bring us into contact with our deeper psyche, the domain of the archetypes – the neurognostic systems that have evolved to facilitate species-specific knowledge and action. More than any other scholar, C.G. Jung spent a lifetime studying archetypal psychology in both his own and his patients' dreams and other experiences, and in the mythologies, iconographies and art of other cultures. His approach has the strength of being grounded in the phenomenology of dream experiences, a grounding that only increased during his career, reflected in his writings from the early days of "Instinct and the Unconscious" in 1919 to the *Mysterium* in 1955. Although his work has had less influence upon anthropology than it should have done, he did take us away from the narrow confines of Freudian dream interpretation to a theoretical position which can handle the kind of impact that "big" dreams have upon polyphasic traditional societies.

A significant percentage of dreams had by traditional folks – and by dreamers here in the West for that matter – have little or nothing to do with "day residue" and everything to do with their spiritual and religious traditions. To the extent that people encounter the archetypes in their "big" dreams, it may be argued that they are experiencing a lot about their greater selves, whether or not they interpret their dreams in that way. In the next chapter we will look at dreaming and the self more closely, and see what difference it might make to the anthropology of dreaming if we take the Jungian archetypal view of culture pattern dreams.

# Chapter 11

# Dreaming and the Self

> ... while cultural and linguistic categories provide one important means by which the self is conceptualized and talked about and must surely influence the way the self is constructed... cultural models and conceptions of the self should not be conflated with the experiential self. Self-concepts may also be derived from one's own personal and social experience. Such individually constituted self-concepts may or may not be widely shared and they may or may not coincide with or reinforce self-concepts which are culturally constituted. Just as one cannot assume that cultural models of the self are merely projections of individual phenomenology, one cannot assume that an individual's experiential self can be reduced to the concepts and terms which are used to talk about it....
>
> Douglas Hollan (1992:287)

When we dream, we experience – can *only* experience – our self, and through our self, extramental reality, either through memory or perhaps through "spooky" communion via a quantum level *morphogenetic field* (Sheldrake 1981). This is as true for the Bororo, the Ongee or the Zulu dreamer as it is for us Westerners; for, all that arises or could ever possibly arise in our theater of mind are the operations of our brain's circuitry: in other words, no brain, therefore no self, no consciousness and no dream (LeDoux 2002:2-3). Thus, when contemporary anthropologists turn their focus toward the role of dreams in the development, construction, experience and knowledge of the self, they are beginning to get at the real ontological status of dreaming, and are on the verge of discovering how so many traditional peoples come to understand the self as a microcosm of existence (see Stephen 1995; Hallowell 1955).

The reader will recall that back in Chapter 3, I described in passing some of the more recent ruminations of anthropologists on the role played by culture and dreaming in the social construction of the self (e.g., Mageo 2003b, 2004, 2006; Hollan 2003b, 2004, 2009; Hiejnen 2010). I noted that, alas, most of these ethnologists fail to follow Murray Wax's seminal injunction that our explanation of dreaming and the self should be grounded first and foremost in the biology and neurobiology of sleep and dreams, and his suggestion that dreams have evolved over millions of years to "deal with the problematics of living and growing" (2004:86). As I read it, anthropology is presently in a muddle with regard to the self (see also Cohen 1994). The definitions of self vary widely and are frequently either fuzzy or limited to a single methodological objective, scope of inquiry, or ideology. Regrettably, many anthropological discussions of the self derive from constructivist ideologies and fail utterly in addressing the organ of the embodied self – the brain. Dombeck (1994:440) recognized this self-muddle and noted how scholars concerned with "personhood" tend to study the "referential aspects of humans," while those concerned with the self concentrate on "interactional, ontological, and reflexive aspects of human experience." In other words, the students of different perspectives on the self often talk past each other.

In order to proceed with an examination of dreaming and the self at a more productive level cross-culturally – that being the explication of the "selfscape" dream (Hollan 2003b, 2004) — we need to delineate what we mean by "self," and to model the concept in such a way that it can be applied ethnographically without leaving behind either the universal neurocognitive processes involved, or the individual-cultural variations of self-experience, self-concept, self-reference or self-presentation (e.g., as brilliantly done by Stephen's 1995 study of the Mekeo self).

There seem to be at least four distinct takes on the "self" used in anthropology, each with variations influenced by selective infusions from outside anthropology – the *phenomenological* approach, the *sociocultural* approach, the *experiential* approach, and the *universalist* or *archetypal* approach. Each of these approaches tends to center upon a discrete data set, and to ignore, exclude or reject alternative sets. Apropos to this book, each suggests a role that dreaming plays in instantiating the self in experience. Let us take each of these in turn and parse-out the meaning of "self" and thus try to untangle the mangle of self so that we can better understand the psychological and cultural nature of dreaming.

**Phenomenological Approach to Self:**

As I discussed back in Chapter 6, any approach to the experiences had cross-culturally is best grounded in phenomenology – that is, the study begins from the position of the phenomenological epoché. Michael Jackson has advocated just such an approach. In his introduction to an edited volume of essays covering both phenomenology and existential aspects of cultural life, Jackson hopes to go beyond the obfuscations generated in postmodernist and poststructuralist debates, and "return to the things themselves," as Edmund Husserl suggested – return to the domain of direct experiences had by people in different societies (Jackson 1996). Chief among his criticisms of non-phenomenological approaches is the confounding of concept and experience – the common practice of forcing native experiences into predigested concepts and distinctions. Unfortunately, few of the articles in that volume are actually phenomenological, but rather experiential (see below).

Fundamental to any Husserlian phenomenology of the self is the ability to realize the phenomenological epoché (Chapter 6). From this state of mind, one then is able to focus awareness on each experience of self as it arises, and determine to what extent it represents a permanent "me." Incidentally, when one does this work, one inevitably realizes that (1) the "watcher" is always distinct from the aspect of self being studied, which in the process has become an object of awareness, (2) the "watcher" itself cannot be reduced to an object, and (3) that every representation of self arising before awareness is impermanent. The full realization of the impermanence of the self in Husserl's system amounts to the "transcendental epoché," and in Buddhist *satipatthana* practice is sometimes referred to as "lesser sainthood." Once one has realized (not merely intellectually theorized) the impermanence of the "self" or any aspect of "self," one is then able to better describe the experiences of self without implying that it is either permanent or part of a permanent ego. As I have argued in Chapter 6, in an ideal world, if all ethnographers would become Husserlian phenomenologists first and fieldworkers second, a lot of the muddle about self would instantly disappear from the ethnographic record.

Suffice to say from the post-epoché standpoint, there is no such thing (self-concepts and cultural metaphors to the contrary) as a permanent self, regardless of the cultural theories of the people being studied (Laughlin 1989; Laughlin and Throop 2009). If this were not the case, then mature contemplatives from different cultural backgrounds could not achieve the same realization of impermanence – and they most emphatically do. The interesting ethnological question is to what extent a people realize the impermanence of the self, either through individual work or through their local theory of the self. Alas, mature phenomenological studies of self cross-culturally are still thin on the ground (but see Spiro 1993 for a very refreshing discussion about experience of the self among Theravada Buddhists in Burma).[1]

**Sociocultural Approach to Self:**

Grounded in George Herbert Mead's social psychology of the self, these studies tend to be constructivist in orientation; that is, self and emotion are considered the products of linguistic and cultural factors operating in the enculturation of the young in each specific society (Erchak 1992; Rosaldo 1984; see Throop 2000 for a comprehensive review). In Margot Lyon's (1995) view, derived from Geertzian interpretive anthropology (Geertz 1973), culture is conceived to be a "complex system of symbols, meanings, categories, models, or schema that structure experience and action" (Lyon 1995:244). Cultural models have a determinative effect upon emotion and the experience of self. Most, if not all constructivist accounts of the self ignore completely the biological and evolutionary aspects of "being in the world" (Csordas 1994b). Moreover, what some of these folks seem to mean by "self" is rather more like the Jungian

---

[1] It was my experience talking with fellow monks in Tibetan Buddhist monasteries in Nepal, as it was Spiro's, while living in a Theravada Buddhist monastery in Burma, that few if any monks "got it" with regard to the realization of *anatta*, the impermanence of the self, and found themselves in contradictory views, still experiencing themselves as seamless entities. The realization of *anatta* is essentially a transpersonal experience, and leaves one's understanding of one's self forever changed (see Throop 2000:42; Laughlin and Throop 1999).

notion of the "persona" which is in effect the public face of the psyche – that little-bitty part of the self that faces the outer world.

**Experiential Approach to Self:**

The experiential approach is grounded to some extent or another in the radical empiricism of William James (Throop 2000:31; see Chapter 6). The father of self anthropology was undoubtedly Irving Hallowell (1955) who wrote an all-important essay in which he tried to bridge between universalist and relativist notions of the self. Self-awareness – that is, one's experience of self as "an object in a world of objects" under specific sociocultural circumstances – is a universal (ibid:75). Everyone on the planet has a sense of themselves, and goes about distinguishing themself from other people and things in the environment. What is it in my experience of the world that is distinctly "me?" Yet, as Hallowell argues (ibid:75):

> Self-awareness in man cannot be taken as an isolated psychological phenomena, however, if we are to understand the full range and depth of its human significance. For it is becoming increasingly apparent that this particularly human phenomenon is the focus of complex, and functionally dependent, sets of linguistic and cultural variables that enter into the personal adjustment of human beings as members of particular societies. At the same time, it is necessary to assume self-awareness as one of the prerequisite psychological conditions for the functioning of any human social order, no matter what linguistic and cultural patterns prevail. If such be the case, the phenomena of self-awareness in our species is as integral a part of a human sociocultural mode of adaptation as it is of a distinctive human level of psychological structuralization.

Since Hallowell there have been innumerable studies of the experience of the self in different cultural contexts (see Throop 2000; Hollan 1992 for references; see also Cohen 1994). Douglas Hollan (ibid:287) reminds us that, just as we have had to keep dream-as-dreamt distinct from dream-as-text in our present analysis, so too do we have to distinguish between culturally loaded self-concepts and the individual's experience of themself, for the two may or may not precisely map onto each other (see epigraph above). Psychological anthropologist C. Jason Throop (2000), as a corrective to the excesses of the constructivist approach, has developed an experiential perspective on emotion and self that more facilitates Hallowell's balanced view. Reminding us that no experience is outside the purview of scientific scrutiny (*à la* James' radical empiricism), Throop points to the failings of the constructivist approach which cannot account for either the structure or the maturation of experience within any given sociocultural environment. Indicating the importance of the transpersonal dimensions of self (see Chapter 12), the experientialist approach he advocates (and which is close to my own) requires that sociocultural influences be, not determinative, but informative (see also Varela 1979 for a consonant view from neuroscience).

**Universalist-Archetypal Approach to Self:**

The universalist, or archetypal approach to the self holds that every normal person on the planet is endowed with a self that is striving for unity (Mageo 2003b:9). Jung's depth psychology of the self is the prime example of this approach, and he has had considerable influence upon some anthropologists (d'Aquili 1975). Another theorist that has had some influence on the anthropology of the self is Heinz Kohut (1971, 1977; Kohut and Wolf 1978; see also Ewing 1990:254; Gay 1983; various in Mageo 2002). Kohut (1913-1981), an Austrian-born American psychoanalyst, extended Freud's work on narcissism and developed the notion of an intrinsically autonomous, bounded self which strives to become unified in relation to empathetic caregivers during childhood, and social relations throughout life. The development of positive self-esteem is dependent upon relationships that mirror back to the developing psyche empathy, worth and caring. Ewing (1990:255), supporting as she does the constructivist position, considers Kohut's model of the self to be the "...least useful for anthropologists studying the self in other cultures."

For Jung the self consists of the entire scope of psychic phenomena. "The self is not only the centre, but also the whole circumference which embraces both conscious and unconscious; it is the center of this totality, just as the ego is the center of consciousness" (Jung 1968a [1944, revised 1958]: para 44). What is routinely misunderstood, however, is that the self never really reaches unity – the unity of self being more an ideal or goal than an actuality (1959 [1951]:31). What often thwarts the developments of true wholeness of the self is the psyche's tendency to project aspects of the unconscious out upon other people or other things – the teacher becomes a symbol of the godhead, the mandala archetype becomes a stained glass window in a temple. These projections are typically laden with emotion, either positive ("I wish I was like him/her!") or negative ("He/she disgusts me – I hate them!"), and have the effect of distorting the development of the complex being projected, and hence the drive to unify the self.

As the reader can see, the various foci of these approaches offer ample opportunity for "talking past each other." And talk past each other they most certainly do. As I made clear in Chapter 1, I will be applying the rule of minimal inclusion in examining the self cross-culturally, thus eliminating the possibility of this dysfunction. By including all levels of causation in our approach, "talking past each other" will not arise.

I have made my position rather clear in the last chapter with regard to dreaming *per se*. I would like to do the same here with the experience of the self. Again, I will use the writings of C.G. Jung as my springboard, for among all of the "fathers" of intellectual thought, Jung's phenomenological approach to the self is closest to realizing the more balanced views of Hallowell, Hollan and Throop in anthropology. From now on I will imply that *self* refers simultaneously to (1) the archetypal (neurognostic) foundations of an embodied self-awareness, (2) the direct experience of the self as distinct from other people and things, and (3) interpretations by the individual or the group of the embodied, self-experience of the individual as informed by what Low (1994) called "embodied metaphors", but which I prefer to call more pointedly, *innervated metaphors* available in one's sociocultural background and language (i.e., one's cultural information pool).[2] To my reading, Jung's account of the self comes closest of any authority to incorporating all these perspectives.

---

[2] The reader will recall that we defined culture in Chapter 2 as a "culture pool" – a pool of information to which members of a society have access.

## Archetypal Self

Engagement with archetypal material in dreams is a dialogue with the self – "self" being the central archetype in Jung's thinking, frequently expressed in dreams, rituals, art and iconography as "superordinate figures" and mandala-like forms (1959 [1951]:31).[3] "The self appears in dreams, myths, and fairytales in the figure of the 'superordinate personality,' such as a king, hero, prophet, savior, etc., or in the form of a totality symbol, such as the circle, square, *quadratura circuli*, cross, etc. (see Figure 11.1). When it represents a *complexio oppositorum* – a union of opposites — it can also appear as a united duality, for instance, in the form of *tao* as the interplay between *yang* and *yin*, or of the hostile brothers (*Mad Magazine's* "spy vs. spy"; see Figure 11.2), or of the hero and his adversary (arch-enemy, dragon), Faust and Mephistopheles, etc. Empirically, therefore, the self appears as a play of light and shadow, although conceived as a totality and unity in which the opposites are united" (Jung 1971:para 790; see also 1959 [1951]:Chap. 4; 1990).

As I have taken pains to point out, cultural anthropologists often fail to understand that the fundamental structures of the organ of culture – the brain – are archetypal in origin. They are made up of neurognostic circuits and systems of circuits, most of which are in place and functioning at birth or within the first six months or so after birth. As I have mentioned earlier (see Chapter 4), the brain is never at any time in its pre- and perinatal development a *tabula rasa* (Laughlin 1991; Laughlin, McManus and d'Aquili 1990:Chap. 9; Pinker 1997, 2003;

---

[3] The mandala as experienced in dreams may not be literally a picture-like image, but an organization of space and objects relative to awareness. For instance, one of the dreams I had while writing this chapter involved me waking up in the dream and seeking a place to urinate (all too common among dreamers of advancing age). I was sleeping in a kind of honey comb mish-mash of entangled sleepers, all of whom were feminine figures. I was looking to place a portable potty amongst us and I suggested to everybody that we could all use the facility – I did not mind if the potty was in my space. I was aware in the dream that my space was located in the middle of this entangled group of feminine images, which upon awakening from the dream I took to be my consciousness centered in mandala-fashion on the various opposing/complimentary and unconscious forces of my anima. The dream was perhaps an invitation to the various components of the unconscious to "let go" into my potty – i.e., to communicate.

Gazzaniga 2000:56; Rakic 1995; LeDoux 2002; Llinás 2001:Chap. 3; Damasio 2010). This is not the same thing as saying that either the self or consciousness is "hard-wired" in any artificial intelligence sense. Neural circuits are neither microchips, nor do they communicate via printed circuits. Genes direct the production and organization of proteins in the developing brain, and experience does indeed influence this process. After all, adaptation to reality is the prime function of the brain as a "regnant" process – a process at the top of a hierarchy of control systems in the body. Yet the role of experience varies with the specific function – experience has little to do with the function of grasping and everything to do with leaning to play a Bach fugue, and little to do with perceiving a world of objects and everything to do with appreciating a painting by Picasso.

While the majority of dreams had by people in any society will be "normal," everyday "little" dreams which are redolent with day residue and reflections of the dreamer's past, the special "big" archetypal dream is "a spontaneous self-portrayal, in symbolic form, of the actual situation in the unconscious" at the time of the dream (Jung, C.G., 1969g [1948]:263). In those societies that encourage engagement with archetypal dreams, there is a tendency for these materials to inform the development of the waking ego of the dreamer. Whereas "little" dreams are perhaps backwards looking toward unresolved conflicts in childhood or events occurring the day before, archetypal dreams among traditional polyphasic peoples tend to be interpreted as *progressive* – as intimately and systemically involved in the future development of the dreamer (Basso 1992). We have seen this role of dreaming in numerous societies where the dream-ego is experienced as one's soul wandering out into the spirit world and engaging with powerful "other-than-human-beings" that communicate information, warn of possible calamities, instruct the dream-ego, and influence the dreamer's future life course.

Such was the case for dreamers among the Kalapalo of Brazil, whom we met in Chapter 7 (ibid:88). The soul wanders and encounters powerful beings that bestow knowledge and power, and are from the Jungian standpoint the manifestation in Kalapalo terms of the Guru archetype (ibid:96):

> The Kalapalo theory of dreaming, the means of interpreting these transitive dreaming experiences, is one that makes explicit reference to the future of the dreamer. Just as their myths do, dreaming provides them with useful models for the formation of new roles and relations, or more simply, new and different feelings towards some problem. Kalapalo interpret their dreaming as a way the self *creates* a goal, rather than as a means of arriving at some satisfactory solution to a distressing problem or the conclusion of some goal.... Through dreaming, a Kalapalo dreamer experiences the self as an actively motivated, symbolically created entity.

Constructivist emphasis upon the sociocultural origins of the self thus miss the other half of self development – engagement with archetypal/neurognostic systems upon which the developing brain depends. In polyphasic cultures, there is an inevitable bivalent pressure upon the development of the self, with the ego mediating the tension between both sociocultural influences from outside and archetypal dream material from inside. As Krippner, Bogzaran and Percia de Carvalho (2002:150) note, "...certain people and activities achieve salience in the dreams of dreamers worldwide because all dreamers share a common humanity and a common physical body." This is simply the adaptational function of the brain in action – constructing a self that is able to adapt to the vicissitudes of inner and outer reality. Anthropologists that miss the archetypal involvement in the developing self will inevitably wander from the truth.

To my reading, Jung was at times as ambiguous about the self as he was about the archetypes. He often conflated the use of the term "self" when referring to variously (1) the organic *potential* for unity of the psyche, (2) the actual process of individuation guided by that unitary imperative, and (3) the archetypal imagery that represents the self in dreams and other ASC. Just as all organs of the body seek unity – or equilibration[4] to use Piaget's (1971) apt term – so too does the brain, both at the level of cellular circuits and models, and at more molar levels of complexes, functions and networks. The brain strives to operate as a unit in its adaptation to extramental reality, but that is a far cry from saying that it always succeeds in reaching functional unity. Many forces from the physical and sociocultural environment influence

---

[4] "Equilibration" is the dynamic form of the more static "equilibrium."

development, and often result in fragmentation of the psyche (i.e., the archetypes, neurognostic models, complexes, so forth).

Marcus and Kiayama (1991), in a classic postmodernist ethnological formulation, consider the notion of an autonomous self as being a Western projection upon traditional societies. They argue that the self is a construct of society's influences, and thus *ipso facto* there can be no underlying structure whose development is being influenced in the process of self development. In effect, the "self" is imposed upon a "blank slate" psyche, and therefore it makes no sense whatever to speak of universal properties of the self or its development cross-culturally. Granted, as they amply demonstrate, different peoples have different concepts of the person and the self, and further, they recognize the interpersonal influences that are involved in self-development. The autonomy of the self in Jungian terms, though rarely mentioned, would from their perspective be beyond the pale.

As a matter of fact, informed advocates of the Jungian or Kohutian views of the self never make the error of thinking of the self as somehow "hard-wired" and fixed. To the contrary, development of the archetypes occurs in the context of adaptational interaction with a real world, so the notion of the self in different societies will differ, some emphasizing the relative autonomy of the self (as among hunting-gathering peoples) while others emphasize the interdependence of selves (as is typical of horticultural peoples). At the actual neurobiological level of development, there is not, nor can there be, a normal self that develops outside the influences of society.

This misunderstanding is nowhere more obvious than in anthropological writings over the last couple of decades (see e.g., various articles in Battaglia's 1995 and Mageo's 2002 edited volumes) that rarely address either the neurobiology or the depth psychology of self with real understanding. These sources are all too often written with a moral or political agenda in mind, and have very little to offer anthropological science. Katherine Ewing (1990) has done a yeoman's job of parsing out the problems in defining "self" in a modern anthropological context. As she notes, "Recent studies by anthropologists of the 'self' are grounded in a relativist paradigm which, if not altogether denying the existence of universals in human experience, is intended to demonstrate that there is much less that is universal than we might have supposed" (ibid:255).⁵ She has argued, quite rightly, that although some folks report experiencing a unitary self, and the "illusion of wholeness" of self in experience is widely spread across cultures, such experiences are actually "fleeting" (1990:252). There exist in most, if not all, societies contingencies that evoke "rapid shifts among inconsistent self-representations" among people in interaction. Although she does not acknowledge the fact, Ewing is reprising the concept of "protean man" as developed in psychiatry some forty years ago by Robert Lifton (1971:298) – the notion being that certain social conditions may produce a "protean style" of self-presentation "characterized by constant shifts in identification and belief."

In fact, entire cosmologies may exhibit this organic and unitary self motif. In the last chapter we visited the Navajo concept of *hózhó*, which is usually translated as "beauty" in English, but which also expresses the ideas of wholeness, unity of opposites, harmony and health. For the Navajo, the natural state of the human being is an organic whole, but this state of unity or equilibration can be and is frequently disrupted by the vicissitudes of daily life, including the contingencies faced by the child while growing up, or a warrior preparing to do battle. To my reading of Jung, he was striving to model the development of the psyche in just this way (Jung 1976:45). The psyche strives for unity and completeness, but the vicissitudes of real life produce fragmentation and culturally influenced selection in the construction of the ego. So the ego, being one complex among many, may not represent this *holistic imperative* (as Gene d'Aquili liked to call it; see Laughlin, McManus and d'Aquili 1990:150; see also Stephen 1995:xii) – it may in fact be off-center due to personal history and enculturation. As Jung himself wrote, "...the general function of dreams is to try to restore our psychological balance by producing dream material that re-establishes, in a subtle way, the total psychic equilibrium" (Jung 1964:34). Along similar lines, Kohut (Kohut and Wolf 1978:414) writes:

> Once the self has crystallized in the interplay of inherited and environmental factors, it aims towards the realization of its own specific programme of action—a programme that is determined

---

⁵ For examples, Ewing cites Clifford Geertz, McKim Marriott, Michelle Rosaldo and Richard Schweder.

by the specific intrinsic pattern of its constituent ambitions, goals, skills and talents, and by the tensions that arise between these constituents. The patterns of ambitions, skills and goals; the tensions between them; the programme of action that they create; and the activities that strive towards the realization of this programme are all experienced as continuous in space and time—they are the self, an independent centre of initiative, an independent recipient of impressions.

We know the archetypal self not only by way of self-reflection in the waking state, but also through the adventures we have in the dream state. In these adventures, imagery arises that may be transformations of the archetypal structure of the self. The transformations can be endlessly various, yet reveal recognizable patterns in retrospect (Jung 1958 [1948]:78-79):

> Already at the very beginning of our dream series the circle appears. It takes the form, for instance, of a serpent, which describes a circle round the dreamer. It appears in later dreams as a clock, a circle with a central point, a round target for shooting practice, a clock that is a perpetuum mobile [perpetual motion], a ball, a globe, a round table, a basin, and so on. The square appears also, about the same time, in the form of a town square or garden with a fountain at the center. Somewhat later the square appears connected with a circular movement: people who walk around in a square, a magical ceremony (the transformation of animals into human beings) which takes place in a square room, in the corners of which are four snakes, and people are again circulating around the four corners; the dreamer driving round a square in a taxi; a square prison cell, an empty square which is itself rotating, and so on.

Jung sometimes speaks of such motifs as "natural symbols" in the sense that in their transformations, they organize and redirect psychic energies, even as they reveal the inner workings of the unconscious psyche (1969j [1948]; e.g., the "libido-symbols" like fire, the sun, etc., see 1956 [1912, revised in 1952]:255) – my own term for natural symbols is "innervated metaphors."

## Self Dreams in Holocultural Perspective

In the last chapter, I introduced the remarkable holocultural study of archetypal dreams carried out by psychoanalyst Vincenza Tiberia (1981) in which she examined five archetypes cross-culturally, one of which was the archetype of the Self (ibid:90-100). She found that Self dreams were uniformly associated with "divine guidance, and the bestowal of power and blessings from beyond" (ibid: 90-91). Again, the variety of imagery illustrates the flexibility of transformation and cultural influences operating in archetypal dreams. The following examples of Self dreams are taken from her study.

A.L. Kroeber (1902/1907:432) wrote down the dream of an Arapaho Indian man who was given guidance:

> He saw himself standing alone on a green prairie.... On his left ...he saw a person seated, dressed entirely in black silk. He thought that this person was the messenger.... Then this person in black spoke to him. He knew all the man's thoughts. He told him of the new world that was to be, and that they were now on a cloud. Then the informant saw the earth below him and the sky above him at an equal distance. The person in black, who was the crow, then showed him a rainbow extending from east to west, and another from south to north. The informant was then taken by him to the spot where the two rainbows crossed one another. There he stood, and the crow told him to look up. He then saw where the father was, and saw the thoughts of all mankind reaching up to him.

A Bedouin commander once prayed for a dream before a battle. "Allah's spokesman" appeared to him and said, "Thy booty is to be a cushion of a litter fastened with a ...rope" (Musil 1928:396-397). He didn't understand the dream and told his fellows about it the next morning. Later in the day they attacked a camp and the commander, "...found himself before the chief's tent where the 'Atfa litter was standing, in which in times of danger the prettiest girl used to be seated in order to encourage the defenders to fight bravely and hold their ground." The commander then understood the dream, and, roping the litter to his saddle, hauled off "their most precious possession, for once the 'Atfa litter is lost it must not be used again."

An Ojibwa Indian dreamed of Jesus (Jenness 1935:48). "After I returned from the war I was ill and unable to do a hard day's work. One night I dreamed that Jesus approached me clothed in a loin cloth and with bleeding wounds as He appears in pictures. I threw myself at His feet and asked for a blessing. Then I awoke and told my friends that Jesus had blessed me and was restoring me to health. I recovered my health and am now as strong as ever."

As with any archetype, the transformations within the dreams may vary endlessly. A Comanche Indian woman (Jones 1972:39) meets a man "who extends his hand while holding a peyote button in his palm. Once she takes the peyote from his hand and holds it with both hands she feels a tingling sensation through her hands and arms that she identifies with 'supernatural power'" (Tiberia 1981:97). An Ashanti man in West Africa (Rattray 1927:196) dreamed he encountered a "... very tall person with an enormous head. ...This person carried three balls of medicine around his neck, one was red, one was white and one was black. The dreamer cried out in his sleep and was awakened. The next day the dreamer went to see a priest who said that the figure in the dream was his 'father's god ...who had come to visit.' He was advised to sacrifice a fowl and did so" (Tiberia 1981:96).

## SELFSCAPE DREAMING

Back in Chapter 3, I mentioned the idea of the "selfscape dream" as developed by psychoanalyst and ethnographer, Douglas Hollan (2003b, 2004, 2007, 2009).[6] These are dreams that "...reflect back to the dreamer how his or her current organization of self relates various parts of itself to itself, its body, and other people and objects in the world" (2004:172). While I only mentioned this idea in passing at the time, I consider it to contain one of the most profound insights in contemporary anthropology of dreaming – the fact of *intra-psychic communication*. The insight, grounded initially in the concept of

---

[6] Hollan (2007:91) was influenced by Heinz Kohut's (1977) notion of "self-state" dreams.

"self-state" dreams of Heinz Kohut (1977:109-110; Tolpin 1983), is that systems within the brain cross-talk and exchange information – that there not only exists communication between conscious and unconscious processes mediating aspects of the self, but that: (1) somatic systems, be they neural circuits or organs, are made up of cells that communicate with each other, (2) this communication is integral to the development of the self, and (3) one of the functions of dreaming is to facilitate communication between neural systems and consciousness, thus participating in the growth, reorganization and equilibration of the psyche. As Hollan (2004:172) writes:

> In my own work, I have tried to bridge the gap between what is universal and what is culturally and individually specific about dreams by focusing on the way particular dreaming processes appear to mediate the dreamer's organization of self and his or her social, emotional, and physical environment. I use the term "selfscape" to refer to emotionally and imaginally vivid dreams that appear to reflect back to the dreamer how his or her current organization of self relates various parts of itself to itself, its body, and other people and objects in the world. These are the dreams that, anywhere in the world, awaken people in the middle of the night or the emotional residues of which carry over into the waking life of the following days, weeks, or years. Such dreams, I argue, provide the mind with an updated map of the self's contours and affective resonances: its relative vitality or decrepitude, its relative wholeness or division, its relative closeness or estrangement from others, its perturbation by conscious and unconscious streams of emotions, and so on. They will be found everywhere in the world because they serve a basic orienting function. Their content, on the other hand, varies considerably, because the relationships of part-self to part-self and of self to world that they map and represent will vary considerably from culture to culture and from person to person, even with the same culture.

To elaborate on Hollan's thinking, it is important to mention that most neural systems in the body receive neural pathways from every place in the body they send neural pathways. That is, interconnections in the brain and nervous system are usually reciprocal – pathways between "part-selves" are a two-way path. It cannot be otherwise, for the body and its nervous system depend upon a vast network of feedback loops. Feedback loops to the outside world operate to maintain adaptational flexibility within a dynamic environment, while feedback loops within the body operate to maintain equilibration and organic unity (also see Rycroft 1979:52-59).

In my opinion, selfscape dreaming is a biopsychological universal, and is the evolutionary consequence of what Stephen J. Gould (1991) termed *exaptation*: namely, the process by which physiological structures either (1) proved adaptive in one way in previous generations and in later generations proved adaptive in new ways, or (2) were not particularly adaptive in earlier generations, but later on proved to be adaptive to new situations. The brain is our organ of exaptation *par excellence*. With its initial complement of neurognostic structures, the developing brain is able to mature in such a way that it resolves the tension between the need to conserve its own integrity and the need to organize itself relative to the sociocultural and physical environment in which it grows (see Piaget 1977, 1985). As we mentioned in Chapter 4, during development there is a great deal of selectivity among the repertoire of neurognostic structures and circuits, only some of which will mature in the course of a lifetime (e.g., Changeux 1985; LeDoux 2003).

Mammalian brains evolved cross-talking circuits to facilitate adaptation to extramental reality, but in higher mammals with more advanced brains, an exaptation took place making cross-talk with consciousness important to adaptation. The different parts of the brain interact during growth and reorganization, and this process becomes expressed by way of innervated metaphors within the dreaming sensorium. Thus, the brain portrays a "movie" about what it is doing at any given time, the "movie" taking the form of a dream, waking dream, vision, etc. (Wax 2004). The movie is normally a form of what Michelle Stephen called "autonomous imagination" – that is, the movie unfolds of its own accord and does not reflect the wishes of the ego. Jung's archetypal dreaming is precisely this kind of selfscape dreaming in which the various archetypes and complexes cross-talk using the most primitive form of symbolic communication, the innervated metaphor. The more aware and interested we become in our dream adventures, the more innervated metaphors accrue (become synaptically connected to) both conscious and unconscious information systems. In time, the unconscious "learns set," as psychologists like to say – i.e., becomes conditioned to communicate with the ego, and vice versa.

This is why experienced dreamworkers find that after a while, the meaning of their dreams becomes increasingly transparent. During selfscape dreams, the brain's sensorium becomes in effect a "theater of mind" in which is played out an imagined portrayal of the brain's ongoing activities. Remember that weird dream I mentioned at the start of the book, the one about having two ears on the right side of my head? To me, the meaning was instantly transparent – I have been unbalanced for some time while researching this book, and have been living a more "left lobe" mental style than is usual for me at this stage in my life. The dream was telling me that I am "listening" to my intellect too much (right ears go to the left side of the brain). In addition, I happen to be a fan of the TV series, *Law and Order: Criminal Intent*, and the character that Vincent D'Onofrio plays is a detective that is quite unbalanced in his life, being highly intellectual and "geeky," but socially challenged. The dual ears and D'Onofrio's hair with which I was trying to cover them are innervated metaphors telling me in dream-speak that I need to get out more — stop being a bookish hermit and increase my social interaction. There are no doubt other interpretations to be made here – as I have said, there is no such thing as a dream with one and only one possible interpretation. But for me, that was a selfscape dream of the first water.

This is also why people who are fully engaged in their dream life over the years tend to become qualitatively different personalities than those who ignore or suppress their dream. From the Jungian view, individuation is facilitated by tracking dreams. For them, the dream is a "spontaneous self-portrayal, in symbolic form, of the actual situation in the unconscious" (Jung 1969c:263), and a conduit of information about the self as it is unfolding.

## Operationalizing Selfscape Dreams

The problem with applying our understanding of selfscape dreams to ethnographic data is that how such dreams are interpreted is generally informed from various local cultural theories of dreaming. We have seen ample evidence that dream interpretation among polyphasic peoples tends toward standardized and institutional oneirocriticism, social repercussions and future orientation. Few societies interpret their dreaming as a personal exploration, or for that matter understand their self in Jungian terms, for they appear more concerned, not with personal individuation *per se*, but with the pragmatics of dreaming for the commonweal. As we have seen, the most common interpretation of dreams featuring the archetypal self is an encounter with an ancestor, a spirit or a god (Mageo and Howard 1996). Applying a selfscape analysis would thus be a kind of etic account – a scientific explanation that may differ entirely from the native understanding.

Hollan illustrates selfscape dreams from his own research among the Toraja of Indonesia and that of Wolfgang Kempf and Elfriede Hermann (2003) among the Ngaing of Papua New Guinea. The Toraja "...were not surprised by our interest in dreams, because the Toraja are one of those groups of people who believe that certain types of dreams can foretell the future. In fact, prophetic dreams—those that are vivid, emotionally charged, and easy to remember—are marked with a special term, *tindo*" (Hollan 2004:175). Moreover, they share dreams quite readily. This dream is from an elder named Nene'na Limbong who was close to death when he recalled a dream he had years before:

> One time I dreamed that my throat had been cut! There was a man who cut my throat. I fell down! And I was frightened. I woke up frightened thinking, "I'm dead!" A man cut me with a machete and I fell down dead and my eyes went dark. Then my body was cut up and distributed to A and B and C [He then whispers in a low, terrified tone of voice], "Oh, this is my body being cut up!" But I could see it happen! I was cut up and distributed [his voice continues low, quiet, horrified], I was very frightened.

When asked the meaning of the dream, the elder replied, "The dream really meant that I would eventually slaughter many buffalo and become an important man" (Hollan 2003:68). For Hollan, this and other dreams collected from the elder signal an internal state of anxiety typical of big men in that society who are born to wealth and social obligations:

Nene'na Limbong's "sacrifice" dream is a good example of a selfscape dream. It demonstrates for us how the manifest content of a dream can point us toward the way in which the nonconscious, dreaming mind is relating and mapping an emerging organization of self relative to its own body, to its relationships with other people, and to the values and social realities of the surrounding world. Obviously this "pointing" is not transparent; it depends on us knowing a lot about the dreamer's past and current life situation and his or her cultural world. Yet despite how obscure the nonverbal language of dream imagery can be, we see how it can reveal rather than obscure aspects of emotional experience and the organization of self.

The methodological problem here is straightforward. There is no independent way of monitoring the elder's anxiety level, except by self-reports. Hence Hollan's analysis, although undoubtedly true given the contingencies facing Nene'na Limbong, is nonetheless tautological. This is almost *always* a problem with psychological-functional explanations (Hempel 1968). The best Hollan – or anyone else without psychometric devices in the field – can do is describe as accurately as possible the personal and social contingencies facing the dreamer at the time of the dream. Hollan gives us this kind of background information that is all too often missing in other ethnographic dream reports, thus making the application of a selfscape analysis to those data rather dicey.

Hollan is on more solid ground with the dreams of the Ngaing. "Dreaming for the Ngaing is an experience of the self. This can be inferred from Ngaing statements with regard to dream experiences, interpreting these, and, when necessary, using them as a springboard to action – statements that in their general formulation constitute a discourse on dreaming" (Kempf and Hermann 2003:63). By reflection upon dream experiences, the Ngaing come to know their "dream-self," spirit or soul, thus expanding their knowledge of their greater self. "A pivotal component of the self, the [soul] is, in everyday situations in the waking life of a normal person, bound to that person with an intimacy that permeates, replenishes, and fortifies. In this state it is manifested as a person's shadow or mirror image" (ibid:64). As with so many peoples, the "dream-self" or soul is conceived by the Ngaing to have the ability to leave the body and wander, thus implying that the self is at least in part independent of the body. Here is a dream reported by a young woman who was being initiated, a process that required ritual seclusion:

> I thought I was in a city. It was a big city! Now it was like I was a child of the whites. . . . Of course I was a black, but a white man adopted me and gave me medicine that turned me into a white. So I always called this man "father," and his wife I always called "mother." Both had adopted me, okay, and this country, well I thought we were in Australia. And then we went into a department store. There you could read "Australia. . . ." Now although I couldn't read what this said, I asked the salesman, "Read it out for me!" and so he did just that. After he had read it out and I had heard it, he said, "You must not go in there and touch the various things on the display counter. Or you'll be put on trial!" Now I clearly heard what was said, but all the same I went and touched the things on the display counter. Then the "security" man came behind my back and seized me. As he seized me, he said to me: "Now you're going off to prison!" (Kempf & Hermann, 2003, p. 75)

When she was questioned about her dream and how she understood it, she said, "... 'How is it that I dream the things I do?' I sat down and thought, and then I said to myself, 'Perhaps it's like this: I went into seclusion and stayed exclusively in this house, and that is just as if I were in prison.' Three weeks in a dream were like one week, and so I said to myself, 'Now I've been here for five and a half weeks, so I dreamed the opposite: three and one, that makes three and a half weeks.' That's what I dreamed" (ibid:75-76). It seems to me very likely that there is more self-reflection and selfscape dreaming of this sort going on among traditional peoples than the ethnographic data would indicate. The problem is methodological, for the usual practice is to merely record dreams and their cultural significance as told, usually without more in-depth clinical interviews of the dreamer. We do have that information for the Ngaing, a people who have been inundated with white Christian missionaries for generations, and we may reasonably infer the presence of racially loaded, psychological tensions independent of dream reports.

I suspect we will eventually conclude that all dreaming that is not completely focused on "day residue" memories will turn out to be selfscape dreams, regardless of how any particular individual or culture interprets their dreaming. This is certainly in accord with a Jungian approach to dreams. The range of archetypal encounters in selfscape dreams will theoretically range from those with "pure" and relatively undeveloped archetypes (like a radiant hero figure), to more developed complexes (like the figure of one's father or mother, or CEO of the company, well-known spiritual figure, a culture hero like Superman, etc.). Let me offer a personal example:

> I dreamed I was in a land full of black people – by black I mean coal-black, not brown. I am the only white person present [thus, the obverse of the young Ngaing woman's dream above] and I am holding a young black child whom I love and am protecting. Two different black babies were "broken" (actually folded backwards upon themselves) by adults before my eyes, and I was aware of anxiety that this not happen to my "ward."

Now, as I will reiterate in Chapter 13, black (or dark brown) human figures always appear for me as messengers from the unconscious.[7] If they are emerging from, say, a tunnel or spiral staircase, they are for me an indicator that I am to receive a message from the depths. In this case, however, it is I who appears to have descended into the depths, a reversal of my more normal symbolism. This indicates to me a more active engagement with the processes of the unconscious, especially those involved in selecting which complexes will develop and which will be "folded-in" upon themselves, thereafter to languish. Perhaps you, the reader, will have other ideas about what this dream means, but it is indicative of my own experience of a selfscape dream in which my anxiety is present in the dream, and stems perhaps from an intense wish to preserve ego-control over my own development – the William Ernest Henley poem "Invictus" comes to mind: "It matters not how strait the

---

[7] You might wish to know that I was reared in the American south and the only black people I knew personally as a child were servants, some of whom had been with our family their whole working lives – hence, my cultural and personal history loading on the symbolism of black people in dreams.

gate, how charged with punishments the scroll, I am the master of my fate: I am the captain of my soul."

I do not mean to imply that selfscape dreaming is an exclusive category in which no influence from the waking world or "day residue" appears. Indeed, the unconscious will assimilate imagery from our experiences in other SOC into the symbolism shared between ego and the greater self. For instance, an old friend of mine, Rodney Malham (personal communication, 27 March 2011), an experienced lucid dreamer and advanced meditator, had the following dream while in Hawaii. It followed two days of early morning swims with wild dolphins in Kealakekua Bay:

> I was floating on the surface of the bay with dolphins swimming below. I came up to near conscious level and imagined this conversation between a mother and young dolphin. The young dolphin asked, " Mother, why do we have anything to do with the humans?" And the mother dolphin replied, "Well little Fin, it started when all beings were together in the great Ocean. At one point, some of the beings decided to try living on the small bits of the planet called land, leaving our brothers and sisters behind to watch over the great Ocean. All was well for many moons, but we started to notice our ancestors had changed and were starting to move about on large leaves and logs. It was when they started to swim again in the ocean that we really knew they were back and they needed us to help them realize the water within all of us, of our shared fluidity. However, the humans seemed to increase in number and their impact on the oceans became noticeable. We started to see them in every bay and at our resting spots, then at the traditional feeding grounds. Firstly they were respectful, but over many generations more of them seemed to be unhappy. We noticed big logs moving faster over the surface and groups of the humans, some dark and moving deeper, others floating and sick. Now we can feel that the humans are not well. We find many of them wanting to be close to us, as if being with us helps them connect with the healing energy of the spirit of the deep. Assisting humans with this, little Fin, is our work and is why we continue to connect with them."

The dream speaks for itself, and is obviously one concerned with the totality and unity of being, and the psychological "glue" that leads to the experience of unity – love and compassion. It may also signal the interaction between conscious (above the sea) and unconscious (in and of the sea) aspects of the psyche.

## The Self and Dreaming in Neuroscientific Perspective

Archetypes and selfscape dreams aside, any view we take about the self as anthropologists should be consonant with what we know about the neurobiology of the self. Depending upon what element of self-awareness we are focusing on, there is a neurophysiology to that element. If we are focusing upon self-representation in narratives, we are obviously limiting our perspective to us humans, being as we are the only ones that talk about ourselves — at times *ad nauseam*. But if we are talking about the distinction that we all make between ourselves and other objects, the neurocognitive systems involved are relatively primitive and shared with other animals (see Bogen 2007; LeDoux 2003).

In fact, Antonio Damasio (1999) has suggested that consciousness requires the automatic, built-in ability to distinguish between self and other objects. Our fundamental sense of self, no matter how we festoon our self-model with memories and associations, moral qualities and social statuses, remains relatively primitive and is present in most SOC, especially in our dreams. Keep in mind that our entire sensory system is "designed" to distinguish what is happening inside our body from what is happening outside our body (i.e., we do not have to think about whether our headache is outside or inside our head). Try a simple phenomenological experiment: stroke one of your hands with the other, and while doing so focus on the sensations this causes. If you are really focused, you should become aware that you are "feeling" the touching both from the inside-out (the stroked hand) and from the outside-in (the stroking hand). You can flip your awareness back and forth between the inside-out perspective and the outside-in perspective. This is possible because there are two different sensory systems involved.

As far as the anthropology of dreaming is concerned, it is far more productive I believe to think in terms of the roots of the self, and the experience of the self relative to non-self, as being a fundamental feature of the primitive organization of our nervous systems. That distinction is a universal given among humans. All the evidence suggests that even as infants we make that distinction (Laughlin 1991; Zelaso, Gao and Todd 2007). Moreover, there is more to our psyche than our ego – a fact apparent to anyone who does depth psychological work on themselves, and who learns to integrate self-related encounters in dreams into one's self-model. How the culture of a dreamer conditions that integration – or individuation in Jung's sense – will vary considerably from society to society, as we have seen. But nowhere is there a society in which people do not distinguish self from other, even though they may emphasize dependence upon others to a varying degree. What we have seen in our study of dreaming so far is that in most polyphasic societies, selfscape dreaming is routinely socially-directed – that is, dreams are interpreted within the society's dream culture, not as encounters with the individual's depths, but rather encounters with a greater transpersonal domain – an experienced reality that is of concern to the society at large. It is by way of the society's cycle of meaning that what might otherwise be taken as a solipsistic venture becomes interpreted as an experience of significant social moment.

## Summary and Segue

There is considerable confusion in anthropology about what constitutes the self, especially in the ranks of constructivist ethnologists that explicitly or implicitly reject any "essentialist" or universal ingredients of the self. We have seen that "self" can refer variously to a social construct and culturally conditioned self-presentation, a domain of experience in which one distinguishes self from other, a unified sense of one's self, a system of archetypes and complexes, a psyche that strives for organic unity. My own opinion is that the social constructivist account of the self is only possible if one excludes evidence from phenomenology, depth psychology and neuroscience – a set of blinders I do not choose to wear. As we have seen, dreaming outside the normal everyday adventures suggested by daily life and processing of memories seem to be encounters with the archetypal depths of one's psyche (or the neurognostic structures of one's brain, if you prefer). These dreams are the ones that rise above the normal and account for many if not most "culture pattern" dreams considered so important in polyphasic societies. The dreams are a domain in which the ego encounters the vastly greater workings of the psyche. These encounters may be with particular archetypes, like the hero, ancestor, guru, demon, etc., or they may be more generalized selfscape dreams in which the state of the psyche is portrayed before the ego like a documentary movie.

This may not be the way the people themselves interpret their dreams. Indeed, they almost certainly will interpret selfscape dreams in terms that make sense to them within their local cycle of meaning. Archetypes will take on the form and presentation of characters – "other-than-human beings" – recognizable within the people's mythopoeic vocabulary. The ancestor archetype becomes our deceased Uncle Harry who has paid us a visit to let us know that everything is all right where he is now, or to warn us that we are going to get sick if we do not change our ways. Such dreams are essentially transpersonal in nature and content, calling as they do upon the resources of the entire psyche instead of the relatively tiny purview of the waking ego. Selfscape dreams may bring one into contact with elements of the self we are either ignorant about, or reject as being "me" – dreams on the order of, "I just wasn't myself today." Moreover, information may be presented to us within the dreamscape that brings our everyday understanding of the world and its machinations into question. This will be the topic we take up in our next chapter. We will look at dreams that may not fit so easily into our materialist, Newtonian understanding of the universe, and our selves as seamless entities.

# Chapter 12

## Transpersonal Dreaming

> Parapsychology plays a subtle part in psychology because it lurks everywhere behind the surface of things. But, as the facts are difficult to catch, their theoretical aspect is still more elusive on account of its transcendent character.
>
> C.G. Jung, *Letters, Volume 1: 1906-1950*

> Why should she give her bounty to the dead?
> What is divinity if it can come
> Only in silent shadows and in dreams?
> Shall she not find in comforts of the sun,
> In pungent fruit and bright green wings, or else
> In any balm or beauty of the earth,
> Things to be cherished like the thought of heaven?
>
> Wallace Stevens, *Sunday Morning*

Transpersonal experiences are those "…in which the sense of self or identity extends beyond (*trans*) the personality or personal to encompass wider aspects of community, culture, and even cosmos. Such experiences have been highly valued across cultures and centuries" (Walsh 2007:5; see also Walsh and Vaughan 1980). Transpersonal psychology emerged as a field of study in the late 1960s (Sutich 1968), followed soon after by transpersonal anthropology (Campbell and Staniford 1978; Laughlin 1989, 1994a, 1994b; Laughlin, McManus and d'Aquili 1990:18; Laughlin, McManus and Shearer 1983, 1994; Lee 1980; see LaHood 2007 for a review). Transpersonal anthropology has flourished since those early beginnings and is now represented by a professional society, the Society for the Anthropology of Consciousness, a section of the American Anthropological Association, which publishes a journal, *Anthropology of Consciousness*. The field is interested in the psychological and cultural dimensions of dreaming, spiritual visions, waking dreams, ethnopharmacology and psychopharmacology, meditation, trance and possession states, mediumship, dissociative states, and other ASC, as well as shamanism, mysticism and other spiritual traditions, paranormal, anomalous and psychic experiences, extrasensory perception (ESP), healing practices and psychotherapies, magic and witchcraft, myth and ritual, etc. As with the study of dreams, the interest in transpersonal phenomena in anthropology goes way back to the work of Andrew Lang and Edward B. Tylor in the 19th century. Lang was, in fact, one of the founding members of the British Society for Psychical Research, the oldest parapsychological research society in the world, and an organization that later drew both Freud and Jung.

We are not interested here in the full range of transpersonal experiences had by folks around the planet – indeed, some anthropologists have filled volumes on that subject (see e.g., Goulet 1998; Goulet and Miller 2007; Young and Goulet 1994; Krippner and Friedman 2010; Cardeña, Lynn and Krippner 2000; Long 1977). But it is necessary right at the start to make one thing very clear with respect to any and all transpersonal experiences: what makes an experience transpersonal is that, however "spooky" or straightforward, it brings into question the individual's self concept or model – one's "cognized self" (Laughlin 1994). A transpersonal experience almost by definition produces *cognitive dissonance*[1] in the individual, and sets the psychological stage for self-transformation. The same experience may be transpersonal to one person and normal to another, and depends upon the state of the experiencing individual's self-knowledge – the first experience of *nirvana* is mind-blowing for a meditator, but is rather ordinary to the enlightened; seeing a ghost may be profoundly transpersonal for a Canadian college student, but may be more commonplace for a rural Chinese (Wing, Lee and Chen 1994). An extraordinary experience encountered by an anthropologist in the field

---

[1] Cognitive dissonance is the cognitive and emotional experience produced by trying to hold conflicting knowledge about one's self or world simultaneously.

may be transpersonal for the fieldworker, and considered ordinary to his/her hosts; for instance, when Bruce Grindal (1983) saw the dead man jump up and play the spirit drums, or when Edith Turner (1994:83) saw a spirit leave a sick man. Such experiences will quite naturally create dissonance in the fieldworker, and may eventually lead to change in their self-knowledge.

More than that, the transpersonal experience may bring their entire set of cultural understandings of self and world into question. As Robert Thurman, an authority on Buddhist practices, notes (as quoted in Mackenzie 1998:115), "What the meditator is doing in those long retreats is a very technical thing. He's not just sitting there communing with the Great Oneness. He's technically going down, pulling apart his own nervous system to become self-aware from out of his own cells. It's like you are using Word Perfect [a computerized word processing program] and you are in the chip. The way you have done that is by stabilizing your mind where you can go down to the dots and dashes, and you've gone down and down even into that." One cannot undergo this intense process without changing – literally, as in changing the synaptic circuitry that is the self.

Transpersonal experiences may also be *paranormal* – that is, they may contain contents that appear to be outside the possibilities allowed by consensus science. For instance, Elkin (1994[1944]:46) reports that some Aboriginal shamans seem to be able to communicate over great distances by focusing their minds on another person. A dream or other experience is paranormal if it involves causation considered to be impossible given our present scientific understanding of physical laws. Hence, as I mentioned in Chapter 9, our inclination as Western-trained, science-minded intellectuals may be to reject as real anything like causation-at-a-distance, backwards causation, or any phenomenon that appears to require such causation – phenomena like telepathy, psychokinesis, prescience, out-of-body experiences, remote viewing, mental control of machines, and so forth. A *scientistic* reaction will be to ignore such phenomena as irrelevant to science – *scientism* being the elevation of scientific theory to the status of an ideology. Ideologies are blind to any evidence that may bring the belief system into question. Whereas the essence of true science is to leave all theory open to disconfirmation.

> If the counteradvocates [skeptics] are rejecting psi evidence based on the assertion that it makes no sense, then likewise the amazing array of modern advancements based on quantum approaches would similarly require rejection, yet our world is undeniably (and increasingly) composed of such innovations. We can only conclude that any *a priori* rejection of psi based on a restriction of what science allows is overly rigid, since science is constantly evolving. (Krippner and Friedman 2011:202)

The common prevalence of scientism in science is the very reason a radical empiricist (Chapter 6) approach is so important. Knee-jerk skepticism is of no use to ethnology, other than as evidence in the study of ideologies and belief systems. We anthropologists are in the business of participating in and describing the life-ways of our hosts, and that may well cause us to bump into phenomena that, for us, appear to be transpersonal and paranormal.

## Transpersonal Dreaming

Our present scope of inquiry, *transpersonal dreaming*, is more limited than the full range of transpersonal experiences. By transpersonal dreams I mean dreams that have the impact upon the individual or the group much as any other type of transpersonal experience, an experience that transcends ego consciousness and may result in change or growth in the psyche of the dreamer (De Becker 1968:Chap. 8). I very explicitly include *paranormal dreaming* within this consideration for four good reasons: (1) the cultural theory of dreaming of many polyphasic societies include what, from our Western viewpoint, are paranormal elements and relations, (2) paranormal dreams may well cause transpersonal reflections by bringing the dreamer's self-understanding into question, (3) radical empiricism requires that any and all dream experiences, whether paranormal or otherwise, must be included within our purview, and (4) this type of dream is not uncommon in the clinical and psychoanalytic literatures (e.g., Totton 2003; Dombeck 1994).

I have already described an example of one of my own transpersonal dreams – the Read Ezekiel dream (Chapter 6). Not only was that dream numinous and memorable, it caused me to reflect on the nature of my self, and my conditioned religious assumptions – it was "way" transpersonal, as my granddaughter might say. Another and more famous example is the experience of Fred Swinney, who later became the healer Graywolf.

> Fred Swinney, a Canadian psychotherapist, was camping in an Ontario forest when he dreamed about animal predators emerging from the woods and devouring him. Awakening in terror, Swinney cast his gaze toward the coals of the campfire; just beyond, he discerned two piercing eyes and the large gray form of a wolf. Surprisingly, fear gave way to total surrender, just as if Swinney had been transformed into a wolf himself. Initially resisting the call, Swinney eventually took the name Graywolf and began working with his clients from a shamanic perspective. (Krippner 1990b:186-187)

We will be focusing on dreams, but as we shall see, under certain circumstances the transpersonal dream may fuzz into other ASC and related considerations (e.g., hallucinogenic drug experiences, transpersonal emotions; see Throop 2000:42). For instance, as we have seen in Chapter 5, when it comes to lucid dreaming, worrying about where a dream leaves off and a vision, meditative trance or other ASC begins may be a pointless exercise, especially if the people being studied do not make the distinction (Hunt 1989; Hunt and Ogilvie 1988) – i.e., it is not always clear whether a shaman is reporting a dream or a trance experience, and for all intents and purposes it doesn't matter. In addition, certain cultural practices, such as ritual procedures, ingestion of psychoactive drugs, meditation, ordeals and incubation, may have an impact upon the transpersonal content and significance of dreams, so the cultural background of transpersonal dreams may be important. For instance, meditators seem to experience more bizarre and archetypal dreams than non-meditators (Hunt and Ogilvie 1988:41). And cultures that routinely use psychoactive drugs may alter dream experiences in ways that become important for their cosmology and symbolism. For instance, Siberian shamans frequently ingested the *Amanita muscaria*, or the Fly Agaric mushroom before entering trance or dreams, and ordinary folk used it for incubating dreams (Devereux 1993:147).

Dreaming among some traditional peoples often confounds our Western consensus understanding of what is normal and what is real (Krippner 1994). As I have taken pains to emphasize, from the cross-cultural perspective what constitutes "normal" and "real" varies enormously. Despite the common psychoanalytic reduction of transpersonal dreaming to "transference," unresolved conflict and other Freudian notions (e.g., Servadio 1966), actual transpersonal dreaming (see Laughlin 1989, 1994a), especially dreaming containing "paranormal" elements such as co-dreaming, precognition, out-of-body experiences, etc. (see Ebon 1966; Littlewood 2004; Ullman 2003; Ullman, Krippner and Alan 2001; Magallón and Shor 1990; Blackmore 1992), is amply illustrated in the ethnographic literature (see Young and Goulet 1994; Goulet and Young 1994; Goulet and Miller 2007; George 1995; Turner 1996).

Katherine Ewing has struggled with the consequences of immersing herself in the culture and practices of Pakistani Sufis. When she entered the field, she did so with the usual objectivist/relativist training we anthropologists receive in graduate school. She arrived equipped with the usual kit of interpretive concepts like "superstition," "latent content," agnosticism, "don't go native," etc. No sooner had she entered the field than she met a Sufi *pir*, or master ("saint," guru) who, being "…the first I had met, told me explicitly that he would come to me while I was sleeping" (Ewing 1994:574). That same night Ewing received a dream visitation:

> At the time, I was living with a Pakistani family who themselves maintained a pious but modernist, pragmatic orientation to the world, an orientation that rejected the "superstitions" of their neighbors and denied the legitimacy of saints. That night I awoke in the middle of the night, so startled from a dream that I sat upright. My awakening woke a young woman sleeping on a cot next to mine. She had visited the saint with me and had been critical of him. I told her about the dream, in which I had seen a white horse approach me. In the dream I had the clear sensation of something touching my thumb, which startled me awake. The young woman declared that it had been the saint, just as he had promised.

Being a dyed-in-the-wool Freudian, she had ready interpretations that avoided taking the dream at face value, or accepting a Sufi explanation for the dream. This had the effect, she admits, of placing her at a distance from her Pakistani hosts. She only began to experience dissonance when she related the dream to a Pakistani psychiatrist who, rather than laughing it off "...suddenly became very serious and wanted to know more about that saint. I found this shift of orientation on the part of a colleague even more jolting than the dream experience itself – I was being socialized into the significance of dreams by a Pakistani whom I had thought shared my interpretive, scientific world, a man whom I regarded as an authority" (ibid:575). She later worked with businessmen and other professional people, including a high court judge, all of whom found no conflict between a Sufi account of dream reality and their roles in modern society. She eventually came to understand that her problem was with the "don't go native" proscription and that accepting the Sufi account of her dream would bring her identity into question – the very definition of a transpersonal experience.

One of the leading figures in the study of transpersonal psychology, both in the laboratory and in the natural world of ethnographic data, is psychologist Stanley Krippner (Krippner 1993, 1994, 2002; Krippner and Combs 2002; Krippner and Friedman 2010). In 1964 he headed-up the dream lab at the famed Maimonides Medical Center in New York City (Krippner 1993, 2001) where he had the opportunity to pursue an enduring interest in the transpersonal dimensions of dreaming (Krippner 1990a, 1990b; Krippner and Thompson 1996; Krippner and Faith 2001; Krippner, Bogzaran and Percia de Carvalho 2002). He has been especially interested in dreaming and shamanism — he notes, "Sometimes, extraordinary dreams reflect a special type of processing, integrating the dream and waking modes of consciousness. Shamanism uses dreams to enhance information transfer to the waking mode, applying this material in healing and other shamanic practices" (Krippner and Combs 2002:80). Of particular use to us are his and his colleagues' reflections on different types of transpersonal dreams in the book, *Extraordinary Dreams and How to Work with Them* (Krippner, Bogzaran and Percia de Carvalho 2002). In the introduction to this book, they tell the story of Dolores who dreamed that someone was knocking at her door. She responded and saw a man through the front door. She asked "What do you want?" and the man said "I want to sleep here tonight." She returned to her bedroom and called 911 and told the emergency operator what had happened. "Oh yes," replied the operator, "we know who he is. His name is Nisrock." Some days later, Dolores visited her local library and found a volume on the unconscious. Opening the book at random, she was surprised to see a drawing labeled "Nisrock, the winged Babylonian god who takes the souls of dreamers to the place of the dream" (ibid:1).

## Experiencing Spiritual Entities and Places in Dreams

Dreams frequently instantiate spiritual entities. This is a fundamental principle in transpersonal methodology, for "supernatural" entities are very often not "supernatural" at all, they are directly experienced in both dreaming and waking life – they are not merely mythopoeic concepts or symbols, they are *real* for the people experiencing them. Thus, when we read in an ethnography that this or that people "believe" in river nixies that cause an illness, very often the term "belief" signals that the anthropologist has not actually seen a nixie, but that his/her host may well have. Paul Devereux (1993:214-215) notes that most "alien abduction" experiences are very likely lucid dreams that have been misinterpreted by monophasic people trying to make sense of their strange experiences. For the record, I think this is a good call, for I myself once interviewed some of John E. Mack's (1995) abduction subjects in an effort to evaluate his program at Harvard,[2] and my strong impression was that they were describing altered states of consciousness, perhaps lucid dreams or waking trances, rather than actual abductions. Many of these abductees have organized themselves into classic cult-like organizations where their highly emotionally-charged transpersonal experiences and spiritual interpretations are socially supported and worked through.

Douglas Hollan (1996:213-214) emphasizes the fact that the Toraja of Indonesia sometimes experience their long-dead ancestors in dreams, and these experiences are taken to be real. When he asked one of his

---

[2] I was a member of the 1999 Study Group, Program for Extraordinary Experience Research, Cambridge Health Alliance, Harvard University.

Toraja friends whether he had seen his dead relatives, his friend replied, "Yes, I have. I've seen my grandmother and my mother and other people who have died... (Did you speak to them?) Some I spoke to and some I didn't, I just saw them... (What does your grandmother say...?) She talks. Sometimes she talks, sometimes she doesn't. But [in the dream] I think that she's still alive. When I awake, [I think], 'Wah, what did I see in my dream?'" (ibid:221). For the Ilahita Arapesh of New Guinea, the "belief" in such entities as ghosts and ancestors is ultimately based upon – or at least confirmed by — direct experience in dreams and waking visions. Donald Tuzin (1975) is one of those ethnologists who has given Edward Tylor's reasoning a serious re-think (see Chapter 2) after considering Arapesh ghost-lore in light of both perception and practice. We do know that there is a common situation in which the dreamer comes partially awake in REM and is aware of sleep paralysis, an experience that, accompanied perhaps by suitable imagery, may be interpreted as a ghost attack. Wing, Lee and Chen (1994) surveyed 600+ Chinese undergraduates and found that 93 percent were familiar with "ghost oppression" while dreaming, and 37 percent said they had experienced such a dream.

Dreams may take one to sacred places – providing experiences that may have a profound influence upon one's life or the eventuality of one's death. Douglas Hollan and Jane Wellenkamp (1996:181) recorded a dream had by one of their Indonesian Toraja hosts, Minaa Sattu, who visited Puya, the land of the dead:

> I went up a mountain first, and then descended [the other side]. I came to a forest... and after that there was some barren ground. A desert. Then I arrived in Puya.... There was a person who came to meet me, but I didn't know his/her name. He/she said, "Why did you come here?" I said, "I want to see my father and mother, because they have been at Puya a long time." The person grabbed me, [saying,] "If you meet with your father and mother, you will die!" My reply was, "I don't care if I die." The person pointed out my father's house.... It was in the mountains.... I wanted to go to his house, but the person forbid me!... He/she said, "Go back!"... I said, "If I can't meet with my father and mother, then show me their water buffalo." The person said, "Your father and

mother's buffalo are there on the mountains, being herded." Then I left Puya.... I arrived in Laka [a nearby village], and I saw [my parents'] buffalo!... Then I arrived at my house. So that's how it was. I've already been there [in Puya].

Minaa Sattu was one of the few Toraja to have visited Puya. Consider what a difference it would make to one's sense of self if one actually were to experience the afterlife – to know with absolute certainty that life continues after death, and continues in a place one has visited, a place much like one's own, peopled by kin and friends.

### Paranormal Dreaming

Among the types of extraordinary dreams covered by Krippner and his colleagues over the years have been telepathic dreams, collective dreams, clairvoyant dreams, precognitive dreams, past lifetime dreams and out-of-body dreams. Many or all of these types of dreams may be transpersonal, depending upon the dreamer and the culture within which the dreamer was reared.

## Telepathic Dreams

Of particular interest to anthropologists are telepathic dreams. These are dreams in which information is received about distant events, the thoughts of others, images via remote viewing, etc. Krippner, Bogzaran and Percia de Carvalho (2002:95) report on a survey done by Posey and Losch (1983-1984) of auditory hallucinations among 375 subjects. They found from surveying their subjects that 71% had heard vocal hallucinations while awake – like having one's name called while alone, hearing one's own voice coming from the back seat of a car, etc. Thirty percent recalled hearing voices while dropping off to sleep (during the hypnagogic) and 14% heard voices when waking up (the hypnopompic). My Read Ezekiel dream would seem to be one of the latter.

The Maimonides experiments into telepathic dreaming and remote viewing followed a pretty standard format (Krippner 1993; Ullman, Krippner and Vaughn 2001:Appendix C; Krippner and Friedman

2010:196-199). A subject was "wired-up" and placed in a soundproof room with a bed. An envelope was then selected at random and taken to a distant room by a researcher who opened the envelope and took out and scanned an art print. The subject's task was to "divine" the image seen by the researcher and incorporate it into his dreams. Later, a group of judges, "…compared the typed dream reports with the total collection of art prints, attempting to identify the print used on the night of each experiment. About two out of three times, we obtained statistically significant results, with odds against chance so great that coincidence was unlikely" (Krippner 2001:xix). An interesting correlation with weather conditions was discovered by neuroscientist, Michael Persinger (Persinger and Krippner 1989), who ran a correlation between the accuracy of subjects "divining" the art print image and weather conditions during each experiment. He found that accuracy increased during relatively calm nights, and decreased during "'stormy' nights marked by high geomagnetic activity" (Krippner and Friedman 2010:198).

Telepathic dreams are not uncommon in the clinical literature. Professor of nursing, Mary-Theresen Dombeck (1994:442-443), reports a dream had by one of her clients, a woman named Cassandra:

> I would like to share a dream, and it's the only time I have ever felt weird about a dream or superstitious or something like that. I had talked to my daughter who was in California and everything was fine on that day. But at two o'clock in the morning, I had this dream that my father-in-law died. It was so intense; and I can't even tell you how he died; I can't remember any of that, but the dream was so intense that I was just shaking and I was sweaty, and it was really a very vivid dream that he had died. I got up in the morning, and didn't say anything to my husband. About two hours later we received the phone call, that he had had a coronary, and that my husband should come down to Virginia.

Cassandra held off telling anyone about the dream because it "it was *so irrational* that I would dream this, and then that it would happen." One can see that this dream, like so many examples that we could list here, was in effect a transpersonal one, for it brought her self view and her cultural understanding of the world into severe question. "It was scary," she reports, "I didn't want anyone to think that I was trying to be a psychic or anything like that." When she did share the dream later on with family members, they could not see why she associated the two events in the first place.

Telepathic dreams are perhaps the most common paranormal dream experiences anthropologists encounter in the field. Additionally, the evidence for their reality is almost always anecdotal (Ryback 1988) – a fact that will put the experimental scientist's teeth on edge. Yet such anecdotal stories are ubiquitous across cultures. For instance, anthropologist David Young (1994) reports that he had visions of human figures entering his bedroom as he awoke from dreaming. When he described these visions to his Cree healer friend, the healer recognized one Amerindian figure as one of his spirit helpers.

Krippner, Bogzaran and Percia de Carvalho (2002:102-103) record a typical telepathic story about a Canadian dreamworker named Parvin who had this dream: "I am back home visiting my mother. She looks as if she is in pain. I take her to give her a bath. Everything looks very real. While I am washing her, my father, who has been dead for five years, appears with a loaf of bread in his hand. He offers the bread to my mother. I try to stop my father, but he keeps insisting that the bread is good for my mother. My mother finally accepts the bread. Next, my mother is gone and I go back to the bath area. I see a small doll resting on the floor. I begin crying loudly and hold the doll in my arms. I wake up sobbing." Disturbed by the dream, Parvin called her mother, only to discover that her mother had died during the night at near the time she was having the dream.

The dream and the actual event need not occur simultaneously – indeed, Jung's experience was that the dream tended to come just before or after the event (Jung 1969i [1952]:443):

> An acquaintance of mine saw and experienced in a dream the sudden death of a friend, with all the characteristic details. The dreamer was in Europe at the time and the friend in America. The death was confirmed next morning by telegram, and ten days later a letter confirmed the details. Comparison of European time with American time showed that the death occurred at least an hour before the dream. The dreamer had gone to bed

late and not slept until about one o'clock. The death occurred at approximately two in the morning. The dream experience is *not synchronous* with the death. Emergences of this kind frequently take place a little before or after the critical event.

Ethnologist Barbara Tedlock is no stranger to transpersonal dreaming. "Beginning as a young child I was deeply interested in my dreams. My earliest dreams, like those of many other children, centered on animals.... . I shared these dreams with my grandmother, who helped me to understand how they related to my spiritual development and the cosmology of her people, the Anishinabe – meaning 'people of good intentions' – who are also known as the Ojibway or Chippewa.... . She actively encouraged my dreaming and worked with my dream stories so as to include me within her cultural world. In this way she passed on to me, a cross-blood child, a northern woodlands dreamscape" (Tedlock 2004:183-184). Tedlock's relationship with her "Granny" was very close. As a child she contracted polio and was laid up for months in an iron lung. Granny stayed by her side during the worst part and told her Ojibwa miracle stories. Granny worked on her throughout her rehab period using traditional remedies. Eventually Tedlock recovered enough to return to school and then on to university (ibid:184):

> One night Granny visited me in a dream and sang, "Thunder Birds on heaps of clouds, they startle me." Then she shook me, and I woke up a little inside my dream. I rose from my bed and walked toward the door. She smiled and said, "Step where I step." And as I did so the night sky reddened, and I realized that I must be dreaming. We walked along silently until we arrived at a large, messy nest filled with serpent bones and bits of eggshells. Granny stirred around in the debris until she found a red feather. "This was the home of a Thunder Bird," she said. When she found what she was looking for – an unbroken light-blue speckled egg – she handed it to me, saying, "Here, take this egg, it will be your medicine power when I am gone." As I stared at the shimmering egg that I held in my cupped hands, Granny slowly faded into lightning-filled clouds. I awoke knowing that she had given me some of her living energy, her medicine knowledge. Then I

realized that she must have died. That morning I stayed home from classes waiting for the phone call. And when it came, I cried uncontrollably for hours. Then I folded and cut out a paper loon (her clan totem) and placed it next to the picture of her I kept on my desk. Each of the next three evenings I went outside at dusk to pray and light a small bonfire to guide her soul southwest to the land of the dead.

## Precognitive Dreaming

As we have seen, people in polyphasic societies focus their attention on dreams that appear to predict future events. The question is, do dream premonitions actually happen, or do they rely merely upon hind-sight interpretation? In Chapter 9, I related the story of the famous Zulu diviner, Ndlulangaye Ngcobo, who saw his teacher in a dream before he met him in the flesh (Sundkler 1948:265-266). What do we make of such a claim? The Toraja of Indonesia look to dreams to foretell pregnancy and the gender of their baby: "Indo'na Sapan dreamed of a big bird that she believes presaged the birth of her second child" (1996:123). Can dreams presage major events in one's life? This is no trivial matter, for these can be dreams that leave a mark upon a person for a lifetime. C.G. Jung (1974:98-99) reported an encounter with a friend of his who was skeptical about his dream-interpretations and who told him of "another idiotic dream" he'd had: "I am climbing a high mountain, over steep snow-covered slopes. I climb higher and higher, and it is marvelous weather. The higher I climb the better I feel. I think 'If only I could go on climbing like this for ever!' When I reach the summit my happiness and elation are so great that I feel I could mount right up into space. And I discover that I can actually do so: I mount upwards on empty air, and awake in sheer ecstasy." Jung warned him to be very careful when he went climbing and not to go alone, and to take guides with him. "Two months later the first blow fell. When out alone, he was buried by an avalanche, but was dug out in the nick of time by a military patrol that happened to be passing. Three months afterwards the end came. He went on a climb with a younger friend, but without guides. A guide standing below saw him literally step out into the air while descending a rock face. He fell on the head of his friend, who was waiting lower down, and both were dashed to pieces far below." As Jung says, "No amount of scepticism and criticism has yet enabled me to regard dreams as negligible occurrences."

Goulet (1994:30) reports a waking dream in which he gained foreknowledge of proper behavior in Dene Tha. He was sitting in a tipi with elders planning a ceremony, and the tipi began to fill up with smoke from the fire. He was wondering what one might do to clear the air when he saw his own double — a distinct image of himself — kneeling at the fire and fanning it with his hat. Then another non-Dene knelt at the fire and started blowing on it. "Immediately, with a loud voice, an elder told him not to blow on the fire, and instructed him to fan the fire with his hat or some other object. The rationale for not blowing on the fire was that such an action would offend spiritual entities and induce a violent wind storm in the camp. Listening to the elder, I realized that I had actually foreseen the proper way of fanning a fire."

Precognitive dreaming may be more common than one might suppose. Krippner, Bogzaran and Percia de Carvalho (2002:96) report on a mail-in questionnaire study done by Palmer (1979) on 354 residents of a town in Virginia, and 268 students at the University of Virginia. Among the other questions asked was: "Have you ever had a rather clear and specific dream that matched in detail an event during or after your dream, and that you did not know about or did not expect at the time of the dream?" One or more dreams of this kind were reported by 36% of the townees and 38% of the students. Two thirds of these dreams were reported as "more vivid" than normal dreams. Around one third of the dreams were confirmed within 24 hours of the dream. In some 20% of the reports, the dreamer said they had told someone else about the dream before the confirmatory event occurred. Telepathic dreaming is thus not uncommon among Americans, despite our more or less monophasic attitudes toward dreaming. In fact, transpersonal experiences generally are more common than mainstream academics would acknowledge. In 1975, A.M. Greeley published a book-length study of various transpersonal experiences in America entitled *The Sociology of the Paranormal*. He concluded by asking that if these experiences were so common, why doesn't sociology pay more attention to them? Why indeed?

As we have seen, dreams are a ubiquitous source of information, not only about the self, but about future events (Goulet 1998:xxvii-xxix). People everywhere want to know what is going to happen before it does. We wake up in the morning and tune-in to the weather report so that we don't go out into foul weather unprepared. But everyone knows how iffy weather reports can be. So too may the precognition of events in a dream be iffy. Many peoples evaluate the accuracy of divinatory dreams by waiting to see if the predicted results actually happen – in other words, they use *post hoc* reasoning (e.g., Jung's mountain climbing story, or the precognitive dreams reported by Palmer 1979, or Krippner 1994).[3]

The Lacandon Maya take a "wait-and-see" attitude toward such dreams. Robert Bruce (1975) demonstrated this attitude by recording dreams and then seeing how the people interpreted the prediction relative to what happened later on – whether or not the dream is confirmed as "predictive." For instance (ibid:45):

> *Dream:* Mateo (Sr.) of Najá dreamed of two domestic pigs, and later of *kitam* (collared peccary).
> *Interpretation:* Foreigners are coming, and there will be two of them... .
> *Confirmation:* Not confirmed... unless (as is often the case) it was remembered long enough to be rationalized upon arrival of the next foreigners, weeks later.

Or again (ibid:49):

> *Dream:* [On June 7] Antonio (first son-in-law of Chan K'in of Najá) dreamed of Augusto de la Cruz, of a Tzeltal family living in El Carmen, coming to sell bread.
> *Interpretation:* The person in question is thought to be of the deer

---

[3] *Post hoc* reasoning, short for the phrase *post hoc ergo propter hoc* ("after this, therefore because of this") is the fallacy of reasoning back from the conclusion to causation in the premise. The fallacy is that just because B follows A does not mean that A *causes* B. Just because Jung's friend dreamed of flying off the mountain does not mean that the dream *caused* his death.

What is really hard for Westerners to get their minds around is the notion that Jung's friend's death may have caused the earlier "precognitive" dream; thus backwards causation.

*Onen*, so may foretell seeing a deer.
*Confirmation:* June 9, K'in Bol (son-in-law in service to Chan K'in of Najá) killed a deer.

Jean-Guy Goulet (1998:155-159) notes that the Dene Tha Indians consider precognition in dreams as commonplace – what they call "knowing with the mind." "Dreaming in this manner, one knows where to go to kill a moose, discerns if a medicine fight has ended with the destruction of the power of the enemy, or learns that deceased relatives are well and happy in the other land." Goulet (ibid:100) tells an interesting story about a Dene Tha woman who quite suddenly suffered insomnia for two nights. She told her sister about it and her sister sent her to a local healer. "The healer responded with the narration of a dream he had had two nights before. The dream was for a woman who was to visit him for help. In the dream the healer set his snares for beavers. Beavers came up to the snares but did not get caught. In his dream he had seen lots of clothes just scattered around; some were burnt, and others were still smoking. There was also a wolf around the area. When he woke up he wondered why he had had that dream. He told the sick woman that most people in the community looked after their things well." The patient then confessed that when her son had refurbished the attic of their house, he had thrown some of her old clothes downstairs. She was told to take care of them, but she didn't. Instead, some kids gathered them up and took them outside and burned them in the yard. The healer then told the patient that she had become ill because she should have done the proper thing, and not just what she felt like doing. In Dene Tha culture, there is a close symbolic association between clothing and the self (ibid:99).

The very idea of dreams actually foretelling future events flies in the face of our own Western materialist biases about causation. As we mentioned in Chapter 9 when discussing magic, the notion that one can "see into the future" violates the Western commonsense model in which event A causes event B, where A happens before B, and not vice versa. Yet, well-controlled scientific experiments have demonstrated both precognition, or "future sight" (Morris 1982; Radin 1997a, 1997b, 2006; Puthoff, Targ and May 1981; Jahn 1981; Bierman and Radin 1997, 1999; Ebon 1966), and causation at a distance and backwards causation (Radin 1997a, 2007; Jahn and Dunne 1987; Rao 2001; see also Laughlin and Throop 2008). For instance, psychologist David Ryback (1988) investigated precognitive dreaming in college students. He administered a questionnaire to over 433 subjects and found that 290 (66.9%) reported some kind of paranormal dream. Although he ended up dropping many of these claims as unfounded, he did conclude that 8.8 % of the population did in fact have precognitive dreams (see also Rhine 1969).

In a series of ingenious experiments, Dean Radin and D.J. Bierman (Radin 1997b, 2007:Chap. 10; Bierman and Radin 1997, 1999) have demonstrated a robust precognition or "presentiment" effect using physiological indicators of "precognitive information" when subjects act before they are presented with a random stimulus. Here's how the experiments work. The subject sits alone in a room in a comfortable chair and is "wired-up" to machines that measure the activity of their autonomic system, and hence their emotional state. When the subject is ready, they push a button and around 7 seconds later a random image is shown on a screen. The image may be of a calming nature, or may be highly emotional (violent or erotic). A computer decides which picture to show *after* the subject pushes the button. Each subject does this a set number of times. Results showed that subjects tend to respond emotionally several seconds *before* the picture appears, and the correlation between emotion and calm vs. highly emotional imagery is significant. Bierman and Scholte (2002) took this research even further by carrying it out on subjects while their brains were being scanned using a functional magnetic resonance imaging (fMRI) machine. Again, they showed that areas mediating appropriate emotion became active before the randomized image was shown.

Keep in mind that this kind of research is by its very nature controversial among Western academics. Arguments rage over whether or not a "presentiment effect" exists or not. It would be interesting to know with absolute certainty that precognitive dreams actually happen or not in experimental situations. But in the sense in which we speak of precognitive or "presentiment" dreams in anthropology, it is less important whether they actually happen and more important that our informants and the societies we research experience presentiments as real and act upon them – an ethnographic reminder of the old W.I. Thomas Theorem: "It is not important whether or not the interpretation is correct – if men define situations as real, they are real in their consequences." As we have seen, most polyphasic societies do believe in precognitive dreaming, however empirical or skeptical they may be of any particular incidence of it. The ethnographic information we have is usually anecdotal descriptions and self-reports.

Take for instance ethnographer Edith Turner's precognitive dream experiences while doing fieldwork among the Iñupiat people of northern Alaska (Turner 1996). On October 5$^{th}$ she records a "waking" dream she had in which she, "...saw a man who was having to carry a whole pile of stuff like window glass – it had something to do with my house" (ibid:38). On November 26$^{th}$, she had an intruder who broke into her basement by breaking a window (ibid:80), and then on December 7$^{th}$ the trash man arrived. "I showed him the sheets of broken glass in the furnace room. He lifted them carefully and carried them out of the house to the truck. Immediately my waking dream of October 5 came back to me – a distinct picture of a man carrying a whole pile of stuff like window glass" (ibid:83). For Turner, this break-in and glass removal were a "disturbance" that were presaged in dream.

## Co-Dreaming

One of the most fascinating types of transpersonal dreaming is the phenomenon of *co-dreaming* (a.k.a., "shared dreaming," "mutual dreaming"); that is, when two or more people share the same dream content at more or less the same time. We have already encountered traditional peoples who are so "into" each other's dreams that co-dreaming may well be happening all the time without the ethnographer being the wiser. Take for instance the intense dream sharing among the Ongee (Pandya 2004) folk of India we discussed in Chapter 7. Some of the ease with which they reach consensus with regard to what the dreams are telling them about events might be the result of not only dream sharing incubation, but co-dreaming as well. In any event, what makes this type of experience so anomalous to Westerners is that the causation involved must be of the "spooky" magical kind (see Chapter 9), as it appears to be an example of "causation at a distance." There are many such anecdotes to be found in the ethnographic literature and elsewhere (see Krippner and Faith 2001).

Shared dreaming is commonplace among the Australian Aborigines. According to Poirier (2003:113):

> In the Wirriman area, it was not uncommon for two individuals to say that they had shared the same dream. Both dreamers usually have shared the same camp overnight and found themselves in the same dream setting and action. There were also instances when, as other dreamers dreamed, they decided to enter yet another person's dream or were attracted to the action occurring in a dream setting. For example, an elderly woman once told me that she feared some male relatives of hers who were sleeping nearby might, during their dreams, have heard her singing sacred-secret songs in her own dream (in this case, men's songs usually forbidden to women); she took great care then in singing very softly. Love magic songs are another example of how dreams are perceived as a space-time of higher receptivity. The beloved will hear a suitor's love song in his or her dreams and thus be attracted to the singer.

Edward W. Kellogg (1997) reported an experience of co-dreaming he had with his friend Harvey Grady. One night in 1994, Kellogg dreamed he was:

> In a sort of archeological dig - in Mexico - I see people digging for gold, peasants, in a sandy Sonoran type desert. We find huge old wagons on the side of the road, from a circus or something, which had bones of elephants and/or lions, etc. I go with the group - realize that I dream, but don't know if they realize it - a sort of virtual reality field trip. I talk with the leaders and they respond. I see [Harvey Grady], and tell him to give me a collect call on waking up to WPR (waking physical reality), if he recalls this dream, and to let me know if he really does participate in a WPR tour at this time. [Harvey] looks like he just shaved off his beard. He shows me some old airplanes in a museum, and I look forward to virtually flying them, although I wonder what

would happen to my physical body if I crash. ...(my lucid dream continues, but I leave [Harvey] behind).

The next morning he called Grady and asked for a report of any dream he might have had, and because it was very similar to his own, asked that Grady write his down and send it to him. This is Grady's dream:

"I remember Ed and three or four other men, whom I knew in the dream but not in daytime, talking about an expedition to explore for probable archeological records, then traveling to an arid desert area with desiccated hills and twisted arroyos, where we split up to search the surface soil for possible artifacts. We also watched for caves. We were dressed appropriately with hats for shade, a little reminiscent of Indiana Jones. The land in the dream was similar to Israel hill country, or arid portions of Arizona, Nevada, or New Mexico. We were searching for ancient artifacts, like (from) Atlantis or Mu. I recognized that the dream dealt only with one part of an ongoing series of the search for evidence of ancient civilizations. In the dream, I felt that we were going through the motions of the search in the astral plane in order to establish energetic templates for the persons who would conduct the search on the physical plane. The energetic templates created from our experiences would guide the search of some physical explorers. Therefore, we went through the motions of the search like actors playing out roles, in order to generate thoughts, emotions, and desires for the template. In the role of explorers, we acted as though we were ignorant and blindly searching for something we had only slight reason to expect might be there. On a higher level, as actors outside of the role, we knew what would eventually be found. We were well aware of the ancient civilizations and their contributions to history and had accepted tasks in helping reveal them to the physical plane. This double level of awareness made the dream more interesting to me.

One of the most remarkable accounts of co-dreaming in the literature is that reported by anthropologist Marianne George (1988, 1995a, 1995b, n.d.) while she was in the field among the Barok people of

New Ireland, New Guinea. Dreaming for the Barok, like so many other peoples, is an important source of knowledge and spiritual power. This is especially so for "big people" – those who attain high status because they master the "tricks" or techniques (*pidiks*) of accessing spiritual power (*lolos*). Chief among those tricks is the art of dreaming. Among the Barok, dreams become real and intent is realized when the dreamer creates the dream images in the real world of conventional, ritualized expressions (*wuo* or *wu*). In this case the dream creation changes and transcends the non-dream reality, and this kind of dreaming is what Barok "big people do" (ibid:30).

Access to power is fundamental to everything important that big people accomplish. Yet power *per se* cannot be directly perceived. "Barok big people told me that in order actually to do something important, one dreams about it first... . What happens in a dream has to do with initiation or clarification of *ara'*, which is "intent, will, or desire." The point of dreaming has to do with having imaginative experiences which express and result in the formation of intent. Thus, dreaming can happen when one is awake as an idea, a meditation, or a daydream, as well as when one is asleep and unconscious" (ibid:30; George n.d.). By intentionally manipulating imagery associated with power, power itself may be accessed and directed to useful purposes – again, the metaphor of the child's magnet and the iron filings comes to mind.

Mimi George first visited New Ireland in 1979. She was living in Kokola where a friend of hers, Tadi, one of four brothers, had arranged for her to live with his family. Her research focus was to study native notions of spiritual power. Tadi was a Barok "big man" (*orong*) and his mother, Kalerian, was a "big woman" (*une tagin*). Kalerian, a woman of about 85, was the matriarch to her family and she took George under her wing, adopting George as her sister. Kalerian lived next to her eldest son, Bore, in whose house George also lived.

> **Co-Dream #1 (1995a:20):** One morning [Kalerian's] third and fourth sons, Alek and Bustaman, came to me while I was waiting for teawater to boil. This was unusual, since this early in the morning they were usually busy in the clan house, where only men go, or in their family cookhouses sharing the fish they had caught before dawn, or feeding their pigs, or getting

ready to go to the gardens. Alek strode directly across the plaza to me and, looking me straight in the eyes, he asked, "Did you understand her?" I looked back at him for more clues, then demanded, "Who?" I had no idea what he was talking about. He looked blank. I tried again nervously, "Say, what?" Alek seemed to steel himself. "My mother [Kalerian] was talking to you last night—She asked me to make sure you understood what she told you." Alek kept a measured tone, and watched me closely. "I did not talk with her last night," I replied, confused. "You do not remember? ...When she came to see you in the night? ... In Tokpisin we call this *griman* (dreaming)." "Oh!" I suddenly felt queasy as I remembered vaguely that she had been in my dreams—though I could not recall specifically what it was about. I just remembered the feeling that there was a problem and she directed me to do something about it, and that even in my dream, I did not take her too seriously. "Ah, yes, I do remember that she was in my dream but I cannot remember much else," I admitted to Alek. "That is why she came to me and to Bustaman too," Alek replied in the calm, clear manner of a kindergarten teacher. Just then Bustaman came out of his house and bounded up to us, grinning and nodding as if all three of us knew what this was about. Alek and Bustaman then described to me exactly what was in my dream, and I knew that what they were saying was true. They repeated to me the exact words that Kalerian had said to me in the dream. I remembered everything with absolute certainty when Alek and Bustaman said those same words to me. I suddenly realized that Alek and Bustaman must have witnessed my dream!

Prior to this dream, George was your average Western dreamer who had trouble remembering dreams and pretty much ignored them when she did. After this dream, however, she devoted herself to remembering her dreams, for, "...there was no getting around the fact that four people had shared the same dream with me. I wondered how one learned to do that, and I hoped that if it ever happened again, I would be able to remember more of the dream without prompting" (ibid:21). When she returned to the field a second time over a year later, it was to discover that her sister Kalerian had died. Yet she continued to have dreams in which Kalerian appeared and gave her information:

**Co-Dream #2 (1995a:23-24):** The third time I went to New Ireland, in 1985, I was interested in learning about one of the oldest known clan house sites in Kokola. It was located far up a mountainside overlooking the sea. It took repeated tries to locate the site – a ten by thirty-foot area. Then I realized that I had no idea where the hearth might be. This was a different sort of clan house site from the ones that were built on the coast after European contact.

That night I had a dream in which the late Kalerian talked to me. When I woke up I remembered little of what she said, but I did remember that she and I were at the old clan house site. She had spoken very intently and pointed among dirt around the roots of a tree that had overgrown one end of the area. Alek joined me for breakfast tea and immediately asked, "Did you understand where she showed you to look?" I stuttered back, "Oh, you mean what Kalerian was telling me in my dream?" The images came flooding back to me. "Yes, I saw her, but I didn't really understand what she meant." Alek looked at me searchingly, then asked carefully, "You want to find the old hearth of that clan house, right?" "Yes!" I agreed, suddenly remembering that I had not succeeded in that effort the day before, and feeling incredibly stupid for not realizing that others had this problem on their minds too. "Well, she showed you where to dig. Did you see the place clearly?" "Yes, I saw…," and I described the layout of the site, and the existence of that big tree root at one end. Alek said, "Yes, that is correct," and he did one better by describing to me the details of the root in this part of the site, though he had not been there with me, nor had he gone there in several years, and no one had talked with him since we returned late the evening before. He could not have known those details except from my dream. "Did you understand her warning?" he then asked me. "What warning?" I felt dense. Alex explained, "She said the far corner of the site is undercut at the cliff edge and if anyone stands there it might landslide.

Don't let the children who are with you go near there." I then did remember lingering in my dream, while Kalerian gestured to the cliff corner with grave concern. I had not understood her clearly then, but now I did with absolute certainty.

That day the children and I went back to the site, and I did assertively keep the children away from the dangerous cliff edge. An adult companion, a European and a hard scientist by training, was also along, and he had not taken my dream seriously. He insisted we should dig at both ends of the site, "In case there were two hearths." First we dug deeply at the opposite end from the one in the dream and found nothing. Then I started to dig among the roots. "It's too hard to dig there," the adult stated, "it will take too long." I dug anyway, with the children helping. Quite soon we found some charcoal, and bagged a sample for dating. It was exactly where Kalerian said it would be.

This is surely one of the least known examples of "psychic archaeology" in the record (see Goodman 1978), and yet it is an instance of the kind of use of dream information to which the Barok avail themselves.

Edith Turner also reports an interesting set of shared dreams described by one of her Iñupiat friends, Jim, a truck driver, who was one of a team of drivers moving a large oil drilling vehicle. The drivers slept in shifts. Jim "woke up" inside a dream to find his two companions, plus a lot of other Iñupiat folks. "I said, 'There are a whole lot of people in this cab' and went to sleep again. I woke up again and the same thing happened the second time. I said, 'There are a *whole lot of people* in this cab.' I never found out exactly who the others were. I had an idea two of them were White. This happened to Eric [another driver] twice, just as it had happened to me. Then it was Eric's turn to drive, and Dicky [third driver] slept, and he woke, and the same thing happened with him, twice. ...When we arrived, and we were sitting down over coffee and doughnuts, it occurred to us that we'd all had the same experience. It's that place; it's always like that: people get lost, lanterns are seen beckoning travelers, and if they go toward them they never come back, and so on" (Turner 1996:219-220).

## What to Make of Transpersonal Dreaming?

Despite the fact that transpersonal dreams are ubiquitous across cultures, even among Western dreamers, accepting the reality of such dreams – especially those with more paranormal content – is problematic for many scientists. The reason for this is, as I have already mentioned, that the causation required for these experiences to be real are of the "spooky" variety. Yet the experiences themselves are real, and for many peoples they have real consequences. No doubt some, perhaps even most precognitive or divinatory dreams are interpreted as such in the clarity of hindsight or fallacious reasoning. But this can hardly be the case when one dreams of a death that is confirmed upon waking. Nor does it explain incidents of co-dreaming. It certainly does not account for the hard experimental evidence of perceptual presentiment.

Would that more ethnographers could have profound transpersonal experiences before entering the field among polyphasic peoples. Indeed, one of the problems in ethnographic accounts of religion and the experiences that give rise to much of religious symbolism, iconography, ritual and textual material, is that the ethnographer rarely experiences first-hand the very ritual techniques geared to incubate such experiences (see Smyers 2002 on this issue) – that is, they rarely participate in the rituals, ingest the drugs, undertake the ordeals and deprivations, or use traditional techniques of dream incubation that drive such experiences. David Young (1994:191) suggests that, "...anthropology is still saddled with a curious blend of relativism and ethnocentrism. The traditional relativism of our discipline has made us tolerant of other modes of thought and behavior, but we don't really take our informants seriously when their worldviews differ radically from our own."

The problem with a lot of skeptical scientists is that they are thinking about causation in antiquated Newtonian terms. Since the advent of quantum physics, evidence has accumulated about the "spooky" kind of causation one finds at the quantum level. If we look to Jung for insights about the physics of the paranormal, we are, alas, doomed to disappointment. Unfortunately for his understanding of quantum physics, Jung was heavily influenced by his friend Wolfgang Pauli (1969a [1946]:229-234) with whom he coauthored a book in 1952 (translated into English as Jung and Pauli 1954) that included Jung's now famous *synchronicity* paper. Pauli accepted Jung's notion of "a causality" — that is, the awareness of coincidences that defy explanation based upon local causation. But Pauli, one of the architects of the Copenhagen interpretation of quantum mechanics, was also wedded to the dualistic account of consciousness and reality that Niels Bohr's[4] thinking required. A major hindrance was that the Copenhagen account would not allow any "hidden variables" to account for observable effects. It is interesting to speculate that had Jung paid more attention to Albert Einstein (who did entertain hidden variables) rather than to Pauli, he might well have reached an altogether different understanding of physics, but even then he probably would not have reached the kind of sophisticated merger of perceptual psychology and quantum physics that, say, David Bohm's (1980, 1990, 1995) insights provide us today. It was Bohm who saw that a more scientific and enlightened view of perception is more consonant with modern quantum physics than with the older Newtonian mechanics.

This is why I brought up the issue of the quantum brain back in Chapter 4. It is entirely possible – although so far unproved – that brains may interact in "spooky" ways via the sea of quantum energies that are within and surround everything in the universe. As we saw in Chapter 4, there is suggestive evidence leading some researchers to hypothesize that brain-quantum sea interactions may operate something like a "quantum computer" (Hameroff 1998; Deutsch 1985; Wallace 1993a, 1993b; Radin 2007). Such information processing would occur at the cellular level, and probably at the synapses of neurons making up neural circuits. These are precisely the synaptic structures linked to consciousness and the self in the writings of some neuroscientists (e.g., Le Doux 2003; Nunez 2010:Chap. 10). The suggestion here is that images arising in one dreaming brain may "cause" images to arise in another dreaming brain via quantum interactions among the cells mediating the imagery in both individuals. If this does prove to be the case, then, because of the peculiar characteristics of relations at the quantum level, spatial distance and temporal relations common to higher-order phenomena may not apply. A mother may well be able to dream of her child's injury or death, regardless of the spatial distance or

---

[4] Neils Bohr (1885-1962) was the Danish physicist who was largely responsible for creating quantum physics.

the exact time difference between them. This may well be an instance of what in quantum physics is known as the Einstein, Podolsky, Rosen effect (also called the EPR system). These three famous physicists demonstrated in a 1935 thought experiment that once two parts of a quantum system are separated, they remain "entangled" and continue to act as a correlated unity no matter how far they travel from each other. EPR-type systems also confound commonsense notions of local causation, for there exists no clear mechanism by which the two parts can "interact" at a distance. Since that time, numerous experiments have upheld the EPR effect, and have thus disconfirmed to some extent the "local" causation assumptions of the more commonsense and classical Newtonian view (e.g., Selleri 1988).

Where does that leave us in relation to the anthropology of dreaming? At the very least modern physics suggests a reasonable electromagnetic field through which telepathic imagery might pass between brains across great distances, and perhaps backwards in time. These notions become scientifically thinkable, even plausible. But curiously enough, that is not the point I wish to leave you with in respect to transpersonal and paranormal dreaming. Rather, the simple fact is that these dream phenomena do seem to occur in the experience and data of ethnographers. Moreover, many of the peoples we work amongst hold these experiences to be reality, and therefore, by the tenets of radical empiricism, they must be addressed. As Ewing (1994), in company with Turner (1993) and George (1995a), make clear, one of the hurdles that has stood in the way of ethnologists fully engaging with transpersonal investigations is the injunction in anthropology against "going native."

This an issue that Edith Turner has taken very much to heart. Because of a number of transpersonal experiences, some of which I have described above, she has come to the conclusion that following the "don't go native" rule in ethnography has the very pernicious effect of putting blinders on the fieldworker. She and her husband Victor Turner gladly donned these blinders in their early field experiences among the Ndembu of Zambia: "Ok, our people believed in spirits, but that was a matter of their different world, not ours. Their ideas were strange and a little disturbing, but somehow we were on the safe side of the white divide and were free merely to study the beliefs. This is how we thought. Little knowing it, we denied the people's equality with us, their 'coevalness,' their common humanity as that humanity extended itself into the spirit world. 'Try out that spirit world ourselves?' No way" (Turner 1993:9). Simply put, describing their hosts' direct experience of spirits as "belief" was tantamount to saying "we will write down what you tell us, but we don't believe you for a minute." After having various transpersonal experiences, she came to the conclusion that ethnographic business as usual would not do when dealing with native experiences of the spirit world (ibid:10):

> Members of many different societies, even our own, tell us they have had experience of seeing or hearing spirits. Let us recall how anthropology has dealt with the question in the past. Mainline anthropologists have studiedly ignored the central matter of this kind of information—central in the people's own view—and only used the material as if it were metaphor or symbol, not reality, commenting that such and such "metaphor" is congruent with the function, structure, or psychological mindset of the society. Clearly this is a laudable endeavor as far as it goes. But the neglect of the central material savors of our old *bete noire*, intellectual imperialism. What is pitiful is the tendency of anthropologists from among the Native peoples themselves to defer to the western view and accordingly draw back from claiming the truth of their own religion. The mission of western anthropologists to explain the system in positivist terms at all costs, which thereby influences a new elite, is oddly similar to the self-imposed task of the more hidebound religious missionaries who are also sworn to eliminate their hosts' religion.... .

Harsh words, but I am afraid they are well earned. We simply do not believe our informants when they tell us they see spirits – "other-than-human beings" in Hallowell's terms. And we do not know what to make of the fact that most of the world's dream cultures hold dreaming to be another domain of reality.

Am I suggesting that we holus-bolus convert to one of the more polyphasic traditional religions? Certainly not. I have already said (Chapter 6) that the phenomenologically grounded ethnographer should take a *perspectivist* view – namely, to acknowledge the reality of the experience had by our hosts, and ideally come to replicate the experience in one's own phenomenology, but bracket and defer until later our own interpretation of the experience. In other words, to cleave to either the native explanation of the experience or the Western positivist account is equally wrongheaded. What we are after here is a competent description of the experience itself – a "return to the things themselves" as Husserl would say. It is the problem of how to access the experience in question that should concern the fieldworker. When it comes to accessing transpersonal experiences, the problem becomes an exercise in applying the approach Ken Wilber advocates in his book *A Sociable God* (1983a). One begins with the injunction "If you want to know this, do this." One goes off and "does this" and observes what happens, what experiences arise. Then one comes back to one's hosts and tells them (if that is appropriate) what one has experienced and see what they have to say about it. One suspends (brackets) one's own system of beliefs so as to get at the entire experience-interpretation aspect of the hosts' cycle of meaning. With respect to dreaming, the fieldworker's task is to develop the skill necessary to access the dream material one's hosts talk about. When one is doing fieldwork among a polyphasic society, the task (for some of us) becomes daunting, but doable. But what one does *not* do is argue with one's hosts that their "belief" in spirits is superstitious, or that a better interpretation of their experiences might be a Jungian one instead of the traditional one.

I am duty-bound to add that pursuing a path of transpersonal experiences is not without consequences in terms of personal change. In any spiritual path there are what might be called *seal experiences* – experiences that take one so far beyond one's previous self-understanding that one cannot go back – that is to say, the experiences change one unalterably — hence such phrases as "before awakening chop wood, after awakening chop wood" in the Zen tradition. The Husserlian phenomenological epoché is one such seal experience, for attaining that state of mind requires learning, and has the effect, intended or unintended, of altering one's self-perception. It is clear from my reading of Husserl that he specifically intended the serious practice of phenomenology to lead to seal experiences that would make a phenomenologically sophisticated science possible. His notion of the "transcendental epoché" is nothing less than the realization of the impermanence of the ego.

In Buddhist iconography, there are the famous traditional paintings of the Buddha's *Parinirvana* where some of those attending are crying and others appear to be in bliss. One intent of the paintings is to demonstrate that after awaking a person knows the illusion of mortality, while the unawakened do not. The implication here is that our native hosts may well have attained seal experiences the fieldworker cannot fathom. It is certainly fair to say that when it comes to transpersonal experiences had in dreams and other ASC, if one hasn't been there, one cannot know, and once one has been there, one cannot know otherwise. As Wilber (1983b:77) notes: "Once an individual transforms to a particular level of consciousness, then he (she) continues to translate both his (her) self and his (her) world according to the basic structures at that level." One's brain mediates one's states of consciousness, and one is only able to reach a new state of consciousness when the circuitry of the brain has transformed into a new configuration. Once the new configuration is developed, there is no going back.

### Summary and Segue

Transpersonal experiences are those that bring the normal everyday ego, or self-representation into question. We may have dreams that present us with transpersonal content, and may have the effect of transforming the knowledge of our self and our view of the world. Some transpersonal dreams may contain information obtained in paranormal ways – e.g., through telepathy, precognition and co-dreaming – perhaps involving rather "spooky" causation. The anthropologist studying dreams must not allow data about such dreams to "fall between the cracks" produced by one's Western, monophasic and positivist standpoint. Wherever possible, the fieldworker needs to privilege the host's claim to have experienced "other-than-human beings" and other spiritual adventures. The experiences are real, regardless of what we as Western scientists care to make of the experiences. Indeed, the brain can portray in living color any cognized reality the individual is capable of knowing.

More than that, the fieldworker should leave him- or herself open to such experiences, perhaps even going so far as to learn the skills necessary to approximate the kind of experiences described by their hosts – "if you want to know this, do this!" The transpersonal approach to native spiritual experiences is a challenge, especially with respect to dreaming for Western fieldworkers who do not normally recall their dreams. As we shall see in the next chapter, this challenge is exacerbated for fieldworkers studying the spiritual practices in the minority of societies with religions that include the practice of full-on dream yogas.

# Chapter 13

## Dream Yogas

> Our revels now are ended. These our actors,
> As I foretold you, were all spirits, and
> Are melted into air, into thin air:
> And like the baseless fabric of this vision,
> The cloud-capp'd tow'rs, the gorgeous palaces,
> The solemn temples, the great globe itself,
> Yea, all which it inherit, shall dissolve,
> And, like this insubstantial pageant faded,
> Leave not a rack behind. We are such stuff
> As dreams are made on; and our little life
> Is rounded with a sleep.
>
> Shakespeare, *The Tempest*

Transpersonal experiences occur among all peoples, and as we have seen, many societies use those experiences to instantiate elements of their worldview, and at the same time evoke conditions conducive to individual development. A system of mythopoeic symbols is frequently embedded in sacred stories and ritual performances which perhaps are amenable to a range of tellings, each geared to the developmental level appropriate to the individual recipient (see e.g., Dan Jorgensen 1980 on the developmental structure of myth among the Telefolmin). As Jeannette Marie Mageo (2003c:23) has noted, "…dreams engage us nightly in what might be called a phenomenological descent into the self." This nocturnal descent is facilitated in part by these images (so-called "cultural schemas") that derive from one's cultural history, one's enculturation, and that "come alive" during one's dreaming. But we have also shown that there are also primordial neurognostic structures (archetypal structures) inherent in the organization of the brain that may also "come alive" in the dream, in effect inviting engagement with consciousness and thereafter with development. Some archetypes present as "pure" and devoid of cultural loading, and some have morphed over time into culturally comprehensible images (see below). In spiritual work, the brain's library of eidetic images becomes a shared language for the different configurations of the ego as they coalesce in different SOC. It is this library of shared knowing that we each carry around between our ears that allows communication between our conscious "I" and our unconscious, and which facilitates whatever extent of integration of the self we have attained. Achieving this internal psychic integration is often *de rigueur* in polyphasic cultures (see e.g., Eggan 1966 on Hopi dreaming and childhood emersion in cultural symbolism; Chidester 2003 on dream interpretation in Zulu religion).

We have further seen that rather specific dream experiences may be incubated using the tools made available by one's culture – the culture's myth-ritual complex, the cultural repertoire of driving mechanisms like fasting, ordeal, psychoactive drugs (or "entheogens;" see Wasson, Kramrisch, Ott and Ruck 1986) and so forth, and the teaching and guidance from elders and gurus. In some of these societies, attaining adulthood, and even one's life-calling may depend utterly upon the dreams one has during developmentally crucial stages of life. It is no coincidence that rituals (i.e., "rites of passage") designed to first de-structure one's experience and then re-structure experience (Turner 1969) are placed by societies at points of life-crisis, for a society may have a great deal at stake in controlling the course of such sensitive moments of personal growth and transformation.

## DREAM YOGAS

Programs of dream incubation and ritual control of experience (Laughlin, McManus, Rubinstein and Shearer 1986) are ubiquitous among the planet's peoples. But among these peoples there are a number that carry the ritual control and exploration of dreaming to the extreme of what we might call *dream yoga*, or what Mary Watkins (1976:20) in her book, *Waking Dream*, called "disciplined dreaming." I am aware that the term "yoga" is from the Sanskrit, and is commonly associated with various forms of Eastern religious practices, but I would like to follow time-honored anthropological tradition and borrow the term "dream yoga" to refer to any cultural program that has developed the ritual control of dreaming into a more complex and elaborate affair than one ordinarily finds among dream cultures. It is not just the classical civilizations of the East that have developed disciplined dream yogas. Such practices may be found all over the world where they are (or *were* in some cases) used to evoke dreams and dream-related development which is taken to instantiate a people's cosmology and guide individuals into the depths of that people's mystery tradition. The whole point of any dream yoga is to *learn how to accomplish, maintain and maximize lucidity in dreams and other ASC.* The purpose for doing so varies across cultures and is dependent upon the local cosmology, dream culture and cycle of meaning.

Wherever one finds meditation paired with dreaming, one is likely to have evidence of a dream yoga (see below for the Kogi), regardless of whether or not intensification of dreaming is the central goal – i.e., training sufficient to maintain higher cognitive processes across the wake-dream boundary. Kelly Bulkeley offers several examples, including those of the ninth century Sufi mystic, al-Tirmidhi, who described the following hypnagogic dream or vision (Bulkeley 2008:208):

> While praying one night, I was overtaken by deep weariness, and as I put my head on the prayer rug, I saw a huge and empty space, a wilderness unfamiliar to me. I saw a huge assembly with an embellished seat and a pitched canopy the clothing and covering of which I cannot describe. And as if it were conveyed to me: "You are taken to your lord." I entered through the veils and saw neither a person nor a form. But as I entered through the veils, awe descended upon my heart. And in my dream I knew with certitude that I was standing in front of Him. After a while I found myself outside the veil. I stood by the opening of the veil, exclaiming: "He has forgiven me!" And I saw that my breath relaxed of the fear.

It was the intense concentration of the trained meditator that produced such a dream (see also Sviri 1999). Lengthy periods of seclusion, dietary restrictions, ascetic practices and meditation produced the type of SOC requisite to such visions. Naturally, the interpretation of the experience was couched in terms consistent with the Kuran.

We have already touched on the role of dreaming in the recruitment and initiation of shamans (Chapter 9). Many such shamanic traditions do involve a program of learning to control dreaming and other ASC (see Sumegi 2008:28-30). One methodological problem we have in the anthropology of dreaming is that the details of these programs are frequently missing in the literature. The common ethnographic situation involves the fieldworker asking questions about shamanism and shamanistic practices without being phenomenologically involved as an apprentice or student. Few ethnographers ever master the skills involved in shamanic dreaming, and thus have little appreciation for how difficult it is to carry ordinary dreaming to the shamanic level of proficiency. Accounts therefore are frequently perfunctory, and we are presented by the abilities of the trained shaman almost as a *fait accompli*. Yet it is obvious, is it not, that if a shaman manifests the ability to remain aware while in lucid dreams and to control his/her intentionality while dreaming, he must have learned to do so? That training would constitute a dream yoga by any reasonable definition.

Barbara Tedlock (1999:96) – who I have mentioned is herself a proficient lucid dreamer – has noted the similarity between Eastern practices and those of many Native American cultures, the latter being, "…a form [of dreaming] as self-conscious as Tibetan Buddhist dream yoga and the Hindu practice of 'dream witnessing' found in Transcendental Meditation. Within both these Asian traditions initiates are taught techniques to enhance lucid dreaming as a form of meditation which is naturally available during sleep. Throughout the Americas shamans talk of experiencing conscious or lucid dreams in which they become aware of dreaming and then, while remaining in the dream state, direct the actions of their souls, shadows, selves, or doubles." As we saw in Chapter 9, these shamans not only may be called to their careers through dreaming, but they must then master the techniques by which they learn to control dream content and intentionality. It is the system of techniques, exercises and progression of realization of the mysteries that is one of the hallmarks of a dream yoga.

Dorothy Eggan described the process of learning that is behind the ease and lucidity with which the Hopi access mythopoeic dreaming (1966:240-241):

> We can now examine the hypotheses that are central to this discussion [of Hopi upbringing]: (a) that the conceptual universe of the Hopi ...was not delimited, as ours is, by notions of time and space which made of dreams an experience apart from reality; and (b) that much of the learning process among the Hopi, especially with reference to religion, involved perception through *imagery derived from dramatic rituals* enacted over and over again before learners, and that this imagery later, according to individual need patterns, could easily be, and frequently was, translated directly into dreams. For as memory, thought, and even perception can be trained by repetitive response to needs through consistent opportunities to satisfy the needs by specific responses, it would seem that, as Murphy [1947:397] suggests, the richness and form of imagery available to a dreamer would depend in part "upon the specific way in which training and broader cultural emphasis have enriched, intensified, or inhibited the imaginal processes of the individual."

Repetition is often the key to techniques for driving both lucidity and intentionality in dreams. The result of such methods is significantly developmental. Not only are the imaginal processes of the brain developed, but so too is the entrainment of these with higher cortical processes, especially the prefrontal cortical executive functions (Chapter 4 and 5).

Mageo (2003b, emphasis mine) remarks along these lines that, "Symbols and symbol systems appropriated from culture ...may be inscribed in the dream. But what about equivalencies between dream images and standardized meanings: aren't they in the interpretation? Parintintin shamans use their culture's dream thesauruses within the dream itself. *By intentionally dreaming of a symbol*, the shaman seeks to create an event in the world that this symbol would ordinarily predict." The Parintintin shaman has to first learn the skill by which such specificity of dream intentionality can occur (Kracke 1992).

Their mythology is replete with imagery, much of it derived initially from dreams, that can be selected and that "comes alive" anew in the dreams of individuals bearing that culture. So integrated are dream content and the origin and elaboration of mythology among some peoples, they may be said to practice "myth-dreams" – a term coined by Burridge (1960:26-30) to cover the blending of mythopoeic symbols with dreaming among Melanesian peoples, especially those involved in cargo cults (also see Stephen 1997).

Let us take the time to reflect that dreaming about an intended image, theme, destination, or problem is not as easy as one might think. Let the reader try this for him/herself. Try making up your mind to dream tonight, say, about what is in the trunk of your car, or a visit to your aunt Jenny, or a flight over your place of work to see if all is as it should be, or if you are a Catholic, a chat with a saint. I doubt you can pull it off. I certainly can't now, although I could have done during the height of my dream yoga practices (see below). A friend of mine, a devout Christian, once mentioned that he was frustrated with his dreaming because he had tried repeatedly to dream of Jesus, but to no avail. This kind of dreaming requires that the intention pass across the wake-sleep boundary – a process we have called elsewhere *cross-phase transference* (or cross-state transference) of symbolic material (Laughlin, McManus and d'Aquili 1990:150-156). Of course, cross-phase transference happens all the time in dreaming – that is where the "day residue" content comes from. But the difference is to what extent can the dreamer choose to dream about a specific object (or image) while awake, recall the intention in a lucid dream state, and proceed to carry out the intention while dreaming. When data surface about a people among whom specialists like shamans are able to dream lucidly at will and direct their gaze at one or another object chosen while awake, we have another hallmark of a dream yoga, by whatever name it is called by the people.

There are some authorities that have hypothesized that imagery of the dream and fantasy variety is going on in the subconscious all the time – perhaps in a continual 90-110 minute *ultradian rhythm*.[1] This was an idea that was first suggested by Nathaniel Kleitman (1963, 1969) and

---

[1] Evidence suggests that all dreaming is influenced by ultradian rhythms (Nielsen 2011a:578).

elaborated by Roger Broughton (1975) – a notion known as the *basic rest-activity cycle* or *BRAC* (see also Othmer, Hayden and Segelbaum 1969). Michele Stephen (1995:99) has re-floated this idea and terms this 24-hour cycling of subconscious dreaming, "autonomous imagination" – by which she means, "...the existence in the mind of a continuous stream of imagery thought that operates mostly outside consciousness and beyond conscious control. Although not usually available to consciousness, it can spontaneously enter consciousness in dreams, and sometimes in waking visions, and is experienced as taking place independently of a person's conscious invention or will." Under the right conditions, this subconscious stream may burble up into consciousness and result in, "...dreams, trance, and possession not merely effecting truths but also the source of a genuine creativity emerging from a distinctive mode of imaginary thought" (Stephen 1997:337). This may well be true, and if so it may mean that the more primitive eidetic functions of our brain are chattering away while our waking ego is mainly aware of sensory experiences and conceptual language.

If a mostly subconscious stream of autonomous imagination is in fact going on 24/7 in our brains, it is a process that may well be at the physiological roots of Jungian "active imagination" (Jung 1997), as well as perhaps many traditional "mystical" techniques, where one may learn to consciously "dip down" as it were into the stream of imagery and experience spontaneous fantasies, not to mention dreams that operate as selfscape representations of what is going on in the unconscious at that moment. However, if autonomous imagination is in fact the case, the practice of dream yoga would seem to reverse the direction of control of content from autonomous streaming while dreaming to intentional control of dream adventures.

## Synesthesia and Dreaming – A Curious Aside

There is a brief tangent I feel we have to take up with respect to dream imagery and autonomous streaming. Imagery occurring subconsciously or arising in dreams may be due to *synesthesia* – that is, sensations arising in one sensory mode automatically give rise to sensations in another sensory mode, as when someone hears color or sees sound. The great composer, Olivier Messiaen, reportedly saw colors when he heard music, whether inside his head or through his ears. Dream images may arise because of other activities going on in the body. We examined this with respect to diagnosis of disease in Chapter 9. But there is a broader sense in which this cross-modal transfer of information may come into play.

Let me offer a personal example. I was once in a lengthy meditation retreat at Samye Ling monastery in southern Scotland – the first major Tibetan Buddhist retreat center in the West. I was given a comfortable room and was brought my meals which I ate in my room. The meals were vegetarian and there were often between 10 and 12 separate cooked foods on my plate – really, the finest veggie cuisine I have ever eaten. As is standard practice, I meditated on the process of eating, at first mainly paying attention to my sense of taste. But before long, I realized that with my eyes closed intense images were arising. With each mouthful of a particular dish, the imagery was either of pink fluffy clouds, or a battlefield — mainly tanks rolling across a desert landscape. This puzzled me until it dawned on me that the chef was possibly offering both yin and yang dishes in each meal. I had never thought of foods in that way. So I asked the server about this and was told the chef indeed very consciously balanced yin and yang foods each meal – a very Taoist approach to meal planning. I then proposed an experiment to which the chef readily agreed. I would receive my plate, sit down to eat and then number each dish from 1 to N on little pieces of paper stuck the foods. I would eat each dish separately and record on a tablet what imagery arose. Number 1 might be pink clouds, number 2 battlefield, number 3 battlefield, and so on. When the chef received my plate back from the server with remnants of each dish and their respective labels, she would make her own list indicating each numbered dish as being either yin or yang. When I compared these lists, I found that my imagery matched unfailingly the yin-yang designation of the food – fluffy pink clouds arose when I was eating yin foods, battle scenes when I was eating yang foods.

This was the first time I realized that there was a direct experiential basis for yin-yang, or female-male, attributions of the type claimed by Eastern mystery traditions. More importantly, it gave me a direct experience of synesthesia, an experience that might point the way to an explanation for very common binary categorizations found cross-culturally, in particular the distinction between "hot" and "cold" diseases, etc. And it showed me that dream and meditation imagery may at times be an expression of non-visual processing of information – processing that might well be organized around binary oppositions.

## A Cahuilla Shaman

Methods for learning to control dream content vary from society to society. A remarkable account of developing this skill is to be found in the memoirs of a Cahuilla (a.k.a., Iviatim) medicine woman named Ruby Modesto to be found in the book, *Not for Innocent Ears: Spiritual Traditions of a Desert Cahuilla Medicine Woman* (Modesto and Mount 1980). Ruby was born in 1913 to her Cahuilla family who lived in the Coachella Valley, the beautiful and arid valley that contains southern California's famous Salton Sea. When she was young, Ruby slept with her family and was told the sacred stories before she fell asleep each night. Her grandfather's Uncle Charlie was a *pul*, or shaman, and told her that shamans are born, not selected. One is chosen in the womb by *Umna'ah*, the Cahuilla's creator god (ibid:25). Each shaman has a dream helper which they contact in a dream that used to be incubated by ingesting the psychoactive plant, Datura (*Datura* spp.), but more recently happens without herbal aids. Ruby's (ibid:26):

> ...helper came spontaneously when I was about ten years old. I dreamed to the 13$^{th}$ level. The way you do that is by remembering to tell yourself to go to sleep in your first level ordinary dream. You consciously tell yourself to lay down and go to sleep. Then you dream a second dream [a dream within a dream]. This is the second level and the prerequisite for real Dreaming. Uncle Charlie called the process "setting up dreaming." You can tell yourself ahead of time where you want to go, or what you want to see, or what you want to learn. On the 3$^{rd}$ level you learn and see unusual things, not of this world. The hills and terrain are different. On both the 2$^{nd}$ and 3$^{rd}$ dream levels you can talk to people and ask questions about what you want to know. During

Dreaming the soul goes out of the body, so you have to be careful. ...When I dreamed to the 13th level, that first time, I was young and didn't know how to get back. Usually I dream to the 2nd or 3rd levels. But that time I kept having different dreams and falling asleep and going to another dream level. That was where I met my helper, *Ahswit*, the eagle. But I was in sort of a coma, asleep for several days. My father tried to bring me back, but couldn't. He had to call my Uncle Charlie who finally managed to bring my spirit back. That was one of his specialties, healing soul loss. When I woke up they made me promise not to Dream like that again, not until I knew how to get back by myself. The way you return is to tell yourself beforehand that you are going to come back (like self-hypnosis [auto suggestion]), later in the dream you have to remember.

Obviously, Ruby was exercising sufficient intentionality in the ordinary dream and transformed the content into another dream ("dream within a dream"), and so forth until she dreamed her way into a trance. What is not clear by her description is whether by "ordinary" dream she was referring to sleep onset (hypnagogic) or the first REM period. In any event, as I have mentioned before, by this point dreaming has become so lucid as to be virtually indistinguishable from a meditation trance (Hunt 1989:181) – a point that Ruby appears to have stumbled upon early in her life.

## Rainbow and the Sun Dance

The Shoshone medicine man credited with revitalizing the Shoshone and Crow Sun Dance after it was outlawed in the 19th century was John Trehero, otherwise known as Rainbow (Fitzgerald 1991:Chap. 8). He received his calling, plus instruction, implements and power from the Chief of the Little People, Seven Arrows, during a three day retreat in a cave. He was fasting and meditating, according to the traditions of his people. On the third day he heard drumming and singing and bells ringing from deeper in the cave. During a lucid dream he was joined by Seven Arrows who invited Trehero to follow him back into the cave so he could show Trehero some things. At first they arrived at a place and saw men gambling on the hoop and arrow game. They wandered back further and came to a cavern where people were betting on horse races. Still further into the cave they arrived at a place where people were betting on the hand game. Seven Arrows indicated that all these gambling games were no good.

They then walked back even further to a place where they could hear a drum beating and saw a tipi. The sides of the tipi were rolled up for ventilation and they could see a sick person who was barely "skin and bones" and a medicine man treating the patient. After the medicine man had completed his ministrations, Seven Arrows told Trehero, "This is what I am going to give you; this is what is good. I know you are sincere and will use your powers only for what is good. I want you to go back now; go back, take up your fasting. You should not use what I am going to give you to do any of the gambling things that you saw back there. Go back home now, and I will tell you later what things I want you to work with. You will be able to help people to get well when they are sick. Now take up your fast and go from the mountain down to that lake and wash up, take a swim" (ibid:56). Seven Arrows led him back to the cave entrance where, as Trehero said to Fitzgerald (ibid:220-221n), "...I saw my body lying there on the ground. I realized then that my vision had not been in the physical world. When I reached my body, I felt as though I was lying down on top of myself, and then I was awake." Trehero did as he was bade and began his career as a healer and he was in touch with Seven Arrows the rest of his life.

It was through the intervention of Seven Arrows that Trehero stopped experimenting with the peyote religion and took up the Sun Dance fulltime. The rest, as they say, is history. "I was going only to the Sun Dances, and I was given more power. I was told what to do, given medicine things, and told how to use them. Seven Arrows gave me all the things I needed to work with. He also told me all the rules and how to run the Sun Dance in the Shoshone way so that our traditional way was restored. It was Seven Arrows and all of the Medicine Fathers who gave me the authority to officiate the Sun Dances every summer among my people" (ibid:59).

## The Kogi Mámas

The Kogi Indians live high in the Sierra Nevada de Santa Marta mountains of Columbia. They are the only surviving remnant of pre-Columbian culture in the Americas, and have one of the most remarkable social structures and cultures in the ethnographic literature. The only ethnographer who has so far been able to study their way of life is Gerardo Reichel-Dolmatoff (1949-1950, 1976). The Kogi are a subsistence agricultural people who are ruled by an elite strata of male priests called *mámas* who undergo what is perhaps one of the most strenuous, years-long spiritual apprenticeships on the planet. A novice is chosen by a máma in trance communion with the Mother-Goddess, or by dream-divination. The family of the chosen baby is notified and at some point during early childhood, the child is taken into the care of the mámas. Then begins a years-long period of training that lasts until the novice is initiated as a new máma during early adulthood. During the many years of training, the novice lives among the family of a máma and never sees the light of day – literally. He sleeps in a ceremonial house during the daylight hours, and only emerges during brief intervals at night for meals and for training, always accompanied by a máma. If the moon is out at night, he has to wear a special hat that blocks out the direct light of the moon. All during the night he is being trained and indoctrinated. He undergoes many of the ritual drivers we have spoken about earlier (Chapter 4), including repetitious chanting, dietary strictures, fasting, rhythmic singing and dancing, total sexual abstinence, meditation and breathing exercises, and ingestion of various psychoactive drugs (about which little is known). "The youth is taught many divinatory techniques, beginning with the simple yes-or-no alternatives, and going on to deep meditation accompanied by exercises of muscular relaxation, controlled breathing, and the 'listening' to sudden signs and voices from within" (1976:280).[2]

The whole point of a novice máma's arduous education is the gradual introduction of direct experience and mastery of ASC, including

---

[2] These voices and signs are quite common to meditation, and are recognized by Tantric Buddhists practitioners as being lawfully related to the type of meditation being done. By reports of these signs, the teacher knows what stage of development the novice meditator has reached.

lucid dreaming, accompanied by proper indoctrination as to the meaning of experiences as they arise. This is a pattern of enculturation anthropologists have recognized in "bush schools" everywhere (e.g., Watkins 1943) – the removal of the novice from normal everyday life, and then a pairing of indoctrination with unfolding experiences, often driven by ritual techniques. For the apprentice máma, this is a long process by which sensory deprivation is accompanied by ritual drivers that evoke inner spiritual experiences in lucid dreams and trance states that, in keeping with our cycle of meaning model, result in the experiential instantiation of the Kogi cosmology, and culminate in union with the divine. As Reichel-Dolmatoff (1976:284-285) writes:

> ...the aim of priestly education is to discover and awaken those hidden faculties of the mind that, at a given moment, enable the novice to establish contact with the divine sphere. The mámas know that a controlled set or sequence of sensory privations eventually produces altered states of consciousness enabling the novice to perceive a wide range of visual, auditory, or haptic hallucinations. The novice sees images and hears voices that explain and extol the essence of being, the true sources of Nature, together with the manner of solving a great variety of common human conflict situations. In this way, he is able to receive instructions about offerings to be made, about collective ceremonies to be organized, or sickness to be cured. He acquires the faculty of seeing behind the exterior appearances of things and perceiving their true nature. ...The entire teaching process is aimed at this slow, gradual building up to the sublime moment of self-disclosure of god to man, of the moment when Sintána or Búnkuasé or one of their avatars reveals himself in a flash of light and says: "Do this! Go there!" Education, at this stage, is a technique of progressive illumination. The divine personification appears bathed in a heavenly light and, from then on teaches the novice at night.

We do not know the exact role of dreaming in this educational process, for no anthropologist has volunteered to enter the training, assuming the mámas would allow such participation. But reading between the lines, the thrust of education is, as Reichel-Dolmatoff says, the mastery of ASC, and this must include evocation and use of lucid dreams, very likely paired with intense meditation. Indeed, it sounds very like the mámas accomplish a 24/7 exploration of dreamed existence, perhaps resulting in one of the most intense and sublime unions between human and the divine among the world's peoples.

## Hindu Dream Yoga

As the above examples illustrate, many dream yogas are designed to evoke transpersonal experiences and to acquire power by way of dream and vision images. On the other hand, there are dream yogas the ultimate intent of which is to transcend perception in either the waking or dreaming life-world. These dream cultures conceive of transcendence as a SOC in which all sensorial activity ceases, leaving awareness with only itself as object – essentially "pure" awareness. Again, the purpose to which this transcendent SOC is put depends upon the particular tradition. When one achieves this SOC, all of the cognitive and eidetic "chatter" has fallen away, and the mind is filled with bliss and tranquility — and more importantly, effortless single-mindedness or concentration. The advantage of this state is that the meditator can direct his/her concentration to any object without being distracted by competing objects.

Hindu yogas are all about realizing that waking/dreaming experience is an illusion created by the mind, and misunderstood as reality. The whole point of Hindu practice is the realization of the true nature of consciousness. George Gillespie (1991:225-226; see also O'Flaherty 1984:Chap. 1) tells us that according to the earliest Upanishadic Hindu tradition, there are four types of consciousness: (1) waking, (2) dreaming, (3) dreamless sleep, and (4) liberation. The first two categories are mundane ones alternately filled with sensory data about the body and the external world (being "awake") and the movie-like imagery of the inner world created and witnessed by the mind ("dreaming"). Both states are equally illusory. Far closer to the goal of liberation is the dreamless sleep state, which I read to be essentially "access concentration." We go into this state every night, but we are conditioned to lose consciousness when in dreamless sleep. The trick in Hindu dream yoga is to maintain lucid awareness after sensory and dream-movie experience stops, for this produces the SOC closest to the realization of liberation. "To experience the fourth [liberation] is to experience the true nature of the Self and to be truly free from the other three states. ...The Self moves from dreamless sleep, its home, to dream and then to waking experience and then returns in reverse order, the way it came. Seen in another way, in dreamless sleep, the senses and mind do not function at all. When the mind works, dreams are created. When both mind and senses are active, it is the waking state" (ibid:226).

A *yogin* (yoga practitioner) is taught certain techniques in order to transcend waking and dreaming phenomena (e.g., Radha 1994:Chap. 23). The techniques boil down to learning to cultivate a mind state that alternates between "choiceless awareness" and single-minded concentration upon one and only one object (usually the breath, but also the rise and fall of the belly, the heartbeat, visualizing a *bindu* (bubble), images of the Divine, etc.). Choiceless awareness is a state in which one watches whatever is happening in the "now" without clinging to, or dialoging with whatever is arising. Single-minded concentration is a state of observing the object of meditation without being distracted by any other object competing for attention. Ideally, these practices "pull the energy rug" out from under the chatter, and as a consequence, the chatter slows down, fades and eventually stops, just leaving the "watcher" and the object being watched (see Gillespie 1985). If the yogin uses dream yoga, this intense and disciplined lucidity continues into the dream states, and both waking and dreaming experiences are transcended, leaving the awareness of dreamless sleep. It is interesting that the Hindu take on dreaming and waking are the opposite of most traditional societies that, as we have seen, consider both equally real. Visualizing images at will and the use of mantra while dreaming are fundamental skills that are easier for some to master than for others (Radha 1994:265). Visualization in the dream state will, as we shall see below, change one's dream life into a field of meditation (Hunt and Ogilvie 1988).

## Tibetan Tantric Buddhist Dream Yoga: A Personal Journey

In order to flesh out what I mean by the more disciplined and extensive uses to which cultures may put to transpersonal dreaming, I would like to share what I can about my exploration of lucid dreaming and Tibetan Tantric Buddhist dream yoga (see Bulkeley 2008:99-108; Tenzin Wangyal Rinpoche 1998; Namkhai Norbu Rinpoche 1992; Laughlin, McManus and Webber 1984).

### Tibetan Tantric Buddhist Dream Yoga

Dreaming, as with all the world's great religions, has been important in Buddhism since its inception some 2500 years ago (Serinity Young 2001; Bulkeley 2008: Chap 3; Evans-Wentz 2005[1951]). The Buddha's mother dreamed of his birth, and the Buddha himself had portentous dreams while still a young prince in his father's household. Later in the development of Buddhist methods, the use of dreaming as a yoga became a powerful tool to propel consciousness toward the ultimate goal of liberation. Tibet inherited the northern Mahayana form of Buddhism that had incorporated many of the Tantric techniques of Hindu traditions. These methods became blended with the Tibetans' own shamanistic *Bön* traditions, and the amalgam culminated in a system of ritual practices designed to incubate or "drive" (Laughlin, McManus and d'Aquili 1990:145-150) alternative states – to my knowledge, a system unequaled in complexity and efficacy among the world's spiritual traditions.

One of those practices is the dream yoga (Tib: *mi-lam*) which is included as one of the so-called Six Yogas of Naropa,[3] revered and emphasized by the Kagyu sect and the Dzogchen teachers of the Nyingma sect of Tibetan Buddhism (Guenther 1963; LaBerge 2003; Bulkeley 2008:99-100; Gillespie 1988a:27; Chang 1991[1963]:52). Integral to the dream yoga are ritual methods for maintaining and enhancing awareness while entering and during dream states. It is

---

[3] I also practiced the other Six Yogas of Naropa to some extent – for a description of some of my experiences exploring the *tumo* or "heat" (psychic energy) yoga, see Laughlin (1994b).

said that a fully accomplished dream yogi remains aware of his/her experience 24 hours a day. This was the system of dream incubation and study that has guided my own dream explorations later in life and to this day.

## Mandala Experiences (From Age 25 - 39)

It all began when I awoke early one morning in 1963 staring at the world through a mandala (in what I later would learn to be a hypnopompic experience; see Gillespie 1987). I don't mean mandala in a trivial metaphoric sense, but quite literally. I came out of sleep and into waking awareness in a state of intense bliss and looking at my bedroom filtered through an exquisitely complex and colorful mandala – like a filter of lace made of the most delicate, complex and multi-hued spider web (perhaps equivalent to Gillespie's "lattice imagery"). It was a living thing and pulsed in synchrony with the rhythm of bliss I felt coursing through my body. The experience lasted for only a few minutes and then subsided. The mandala image and intensity of bliss faded at the same time. It is hard to describe the complexity of the image, for no matter how proficient an artist I might have been, there is no way I could have ever rendered the image accurately on paper. It was made up of hundreds of thousands of fine, radiant colored lines, like a multicolored, pulsing curtain made of pure energy hanging in front of my eyes. The ambient light in my bedroom was dim, but I could discern the normal objects in the room through the gauze-like filter of the mandala. As the term implies, the mandala had a distinct center and radians from the center outward to the periphery.

This experience scared me. In fact, I became furious with a friend with whom I had coffee the night before, thinking that she had maliciously spiked my beverage with some kind of drug. As absurd as it was, that was the only interpretive frame I had at the time to make sense of the experience. As it turned out, this was the first of many such experiences that I was to have over the years, and I quite naturally became very curious about my dream phenomenology. The experiences in those early days were always spontaneous, and I had no notion that

I could willfully produce them. They were essentially hypnopompic images and they all shared a common structure:

- *The Visual Aspect.* An intense, pulsing visual experience consisting of an intricate pattern of brightly colored, nearly infinitesimal lines – the total configuration corresponding to a classical mandala (i.e., manifests a definite center, is symmetrical about that center, is circular while at the same time "quaternary;" see Argüelles and Argüelles, 1972). The pattern is so intense that it may be perceived for a few minutes or longer after awakening with the eyes open or closed, even in a lighted environment.
- *The Affective Aspect.* An intense and active state of pulsing euphoria not associated with the ingestion of drugs. This affective state corresponds in intensity and decay rate with the visual aspect, and is a similar state of bliss I later learned to that experienced under deep meditation or trance.

Over the years I have spoken with a few people who have had similar experiences of mandalas in their waking consciousness – usually during meditation sessions – and many more people who recall mandala motifs arising in their dreams. The direct experience of spontaneous, eidetic mandala imagery while people are awake, however, appears to be a fairly rare event.[4] I am still not clear as to whether or not this kind of mandala experience occurs in all persons during their dream life, or merely in a significant few. But that it is experienced by some people in all societies is quite likely, for the mandala motif in company with other images expressing the wholeness of the self is – as C.G. Jung (1951/1959) noted in *Aion* – a virtual cultural universal. The appearance of the mandala motif in religious and nonreligious symbolism is very widespread among the world's societies. It is present in the iconography of Buddhist sects, the Australian aborigines, various plains Indian groups, in Western Christianity, to mention but a few examples (see Krippner 1997; TenHouten 1993).

Jung was, as it turned out, as fascinated with mandalas as I, and for very much the same reasons. But I was unaware of Jung or of his

---

[4] Other kinds of images arising in the hypnopompic are not uncommon; see Young (1994) who had similar "waking dream" images after waking.

interest during those early years of spontaneous transpersonal episodes and later drug-assisted explorations of mandalas. My first encounter with Jung and his study of mandala symbolism was profound and significant. A decade after my own first mandala experience, I was browsing in a book store and found a copy of Jung's book, *Mandala Symbolism* (1969f). As I leafed through the book's plates, I was struck by the remarkable similarity between four of those images and my own mandala experiences. So I bought the book, and only later did I discover in an editorial footnote that the four plates I had identified were the very four, and the only four, that Jung himself painted from his own dream recall. This remarkable correspondence naturally led me to study closely all of Jung's writings pertaining to the mandala, and then everything else he wrote bearing on depth psychology and extraordinary dream experiences.

In a number of places, C.G. Jung (e.g., 1964) points to the scientific significance of the mandala motif in dreams and religious symbolism around the world. Jung (1969a:3) described the phenomenon as follows:

> The Sanskrit word mandala means "circle" in the ordinary sense of the word. In the sphere of religious practices and in psychology it denotes circular images, which are drawn, painted, modeled, or danced. Plastic structures of this kind are to be found, for instance, in Tibetan Buddhism, and as dance figures these circular patterns occur also in Dervish monasteries. As psychological phenomena they appear spontaneously in dreams, in certain states of conflict, and in cases of schizophrenia. Very frequently they contain a quaternity or a multiple of four, in form of a cross, a star, a square, an octagon, etc. In alchemy we encounter this motif in the form of *quadratura circuli*.

As we saw in Chapter 12, Jung firmly believed in the existence of the universal or "collective" unconscious, as well as in the fundamental tendency of humans to reason by constructing binary oppositions, or *antinomies*. Jung felt the mandala to be the key to human symbolism because it is a primal archetype, and as such it often represents both the self and the unification or nexus of all possible oppositions (Jung

1959[1951]: 31; see also Laughlin 2001).[5] Among other contexts, the mandala is encountered by the conscious ego through dreaming. The mandala symbol is a virtual cultural universal, appearing as it does in traditional art, iconography, myth and dreaming among peoples all over the planet (see e.g., Ridington and Ridington 1970:51 on the mandala in Dunne-za cosmology).

## Tibetan Dream Yoga (From Age 39+)

Between the ages of 25 and 39, I had yet to hear of Tibetan dream yoga, but I had learned to enhance and explore my dream life, and had become an occasional lucid dreamer – that is, I would wake up while dreaming and know that I was dreaming and that I had a certain amount of control over what happened in the dream. I had done all the usual things – I learned that the only thing necessary to increase dream recall and lucidity was to develop an intense interest in my dreams, to put a tablet of paper and a pen next to my bed and write down every scrap of dream I could recall immediately after waking. I drank half a glass of water before falling asleep and finished the glass of water upon waking. I would fall asleep focusing upon my intention to become more aware of my dreams, or upon a problem I wished to solve with the help

---

[5] Selfscape Dream had while writing this chapter (3/25/11): I am a member of a group, one of four that were organized around a center and each to a quarter of the space. I have become the leader of my group and seem to have a special relationship with the group in the opposite quadrant to mine. I considered the leader of the opposite group to be a dull fellow and easily manipulated, so I fomented a plan to take over all the groups. But then the "boss" showed up whom I introduced jokingly as the "uber" something. I asked if I could speak to him alone, back in my own group, intending to communicate my plan to him, but the "uber" resisted going off with me as he was standing in the middle between all the groups. I told him my plan anyways, and he responded, "But what of art, of music…?" and some other finer things. Then he became abusive all of a sudden and I angry, and I struck out at him and woke up. My immediate thought was of the obvious mandala-like spatial format of the groups and relations between groups, and the "special" complimentary relationship I had with my opposite in the other group. It seems that I, as spokesman for my group, was trying to usurp (was positively greedy for) the role of "uber," of leader of the whole — in other words, my dream ego complex was trying to hog control of the whole self. I was reminded by the real "uber" that there was more to myself than control by one unbalanced ego.

of the "depths." All of these techniques had deepened my conscious involvement and lucidity in my dream life by the time I was introduced to Tibetan dream yoga when I was around 40 years old.

When I encountered Tibetan dream yoga, I changed my incubation practice to a more active meditation (see Tenzin Wangyal Rinpoche 1998:Chap. 5 for a description of dream yoga methods). My only instruction at the time came from my new teacher[6] and what I could glean from the few books available at the time, mainly those by Garma C.C. Chang (1991[1963]), W.Y. Evans-Wentz (1958) and Herbert Guenther (1963). I began my nightly meditation by going to bed before I was actually tired. I concentrated first upon a neon red English letter 'A' at the base of my throat (Tibetans use their letter corresponding to the "ah" phone in the "throat chakra"), and later simplified this image to a red *bindu* (Tib: *Tig Le*) or radiant bubble the size of a pea at the base of my throat (Chang 1991[1963]:61). At the same time I chanted "ahhhhhh" softly in my throat, and later learned to do this sublingually in my head. Using these simple techniques, I was able to enter sleep onset – the hypnagogic state (Chapter 4) — in an alert, energized and focused state of awareness, and eventually found that the hypnagogic, lasting but a few seconds in normal sleep onset, began to stretch out into minutes. I was eventually able to remain in the hypnagogic "hallucinogenic" state for up to a half hour, and experienced intense kaleidoscopic imagery which began as a kind of gorgeous two dimensional slide show, but then deepened into dynamic, four dimensional experiences. Many of the "signs" and "voices" I mentioned above with respect to Kogi meditation arose. As I intimated, meditation texts in the Buddhist tradition list many such images as lawfully associated "signs" of maturation in any distinct meditation. Meditation on the breath produces one set of signs, meditation on water another set of signs, and so on. Because of the kind of meditation I was doing, mandala-like imagery arose. The rather two dimensional mandalas I first encountered in the hypnagogic (and earlier in the hypnopompic) became dynamic tunnels down which I would travel and that led to various events, places and landscapes (see

---

[6] My teacher at the time was Venerable Tarchin Hearn who was then an ordained Tibetan Buddhist monk and resident teacher at the Crystal Staff house in Ottawa, Ontario. At this writing (2011) he is the resident meditation master at the Wangapeka Study and Retreat Center in New Zealand.

Green 1968:60-61 for a similar tunneling experience). One thing I learned was that my earlier mandala experiences constituted a symbolic "calling," that is, an invitation from the depths of the psyche to engage in an inner exploration. Once the mandalas succeeded in gaining my undivided attention, they morphed into portals into the spiritual realm. I also learned what the phenomenology of a *bardo* is like to Tibetan Buddhists, the dream equivalent of the intermediate state of being between this life and the next, as described in the *Bardo Thodol*, or the *Tibetan Book of the Dead* (Sumegi 2008:82).[7]

However, no matter how concentrated my mind state entering the hypnagogic, I could not remain conscious more than about half an hour, and when I became fatigued I would inevitably lose consciousness and enter normal sleep. My dream recall and rate of lucid dreaming increased markedly due to this more intense meditative practice – I recorded lucid experiences of some sort almost nightly (see Tenzin Wangyal Rinpoche 1998:Chap. 6 on enhanced lucidity) — but I could not approximate the unbroken awareness throughout the sleep cycle that dream yogis have described. At some point – after I had turned 41 – I concluded I had to "up the ante" somewhat and stop trying to stay awake while sleeping in the prone position. It was obvious to me that I was struggling against a lifetime's conditioning to lose consciousness when I lay down, so I became determined not to lie down at all. So I began sitting in half-lotus posture with my back in a corner and meditated my way into the hypnagogic. This worked to some extent in prolonging the hypnagogic and even entering deep lucid dreaming, but again, the conditioning was too strong and I would wake up after a sleep cycle or two lying flat out and realizing that I had lost consciousness. I even tried the Tibetan trick of using a meditation strap to keep myself in proper posture, but to no avail (see Evans-Wentz 2005[1951]:xviii).

I finally decided to rig things so that it was impossible for me to lie down during the night. I built a box out of plywood approximately four feet square and higher than my shoulders when sitting in half-lotus. I lined the bottom and sides of the box with foam sheets thick

---

[7] Incidentally, it became very interesting to me as an anthropologist that *there are no phenomenal experiences described for the bardo of dying that cannot be had in a dream bardo*, leading me to the hypothesis that Tibetan yogis in ancient days projected their living dream experiences upon the process of dying.

enough that it made the inside rather round, soft and snug. The corner facing me was open as the two sides that would have met to form the corner extended only half the length of the side of the bottom. This left a corner at my back and two angles on each side for my knees to fit in snugly, and an opening in front of me to enter the box and to lay things (water, tablet and pen, rosary, so forth) within easy reach on the floor. Thus began a rather crazy time in my life due to the most intense dreamwork I have ever undertaken. I slept sitting up for months, and though I was never able to remain conscious throughout the night, I spent much of my sleep in lucid dreaming, wafting in and out of the waking and dream states and recording experiences on paper as I could.

Apropos to Buddhism generally (Obeyesekere 1990:65), and Tibetan yoga techniques in particular (Sumegi 2008:81), I began thinking of dreaming as reality and waking as dreaming – which, considering I was a university professor at the time with a full class-load, made my lectures rather strange I am sure. Ideally, this practice should be done in retreat circumstances in which one is learning to cultivate *samadhi* or *rigpa* in all states of consciousness, thus making meditating one's way into dream states so much easier (e.g., see Tenzim Palmo's retreat experiences in Mackenzie 1998:119). In any event, the goal from the Tibetan Buddhist point of view is to realize that *all states of consciousness are illusory* (Sumegi 2008), or products of the mind driven by karma, and the ultimate goal is the experience of Nirvāna – that is, the realization of the essence of mind that projects or "builds" all these illusory "realities." True to the method's intent, my waking life really did take on the feeling and surreal qualities of the dream state, and the lucidity I attained in dream states was far more vivid and "real" than the waking state.[8]

Throughout it all there was recognition that I was in and out of what the Tibetan teachers call *rigpa*, or non-dual awareness. I was acutely aware

---

[8] Tibetan yogis use this kind of practice as a way to recondition the mind to think of all phenomenal states as being illusory – all episodes in the unfolding of *Sangsāra*. It was only much later that I learned that my preceptor and meditation master in Nepal, the Shakya lama Chogye Trichen Rinpoche, had taken one of the "secret vows", and never lay down at night, a fact to which I can attest as I was near him for months at a time at his monastery in Lumbini, and he occupied a room with only a screen door to the hallway. No matter what time of night I was wandering by his room, he was sitting up and either chanting or nodding off.

that whether "awake" or "dreaming," my mind was generating a movie which might or might not correspond very closely with extramental reality. It was only later on in my "insight" practice that I fully came to realize that our phenomenal world is constructed by our brain as a flickering field of particles (granules, pixels, *yods*, dots; see Laughlin, McManus and d'Aquili 1990:108-112), regardless of state of consciousness.

The experiences I had during and before using the sleeping box were not always pleasant ones — far from it in fact. Many were dark and disturbing, and some downright frightening. My sense of self during the early months was like that of a committee in a boardroom without a CEO, then after a point I knew who the real CEO was – not an entity, but a "complex above complexes," as Jung would say, or as A.N. Whitehead put it, a "presiding occasion." Because I was as much a Jungian as a Buddhist, I interpreted these ordeals as the result of my having tapped into the deeper levels of my unconscious self, which, because of my conditioned "neurotic" fear, took threatening forms. Different complexes warred with each other for control of consciousness – all of them affectively charged either positively (sometimes ecstatically) or negatively (fear, anxiety, revulsion, self-hate). Again, my Buddhist studies came in handy, for I took up another Tibetan practice; that being to consciously transform my dream-ego into a particular semi-fierce "deity" which I had been assigned by one of my teachers – my *yidam*, or personal protector, was called *Mahamaya*, the Great Sorcerer, who is depicted on Tibetan paintings (*thangka*) as a huge light blue figure dancing in flames with four multicolored heads, each with a mouth with fangs and two red eyes and a "third eye" just for good measure, two sets of arms with hands holding various implements, clothed in a tiger skin and wearing a necklace of human skulls. I cannot think of a better dream body when encountering the demons of the depths. After some practice I was able to assume this dream body, and this practice alone transformed encounters with the unconscious to a less terrifying tone.

During this period I experienced "rebirthing," as some New Age folks like to call it. I spontaneously "recalled" and re-experienced my birth, which had been traumatic due to the fact that my mother was drugged and I was apparently removed forcefully from the womb using forceps – all this compounded by anoxia. The sequence of dreamed birth experiences took many months to fully unfold, and were very much involved with body witness and affect, especially hunger, anoxia and terror. During the sleeping box period, I kept a bowl of condensed milk on hand to bathe my mouth during the night, thus "feeding" the traumatized infant within my unconscious. That infant never really integrated within my personality. "Baby Denny" is every bit the Jungian complex, a rather encystized part of my being that is still with me in my seventies. But thanks to that early yoga work, I came to know him intimately and his effects upon my mood and body kinetics lessened over time. I also experienced full-blown demons, and once the devil himself climbing up a spiral staircase with his minions following behind him.

Many of the characters and objects I encountered during these years of intense dreaming were archetypal images (Chapter 10; see also Laughlin 1996, 2001; Kruger 1985). One of the hallmarks of encountering archetypes for the first time is that they often present as "pure" eidetic images with little, if any, cultural overlay. With repeated encounters the images begin to incorporate cultural and personal attributes, like hair-dos, Western clothing, Western gestures and mannerisms, so forth. Objects lose their universal form and become common everyday objects – pure bubbles may become wine glasses or milk bottles, geometric forms may become gem stones, and so forth. In other words, the archetypal image shows development as it becomes more familiar, adapts to waking cultural expectations, and takes its place within the library of shared symbols and meanings available to both the waking/dreaming ego and the unconscious. One begins to recognize human images as being like people one has known. When they first present, archetypal human forms may take the appearance of "radiant" beings, whether positive (god/goddess) or negative (demonic). They are beings of light and no substance, perfect in every way (no flaws, blemishes, asymmetries, pores, etc.).[9] Archetypal radiant beings were more complete, more beautiful or repulsive, and way more numinous than anything in the waking "real" world could ever be.

---

[9] I had learned early on in doing Tibetan style "arising" yoga that when one internalizes an external image or object – perhaps using a picture or object in the outer world to gaze at and then shut the eyes and hold the image before the mind's eye – the eidetic image tends to perfect itself. Any blemishes, cracks, splotches, etc. tend to vanish and one is left with a perfected inner version of the outer, "real" image upon which to meditate.

Moreover, when they first present they may be accompanied by a sense of numinosity, power and the feeling of ecstatic bliss. These feelings too dissipate as the radiant being develops over time and takes its place in the library of internally shared symbols.

Being a heterosexual male, the goddess figures I encountered were lovelier than any real woman could ever be in the flesh (Laughlin 2001). They were perfect (as viewed with the sensitivities of my particular dream ego), garbed in veils of light, and able to morph into other forms before my mind's eye. Sometimes they would initially present as radiantly beautiful feminine forms and then morph into something bestial, repulsive and scary. I recall one dream in which such a lovely goddess figure came toward me and as she entered a gate in a picket fence that had been between us, she morphed into a demon of dull gray with leathery wings, fangs and threatening eyes. She spread her wings and flew at me and over my head. It was during the course of many such dreams that I learned where traditional peoples get the notion that gods, goddesses and spirits are real. I also learned what the Kuma of New Guinea mean by asserting that evil can well be disguised by attractive features (Reay 1962). Had I not been as much a Jungian as a Buddhist, I might well have interpreted these encounters as communion with the gods, demons or ancestors. I also learned how people may get the notion that people and animals may be shape-shifters, morphing freely from form to form as the underlying archetype manifests its various visual and affective facets.

Coitus was another archetypal motif I encountered often, especially in the beginning before it got so utterly boring that the mind stopped producing the images. I recall dreaming of rocky landscapes with naked couples and groups made up of radiant figures making love in every conceivable position and using every possible technique. I learned that if I shifted my energies (*chi*, *prana*, or *tumo*) from my lower body and genital area up to my heart or head, the imagery would likewise shift to some other symbolic motif. In other words, it was possible in these dreams to willfully modify how my libido presented from sexual arousal to the experience of non-sexual love and communion with whatever arose before my mind's eye. There was a time when I played with flipping the energies back and forth between these two poles – between sexual arousal and loving-kindness (*metta*), and the imagery that arose would change accordingly. Also, if I sent the energies into the crown of my head, I could generate intense light experiences, and at times experience myself discorporate into a million radiant particles. For Tibetan Tantric yogis, it is this willful control of psychic energy (*tumo*, or *dumo*) that is one of the important skills to master in this kind of work, and hence sexual abstinence is encouraged or required so as to remove external stimuli and internalize the distribution of psychic energy (see Laughlin 1994b on Tibetan *dumo* practice; for descriptions of psychic energy experiences among other peoples see Tedlock 1981 on the Quiché Maya; Lederman 1991 for Malay shamans; Brown 1992 for the Aguaruna; Katz for the Kalihari Bushmen). When one can direct psychic energy to the different *chakras*, those energies may be used to forward other, more advanced meditative practices, all leading to insight and eventual liberation. In this case, for instance, if one can transform sexual energy into loving-kindness in the dream state, one has thus entered a fearless state appropriate to encountering otherwise scary aspects of one's being – knowledge of this being another "seal" experience (Chapter 12).

Experiences had in lucid dreams would sometimes inform me of the real mystery behind meditative practices done in waking state. One of the "foundation" practices in Tibetan Buddhism is to complete 100,000 repetitions of deep prostrations to the guru. This is accomplished while standing before an altar, or while visualizing the guru, and then moving from a standing start to a fully prostrated position. I was well into this practice when I had a lucid dream in which I was starting a prostration before a colorful altar at the end of an in-breath and by the time I had reached the end of the out-breath and completed the prostration, my dream body had discorporated and my consciousness expanded into a vast, infinite plenum void, accompanied with intense ecstasy. When I awoke, it was with the certain understanding that if one were to do a prostration properly, only one repetition would do the trick to evoke the transcendental mind state toward which the practice is pointing.

I do not recall ever having a precognitive dream, or co-dreaming with anyone. I did have two different "past lifetime" dreams in which I recognized myself in another human form from another era of history. The quality of these dreams was quite unique as they were in black-grey-white tones and were like the old black and white, documentary-style

Pathé News films of the '40s and '50s. I have never had another dream quite like them. The imagery emerged in both cases out of a mist or cloud and into crystal clarity. Both figures were warriors, one from the East long ago, and the other a naval officer on the bridge of an early 20$^{th}$ century German warship (I recognized his uniform when he turned around and stared at me). But as I do not believe in an afterlife or in reincarnation, I concluded that the certainty with which I identified with these forms was just part of the illusion. In other words, how I interpreted these apparitions within the dreams was determined in part by my interpretive frame. And I can well understand how someone of another culture might have understood these experiences as visitations from ancestors, or as glimpses into the dreamer's own past lifetimes.

Out-of-body experiences were commonplace in dreams during the sleeping box period. I could look down at my physical self in the box, and consciously leave my body to wander about and then return to it – just as described in other chapters for dreamers in traditional societies. I recall the first time I consciously left my body in this way. I was in my body at the beginning of an in-breath, and was floating near the ceiling at the end of the in-breath. My first thought was, "How am I going to get down from here?" – immediately followed by an urge to test whether I was actually out of my body. I slipped my hand under my rear, and as I felt the padding under me, my dream ego was immediately back in my normal body awareness. I never tested the experience again, always interpreting that my out-of-body experience was another part of the movie unfolding between my ears (see Blackmore 2005 on this issue). But I also became aware over time that many of my fellow Tantric practitioners uncritically assumed they were really out of their bodies and floating around "out there," not "in here" between the ears.

One of the most profound discoveries during my dreamwork was that if I needed guidance or an answer to a burning question, the dream content would often present an answer or offer guidance. Once while staying in Chogye Rinpoche's monastery in Lumbini, Nepal, I was beset with demons during the night, which reflected a state of depression, anxiety and alienation (in hindsight, a lovely dose of culture shock). In desperation I called out mentally to Rinpoche, and almost immediately I was looking over Rinpoche's shoulder (in the lucid dream) and saw that he was concentrating upon a mirror upon which energy formed and dissipated like clouds of colorful rice grains.[10] I was immediately reminded that all the scary demons were but illusions made of dots, and the fear and alienation vanished, and I could return to the equanimity of *rigpa*. Tiberia (1977:87), citing Bell (1931:25), described a similar experience had by a Tibetan monk: "The monk was fasting in the mountains and could not keep warm because he did not know the proper meditational technique. He prayed earnestly to his 'guru' and eventually some women appeared to him one night in a vision. They instructed him in physical and breathing exercises through which he could keep warm."

## My Interpretive Frame

I could go on and on relating dream-vision experiences whilst practicing the dream yoga, but I would like to spend the rest of the chapter discussing my interpretive frame. This is obviously important given what I said in Chapter 7 about the cycle of meaning. While I benefited from my Buddhist teachers, my interpretive frame was quite different than traditional Buddhist accounts or technical use of experience. The uses to which dream yoga is put in "The Teaching" is quite different from the use to which I put the experiences as a neuroanthropologist. For Tibetan Buddhists, the interpretation of experiences had in dreams is always couched in terms of textual material or "whispered" teachings from their *lama* (guru), and the ultimate goal of liberation. For me, the exploration was about the range of experienced "realities" that my brain could construe for its own consumption – the brain as producer, director and stage, as well as audience for the movie unfolding in various states of consciousness. Mind you, in this respect the neuropsychology of dreaming and waking states is quite consonant with Buddhist psychology. All phenomenal experiences are illusion – a symbolic play that represents either internal or external extramental reality, and as such

---

[10] Rice on a mirror was already meaningful to me because I had completed the 100,000 repetitions of the mandala offering practice which is part of the foundation practices in Tibetan meditation (see Chapter 5 for a description of the practice), as well as a common motif in many shamanic traditions (see MacDonald, Cove, Laughlin and McManus 1988).

"...exemplify the nature of the phenomenal world – fleeting, changeable, insubstantial, not ultimately valuable or reliable" (Sumegi 2008:79).

My interpretive bias with regard to dream symbolism and the self was distinctly Jungian. Out-of-body experiences that fellow meditators would routinely interpret as veridical reality I would interpret as metaphorical and occurring entirely within my brain and physical body. With respect to the relevance of lucidity to the anthropological study of dreaming, it became clear to me that much of the meaning of a dream was in fact present and a part of the dream, and did not require a "demythologizing" post-dreaming analysis of the kind influenced by Freudian dreamwork. In Erica Bouguignon's term, my dreaming was "pre-interpreted;" i.e., the dream was meaningful in and of itself, and that meaning was carried over into the post-dreaming, waking state as a memory just as integral to the dream as the feelings and imagery. For researchers undertaking this kind of intense dreamwork, the ego becomes effectively a multi-state system of awareness – in other words, a kind of "meta-ego" that traverses in an unfragmented awareness through different states of consciousness. In other words, this work is fundamentally transpersonal, as one becomes changed in the doing of it.

The understanding that lucid dreaming can be preinterpretive led quite naturally to the hypothesis that the more the prefrontal cortex becomes involved as a component in the structure of dreaming, the less important "latent" content – that is, motivations and material projected on dream content from the waking state – is to the dreamer. The meaning of the dream is apparent within the dream itself, and that meaning invites further reflection and thought after the fact – much as does myth. What becomes relevant to the dreamer is the pre-interpreted information within the dream, rather than understanding imposed by hindsight from outside the dream. It also became quite clear to me that where "dreaming" left off and "trancing" began became very fuzzy indeed – in fact became a rather useless distinction. This is one difference I think between meditating one's way into dreaming and merely waking up in a dream characteristic of the more common lucid dream. Meditation leading to extended hypnagogic experiences is rather more a trance state than sleep onset in the usual sense of the term. Yet the lucid dreams I enjoyed later in the night were presumably REM dreams, although I have no independent confirmation of that.

### Summary and Segue

We have examined dreaming cross-culturally from all sorts of perspectives. We have described a number of dream cultures and ritual practices used by peoples to enrich their dream experiences, and draw them into their society's cycle of meaning and worldview. Hopefully, we have broadened our understanding of the range of experiences had by people in more polyphasic societies – those who encourage their members to engage with their dreaming for personal and social purposes. In this chapter we focused on those few societies that maximize the potential uses of dreams as a window into the sublime, into the depths, or as a field of phenomenology. There would seem to be a qualitative difference between the lucidity of dreaming where awareness is maintained across the wake-sleep boundary and the lucidity when one "wakes up" in a dream. For one thing, complex intention may be maintained in the former, whereas it must be remembered in the latter.

It is now time to shift our orientation from the ethnography of dreaming to a more theoretical account of dreaming as a universal human phenomenon. The next section of the book will begin with a neuroanthropological theory of dreaming in which we integrate what we have come to know about both the universal properties of dreaming and the cross-cultural variation in dreams with what we know about how the brain works and has evolved. After that we will present a discussion of the role of dreaming in the modern world.

PART THREE

# A Neuroanthropology of Dreaming

# Chapter 14

# A Neuroanthropology of Dreaming

> In any case, although anthropologists have made some interesting contributions to the literature on dreaming, more could be done. There is a need for a theory that lends itself to a cross-cultural, comparative study of dreams. Such a theory would have to acknowledge what we know about the evolutionary, neurobiological substrates of dreaming common to all humans. But as anthropologists have suggested, it also would need to account for the complex ways in which the mind and dreams are affected by social and cultural experience, including the ways in which the narrating of dreams may feed back into the way they are felt and experienced.
>
> Douglas Hollan (2004:171-172)

Dreaming, first and foremost, is a product of the activity of our brain while we are asleep (Fiss 1986). As we saw in Chapter 4, each and every SOC is mediated by a discrete and dynamic organization of neural circuits that operate more or less in parallel, and that come together to produce the on-going "movie" of our perceptual and imaginal mind. Our *brainmind* (as Earl Count 1958 liked to call it) has evolved over millions of years, and has developed during the course of each of our lives — a process of cellular growth and refinement that began before we were born and that will continue until our death. Our evolutionary past has assured that in each of our brains, species-typical neurognostic (or archetypal) structures emerge early in development which, after further development, mark each and every human being as a bearer of a uniquely human mind (Edith Turner 1986). By the same token, as we have seen in Part 2, the variation in dreaming and dream interpretation across cultures is considerable. Each society leaves its mark on the developing brainmind of its members – its "culture-bearers" — thus obscuring the underlying universal patterns of mentation that form the foundation of every normal human's consciousness. What we dream about, how we interpret our dreams, the social import of dreams, the reality or unreality of events in dreams, to what extent they augur the future or offer us useful information about ourselves and our environment – all of these aspects are heavily influenced by our culture. Our culture channels the physiological development of our minds, in both dreaming and waking states, along the paths considered appropriate and useful by society.

In an evolutionary sense, "culture" is anthropology's shorthand for plasticity of human neural development. Socially influenced learning and flexibility of cognition and behavior are not unique to humans, nor are they dependent upon human culture, but the complexity, as well as the enormous variety of meanings and behaviors exhibited by humans are culturally dependent. All primates learn to do things with their hands, like use hammer stones and clubs, tease termites out of their mounds, swing through the forest canopy, groom each other. However, none but humans can perform surgery, play a Bach prelude, perform sleight of hand tricks, or type manuscripts. In fact, if you consider the skill exhibited by high wire acrobats, we humans are even the world's best primate brachiators. The fact that we have been able to adapt ourselves to life on the moon, however briefly, and the depths of the ocean, in addition to every niche on the planet that might conceivably sustain us is testament enough to the successful strategy of enhanced neural plasticity.

In this chapter I want to pull all the elements we have discussed together into a coherent, general account of the evolutionary neurobiology and the ethnology I have surveyed in the first two parts of the book. I want to show why and how dreaming evolved, and how the cultural loading upon the development of dreaming and social interpretation of dreams came to be important in human evolution. And I want to do this without giving either the neurobiology or the ethnology of dreaming short shrift.

## Evolution of the Dreaming Brain

We know that all placental mammals dream, including all primates. Our species *Homo sapiens sapiens* is one of roughly 350 known primate species (Matsuzuwa 2010:6), all of whom dream (Zepelin 1989). Thus, we may infer that our primate ancestors living during the Miocene period 14 million years ago (or more) also dreamed. I cannot imagine we will ever know what Miocene apes dreamed about, but on the current evidence, we can be reasonably sure that they did not have language, and thus could not share their dreams with one another any more than wild chimpanzees can today. They probably were incapable of going on intentional adventures in their dreaming, adventures that would allow them to access information of practical importance when they awoke. Therefore, dreaming was no doubt of as little social or cultural importance to Miocene apes as it is to present day apes. So far as we know now, humans are the only species capable either of communicating dream content with others, or of socially incubating, interpreting and using dream content in a public manner. It is obvious, therefore, that when we are addressing the evolution of dreaming, we are really talking about two issues; namely, (1) how and why dreaming as a SOC evolved among animals in the first place, and (2) how the ability to share subjective states evolved as a function of the evolution of communication.

## The Origin and Function of the Sleeping Brain

The evolution of the animal kingdom began with the origin of single cell creatures who very likely also experienced their environment in some very rudimentary way. Single cell animals adapt to their environment by moving in space over time. That means there must be some mechanism, however primitive, of internally depicting their environment as information, and acting in accord with that information. We know that single cell critters like euglena, amoebas and paramecia have the ability to sense variations of light and chemistry and move accordingly. "Experience" (a crude and simple "movie;" see Chapter 4) first arose as an adaptation to a dynamic environment within which animals had to find food and avoid dangers. J.R.R. Tolkien's *Ents* aside, land plants do not adapt to their environments by moving their position in space, and thus may not have evolved the mechanisms necessary for mediating experience.[1] Thus far there is no good evidence that unicellular animals sleep, much less dream.

The emergence of multicellular animals further developed the reliance upon experiencing and moving in space over time. They had to develop mechanisms for controlling and coordinating somatic activities so that potentially autonomous cells did not render concerted action impossible. This necessity eventually led to the specialization of control cells that evolved into neurons and eventually simple neural nets (or circuits) typical of creatures like the jellyfish (Sanes, Reh and Harris 2005:Chap. 1). As animal species increased in size and cellular complexity, so too did the neural networks become more complex in order to maintain control of otherwise autonomous somatic systems (Sporns 2010:142-148). Eventually, these primitive neural circuits formed a neural tube with multiple sensory organs (typical say of triploblastic worms like those that evolved a billion years ago; see Ghysen 2003). It is thus very likely that experience mediated by a primitive nervous system – a system that included awareness of a multi-modal sensorium – arose in the earliest stages of multicellular animal evolution (see Crist 2002 on Darwin's fascinating research demonstrating "intelligence" and experience in earthworms).

It is very unlikely that animals with such primitive sensoria actually dreamed – but it also seems probable that we will never know for sure. In my opinion, dreaming had to await the proliferation of networks made up of special neurons sufficient to produce alternative states of awareness. So that we are on the same page here, there are three types of neurons in the mammalian brain: (1) *afferent neurons* that carry sensory information from sense organs into the sensory association brain centers, (2) *efferent neurons* that carry commands from within the brain's control areas out to organs and muscles, and (3) *interneurons* (or *local circuit neurons*; Sporns 2010:3) that connect to each other to form local circuits. These are cells that neither deliver sensory data from the surfaces of our body or organs, nor carry commands to muscles and

---

[1] Some plants are phototropic, and thus have a rudimentary ability to orient their leaves to maximize sunlight. Also, there is some evidence that a plant's root systems may communicate within the system to maximize nutriment.

organs, but inhabit an intermediate space between those information-in, information-out functions.

Simple local circuits make our reflexes work. When the doctor taps you on the knee with her little hammer, it is the reflexes in your spinal cord that transform sensory input into action. More complex systems of interneurons comprise the sensory association areas, memory circuits and higher cortical functions that intervene between sensory input and action. There are many times the number of interneurons relative to afferent and efferent neurons in the brains of more advanced animals, and the higher on the evolutionary scale, the higher that proportion of interneurons becomes. Interneurons organize to mediate experiential models (or "schemas") of extramental reality (Hensch 2005).[2] In other words, without the emergence of interneurons intervening between sensory input and behavioral output, complex experience (our inner "movie") as we humans know it would not be possible. Not only that, but the physiological necessity of dreaming would never have arisen in phylogenesis.

The pattern throughout animal phylogenesis is towards an increase of body size, and complexity and flexibility of neural control in adaptation to the environment (Sporns 2010:Chap. 14). Maximal control requires that neural systems not only respond to sensed changes in the environment, but they also must be able to feed-forward in anticipation of events yet to come (Miller, Galanter and Pribram 1960). When we are walking, we take our next step in anticipation that a solid ground will be there to meet our footfall. We may be wrong of course, and may well step off the edge of a cliff. This is because we, like all animals, operate upon our inner models of reality and not upon extramental reality itself. Thus, there is an adaptive advantage for an animal to accurately predict events in the near future. Interneurons emerged perhaps a billion years ago and then evolved into local circuits and systems of circuits that required both greater numbers of interneurons, and an increasing variety of types of interneurons that became specialized in their form and function, thereby making possible more refined circuits and inner models of ever greater complexity and flexibility.

---

[2] I prefer the term "model" to the old gestalt "schema" used so effectively by Piaget. These earlier theorists had no way to ground the organization of representations of reality in neuroscience, but we now do. My use of model implies a neurophysiological structure that mediates experience of the self or extramental reality.

As nervous systems became more complex, there appeared an advantage of periodically entering a metabolic period of "down time" – a lethargic, sleep-like state in which an organism channels energy resources away from dealing with the external world, and toward internal growth and development. This sleep-like state among creatures with brains must have arisen very early in evolution, for it has been demonstrated in simple invertebrates like round worms (e.g., *Caenorhabditis elegans;* see Raizen *et al.* 2008). This suggests that brains from the earliest, most primitive period of their inception have required sleep in order to maximize adaptation, a process that involves changes in synaptic interconnections to maintain neural plasticity and accuracy of modeling. Moreover, fruit flies (*Drosophila melanogaster*) not only require intermittent sleep, but demonstrate the same repercussions of experimental sleep deprivation as humans and other mammals – the longer they are deprived, the longer they sleep when allowed to do so (Zimmerman *et al.* 2006; Huber *et al.* 2004).

As I have already presented data and theoretical considerations pertaining to the function of sleep in Chapter 4, I will merely remind the reader that sleep functions to facilitate the transformations in neural organization required for on-going adaptation to the environment. Because the brain is a trophic and self-regulating system, sleep operates to potentiate, store, associate, change and develop the structures that mediate memories and other processes (Katz and Shatz 1996; LeDoux 2003: Chap. 5). Sleep funnels finite metabolic resources into the growth of new synaptic connections between nerve cells and thus is essential to intuitive and creative problem-solving (Hobson and Wohl 2005:15). So important is sleep to the optimal functioning of the animal brain that it outweighs the considerable disadvantage of enhanced vulnerability during lethargic "down time."

## The Origin and Functions of the Dreaming Brain

As was already discussed in Chapter 4, we know that all placental mammals (Zepelin 1989) and passerine birds (Low *et al.* 2008) both sleep and dream. Reptiles, the common ancestors of mammals and birds, do show evidence of sleep as well as slow-wave EEG activity, and there is now some evidence as well of REM-type, low voltage, fast wave activity in reptiles of the kind that is typical of dreaming in higher animals (Siegel 1999, 2005). And as we know, most vivid and lucid dreaming occurs during REM periods among humans (although dreaming is also reported during NREM). It is curious that smaller animals (e.g., rats) tend to require more REM sleep than larger animals (e.g., elephants), and those mammals that are born while still helpless ("altricial" births) exhibit more REM than those born able to fend for themselves ("precocial" births; Siegel 1999). Cetacea, like the Bottlenose Dolphin, enter sleep by alternating each hemisphere of their brain, thus reducing somatic atonia and allowing them to surface in order to breathe while asleep.

The relationship between experiencing during sleep and the structure of REM and NREM sleep stages is problematic at this point, for it is not altogether clear whether or not there exist qualitative distinctions between REM dreams and NREM dreams (see Chellappa *et al.* 2011; Nielsen 1999). An example of a difference in quality is that nightmares tend to happen during REM and so-called "night terrors" happen during NREM (McNamara 2008:14).[3] What is clear is that dreaming goes on intermittently throughout the stages of sleep, while the changes in neural activity during different sleep stages may subserve a variety of neurobiological functions in addition to mediating dream "movies." Some researchers are beginning to distinguish among the various kinds of "mentation" that may go on in sleep, but for our purposes I have limited our concern to dreaming in the normal sense of the term — that is, experiences involving pseudo-perceptual content.

All-in-all, there is probably no way we can discover with certainty just when dreaming – that is, experiencing while asleep – first arose in phylogenesis. But I am going to suggest a simple hypothesis that would go a long way in answering that question. My suggestion is that dreaming arose when sleeping brains evolved, long before the REM-type sleep stage emerged. In other words, when the first brains evolved that required the metabolically lethargic down-time for optimal functioning, dreaming arose as a byproduct. Why do I propose this

---

[3] Night terrors usually happen to children who will wake up – perhaps sit up in bed — in a state of great dread and often screaming, and may be either hallucinating or have no dream recall at all (Santomauro and French 2009).

idea? Simple really, for as I just mentioned, it is now clear that the inception of dreaming did not require the evolution of REM-type sleep stages. Moreover, much of the confusion about the functions of dreaming stem from the erroneous idea that when critters sleep, they are sort of "switched off," only to be "switched on" again when they awake. This view is the consequence of an over-mechanical understanding of how brains work.

When we sleep, that does not mean that our brains turn off. Brains are made of cells, and individual cells do not sleep. Systems of cells (like those that control voluntary muscle systems) may be inhibited while the brain goes on experiencing, thus justifying the old label "paradoxical sleep," but that does not mean that the cells involved are "switched off" like microchips. Indeed, neurons and support cells may remain quite active during sleep, and my hypothesis is that when systems of cells that mediate experience in waking life become active during sleep, they will produce "pseudo-perceptual" imagery (Wallace 1951) within the sensorium of the brain and hence the organism dreams. These experiential cell-systems (networks, or models) become active for all the reasons we discussed in Chapter 4: facilitation of growth and development, establishing new synaptic connections, intra-psychic cross-talk facilitating reorganization and autoregulation, running simulations of the perceptual world, especially those involving threatening events, and rehearsal of adaptive responses. There may well have been early selection in favor of animals that entrained awareness to the systems mediating dreaming, especially where rehearsal or simulation was involved (Donald 1995). This is sheer speculation on my part, but it is not an improbable scenario to imagine. Integration of awareness with rehearsed responses to environmental contingencies would have provided a powerful anticipatory function for adaptation.

## Evolution of the Symbolic Process and Dreaming

If I am correct, direct selection in favor of experiencing while sleeping began when dreaming became coupled to reality simulation, rehearsal and awareness (Revonsuo 2000, 2006; Nielsen 2011b; Donald 1995), and this would have happened very early in phylogenesis. While dreaming probably arose as a byproduct of sleeping, at some later point it became an *exaptation* – that is, a structure selected for originally because of one function becomes selected for because of another function later on (see Gould 1991). To better understand the significance of this shift in functioning, we should understand something more about images as symbols (see Chapter 4). All experiencing brains from their earliest inception would have operated upon what I and my colleagues have called elsewhere the *symbolic process* (Laughlin, McManus and d'Aquili 1990:163)[4] – the process by which images arising in perception and pseudo-perception are synaptically associated with fields of information in memory. (Remember the children's magnet and iron filings model?) Selection for complexification of the symbolic process involving experience would have been nearly immediate, I should think, and would have resulted in an increasing proportion of interneurons specialized to that function. It would not have taken long (in terms of evolutionary time) for selection to favor complexity of the symbolic process, and with it the complexification of dream imagery, and the integration of dreaming and waking cognition, however primitive.

Much of the symbolic function in higher mammals is mediated by cortical structures of the brain. It is very common for people to think of the cortex as a recent innovation in evolution, but this is not the case, as the primitive cortex and its precursors date way back to the brains of invertebrates living during the Precambrian era, some half a billion years ago or more (Tomer *et al.* 2010). Part of the confusion about this issue is semantic. The outermost surface of the invertebrate brain is called the *mushroom body*, a structure found in the brains of many worms and arthropods today that mediates learning and memory – the two most important precursor functions to the selection for the symbolic process in evolution. All vertebrates have a similar layer of neural surface tissue that is called the *pallium*, which serves the same function, shares the same genetics as the invertebrate mushroom body, and dates back to roughly 360 million years ago (Jarvis 2009). It is

---

[4] "The symbolic process is that function of the nervous system by which the neural network mediating the whole [meaning of something] is entrained by and to the network mediating the part [image of that something]; that is, the mechanism by which the neurocognitive model of [reality] is evoked by partial sensory information stimulated by [that reality]" (Laughlin, McManus and d'Aquili 1990:163).

also much more complex and advanced in birds and lower mammals than was once thought, due to the mistaken notion that the pallium consisted only of what we would call the basal ganglia in the human brain (Jarvis 2004). The pallium expanded and complexified over time and became the cerebrum of lizards, and then birds and mammals between 220 and 280 million years ago. This suggests that experience included symbolic processing from nearly the inception of sleeping brains. Hence, symbolic imagery has been fundamental to dreaming since at least the beginning of the Cambrian some 540 million years ago. At some unknown point thereafter, the symbolic process mediating dreaming became paired with rehearsal (Parman 1979; Revonsuo 2000) of schemes with adaptational effects in the waking state. This shift in function would have lead to exaptation and direct selection in favor of dreaming.

## Assimilation and Accommodation

There are two demands placed upon the symbolic process no matter how advanced or primitive the brain. Jean Piaget called these demands *assimilation* and *accommodation* (Piaget 1977, 1980; see also Block 1982). Neural models of extramental reality must be open both to the assimilation of information from reality (adjust practice to models), and to the accommodation of internal structures to the evidence from reality (adjust models to practice). It is the adjustment of internal models both to reality and to changes of circuits within the brain that produces some of the experiences had while dreaming. It also is the adaptational process that produces creativity and problem-solving while dreaming (Cartwright 1986). This reciprocal adjustment process is ongoing from cradle to grave, and is one we inherited from the long distant phylogenetic past. All brains that mediate experience would operate in the same way symbolically, regardless of how ancient or primitive they may be. Internal models must both anticipate events in waking life (that is why they are adaptive in the first place) and must be capable of growth and change in order to develop and maintain models that are adaptive to a dynamic reality over time. For example, James L. Gould (1986; see also Seeley 2010) has shown that honeybees operate upon an internal cognitive map of their landscape, and that the younger the worker bee, the closer it remains to the hive in its foraging. It takes time for its cognized landscape to develop such that it can effectively forage further afield and unfailingly find its way home.

It would be immediately advantageous to an animal for a perceptual/pseudo-perceptual image to "stand for," to evoke its meaning field stored in memory, and to be the basis of action, rather than have to seek more information from the environment before acting. As Seligman and Hager (1972) pointed out years ago, some images are already "wired-into" the brains of animals so that only one or a few sensory encounters with the corresponding bit of reality will suffice to activate inherent (archetypal, neurognostic) meaning and response schemes – often little more than a step up from reflex loops in simpler animals. As these would be primitive animals whose brains nonetheless mediate some simple form of experience – i.e., provide the animal an internal "theater of mind" – these images would also arise in dreams and perhaps be involved in simulations and rehearsals.

## Reality and Reality Testing

I am not constructing a solipsistic theory here. Rather, the theory requires a kind of evolutionary and scientific realism (Devitt 1991:Chap. 7) – that is, the presumption of an extramental reality that is both sensible and invisible to the animal. All animals with brains operate upon their own inner cognized world – a world of experience mediated by their system of neural models (Laughlin and d'Aquili 1974; Donald 1991). How then does an animal know when an experience is real? Furthermore, how does an animal "true-up" its models so that they are more accurate and adaptive? The answer is, brains are neurognostically "pre-wired" to accept the limits of extramental reality while they are awake – limits that exhibit the twin qualities of obduracy and affordancy. The term *obduracy* is given a very moralistic definition in the dictionary, but in metaphysics the term generally means the *characteristic of reality to resist the will and intentions of the psyche*. If we try to walk through a wall without the benefit of a door, we will come up against the obdurate nature of reality. While we may dream that we are flying without mechanical help, attempts to do so in reality might prove disastrous. Much of early development in the baby has to do with exploring the somatosensory limits of obduracy – the obduracy of the baby's environment and of his/her own body (Piaget, 1980).

The other quality of extramental reality is *affordancy,* a term coined by the great perceptual psychologist, James J. Gibson (1979, 1982), to conceptualize the active interaction between experience and what is allowed by extramental reality. "Roughly, the affordances of things are what they furnish, for good or ill, that is, what they *afford* the observer" (1982, p. 401). Again, "…the *affordances* of the environment are what it *offers* the animal, what it *provides* or *furnishes*, either for good or ill" (1979, p. 127, emphasis by Gibson). The development of knowledge about the world is a process of interaction in which things in reality *afford* the experiencing animal particular qualities relative to the animal's ability to model and utilize its environment. Obviously then, the affordances of things in the world depend upon the structure of the animal. A stick laying over a stream may afford adequate support for a squirrel or an ant wishing to cross over, but not for a large dog. Flowers afford electromagnetic information in the ultraviolet range for honeybees, but not for people.

Obduracy and affordancy are actually obverse qualities of extramental reality in relation to the structure and limitations of the animal's body and its nervous system. Both the body and the world present obdurations and affordances that condition our intentionality, and thus operate to limit, guide and inform our learning about our body and our world. We encounter these qualities daily, as do all animals with neurocognitive systems. We only become aware of them when we run up against either resistance to our intentions or new opportunities. Once we have adapted to (adjusted our neural models of) obdurate and affordant aspects of the world, we generally lose awareness of the distinction between our experience of reality and extramental reality itself.

What makes dreaming real for animals are not the obduracy and affordancy of outer reality as experienced in the waking state, but the obduracy and affordancy of the animal's own extramental body, the functions of its nervous system and the latter's imaging capabilities (e.g., honeybees may dream in ultraviolet and electric eels may dream of non-visual electromagnetic fields, but we cannot do either). Dreams afford the revelation of the hidden, the invisible – the causal connections between things that are often unavailable to waking awareness. The underlying forces that may cause things to happen — but like the wind, remain outside of waking perception — may become sensible in dreams because we can imagine them without bumping up against sensory obduracy. In other words, dreaming facilitates construction and rehearsal of alternative solutions to a problem – creative response possibilities – without immediate censure from outer reality.

Susan Parman (1979) was spot-on when she linked the selection for dreaming with selection for play. As with sleeping and dreaming, we now know that play arose much earlier in phylogenesis than was previously thought (Burghardt 2006). Play is virtually ubiquitous among mammals and some birds. There is some evidence of play among reptiles as well, including Lazell and Spitzer (1977) for crocodiles, Burghardt (1998; Burghardt, Ward and Rosscoe 1996) for turtles and Burghardt (1982) for chameleons. Playing with objects has been demonstrated among octopuses by Kuba *et al.* (2006) – no surprise really, for the octopus is the largest brained invertebrate in the world. I myself have kept many different species of tarantulas – the most neurophysiologically advanced land invertebrates – and have never observed play behavior, although I did place novel objects in their tanks. The problem with lower animals is that it is very hard to tell when they might be playing, so future research may well push the evolutionary origins of play back even further into early evolution. But at this point it seems very likely that selection for dreaming predated selection for play by millions of years.

In any event, like play, dreaming facilitates creative neural modeling. Models are elaborated in creative ways, and then these new possibilities are tested in the crucible of extramental reality – they are literally "trued-up" relative to reality (Donald 2011:137-148). This testing function of neural models was discussed by George Miller and his colleagues (Miller, Galanter and Pribram 1960; see also Pribram 1971, 1980) who suggested that neural models undergo a reality test they called the *T.O.T.E.* or the "test, operate, test, exit" process. The organism "tests" (seeks sensory information about a problem it faces in the world), "operates" (applies the model as action in the world), "tests" again (seeks sensory information about the efficacy of the operation) and either returns to the "operates" phase, or moves on to "exit" (habituation and moving on from the problem). In other words, all organisms act in the world of reality by operating upon their internal models of reality. The obduracy of reality may resist the efficacy of actions precipitated by the organism's neural models, and if the organism does not die, it has to reformulate its models until they conform as much as possible to reality. When the model anticipates affordancy accurately, the organism's activity works and the problem of obduracy has been cognitively transformed into affordancy – the problem is solved. Dreaming on this account is a sleep function that maximizes plasticity of model construction, and thus maximizes alternative action possibilities while awake – all within the structural constrains and possibilities of the particular organism's nervous system.

## The Great Divide

Speaking of structural constraints, one of the problems we have in empathizing with dreaming among other animals is that there has been a quantum leap from the brainminds of Miocene apes, or even hominins of 2.5 million years ago, to the brainminds of humans today. We should note that the sheer amount of cortical tissue has increased "several hundredfold" from the earliest primates to modern humans (Koch 2004:70). Also, our hominin ancestors became extinct long ago, and all we have left are brain endocasts made from inside their petrified skulls to give us some gross pictures of what the surfaces of their brains might have looked like (Falk 2004). Ralph Holloway (1995) has argued that the reorganization of the ape brain into the earliest hominin configuration occurred between 3 to 4 million years ago, long before there is any evidence of language-related cortical changes. But this argument has been disputed by Tobias (1995:64), Falk (2004:32-35) and many others. What is certain is that the earliest hominin endocasts show that they are of the same size as those of apes. Later on, creatures like *Homo habilis* (living in Africa about 2 million years ago) were clearly tool users and had become capable of fashioning stone tools of such complexity that no other animal would have been able to make or master them, much less would have been clever enough to retain them at hand for future use. Their speech-related cortical structures (e.g., Broca's area) had also taken on a distinctly human form. But more important, the size and configuration of the frontal lobes, and especially of the prefrontal cortex, outstripped all other features in the evolving hominin line. Our species, *Homo sapiens sapiens*, came on the scene around 100,000 years ago, and has a brain that features a PFC that is proportionally larger and more complex than any previous hominin (Jerison 1973, 1985; Rilling and Insel 1999; Bering and Bjorklund 2007; Geary 2007:230).

Some of these ancestors were truly intermediate between early apes and us. If only we had a living community of *Homo erectus* around for us to ask endless questions, and put through fMRI studies, we might be further ahead in our understanding of the differences between our minds and theirs with respect to neocortical functions. Even if we had just one *Homo erectus* "bog man" with an intact, preserved brain, we would be light years beyond our present understanding. But alas we do not, and so we are left to ground our extrapolations on the available and very limited data. As a shorthand way of illustrating the difference in the size of the human brain relative to over-all body size, we use what Jerison (1973; Coolidge and Wynn 2009:75) called the *encephalization quotient*, or EQ. EQ is a rough measure of the size of the brain relative to body size as one would expect them to be. An EQ of 1.0 means that brain size is average relative to body size if all that has changed is an increase in the animal's size. The chimpanzee has an EQ of 2.4, whereas *Australopithecus afarensis*, a hominin living 3 million years ago has an EQ of 3.1, which means that selection for bigger brains irrespective of body size was operating along the ape line, and especially the hominin line. *Homo habilis* had an EQ of 4.0, *Homo erectus* of 5.5 and modern humans have an EQ of 7.6 (Tobias 1987). These figures indicate not only selection for brain over and above larger body size, but also for vast changes in the organization of mental functions from the beginning of the hominin line to humans today (in this respect, Holloway was undoubtedly correct).

In my opinion, the most important function of the human prefrontal cortex with respect to unique human cognitive abilities is the construction and empirical testing of *plans* (Miller, Galanter and Pribram 1960; Fuster 2008:4; Miller and Cohen 2001; Coolidge and Wynn 2009:13-14). Plans are neurocognitive meta-models that bind time, establish linked serial operations, and make the organization of goals possible. I began to write this book over a year ago, and I am still at it. This is in part because I could organize my on-going activities in such a way that they make realizing such a long-term goal possible. So far as we know, we are the only animal that can do this. It is true that the anthropoid apes can follow goals for short durations – for example, when a chimpanzee walks away from a termite mound to seek and prepare a sticky twig, walks back again to the mound and places the twig in the opening and waits while termites get stuck on the twig's resin, then pulls the twig out and eats the trapped termites. This is a plan that can take a half hour or so to complete. Moreover, young chimps learn this skill from watching adults. This is no less a plan for a chimp than my writing this book is for me, but the human plan can bind time for hours, days, even years — not just minutes. Plans are inherently future oriented and are thus obviously advantageous in an evolutionary sense. I have already implied that all creatures with brains feed-forward into the future, at least in terms of anticipating the next few moments (see Laughlin and Throop 2008). In addition, Gene d'Aquili and I (Laughlin and d'Aquili 1974) argued that the fact of tool retention was as important as tool manufacture in the archeological record, for it indicates the expansion of planning way into the future. Some wild chimpanzees use clubs very effectively in defense (Kortlandt 1963), but despite the fact that forest dwelling chimps are commonly attacked by leopards and do use clubs to defend themselves (Boesch 1991), none have been observed to carry a shillelagh in the event it might be useful in the next attack.

It is important to note that the prefrontal lobes do *not* send the commands for specific actions directly, but rather organize those action schema into a temporal queue (Fuster 2008:335). Entrainment of PFC planning and executive functions to the neural structures mediating dreaming is what makes lengthy, goal-directed adventures possible in dreams of a more lucid character. It is just possible that a chimpanzee could dream an adventure in which he had to do this before he did that to bring about a temporal goal, but only if it was a simple set of acts similar to preparing a termite fishing twig. On the other hand, a wild chimp cannot express that dream to others as a story. The chimp certainly has the intelligence to plan (Premack 1976), but his neocortex is not wired to learn speech. We now know that chimpanzees can learn symbolic communication, but only by way of the visual system. By comparison, a traditional polyphasic dreamer might go on lengthy dream adventures, perhaps to the land of the dead and back, and be able to spin a story of multiple, many-faceted events in a coherent narrative with immediate social portent.

## Cross-Over, Lateralization and Dreaming

Neuropsychologists have established that the human brain is lateralized in both its architecture and its functions. Generally speaking, our brain is designed so that right and left lobe functions are complimentary and both contribute to complex functions. As we saw in Chapter 4, there is some evidence that the right hemisphere specializes in mediating lucidity, while the left hemisphere (in most people) mediates language. But we also saw that mediation of pseudo-perceptual imaging is far from that clear-cut. It depends upon what aspects of imaging one is discussing. What is clear is that the organization of the brain across the hemispheres is fundamental to our understanding of dreaming, especially among human beings.

Neither the *functional lateralization*, nor the *decussation* (cross-over of senses and motor control from the right side of the body to the left side of the brain, and vice versa) are unique to the human brain. Far from it, as they are fundamental organizational principles upon which all vertebrate brains are structured. Both are very ancient features in the evolution of the vertebrate nervous system (Rogers 2000; Shinbrot and Young 2008). It follows that each feature must have been in some way advantageous to survival. The decussation of sensory and behavioral tracts to the opposite side of the brain would appear to provide three-dimensional topological stability. Shinbrot and Young (2008:1278) report that, "… we examine constraints imposed by topology on the ways that a three dimensional processor and environment can be wired together in a continuous, somatotopic, way. We show that as the number of wiring connections grows, decussated arrangements become overwhelmingly more robust against wiring errors than seemingly simpler same-sided wiring schemes."

Functional lateralization of the brain also appears to provide adaptive advantages for vertebrates (Vallortigara, Rogers and Bisazza 1999). Lateralization in mammals and birds appears to facilitate the ability to track the environment for predators with the right side of the brain while the left side is busy completing some task like hunting and pecking grain. In a number of studies, the right eye and left hemisphere of birds, fish and other animals appear to be specialized in categorizing stimuli and making considered (hence delayed) decisions. As Rogers notes, "The opposite lateralizations for aggressive and feeding responses may, of course, reflect underlying hemispheric specializations for perceptual processing and for rapid versus considered responding. In other words, there may be a general tendency for the left hemisphere to process information based on categories and to make considered decisions before responding, whereas the right hemisphere attends to novelty and the immediate, unsorted features of a stimulus and so controls rapid responses" (ibid:239). Based upon the now famous split-brain studies[5] among human subjects (Sperry 1974, 1982; Levy 1972; Levy-Agresti and Sperry 1968), neuroscientists now take the lateralization of functions, and the different qualities of consciousness mediated by the two hemispheres of the brain as a given (Gazzaniga 2000; Gazzaniga & LeDoux, 1978; LeDoux 2003:304; McGilchrist 2009; Hellige 1993).

Considering that functional lateralization of the vertebrate brain and decussation of sensory and motor systems has no direct correlation with dreaming (except for perhaps lucid dreaming with REM and right lobe activity), why then have I raised the issue? For the simple reason that though both hemispheres do seem to be involved in mediating dreams, specific cognitive and communicative functions are lateralized, and that lateralization would seem to involve the ancient specialization of the two hemispheres for complimentary responses to stimuli. Namely, the left hemisphere specialization for categorization and considered decision making would seem to have been a preadaptation (exaptation) for the emergence of language.

Language is inherent to our species. All normal humans develop language more or less automatically and require little or no encouragement to do so – the development of language being

---

[5] The tissues that connect the two sides of the brain were surgically severed to relieve the symptoms in a number of patients suffering from extreme epilepsy.

an inherent product of human neurocognitive development (Pinker 1994, 1997; Gazzaniga 2000:58). Whereas we once thought that language functions are lodged solely in the left hemisphere for most people, we now know that the extent of hemispheric dominance depends on which language function is being addressed (Hellige 1993:68-73). "The left hemisphere seems dominant for producing overt speech, phonetic decoding, using syntax, and certain (but not all) semantic processes. The right hemisphere seems dominant for using the pragmatic aspects of language, integrating information across sentences, and using context" (ibid:110). Language processing thus requires mediation by many areas of cortex from the prefrontal lobes back to the inferior parietal lobule, and is distributed over both hemispheres (see Figure 4.1).

By language I do not mean merely vocal communication, for songbirds also appear to have natural vocal communication which is mediated by their left lobes (Jarvis 2004). I am more concerned with that aspect of human communication that involves concepts (see Carey 2009). For present purposes, a *concept* is a mental category that can be communicated by speech (or in later stages of human evolution, gesturally, haptically or visually). Neurobiologically speaking, the ability to conceptualize is a later stage in the evolution of the symbolic process, and a communicative refinement of the capacity to categorize. Thinking about things in a human way – that is, thinking in words in your head, or carrying out deductive reasoning – requires concepts and language (Edelman and Tononi 2000:196; Bickerton 2009:204-209; Fuster 2003:227), and the left hemisphere does appear to be dominant for linking concepts with overt speech, and with deductive reasoning. But keep in mind that cognition (non-linguistic thought, knowing, intuiting) about things only requires categories, with or without the ability to communicate with them (Fitch 2010:Chap. 4; also the case of Brother John below). An animal categorizes (a left lobe specialization, as we have seen above) sensory information so that identification of an object in the world is linked quickly to an adaptively appropriate response. Moreover, animals are able to perform mental operations upon those categories. But while many birds and other animals can communicate their intentions to conspecifics, as far as we know now only humans can communicate conceptual information using vocalizations.

The ability to do this would have been a very important evolutionary watershed, and may have occurred somewhere around the time of *Homo habilis* as much as 2.5 million years ago. But again, we are hampered by the "great divide" and have no real way of knowing when the first two hominins linked an utterance with an object in the world. If one holds loosely to the notion that ontology recapitulates phylogeny, which to an extent I do (Gould 1977; Dor and Jablonka 2010), then early hominin language would have taken the form of one word utterances similar to those of young children today. The importance of the inferior parietal lobule is that it is an area of cortex that lies at the boundary of multiple sensory association areas – it is the association area of association areas, so to speak. It is the main part of the brain where information from different sensory modalities joins to form categories, and then concepts.[6]

Our ability to conceptualize has evolved markedly over the course of hominin evolution to the point where we can communicate concepts that categorize abstract ideas such as imaginary objects that have no perceptual reality, or use sensory objects as metaphors for non-sensory ideas ("House of Windsor" for the British monarchy, "Big Bang" for the origin of the universe). We can conceptualize parts of speech and clusters of embedded categories ("bird" contains the category "songbird" which contains "parakeet" which contains my particular parakeet named Raffles). We can order events in time through the use of tensing and other signals. And, most importantly, we can describe events in great detail and considerable accuracy and thus are able to share experiences vicariously. This latter facility is the one that changed the role of dreaming in hominin life.

## Sharing Vicarious Experience

It happened more or less this way. Before some point in our evolution, our hominin ancestors, like all mammals before them, experienced reality in both waking and sleeping life, and they took experiences at their face

---

[6] What I am getting at is that category X is linked to a discrete pattern of sound A, while category Y is linked to a discrete sound B. The area most identified with combining these categories is the *inferior parietal lobule* (see Figure 4.1) on the left hemisphere of most human brains (Geschwind and Galaburda 1984).

value. Their experiences were real. We don't know if what they dreamed about influenced what they did individually in waking life any more than we know if our pet dogs and cats have spill-over from their dreams into their waking lives. I think it is pretty doubtful that much more than mood passes over, for this is a matter of time binding again. We do not know to what extent early hominins were able to stretch the duration of memories beyond the ongoing, unfolding experiential epoch (Chapter 4). Experiments with primates in the wild show that chimps, for instance, will demonstrate *neophilia* (remain curious about novel objects) much longer than, say, monkeys, but this curiosity is still only a matter of minutes (see e.g., Menzel 1966, 1971; Bergman and Kitchen 2009).

What we can be sure of is that dreaming remained purely subjective, for there was no system of communication complex enough to share dreams with each other. Meanwhile, the hominin PFC became more and more complex, and grew in relation to other parts of the nervous system. The more advanced the PFC and associated structures became, the smarter the species became — the more individuals were able to comprehend and model causation, memories of events in temporal sequence, and anticipation of future events – all within the bounds of their individual subjectivities. This set the stage for a major revolution in hominin phylogenesis. That revolution occurred when *individual subjectivities became so complex that their comprehension transcended immediate perceptual reality.* Now, the internal cognized worlds of individuals could diverge to such an extent that consensus reality and the powerful social adaptations that had served our ancestors well as social primates (Wilson 1975) might become weakened. Individuals within the group would be operating upon different cognized worlds, and concerted action would become harder to mount – like trying to get a group of untreated psychotics to work together for a common goal.

However this expansion of consciousness played out on the Pleistocene ground, there would have been a new and decided selective advantage for communication of vicarious experience (Laughlin and d'Aquili 1974). A new loading must have been placed on what had heretofore been merely the association of utterances and objects. Simple one word utterances of an early hominin "protolanguage"[7] (whatever form that would have taken;

---

[7] I am purposely avoiding the arguments about hominin protolanguages for all the reasons Fitch (2010:Chap. 15) covers in his excellent summary of theories.

see Fitch 2010:Chap. 12) would not have been sufficient to carry that information load, for merely labeling a category would not have allowed sharing of increasingly complex mental operations. But fortunately, the cortical processes that were evolving and making mental planning more complex also made grammar possible – that is, the stacking of utterances over time into two-word, three-word and multi-word expressions that could more accurately communicate vicarious experience using the magic of syntax (Pinker 1995; Fuster 2008:193). In other words, language and cognitive complexity in humans evolved in tandem (Bloom 1998). This is an answer to the intriguing question that an elementary school student once asked anthropologist Terrence Deacon (1997); namely, if non-human animals do not have full-blown languages, why then do they not have "simple" languages? At the time Deacon had no real answer to this question. But after studying the question he later produced a book-length answer. I will let readers read Deacon's answer for themselves. My answer to the question is the same that Gene d'Aquili and I gave in our first book *Biogenetic Structuralism* back in 1974 – what we then called the problem of the "cognitive extension of prehension."

Selection would have been for both neural functions – for both comprehension that was no longer constrained by immediate perception, and for communication of that comprehension between group members (Pinker 1997; but cf. Bickerton 2009:12-13). They were two aspects of the same process. Selection for language could not have happened without the backdrop of cognitive complexity. Advanced cognition would not have been selected for alone, because, with a lack of communication, hominin social adaptation would have been diminished. When did all this happen? That is anyone's guess. One can argue for a variety of origin points. It could have begun in earnest as early as the age of *Homo habilis*. Perhaps it began even earlier, for there is some evidence that one of the language-related cortical features detected on brain endocasts – the so-called Broca's area – shows significant Homo-like development in *Australopithecus* (Holloway 1972, 1995). Certainly it was well established by the time of *Homo heidelbergensis* some 600,000 years ago (Coolidge and Wynn 2009:174). In any event, the emergence of language would have made the coordination of social action much more flexible than before. But more importantly, it allowed individuals to share their subjective worlds to an extent never before possible among social animals.

The answer to Deacon's question? There are no "simple" languages among non-human animals precisely because there was no selection for them.[8] Animals do not have simple languages because there is no selection for sharing vicarious experience – yet they do communicate in ways that facilitate their own distinct adaptations in response to the vicissitudes of their respective niches (Bickerton 2009). It is well to note that the song of many birds exhibits many parallels with speech (Hultsch and Todt 2004:101) – both require learning, both depend on "perception, memorization and imitation," and both are best learned during sensitive periods in the development of the brain. Both also communicate information of adaptive use to the animal. But birdsong does *not* communicate vicarious experience because thus far no social avian brain has evolved to the point where their inner cognized world transcended perceptual reality and put their social adaptations in jeopardy.

## The Evolution of Dream Sharing and Dream Culture

Here is the point of my discussion of hominin mental and linguistic evolution – and thank you for being so patient in waiting for it: The byproduct of the selection for communication of vicarious waking experience was *the sharing of all forms of experience, no matter the SOC in which experience arose.* Selection for intersubjective sharing of waking experience *ipso facto* resulted in the potential sharing of dream experience as well. For the first time in phylogenesis, pure subjectivity became socially accessible. Beyond doubt, early hominins experienced their dreaming as being as real as their waking experiences. After all, as we have seen, people in most human societies today consider their dream experiences as real. Consider how little information would be necessary to express a dream to another. For instance, let us speculate that all an ancient ancestor would need to say is "night I hunt" (with perhaps a gesture backwards meaning "last") to communicate that I had gone hunting last night in my dreams rather than intending to do so tonight in my dreams. As virtually everyone in the group would have themselves dreamed of hunting at one time or another, it would have

---

[8] The jury is still out, in my opinion, on whether or not dolphins, or other *Cetacea* have something like language (see Hillix and Rumbaugh 2010:Chap. 13).

been understood because it would have penetrated to the memories of the audience. All that would be required perhaps is the ability to make three-word utterances.

These early dream sharers would surely have puzzled about the meaning of such experiences, and a theory would have been developed and communicated down through the generations. Let us remember that the "effort after meaning" (Chapter 7) is universal among animals with brains. If I dream of a successful hunt, and my dreams are real, where is the game that I killed? At some point our ancestors understood that the hunting dreams must be portents: That it had not happened yet in waking reality, or that it was a sign for something else that is about to happen. Dream experiences laid bare the normally invisible causal forces, and thus allowed experientially grounded foreknowledge. If I dream that my dead mother visited me and told me some interesting things, then what does physical death observed in waking life really mean? If my mother is dead and I can still visit with her, where did she go and how did she go? These and many other existential questions would have arisen as a consequence of dream sharing. Prior to the ability to share, dreaming would have remained within the confines of the individual's subjectivity, and hence beyond social processes of interpretation and symbolic/ritual control. After dream sharing became commonplace, dreaming and its attendant existential questions would have become part of the social process. That social process would increasingly be oriented toward conditioning and controlling the consciousness of group members so that everybody was (ideally at least) operating on a consensus reality (Edith Turner 1986; Bickerton 2009:159).

Dreaming, in other words, became part of the mental reality conditioned by hominin culture. I am not going to get into the silly arguments over whether non-human animals have either consciousness or culture, for that is not a topic within the purview of this book (see Laland and Galef 2009; Mcgrew 2010; for serious discussions of this issue). Suffice it to say that many of the difficulties with the issue have to do with definitions of "consciousness" or "culture" – ethologists define the terms so that it includes the awareness, experience, social behavior and cognition of non-human animals (e.g., Thompson 1994:98-99), and humanist anthropologists define them so that they can only apply in principle to human beings and their societies (e.g., culture or self-reflection requires language). I have previously (Chapter 2) defined culture for purposes relevant to the present topic as a pool of information available to group members. This definition does not exclude culture among non-human animals.

Indeed, I take it as an empirical given that other animals besides humans exhibit culture as an adaptive strategy. Socially shared information does not require language (Tomasello 2010:22). Obviously, animals coordinate their movements and behaviors without language, sometimes with the use of gestural and vocal skills that are either inherent or learned in part by mimicking the behavior of others. Culture – in the sense of behavior and skills that are invented, socially shared, typical of specific groups and transmitted down through the generations – has been demonstrated for chimpanzees and Macaque monkeys (Quiatt and Itani 1994; Whiten and Boech 2001). Utterances are often linked to environmental contingencies and the ability to perceptually distinguish, categorize and communicate information (e.g., a Vervet monkey with a discrete utterance that is interpreted by everybody as "danger on the ground, head for the trees;" Seyfarth, Cheney and Marler 1980). Alarm calls of different types made by birds can be picked up and correctly understood by monkeys for their own use. Putty-nosed monkeys have now been shown to combine specific calls in a semantic sequence meaningful to the animals in the wild (Arnold and Zuberbühler 2006), an ability long known for some birds (W. John Smith 1980:188). Wild chimpanzees seem to rely most heavily upon a complex gestural system, and less upon calls, but even call systems are remarkably rich in the transmission of information. Slocombe and Zuberbühler (2010:204) have suggested that "...chimpanzee listeners may be able to draw inferences about their social and ecological world that they cannot see."

Turning to humans, and drawing on a case description by Lecours and Joanette (1980), Merlin Donald (2001:69) describes an interesting syndrome called "paroxysmal aphasia" which inflicts a patient with the intermittent loss of language-related abilities. Writing about one such patient, a monk named Brother John, Donald notes: "His language, including speech comprehension, speaking, reading, writing, and 'inner speech,' which is the habit of silently talking to oneself, was globally impaired." Yet Brother John remained fully conscious, most of his cognitive functions were normal, including self-reflection and self-evaluation. He carried around a portable radio tuned to a talk station so that when he began to understand speech, he knew he was on the mend. The point is, neither consciousness nor self-awareness, self-reflection or self-representation require language. They are mediated elsewhere than the language-specific structures of the brain. Self-representation – that is, how an animal conceives of itself only requires categorical thinking, not language. All that is needed, in other words, for the "sense of self" to be present in consciousness is a neural model of the self that is open to modification and development in interaction with the physical and social environment. It is entirely likely that non-human animals, especially big-brained social animals, are born with self-awareness and subsequently develop models of their self informed in part by dreaming. The fundamental metaphysical problem thwarting acceptance of this view among some scientists is Cartesian in origin (Terrace and Metcalf 2005) – that is, linking the development of the self with the ability to think in words.

Only language, however, would have provided a social window into the pure subjectivity of dreaming among animals. Obviously, individuals cannot directly observe one another's dream adventures. A glimpse into the domain of the other's subjectivity had to await the evolution of a language of sufficient complexity that experience (not just objects and augmentation of simple intentions) could be vicariously shared. Brother John would no doubt have been able to dream, but language comprehension within the dream would have been lost for the duration of the episode. More to the point, *he could not share his dreams with anyone.* With the sharing via language innovation, theories of dreaming would have quickly emerged as part of the group's cultural information pool, along with a consensus understanding of the significance of dreaming and its manifest content.

Does this mean that Edward B. Tylor was right after all (see Chapter 2) when he reasoned that our primitive ancestors made a metaphysical mistake in considering their dreams as real? If so, it would mean that most traditional peoples on the planet today repeat the same fundamental error. Whereas I do think there is some merit in placing dreaming at the root of animistic religious convictions (see Chapter 3; see also Nurit Bird-David 1999; Nielsen 1991) – how could it be otherwise? – the presumption that people cannot tell the difference between waking and dreaming is nonsense. As with all natural categories, each discrete SOC is recognizable by its qualities, has fuzzy boundaries, and often overlaps with other categories of experience (Rosch 1977; Rosch et al. 1976). Normal human language communicates using natural categories elevated by the symbolic process into concepts. Moreover, the structure of particular languages impresses itself upon dreams. When a dream is being reported and shared, it naturally takes on the form of a narrative. But a polyphasic audience knows the difference between the dream story they are hearing and the dream-as-dreamt that inspired the story because they've all been there. They know they normally cannot fly when awake and may do when dreaming. They know that their dead ancestors normally don't appear during waking life, but may do in a dream. What polyphasic peoples also know is that they can "end run" the obdurate nature of the waking world in their dreams, and thus are able to obtain information not otherwise available to them – information about events distant in space and time, especially events yet to materialize.

As we have seen, Western science has problems with paranormal phenomena, but traditional peoples do not. And the question of whether or not access to paranormal information – derived via telepathy, co-dreaming, precognition, or whatever – is actually possible is, as far as I am concerned, still wide open. Frankly, it is hard for me to understand how our hominin ancestors and our own modern species could have sustained such self-delusion if paranormal phenomena are a total fiction, when in all other ways people hold to a kind of empirically grounded, cultural pragmatism (see Kroeber 1952:402). As we have seen, the human brain is organized to test its models in the crucible of experienced reality. Remember, for instance, the "wait-and-see" attitude of Bruce's Lacandon friends with respect to whether or not their dreams were accurate in foretelling events in the future (Chapter 12; Bruce 1975).

Perhaps more important than access to paranormal information, but perhaps harder for many monophasic Westerners to grasp, is the access to archetypal models of reality. All brains, regardless of species, are structured neurognostically; that is, they are genetically endowed with a system of rudimentary knowledge upon which their development depends. Taken as a whole, the neurognostic structure of the brain predetermines how we come to know what we know about our self and our world. We are no different in that respect than the chimpanzee (Lonsdorf, Ross and Matsuzawa 2010) or honeybee (Seeley 2010). We are born with species-specific knowledge (our "biogram," to use Count's term) and that knowledge conditions our experience while dreaming or awake.[9] The species-specific structure not only provides nascent knowledge, but also forms the limits of any species' neurocognitive development. This is a kind of inner obduracy that conditions our understanding of anything. Dream experience, because it is freed from the press of sensory perception, becomes an internalized theater for the expression of those aspects of the self that are suppressed in the interests of adaptation during waking life. It is no coincidence that virtually all intact polyphasic cultures have worldviews that are cosmological in structure, and that are publically displayed as myths and performance. Their worldviews are on the whole metaphysically accurate, for they are the expressions, through symbolic media of the microcosmic organization of the brain – an organization that was selected for over millions of years to optimize the truth of its models of the world. The brain inherently knows that the world is made up of objects and movements and relations and causes, that experience unfolds moment by moment, and that everything is implicated in and entangled with everything else (Varela, Thompson and Rosch 1991; Bohm and Hiley 1995; Laughlin and Throop 2001).

Thus dreaming operates as, among other things, a complement to the more parochial demands of waking adaptation. Dreaming "trues-up" models in their relationship *both* to external reality *and* the self – an exercise of the brain's inherent "effort after truth" we spoke about in Chapter 7. The sleeping brain expends its metabolic resources running scenarios, rehearsing schemes, developing and refining plans and solving problems. It also creates for itself a safe haven for

---

[9] My argument here is similar to those made by evolutionary psychologists. However, one problem I have with evolutionary psychology is that "adaptation" is usually defined solely with respect to natural selection and *external extramental reality*; that is, adaptation is always something that happens in relation to the external world, not the internal world of the body and its brain. This excludes the use of the term adaptation in a more Piagetian (e.g., Piaget 1980) sense of neural structures also adapting to the internal organization of the nervous system.

cross-talk among archetypal structures that contain information of a metaphysically different kind – the kind that is understood by peoples as "spiritual." From time to time these archetypal dream fields may erupt into consciousness and become the "big" dreams, the culture pattern dreams we spoke about in Chapters 9 and 10. These experiences have the effect developmentally of keeping the waking ego in check – keeping the ego in the vicinity, as it were, of the center of the self.

With the advent of language, these spiritual, transpersonal and timelessly veridical experiences became socially available, and were brought under the influence of social interpretations and ritual control – in other words, dreaming became part of the group's cycle of meaning. Dreaming became a (perhaps, as Tylor might have argued, *the*) major source of information about the invisible world of spiritual essence, causality and intentionality. And if it proves to be the case that some of the more paranormal information obtained in dreams derives from cellular interaction with the quantum sea, then the social sharing of that information might have had a significant impact upon cultural adaptation.

## DREAMING, SELF-REFLECTION AND CULTURAL VARIATION

It should be evident to the reader by now that I tend to reject out-of-hand any definition of brain functions and their artifices that *in principle* apply solely to human beings. Phenomena *must* be defined so that they may be explored and compared across species. Moreover, there is no such thing as a neurophysiological structure that did not evolve from its anlage.[10] Language evolved, it did not pop into existence holus bolus from nowhere. Likewise, dreaming has evolved as a function of the evolution of the brain and its adaptational processes. And learned variation in thought and action has evolved as a consequence of selection for neurocognitive complexity, not merely as a result of language. It will not surprise the reader, therefore, that I am also suspicious of any suggestion that the existence of the self had to await the evolution of language, human culture or social construction (see Edelman and

---

[10] An "anlage" (pl. "anlagen") is a precursor structure that forms the foundation for future development or evolution (see Count 1973 on the anlagen for the human biogram).

Tononi 2000:199). Nor for obvious reasons will I consider any approach to the self that is not grounded (or ground-able) in neurobiology and evolutionary biology. The science of consciousness has gone way beyond dualistic and constructivist takes on depth psychology and the self (Csordas 1994b; Damasio 2010; Korzeniewski 2011; LeDoux 2003; Llinás 2001; Wax 1998).

Dreaming is the brain experiencing itself (its self) during sleep, and is mainly the expression of what is happening at that moment in the depths. As Jung noted, dreaming is a "...spontaneous self-portrayal, in symbolic form, of the actual situation in the unconscious... ." (1969c:263). In its development, the self is conditioned by both genetic inheritance and by environmental press, and especially its interactions with the local sociocultural environment.

## The Nature of Self-Awareness

One of the most difficult questions neurobiologists and ethologists have asked themselves is: When did self-awareness first arise in phylogenesis? As usual, the answer depends on how one defines "self." (Please, no anthropocentric definitions need apply!) For our purposes (see Chapter 11), the self refers to the sum total of archetypes (neurognostic structures) in a creature's psyche. Self-awareness then would be awareness of the functioning of some of the parts of the psyche. One can immediately see that, as we cannot get into the minds of non-human animals, we cannot know to what extent they are aware of themselves as either a psyche or as a conscious mind. But the "sense of self," however it manifests in the animal's experience of themselves, would perform the function of distinguishing self from Other.

Ethologists have used various tricks to test for self-awareness in animals. The most common is the use of mirrors to detect self-recognition (Gallup 1982, 1994; Parker, Mitchell and Boccia 1994). If one places a mirror in a primate's (or another animal's) cage and waits for the animal to habituate to its presence, and then put a dab of red paint on its forehead while it's asleep, will the animal be able to recognize it has paint on its forehead when it looks in the mirror? In short, chimpanzees will immediately touch their foreheads when they see the face with the red dot in the mirror, and monkeys will not. The implication is that chimps recognize themselves in the mirror, and monkeys think their reflection is of another animal. Therefore, chimps have self-awareness and monkeys do not (Parker and McKinney 1999:154-157).

Many authorities accept this view uncritically (e.g., McGilchrist 2009:87). But the fallacy of this kind of approach should be obvious once one thinks about it. No animal in the wild would depend upon self-recognition in mirrored surfaces to develop self-awareness or a "sense of self" – especially not in the way I am using the term "self." It's Emil Menzel's (1967) cautionary story all over again. The experientialist's facial recognition task makes no sense with respect to the natural niches in which the animals evolved. Animals in the wild do not use mirrored surfaces to study themselves. Rather, they know themselves from the inside out, so to speak. Yes, self-recognition in mirrors (or its absence) is interesting, and perhaps even significant, but it does not answer the key question: When did self-awareness arise in evolution and what role, if any, did dreaming fulfill in that process. My answer will again have to be speculative. I think that the cognitive and perceptual distinction of self from Other is neurognostic and very ancient – a primitive perceptual-ecological feature of experience. The only sensible account of the origins of the sense of self and self-knowledge is ecological (Gibson 1979; Neisser 2006; Butterworth 1995). As with dreaming, we must distinguish between (1) *self experience*, or *self-awareness* (which I believe is "wired-in" to all primate brains, and probably all vertebrate brains; Damasio 1999; see Chapter 4), (2) the *categorization of the embodied self* (which is also pre-linguistic) and (3) the *concept of self* which can only arise in humans due to their culture and language abilities (thus allowing *self-reference* in narratives; see Neisser 2006).

It goes almost without saying that any animal with self-awareness while awake may be self-aware while dreaming. Remember, the self is compositional (see Chapter 4). It is a system, not a thing. There is no little homunculus inside our brain with "me" stenciled on its t-shirt (see Neisser 2006:3). In addition, most of the self's operations occur unconsciously. Hence, self-experience in dreams can only be awareness of those bits of the self that, at that time, are expressing themselves in imagery, emotion, relations among images and self-knowledge. My hunch is that all animals that have dreaming brains also experience the "searchlight" intentionality of self-awareness, however primitive that function might be. I would strongly disagree with Joseph LeDoux (2002:27-28) who, while acknowledging that animals have selves, muddles the picture somewhat by reserving "self-awareness" to those animals with an "explicit" notion of themselves – that is, they have a "self-concept" that allows them to be conscious of themselves. He seems to retain a qualitative distinction between humans and all other animals, much as anthropologists tend to do (ibid:28). The trouble is that if concepts require language for communication, then *ipso facto* no animals can have self-awareness *in principle*. This just won't do, for we have seen that human beings like Brother John, while bereft of their linguistic systems, are still self-aware. Moreover, self-awareness and social cognition is mediated by non-language related, right hemisphere cortical and sub-cortical systems in both humans and non-human animals (see Schore 2003 on the importance of the right hemisphere orbitofrontal cortex in developing and mediating the sense of self; see also Geary 2007:243). The inherent sense of self present in the midst of experiencing, often associated with emotion, self-related memories and perceptions of one's body combine to mediate subjective self-awareness (Changeux 2002:86). Perception of the body comes via *proprioception* (knowledge of the various body parts and their relations with each other in space), *interoception* (internal body sensations like hunger, pain, stretching, etc.) and *exteroception* (external sensing of the body and its position in space). All vertebrates have this self-awareness to some extent. Whether it is primitive or more advanced depends in part upon the complexity of memory.

Language is simply not required for self-awareness. Nor is it required for *consciousness*, which is self-awareness within the total experience of the world while awake, or pseudo-perception of the imaginal world while sleeping (Fuster 2008:376-377; Damasio 1999; Dietrich 2007:207-213). Human self-awareness and consciousness are indeed influenced by language, both in waking and dreaming experience. I not only experience myself, I can think about myself using talk-think, and I can talk about myself with others. Non-human animals can also experience themselves and their interactions with the world – in other words, they are conscious. They can category-think about themselves just as they can abut any other object, but have no way of communicating that thinking to others. My argument is that all animals with brains dream and that the inner "theater of mind" is structured much the same way it is for us humans – dreaming is experienced from a point of view, from a "standpoint" (Ger: *Standpunkte*; see Brentano 1973[1874]). The "searchlight" of awareness from a point of view is, I suspect, universal to brains. I am witnessing my dreaming from behind my eyes, whether or not I am aware of my body. I am either passively watching what is happening, taking part in what is happening or am absorbed in what is happening to such an extent that the distinction between "me" and the happening dissolve. Most dreaming among Westerners is of the first two kinds. Some lucid dreaming may generate sufficient concentration that the third type – absorption in the dream object – may occur. This is probably the case for all vertebrates, and perhaps other animals as well. Like we humans, vertebrates are watching their archetypal selves being expressed in dream experiences, although probably only human beings are potentially capable of the self-reflection requisite to understanding what is going on, or why. I say "potentially," for it seems to me that most humans never come to understand this about themselves and their dreaming. A major barrier to attaining empirical self-understanding in this kind of advanced phenomenological way is culture.

## Culture as Universal and as Variety

Human society and culture are marked by both universal neuropsychological processes and a great variety of patterns and nuances of meanings that influence the development of the self (Brown 1991; Wiredu 1996; Parker, Mitchell and Boccia 1994). As Robert Hinde (1995:189) noted: "...universals must be thought of as characters potentially present in all humans (or in all members of a particular age/sex class), actually present in most, but variable between individuals in some degree." He offers a lengthy list of such universals (ibid:190), including those involved in perception, motor activities, responses to specific stimuli, motivation, cognitive processes, predisposition to learn in certain ways, language development and certain aspects of relationship. In addition, the development of cognitive maps of the physical environment is universal to all people and thus to all cultures (Stea, Blaut and Stephens 1996). There are universal patterns to aggression, manufacture, use and retention of tools and anticipation of the future (Mitchell and Boccia 1994), emotions and their expressions (Laughlin and Throop 1999), traditional cosmologies (Laughlin and Throop 2001), ritual behavior (d'Aquili, Laughlin and McManus 1979), art (Ramachandran 2005; Dissanayake 1992) and religious systems (Murdock 1955). Anthony Stevens (1982:23), citing Murdock (1945) and Fox (1975), lists the following universal aspects of culture:

> ...no human culture is known which lacked laws about ownership, inheritance and disposal of property, procedures for settling disputes, rules governing courtship, marriage, adultery, and the adornment of women, taboos relating to food and incest, ceremonies of initiation of young men, associations of men which exclude women, gambling, athletic sports, co-operative labor, trade, the manufacture of tools and weapons, rules of etiquette prescribing forms of greeting, modes of address, use of personal names, visiting, feasting, hospitality, gift-giving, and the performance of funeral rites, status differentiation on the basis of a hierarchical social structure, superstition, belief in the supernatural, religious rituals, soul concepts, myths and legends, dancing, homicide, suicide, homosexuality, mental illness, faith healing, dream interpretation, medicine, surgery, obstetrics, and meteorology. The list could go on.

Indeed it could go on and on, but it is also the case that each and every universal pattern listed above gives rise to a range of cultural variations. For instance, the categories of kin covered under incest proscriptions varies widely across cultures (Wolf and Durham 2004), as does marriage (Stockard 2001), performance (Schechner 2006; Schechner and Turner 1985), astronomy (Selin 2001), and virtually any other cultural category one can name. One of the errors we anthropologists make is drawing an absolute distinction between innate and learned elements (Hinde 1991). When we understand how the brain works, it is much easier for us to see how universal proclivities may be suppressed or be elaborated through development and learning.

So it is with dreaming. As we have seen, there are universal processes operating in both dreaming and dream cultures. If you have followed me on the neurobiology of archetypes and the self, and understand that much of dreaming is the brain experiencing the symbolic expression of what is going on within itself, then you will see immediately that there must be universal patterns and motifs in the manifest content of dreams. This is because every person's self develops from neurognostic structures within their fetal brain. Be that as it may, we have seen many common and universal motifs crop up in our cross-cultural survey of dreaming. Visits with deceased ancestors, flying and OBEs, mandala-like geometrical forms, shape-shifting beings, journeys to spiritual places, violent struggles, snakes and other totemic animals, witches, ghosts, spirits that cause and heal sickness, near death experiences, visits to the afterworld, encounters with teachers or gurus, anima and animus figures, marriage, death, and so forth inhabit the dreaming of peoples all over the planet. Yet in every case, the motif will tend to be colored by cultural conditioning. Who is marrying whom, the species of snake, the place to which one is flying, what nastiness the witch is bent on doing, what category of deceased kin visits during slumber, all of these things vary depending upon the conditioning and information available in the culture.

Perhaps one of the most important things we have learned over the middle section of this book is that the quality, complexity, vividness and intentionality of dreaming depends a lot on how involved the prefrontal cortex (PFC) is in the neural network mediating dreaming. We have seen that PFC involvement can be fortuitous, as when lucid dreams occur spontaneously even among monophasic peoples who ordinarily pay little attention to their dream life. But we have also seen that intentional entrainment of PFC functions to dreaming consciousness produces the lucidity that polyphasic peoples take for granted in their dreaming. In a sense, the "normal" dreaming we Westerners take for granted is actually quite primitive compared to lucid dreaming. I mean this literally – dreaming bereft of PFC mediation is a kind of throwback to the dreaming of hominins prior to the evolution of language. Present are pseudo-perceptual hallucinations, surreal bizarreness, nonsensical events, and truncated and episodic memories associated with little if any thought, image-based meaning or intentionality.

The cultural theory of dreaming among polyphasic folks very commonly drives and informs lucidity by way of the society's cycle of meaning. Standardized interpretations, ritualized incubation techniques, social expectations, the universal desire to foretell events before they happen, all combine to enrich and condition the experiences people have while sleeping. For many polyphasic peoples, the higher cortical functions come into play, thus allowing dreams to be influenced by waking intentions (vision quests, oracles, intentional journeys), time-binding, and by thought-while-dreaming, including self-reflection, all of which in turn generates information that is carried by memory into waking life, and vice versa. Perhaps we will never know to what extent episodic memories of dream experiences actually influence individual chimps, elephants or dolphins, but that capacity coupled with social sharing via language caused a profound alteration of social consciousness, social action and way of life for humans.

## SUMMARY AND SEGUE

We have seen how long and complex has been the evolutionary road to human dreaming. Because of language and culture, the individual subjectivity of dreaming became accessible to our forebears – one of the landmark revolutions in our evolution. Dreaming throughout antiquity, and for most peoples today, constitutes one of the main ways that the adaptations required by the environment are complemented by operations internal to the psyche that seek unity and equilibration. We have resisted any attempt to define dreaming, self-awareness or consciousness in anthropocentric terms, for such approaches thwart an evolutionary and neurobiological account of the human psyche. While it is true that we are hampered by the "great divide" between modern humans and our distant hominin ancestors, this lack of living representatives of past hominins cannot be used to support dualistic thinking about dreaming. The "great divide" does not equal a wide Rubicon between nature and nurture.

What I have done in this chapter is develop a neuroanthropological theory of dreaming that places humans within the general process of biological evolution, especially the evolution of sleep and dreaming. There are universal properties of dreaming that we carry into our contemporary life, and how we position ourselves in relation to our biological natures has a lot to do with the kind of life-worlds we experience. In the next chapter we will explore the role of dreaming in contemporary life, and suggest some of the tragic costs some of us pay for ignoring our dreaming. We will also cover some of the dreamwork movements that have arisen to perhaps balance the lives of monophasic peoples.

# Chapter 15

# Dreaming in the Modern Age

> Anthropologists can make an important contribution to the field of dream research and to the grassroots effort to change our Western cultural attitude toward dreams. Besides expanding the scope of cross-cultural research on dreams and increasing our knowledge of the cultural context of dreaming, anthropologists can offer practical support for the changes that are occurring in the settings and methods of dream sharing.
>
> Deborah Jay Hillman (1999:84-85)

> Ideologies have no heart of their own. They're the whores and angels of our striving selves.
>
> John le Carré

On January 8, 2011, a 22 year old man named Jared Lee Loughner allegedly shot a United States congresswoman and 18 other people during an outdoor meeting in Tucson, Arizona. The legislator survived, but six others died. At the time of this writing, a federal judge has ruled that Loughner is mentally incompetent to stand trial due to schizophrenia. Comments by those who know the young man leave one in little doubt he was mentally disturbed and likely psychotic. He apparently drove himself deeper into a dissociative state with a variety of psychoactive drugs, including magic mushrooms, salvia, cannabis and LSD. What makes this story relevant to our present topic is that Loughner was "obsessed" with lucid dreaming. Days ahead of the shootings, he left a series of observations about dreaming on *YouTube*, including a video in which he made the statement: "I am a sleepwalker — who turns off the alarm clock." There is reason to believe he kept a dream diary. Journalists were quick to do their homework on lucid dreaming, citing Stephen LaBerge's websites and interviewing psychologists like Dr. Gary Schwartz, a professor of psychology and neurology at the University of Arizona, who is quoted as saying: "For individuals who become not just gifted lucid dreamers but become obsessed with lucid dreaming and prefer lucid dreaming more than regular life, it becomes potentially dangerous to them and society."[1] Commentators have even raised the interesting question as to whether Loughner thought that he was in a lucid dream at the time of the incident.

However the Loughner case eventually plays out in mental facilities and the courts, it does raise questions about dreaming and mental health. On a still wider scope, it suggests questions about the role and significance of dreaming in the modern age. Have modern humans evolved beyond the need for dreaming? Are there ways of making our dream life relevant to today's social relations and information age culture? Is dreaming necessary for spiritual fulfillment, and if so, how does one go about it? Are there subcultures in modern societies that appear more like polyphasic traditional peoples? How would widespread reintroduction of polyphasic culture impact modern society? These are some of the questions I will address in this chapter. What I will *not* do is present a lengthy summary or discussion of distortions of sleep and dreaming correlated with psychopathologies generally, or the use of dreaming in various medical treatments and psychotherapies. This has been done extensively elsewhere (see Palagini and Rosenlicht 2011; Kryger, Roth and Dement 2011).

## Dreaming and Mental Health

We have seen in Chapter 9 that dreaming is directly involved with physical and mental health among many traditional peoples. Dreaming is a window into the soul which can be attacked or stolen, thus causing sickness. Shamans all over the planet are recruited into community service by dreams, and healers use dreaming to diagnose and cure diseases. Peoples learn to avoid danger and illness by paying

---

[1] Quoted from an ABC World News story of January 11, 2011.

attention to what their dreams augur for the future. We have also seen that modern science has confirmed that dreams can express actual physical injury and disease (e.g., Haskell 1985; Daruna 2004). People since the beginning of the Upper Paleolithic have probably viewed dreams as a portal into the sublime – a vast spiritual place where they could become centered and connected with something greater than themselves. The perils and benefits of engaging this divine space are expressed within the majority of traditional dream cultures as reported in the ethnographic record.

The manifest content of dreams is used by many cultures to indicate various mental conditions that sometimes need immediate intervention to correct. As I mentioned in Chapter 7, Anthony F.C. Wallace (1958) reconstructed the dream theory of the 17$^{th}$ century Iroquois people which held that dreams were considered to be an expression of the emotionally-laden desires of the soul. These desires had to be either literally or symbolically fulfilled in waking life in order to avoid illness and other possible calamities. Modern polysomnographic[2] research shows that people who suffer from serious depression also show multiple distortions of normal sleep and dream patterns, including reduced slow wave sleep, a shortened REM latency (time between sleep onset and first REM period), a lengthening of the first REM period and increase in REM density (the number of eye movements per minute; see Palagini and Rosenlicht 2011:182). It is not yet known for sure whether sleep/dream disturbance is a cause or an effect of mental illness.

More to the point, numerous researchers have pointed to the similarities between dreaming and various forms of psychosis (mental disease producing loss of contact with reality; e.g., dissociative delusions accompanying schizophrenia, some forms of clinical depression and bipolar disorder; see Benson and Feinberg 2011; Fuster 2003:256). Loss of contact with reality may consist of seeing or hearing things that "aren't there," and thought disorders (e.g., paranoid interpretations of actually benign sensory events) that produce inaccurate, maladaptive and self-destructive delusions. All too often, authorities like Freud (2010 [1899]), Hobson (1994:Chap. 1, 2001:231-233) and others

---

[2] Polysomnography is the use of multiple electronic measures of biophysical activity in the sleeping brain.

influenced by psychoanalysis have equated dreaming with psychotic delusions. Such hypotheses generally either focus on the bizarreness of manifest content, or ignore content altogether and reason from deduced latent "delusional" processes producing dreams. These notions seem to reflect the arguments once held by psychological anthropologists that shamanic trance states and prophetic dreams were a form of schizophrenia among traditional peoples – a view that has now been largely repudiated (see Noll 1983). The error made by these and other monophasically-biased approaches (see Crick and Mitchison 1983 for an extreme example) to the functions of dreaming is that they fail to acknowledge the role of dreaming as an expression of internal activities of the self – their "selfscape-ness." Their central idea is that when consciousness is disconnected at sleep onset from the external sensory world – thus allowing "paradoxical sleep" – consciousness promptly becomes delusional and goes mad. This entire book stands as a corrective against this kind of blatant ethnocentrism – the product of monophasic science trying to explain polyphasic experience and culture (see also Randal *et al.* 2008). Normal dreaming is not dissociation, but a shift to association with the inner self.

What does this have to do with lucid dreaming and the plight of young Loughner? So far we know very little about his childhood, but while it is undoubtedly an oversimplification, we can say that many people who have been traumatized have trouble coping with extramental reality in their waking life and may withdraw (dissociate) from that reality in the sense that their ability to test their models of themselves and the world against the obduracy and affordancy of reality becomes compromised and dysfunctional (Feinberg and Guazzeli 1999; Benson and Feinberg 2011; van der Hart, Nijenhuis and Steele 2006:1-7). When this happens, clinicians tell us that sleep patterns become very disturbed, occasionally including a reversal of sleep to daytime and insomnia at night. Reports by those who know Loughner say that something changed in him and he became increasingly withdrawn, antisocial and delusional. If he is indeed schizophrenic, then what we can say without a shred of doubt is that *the last thing* he should have been doing was driving his dreaming into greater lucidity. This is an object lesson to those in our society that are proselytizing about the positive benefits of intense involvement in lucid dreaming.

## Control and Dreaming

Remember what we said back in Chapter 5, that Western lucid dreaming researchers emphasize self-awareness and *control over dream events* as the definitive characteristics of lucid dreaming? Control is the key here, for when we normally dream, things just happen to us as watchers or participants. We have little or no control over the course of events. But then most of us feel more or less in control of our waking lives, so that there is that added distinction between our dream experiences and our waking experiences, and we are not usually motivated to seek control in other SOC. But in lucid dreaming, we can learn to gain control over the activities of our dream ego and over experienced events, while at the same time the obduracy and affordancy of the external world are kept at bay. A person with a weak ego can experience themselves as powerful, even a superhero if they gain sufficient lucidity. I personally felt quite powerless as a child and recall dreaming repeatedly that I was Superman (my favorite radio show at the time). Trouble was, for a very long time I could not fly – I was always held back by a rope or something tied to the ground. I recall vividly the first time I did fly in my dreams, as well as the feeling of exhilaration that accompanied the sense of freedom and power this gave me.

David Geary (2005:3, 7) has placed the *motivation to control* squarely at the center of cognitive evolution. "…[T]he brain and mind of all species have evolved to attend to and process the forms of information, such as the movement patterns of prey species, that covaried with survival and reproductive prospects during the species' evolutionary history. These systems bias decision making and behavioral responses in ways that allow the organism to attempt to achieve access to and control of these outcomes" (ibid:7). There is a drive to know self and world in a way that allows cognitive and behavioral mastery over events. Gene d'Aquili liked to call this drive the "cognitive imperative" (Laughlin and d'Aquili 1974:114) for individual neurocognition, while A.L. Kroeber (1952:152, 402) called it "reality culture" at the collective level.[3] Systematic failure

---

[3] *Reality culture* is "…concerned with finding out, mastering, and directing nature – and sometimes mastering and directing fellow-men as well. Technology, the useful arts, ways of successful practical living, are avenues by which reality culture is expressed" (Kroeber 1952:402).

to perceive oneself as controlling intentions and objectives in waking life can produce severe psychopathology, including profound depression and dissociation from the outer world. Children are especially vulnerable to adverse childrearing practices and traumas that later on produce clinical depression and dissociation disorders (Schäfer, Ross and Read 2008).

As we have seen throughout this book, dreaming feeds into this universal drive for mastery at both the individual and collective levels in most human societies, and has probably done so for tens of thousands of years. Dreaming allows people to reveal causation, take remedial actions, seek and retain important information about future events, remove uncertainty about the intentions of others, seek guidance upon one's life course, overcome the apparent finality of the death of loved ones, discover the causes and cures of sickness, bring one's own life experience into accord with the sacred stories, instantiate in direct experience the existence of one's soul and bring self-understanding into accord with the species-specific wisdom of the archetypal self. All of these functions, amply evidenced in the ethnography of dreaming and dream cultures, have to do with maintaining the individual's sense of control.

## Dreaming and Sanity

But what about dreaming in our modern, post-industrial world? Most of us pay little attention to our dreams. How does this affect our individual and collective motivation to control? It is here that we must re-emphasize that adaptation has *two* meanings, not just one. There is adaptation to the local environment, and adaptation of neural models to the internal reality of the self. This is where monophasic scientific theories of consciousness so often go awry. "Awake" is what we call our conscious engagement with the external world, while "dreaming" is our conscious engagement with the inner world of being. In other words, *waking life focuses energies and resources on adaptation to the local environment, while dreaming life focuses on adaptation to the demands of the global self, and through the archetypal structure of the self, the cosmos.* Waking "trues-up" models to local conditions; dreaming "trues-up" models relative to the entire self and cosmos. Thus, dreaming operates among polyphasic peoples to balance the two poles of adaptation. Local waking adaptations are integrated with the inner world of the self during dreaming, and information about and from the self attained while dreaming (however interpreted by the local dream theory) is applied locally when awake. If someone becomes dissociated from the normal process of waking adaptation to reality and withdraws into sleeping or waking dreams, then the person's energies and resources become out of balance favoring inner adaptation. Balance between the demands of each pole of adaptation is requisite to individual sanity.

Is it possible for an entire society to be so unbalanced in adaptation that they are less than sane? Can it be that a particular culture's adaptation can condition the development of the individual ego so far out of synch with the self that the social cost is a high percentage of psychopathology? The great sociologist and psychoanalyst, Erich Fromm (1900-1980), certainly thought so. In his magnum opus, *The Sane Society* (1955;23), Fromm took a position antithetical to constructivist notions of mental health – that is, that mental health can only be defined or evaluated from within the norms of any particular society. His view was that mental aberrations, including delusions, can, by way of cultural conditioning, become shared by all or a significant proportion of the members of a society. He noted that:

> What is so deceptive about the state of mind of the members of a society is the "consensual validation" of their concepts. It is naively assumed that the fact that the majority of people share certain ideas or feelings proves the validity of these ideas and feelings. Nothing is further from the truth... Just as there is a *folie à deux* [mental disorder shared by two closely related people] there is a *folie à millions* [mental disorder shared by millions]. The fact that millions of people share the same vices does not make these vices virtues, the fact that they share so many errors does not make the errors to be truths, and the fact that millions of people share the same form of mental pathology does not make these people sane.

Mental health for Fromm is equated with reaching full maturity within the constraints imposed by our species' nature. On this account, some societies can be seen to thwart full maturity in individuals, while others nurture and encourage it.

To the extent that a society thwarts the natural development of psychological maturity, it may be considered as relatively *un-sane*.[4] An un-sane society is one in which mental defects are culturally patterned (ibid:23) – they are common within the society and caused by enculturation in interaction with the society's normative conditions of life. A *socially patterned defect* is common enough that, "The individual shares it with many others; he is not aware of it as a defect, and his security is not threatened by the experience of being different, of being an outcast, as it were. What he may have lost in richness and in a genuine feeling of happiness, is made up by the security of fitting in with the rest of mankind – *as he knows them*" (ibid:23; emphasis Fromm's). My contention is that many modern post-industrial societies are relatively un-sane. I am speaking about societies, like those in North America, South America, Europe, Japan and China,[5] that are now primarily monophasic materialist cultures in which people are encouraged to expend their lives in a perpetual state of uncertainty, competition, struggle and stress, and that tend also to eschew involvement in their dream life (see also Wax 2004). As educator and dream researcher, Jeremy Taylor (1996:139-140), has written:

> As a species, *Homo sapiens* is in trouble. The toxic by-products of our voracious technologies are polluting the soil, air, and water to such an extent that the ability of the planet to continue supporting complex mammalian life appears to be in jeopardy. Our social, political, religious, and cultural institutions, East and West, are breaking down at a rapid rate and everywhere men, women, and particularly children seem filled with an increasing sense of hopelessness, coupled with a feeling of spiritual emptiness and an absence of broader vision, purpose, and connection with anything worthy of the name divine.

---

[4] The term "un-sane" has been attributed to psychologist Philip S. Graven.

[5] None of these societies were monophasic during earlier eras of their respective histories; see Chapter 2.

For instance, the picture of mental health in the United States today is grim.[6] Most households in the US have personally experienced the toll taken by mental illness. The cost of illness, as well as death due to mental illness (e.g. suicide), is staggering throughout the industrialized world (Murray and Lopez 1996): "Among developed nations, including the United States, major depression is the leading cause of disability. Also near the top of these rankings are manic-depressive illness, schizophrenia, and obsessive-compulsive disorder". Depending upon how one defines mental illness, at least one in five people in the United States suffers from some sort of mental illness. That is roughly 44 million people! Of those, 7,216,000 on average suffer from anxiety disorders, 3,124,000 from serious mood disorders and 572,000 from schizophrenia and related thought disorders. And these are just the serious disorders that are reported and treated. The majority of anxiety and depression sufferers in the US go unreported and untreated. Depression and anxiety are so common in our population that, painkillers aside, anti-anxiety and anti-depression drugs are the most common psycho-pharmaceutical prescriptions. In 2009, the most popular psychiatric drug was the anti-anxiety pill, *Xanex* (44,029,000 prescriptions), while *Lexapro*, a depression-anxiety drug sold 27,698,000 prescriptions – and the latter is only one of many anti-depression drugs available.[7] "Lost productive time among U.S. workers due to depression is estimated to be in excess of $31 billion per year. Depression frequently co-occurs with a variety of medical illnesses such as heart disease, cancer, and chronic pain and is associated with poorer health status and prognosis. It is also the principal cause of the 30,000 suicides in the U.S. each year. In 2004, suicide was the 11th leading cause of death in the United States, third among individuals 15-24."[8]

---

[6] Statistics on mental health in the United States are taken from: U.S. Department of Health and Human Services. *Mental Health: A Report of the Surgeon General.* Rockville, MD: U.S. Department of Health and Human Services, Substance Abuse and Mental Health Services Administration, Center for Mental Health Services, National Institutes of Health, National Institute of Mental Health, 1999. The document may be found on-line at: http://www.surgeongeneral.gov/library/mentalhealth/toc.html.

[7] Statistics taken from John M. Grohol, "Top 25 Psychiatric Prescriptions for 2009," (http://psychcentral.com/lib/2010/top-25-psychiatric-prescriptions-for-2009/)

[8] Quoted from "Ranking America's Mental Health: An Analysis of Depression Across the States" at http://www.nmha.org/go/state-ranking.

Depression is influenced by many factors, including genetic proclivities, developmental challenges and life exigencies (Plomin 1996). Genetic vulnerability aside, the most common risk factor for depression and related sequelae is stress. *Stress* is of two types, *eustress*, the kind of challenge from the environment necessary for peak neurocognitive efficiency, and *distress*, the kind of environmental press that overwhelms the nervous system and decreases efficiency (Selye 1974). A person encountering eustress is left with feelings of satisfaction, accomplishment, well being and happiness. But in the more common meaning of the term "stress," distress happens when environmental contingencies overwhelm the ability of the organism to adapt, resulting in systematic loss of control and mastery. Chronic distress leads to maladaptive behaviors, poor health, and mood and thought disorders. A common source of stress in our modern world is the systematic failure of expectations and an accompanying sense of helplessness. There is a chronic mismatch between the world as expected and sensory feedback about the world as it really is. For instance, if one experimentally puts non-human primates in situations in which their expectations fail, it will eventually produce profound depression (Mineka 1982).

For a specific example of the relationship between capitalist culture and anxiety-depression and related health issues, the United States is presently in the midst of an epidemic of obesity. Medical scientists have now pinned this epidemic to the stressful way of life that is endemic to today's capitalist, post-industrial society. Wisman and Capehart (2010:975) write that obesity, "…is traceable in part to increasing insecurity and stress in an environment in which there is ever-greater availability of fat and sugary foods. The social gradient of obesity is due to a social gradient of insecurity. The logic of evolution as well as a growing number of studies suggests that insecurity and stress enhance appetite for fatty and sweet foods, with weight gain resulting. The availability of such foods is thus in good part demand-driven, a consequence of rising insecurity and stress stemming from capitalism's ever-more robust creative-destruction. Consequently the prescription that we need more economic growth to become richer, even if this entails greater insecurity and stress, is bad medicine." It is interesting to reflect upon the words John Stewart Mill wrote over 160 years ago about the capitalist/industrial society he was watching evolve around him: "I confess I am not charmed with the ideal of life held out by those who think that the normal state of human beings is that of struggling to get on; that the trampling, crushing, elbowing, and treading on each other's heels, which form the existing type of social life, are the most desirable lot of humankind, or anything but the disagreeable symptoms of one of the phases of industrial progress" (Mill 1973[1848]:748).

To make mental health matters even worse, people in the United States and elsewhere in the "developed" world are increasingly sleep and dream deprived – again, a consequence of our high stress way of life (Jean-Louis, Kripke and Anconi-Israel 2000). This pattern of deficit extends to our children and adolescents.[9] The deleterious effects of systematic sleep and dream deprivation are serious, and have been linked to obesity and diabetes (Knudson *et al.* 2007), loss of vigilant attention and response time (Lim and Dinges 2008), cardiac morbidity (Mullington *et al.* 2009) and deficits in neurocognitive and higher cortical functions (Durmer and Dinges 2005), to mention but a few. Sleep and dreaming are often considered a waste of time in a monophasic and materialist society, resulting in what chronobiologist Charles Czeisler (2006) calls "sleep machismo," the willingness to give up sleep in the favor of more valuable goals.

I would like to suggest that the movement toward a materialist economy and the concomitant loss of sleep and awareness of one's dream life are not coincidental, but systemically entangled (see Bulkeley 1995:158). The loss of involvement with dreaming is part and parcel to the "false consciousness" that makes such politico-economic systems work – *false consciousness* being a culturally conditioned awareness that:

> ...serves to perpetuate inequality by leading members of a subordinate group to believe that they are inferior, deserving of their plight, or incapable of taking action against the causes of their subordination. ...the holding of false or inaccurate beliefs that are contrary to one's own social interest and which thereby contribute to the maintenance of the disadvantaged position of the self or the group (Jost 1995:400).

---

[9] National Sleep Foundation, Summary of findings: 2005 Sleep in America Poll.

A capitalist culture seems to require that everyone be focused primarily on the material conditions of life as the principal font of real value – even at the expense of sleep deprivation and its sequelae. I suspect that most people who are raised in a monophasic culture, with its disattention to things mystical or spiritual, develop egos that are far off-balance in the Jungian sense – not in tune with the depth dynamics of their own psyches. They will experience dreams that express this lack of balance, but they typically are not prepared to pay attention to or understand them, unless they enter a course of psychotherapy that introduces them to some kind of dreamwork. Thus, materialist cultures leave most of their people with a kind of "thirst" for the spiritual that can and does lead to various movements and subcultures offering people methods to slake their thirst for the sublime and spiritual health.[10]

Art is particularly sensitive to this kind of psychological flux in society (Laughlin 2004b). The swing toward complementarity may be presaged in the iconoclasm of modern art, especially in the art of the "surrationalist" movements that have forsaken any semblance of "realism" (Kandinsky 1977 [1914],1982:758). This reversal in art, sometimes explicitly associated with dream exploration, as in the surrealist movement (Bradley 1997), may be a reaction to the lived experience of most people in modern materialist society whose preoccupation with making a living and raising families is done within the off-balanced system of false consciousness requisite to maintaining materialist values.

## Dreaming in Modern Society

The organism seeks to heal itself. This is as true of humans as it is for any other animal. Animals are known to self-medicate and show extraordinary dietary and therapeutic wisdom (Huffman 2003), as are humans (Solomon Katz 1990). Given the chance, both non-human animals and humans alike will seek to heal themselves from the effects of psychological distress. In my opinion, one of the most notable examples of the inherent drive to health is the modern dreamwork

---

[10] I use health in its traditional and literal meaning, derived from the same root as "hail," "whole," "holy," "wholesome," and so forth.

movement (see Ullman 2006[1996]; Ullman and Limmer1999; Ullman and Zimmerman 1989[1979]; Deborah Hillman 1999; Bulkeley 1994: Appendix 1; Taylor 2009: Chap. 6, 1983:Chap. 9).

## The Dreamwork Movement

Interest in dreaming, and the personal and social use of dreams has been growing in Western society for several decades – due in part to the leadership of the late psychiatrist, Montague Ullman and his colleagues. Ullman and Zimmerman published a landmark book in 1979 entitled *Working with Dreams* that began the process of disentangling dream exploration from its long association with psychotherapy. This set in motion a wave of culture change back in the direction of polyphasic culture, at least for some small subcultures among Western societies. With the advent of the Internet, people interested in meeting fellow dreamers, and in seeking guidance and help interpreting their dreams are but a "click" away from sites offering counseling, companionship, interaction and expertise relating to sleep, dreaming and spirituality. At the present time, online sites like The Dream Tribe ("engage your inner healer"), The Dream Star Institute ("dream analysis mentoring and certification"), Facebook's Dream Talk ("the talking circle for dreamers"), Electric Dreams ("John Herbert's pioneering online research and dream groups") and Cyber Dream Work ("interactive dreamwork in cyberspace") inhabit the ether. In addition, there are numerous C.G. Jung Societies throughout the world and on the Internet, as well as "neo-shamanic" groups such as online Neo-Shamanism websites ("ancestral and modern shamanism for our evolution") and Michael Harner's Foundation for Shamanic Studies ("dedicated to the preservation, study, and teaching of shamanic knowledge for the welfare of the planet and its inhabitants"). It is the information age after all, and sources of information, self-help guidance and social contact are widely available – but as in all things in the marketplace, *caveat emptor* ("let the buyer beware").

Montague Ullman's (2006[1996]) approach was largely group oriented, for there was a concern for the safety and support offered by fellow dream explorers (something that young Loughner apparently did not have or seek). "Can dreamwork be extended safely and effectively beyond the confines of the psychotherapist's consulting room? We felt that it could, and we described a group approach to working with dreams that could meet the standards of responsible dreamwork *and could also be entrusted to an interested public*" (Ullman and Limmer 1999:ix, emphasis mine). After reading about dreaming and dream cultures from around the globe, don't you find this latter statement remarkable? Have our Western societies become so alienated from their dream life that serious caution need be exercised in re-introducing people to their own natural faculties? As we have seen above in discussing the Loughner case and the actual dangers posed by weak or traumatized egos and dissociation, Ullman's caution was both pragmatic and justified. Healing in the sense that we mean here results in nothing less than a transformation of the previously monophasic ego toward a polyphasic one. I recall overdoing my Tibetan Tantric *dumo* (*kundalini*) breathing practice once at the beginning of my Tibetan meditation work (Laughlin 1994b) and managed to knock myself unconscious. When I came to, I was disoriented and panicky. Fortunately, I had been doing the breathing exercise at a Buddhist center and one of the leaders held my hand and commiserated with me until I returned to normal. Needless to say, that was one dumb mistake I never repeated.

It is anthropologically interesting that Ullman (Ullman and Limmer 1999) emphasized two factors in advocating group dreamwork, the "safety factor" and the "discovery factor." The first factor is the social support for an essentially subjective exploration – the dreamer is to feel safe and secure within the group setting (see also Taylor 2009:Chap. 6). The second factor is that people need guidance in understanding dream symbolism and what symbolism reveals about one's psyche. As we have seen in this book, all intact polyphasic cultures offer both of these factors for their people. But in polyphasic societies, the individual has been enculturated as a polyphasic ego from childhood.

In Ullman's dreamwork, certain ethnocentric beliefs and attitudes are quite evident. For instance, Ullman (1999:6) rightly notes that working with dreams requires dream sharing, but he also emphasizes: (1) that the dreamer is alone in his/her subjectivity, and (2) that people and other beings encountered in dreams are to be understood as metaphors. As we have seen in the previous chapters, traditional polyphasic peoples take dreaming to be real, and consider characters encountered during dreaming to be real, even if they are deceased – hence they are not alone in their subjectivity, despite the simultaneous realization that dreams may need to be socially shared and interpreted. Ullman's psychotherapeutic orientation to dreamwork derives from his training as a Western psychoanalyst, and informs the dream culture that underlies this kind of exploration (see various articles in Ullman and Limmer 1999). The intent of this sort of dreamwork is more about emotional healing, and less about a communion with the spiritual world. Hence, the therapeutically-oriented, cultural dream theory takes on the attributions and psychological trappings of various clinical theories (see Dombeck 1991:21; Edgar 1995). This approach to dreamwork represents the easiest incorporation of dreaming into what remains essentially a monophasic culture.

One may also encounter dreamwork from within one of the established religions. Many of those interested in dreaming and religion today focus on the use of dreaming in pastoral care (Bulkeley 2000; Haden 2011; Hunt-Meeks 1983). Indeed, there has been a lengthy history to the use of dreamwork in the Judeo-Christian tradition. As Savary, Berne and Williams (1984:1) demonstrate, it is possible to "…present a comprehensive method for using your dreams to connect you with God, yourself, and the believing community." They trace the history of dreaming in *New Testament* times, address the early rejection of dreamwork by the church, and discuss the return to dreamwork in the 20th century and modern methods for enriching a Christian-oriented spirituality through attention to dreaming. In doing this, they isolate numerous methods that can be used to beef-up one's dreaming and bring dreams into dialogue with one's faith.

Llewellyn Vaughan-Lee (1994) has shared his experiences doing dreamwork among a Sufi group. People meet to support each other on the path, "for the purpose of transformation beyond the ego" (ibid:xii), and to tap into the one great source of energy, the Self. "Channeling the energy of the Self, such a group becomes a point of light, bringing the nourishment, and wholeness of the Self into the world of time and space" (ibid:xiv). The dreamwork is done within this context by relating dream content with spiritual stories – the famous teaching stories of the Sufi masters. Dreams themselves are considered stories within which there lies a "thread" that is our inner spiritual journey. Here is the way that Vaughan-Lee (ibid:3) describes Sufi dreamwork: "To work with dreams is to work with the symbolic substance that underlies our life. The images and symbols that come to us in dreams are not idle fantasies, but point to a reality that is deeper than the reality of the outer world. Almost all processes of inner growth and transformation depend upon working with this symbolic stratum of the psyche. It forms the embryo from which we are reborn." To my reading, Sufi dreamwork is very compatible with Jungian dreamwork.

Anthropologists have done a fair job of researching image work generally, and the dreamwork movement specifically (Edgar 2004). Deborah Jay Hillman, herself a lucid dreamer (1984), studied some of Ullman's dreamwork groups and other groups in and around New York City (1990, 1994). Just as Barbara Tedlock and other exceptional ethnographers have found in their approach to dreaming in diverse societies (Nuttall 2007:348; Goulet 1994; Tedlock 1991; see Chapter 6), Hillman found that her own proficiency as an experienced dreamer stood her in good stead with her informants – in fact, her dreaming was quite indispensable in the field (1994:79). She centered her efforts on what she calls "grassroots" groups. She suggested that, "…we view as grassroots efforts all community-based, nonclinical dream groups organized by and for lay people (in the traditional sense). These run the gamut from informal, leaderless groups that are free to groups offered by the 'new' dreamwork professionals, for a fee" (1990:15). The motivations of people seeking such groups covers a spectrum from the wish to heal to the deep desire to connect with the Divine. The social structure of groups ranges widely in size, gender, ethnicity and complexity. Membership may be an informal association of people with a common interest in dreaming, or may be by recruitment. They may be sponsored by churches, schools, community centers and the like, or by lists and blogs on the Internet. These days the *Dream Network* (established in 1982) and its journal are online and continue to facilitate communication and local group organizations. There are groups centered on special interests, such as artist's and women's groups (ibid:16). Interests and approaches to dreamwork vary widely, but, "[b]roadly speaking, the goal of nonclinical dreamwork is to foster an appreciation of dreams and to make them more available as useful resources for waking life. Differences exist in the ways that sense of appreciation is engendered and in the waking domains to which the dreams are most assiduously applied. Generally, it is the psychological and spiritual dimensions of the dream that receive the greatest attention. For although dreams contain a wealth of social and cultural information, these aspects are rarely explored in dreamwork settings, at least not explicitly" (ibid:17).

Hillman distinguishes between two styles of interaction, either or both of which may be present in any specific group. She terms one type as the "study group" format in which participants share their dreams in an informal and conversational setting. There may be discussions of techniques of incubating dreams, approaches to interpretation, sharing of meaning, that sort of thing. The second style is the "experiential" format which is more formally structured and in which members use specific techniques for guiding and eliciting deeper understanding of dreaming (Ullman's program above fits into this category).

Against the backdrop of a monophasic culture, the dreamwork movement has its work cut out for it. There is reason to suppose that the rise of this non-clinical grassroots movement may shift the personal dream theories of individuals and even sub-cultures toward a more polyphasic comprehension of consciousness. The movement is anything but monolithic, however, for the motivations of dreamwork advocates are as complex as the society they live in. "Factors such as intracultural variations in dream theory, the nature and interpretation of the dream itself, the personal attributes of the dreamer and his relationships with other people all influence the motivation, timing, content, degree of reciprocity, and implications of dream narration" (Collins 1984:3). In addition, we must keep in mind that the monophasic nature of capitalist, post-industrial false consciousness has not been the mere product of a random historical drift in culture change. Rather, it is endemic to this type of politico-economic system. One may expect resistance to changes in self-awareness, materialist values and goals, and adaptational traditions by such social systems – even from entrenched ideologies within institutional religious organizations. Still, even within such a conservative establishment as institutional Christianity, the movement has made inroads into pastoral care and counseling (Haden 2011; Bulkeley 2000; Krippner, Bogzaran and de Carvalho 2002:154).

It is significant, I think, that much of the organized dreamwork movement is oriented toward healing, whether it be closely associated or not with the psychotherapeutic industry or pastoral care. This is precisely what one might expect as a compensatory symptom of an un-sane society. In other words, the organization of consciousness, the enculturation into a society's value system, the daily demands of the marketplace and so forth tend to be conditioned by the political and economic ideologies dominant in the society. As Louis Althusser (2010[1968]; Resch 1992:53), borrowing from Engles, has argued, any economic system exercises *determination in the last instance* — meaning that the historical relationship between the political and economic structures of a society has causal primacy over the conditioning of consciousness within any particular society. No matter how "weird" were my experiences while practicing Tibetan dream yoga (Chapter 13), I still had to retain a flexibility of mind that enabled me to go to work and teach classes. I often wondered at the time what I would have done had I still been a longshoreman having to face loading greasy cowhides into the holds of Japan-bound freighters. In order for a person to step away from their cultural conditioning they must replace their monophasic worldview with something quite different – and yet they must be able to adapt to the real local world. An old Zen Buddhist saying comes to mind: before awakening chop wood, after awakening chop wood.

## Modern Dreamwork and the Cycle of Meaning

Let us return to the cycle of meaning model and the relations between worldview, mythopoeic symbolism and dream experience (see Chapter 7). Modern materialist societies rarely provide a true cosmology for their members. We may intellectually or scientifically understand that the universe is a single system made up of subsystems and sub-subsystems, etc. (i.e., the "cosmos"), but this has little practical value in our daily lives (unless one happens to follow astrology). Hardly anyone in the West cares where the Pleiades constellation is in the night sky, assuming they know what the Pleiades is in the first place. Yet many traditional cultures will schedule annual economic activity and travel based upon the movement of the Pleiades and other constellations. Part of what it means to have a full-on spiritual culture is that the world of experience in all SOC *is understood as a living cosmology*. This is why dreaming, dream sharing and dream interpretation have been so closely associated with mythology in traditional societies, but only with certain psychotherapies in our modern Western zeitgeist. According to monophasic dream theory, dreams are not a window into the spiritual world or the soul, but only into our individual, possibly disturbed psyche. As we have seen, nothing could be further from the truth. As Adam Kuper (1979:661) wrote, "…the reasoning of the unconscious and the logic of mythical thought are both not only rigorous but also similar in kind, perhaps revealing deep and significant features of human mental processes."

As David Feinstein (1986, 1990) and Stanley Krippner (Feinstein and Krippner 2009[1988]:285-291) have so aptly emphasized, effective dreamwork necessitates the construction of a cycle of meaning within which dream conflicts and other experiences generate meaning and become integrated within a more polyphasic, symbolic understanding of the self and the world. This is no easy task. It takes dedication, determination and a hell of a lot of hard work and time. At the heart of the new cycle of meaning is myth (Chapter 7). "Dreaming and myth always address the deeper realities of our lives below the surface of appearance" (J. Taylor 1996:140). As Feinstein puts it, "Your personal mythology interprets the past, defines the present, and offers guidance for the future. Myths …are *not* falsehoods; they are the lens through which the human psyche perceives and organizes reality. Mythic thought, with its compelling symbolism and narrative, is the natural language of the psyche. A personal myth is a complex of images, emotions, and concepts, organized around a core theme that addresses at least one of the domains within which mythology traditionally functions" (1990:21; Feinstein's emphasis).

The problem is, where does a new personal cycle of meaning and mythology come from? Does one develop one's own system from within the context of a psychotherapeutic relationship? Does one embrace another society's cycle of meaning – for instance, does one engage in so-called Senoi dreamwork,[11] Tibetan dream yoga (Chapter 13), the

---

[11] Senoi dreamwork takes its name from a small Malaysian hunting and gathering society who were supposed to use lucid dreaming in healing – a claim that turned out to be a hoax; see Domhoff, G.W., 2003. "Senoi Dream Theory: Myth, Scientific Method, and the Dreamwork Movement." unpublished paper retrieved from the Internet: http://dreamresearch.net/Library/senoi.html.

Native American medicine wheel,[12] or perhaps neo-shamanism (see below)? Indeed, one of the main motives behind "ethnotourism"[13] is to seek an authentic alien cultural experience upon which to base one's spiritual quest. Does one join a local group, such as one of the numerous C.G. Jung societies, or perhaps an online network? Maybe one may take charge and develop a new spiritual study group in dialogue with others?[14] Is the guidance of a master necessary or vital to one's quest? Or does one turn inward for guidance and meaning and allow the psyche or spiritual world to speak for itself? Feinstein and Krippner (2009[1988]) have worked out a program for teaching people to develop their own mythology. The method is based upon applying four universal aspects of myth: biology, culture, personal history and transcendent experiences (Feinstein 1990:23):

- **Biology**: "[T]he capacities for symbolism and narrative are rooted in the structure of the brain, information and attitudes are neurochemically coded, temperament and hormones influence belief systems." Mythology is, in other words, structured by neurognosis – it is archetypal by nature.
- **Culture**: "[T]he individual's mythology is, to an extent, the culture's mythology in microcosm." If one is raised a Muslim, then part of one's personal mythology will be influenced by that religious tradition.
- **Personal History**: "[E]very emotionally significant event leaves a mark on one's developing mythology." This includes traumatic events, especially in childhood. Indeed, in Buddhism there is the saying, "the greater the suffering, the greater the awakening."
- **Transcendent Experiences**: "[T]hose episodes, insights, and visions that have a numinous quality, expand a person's perspective,

---

[12] See *Dancing with the Wheel: The Medicine Wheel Workbook*, by Sun Bear, Wabun Wind and Crysalis Mulligan.

[13] The ethnotourism industry caters to people who wish to live with an indigenous society for a while and participate in their daily lives and rituals. This includes "ayahuasca tourism" in which people pay to travel to one of the ayahuasca-using groups in South America to participate in religious ceremonies.

[14] My mother, Martha Laughlin, joined her local "psi group" which met monthly to discuss various aspects of spiritual knowledge and practice. I visited with them many times and taught them how to meditate.

and inspire more enlightened behavior." One enters the domain of transpersonal and polyphasic dream experiences in which the symbolism in one's personal mythology takes on a deeper and ego-expanding meaning.

Feinstein and Krippner view the establishment of a new personal mythology as a dialectical process by which one's old and spiritually dissatisfying mythology is juxtaposed "by a counter-myth generated to compensate for the old myth's limitations" (ibid:24). From this counter-position of the two myths, a new Hegelian synthesis emerges as the maturity of one's dream and other ASC experiences develop.

Dreamwork is often integral to neo-shamanic practice (Chidester 2008b). *Neo-shamanism* ("contemporary shamanism") is a New Age spiritual movement that draws heavily on the ethnographic literature about indigenous religions (see Chapter 9; see also Townsend 1988, 2004; DuBois 2009:Chap. 14; Taylor and Piedilato 2002), particularly on the teachings and writings of anthropologist, Michael Harner whose work with Jivaro Indian shamans (1973) led to his publishing *Way of the Shaman* (1990[1980]) – one of the "bibles" of the movement. Among other influential notions, Harner has parsed the universal aspects of traditional shamanism and has distilled them into what he calls "core shamanism" – a set of concepts and techniques, including dream incubation, that can be used by anyone as a basis for their own spiritual practice.

Similarly, *neo-paganism* movements – including *Wicca* — use dreaming in their practices. Neo-paganists may trace their roots back to the works of Aleister Crowley (1875-1947), a very controversial English mystic and one of the leading lights of the Hermetic Order of the Golden Dawn tradition of the Western mysteries. Crowley was also the founder of the Thelema religious cult which survives today and which also practices dream incubation. Each of these New Age dream approaches to spiritual experiences comes equipped with a variety of textural, symbolic, ritual and interpretive frameworks with which one may build a personal mythology and cycle of meaning. Interpretive frameworks may derive from shamanic lore, Freudian, Jungian or Gestalt psychology, the Western mysteries tradition, or esoteric Christianity, Sufism, Kabbalah, Buddhism, etc. Ritual practices run the gamut from drumming to "holotropic breath work," from transpersonal psychotherapeutic techniques to psychic healing, from formal meditation to lucid dream incubation.

Two pitfalls often lay along the spiritual path chosen by New Age practitioners. The first is the ever-present temptation to accept some religious ideology as "the one true belief." An *ideology* is a knowledge system that admits of no exceptions to doctrine. It refers to a closed and rigidly conservative system of belief which professes to understand all possible transpersonal experiences, and offers dream and other ASC interpretations that reflect back upon itself in an inevitably self-referential way. An ideological practice is equipped with a totally closed cycle of meaning which allows no new positive feedback into its system of knowledge, and no possibility of empirical disconfirmation. Thus, ideologies effectively dumb-down the more creative and free-wheeling explorations that naturally arise during the course of spiritual journeys of self-discovery. Religious ideologies abound on the planet and include much that is called "born again" evangelical Christianity, Islamic fundamentalism and Salafist jihadism, as well as the worst excesses of such cults as Scientology, the Unification Church, the Great White Brotherhood, and the like.

The second pitfall is the natural, and even archetypal projection of guru-status on teachers. Spiritual seekers from monophasic cultures are especially vulnerable to being manipulated by charlatans[15] and false prophets. The central question a novice needs to ask themselves is whether or not they really need a guru or spiritual master. Each of us has within our archetypal natures an "inner guru," and it is this sense of "teacher" that we may project outwards upon another person who we perceive to embody knowledge, maturity, wisdom, or spiritual enlightenment, perfection and power – this is why we recognize gurus, priests, pastors, rabbis, mullahs, shamans, doctors and the like. I am *not* meaning to imply that there are no people who may know more about our spiritual path than we do – as some wise person once said, the master is someone that started out on the path before you did. I am talking about the psychodynamics by which we may be led to project "teacher" on a con artist. They *seem* to walk the walk and talk the talk, but do they live the life of the enlightened? Have they actually accomplished what they

---

[15] The word "charlatan" comes from the French, which in turn came from the Italian *ciarlatano* meaning a "quack" or "fraud."

claim to have done? The best advice I can offer is no better than that attributed to Jesus when he said "Ye shall know them by their fruits. Do men gather grapes of thorns, or figs of thistles" (Matthew 7:16)? Does your prospective guru take sexual liberties with young men and women among his/her flock of devotees? Does the "master" use money you give him/her to buy a fleet of Rolls Royces – one for each day of the month? Perhaps this person is a teacher, but may not be "living the life" of the enlightened. The term *arhat* (Pali: *arahant*) in Buddhism is used to label an awakened person, one who has overcome all the obstacles to enlightenment. However, it sometimes also means one who has "no secrets," no secret life – in other words, "what you see is what you get."

Does a person *need* a guru to do dreamwork? The answer is a big-fat, conditional "NO!" After all, a Baptist preacher named George Gillespie (1988b) discovered he was having lucid dreams when he was 41, and continued to explore and experiment with dreams for years without a guru to guide him. But I said "conditional," and the condition is this – how intensely does one intend to follow the path of dreamwork? If the intent is to increase awareness of one's dreams and write them down, puzzle over their meaning and maybe share them with other dreamers, then no, one does not *require* a teacher to be safe. But if one intends to practice one of the dream yogas full-on, carry out lengthy retreats or use powerful ritual drivers in their practice, then they would be well-advised to seek a guide. And if the dreamwork involves healing oneself, then guidance of a psychotherapist or other healer might be safer and more productive. My stipulation is this: Avoid any and all ideologies, whether they be scientific, psychotherapeutic or religious. Ideologies put an end to questions — transcendent dreaming raises questions.

## Jungian Dreamwork

As you may have noticed, I am particularly fond of C.G. Jung's approach to the depth psychology of dreaming (see also Bulkeley 1994: Chap. 5; Bogart 2009). This is not just a personal preference on my part. Of all the competing Western psychological theories of dreaming, Jung's is *the most consonant with both the neuropsychology and the anthropology of dreaming.* In other words, Jung's theory of dreaming allows us to bridge between what we know about how the brain works, and the cross-cultural data about dreaming, dream theories, culture pattern dreaming, dream sharing and interpretation, mythological consequences of social dreaming and the development of the dreaming psyche. The Jungian approach emphasizes the role of dream awareness in the individuation of the self – a view that is light years beyond the understanding of more ethnocentric Freudian accounts, some of which treat the manifest content of dreams as merely a form of delirium (e.g., Hobson 1994). In Chapters 10 and 11 we discussed the Jungian theory of archetypes and the self, and explored how dreaming operates as a window on the self – something like Hollan's "selfscape" dreams. Apropos to the present discussion, Jungian depth psychology has developed methodologies for both the phenomenological exploration of dreaming (Singer 1990; Mattoon 1978; White-Lewis 2001; Henriques 2004; Johnson 1986; Bogart 2009) and the exploration of dream motifs arising in waking consciousness (Jung 1968f:194, 1997; von Franz 1997[1979]; Price-Williams 1992:247; Mattoon 1978:149; Watkins 1976:42-50; Mageo 2001; Johnson 1986), methods that are quite appropriate for modern dreamwork.

Jung's method of *active imagination* (see Chapter 10) is simple enough in principle, but very hard to realize – and in the hands of someone as loosely wired as Jared Loughner is reputed to be, can be quite dangerous. The method is nothing more nor less than Jung's rediscovery of the ancient Tibetan Tantric "arising yoga" meditation, which is the intense, one-pointed concentration upon an image until that image "comes alive" in consciousness (see Chapter 13 for my own experiences with this type of meditation). The images used in Buddhist meditation, however, usually come from a textual description (as in Theravada *kasina* practice), a description by one's guru, or a painting (such as a Tibetan *tangka*), whereas the images used in Jungian active imagination derive from one's own dreams, visions or fantasies – in other words, generated out of one's own imagination. The "pith instructions" (Tib: *mengakdé*) are essentially the same: choose an auspicious image and develop one's concentration upon it until it takes on a life of its own (see Laughlin, McManus and Webber 1984 for more details about the Tibetan system). In Jungian dreamwork this process is understood as the conscious ego establishing a dialogue with the archetypal stratum of the psyche expressed in the dream, fantasy image, sand play game, storybook, or some mythological source. This is a process the Germans call *betrachten* which can be taken to mean "...making something pregnant [with power and meaning] by giving it your attention" (Chodorow 1997:7). Active imagination is indeed "active," and requires skill, persistence and effort (see Johnson 1986 for a guide).

To offer an example of how the method may be used, over the last several months, I have had recurring *anima* dreams – by which I mean the predominant presence of female figures, most of whom I do not know. Very recently, the motif has shifted somewhat to include direct interaction with a female character. Upon waking I generally spend time concentrating upon the eidetic images I recall from these dreams and take note of any spontaneous fantasies, intuitive associations, and especially emotions that *arise* (get it, "arising" yoga?). I just note what associations pop into consciousness, and then get on with my day. Well, over the last week or so (as I write this), these interactions have included the knowledge of being "married" to the female figure – the "marriage archetype" we discussed in Chapter 10. In one dream I was married to the female and experiencing physical intimacy (but not sexual arousal) with her. In my meditation on the imagery, a distinct feeling of fulfillment and well-being arose. I interpret this pattern of imagery over the last months as having to do with what Jung (1970 [1955/56]) termed the *conjunctio*, the "holy wedding." But naturally if I were an Ongee, a Lacandon or a Barok I would be interpreting the imagery in different terms, and as related to a different knowledge system. It is always well to remember *that there is no such thing as an experience that admits to one and only one interpretation*. This dictum goes a long way in protecting us from either inflating our ego, or being trapped by an ideological belief system. It also respects the transcendental nature of dream experiences relative to our understanding – there always being more to know about dreams and the self that generates them than we can ever know.

The Jungian interpretive frame is that of the Western European alchemical tradition. There is an interesting irony here. Jung (for various personal reasons) was highly suspicious of Westerners buying into any Oriental spiritual frame of reference (Jung 1965 [1961]). Instead, he went in search of his own – his was a case of experience overrunning an outmoded worldview.[16] He found an interpretive system in the symbolism of latter day alchemy (1967, 1968a). Now, Jungians tend to couch their dream and fantasy interpretations in Jungian terms – in either Jung's archetypal psychology, or in his reconstituted alchemical cosmology. But what is often not said is that, just like Tibetan Buddhism or Sufism, one may apply Jungian methods, but not necessarily accept Jung's frame of reference. Just because Jung found Eastern frames inappropriate for Westerners, we need not. Indeed, while advocating for a more Western interpretive frame, Jung nonetheless held that mystical experiences were much the same across cultures (see Hunt 1989: Appendix for relevant empirical data). The difference is how such experiences are viewed, evaluated, understood and modeled by culture:

> For the [traditional person], the phenomenon of spirits is direct evidence for the reality of a spiritual world. If we inquire what these spirit phenomena mean to him, and in what they consist, we find that the most frequent phenomenon is the seeing of apparitions, or ghosts. It is generally assumed that the seeing of apparitions is far commoner among [traditional folks] than among civilized people, the inference being that this is nothing but superstition, because civilized people do not have such visions unless they are ill. It is quite certain that civilized man makes much less use of the hypothesis of spirits than the [traditional], but in my view it is equally certain that psychic phenomena occur no less frequently with civilized people than they do with [traditional people]. The only difference is that where the [traditional person] speaks of ghosts, the European speaks of dreams and fantasies and neurotic symptoms, and attributes less importance to them than the [traditional person] does. (Jung 1969h [1948]:303)

As Paul Ricoeur once said, "symbols invite thought," and thought produces meaning and realization. A difference between monophasic

---

[16] Since the publication of Jung's *Red Book* (2009), one can appreciate the difference that discovering the alchemical system made in his understanding of dream symbolism.

and polyphasic peoples is the amount of thought they give to mystical symbolism arising in dreams (Whiteman 1961). In any event, the reader wishing to explore more about the Jungian approach to dreamwork might wish to read Thomas Kirsch's unique book, *The Jungians* (2000) which presents a detailed history of the Jungian movement worldwide. In that book you can find out about Jungian institutes, analytical psychology clubs and so forth.

## THE CHALLENGE OF DREAMING IN THE MODERN WORLD

Theoretically speaking, any frame of reference that (1) views dreaming as "real" in some sense, (2) treats dream elements as symbolic and meaningful, and (3) keeps waking life grounded in perceptual reality, might do. That is precisely the pattern we have seen with traditional peoples all over the planet. Their engagement in their dream life, far from being delusional or dissociative, is brought into their daily lives and, if anything, tends to be in aid of *both* waking adaptation *and* developing a mature spiritual self. But traditional peoples are raised within an intact cycle of meaning, while we Westerners typically face the problem of "rolling" our own (see Bulkeley 1994: Chap. 13; Bosnak 2007). This is where some caution is in order, for there are spiritual paths and then there are spiritual paths. The wise will seek an interpretive frame (1) that will carry one beyond mundane "dream book" interpretations, (2) that at the very least avoids the pitfalls of ideology and false prophets, and (3) that has as its goal the integration of dream awareness and knowledge within the context of the individuation of the self. Jungian dreamwork is one such path, but there are many others (see Hudson 1985 for a very useful method based on poetic analysis) — some of which are, as we have seen, associated with the great religions, or with one of the Western mysteries traditions.

Harry Hunt, citing a comment by Liam Hudson (1985), raised the interesting question, "If dreaming becomes more and more mundane and even subjectively ceases in the lives of many modern adults, then could this same fate not become general – as a postmodern but not post-money mentality works its way pervasively through peoples lives" (1989:218)? He thinks this scenario unlikely, as do I. As we have seen, dreaming is "wired-in" – the experience of neurobiological processes that have evolved over millions of years. As far as we know, there exist no "racial" or ethnic variations in the essential structure of the human brain – only different courses of development and maturation. All people dream and do so with the same neurocognitive structures. Indeed, they *must* dream, whether or not they pay any attention to their dream content. My position goes farther than Hunt's, however, for my (and Jung's) experience tells me that there are two types of people in the world, those who participate in a conscious way in their unfolding self-development and those who do not – maturation (individuation) occurs whether or not one is aware of the process, but the person who consciously participates in their own development becomes a qualitatively different person. Modern society is full of people who pay little attention to their individuation – a sad state of affairs, in my estimation. Culture makes all the difference, and when a society conditions its members to disattend dreaming – the natural window upon the self — it is essentially predisposing its members away from full participation in self-development and, in the sense that I spoke of above, toward un-sanity.

The real challenge for people in the modern, post-industrial age is *not* how to get along without dream awareness, but how to re-establish an intimate connection with their dream life and thereby themselves – perhaps even their souls or spiritual natures (however understood or talked about) – and thus integrate their entire range of experiences into a polyphasic consciousness. The challenge is that they have to do this in a way that does not jeopardize their ongoing adaptation to external reality. We do not need any more Jared Lee Loughners than our un-sane society is already producing. It would help a lot if my fellow anthropologists could form an educational vanguard in this respect, for they tend to be more sensitive as a group to the nuances of cultural difference among peoples, and should be in a position to help formulate a corrective to the un-sanity around them. But alas, anthropologists are people and people are the products of their own conditioning.

There are exceptions within our ranks. Anthropologist and economic development specialist, Tara Lumpkin (2001) has been impressed by the destructive effects of spreading materialist culture with its attendant monophasic values. She has argued that the developing world is losing (as we have already done) not only "... (1) *biodiversity* (biocomplexity) in environments and (2) *cultural diversity* in societies, we also are losing (3) *perceptual diversity* in human cognitive processes. All three losses of diversity (bio, cultural, and cognitive) are interrelated" (ibid:37; emphasis mine). False consciousness is accomplished by a narrowing of perspective to the point where people cannot keep a holistic, ecological and cosmological worldview squarely in mind. When people lose the ability to comprehend how everything is entangled in a vast, unified ecological system, and how human well-being depends upon the biodiversity of plants and animals, they become vulnerable to the unintended and pernicious consequences of their actions upon the environment. Losing the "spiritual" or "sublime" dimensions of reality in the wholesale conversion to materialist culture is the same thing as losing touch with the entangled totality of existence.

The polyphasic culture – including involvement in dream life — so common to most traditional peoples on the planet is necessary for the maintenance of perceptual diversity, according to Lumpkin. She argues (ibid:39) that:

> ...when a culture restrains perceptual diversity, that same culture reduces human adaptability, which, in turn, leads to human beings living unsustainably. Unsustainable lifestyles result in ecological destruction, including destruction of biodiversity (or biocomplexity). In a feedback loop, degraded environments offer fewer choices to human beings for adaptability, and a downward spiral commences. If, indeed, perceptual diversity promotes human adaptability and indirectly promotes healthy environments, then perceptual diversity has a practical application in everyday life. Yet the value of perceptual diversity is not acknowledged by international development experts, who insist that only a monophasic worldview is valid. In fact, one of the steps to development is for a culture to jettison its perceptual diversity in favor of a specialized approach based on the scientific method and economic progress. The scientific method only acknowledges monophasic consciousness. The method is a specialized system that focuses on studying small and distinctive parts in isolation, which results in fragmented knowledge.

The method also results in the loss of the direct experience of the spiritual and sublime. Loss of dream awareness *is* loss of perceptual diversity in its most natural state. We have seen that evolution has favored perceptual diversity in animals over the course of hundreds of millions of years. Curious, is it not, that only in materialist culture do we turn our backs so fundamentally upon our very nature.

There are dream researchers who have thought deeply about the relevance of dreaming to the spiritual lives of people in the modern age. Psychologist, Kelly Bulkeley (see 1994, 1995, 1996a, 1996b), is one of those. Steeped in the ethnography of dream cultures, he brings those data to bear on the relevance of what he calls *spiritual dreaming* in modern society. Spiritual dreams are, "…those dreams that bring people experientially closer to the powers of the sacred and that speak to their ultimate existential concerns. These dreams do not, however, always have traditionally religious imagery. A person may have a dream that is profoundly spiritual in its symbolism, emotional impact, and existential meaning, even though the dream *appears* on the surface to be quite ordinary and unremarkable" (1995:3; emphasis Bulkeley's). In his analysis of spiritual dreams across cultures and within modern society, he has shown that dreaming offers a universal window to the sacred and sublime dimensions of reality. He has also shown that whether or not that window onto spiritual opportunity is acknowledged or not depends on cultural conditioning and on personal development – the old Biblical phrase comes to mind: "For many are called, but few are chosen" (Matthew 22:14).

I would argue with considerable evidence that the capacity to enter the spiritual domain is in our very nature, and that turning our back to that sublime invitation is counter to that nature – but part and parcel to false consciousness. Just as dreaming is a natural process, so too is the journey into the depths of our being. In my own life I have learned that the truth is indeed "closer than my nose," and that all I needed to do is answer the call. For me the call of the sublime came in dreams (see Chapter 13). Similar to Jung who considered the forest as an archetype of the unconscious, Bulkeley likes to use the metaphor of the wilderness when referring to the spiritual dimensions of dreaming. As an "architectural structure" may be used as a metaphor for rational theory construction, says Bulkeley (1994:23), the metaphor of the "wilderness" best fits the spiritual dimension entered in our dream life. The "wilderness of dreams" is "...a dark, mysterious region, a region about which little is known but much is fancied. The researchers who have journeyed there have brought back fantastic tales of strange beings, breathtaking wonders, and paralyzing terrors" (ibid:24). It is an excellent metaphor, for as Jung taught, each person must enter the forest of the unconscious at the place they find most dark and frightening to themselves. Dreaming offers each person a window into the depths, but precisely what part of the depths is glimpsed through the window varies with the person.

## Childrearing Values and Education

With rare exceptions, public school education programs pay scarce attention to dreaming – the very place and age range where dreamwork would prove most effective in facilitating global culture change (see King, Welt and Bulkeley 2011). However we as individual dreamers answer the call of the depths, the only way to ensure a more global change in culture away from capitalist/materialist false consciousness and toward a more balanced and "sane" polyphasic orientation is to change our patterns of childrearing and education (see Bulkeley 1994:219-220; Hunt 1989:218-219; Garfield 1985). This is a tall order, for as I have said, the political economy of a materialist society tends to determine "in the last instance" parental attitudes and practices, and primary/secondary school curricula. Liberal curricula geared to educating "the whole person" quickly succumb to pressures for standardized and market-driven cognitive skills. As I write this, hundreds of thousands of jobs go wanting in the high tech manufacturing field, and there is great pressure by industry for secondary schools to provide job-relevant skills. Determination in the last instance can be overcome with sufficient awareness, for as I say, materialist attitudes and activities are not the product of some grand conspiracy, but rather the product of culture history – the "we do it this way because our parents and their parents and grandparents before them did it this way" kind of history. All it really takes is for parents to change their attitudes to include interest in and encouragement of their children's dreaming. Exchanging dreams with children, talking to them about dreaming and raising questions about dream motifs and adventures will help condition them to retain awareness of what is, after all, a natural process. Parents can encourage their children to paint their dreams, or write down their dreams like short stories in a journal. Just as developing an interest in one's dreams is all that is required to increase dream recall in adults, showing sustained interest in a child's dreaming is all that is required to keep them in touch with their dream life, and potentially their spiritual life.

Changing school systems to follow suit is more challenging, for elementary school curricula are often under the thumb of school boards and political functionaries who may consider dream-related units and courses to be non-productive and a waste of time. Convincing school administrators on the idea that dreaming is just as important as math and science will be a hard sell under the present climate of curriculum standardization, political conservatism and shrinking revenues. Yet some have succeeded in introducing dreamwork curricula and have learned valuable lessons teaching dreaming to school kids. Jungian analyst Jane White-Lewis (1996) had the opportunity to teach high school dream courses in Connecticut. She experimented with a variety of methods for interesting inner city kids in dreaming, including playing with images cut out of magazines to get them engaged with images as symbols, psychodrama in which dream motifs were acted out, active imagination on someone's dream theme, keeping a dream journal, discussing dreams in literature and other forms of art, as well as in television programs. She reports that, "…teaching the dream courses at the High School in the Community has become an important part of my life. This experience has had an enormous impact on me; I suspect the same is true for many of my students. And, of course, the effect of introducing dream studies into the curriculum [has] been felt beyond my particular classes" (ibid:11-12). Of course, hers was one high school out of the estimated 36,000+ public and private secondary schools in the United States.[17] As I say, it's a tall order.

---

[17] Figures from the Digest of Education Statistics, 2001, Table 89.

## Summary and Segue

It can be argued that modern post-industrial societies tend to produce un-sane populations – multitudes of people who are unbalanced in their adaptation to the destructive stress of daily existence. One of the symptoms of this un-sanity is the loss of contact between the waking ego and the depths of the self, a contact that requires involvement in dream experiences and information. Cultures generally resist change, and modern materialist societies are no different in this respect. Devaluation of dreaming and other spiritually efficacious experiences is part of the foundation of "false consciousness" required by capitalist/materialist political economies. Materialist cultures require that the focus of awareness be upon the material conditions of waking life and away from involvement with the inner being which is the only road to spiritual maturation.

Another symptom of societal un-sanity is the emergence of various forms of organized dream movements. People have been left with an unquenched thirst for spiritual fulfillment, and the drive for health and balance results in a kind of rebound from extreme materialism into explorations of the inner life, and an approximation of traditional, polyphasic ways of life. We have seen that there are numerous approaches to re-involving oneself in our dreaming life-world, including psychotherapies and non-clinical dreamwork movements. We have cautioned the novice against uncritical acceptance of ideologies and gurus, but have extolled the benefits of reintegrating dream consciousness into one's life.

We will now conclude our exploration of dreaming, dream culture and the dreaming brain by re-emphasizing the value of merging neuroscience and anthropology in the study of cross-cultural phenomena like dreaming. We will also summarize the more important universal aspects of dreaming across cultures, and suggest some ways that ethnographers and other dream researchers may strengthen their own skills as dreamers.

# Chapter 16

## Conclusion

> As far as we can discern, the sole purpose of human existence is to kindle a light in the darkness of mere being.
>
> C. G. Jung, *Memories, Dreams, Reflections*

> Do not believe in anything simply because you have heard it. Do not believe in anything simply because it is spoken and rumored by many. Do not believe in anything simply because it is found written in your religious books. Do not believe in anything merely on the authority of your teachers and elders. Do not believe in traditions because they have been handed down for many generations. But after observation and analysis, when you find that anything agrees with reason and is conducive to the good and benefit of one and all, then accept it and live up to it.
>
> Buddha, *Kalama Sutta*

Polyphasic peoples all over the world take full advantage of their dreaming life-world. They, like everybody else, spend approximately a third of their lives asleep, but unlike most of us raised in materialist, post-industrial societies, they do not spend this time pretty much unconscious. When one thinks about it, if one has to spend all that time asleep, why not enjoy the movie? It is curious that so many of us remain unconscious while asleep. It is not a coincidence that our upbringing denies and blocks out that aspect of our psychological natures. If I am correct, the lack of dream involvement is part of the conditioning into false consciousness that a capitalist, post-industrial political economy requires. The reader may wish to try a thought experiment: Imagine what would happen to our society and way of life if everybody suddenly started dreaming more lucidly. Might it have the effect of re-directing the focus of consciousness away from the everyday grind of making a living and toward a whole new domain of spiritual question and experience? How would this change parental interaction with their children? Would this reorientation of consciousness during development ameliorate the rampant psychopathology inflicting people in our society? I have no way of knowing for sure what the effects might be, but it would be really interesting to find out, wouldn't it?

One thing we can say for sure is that society will not revert to something like a traditional polyphasic system. There has never been a modern society yet that, having once lost its polyphasic dream orientation, became polyphasic again. Subcultures have arisen in these societies, as we have noted in the last chapter, but these are the result of counter-cultural movements, none of which have thus far replaced an entire materialistic and monophasic culture. Hence, one may only speculate about what such a society might look like, but one can easily slip into imagining an unrealistic, utopian ideal. My hunch is that such a society would be an evolutionary advance over any of the sociocultural systems that have existed before. It would truly be a "post-modern" society.

## Common Patterns in the Ethnography of Dreaming

The reader may have noticed some recurrent patterns among dreaming cultures, many of which were typical of Western dream cultures in the ancient past (Kruger 2005). Above all, dreaming appears to be more lucid among polyphasic folk than we consider normal in our societies. Many of these patterns are pegged to greater lucidity. Let me summarize these patterns (see also Bulkeley 1996b; Hall and Van de Castle 1966), many of which are due in part to the neurocognitive universals noted in Chapter 14. The categories below are naturally fuzzy ones and thus will overlap:

- **Dreams are real.** Polyphasic peoples consider experiences had while dreaming as real in some sense – not as unreal as industrial and post-industrial folk tend to do. Moreover, the dream world and waking world have permeable boundaries such that intentions and information available in the one can cross into the other by way of memory and perhaps narration.

- **Prophetic dreaming.** My impression is that most polyphasic societies look to dreaming as a means of predicting future events. In many societies, specific strategies are employed in response to dreams auguring misfortune or calamity. I suspect that people in all such societies will apply a "wait and see" attitude to many potentially divinatory dreams, and will attribute accuracy of prediction to those whose dreams have proven prescient in the past.
- **Dream ego as soul.** The dream ego, or quasi-perceptual point of view, is considered to be one's soul or spiritual essence freed from the body and able to wander around in the spirit world. Sometimes soul journeys are intentional and take one to places and encounters with spirit beings from which information is retrieved that may be of use in the waking world. In some societies this ability is attributed to shamans, and in others everybody has this facility. Dreaming is probably the primary venue in which people have out-of-body experiences, adding evidence that soul and body are ontologically separable.
- **Spirit beings.** Peoples will tend to interpret characters arising in dreams as spirits, ghosts, demons, angels, familiars, guides and other sacred "other than human" beings. Dreams are real, so therefore the characters that one encounters in dreams are real. Sometimes the beings are an expression of normally invisible causal factors – for instance, the spirit causing or curing a disease, or a witch attack. Encounters with spirit beings while dreaming is the main source of knowledge behind animistic attributions in the waking state, as well as a society's mythological characters and interactions. Some encounters with the spirit world may be so numinous that they are taken as communion with gods and other divine beings.
- **Communing with the Dead.** Visits by or to deceased ancestors are quite common and are taken as evidence that there is some kind of afterlife. Conversations with dead relatives are often the source of valuable guidance and information about coming events. Ancestors may be considered as intermediaries between the living and the divine, often resulting in an ancestor cult. They may live

in a specific place in the spiritual world – for instance, a village or mountain of the dead.
- **Dreams as oracles.** It is common for young people to go on vision quests or to incubate dreams to answer key questions in their lives, to find out what one's career will be, to attain blessings or powers from spirit beings, to seek the causes of untoward events and illnesses, etc. Sometimes the society requires this kind of intense dialogue with the spiritual realm before one is considered an adult.
- **Problem-solving and creativity.** Many societies recognize dreaming as a source of creative insight and problem solving. New songs, rituals and mythopoeic themes may be derived from dreams. Artistic and ornamental motifs may suggest themselves as well in dreams. People confronting problems will often "sleep on it" – thus incubating dreamed solutions.
- **Medical dreaming.** Shamans and healers will often find their calling through their dreams, and then use dreaming as a diagnostic and curing tool. If a disease is caused by soul loss, the healer may go off in search of the soul and retrieve it in order to heal the patient's affliction. The disease may also be due to a foreign object cast by witchcraft into the body of the patient, and dream diagnosis is used to reveal the hidden cause and the perpetrator of the sorcery.
- **Dream sharing and social interpretation.** What makes human dreaming so distinct is that we are able to share our dreams with others. In many societies, dream interpretation is linked to dream sharing, and in such situations, a standardized, rather conservative process of interpretation is used. Sometimes attributions involve a complex hermeneutic process involving oneirocritics and dream book type interpretive systems. It is very common for specific dream motifs to be linked with specific behavioral outcomes in waking life.
- **Dream power.** Dreams may make spiritual power resources visible and accessible. Indeed, there are activities like going into battle or hunting that will not happen without the right power. The source of power might be a sacred landmark, a spirit or some other propitious source experienced in auspicious dreams.
- **Emotional conflict.** The often deep-seated conflict felt about life's situations can play out in dreams. These may present as recurrent

nightmares, incubus attacks and other negative scenarios perhaps associated with trauma. In many societies these dreams may be considered symptomatic of disease or witchcraft.
- **"Big" dreaming.** Virtually all societies recognize certain dreams as more important than others. These are the "big," or culture pattern dreams. These are dreams that are numinous, archetypal in origin and associated with great portent, either for the dreamer or the society. The characters or events in these dreams often relate to the society's mythology. It is through "big" dreams (and other ASC) that sacred stories may be instantiated in direct experience.

There are other commonplace dream patterns found cross-culturally, but these seem to me to be the ones most easily supported by ethnographic evidence. Many of these elements, like the quest for power in dreams, have direct effects upon individual and social waking activity. Dreaming is often as relevant as waking experience for polyphasic peoples, and the two SOC seem to be thoroughly entangled and tend to complement each other, feeding information and understanding back and forth in a mutually reciprocal way. In a polyphasic society, the cosmological worldview depends upon both primary states, the one for getting local and material things done, the other for cosmic understanding, portent and power.

## THE ANTHROPOLOGY OF DREAMING GOING FORWARD

The reader may now have a better appreciation for the peculiarities of contemporary anthropology – features of the discipline one should understand when reading the rich literature on other peoples' ways of life. Anthropologists have amassed a library full of information about dreaming and dream cultures over the last century and a half of its existence. It is hard to predict where the anthropology of dreaming will go in the future. For one thing, as I mentioned in Chapter 3, anthropology is a pre-normal, naturalistic science that is vulnerable to political and ideological fads. One cannot predict when the next "ism" will arise, or how influential it will be on theory and methods in the discipline. What I can share with the reader are my views on where the anthropological study of dreaming *should* go in the future in order to (1) realize the goal of anthropology becoming a mature "normal" science, and (2) optimize the value of data on dreaming generated by ethnographic fieldwork.

At the expense of repeating myself, anthropology has scant chance of becoming a normal science until it grounds itself thoroughly in evolutionary biology (including primate ethology) and neurophysiology (Count 1958, 1990). Without this grounding, there is no physical structure to account for human psychological and cultural universals, or for the development and plasticity underlying apparent cultural variation. The immaturity of ethnology in this respect is very apparent in the contemporary paucity of really interesting and compelling theory. As the late ethnologist, Roy Rappaport, in a fit of exasperation once told me over a beer, "anthropological theory has become moribund." This is especially noticeable in the ethnology of dreaming where descriptions of dream cultures are still more often than not couched at the level of "beliefs" and institutions. As we saw in Chapter 6, one of the major hindrances to ethnographers studying ASC cross-culturally is the pervasive monophasia of Western cultural conditioning. The really great ethnographers of dreaming almost always have been intensely involved in their own dream life. W.H.R. Rivers, Barbara Tedlock, Deborah Jay Hillman, Jean-Guy Goulet, Robert Bruce, J.S Lincoln and others I could name have produced research that is qualitatively better, "thicker" and more enduring than others precisely because they were experienced dreamers as well as anthropologists. They came equipped into the field with the phenomenological maturity to comprehend the essential subjectivity of dreaming lying behind dream narratives and social responses to shared dreams. Moreover, they immediately intuit the potential for people having profound spiritual experiences while dreaming.

One of the lessons I wish young ethnographers to take away with them is that, if they are contemplating doing fieldwork among polyphasic peoples, and if they judge that they themselves are deficient in dream awareness, or in experiences of other ASC, that they will undertake to re-train themselves so that their own dreaming may approximate the maturity of their informants'. Also, many ethnographers who are experienced dreamers have found this ability indispensable in the field. It is not hard to learn to remember one's dreams, and should be considered a skill that is at least as important as learning non-parametric statistics, or how to make a kinship chart. "Observation of participation" (as Barbara Tedlock 1991b calls it) in dream cultures requires a minimum of dreaming competence lest the ethnographer go seriously awry at the phenomenological level.

How one goes about training oneself as a dreamer – whether a student of anthropology or not — will largely depend on individual initiative, as university dreaming curricula are thin on the ground. For some neophytes, involvement in one of the myriad dreamwork groups might do the trick. The enthusiasm of experienced dreamers kind of "rubs off" for some people. For fieldwork training purposes, it really does not matter the orientation of the group; it is gaining the skill and experience that counts in the field. Other beginners may choose to learn to recall their dreams by themselves. There are a number of self-help books and courses available, some of which I have mentioned in previous chapters, and all of the ones I would recommend are written by experienced dreamers and teachers. Celia Green's *Lucid Dreams* (1968) is a classic, as are Ann Faraday's *Dream Power* (1972), Gayle Delaney's *Living Your Dreams* (1979), Patricia Garfield's *Creative Dreaming* (1974), and Krippner and Dillard's *Dreamworking: How to Use Your Dreams for Creative Problem Solving* (1988). Stephen LaBerge's *Lucid Dreaming: A Concise Guide to Awakening in Your Dreams and in Your Life* (2009), Bosnak's *Embodiment: Creative Imagination in Medicine, Art and Travel* (2007), Robert Waggoner's *Lucid Dreaming: Gateway to the Inner Self* (2009) and Paul and Charla Devereux's *Lucid Dreaming: Accessing Your Inner Virtual Realities* (2011) are excellent introductions to lucid dreaming methods, while Robert Hoss' *Dream Language* (2005) and Feinstein and Krippner's *Personal Mythology* (2008) offer rather complete courses in dreaming. The Ullman-Zimmerman approach is covered nicely in their *Working with Dreams* (1989[1979]). Chapter four of Jeremy Taylor's *The Wisdom of Your Dreams* (2009; see also Taylor 1983) is an excellent short introduction to dream recall — full of tips and essentials. Parents wishing to work with their children might wish to read Patricia Garfield's *Your Child's Dreams* (1984). For those inclined to follow a more Jungian path, I can recommend Robert Bosnak's *A Little Course in Dreams* (1988), Jeremy Taylor's *Dream Work* (1983) and Greg Bogart's *Dreamwork and Self-Healing* (2009), although some of these sources may take you deeper into a confrontation with the unconscious than you may wish to go. Remember, Jungian dreamwork is usually applicable to people after they reach their mid-life.

Above all else, I hope that this book has broadened the reader's perspective on the fascinating and mysterious world of dreaming. Indeed, one major lesson for those readers who are avid dreamers is that you are not abnormal relative to most people on earth, but perhaps only in the context of your local society. I also hope this book will help to disparage the largely negative attitude of most Westerners towards dreams and the terribly mistaken view that manifest dream content is crazy, meaningless or useless. The book will have been worth the writing if the reader can now appreciate that dreaming is a window available to everyone who wishes to explore their spiritual depths, their self and the rich and unbounded universe of symbolic entanglement. All one has to do is take the plunge and perhaps one day come to the direct realization behind the mystical formula in Matthew 7:7, "Ask and it will be given to you; seek and you will find; knock and the door will be opened to you." Yes, really!

# Bibliography

Alfinito, Eleonora and Giuseppe Vitiello, 2000. "Formation and Life-Time of Memory Domains in the Dissipative Quantum Model of Brain." *International Journal of Modern Physics* B14 (2000) 853-868; Erratum 1613.

Althusser, Louis, 2010[1968]. *For Marx.* New York: Verso.

Alvarado, Carlos S., 2000. "Out-of-Body Experiences." in Etzel Cardeña, Steven Jay Lynn and Stanley Krippner (eds), *Varieties of Anomalous Experience: Examining the Scientific Evidence.* Washington, DC: American Psychological Association, pp. 183-218.

Amodio, David M. and Chris D. Frith, 2006. "Meeting of Minds: the Medial Frontal Cortex and Social Cognition." *Nature Reviews Neuroscience* 7:268-277.

Anch, A. Michael, Carl P. Browman, Merrill M. Mitler and James K. Walsh, 1988. *Sleep: A Scientific Perspective.* Englewood Cliffs, NJ: Prentice-Hall.

Argüelles, J.A. and M. Argüelles, 1972. *Mandala.* Berkeley: Shambhala.

Arnold, K. and K. Zuberbühler, 2006. "Language Evolution: Semantic Combinations in Primate Calls."*Nature* 441:303.

Arnold-Forster, Mary, 1921. *Studies in Dreams.* New York: Macmillan.

Aserinsky E. and Kleitman N., 1953. "Regularly Occurring Periods of Eye Motility, and Concomitant Phenomena, during Sleep." *Science* 118: 273–274

Ashok and Skafte, Peter, 2001[1992]. "Interview With a Killing Shaman." in J. Narby and F. Huxley (eds), *Shamans Through Time.* New York: Tarcher, pp. 234-237.

Astuti, Rita, and Paul L. Harris, 2008. "Understanding Mortality and the Life of the Ancestors in Rural Madagascar." *Cognitive Science* 32:713-740.

Atran, Scott and Douglas Medin, 2008. *The Native Mind and the Cultural Construction of Nature.* Cambridge, MA: MIT Press.

Barkow, Jerome, Leda Cosmides and John Tooby (eds), 1992. *The Adapted Mind: Evolutionary Psychology and the Generation of Culture.* Oxford: Oxford University Press.

Barrett, Deirdre, 1991. "Flying Dreams and Lucidity: An Empirical Study of Their Relationship." *Dreaming: Journal of the Association for the Study of Dreams* 1(2):129-134.

Barrett, Deirdre (ed), 1996. *Trauma and Dreams.* Cambridge, MA: Harvard University Press.

Barrett, Deirdre, 2001. *The Committee of Sleep: How Artists, Scientists, and Athletes Use Dreams for Creative Problem Solving.* Amazon.com: Oneiroi Press.

Barrett, Deirdre, 2007. "An Evolutionary Theory of Dreams and Problem-Solving." in Deirdre Barrett and Patrick McNamara (eds), *Cultural and Theoretical Perspectives, Volume 3* of *The New Science of Dreaming.* Westport CT: Praeger, pp. 133-154.

Barrett, Deirdre and Patrick McNamara (eds), 2007. *The New Science if Dreaming: Cultural and Theoretical Perspectives.* Westport, CT: Praeger.

Bartlett, F.C. 1932. *Remembering: A Study in Experimental and Social Psychology.* Cambridge: Cambridge University Press.

Basso, Ellen B., 1992. "The Implications of a Progressive Theory of Dreaming." in Barbara Tedlock (ed), *Dreaming: Anthropological and Psychological Interpretations.* Cambridge: Cambridge University Press, pp. 86-104.

Bastide, Roger, 1966. "The Sociology of the Dream." in G.E. von Grunebaum and R. Caillois (eds), *The Dream and Human Societies.* Berkeley: University of California Press, pp. 199-211.

Batchelor, J., 1927. *Ainu Life and Lore*. Tokyo: Kyobunkwan.

Battaglia, Debbora (ed), 1995. *Rhetorics of Self-Making*. Berkeley: University of California Press.

Beck, Friedrich, 1994. "Quantum Mechanics and Consciousness." *Journal of Consciousness Studies* 1(2):253-255.

Beck, Friedrich and John C. Eccles, 1992. "Quantum Aspects of Brain Activity and the Role of Consciousness." *Proc. Natl. Acad. Sci.* USA 89:11357-11361.

Belicki, Kathryn and Marion A. Cuddy, 1991. "Nightmares: Facts, Fictions and Future Directions." in Jayne Gackenbach and Anees A, Sheikh (eds), *Dream Images: A Call to Mental Arms*. Amityville, NY: Baywood, pp. 99-126.

Bell, C.A., 1931. *The Religion of Tibet*. Oxford: Clarendon Press.

Bellah, Robert N., 1964. "Religious Evolution," *American Sociological Review* 29:358-374.

Benedetti, Fabrizio, 2008. *Placebo Effects: Understanding the Mechanisms in Health and Disease*. Oxford: Oxford University Press.

Benedict, Ruth Fulton, 1922. "The Vision in Plains Culture." *American Anthropologist* 24(1):1-23.

Benington, Joel H., 2000. "Sleep Homeostasis and the Function of Sleep." *Sleep* 23(7):959-966.

Benington, Joel H. and Marcos G. Frank, 2003. "Cellular and Molecular Connections Between Sleep and Synaptic Plasticity." *Progress in Neurobiology* 69:71–101.

Benington, Joel H. and H. Craig Heller, 1995. "Restoration of Brain Energy Metabolism As the Function of Sleep." *Progress in Neurobiology* 45:347-360.

Bennett, Wendell C. and Robert C. Zingg, 1976. *The Tarahumara: An Indian Tribe of Northern Mexico*. Glorieta, NM: Rio Grande Press.

Benson, Kathleen L. and Irwin Feinberg, 2011. "Schizophrenia." in M.H. Kryger, T. Roth and W.C. Dement (eds), *Principles and Practice of Sleep Medicine*, 4th edition. Philadelphia: Elsevier, pp. 1501-1511.

Bering, Jesse M. and David F. Bjorklund, 2007. "The Serpent's Gift: Evolutionnary Psychology and Consciousness." in P. D. Zelazo, M. Moscovitch, & E. Thompson (eds), *Cambridge Handbook of Consciousness*. New York: Cambridge University Press, pp. 597-629.

Bharati, Agehananda, 1975. *The Tantric Tradition*. New York: Samuel Weiser.

Bergman, Thore J. and Dawn M. Kitchen, 2009. "Comparing Responses to Novel Objects in Wild Baboons (*Papio ursinus*) and Geladas (*Theropithecus gelada*)." *Animal Cognition* 12:63-73.

Bickerton, Derek, 2009. *Adam's Tongue: How Humans Made Language, How Language Made Humans*. New York: Hill and Wang.

Bierman, Dick J. and Dean I. Radin, 1997. "Anomalous Anticipatory Response on Randomized Future Conditions." *Perceptual and Motor Skills* 84 (2): 689–690.

Bierman, Dick J. and Dean I. Radin, 1999. "Conscious and Anomalous Nonconscious Processes: A Reversal of the Arrow of Time?" in Stuart R. Hameroff, Alfred W. Kaszniak (eds), Toward a Science of Consciousness III: The Third Tucson Discussions and Debates. Cambridge, MA: MIT Press. pp. 367–386.

Bierman, Dick J. and H. Steven Scholte, 2002. "A fMRI Brain Imaging Study of Presentiment." unpublished manuscript.

Bird-David, Nurit, 1999. "Animism" Revisited Personhood, Environment, and Relational Epistemology." Current Anthropology 40(supplement):S67-S91.

Bischof, Marco, 1994. "The History of Bioelectromagnetism." in Mae-Wan Ho, Fritz-Albert Popp and Ulrich Warnke (eds), *Bioelectrodynamics and Biocommunication*. London: World Scientific.

Blackmore, Susan J., 1990. "Dreams that Do What They're Told." *New Scientist* 125(1698):48.

Blackmore, Susan J., 1992. *Beyond the Body*. Chicago, IL: Academy Chicago Publishers.

Blackwood, Beatrice, 1935. *Both Sides of Buka Passage: An Ethnographic Study of Social, Sexual, and Economic Questions in the North-Western Solomon Islands.* Oxford: Clarendon Press.

Blainey, Mark, 2010. "Towards an Ethnometaphysics of Consciousness: Suggested Adjustments in SAC's Quest to Reroute the Main(Stream)." *Anthropology of Consciouess* 21(2):113–138.

Blanke, Olaf, Theodor Landis, Laurent Spinelli and Margitta Seeck, 2004. "Out-of-Body Experience and Autoscopy of Neurological Origin." *Brain* 127(2):243-258.

Blanke, Olaf, Christine Mohr, Christoph M. Michel, Alvaro Pascual-Leone, Peter Brugger, Margitta Seeck, Theodor Landis, and Gregor Thut, 2005. "Linking Out-of-Body Experience and Self Processing to Mental Own-Body Imagery at the Temporoparietal Junction." *Journal of Neuroscience* 25(3):550-557.

Block, Jack, 1982. "Assimilation, Accommodation, and the Dynamics of Personality Development." *Child Development* 53:281-295.

Bloom, Paul, 1998. "Some Issues in the Evolution of Language and Thought." in Denise Dellarosa Cummins and Colin Allen (eds), *The Evolution of Mind.* Oxford: Oxford University Press, pp. 204-223.

Boas, Franz, 1930. "I Desired To Learn the Ways of the Shaman." in *The Religion of the Kwakiutl.* New York: Columbia University Press.

Boas, Franz, (1938 [1910]). *The Mind of Primitive Man* (revised edition). New York: Macmillan.

Boas, Franz, (1940 [1896]). "The Limitations of the Comparative Method of Anthropology." in Franz Boas, Race, Language and Culture. New York: Macmillan, pp. 270-280.

Boas, Franz, 1966. *Kwakiutl Ethnography* (edited by Helen Codere). Chicago: University of Chicago Press.

Boas, Franz, 1974 [1889]. "On Alternating Sounds." in George W. Stocking, Jr. (ed), *A Franz Boas Reader: The Shaping of American Anthropology, 1883-1911.* Chicago: The University of Chicago Press, pp. 72-76.

Bogart, Greg, 2009. *Dreamwork and Self-Healing: Unfolding the Symbols of the Unconscious.* London: Karnac.

Bogen, Joseph E., 2007. "The Thalamic Intralaminar Nuclei and the Property of Consciousness." in P. D. Zelazo, M. Moscovitch, & E. Thompson (eds), *Cambridge Handbook of Consciousness.* New York: Cambridge University Press, pp. 775-807.

Bogoras, H., 1904-1909. *The Chukchee.* New York: G.E. Stechert.

Bohm, David, 1980. *Wholeness and the Implicate Order.* Boston: Routledge and Kegan Paul.

Bohm, David, 1990. "A New Theory of the Relationship of Mind and Matter." *Philosophical Psychology* 3(2/3):271.

Bohm, David and Basil J. Hiley, 1995. *The Undivided Universe: An Ontological Interpretation of Quantum Theory.* New York: Routledge.

Bond, James D. and Gerald C. Huth, 1986. "Electrostatic Modulation of Electromagnetically Induced Nonthermal Responses in Biological Membranes." in Felix Gutmann and Hendrik Keyzer (eds), *Modern Bioelectrochemistry.* New York: Plenum. pp. 289-313.

Bootzin, Richard R., John F. Kihlstrom and Daniel L. Schacter (eds), 1990. *Sleep and Cognition.* Washington, DC: American Psychological Association.

Bosnak, Robert, 1988. *A Little Course in Dreams.* Boston: Shambhala.

Bourguignon, Erika, 1954. "Dreams and Dream Interpretation in Haiti." *American Anthropologist* 56(2 - Part 1):262-268.

Bourguignon, Erika, 1972. "Dreams and Altered States of Consciousness in Anthropological Research." in Francis L.K. Hsu (ed), *Psychological Anthropology* (second edition). Cambridge, MA: Schenkman, pp. 403-434.

Bourguignon, Erika, 1973. *Religion, Altered States of Consciousness, and Social Change.* Columbus, Ohio: Ohio State University Press.

Bourguignon, Erika, 2003. "Dreams That Speak: Experience and Interpretation." in Jeannette Marie Mageo (ed), *Dreaming and the Self: New Perspectives on Subjectivity, Identity, and Emotion.* Albany, NY: State University of New York Press, pp. 133-153.

Bourguignon, Erika and T.L. Evascu, 1977. "Altered States of Consciousness within a General Evolutionary Perspective: A Holocultural Analysis." *Behavior Science Research* 12(3), 197-216.

Bradley, Fiona, 1997. *Surrealism.* Cambridge: Cambridge University Press.

Braun, A. R., T. J. Balkin, N. J. Wesensten, R. E. Carson, M. Varga,1 P. Baldwin, S. Selbie, G. Belenky and P. Herscovitch, 1997. "Regional Cerebral Blood Flow Throughout the Sleep–Wake Cycle." *Brain* 120:1173–1197.

Brentano, F., 1874. *Psychologie vom empirischen Standpunkte* (1973 trans. by A. Rancurello et al.). New York: Humanities Press.

Brereton, Derek P., 2000. "Dreaming, Adaptation, and Consciousness: The Social Mapping Hypothesis." *Ethos* 26(3):379-409.

Britton, Thomas C. and K. Ray Chaudhuri, 2009. "REM Sleep Behavior Disorder and the Risk of Developing Parkinson Disease or Dementia." *Neurology* 72(15):1294-1295.

Brock, Harald Beyer, 2000. "Yellow Crocodiles and Bush Spirits: Timpaus Islanders' Conceptualization of Ethereal Phenomena." *Ethos* 28(1):3-19.

Brooke, Roger (ed), 1999. *Pathways into the Jungian World: Phenomenology and Analytical Psychology.* New York: Routledge.

Brough, John B. and Embree, Lester (eds ), 2000. *The Many Faces of Time.* Dordrecht: Kluwer.

Broughton, Roger, 1975. "Biorhythmic Variations in Consciousness and Psychological Functions." *Canadian Psychological Review* 16(4):217-239.

Brown, Donald E., 1991. *Human Universals.* New York: McGraw-Hill.

Brown, Michael, 1992. "Ropes of Sand: Order and Imagery in Aguaruna Dreams." in Barbara Tedlock (ed), *Dreaming: Anthropological and Psychological Interpretations.* Cambridge: Cambridge University Press, pp. 154-170.

Bruce, Robert D., 1975. *Lacandon Dream Symbolism: Dream Symbolism and Interpretation Among the Lacandon Maya of Chiapas, Mexico.* Perugino, Mexico: Ediciones Euroamericanas Klaus Thiele.

Bulkeley, Kelly, 1994. *The Wilderness of Dreams: Exploring the Religious Meanings of Dreams in Modern Western Culture.* Albany, NY: State University of New York Press.

Bulkeley, Kelly, 1995. *Spiritual Dreaming: A Cross-Cultural and Historical Journey.* New York: Paulist Press.

Bulkeley, Kelly (ed), 1996a. *Among All These Dreamers: Essays on Dreaming and Modern Society.* Albany: State University of New York Press.

Bulkeley, Kelly, 1996b. "Dreaming as a Spiritual Practice." *Anthropology of Consciousness* 7(2):1-15.

Bulkeley, Kelly, 1997. *An Introduction to the Psychology of Dreaming.* New York: Praeger.

Bulkeley, Kelly, 2000. "Dream Interpretation: Practical Methods for Pastoral Care and Counseling." *Pastoral Psychology* 49(2):95-104.

Bulkeley, Kelly (ed), 2001. *Dreams: A Reader on the Religious, Cultural, and Psychological Dimensions of Dreaming.* New York: Palgrave.

Bulkeley, Kelly, 2008. *Dreaming in the World's Religions.* New York: New York University Press.

Bulmer, R.N.H., 1965. "The Kyaka of the Western Highlands." in P. Lawrence and M.J. Meggitt (eds), *Gods Ghosts and Men in Melanesia.* Melbourne: Oxford University Press, pp. 132-161.

Bunzel, Ruth, 1952. *Chichicastenango: A Guatamalan Village*. Locust Balley, NY: J.J. Augustin.

Burghardt, Gordon M., 1998. "The Evolutionary of Play Revisited: Lessons from Turtles." in M. Bekoff and J. A. Byers (eds), *Animal Play: Evolutionary, Comparative, and Ecological Perspectives*. New York: Cambridge University Press, pp. 1 – 26.

Burghardt, Gordon M., 2006. *The Genesis of Animal Play: Testing the Limits*. Cambridge, MA: MIT Press.

Burghardt, Gordon M., Brian Ward and Roger Ross\coe, 1996. "Problem of Reptile Play: Environmental Enrichment and Play Behavior in a Captive Nile Soft-shelled Turtle, *Trionyx triunguis*." *Zoo Biology* 15(3):223–238.

Burridge, Kenelm, 1960. *Mambu: A Melanesian Millennium*. Princeton, NJ: Princeton University Press.

Burridge, Kenelm, 1969. *Tangu Traditions*. Oxford: Oxford University Press.

Burridge, Kenelm, 1972. "Cargo." in Pierre Maranda (ed), *Mythology*. Harmondsworth: Penguin, pp. 127-135.

Burridge, Kenelm, 1973. *Encountering Aborigines*. New York: Pergamon.

Buss, David M., 2004. *Evolutionary Psychology: The New Science of the Mind*. Boston: Pearson.

Butterworth, George, 1995. "An Ecological Perspective on the Origin of Self." in José Luis Bermúdez, Anthony Marcel and Naomi Eilan (eds), *The Body and the Self*. Cambridge, MA: MIT Press, pp. 87-106.

Cacioppo, John T., Gary G. Berntson, Shelley E. Taylor, and Daniel L. Schacter (eds), 2002. *Foundations in Social Neuroscience*. Cambridge, MA: M.I.T. Press.

Cacioppo, John T., Penny S. Visser and Cynthia L. Pickett (eds), 2005. *Social Neuroscience: People Thinking about Thinking People*. Cambridge, MA: M.I.T. Press.

Cahen, Roland, 1966. "The Psychology of the Dream." in G.E. von Grunebaum and R. Caillois (eds), *The Dream and Human Societies*. Berkeley: University of California Press, pp. 119-143.

Cai, Jianming, Gian Giacomo Guerresch, and Hans J. Briegel, 2010. "Quantum Control and Entanglement in a Chemical Compass." *Physical Review Letters* 104(22): id. 220502.

Campbell, R.L. and P.S. Staniford, 1978. "Transpersonal Anthropology." *Phoenix: The Journal of Transpersonal Anthropology* 2(1):28-40.

Cann, D.R. and D.C. Donderi, 1986. "Jungian Personality Typology and the Recall of Everyday and Archetypal Dreams." *Journal of Personality and Social Psychology* 50(5):1021-1030.

Cardeña, Etzel, Steven Jay Lynn and Stanley Krippner (eds), 2000. *Varieties of Anomalous Experience: Examining the Scientific Evidence*. Washington, D.C.: American Psychological Association.

Carey, Susan, 2009. *The Origin of Concepts*. Oxford: Oxford University Press.

Cartwright, R. 1986. "Affect and Dream Work from an Information Processing Point of View." *Journal of Mind and Behavior* 7:411-428.

Casey, Edward S., 2000. *Imagining: A Phenomenological Study* (second edition). Bloomington: University of Indiana Press.

Cassirer, Ernst, 1957. *The Philosophy of Symbolic Forms*. Vol. 3: *The Phenomenology of Knowledge*. New Haven, CT: Yale University Press.

Casto, Kira Lynn, Stanley Krippner and Robert Trartz, 1999. "The Identification of Spiritual Content in Dream Reports." *Anthropology of Consciousness* 10(1):43-53.

Chang, Garma C.C., 1991[1963]. *Teachings of Tibetan Yoga*. Secaueus, New Jersey: The

Citadel Press.

Chang, Jiin-Ju, Joachim Fisch and Fritz-Albert Popp (eds), 2010. *Biophotons*. New York: Springer.

Changeux, Jean-Pierre, 1985. *Neuronal Man: The Biology of Mind*. Oxford: Oxford University Press.

Chapple, Elliot D., 1970. *Culture and Biological Man*. New York: Holt, Rinehart and Winston.

Chapple, Eliot D. and Carleton S. Coon, 1942. *Principles of Anthropology*. New York: Holt, Rinehart and Winston.

Charsley, S.R., 1973. "Dreams in an Independent African Church." *Africa: Journal of the International African Institute* 43(3):244-257.

Chellappa, Sarah Laxhmi, Sylvia Frey, Vera Knoblauch and Christian Cajochen, 2011. "Cortical Activation Patterns Herald Successful Dream Recall after NREM and REM." *Biological Psychology* (in press).

Chidester, David, 2008a. "Dreaming in the Contact Zone: Zulu Dreams, Visions, and Religion in Nineteenth-Century South Africa." *Journal of the American Academy of Religion* 76(1):27-53.

Chidester, David, 2008b. "Zulu Dreamscapes: Senses, Media, and Authentication in Contemporary Neo-Shamanism." *Material Religion: The Journal of Objects, Art and Belief* 4(2):136-158.

Clare, John and Ali Zarbafi, 2009. *Social Dreaming in the 21$^{st}$ Century: The World We are Losing*. London: Karnac.

Clifford, J. and G. Marcus, (eds), 1986. *Writing Culture: The Poetics and Politics of Ethnography*. Berkeley, CA: University of California Press.

Codrington, Robert Henry, 2005 [1891]. *The Melanesians: Studies in Their Anthropology and Folklore*. Elibron Classics Replica Edition of the original Oxford: Clarendon Press edition.

Cohen, Anthony P., 1994. *Self Consciousness: An Alternative Anthropology of Identity*. London: Routledge.

Colby, Kenneth Mark, 1963. "Sex Differences in Dreams of Primitive Tribes." *American Anthropologist* 65:1116-1122.

Collins, Kathleen, 1984. "Anthropology of Dreaming in America." *ASD Newsletter* 1(4):1, 3.

Conrad, Michael, 1994. "From Brain Structure to Vacuum and Back Again: The Great Chain of Being Model." Nanobiology 3:99-121.

Constantinides, Pamela, 1977. "'Ill at Ease and Sick at Heart': Symbolic Behavior in a Sudanese Healing Cult." in I. M. Lewis (ed), *Symbols and Sentiments*. London: Academic Press, pp. 61-84.

Coolidge, Frederick L. and Thomas Wynn, 2009. *The Rise of Homo sapiens: The Evolution of Modern Thinking*. Chichester, West Sussex: Blackwell and Wiley.

Cooper, Guy H., 1984. *Development and Stress in Navajo Religion*. Stockholm: Almquist and Wiksell.

Cooper, John M., 1956. *The Gros Ventres of Montana*, Part 2: *Religion ad Ritual*. Washington: Catholic University of America.

Corballis, Michael C., 2011. *The Recursive Mind: The Origins of Human Language, Thought, and Civilization*. Princeton, NJ: Princeton University Press.

Corbin, Henry, 1969. *Alone With The Alone: Creative Imagination in the Sufism of Ibn 'Arabi*. Princeton, NJ: Princeton University Press.

Cosmides, L. & Tooby, J., 1995. "From Function To Structure: The Role of Evolutionary

Biology and Computational Theories in Cognitive Neuroscience." in M. S. Gazzaniga (ed), *The Cognitive Neurosciences*. Cambridge, MA: MIT Press.

Count, Earl W., 1958. "The Biological Basis of Human Sociality." *American Anthropologist* 60: 1049-1085.

Count, Earl W., 1960. "Myth as World View." in S. Diamond (ed), *Culture in History*. New York: Columbia University Press.

Count, Earl W., 1973. *Being and Becoming Human*. New York: Van Nostrand Reinhold.

Count, Earl W., 1990. "Interview with Earl W. Count." *Neuroanthropology Network Newsletter*, 3(1), 5-8.

Cove, John J., 1987. *Shattered Images: Dialogues and Meditations on Tsimshian Narratives*. Ottawa, Canada: Carleton University Press.

Craig, P. Erik, 1987. The Realness of Dreams." in Richard A. Russo (ed), *Dreams Are Wiser Than Men*. Berkeley, CA: North Atlantic Books, pp. 34-57.

Crane, Tom and Sarah Patterson, 2000. *History of the Mind-Body Problem*. London: Routledge.

Crick, F. and G Mitchison, 1983. "The Function of Dream Sleep." *Nature* 304(5922):111-114.

Crist, Eileen, 2002. "The Inner Life of Earthworms: Darwin's Argument and Its Implications." in Marc Bekoff, Colin Allen and Gordon M. Burghardt (eds), *The Cognitive Animal: Empirical and Theoretical Perspectives on Animal Cognition*. Cambridge, MA: MIT Press, pp. 3-8.

Crocker, Jon Christopher, 1985. *Vital Souls: Bororo Cosmology, Natural Symbolism, and Shamanism*. Tucson, AZ: University of Arizona Press.

Csikszentmihalyi, Mihaly, 2008. *Flow: The Psychology of Optimal Experience*. New York: Harper.

Csordas, Thomas J., 1990. "Embodiment as a Paradigm for Anthropology" *Ethos* 18:5-47.

Csordas, Thomas J., 1993. "Somatic Modes of Attention." *Cultural Anthropology* 8:135-56

Csordas, Thomas J. (ed), 1994a. *Embodiment and Experience: The Existential Ground of Culture and Self.* Cambridge: Cambridge University Press.

Csordas, Thomas J., 1994b. "Introduction: The Body as Representation and Being-in-the-World." in Thomas Csordas (ed), *Embodiment and Experience: The Existential Ground of Culture and Self.* Cambridge: Cambridge University Press, pp. 1-24.

Csordas, Thomas J., 1994c. *The Sacred Self: A Cultural Phenomenology of Charismatic Healing*. Los Angeles: University of California Press.

Cummins, Denise Dellarosa and Colin Allen (eds), 1998. *The Evolution of Mind*. Oxford: Oxford University Press.

Czaplicka, Marie Antoinette, 1914. *Aboriginal Siberia: A Study in Social Anthropology*. Oxford: Oxford University Press.

Czeisler, Charles A. 2006. "Sleep Deficit: the Performance Killer – A Conversation with Harvard Medical School Professor Charles A. Czeisler." *Harvard Business Review* 84(10):53-69.

Dadosky, John, 1999. "Three Diné Women on the Navajo Approach to Dreams." *Anthropology of Consciousness* 10(l):16-27.

Dainton, Barry, 2006. *Stream of Consciousness: Unity and Continuity in Conscious Experience* (revised paperback edition). London: Routledge.

Damasio, Antonio, 1999. *The Feeling of What Happens: Body and Emotion in the Making of Consciousness*. New York: Harcourt.

Damasio, Antonio, 2010. *Self Comes to Mind: Constructing the Conscious Brain*. New York: Pantheon.

D'Andrade, Roy G., 1961. "Anthropological Studies of Dreams." in Francis L.K. Hsu (ed), *Psychological Anthropology* (first edition). Homewood, IL: Dorsey, pp. 296-332.

D'Andrade, Roy G., 1984. "Cultural Meaning Systems." in Richard A. Shweder and Robert A Levine (eds), *Culture Theory: Essays on Mind, Self, and Emotion*. Cambridge: Cambridge University Press, pp. 88-119.

D'Andrade, Roy G., 1995. *The Development of Cognitive Anthropology*. Cambridge: Cambridge University Press.

D'Aquili, Eugene G., 1972. *The Biopsychological Determinants of Culture*. Reading, MA: Addison-Wesley.

D'Aquili, Eugene G., 1975. "The Influence of Jung on the Work of Claude Lévi-Strauss." *Journal of the History of the Behavioral Sciences* 11(1):41-48.

D'Aquili, Eugene G., Charles D. Laughlin & John McManus (eds), 1979. *The Spectrum of Ritual*. New York: Columbia University Press.

D'Aquili, Eugene G. & A.B. Newberg, 1999. *The Mystical Mind: Probing the Biology of Religious Experience*. Minneapolis: Fortress Press.

Davidson, J.M., 1976. "The Physiology of Meditation and Mystical States of Consciousness." *Perspectives in Biology and Medicine* 19: 345-379.

Deacon, Terrence W., 1997. *The Symbolic Species: The Co-Evolution of Language and the Brain*. New York: Norton.

De Becker, Raymond, 1968. *The Understanding of Dreams and Their Influence on the History of Man*. New York: Bell Publishing.

Delaney, Gayle, 1979. *Living Your Dreams*. New York: Harper and Row.

Dentan Robert Knox, 1986. "Ethnographic Considerations in the Cross-Cultural Study of Dreaming." in Jayne Gackenbach (ed), *Sleep and Dreams: A Sourcebook*. New York: Garland Reference Library, pp. 317-358.

Dentan, Robert Knox and Laura J. McClusky, 1993. "'Pity the Bones by Wandering River Which Still in Lovers' Dreams Appear as Men.'" in Allan Moffitt, Milton Kramer and Robert Hoffman (eds), *The Function of Dreaming*. Albany, NY: State University of New York Press, pp. 489-548.

De Saint Denys, Hervey, 1982 [1867]. *Dreams and How To Guide Them*. Trans. by N. Fry. London: Duckworth.

Descola, Philippe, 1989. "Head-Shrinkers versus Shrinks: Jivaroan Dream Analysis." *Man* 24(3):439-450.

Deutsch, D., 1985. "Quantum Theory, the Church-Turing Principle and the Universal Quantum Computer." *Proceedings of the Royal Society of London* A 400:97-117.

Devereux, George, 1937. "Mohave Soul Concepts." *American Anthropologist* 39(3):417-422.

Devereux, George, 1969. *Reality and Dream: Psychotherapy of a Plains Indian* (second edition). Garden City, NY: Doubleday.

Devereux, George, 1957. "Dream Learning and Individual Ritual Differences in Mohave Shamanism." *American Anthropologist* 59:1036-1045.

Devereux, Paul, 1992. *Symbolic Landscapes*. Sumerset, England: Gothic Image Publications.

Devereux, Paul, 1993. *Shamanism and the Mystery Lines: Ley Lines, Spirit Paths, Shape-Shifting and Out-of-Body Travel*. St. Paul, MN: Llewellyn.

Devereux, Paul, 1997. *The Long Trip: A Prehistory of Psychedelia*. New York: Penguin.

Devereux, Paul, 2000. *The Sacred Place*. London: Cassell.

Devereux, Paul, 2005. "Dreaming of Time Past." *Freemasonry Today* 32.

Devereux, Paul, 2010. *Sacred Geography: Deciphering Hidden Codes in the Landscape*. London: Octopus.

Devereux, Paul and Charla Devereux, 2011. *Lucid Dreaming: Accessing Your Inner Virtual*

*Realities*. Australia: Daily Grail Publishing.

Devitt, Michael, 1991. *Realism and Truth* (second edition). Princeton, NJ: Princeton University Press.

DeWalt, Kathleen M., 2010. *Participant Observation: A Guide for Fieldworkers* (second edition). Lanham, MD: AltaMira.

Dietrich, Arne, 2003. "Functional Neuroanatomy of Altered States of Consciousness: The Transient Hypofrontality Hypothesis." *Consciousness and Cognition* 12:231-256.

Dietrich, Arne, 2007. *Introduction to Consciousness: Neuroscience, Cognitive science, and Philosophy*. New York: Palgrave Macmillan.

Dilley, Roy M., 1992. "Dreams, Inspiration and Craftwork Among Tukolor Weavers." in M.C. Jedrej and Rosalind Shaw (eds), *Dreaming, Religion and Society in Africa*. Leiden: E.J. Brill, pp. 71-85.

Dilthey, Wilhelm, 1977. *Dilthey: Selected Writings*. H. P. Rickman (ed and trans), Cambridge: Cambridge University Press.

Dinges, David F., 1990. "Are You Awake? Cognitive Performance and Reverie During the Hypnopompic State." in Richard R. Bootzin, John F. Kihlstrom and Daniel L. Schacter (eds), *Sleep and Cognition*. Washington, DC: American Psychological Association, pp. 159-175.

Dissanayake, Ellen, 1988. *What Is Art For?* Seattle, WA: University of Washington Press.

Dissanayake, Ellen, 1992. *Homo Aestheticus: Where Art Comes From and Why*. Seattle: University of Washington Press.

Dombeck, Mary-Therese B., 1991. *Dreams and Professional Personhood*. Albany, NY: State University of New York Press.

Dombeck, Mary-Therese B., 1994. "The Telling and Interpretation of Psychic Dreams: The Interpreted/Interrupting Self." *Ethos* 22(4):439-459.

Domhoff, G. William, 1996. *Finding Meaning in Dreams: A Quantitative Approach*. New York: Plenum.

Domhoff, G. William, 2003. *The Scientific Study of Dreams: Neural Networks, Cognitive Development, and Content Analysis*. Washington, D.C.: American Psychological Association.

Donald, Merlin, 1991. *Origins of the Modern Mind*. Cambridge, MA: Harvard University Press.

Donald, Merlin, 1995. "The Neurobiology of Human Consciousness: An Evolutionary Approach." *Neuropsychologia* 33(9):1087-1102.

Donald, Merlin, 2003. *A Mind So Rare: the Evolution of Human Consciousness*. New York: Norton.

Dor, Daniel and Eva Jablonka, 2010. "Plasticity and Canalization in the Evolution of Linguistic Communication: An Evolutionary Developmental Approach." in Richard K. Larson, Viviane Déprez and Hiroko Yamakido (eds), *The Evolution of Human Language: Biolinguistic Perspectives*. Cambridge: Cambridge University Press, pp. 135-147.

Dourley, John P., 1984. "Jung and the Coincidence of Opposites: God, Universe and Individual." *University of Ottawa Quarterly* 54(2):37-51.

Dow, James, 1986a. "Universal Aspects of Symbolic Healing: A Theoretical Synthesis." *American Anthropologist* 88(1):56-69.

Dow, James, 1986b. *The Shaman's Touch: Otomi Indian Symbolic Healing*. Salt Lake City, UT: University of Utah Press.

DuBois, Thomas A., 2009. *An Introduction to Shamanism*. Cambridge: Cambridge University Press.

Durkheim, Émile, 1995 [1912]. *The Elementary Forms of Religious Life*, translation Karen E, Fields. New York: The Free Press.

Durmer, Jeffrey S., and David F. Dinges, 2005. "Neurocognitive Consequences of Sleep Deprivation." *Seminars in Neurology* 25(1):117-129.

Ebbesson, Sven O.E., 1984. "Evolution and Ontogeny of Neural Circuits." *Behavioral and Brain Sciences* 7:321-331

Ebon, Martin, 1966. "Parapsychological Dream Studies." in G.E. von Grunebaum and R. Caillois (eds), *The Dream and Human Societies*. Berkeley: University of California Press, pp. 163-177.

Edelman, Gerald M. and Giulio Tononi, 2000. *A Universe of Consciousness: How Matter Becomes Imagination*. New York: Basic Books.

Edgar, Iain, 1995. *Dreamwork, Anthropology and the Caring Professions: A Cultural Approach to Dreamwork*. Aldershot, UK: Avebury.

Edgar, Iain, 1999. "Dream Fact and Real Fiction: The Realization of the Imagined Self." *Anthropology of Consciousness* 10(l):28-42.

Edgar, Iain, 2004a. *Guide to Imagework: Imagination-Based Research Methods*. London: Routledge.

Edgar, Iain, 2004b. "Imagework in Ethnographic Research." in Sarah Pink, László Kürti and Ana Isabel Afonso (eds), *Working Images: Visual Research and Representation in Ethnography*. L:ondon: Routledge, pp. 90-106.

Edgar, Iain and David Henig, 2010. Istikhara: The Guidance and Practice of Islamic Dream Incubation Through Ethnographic Comparison." *History and Anthropology* 21(3):251–262.

Edinger, Edward F., 1972. *Ego and Archetype: Individuation and the Religious Function of the Psyche*. New York: G.P. Putnam's Sons.

Edinger, Edward F., 1985. *Anatomy of the Psyche: Alchemical Symbolism in Psychotherapy*. La Salle, IL: Open Court.

Edinger, Edward F., 1995. *The Mysterium Lectures: A Journey Through C.G. Jung's Mysterium Coniunctionis*. Toronto, Canada: Inner City Books.

Eggan, Dorothy, 1949. "The Significance of Dreams for Anthropological Research." *American Anthropologist* 51:177-198.

Eggan, Dorothy, 1955. "The Personal Use of Myth in Dreams." *American Anthropologist* 57:

Eggan, Dorothy, 1961. "Dream Analysis." in Bert Kaplan (ed.), *Studying Personality Cross-Culturally*. Evanston, IL. Row, Peterson.

Eggan, Dorothy, 1966. "Hopi Dreams in Cultural Perspective." in G.E. von Grunebaum and R. Caillois (eds), *The Dream and Human Societies*. Berkeley: University of California Press, pp. 237-265.

Eggan, Fred,1954. "Social Anthropology and the Method of Controlled Comparison." *American Anthropologist* 56:743-763.

Eichwald, C. and F. Kaiser, 1993. "Model for Receptor-Controlled Cytosolic Calcium Oscillations and for External Influences on the Signal Pathway." *Biophysical Journal* 65:2047-2058.

Eliade, Mircea, 1963. *Myth and Reality*. New York: Harper and Row.

Eliade, Mircea, 1964. *Shamanism: Archaic Techniques of Ecstacy*. Princeton, N.J.: Princeton University Press.

Eliade, Mircea, 1966. "Initiation Dreams and Visions among the Siberian Shamans." in G.E. von Grunebaum and R. Caillois (eds), *The Dream and Human Societies*. Berkeley: University of California Press, pp. 331-340.

Elkin, A.P., 1994[1944]. *Aboriginal Men of High Degree: Initiation and Sorcery in the World's Oldest Tradition*. Rochester, VT: Inner Traditions.

Elwin, V., 1991[1947]. *The Muria and Their Ghotul*. Bombay: Oxford University Press.

Epstein, Mark, 2004. *Thoughts Without A Thinker: Psychotherapy from a Buddhist Perspective*. New York: Basic Books.

Erchak, G.M., 1992. *The Anthropology of Self and Behavior*. Piscataway, NJ: Rutgers University Press.

Erlacher, Daniel and Heather Chapin, 2010. "Lucid Dreaming: Neural Virtual Reality As a Mechanism for Performance Enhancement." *International Journal of Dream Research* 3(1):7-10.

Erlacher, Daniel and M. Schredl, 2008. "Do REM (Lucid) Dreamed and Executed Actions Share the Same Neural Substrate?" *International Journal of Dream Research* 1:7-13.

Erlacher, Daniel and M. Schredl, 2010. "Frequency of Sport Dreams in Athletes." *International Journal of Dream Research* 3(1):91-94.

Evans-Pritchard, E.E., 1937. *Witchcraft, Oracles and Magic Among the Azande*. Oxford: Oxford University Press.

Evans-Wentz, W.Y., 1958. *Tibetan Yoga and Secret Doctrines*. London: Oxford University Press.

Evans-Wentz, W.Y., 2005[1951]. *Tibet's Great Yogi Milarepa*. Delhi: Winsome Books India.

Everson C.A., B.M. Bergmann and A. Rechtschaffen, 1989. "Sleep Deprivation in the Rat: III. Total Sleep Deprivation." *Sleep* 12(1):13-21.

Ewing, Katherine P., 1990. "The Illusion of Wholeness." *Ethos* 18(3):251-278.

Ewing, Katherine P., 1994. "Dreams from a Saint: Anthropological Atheism and the Temptation to Believe." *American Anthropologist* 96(3):571-583.

Ewing, Katherine P., 2000. "Dream as Symptom, Dream as Myth: A Cross-Cultural Perspective on Dream Narratives." *Sleep and Hypnosis* 2(4):152-159.

Faber, P.A., G.S. Saayman, and S.W. Touyz, 1978. "Meditation and Archetypal Content of Nocturnal Dreams." *Journal of Analytical Psychology* 23:1-22.

Fabrega, Horacio and Daniel Silver, 1970. "Some Social and Psychological Properties of Zinacanteco Shamans." *Behavioral Science* 15(6):471-486.

Falk, Dean, 2004. *Braindance: New Discoveries About Human Brain Evolution*. Gainesville, FL: University Press of Florida.

Faraday, Ann, 1972. *Dream Power*. New York: Berkeley Books.

Fausto, Carlos, 2004. "A Blend of Blood and Tobacco: Shamans and Jaguars Among the Parakanã of Eastern Amazonia." in Neil L. Whitehead and Robin Wright (eds), *In Darkness and Secrecy: The Anthropology of Assault Sorcery and Witchcraft in Amazonia*. Durham, NC: Duke University Press, pp. 157-178.

Faye, J., 1989. *The Reality of the Future: An Essay on Time, Causation and Backward Causation*. Odence: Odense University Press.

Feinberg, I., 1969. "Effects of Age on Human Sleep Patterns." in A. Kales (ed)., *Sleep: Physiology and Pathology*. Philadelphia: Lippincott, pp. 39-52.

Feinberg, I. and M Guazzelli, 1999. "Schizophrenia – A Disorder of the Corollary Discharge Systems That Integrate the Motor Systems of Thought with the Sensory Systems of Consciousness." *The British Journal of Psychiatry* 174:196-204.

Feinstein, David, 1986. "Myth-Making Activity Through the Window of the Dream." *Psychotherapy in Private Practice* 4(4):119 - 135.

Feinstein, David, 1990. "The Dream as a Window on your Evolving Mythology." in Stanley Krippner (ed), *Dreamtime and Dreamwork*. Los Angeles: Tarcher, pp. 21-33.

Feinstein, David and Stanley Krippner, 2009[1988]. *Personal Mythology: Using Ritual, Dreams, and Imagination to Discover Your Inner Story.* Fulton, CA: Energy Psychology Press.

Feyerabend, Paul, 2010. *Against Method: Outline of an Anarchistic Theory of Knowledge* (4th edition). New York: Verso.

Fine, Gary Alan and Laura Fischer Leighton, (1993. "Nocturnal Omissions: Steps Toward a Sociology of Dreams." *Symbolic Interaction* 16(2):95-104.

Firth, Raymond, 2001. "Tikopia Dreams: Personal Images of Social Reality." *Journal of the Polynesian Society* 110(1):7-29.

Fischer, Manuela, Peter Bolz, Susan Kamel and Emily Schalk (eds), 2007. *Adolf Bastian and His Universal Archive of Humanity: The Origins of German Anthropology.* Zürich: Georg Ohms.

Fiss, Harry, 1986. "An Empirical Foundation for a Self Psychology of Dreaming." *the Journal of Mind and Behavior* 7(2/3):161-192.

Fitch, W. Tecumsey, 2010. *The Evolution of Language.* Cambridge: Cambridge University Press.

Flanagan, Owen, 1995. "Deconstructing Dreams: The Spandrels of Sleep." *The Journal of Philosophy* 92(1):5–27.

Flannery, Regina and Mary Elizabeth Chambers, 1985. "Each Man Has His Own Friends: The Role of Dream Visitors in Traditional East Cree Belief and Practice." *Arctic Anthropology* 22(1):1-22.

Fortune, R.F., 1963 [1932]. *Sorcerers of Dobu.* New York: Dutton.

Fortune, R.F., 1969 [1935]. *Manus Religion: An Ethnological Study of the Manus Natives of the Admiralty Islands.* Lincoln: University of Nebraska Press.

Foster, George M., 1973. "Dreams, Character, and Cognitive Orientation in Tzintzuntzan." *Ethos* 1(1):106-121.

Foulkes, David, 1982. *Children's Dreams: Longitudinal Studies.* New York: John Wiley.

Foulkes, David, 1985. *Dreaming: A Cognitive-Psychological Analysis.* Hillsdale, NJ: Erlbaum.

Foulkes, David, 1999. *Children's Dreaming and the Development of Consciousness.* Cambridge, Mass.: Harvard University Press.

Fox, Oliver, 1962. *Astral Projection: A Record of Out-of-the-Body Experiences.* Secaucus, NJ: Citadel.

Fox, Robin, 1975. *Encounter With Anthropology.* London: Peregrine.

Frank, Marcos G. and Joel H. Benington, 2006. "The Role of Sleep in Memory Consolidation and Brain Plasticity: Dream or Reality?" *Neuroscientist* 12(6):1–12.

Freidel, David, Linda Schele and Joy Parker, 1995. *Maya Cosmos: Three Thousand Years on the Shaman's Path.* New York: Harper.

Freud, Sigmund, 2010 [1899]. *The Interpretation of Dreams.* Charlotte, NC: IAP.

Frohlich, Herbert, 1968. "Long Range Coherence in Biological Systems." *International Journal of Quantum Chemistry* 2:641-649.

Frohlich, Herbert, 1980. "The Biological Effects of Microwaves and Related Questions." *Adv. Electron. Electron Phys.* 53:85-152.

Frohlich, Herbert, 1986. "Coherent Excitation in Active Biological Systems." in Felix Gutmann and Hendrik Keyzer (eds), *Modern Bioelectrochemistry.* New York: Plenum. pp. 241-261.

Frohlich, Herbert and F. Kremer, 1983. *Coherent Excitations in Biological Systems.* New York: Springer-Verlag.

Fuster, Joaquin M., 2003. *Cortex and Mind: Unifying Cognition.* Oxford: Oxford University Press.

Fuster, Joaquin M., 2008. *The Prefrontal Cortex* (4th edition). London: Elsevier.

Gackenbach, Jayne (ed), 1986. *Sleep and Dreams: A Sourcebook*. New York: Garland Reference Library.

Gackenbach, Jayne, 1991a. "Introduction." in Jayne Gackenbach and Anees A, Sheikh (eds), *Dream Images: A Call to Mental Arms*. Amityville, NY: Baywood, pp. 1-14.

Gackenbach, Jayne, 1991. "A Developmental Model of Consciousness in Sleep: From Sleep Consciousness to Pure Consciousness." in Jayne Gackenbach and Anees A, Sheikh (eds), *Dream Images: A Call to Mental Arms*. Amityville, NY: Baywood, pp. 287-308.

Gackenbach, Jayne and Jane Bosveld, 1989. *Control Your Dreams*. New York: Harper and Row.

Gackenbach, Jayne and Stephen LaBerge (eds), 1988. *Conscious Mind, Sleeping Brain*. New York: Plenum.

Gackenbach, Jayne and Anees A, Sheikh, 1991. *Dream Images: A Call to Mental Arms*. Amityville, NY: Baywood.

Gallup, Gordon G., 1982. "Self Awareness and the Emergence of Mind in Primates." *American Journal of Primatology* 2:237-248.

Gallup, Gordon G., 1994. "Self-Recognition: Research Strategies and Experimental Design." in Sue Taylor Parker, Robert W. Mitchell and Maria L. Boccia (eds), *Self Awareness in Animals and Humans: Developmental Perspectives*. Cambridge: Cambridge University Press, pp. 35-50.

Gandhi, M.K., 1957. *My Autobiography*. Ahmedabad, India: Navahvan.

Garfield, Patricia, 1974. *Creative Dreaming*. New York: Simon and Schuster.

Garfield, Patricia, 1984. *Your Child's Dreams*. New York: Ballantine.

Garro, Linda C., 2007. "'Effort After Meaning' in Everyday Life." in Conerly Casey and Robert B. Edgerton (eds), *A Companion to Psychological Anthropology: Modernity and Psychocultural Change*. Oxford: Blackwell, pp. 48-71.

Gay, Volney P., 1983. "Ritual and Self-Esteem in Victor Turner and Heinz Kohut." *Zygon* 18(3):271-283.

Gazzaniga, Michael S., 2000. *The Mind's Past*. Berkeley, CA: University of California Press.

Gazzaniga, Michael S. and Joseph E. LeDoux, 1978. *The Integrated Mind*. New York: Plenum.

Geary, David C., 2005. *The Origin of Mind: Evolution of Brain, Cognition and General Intelligence*. Washington, DC: American Psychological Association.

Geertz, Clifford, 1984. "'From the Native's Point of view': On the Nature of Anthropological Understanding." in R.A. Shweder and R.A. Levine (eds), *Cultural Theory: Essays on Mind, Self, and Emotion*. Cambridge: Cambridge University Press, pp. 123-136.

Geertz, Clifford, 1973. *The Interpretation of Cultures*. New York: Basic Books.

Geertz, Clifford, 1983. *Local Knowledge*. New York: Basic Books.

Gell, Alfred, 1977. "Magic, Perfume, Dream." in I. M. Lewis (ed), *Symbols and Sentiments*. London: Academic Press, pp. 25–38.

Gell, Alfred, 1998. *Art and Agency: An Anthropological Theory*. Oxford: Clarendon.

Gellhorn, Ernst, 1967. *Principles of Autonomic-Somatic Integration*. Minneapolis: University of Minnesota Press.

Gellhorn, Ernst and W.F. Kiely, 1972. "Mystical States of Consciousness: Neurophysiological and Clinical Aspects." *Journal of Nervous and Mental Diseases* 154:399-405.

Gellhorn, Ernst and G.N. Loofbourrow, 1963. *Emotions and Emotional Disorders*. New York: Harper and Row.

George, Marianne, 1988. *"A Wosak Maraluon!" The Barok Pidik of Hidden Power, and the Ritual Imaging of Intent and Meaning*. Unpublished doctoral dissertation, Department of Anthropology, University of Virginia.

George, Marianne, 1995a. "Dreams, Reality, and the Desire and Intent of Dreamers As Experienced By a Fieldworker."*Anthropology of Consciousness* 6(3):17-33.

George, Marianne, 1995b. "In a Pig's Eye: Learning from Tattoos and Dreams Among the Barok." *The World and I* (electronic magazine at www.worldandI.com), November 1995 issue, pp. 189-200.

George, Marianne, n.d. *Seeking the Hidden: Finding Women's Power: Spiritual Process, Female Images, and Religious Experience As Learned Among the Barok of New Ireland, PNG.* Unpublished manuscript.

Geschwind, N. and A.M. Galaburda, 1984. *Cerebral Dominance.* Cambridge, MA: Harvard University Press.

Ghysen, Alain, 2003. "The Origin and Evolution of the Nervous System." *International Journal of Developmental Biology* 47:555-562.

Gibson, James, 1979. *The Ecological Approach to Visual Perception.* Boston: Houghton Mifflin.

Gibson, James, 1982. "Notes on Affordances." in Edward Reed and Rebecca Jones (eds), *Reasons For Realism.* Hillsdale, NJ: Lawrence Erlbaum, pp. 401-430.

Gillespie, George, 1985. "From Lucid Dream to Dreamless Sleep." *ASD Newsletter* 2(4):6-10.

Gillespie, George, 1988a. "Lucid Dreams in Tibetan Buddhism." in Gackenbach, Jayne and Stephen LaBerge (eds), *Conscious Mind, Sleeping Brain.* New York: Plenum, pp. 27-35.

Gillespie, George, 1988b. "Without a Guru: An Account of My Lucid Dreaming." in Gackenbach, Jayne and Stephen LaBerge (eds), *Conscious Mind, Sleeping Brain.* New York: Plenum, pp. 343-350.

Gillespie, George, 1991. "Early Hindu Speculation about Dreams: Implications for Dream Yoga." in Jayne Gackenbach and Anees A, Sheikh (eds), *Dream Images: A Call to Mental Arms.* Amityville, NY: Baywood, pp. 225-230.

Gillespie, George, 1997. "Hypnopompic Imagery and Visual Dream Experience." *Dreaming* 7(3):187-194.

Globus, Gordon, 1987. *Dream Life, Wake Life: The Human Condition Through Dreams.* Albany, NY: State University of New York Press.

Globus, Gordon, 1998. "Self, Cognition, Qualia and World in Quantum Brain Dynamics." *Journal of Consciousness Studies* 5(1):34-52.

Goodenough, Ward H., 1954. "Cultural Anthropology and Linguistics." In Dell Hymes (ed), *Language in Culture and Society.* New York Harper & Row, pp. 36-39.

Goodenough, Ward H., 1971. *Culture, Language, and Society.* Reading, MA: Addison-Wesley.

Goodman, Jeffrey, 1978. *Psychic Archaeology.* London: Wildwood House.

Gough, K.,1961. "Nayar: Central Kerala." in D.M. Schneider and K. Gough (eds), *Matrilineal Kinship.* Berkeley: University of California Press.

Gould, James L., 1986. "The Locale Map of Honey Bees: Do Insects Have Cognitive Maps?" *Science* 232:861-863.

Gould, Stephen J., 1977. *Ontogeny and Phylogeny.* Cambridge: Harvard University Press.

Gould, Stephen J., 1991. "Exaptation: A Crucial Tool for an Evolutionary Psychology." *Journal of Social Issues* 47:43-65.

Goulet, Jean-Guy, 1987. "Ways of Knowing: Towards a Narrative Ethnography of Experiences among the Dene Tha." *Journal of Anthropological Research* 50(2):113-139.

Goulet, Jean-Guy, 1994. "Dreams and Visions in Other Lifeworlds." in David E. Young & Jean-Guy Goulet (eds), *Being Changed by Cross-Cultural Encounters.* Peterborough,

Ontario: Broadview Press, pp. 16-38.

Goulet, Jean-Guy, 1998. *Ways of Knowing: Experience, Knowledge, and Power Among the Dene Tha*. Lincoln, NE: University of Nebraska Press.

Goulet, Jean-Guy and David Young, 1994. "Theoretical and Methodological Issues." in David E. Young & Jean-Guy Goulet (eds), *Being Changed by Cross-Cultural Encounters*. Peterborough, Ontario: Broadview Press, pp. 298-335.

Goulet, Jean-Guy and Bruce Granville Miller, 2007. *Extraordinary Anthropology: Transformations in the Field*. Lincoln, NE: University of Nebraska Press.

Graham, Laura R., 1994. "Dialogic Dreams: Creative Selves Coming into Life in the Flow of Time." *American Ethnologist* 21(4):723-745.

Graham, Laura R., 2003. *Performing Dreams* (second edition). Tucson, AZ: Fenestra.

Gray, Jeffrey A., 1982. *The Neuropsychology of Anxiety: An Enquiry into the Functions of the Septo-Hippocampal System*. Oxford: Clarendon Press.

Greeley, A.M. (1975) *The Sociology of the Paranormal*. Beverley Hills: Sage Publications.

Green, Celia, 1968. *Lucid Dreams*. Oxford: Institute of Psychophysical Research.

Green, Maurice R., Montague Ullman and Edword S. Tauber, 1995. "Dreaming and Modern Dream Theory." in Judd Marmor (ed), *Modern Psychoanalysis: New Directions and Perspectives*. Piscataway, NJ: Transaction Publishers.

Greenwood, Susan, 2009. *The Anthropology of Magic*. Oxford: Berg.

Gregor, Thomas, 1981. "'Far, Far Away My Shadow Wandered...': The Dream Symbolism and Dream Theories of the Mehinaku Indians of Brazil." *American Ethnologist* 8(4):709-720.

Grim, John A., 1983. *The Shaman: Patterns of Religious Healing Among the Ojibway Indians*. Norman, OK: University of Oklahoma Press.

Grimes, Ronald L., 2010. *Beginnings in Ritual Studies* (3rd edition). CreateSpace.

Grindal, Bruce T., 1983. "Into the Heart of Sisala Experience: Witnessing Death Divination." *Journal of Anthropological Research* 39(1):60-80.

Groark, Kevin P., 2009. "Discourses of the Soul: The Negotiation of Personal Agency in Tzotzil Maya Dream Narrative." *American Ethnologist* 36(4):705–721.

Grundler, W., F. Kaiser, F. Keilmann and J. Walleczek, 1992. "Mechanisms of Electromagnetic Interaction with Cellular Syustems." *Naturwissenschaften* 79:551-559.

Gu, Q. and Fritz-Albert Popp, 1993. "Biophoton Physics: Potential Measure of Organizational Order." in Ernst G. Jung (ed), *Biological Effects of Light*. Berlin: Walter de Gruyter.

Guenther, Herbert V., 1963. *The Life and Teaching of Naropa*. Oxford: Oxford University Press.

Guthrie, S., 1993. *Faces in the Clouds: A New Theory of Religion*. Oxford: Oxford University Press.

Haden, Bob, 2011. "How Dreams Are Helpful To Me as a Priest, Pastoral Counselor and Spiritual Director." *Dream Network Journal* 30(1):9.

Halifax, Joan, 1979. *Shamanic Voices: A Survey of Visionary Narratives*. New York: Penguin.

Hall, Calvin S., 1953. *The Meaning of Dreams*. New York: Harper.

Hall, Calvin S. and Bill Domhoff, 1963a. "Aggression in Dreams." *International Journal of Social Psychiatry* 9: 259-267.

Hall, Calvin S. and Bill Domhoff, 1963b. "A Ubiquitous Sex Difference in Dreams." *Journal of Abnormal Social Psychology* 66:278-280.

Hall, Calvin S. and Bill Domhoff, 1964. "Friendliness in Dreams." *Journal of Social Psychology* 62:309-314.

Hall, Calvin S. and Robert L. Van de Castle, 1966. *The Content Analysis of Dreams*. New York: Appleton-Century-Crofts.

Hallowell, A. Irving, 1955. "The Self and Its Behavioral Environment." in A. Irving Hallowell (ed), *Culture and Experience*. Philadelphia, PA: University of Pennsylvania Press.

Hallowell, A. Irving, 1976. "The Role of Dreams in Ojibwa Culture." in A. Irving Hallowell, *Contributions to Anthropology*. Chicago: University of Chicago Press, pp. 449-471.

Hallowell, A. Irving, 2002. "Ojibwa Ontology, Behavior, and World View." in Graham Harvey (ed), *Readings in Indigenous Religions*. New York: Continuum, pp. 17-49.

Hameroff, Stuart R., 1994. "Quantum Coherence in Microtubules: A Neural Basis for Emergent Consciousness?" *Journal of Consciousness Studies* 1(1):91-118.

Hameroff, Stuart R., 1998. "Quantum Computation in Brain Microtubules? The Penrose–Hameroff 'Orch OR' Model of Consciousness." *Philosophical Transactions of the Royal Society of London* A 356(1743):1869-1896.

Hamilton, Mary, 1906. *Incubation: Or, the Cure of Disease in Pagan Temples and Christian Churches*. London: W.C. Henderson and Son.

Harding, D.E., 1986. *On Having No Head: Zen and the Re-Discovery of the Obvious*. London: Arkana.

Harner, Michael J., 1962. "Jivaro Souls." *American Anthropologist* 64:258-272.

Harner, Michael J., 1973. *The Jivaro*. Garden City: Doubleday.

Harner, Michael J., 1990[1980]. *The Way of the Shaman*. New York: HarperOne.

Harris, Judith Rich, 2007. *No Two Alike: Human Nature and Human Individuality*. New York: W.W. Norton.

Harris, William V., 2009. *Dreams and Experience in Classical Antiquity*. Cambridge, MA: Harvard University Press.

Hartmann, Ernest, 2007. "The Nature and Function of Dreaming." in Deirdre Barrett and Patrick McNamara (eds), *Cultural and Theoretical Perspectives*, Volume 3 of *The New Science of Dreaming*. Westport CT: Praeger, pp. 171-192.

Hartmann, Ernest, 2011. *The Nature and Functions of Dreaming*. Oxford: Oxford University Press.

Haskell, Robert, 1985. "Dreaming, Cognition, and Physical Illness: Part I." *Journal of Medical Humanities* 6(1):46-56.

Haule, John Ryan, 2010. *Jung in the 21$^{st}$ Century*, Volume 1: *Evolution and Archetype*. New York: Routledge.

Headland, Thomas, Kenneth Pike, and Marvin Harris (eds), 1990. *Emics and Etics: The Insider/Outsider Debate*. Thousand Oaks, CA: Sage Publications.

Hebb, Donald O., 1949. *The Organization of Behavior*. New York: Wiley.

Heelas, Paul, 1996. *The New Age Movement*. Cambridge, MA: Blackwell.

Heidegger, Martin, 1977. "The Question Concerning Technology." in *Basic Writings* (trans. by D. Krell). New York: Harper and Row.

Heijnen, Adriënne, 2010. "Relating Through Dreams: Names, Genes and Shared Substance." *History and Anthropology* 21(3):307-319.

Heijnen, Adriënne and Iain Edgar, 2010. "Imprints of Dreaming." *History and Anthropology* 21(3):217-226.

Hellige, Joseph B., 1993. *Hemispheric Asymmetry: What's Right and What's Left*. Cambridge, MA: Harvard University Press.

Hempel, Carl, 1968. "The Logic of Functional Analysis." in May Brodbeck (ed), *Readings in the Philosophy of the Social Sciences*. New York: Macmillan.

Henriques, Marika, 2004. "'The Lions Are Coming': The Healing Image in Jungian Dreamwork." *British Journal of Psychotherapy* 20(4):513–526.

Hensch, T.K., 2005. "Critical Period Plasticity in Local Cortical Circuits." *Nature Reviews Neuroscience* 6:877–888.

Herdt, Gilbert H., 1977. "The Shaman's 'Calling' Among the Sambia of New Guinea." *Journal de la Société des Océanistes* 33:153-167.

Herdt, Gilbert H., 1992. "Selfhood and Discourse in Sambia Dream Sharing." in Barbara Tedlock (ed), *Dreaming: Anthropological and Psychological Interpretations*. Cambridge: Cambridge University Press, pp. 55-85.

Herr, Barbara, 1981. "The Expressive Character of Fijian Dream and Nightmare Experiences." *Ethos* 9(4):331-352.

Hewitt, Daryl E., 1988. "Induction of Ecstatic Dreams." *Lucidity Letter* 7(1):64-66.

Hillix, W.A. and Duane Rumbaugh, 2010. *Animal Bodies, Human Minds: Ape, Dolphin, and Parrot Language Skills*. New York: Kluwer.

Hillman, Deborah Jay, 1984. "Lucid Dream Consciousness: A Subjective Account." *Dream Network Bulletin* 3(5):1-5.

Hillman, Deborah Jay, 1990. "The Emergence of the Grassroots Dreamwork Movement." in Stanley Krippner (ed), *Dreamtime and Dreamwork*. Los Angeles: Tarcher, pp. 13-20.

Hillman, Deborah Jay, 1999. "Dream Work and Field Work: Linking Cultural Anthropology and the Current Dream Work Movement." in Montague Ullman and Claire Limmer (eds), *The Variety of Dream Experience* (second edition). Albany, NY: State University of New York Press, pp. 65-89.

Hillman, James, 1985. *Archetypal Psychology: A Brief Account*. Dallas, TX: Spring Publications.

Hinde, Robert A., 1991. "A Biologist Looks at Anthropology." *Man* (New Series) 26(4):583-608.

Hinde, Robert A., 1995. "Individuals and Culture." in Jean-Pierre Changeux and Jean Chavaillon (eds), *Origins of the Human Brain*. Oxford: Clarendon, pp. 186-197.

Ho, Mae-Wan, Fritz-Albert Popp and Ulrich Warnke, 1994. *Bioelectrodynamics and Biocommunication*. London: World Scientific.

Hobson, J. Allan, 1988. *The Dreaming Brain*. New York: Basic Books.

Hobson, J. Allan, 1989. *Sleep*. New York: Scientific American Library.

Hobson, J. Allan, 1994. *Dreaming as Delirium: How the Brain Goes Out ofg Its Mind*. Cambridge, MA: MIT Press.

Hobson, J. Allan, 1999. *Consciousness*. New York: Scientific American Library.

Hobson, J. Allan, 2001. *The Dream Drugstore*. Cambridge, MA: MIT Press.

Hobson, J. Allan, 2002. *Dreaming: An Introduction to the Science of Sleep*. Oxford: Oxford University Press.

Hobson, J. Allan, 2007. "States of Consciousness: Normal and Abnormal Variation." in P. D. Zelazo, M. Moscovitch, & E. Thompson (eds), *Cambridge Handbook of Consciousness*. New York: Cambridge University Press, pp. 435-444.

Hobson, J. Allan, 2009. "The Neurobiology of Consciousness: Lucid Dreaming Wakes Up." *International Journal of Dream Research* 2(2):41-44.

Hobson, J. Allan, Edward F. Pace-Schott and Robert Stickgold, 2003. "Dreaming and the Brain: Toward a Cognitive Neuroscience of Conscious States." in Edward F. Pace-Schott, Mark Sohms, Mark Blagrovde and Stevan Harnad (eds), *Sleep and Dreaming: Scientific Advances and Reconsiderations*. Cambridge: Cambridge University Press, pp. 1-50 .

Hobson, J. Allan and Hellmut Wohl, 2005. *From Angels to Neurons: Art and the New Science of Dreaming.* Fidenza, Italy: Mattioli 1885.

Hollan, Douglas, 1989. "The Personal Use of Dream Beliefs in the Toraja Highlands." *Ethos* 17(2):166-186.

Hollan, Douglas, 1992. "Cross-Cultural Differences in the Self." *Journal of Anthropological Research* 48():283–300.

Hollan, Douglas, 1996. "Cultural and Experiential Aspects of Spirit Beliefs Among the Toraja." in Jeannette Marie Mageo and Alan Howard (eds), *Spirits in Cultures, History, and Mind.* New York: Routledge, pp. 213-235.

Hollan, Douglas, 2003a. "The Cultural and Intersubjective Context of Dream Remembrance and Reporting." in Roger Ivar Lohmann (ed), *Dream Travelers: Sleep Experiences and Culture in the Western Pacific.* New York: Palgrave, pp 169-187.

Hollan, Douglas, 2003b. "Selfscape Dreams." in Jeannette Marie Mageo (ed), *Dreaming and the Self: New Perspectives on Subjectivity, Identity, and EmotionI.* Albany, NY: State University of New York Press, pp. 61-96.

Hollan, Douglas, 2004. "The Anthropology of Dreaming: Selfscape Dreams." in Charles Stewart (ed), *Anthropological Approaches to Dreaming*, Special issue. *Dreaming* 14(2-3):170-182.

Hollan, Douglas, 2007. "Dreaming in a Global World." in Conerly Casey and Robert B. Edgerton (eds), *A Companion to Psychological Anthropology: Modernity and Psychocultural Change.* Oxford: Blackwell, pp.90-102.

Hollan, Douglas, 2009. "The Influence of Culture on the Experience and Interpretation of Disturbing Dreams." *Culture, Medicine and Psychiatry* 33:313–322.

Hollan, Douglas and Jane C. Wellenkamp, 1996. *The Thread of Life: Toraja Reflections on the Life Cycle.* Honolulu: University of Hawaii Press.

Holloway, Ralph L., 1972. "Australopithecine Endocasts, Brain Evolution in the Hominoidea, and a Model of Hominid Evolution." in R. Tuttle (ed), *The Functional and Evolutionary Biology of Primates.* Chicago: Aldine.

Holloway, Ralph L., 1995. "Toward a Synthetic Theory of Human Brain Evolution." in Jean-Pierre Changeux and Jean Chavaillon (eds), *Origins of the Human Brain.* Oxford: Clarenden, pp. 42-60.

Honegger, Barbara, 1979. "A Shamanistic Seed-Dream Interpretation: The Bird-man Mural at Lascaux." Phoenix: New Directions in the Study of Man 2(2): 5-12.

Horne, J.A., 1985. "Sleep Function, with Particular Reference to Sleep Deprivation." *Annals of Clinical Research* 17:199-208.

Hoss, Robert J., 2005. *Dream Language: Self-Understanding through Imagery and Color.* Ashland, OR: Innersource.

Howes, David, 1991. *The Varieties of Sensory Experience.* Toronto: University of Toronto Press.

Hu, Peter, Melinda Stylos-Allan and Matthew P. Walker, 2006. "Sleep Facilitates Consolidation of Emotional Declarative Memory." *Psychological Science* 17(10):891-898.

Huber, R. *et al.*, 2004. "Sleep Homeostasis in Drosophila Melanogaster." *Sleep* 27(4):628-39.

Hudson, Liam, 1985. *Night Life: The Interpretation of Dreams.* New York: St. Martin's Press.

Huffman, M.A., 2003. "Animal Self-medication and Ethno-medicine: Exploration and Exploitation of the Medicinal Properties of Plants." *Proceedings of the Nutrition Society* 62(2):371-81.

Hufford, D.J., 1982. *The Terror that Comes in the Night: An Experience-Centered Study of Supernatural Assault Traditions.* Philadelphia: University of Pennsylvania Press.

Hultkrantz, A., 1973. "Ecological and Phenomenological Aspects of Shamanism." in V.

Dioszegi and M. Hoppel (eds), *Shamanism in Siberia*. Budapest: Akademiai Kiado.

Hultsch, Henrike and Dietmar Todt, 2004. "Learning to Sing," in Marler, Peter R. and Hans Slabbekoorn (eds), *Nature's Music: The Science of Birdsong*. New York: Academic Press, pp. 80-107.

Hume, Lynne, 1999. "On the Unsafe Side of the White Divide: New Perspectives on the Dreaming of Australian Aborigines." *Anthropology of Consciousness* 10(1):1-15.

Hunt, Harry T., 1989. *Multiplicity of Dreams: Memory, Imagination and Consciousness*. New Haven, CT: Yale University Press.

Hunt, Harry T. and Robert D. Ogilvie, 1988. "Lucid Dreams in their Natural Series: Phenomenological and Psychophysiological Findings in Relation to Meditative States." in Jayne Gackenbach and Stephen LaBerge (eds), *Conscious Mind, Sleeping Brain*. New York: Plenum, pp. 389-418.

Hunt, Harry T., R. Ogilvie, K. Belicki, D. Belicki, and E. Atalick, 1982. "Forms of Dreaming." *Perceptual and Motor Skills* 54:559-633.

Hunt-Meeks, Swanee, 1983. "The Anthropology of Carl Jung: Implications for Pastoral Care." *Journal of Religion and Health* 22(3):191-211.

Husserl, Edmund, 1964 [1928]. *The Phenomenology of Internal Time-Consciousness*. Bloomington: Indiana University Press.

Husserl, Edmund, 1970 [1937]. *The Crisis in European Sciences and Transcendental Phenomenology*. Evanston: Northwestern University Press.

Iacoboni, M., M.D. Lieberman, B.J. Knowlton, I. Molnar-Szakacs, M. Moritz, C.J. Throop and A.P. Fiske, 2004. "Medial Prefrontal and Parietal Activation while Watching Social Interactions Compared to a Resting Baseline." *NeuroImage* 21:1167-1173

Irwin, Lee, 1994. *The Dream Seekers: Native American Visionary Traditions of the Great Plains*. Norman, OK: University of Oklahoma Press.

Jackson, Michael, 1989. *Paths Toward a Clearing: Radical Empiricism and Ethnographic Inquiry*. Bloomington: Indiana University.

Jackson, Michael, 1996. "Introduction: Phenomenology, Radical Empiricism, and Anthropological Critique." in Michael Jackson (ed), *Things as They Are: New Directions in Phenomenological Anthropology*. Bloomington: Indiana University Press, pp. 1-50.

Jahn, Robert G. (ed), 1981. *The Role of Consciousness in the Physical World*. Washington, D.C.: American Association for the Advancement of Science.

Jahn, Robert G., Paul Devereux & Michael Ibison, 1996. "Acoustical Resonances of Assorted Ancient Structures." *Journal of the Acoustical Society of America* 99(2), 649-658.

Jahn, Robert G. and Brenda J. Dunne, 1987. *Margins of Reality: The Role of Consciousness in the Physical World*. New York: Harcourt Brace Jovanovich.

James, William, 1890. *The Principles of Psychology*. New York: Henry Holt & Co.

James, William, 1976 [1912]. *Essays in Radical Empiricism*. Cambridge, MA: Harvard University Press.

James, William, 1904a. "Does 'Consciousness' Exist?" *Journal of Philosophy, Psychology, and Scientific Methods* 1:477-491.

James, William, 1904b. "A World of Pure Experience." *Journal of Philosophy, Psychology, and Scientific Methods* 1:533-543.

Jarvis, Erich D., 2004. "Brains and Birdsong." in Marler, Peter R. and Hans Slabbekoorn (eds), *Nature's Music: The Science of Birdsong*. New York: Academic Press, pp. 226-271.

Jarvis, Erich D., 2009. "Evolution of the Pallium in Birds and Reptiles." in M.D. Binder, N. Hirokawa, U. Windhorst and As-e Butler (eds), *Encyclopedia of Neuroscience*. Berlin: Springer-Verlag, pp. 1390–1400.

Jaspars, J., M. Hewstone and F.D. Fincham, 1983. "Attribution Theory and Research: The State of the Art." in J. Jaspars, F.D. Fincham and M. Hewstone (eds), *Attribution Theory and Research: Conceptual, Developmental and Social Dimensions*. New York: Academic Press.

Jean-Louis, G., D.F. Kripke and S. Anconi-Israel, 2000. "Sleep and Quality of Well-being." *Sleep* 23(8):1115-1121.

Jedrej, M.C., 1992. *Dreaming, Religion and Society in Africa*. Leiden: Brill.

Jenness, Diamond, 1935. *The Ojibwa Indians of Perry Island: Their Social and Religious Life*. Ottawa: National Museum of Canada Bulletin No. 78, Anthropological Series No. 17.

Jerison, Harry J., 1973. *Evolution of the Brain and Intelligence*. New York: Academic Press.

Jerison, Harry J., 1985. "On the Evolution of Mind." in D.A. Oakley (ed), *Brain and Mind*. New York: Methuen.

Jibu, Mari, Scott Hagan, Stuart R. Hameroff, Karl H. Pribram and Kunio Yasue, 1994. "Quantum Optical Coherence in Cytoskeletal Microtubules: Implications for Brain Function." *BioSystems* 32:95-209.

Jibu, Mari and Kunio Yasue, 1995. *Quantum Brain Dynamics and Consciousness: An Introduction*. Amsterdam: Benjamins.

Jibu, Mari and Kunio Yasue, 2004. "Quantum Brain Dynamics and Quantum Field Theory." in Gordon G. Globus, Karl H. Pribram, Giuseppe Vitiello (eds), *Brain and Being: At the Boundary Between Science, Philosophy, Language and Arts*. Amsterdam: Benjamins, pp. 255-290.

Jilek, Wolfgang G., 1982. "Altered States of Consciousness in North American Indian Ceremonials." *Ethos* 10(4):326-343.

Jochelson, W., 1975 [1908]. *The Koryak*. Volume 6 of the *Jesup North Pacific Expedition*. New York: AMS Press.

Johnson, Kenneth E., 1978. "Modernity and Dream Content: A Ugandan Example." *Ethos* 6(4):212-220.

Johnson, Robert A., 1986. *Inner Work: Using Dreams and Active Imagination for Personal Growth*. San Francisco, CA: Harper.

Jones, David E., 1972. *Sanapia: Comanche Medicine Woman*. New York: Hold, Rinehart and Winston.

Jones, Ernest, 1951. *On the Nightmare*. New York: Liveright.

Jorgensen, Dan, 1980. "What's in a Name: The Meaning of Nothingness in Telefolmin." *Ethos* 8(4):349-366.

Jorgensen, Joseph G., 1972. *The Sun Dance Religion*. Chicago: University of Chicago Press.

Jorgensen, Joseph G., 1983. "Comparative Traditional Economics and Ecological Adaptations." in A. Ortiz (ed), *Southwest, Handbook on North American Indians*, Vol. 10, pp. 684-710. Washington, D.C.: Smithsonian Institute.

Jorgensen, Joseph G. and Eric Wolf, 1970. "Anthropology on the Warpath." *The New York Review of Books* 15(9).

Joseph, Rhawn, 1992. *The Right Brain and the Unconscious*. New York: Plenum.

Jost, John T., 1995. "Negative Illusions: Conceptual Clarification and Psychological Evidence Concerning False Consciousness." *Political Psychology* 16(2):397-424.

Juergens, Heinrich, 1953. *Traum-Exerzitien*. Freiburg: Bauer.

Jung, C.G., 1933. *Modern Man in Search of a Soul*. New York: Harcourt.

Jung, C.G., 1953 [orig. pub. 1943/45]). *Two Essays on Analytical Psychology*. London: Routledge & Kegan Paul.

Jung, C.G., 1954a [orig. pub. 1931]). "Introduction to Wickes's 'Analyse der Kinderseele'." in *The Development of Personality*. London: Routledge and Kegan Paul, pp. 39-46 (Collected Works No. 17).

Jung, C.G., 1954b [1931]. *The Development of Personality*. London: Routledge and Kegan Paul, pp. 39-46 (Collected Works No. 17).

Jung, C.G., 1954c[1924]. "Analytical Psychology and Education." in *The Development of Personality*. Princeton, NJ: Princeton University Press, (Collected Works No. 17).

Jung, C.G., 1956 [orig. pub. 1912, revised in 1952]). *Symbols of Transformation: An Analysis of the Prelude to a Case of Schizophrenia*. London: Routledge and Kegan Paul (Collected Works No. 5).

Jung, C.G., 1958 [1948]. *Psychology and Religion: West and East*. New York: Pantheon Books (Collected Works No. 11).

Jung, C.G., 1959 [1951]. *Aion: Researches into the Phenomenology of the Self*. Princeton, NJ: Princeton University Press (Collected Works No. 9).

Jung, C.G., 1960. *The Psychogenesis of Mental Disease*. Princeton, NJ: Princeton University Press (Collected Works No. 3).

Jung, C.G., 1964. *Man and His Symbols*. New York: Doubleday.

Jung, C.G., 1965 [1961]. *Memories, Dreams, Reflections*. New York: Vintage Books.

Jung, C.G., 1967. *Alchemical Studies*. Princeton, NJ: Princeton University Press, (Collected Works No. 10)

Jung, C.G., 1968a [1944, revised 1958]. *Psychology and Alchemy*. Princeton, NJ: Princeton University Press, (Collected Works No. 12).

Jung, C.G., 1968b [1934, revised 1954]. "Archetypes of the Collective Unconscious." in *The Archetypes and the Collective Unconscious*. Princeton, NJ: Princeton University Press, pp. 3-41 (Collected Works No. 9).

Jung, C.G., 1968c [1936/37]. "The Concept of the Collective Unconscious." in *The Archetypes and the Collective Unconscious*. Princeton, NJ: Princeton University Press, pp. 42-53 (Collected Works No. 9).

Jung, C.G., 1968d [1936]. "Concerning the Archetypes, with Special Reference to the Anima Concept." in *The Archetypes and the Collective Unconscious*. Princeton, NJ: Princeton University Press, pp. 54-72 (Collected Works No. 9).

Jung, C.G., 1968e [1940]. "The Psychology of the Child Archetype." in *The Archetypes and the Collective Unconscious*. Princeton, NJ: Princeton University Press, pp. 151-181 (Collected Works No. 9).

Jung, C.G., 1968f. *Analytical Psychology*. London, Routledge & Kegan Paul.

Jung, C.G., 1969a [1946]. "On the Nature of the Psyche." in *The Structure and Dynamics of the Psyche*. Princeton, NJ: Princeton University Press, pp. 159-234 (Collected Works No. 8).

Jung, C.G., 1969b [1931]. "The Stages of Life." in *The Structure and Dynamics of the Psyche*. Princeton, NJ: Princeton University Press, pp. 387-403 (Collected Works No. 8).

Jung, C.G., 1969c [1949]. "Forward." in *The Origins and History of Consciousness*, Erich Neumann. Princeton, NJ: Princeton University Press, pp. xiii-xiv.

Jung, C.G., 1969d [1919]. "Instinct and the Unconscious." in *The Structure and Dynamics of the Psyche*. Princeton, NJ: Princeton University Press, pp. 129-138 (Collected Works No. 8).

Jung, C.G., 1969e [1948]. "On the Nature of Dreams." in *The Structure and Dynamics of the Psyche*. Princeton, NJ: Princeton University Press, pp. 281-300 (Collected Works No. 8).

Jung, C.G., 1969f. *Mandala Symbolism*. Princeton, N.J.: Princeton University Press.

Jung, C.G., 1969g [1948]. "General Aspects of Dream Psychology." in *The Structure and Dynamics of the Psyche*. Princeton, NJ: Princeton University Press, pp. 237-280 (Collected Works No. 8).

Jung, C.G., 1969h [1948]. "The Psychological Foundation of the Belief in Sprits." in *The Structure and Dynamics of the Psyche*. Princeton, NJ: Princeton University Press, pp. 301-318 (Collected Works No. 8).

Jung, C.G., 1969i [1952]. "Synchronicity: An Acausal Connecting Principle." in *The Structure and Dynamics of the Psyche*. Princeton, NJ: Princeton University Press, pp. 417-519 (Collected Works No. 8)

Jung, C.G., 1969j [1948]. "On Psychic Energy." in *The Structure and Dynamics of the Psyche*. Princeton, NJ: Princeton University Press, pp. 3-66 (Collected Works No. 8).

Jung, C.G., 1970 [1955/56]. *Mysterium Coniunctionis: An Inquiry into the Separation and Synthesis of Psychic Opposites in Alchemy*. Princeton, NJ: Princeton University Press (Collected Works No. 14).

Jung, C.G., 1971. *Psychological Types*. Princeton, N.J.: Princeton University Press (Collected Works No. 6).

Jung, C.G., 1974. *Dreams*. Princeton, N.J.: Princeton University Press.

Jung, C.G., 1990. *The Undiscovered Self*. Princeton, N.J.: Princeton University Press.

Jung, C.G., 1997. *Jung on Active Imagination* (edited by Joan Chodorow). Princeton, NJ: Princeton University Press.

Jung, C.G., 2009. *The Red Book: Liber Novus*. New York: Norton.

Kaiser, F., 1978. "Coherent Oscillations in Biological Systems. Parts I and II." *Z. Naturforsch* 33a:294-304, 418-431.

Kahan, Tracey L., Stephen LaBerge and Lynne Levitan, 1997. "Similarities and Differences between Dreaming and Waking Cognition: An Exploratory Study." *Consciousness and Cognition* 6:132-147.

Kahn, David, 2007. "Metacognition, Recognition, and Reflection while Dreaming." in Deirdre Barrett and Patrick McNamara (eds), *Biological Aspects*, Volume 1 of The *New Science of Dreaming*. Westport CT: Praeger, pp. 245-268.

Kalsched, Donald, 1996. *The Inner World of Trauma: Archetypal Defenses of the Personal Spirit*. New York: Routledge.

Kandinsky, Wassily, 1977 [1914]. *Concerning the Spiritual in Art*. New York: Dover.

Kandinsky, Wassily, 1982. *Kandinsky: Complete Writings on Art*. Volume 2 (1922-1943). Boston: G.K. Hall.

Kappeler, Peter M. and Joan B. Silk (eds), 2010. *Mind the Gap: Tracing the Origins of Human Universals*. Berlin: Springer-Verlag.

Kassam, Aneesa, 1999. "On Becoming an Oromo Anthropologist: Dream, Self and Ritual Three Interpretations." *Anthropology of Consciousness* 10(2-3):1-12.

Katz, L.C. and C. J. Shatz, 1996. "Synaptic Activity and the Construction of Cortical Circuits." *Science* 274:1133-1138.

Katz, Richard, 1982. *Boiling Energy: Community Healing Among the Kalahari Kung*. Cambridge, MA: Harvard University Press.

Katz, Solomon H., 1990. "An Evolutionary Theory of Cuisine." *Human Nature* 1(3):233-259.

Kellogg, E.W., 1997 "Mutual Lucid Dream Event." *Dream Time* 14(2):32-34.

Kempf, Wolfgang and Elfriede Hermann, 2003. "Dreamscapes: Transcending the Local in Initiation Rites Among the Ngaing of Papua New Guinea." in R. I. Lohmann (ed), *Dream Travelers: Sleep Experiences and Culture in the Western Pacific.* New York: Palgrave, pp. 61–86.

Kennedy, John G. and L.L. Langness, 1981. "Introduction." *Ethos* (special issue on dreaming) 9(4):249-257.

Kilborne, Benjamin, 1981. "Pattern, Structure, and Style in Anthropological Studies of Dreams." *Ethos* 9(2):165-185.

Kilborne, Benjamin, 1990. "Ancient and Native Peoples' Dreams." in Stanley Krippner (ed), *Dreamtime and Dreamwork: Decoding the Language of the Night.* Los Angeles: Tarcher, pp. 194-213.

Kilborne, Benjamin, 1992. "On Classifying Dreams." in Barbara Tedlock (ed), *Dreaming: Anthropological and Psychological Interpretations.* Cambridge: Cambridge University Press, pp. 171-193.

Kilbride, Philip K., 1973. "Modernization and the Structure of Dream Narratives Among the Baganda." in M. Robbins and P.K. Kilbride (eds), *Psycho-Cultural Change in Modern Buganda. Nkanga 7,* Kampala: Makerere Institute of Social Research.

King, Philip, Bernard Welt and Kelly Bulkeley, 2011. *Dreaming in the Classroom: Practices, Methods, and Resources in Dream Education.* Albany, NY: State University of New York Press.

Kirsch, Thomas B., 2000. *The Jungians: A Comparative and Historical Perspective.* London: Routledge.

Kirtsoglou, Elisabeth, 2010. "Dreaming the Self: A Unified Approach towards Dreams, Subjectivity and the Radical Imagination." *History and Anthropology* 21(3):321–335.

Klein, Stephen B. and B. Michael Thorne, 2007. *Biological Psychology.* New York: Worth.

Kleitman, Nathaniel, 1963. *Sleep and Wakefulness.* Chicago: University of Chicago Press.

Kleitman, Nathaniel, 1969. "Basic Rest-Activity Cycle in Relation to Sleep and Wakefulness." in A. Kales (ed), *Sleep: Physiology and Pathology.* Philadelphia: Lippincott.

Kluger, H.Y., 1975. "Archetypal Dreams and 'Everyday' Dreams: A Statistical Investigation into Jung's Theory of the Collective Unconscious." *The Israel Annals of Psychiatry and Related Disciplines* 13(1):6-47.

Knutson, Kristen L., Karine Spiegel, Plamen Penev and Eve Van Cauter, 2007. "The Metabolic Consequences of Sleep Deprivation." *Sleep Medicine Reviews* 11(3):163-178.

Koch, Christof, 2004. *The Quest for Consciousness: A Neurobiological Approach.* Englewood, CO: Roberts.

Kockelmans, J.J., 1967. *Phenomenology: The Philosophy of Edmund Husserl.* Garden City, New York: Doubleday.

Koepping, Klaus-Peter, 1983. *Adolf Bastian and the Psychic Unity of Mankind: The Foundations of Anthropology in Nineteenth Century Germany.* St. Lucia: University of Queensland Press.

Koepping, Klaus-Peter, 2007. Bastian and Lévi-Strauss: From 'Entelechy' to 'Entropy' as 'Scientific' Metaphors for Cultural Teleologies." in Manuela Fischer, Peter Bolz, Susan Kamel and Emily Schalk (eds), *Adolf Bastian and His Universal Archive of Humanity: The Origins of German Anthropology.* Zürich: Georg Ohms, pp. 23-31.

Kohl, Johann Georg, 2009 [1860]. *Kitchi-Gami: Wanderings Round Lake Superior.* General Books.

Kohler, M., 1941. *The Izangoma Diviners.* Pretoria: Union of South Africa Government Printer.

Kohut, Heinz, 1971. *The Analysis of the Self.* New York: International Universities Press.

Kohut, Heinz, 1977. *The Restoration of the Self.* New York: International Universities Press.

Kohut, Heinz and Ernest S. Wolf, 1978. "The Disorders of the Self and Their Treatment: An Outline." *International Journal of Psychoanalysis* 59:413-425.

Kortooms, Toine, 2002. *Phenomenology of Time: Edmund Husserl's Analysis of Time-Consciousness.* Dortrecht: Kluwer.

Korzeniewski, Bernard, 2011. *From Neurons to Self-Consciousness: How the Brain Generates the Mind.* Amherst, NY: Humanity Books.

Kosslyn, Stephen M., 1994. *Image and Brain: The Resolution of the Imagery Debate.* Cambridge, MA: MIT Press.

Kottak, Conrad, 2008. *Anthropology: The Exploration of Human Diversity.* New York: McGraw-Hill.

Kracke, Waud H., 1979. "Dreaming in Kagwahiv: Dream Beliefs and Their Psychic Uses in an Amazonian Indian Culture." *Psychoanalytic Study of Society* 8:119-171.

Kracke, Waud H., 1991. "Languages of Dreaming: Anthropological Approaches to the Study of Dreaming in Other Cultures." in Jayne Gackenbach and Anees A, Sheikh (eds), *Dream Images: A Call to Mental Arms.* Amityville, NY: Baywood, pp. 203-224.

Kracke, Waud H., 1992. "Myths in Dreams, Thought in Images: An Amazonian Contribution to the Psychoanalytic Theory of Primary Process." in Barbara Tedlock (ed), *Dreaming: Anthropological and Psychological Interpretations.* Cambridge: Cambridge University Press, pp. 31-54.

Kracke, Waud H., 2003. "Dream: Ghost of a Tiger, A System of Human Words." in Jeannette Marie Mageo (ed), *Dreaming and the Self: New Perspectives on Subjectivity, Identity, and Emotion.* Albany, NY: State University of New York Press, pp. 155-164.

Kreitler, Shulamith and Hans Kreitler, 1989. "Horizontal Decalage: A Problem and Its Solution." *Cognitive Development* 4(1):89-119.

Krige, Eileen Jenson, 1965. *The Social System of the Zulus.* Pietermaritzburg, South Africa: Shuter and Shooter.

Krippner, Stanley (ed), 1990a. *Dreamtime and Dreamwork: Decoding the Language of the Night.* Los Angeles: Tarcher.

Krippner, Stanley, 1990b. "Tribal Shamans and Their Travels into Dreamtime." in Stanley Krippner (ed), *Dreamtime and Dreamwork: Decoding the Language of the Night.* Los Angeles: Tarcher, pp. 185-193.

Krippner, Stanley, 1993. "The Maimonides ESP-Dream Studies." *Journal of Parapsychology* 57:39-53.

Krippner, Stanley, 1994. "Waking Life, Dream Life, and the Construction of Reality." *Anthropology of Consciousness* 5(3):17-23.

Krippner, Stanley, 1997. "The Role Played by Mandalas in Navajo and Tibetan Rituals." *Anthropology of Consciousness* 8(1):2-31.

Krippner, Stanley, 2001. "Introduction to Third Edition." in Ullman, Montague, Stanley Krippner and Alan Vaughan (eds), *Dream Telepathy: Experiments in Nocturnal Extrasensory Perception.* Charlottesville, VA: Hampton Roads, p. xix-xxiv.

Krippner, Stanley, 2002. "Conflicting Perspectives on Shamans and Shamanism: Points and Counterpoints." *American Psychologist* 57(11):962-977.

Krippner, Stanley, Fabiba Bogzaran and André Percia de Carvalho, 2002. *Extraordinary Dreams and How to Work with Them.* Albany, NY: State University of New York Press.

Krippner, Stanley and Allan Combs, 2002. "The Neurophenomenology of Shamanism." *Journal of Consciousness Studies* 9(3):77–82.

Krippner, Stanley and Joseph Dillard , 1988. *Dreamworking: How to Use Your Dreams for Creative Problem Solving.* New York: Bearly Books.

Krippner, Stanley and Laura Faith, 2001. "Exotic Dreams: A Cross-Cultural Study." *Dreaming* 11(2):73-82.

Krippner, Stanley and Cheryl Fracasso, 2011. "Dreams, Telepathy, and Various States of Consciousness." *NeuroQuantology: An Interdisciplinary Journal of Neuroscience and Quantum Physics* (Special issue on *Dreams, Telepathy and Various States of Consciousness*) 9(1). [and electronic journal available at: http://www.neuroquantology.com/]

Krippner, Stanley and Harris L. Friedman (eds), 2010. *Debating Psychic Experience: Human Potential or Human Illusion*. Santa Barbara, CA: Praeger.

Krippner, Stanley and April Thompson, 1996. "A 10-Facet Model of Dreaming Applied to Dream Practices of Sixteen Native American Cultural Groups." *Dreaming* 6(2):71-96.

Kroeber, Alfred L., 1902/1907. *The Arapaho*. American Museum of Natural History, Bulletin 18:i-xiv, 1-229, 279-466.

Kroeber. Alfred L., 1917. "The Superorganic." *American Anthropologist* 19:163-213.

Kroeber, Alfred L., 1952. *The Nature of Culture*. Chicago: University of Chicago Press.

Kroeber, Alfred L. and Clyde Kluckhohn, 1952. "Culture: A Critical Review of Concepts and Definitions." *Papers of the Peabody Museum of American Archaeology and Ethnology* 65.

Kruger, Steven, 2005. *Dreaming in the Middle Ages*. Cambridge: Cambridge University Press.

Kruger, Y., 1985. "Archetypal Dreams and "Everyday" Dreams." *The Israel Annals of Psychiatry and Related Disciplines* 13(1): 6-47.

Kryger, M.H., T. Roth and W.C. Dement (eds), 2011. *Principles and Practice of Sleep Medicine*, 4th edition. Philadelphia: Elsevier.

Kuba, Michael J., Ruth A. Byrne, Daniela V. Meisel and Jennifer A. Mather, 2006. "When Do Octopuses Play? Effects of Repeated Testing, Object Type, Age, and Food Deprivation on Object Play in *Octopus vulgaris*." *Journal of Comparative Psychology* 120(3):184–190.

Kuiken, Don and Shelley Sikora, 1993. "The Impact of Dreams on Waking Thoughts and Feelings." in Allan Moffitt, Milton Kramer and Robert Hoffman (eds), *The Function of Dreaming*. Albany, NY: State University of New York Press, pp. 419-476.

Kunzendorf, Robert G., 2007. "'Symbolic' Images in Dreams and Daydreams." in Deirdre Barrett and Patrick McNamara (eds), *Cultural and Theoretical Perspectives*, Volume 3 of The *New Science of Dreaming*. Westport CT: Praeger, pp. 155-170.

Kuper, Adam, 1979. "A Structural Approach to Dreams." *Man* (NS) 14(4):645-662.

Kuper, Adam, 1983. "The Structure of Dream Sequences." *Culture, Medicine and Psychiatry* 7:153-175.

Kuper, Adam, 1986. "Structural Anthropology and the Psychology of Dreams." *Journal of Mind and Behavior* 7(2-3):333-344.

Kuper, Adam and A.A. Stone, 1982. "The Dream of Irma's Injection: A Structural Analysis." *American Journal of Psychiatry* 139:1225-1234.

Kushida, Clete A., 2005. *Sleep Deprivation: Basic Science, Physiology and Behavior*. New York: Marcel Dekker.

Kuznar, Lawrence A., 2008. *Reclaiming a Scientific Anthropology* (second edition). London: Altimira Press.

La Barre, Weston, 1980. *Culture in Context: Selected Writings of Weston La Barre*. Durham, NC: Duke University Press.

LaBerge, Stephen, 1980. "Lucid Dreaming as a Learnable Skill: A Case Study." *Perception and Motor Skills* 51:1039-1042.

LaBerge, Stephen, 1985. *Lucid Dreaming*. Los Angeles: Tarcher.

LaBerge, Stephen, 1990. "Lucid Dreaming: Psychophysiological Studies of Consciousness during REM Sleep." in R.R. Bootzen, J.F. Kihlstrom, and D.L. Schacter (eds), *Sleep and Cognition.* Washington, D.C.: American Psychological Association (pp. 109-126).

LaBerge, Stephen, 1994. "The Stuff of Dreams." *Anthropology of Consciousness* 5(3):28-30.

LaBerge, Stephen, 2003. "Lucid Dreaming and the Yoga of the Dream State: A Psychological Perspective." in Alan B. Wallace (ed), *Buddhism & Science: Breaking New Ground.* Columbia Series in Science and Religion. New York: Columbia University Press.

LaBerge, Stephen, 2009. *Lucid Dreaming: A Concise Guide to Awakening in Your Dreams and in Your Life.* Boulder, CO: Sounds True.

LaBerge, Stephen, 2010. "Signal-Verfied Lucid Dreaming Proves that REM Sleep Can Support Reflective Consciousness." *International Journal of Dream Research* 3(1):26-27.

LaBerge, Stephen and Donald J. DeGracia, 2000. "Varieties of Lucid Dreaming Experience." in R.G. Kunzendorf and B. Wallace (eds), *Individual Differences in Conscious Experience.* Amsterdam: John Benjamins, pp. 269-307.

LaBerge, Stephen and Jayne Gackenbach, 1987. "At Home Research Project: Lucid Dreaming Exercises and Questionnaire." *Lucidity Letter* 6(1).

LaBerge, Stephen, Lynne Levitan and William C. Dement, 1986. "Lucid Dreaming: Physiological Correlates of Consciousness During REM Sleep." *Journal of Mind and Behavior* 7(2-3):251-258.

LaBerge, Stephen, L. Nagel, W. Dement and V. Zarcone, 1981. "Lucid Dreaming Verified by Volitional Communication During REM Sleep." *Perceptual and Motor Skills* 52:727-732.

LaBerge, Stephen and H. Rheingold, 1990. *Exploring the World of Lucid Dreaming.* New York: Ballantine.

LaHood, Gregg, 2007. "One Hundred Years of Sacred Science: Participation and Hybridity in Transpersonal Anthropology." *Re-Vision* 29(3):37-48.

Laland, Kevin N. and Bennett G. Galef (eds), 2009. *The Question of Animal Culture.* Cambridge, MA: Harvard University Press.

Lang, Andrew, 1897. *The Book of Dreams and Ghosts.* London. Longmans.

Lang, Andrew, 1909. *The Making of Religion* London: Longmans, Green and Co.

Lather, Patti, 2001. "Postmodernism, Post-Structuralism and Post(Critical) Ethnography: Of Ruins, Aporias and Angels." in Paul Atkinson, Amanda Coffey, Sara Delamont, John Lofland and Lyn Lofland (eds), *Handbook of Ethnography.* New York: Sage, pp. 477-492.

Laughlin, Charles D., 1972. "*Kenisan*: The Economic and Social Ramifications of the Ghost Cult Among the So of Northeastern Uganda." *Africa* 42(1):9-20.

Laughlin, Charles D., 1988. "The Prefrontosensorial Polarity Principle: Toward a Neurophenomenology of Intentionality." *Biology Forum* 81 (2): 243-260; Japanese version in *Foundation of Structuralist Biology* (ed. by K. Ikeda). Tokyo: Kaimeisha.

Laughlin, Charles D., 1989. "Transpersonal Anthropology: Some Methodological Issues." *Western Canadian Anthropologist* 5:29-60.

Laughlin, Charles D., 1991. "Pre- and Perinatal Brain Development and Enculturation: A Biogenetic Structural Approach." *Human Nature* 2(3), 171-213.

Laughlin, Charles D., 1992. "Time, Intentionality, and a Neurophenomenology of the Dot." *The Anthropology of Consciousness* 3(3-4): 14-27.

Laughlin, Charles D., 1993. "Fuzziness and Phenomenology in Ethnological Research: Insights from Fuzzy Set Theory." *Journal of Anthropological Research* 49(1): 17-37.

Laughlin, Charles D., 1994a. "Transpersonal Anthropology, Then and Now." *Transpersonal Review* 1(1):7-10.

Laughlin, Charles D., 1994b. "Psychic Energy and Transpersonal Experience: A Biogenetic Structural Account of the Tibetan Dumo Practice." in David E. Young & Jean-Guy Goulet (eds), *Being Changed by Cross-Cultural Encounters*. Peterborough, Ontario: Broadview Press, pp. 99-134.

Laughlin, Charles D. 1994c. "Apodicticity: The Problem of Absolute Certainty in Transpersonal Anthropology." *Anthropology and Humanism* 19(2): 1-15.

Laughlin, Charles D., 1996. "Archetypes, Neurognosis and the Quantum Sea." *Journal of Scientific Exploration* 10(3):375-400.

Laughlin, Charles D., 1997a. "The Nature of Intuition: A Neuropsychological Approach." in Robbie E. Davis-Floyd and P. Sven Arvidson (eds), *Intuition: The Inside Story*. New York: Routledge, Pp. 19-37.

Laughlin, Charles D., 1997b. "Body, Brain, and Behavior: The Neuroanthropology of the Body Image." *Anthropology of Consciousness* 8(2-3):49-68.

Laughlin, Charles D., 1997c. "The Cycle of Meaning: Some Methodological Implications of Biogenetic Structural Theory." in S. Glazier (Ed.), *Anthropology of Religion: Handbook of Theory and Method*. Westport, CT: Greenwood Press, pp. 471-488.

Laughlin, Charles D., 2001. "Mandalas, Nixies, Goddesses, and Succubi: A Transpersonal Anthropologist Looks at the Anima." *International Journal of Transpersonal Studies* 20:33-52.

Laughlin, Charles D., 2004a. "Art and Spirit: Brain, the Navajo Concept of Hozho, and Kandinsky's 'Inner Necessity'." *International Journal of Transpersonal Studies* 23: 1-20.

Laughlin, Charles D., 2004b. "Navajo Shamanism." in Mariko Namba Walker & Eva Jane Neumann Fridman (eds), *Shamanism: An Encyclopedia of World Beliefs, Practices, and Culture*, Vol. I. Santa Barbara, CA: ABC-CLIO, pp. 318-323.

Laughlin, Charles D. and Elizabeth Allgeier, 1979. *An Ethnography of the So of Northeastern Uganda*, (2 vols.). New Haven: HRAF Press.

Laughlin, Charles D. and Eugene G. d'Aquili, 1974. *Biogenetic Structuralism*. New York: Columbia University Press.

Laughlin, Charles D. and Johannes H.N. Loubser, 2010. "Neurognosis, the Development of Neural Models, and the Study of the Ancient Mind." *Time & Mind* 3(2):135-158.

Laughlin, Charles D. and John McManus, 1982. "The Biopsychological Determinants of Play and Games," in R.M. Pankin (ed), *Social Approaches to Sport*. New York: Fairleigh Dickinson University Press.

Laughlin, Charles D. and John McManus, 1995. "The Relevance of the Radical Empiricism of William James to the Anthropology of Consciousness." *Anthropology of Consciousness* 6(3):34-46.

Laughlin, Charles D., John McManus and Eugene G. d'Aquili, 1990. *Brain, Symbol and Experience: Toward a Neurophenomenology of Consciousness*. New York: Columbia University Press.

Laughlin, Charles D., John McManus and Jon Shearer, 1983. "Dreams, Trance and Visions: What a Transpersonal Anthropology Might Look Like." *Phoenix: The Journal of Transpersonal Anthropology* 7(1/2):141-159.

Laughlin, Charles D., John McManus and Jon Shearer, 1993. "Transpersonal Anthropology." in R. Walsh and F. Vaughan (eds), *Paths Beyond Ego: The Transpersonal Vision*. Los Angeles, CA: Tarcher, pp. 190-195

Laughlin, Charles D., John McManus and C.D. Stephens, 1981. "A Model of Brain and Symbol." *Semiotica* 33(3/4): 211-236.

Laughlin, Charles D., John McManus and Mark Webber, 1984. "Neurognosis, Individuation, and Tibetan Arising Yoga Practice." *Phoenix: The Journal of Transpersonal Anthropology*

8(1/2):91-106.

Laughlin, Charles D., John McManus, Robert A. Rubinstein and Jon Shearer, 1986. "The Ritual Control of Experience." in Norman K. Denzin (ed), *Studies in Symbolic Interaction* (Part A). Greenwich, Conn.: JAI Press.

Laughlin, Charles D. and C. Jason Throop, 1999. "Emotion: A View from Biogenetic Structuralism." in A.L. Hinton (ed), *Biocultural Approaches to the Emotions*. Cambridge: Cambridge University Press, pp. 329-363.

Laughlin, Charles D. and C. Jason Throop, 2001. "Imagination and Reality: On the Relations Between Myth, Consciousness, and the Quantum Sea." *Zygon* 36(4):709-736.

Laughlin, Charles D. and C. Jason Throop, 2006. "Cultural Neurophenomenology: Integrating Experience, Culture and Reality Through Fisher Information." *Journal Culture & Psychology* 12(3): 305-337.

Laughlin, Charles D. and C. Jason Throop, 2008. "Continuity, Causation and Cyclicity: A Cultural Neurophenomenology of Time-Consciousness." *Time & Mind* 1(2): 159-186.

Laughlin, Charles D. and C. Jason Throop, 2009. "Husserlian Meditations and Anthropological Reflections: Toward a Cultural Neurophenomenology of Experience and Reality." *Anthropology of Consciousness* 20(2):130-170.

Laughlin, Robert M., 1976. *Of Wonders Wild and New: Dreams from Zinacantán*. Washington, DC: Smithsonian Contributions to Anthropology No. 22.

Lavie, Peretz and Orna Tzischinsky, 1985. "Cognitive Asymmetry and Dreaming: Lack of Relationship." *The American Journal of Psychology* 98(3):353-361.

Lazell, J. D., and N.C. Spitzer, 1977. "Apparent Play in an American Alligator." *Copeia* 1977(1): 188-189.

Lecours, André Roch and Yves Joanette, 1980. "Linguistic and Other Psychological Aspects of Paroxysmal Aphasia." *Brain and Language* 10(1):1-23.

Lederman, Carol, 1988. "Wayward Winds: Malay Archetypes, and Theory of Personality in the Context of Shamanism." *Social Science and Medicine* 27(8):799-810.

Lederman, Carol, 1991. *Taming the Wind of Desire: Psychology, Medicine and Aesthetics in Malay Shamanistic Performance*. Berkeley: University of California Press.

LeDoux, Joseph, 2003. *Synaptic Self: How Our Brains Become Who We Are*. New York: Penguin.

Lee, Shirley, 1980. "Association for Transpersonal Anthropology." *Phoenix: The Journal of Transpersonal Anthropology* 4 (1 and 2): 2-6.

Lee, S.G., 1958. "Social Influence in Zulu Dreaming." *Journal of Social Psychology* 47:265-283.

Leong, F., 2009. *Beginners Guide To Lucid Dreaming Techniques - Everything You Need To Know To Be Able To Choose What You Do In Your Dream!* Amazon.com Kindle digital book.

Lett, James, 1997. *Science, Reason, and Anthropology: The Principle of Rational Inquiry*. New York: Rowman & Littlefield.

Levine, Julia, 1991. "The Role of Culture in the Representation of Conflict in Dreams : A Comparison of Bedouin, Irish, and Israeli Children." *Journal of Cross-Cultural Psychology* 22: 472-490.

LeVine, Robert A. (ed), 1966. *Dreams and Deeds: Achievement Motivation in Nigeria*. Chicago: University of Chicago Press.

LeVine, Sarah, 1981. "Dreams of the Informant About the Researcher: Some Difficulties Inherent in the Research Relationships." *Ethos* 9(4):276-293.

LeVine, Sarah, 1982. "The Dreams of Young Gusii Women: A Content Analysis." *Ethnology*

21(1):63-77.

Lévi-Strauss, Claude, 1963. "The Sorcerer and His Magic." in *Structural Anthropology*, Vol. 1. London: Peregrine, Chap. 9.

Lévi-Strauss, Claude, 1964. *Mythologiques: Le Cru et le Cuit*. Paris: Plon.

Levitan, L., S. LaBerge, D.J. DeGracia, and P.G. Zimbardo, 1999. "Out-of-Body Experiences," Dreams, and REM sleep." *Sleep and Hypnosis* 1(3):186-196.

Levtzion, Nehemia, 1979. *Conversion to Islam*. New York: Holmes and Meier.

Levy, J., 1972. "Lateral Specialization of the Human Brain: Behavioral Manifestations and Possible Evolutionary Basis." in J.A. Kiger (ed), *The Biology of Behavior*. Corvallis: Oregon State University Press.

Levy-Agresti, J. and Roger W. Sperry, 1968. "Differential Perceptual Capacities in Major and Minor Hemispheres." *Proceedings of the National Academy of Science* 61:1151-1154.

Levy-Bruhl, Lucien., 1923. *Primitive Mentality* (1966 edition). Boston: Beacon Press.

Lewis-Williams, J.D., 1987. "A Dream of Eland: An Unexplored Component of San Shamanism and Rock Art." *World Archaeology* 19(2):165-177.

Lewis-Williams, J.D., 2002. *A Cosmos In Stone: Interpreting Religion and Society Through Rock Art*. Lanham, MD: AltaMira.

Lewis-Williams, J.D. and T. A. Dowson, 1988. "The Signs of All Times: Entoptic Phenomena in Upper Paleolithic Art." *Current Anthropology* 29(2):201-245.

Lex, Barbara W., 1979. "The Neurobiology of Ritual Trance." in Eugene G. d'Aquili, Charles D. Laughlin and John McManus (eds), *The Spectrum of Ritual*. New York: Columbia University Press.

Lifton, Robert Jay, 1971. "Protean Man." *Archives of General Psychology* 24(4):298-304.

Lim, J. and D.F. Dinges, 2008. "Sleep Deprivation and Vigilant Attention." *Annals of the New York Academy of Sciences* 1129:305–322.

Lincoln, J.S. 1935. *The Dream in Primitive Culture*. London: Cresset.

Linnekin, Jocelyn and Lin Poyer, 1990. *Cultural Identity and Ethnicity in the Pacific*. Honolulu, HI: University of Hawaii Press.

Littlefield, Richard and David Neumeyer, 1992. "Rewriting Schenker: Narrative-History-Ideology." *Music Theory Spectrum* 14(1):38-65.

Littlewood, Roland, 2004. "From Elsewhere: Prophetic Visions and Dreams among the People of the Earth." in Stewart, Charles (ed), *Anthropological Approaches to Dreaming*, Special issue. *Dreaming* 14(2-3):94-106.

Llinás, Rodolfo R., 2001. *I of the Vortex: From Neurons to Self*. Cambridge, MA: MIT Press.

Locke, Ralph G. and Edward F. Kelly, 1985. "A Preliminary Model for the Cross-Cultural Analysis of Altered States of Consciousness." *Ethos* 13(1):3-55.

Lockwood, Michael, 1989. *Mind, Brain and the Quantum*. Oxford: Basil Blackwell.

Lohmann, Roger Ivar, 2000. "The Role of Dreams in Religious Enculturation Among the Asabano of Papua New Guinea." *Ethos* 28(1):75–102.

Lohmann, Roger Ivar (ed), 2003a. *Dream Travelers: Sleep Experiences and Culture in the Western Pacific*. New York: Palgrave.

Lohmann, Roger Ivar, 2003b. "Introduction: Dream Travels and Anthropology." in Roger Ivar Lohmann (ed), *Dream Travelers: Sleep Experiences and Culture in the Western Pacific*. New York: Palgrave, pp. 1-17.

Lohmann, Roger Ivar, 2004. "Dreams and Shamanism (Papua New Guinea)." in Mariko Namba Walters and Eva Jane Neumann Fridman (eds), *Shamanism: An Encyclopedia of World Beliefs, Practices, and Cultures* (2 volumes). Santa Barbara, CA: ABC-CLIO,

Volume 2, pp. 865-869.

Lohmann, Roger Ivar, 2007. "Dreams and Ethnography." in Deirdre Barrett and Patrick McNamara (eds), *Cultural and Theoretical Perspectives,* Volume 3 of The *New Science of Dreaming.* Westport CT: Praeger, pp. 35-70.

Lohmann, Roger Ivar, 2010. "How Evaluating Dreams Makes History: Asabano Examples." *History and Anthropology* 21(3):227-249.

Long, Joseph K. (Ed), 1977. *Extrasensory Ecology: Parapsychology and Anthropology.* Metuchen, NJ: Scarecrow.

Lonsdorf, Elizabeth V., Stephen R. Ross and Tetsuro Matsuzawa, 2010. *The Chimpanzee Mind: Ecological and Experimental Perspectives.* Chicago: University of Chicago Press.

Lorand, Sandor, 1974. "Dream Interpretation in the Talmud (Babylonian and Graeco-Roman Period)." in Ralph L. Woods and Herbert B. Greenhouse (eds), *The New World of Dreams.* New York: Macmillan, pp. 150-158.

Low, Philip Steven, Sylvan S. Shank, Terrence J. Sejnowski, and Daniel Margoliash, 2008. "Mammalian-Like Features of Sleep Structure in Zebra Finches." *Proceedings of the National Academy of Sciences* (USA) 105(26):9081-9086.

Low, Setha M., 1994. "Embodied Metaphors: Nerves As Lived Experience." in Thomas Csordas (ed), *Embodiment and Experience: The Existential Ground of Culture and Self.* Cambridge: Cambridge University Press, pp. 139-162.

Lowie, Robert H., 1915. "The Sun Dance of the Crow Indians." *Anthropological Papers of the American Museum of Natural History* 16:1-50.

Lumpkin, Tara W., 2001. "Perceptual Diversity: Is Polyphasic Consciousness Necessary for Global Survival?" *Anthropology of Consciousness* 12(1 -2):37-7O

Lutz, Antoine, John D. Dunne and Richard J. Davidson, 2007. "Meditation and the Neuroscience of Consciousness." in P. D. Zelazo, M. Moscovitch, & E. Thompson (eds), *Cambridge Handbook of Consciousness.* New York: Cambridge University Press.

Lyon, Margot L., 1995. "Missing Emotion: The Limitations of Cultural Constructivism in the Study of Emotion." *Cultural Anthropology* 10(2):244-263.

MacDonald, George F., John Cove, Charles D. Laughlin and John McManus, 1988. "Mirrors, Portals and Multiple Realities." *Zygon* 23(4):39-64.

Mack, John E., 1970. *Nightmares and Human Conflict.* Boston: Little, Brown.

Mack, John E., 1995. *Abduction: Human Encounters with Aliens.* New York: Ballantine Books.

MacKenzie, Vicki, 1998. *Cave in the Snow: Tenzim Palmo's Quest for Enlightenment.* New York: Bloomsbury.

Magallón, Linda Lane and Barbara Shor, 1990. "Sharing Dreaming: Joining Together in Dreamtime." in Stanley Krippner (ed), *Dreamtime and Dreamwork: Decoding the Language of the Night.* Los Angeles: Tarcher, pp. 252-260.

Mageo, Jeannette Marie, 2001. "Dream Play and Discovering Cultural Psychology." *Ethos* 29:187–217.

Mageo, Jeannette Marie (ed), 2002. *Power and the Self* (Publications of the Society for Psychological Anthropology). Cambridge: Cambridge University Press.

Mageo, Jeannette Marie (ed), 2003a. *Dreaming and the Self: New Perspectives on Subjectivity, Identity, and Emotion.* Albany, NY: State University of New York Press.

Mageo, Jeannette Marie, 2003b. "Theorizing Dreaming and the Self." in Jeannette Marie Mageo (ed), *Dreaming and the Self: New Perspectives on Subjectivity, Identity, and Emotion.* Albany, NY: State University of New York Press, pp. 3-22.

Mageo, Jeannette Marie, 2003c. "Subjectivity and Identity in Dreams." in Jeannette Marie Mageo (ed), *Dreaming and the Self: New Perspectives on Subjectivity, Identity, and Emotion.* Albany, NY: State University of New York Press, pp. 23-40.

Mageo, Jeannette Marie, 2004. "Toward a Holographic Theory of Dreaming." *Dreaming* 4(2–3):151–169

Mageo, Jeannette Marie, 2006. "Figurative Dream Analysis and U.S. Traveling Identities." *Ethos* 34(4): 456–487.

Mageo, Jeannette Marie and Alan Howard (eds), 1996. *Spirits in Culture, History, and Mind*. New York: Routledge.

Magoun, H. W., 1952. "An Ascending Reticular Activating System in the Brain Stem." *Ama Archives of Neurology and Psychiatry* 67(2):145–154.

Malamud, J.R.,1979. *The development of a training method for the cultivation of "lucid" awareness in fantasy, dreams, and waking life* (doctoral dissertation). Ann Arbor, Michigan: University Microfilms International, Order No. 8010380.

Malinowski, Bronislaw, 1927. *Sex and Repression in Savage Society*. New York: Harcourt-Brace.

Malinowski, Bronislaw, 1987 [1929]. *The Sexual Life of Savages*. Boston, MA: Beacon Press.

Mannheim, Bruce, 1992. "A Semiotic of Andean Dreams." in Barbara Tedlock (ed), *Dreaming: Anthropological and Psychological Interpretations*. Cambridge: Cambridge University Press, pp. 132-153.

Maguet, Jacques, 1971. *Introduction to Aesthetic Anthropology*. New York: Addison-Wesley Module.

Maguet, Jacques. 1986, *The Aesthetic Experience*. New Haven: Yale University Press.

Marcus, Hazel R. and Shinobu Kitayama, 1991. "Culture and the Self: Implications for Cognition, Emotion, and Motivation." *Psychological Review* 98(2):224-253.

Marjasch, Sonja, 1966. "On the Dream Psychology of C.G. Jung." in G.E. von Grunebaum and R. Caillois (eds), *The Dream and Human Societies*. Berkeley: University of California Press, pp. 145-161.

Massé, H., 1938. *Croyances et coutumes persanes (Persian Beliefs and Customs)*. Paris: Librairie Orientale et Americaine.

Matsuzuwa, Tetsuro, 2010. "The Chimpanzee Mind: Bridging Fieldwork and Experimental Work." in Elizabeth V. Lonsdorf, Stephen R. Ross and Tetsuro Matsuzawa (eds), *The Mind of the Chimpanzee: Ecological and Experimental Perspectives*. Chicago, IL: University of Chicago Press, pp. 1-19.

Mattoon, M.A., 1978. *Applied Dream Analysis: A Jungian Approach*. Washington: Wilson and sons.

Mauss, Marcel, 1969 [1924]. *The Gift*. London: Cohen and West.

Mavromatis, Andreas, 2010[1987]. *Hypnagogia: The Unique State of Consciousness between Wakefulness and Sleep*. London: Thyrsos.

McCauley, Robert N. and E. Thomas Lawson, 1984. "Functionalism Reconsidered." *History of Religions* 23(4):372-381.

McClelland, J.L. and D.E. Rumelhart (eds), 1986. *Parallel Distributed Processing*, Vol 2: *Psychological and Biological Models*. Cambridge, MA: MIT Press.

McCormick, L. et al., 1997. "REM Sleep Dream Mentation in Right Hemispherectomized Patients." *Neuropsychologia* 35(5):695-701.

McGilchrist, Iain, 2009. *The Master and His Emissary: The Divided Brain and the Making of the Modern World*. New Haven, CT: Yale University Press.

McGrew, W.C., 2010. "New Theaters of Conflict in the Animal Culture Wars: Recent Findings from Chimpanzees." in Elizabeth V. Lonsdorf, Stephen R. Ross and Tetsuro Matsuzawa (eds), *The Mind of the Chimpanzee: Ecological and Experimental Perspectives*. Chicago, IL: University of Chicago Press, pp. 168-177.

McManus, John, Charles D. Laughlin and Jon Shearer, 1993. "The Function of Dreaming in the Cycles of Cognition." in Allan Moffitt, Milton Kramer and Robert Hoffman (eds), *The Function of Dreaming*. Albany, NY: State University of New York Press, pp. 21-50.

McNamara, Patrick, Jill Clark and Ernest Hartmann, 1998. "Handedness and Dream Content." *Dreaming* 8(1):15-22.

McNamara, Patrick, 2008. *Nightmares: The Science and Solution of Those Frightening Visions during Sleep*. New York: Praeger.

McNamara, Patrick, Deirdre McLaren, Dana Smith, Ariel Brown and Robert Stickgold, 2005. "A "Jekyll and Hyde" Within Aggressive Versus Friendly Interactions in REM and Non-REM Dreams." *Psychological Science* 16(2):130-136.

McNeley, James K., 1981. *Holy Wind in Navajo Philosophy*. Tucson, AR: University of Arizona Press.

Mead, Margaret, 1952. "Some Relationships Between Social Anthropology and Psychiatry." in Franz Alexander and Helen Cross (eds), *Dynamic Psychiatry*. Chicago, IL: University of Chicago Press.

Meggitt, M.J., 1962. "Dream Interpretation Among the Mae Enga of New Guinea." *Southwestern Journal of Anthropology* 18(3):216-229.

Meggitt, M.J., 1965. "The Mae Enga of the Western Highlands." in P. Lawrence and M.J. Meggitt (eds), *Gods Ghosts and Men in Melanesia*. Melbourne: Oxford University Press, pp. 105-131.

Meier, Carl Alfred, 1966. "The Dream in Ancient Greece and Its Use in Temple Cures (Incubation)." in G.E. von Grunebaum and R. Caillois (eds), *The Dream and Human Societies*. Berkeley: University of California Press, pp. 303-320.

Meier, Carl Alfred, 1967. *Ancient Incubation and Modern Psychotherapy*. Evanston, IL: Northwestern University Press.

Meier, Carl Alfred, 2009. *Healing Dream and Ritual: Ancient Incubation and Modern Psychotherapy*. Einsiedeln, Switzerland: Daimon Verlag.

Menzel, Emil W.,1966. "Responsiveness to Objects in Free-ranging Japanese Monkeys." *Behaviour* 26:130–150.

Menzel, Emil W., 1967. "Naturalistic and Experimental Research on Primates." *Human Development* 10: 170-186.

Menzel, Emil W., 1971. "Group Behavior in Young Chimpanzees: Responsiveness To Cumulative Novel Changes in a Large Outdoor Enclosure." *Journal of Comparative and Physiological Psychology* 74:46–51.

Merleau-Ponty, Maurice, 1962. *Phenomenology of Perception*. London: Routledge and Kegan Paul.

Merrill, William, 1992. "The Ramámuri Stereotype of Dreams." in Barbara Tedlock (ed), *Dreaming: Anthropological and Psychological Interpretations*. Cambridge: Cambridge University Press, pp. 194-219.

Mershin, A., D.V. Nanopoulos and E.M.C. Skoulakis, 1999. "Quantum Brain?" *Proceedings of the Academy of Athens* 74A:1-37.

Metzinger, Thomas, 2009. *The Ego Tunnel: The Science of the Mind and the Myth of the Self*. New York: Basic Books.

Michell, J.F., 1979. *Simulacra: Faces and Figures in Nature*. London: Thames & Hudson.

Mill, John S., 1973[1848]. *Principles of Political Economy*. Clifton, NJ: Augustus M. Kelly.

Miller, E.K. and J.D. Cohen, 2001. "An Integrative Theory of Prefrontal Cortex Function." *Annual Review of Neuroscience* 24:167-202.

Miller, G.A., E.H. Galanter and K.H. Pribram, 1960. *Plans and the Structure of Behavior*.

New York: Holt, Rinehart and Winston.

Mineka, S., 1982. "Depression and Helplessness in Primates." in H.E. Fitzgerald, J.A. Mullins and P. Gage (eds), *Child Nurturance*, Vol. 3: *Studies of Development in Nonhuman Primates*. New York: Plenum.

Modesto, Ruby and Guy Mount, 1980. *Not for Innocent Ears: Spiritual Traditions of a Desert Cahuilla Medicine Woman*. Angeles Oaks, CA: Sweetlight.

Moerman, Daniel E., 1979. "Anthropology of Symbolic Healing." *Current Anthropology* 20(1):59-80.

Moerman, Daniel E., 2002a. "Deconstructing the Placebo Effect and Finding the Meaning Response." *Annals of Internal Medicine* 136(6):471-476.

Moerman, Daniel E., 2002b. *Meaning, Medicine, and the "Placebo Effect."* Cambridge: Cambridge University Press.

Moffitt, Alan, Robert Hoffman, Roger Wells, R. Armitage, R. Pigeau and Jon Shearer, 1982. "Individual Differences Among Pre- and Post-Awakening EEG Correlates of Dream Reports Following Arousals from Different Stages of Sleep." *The Psychiatric Journal of the University of Ottawa* 7(2):111-125.

Moffitt, Alan, Milton Kramer and Robert Hoffman (eds), 1993. *The Functions of Dreaming*. Albany, NY: State University of New York Press.

Moorcroft, William H., 2003. *Understanding Sleep and Dreaming*. New York: Kluwer Academic.

Morgan, William, 1932. "Navajo Dreams." *American Anthropologist* 34(3): 390-405.

Morinis, E.A., 1982. "Levels of Culture in Hinduism: A Case Study of Dream Incubation at a Bengali Pilgrimage Centre." *Contributions to Indian Sociology* (NS) 16(2):255-270.

Morris, R. L., 1982. "Assessing Experimental Support for True Precognition." *Journal of Parapsychology* 46: 321–336

Mota-Rolim, Sérgio A., Daniel Erlacher, Adriano B.L. Tort, John F. Araujo1 and Sidarta Ribeiro, 2010. "Different Kinds of Subjective Experience during Lucid Dreaming May Have Different Neural Substrates." *International Journal of Dream Research* 3(1):33-36.

Mould, Richard A., 2003. "Quantum Brain States." *Foundations of Physics* 33(4):591-612.

Mullington, Janet M., Monika Haack, Maria Toth, Jorge M. Serrador and Hans K. Meier-Ewert, 2009. "Cardiovascular, Inflammatory, and Metabolic Consequences of Sleep Deprivation." *Progress in Cardiovascular Diseases* 51(4):294-302.

Munn, Nancy D., 1973. *Walbiri Iconography: Graphic Representation and Cultural Symbolism in a Central Australian Society*. Ithaca: Cornell University Press.

Munn, Nancy D., 1990. "Constructing Regional Worlds in Experience: Kula Exchange, Witchcraft and Gawan Local Events." *Man* (NS) 25(1):1-17.

Murdock, George Peter, 1945. "The Common Denominator of Culture." in Ralph Linton (ed), *The Science of Man in the World Crisis*. New York: Columbia University Press.

Murdock, George Peter, 1955. Universals of Culture. in E.A. Hoebel, J.D. Jennings and E.R. Smith (eds), *Readings in Anthropology*. New York: McGraw-Hill.

Murphy, Gardner, 1947. *Personality: A Biosocial Approach to Origins and Structure*. New York: Harper.

Murray, C.L., and A.D. Lopez (eds), 1996. *The Global Burden of Disease: A Comprehensive Assessment of Mortality and Disability from Diseases, Injuries, and Risk Factors in 1990 and Projected to 2020*. Cambridge, MA: Harvard University.

Musil, Alois, 1928. *The Manners and Customs of the Rwala Bedouins*. New York: American Geographical Society, Oriental Explorations and Studies 6.

Myers, L. Daniel, 2004. "Great Basin Hinters and Gatherers." in Mariko Namba Walters and Eva Jane Neumann Fridman (eds), *Shamanism: An Encyclopedia of World Beliefs, Practices, and Cultures* (2 volumes). Santa Barbara, CA: ABC-CLIO, Volume 1, pp. 292-296.

Nader, Kathleen, 1996. "Children's Traumatic Dreams." in Deirdre Barrett (ed), *Trauma and Dreams*. Cambridge, MA: Harvard University Press, pp. 9-24.

Nakashima Degarrod, Lydia, 2004. "Dreams and Visions." in Mariko Namba Walters and Eva Jane Neumann Fridman (eds), *Shamanism: An Encyclopedia of World Beliefs, Practices, and Cultures* (2 volumes). Santa Barbara, CA: ABC-CLIO, Volume 1, pp. 89-94.

Narby, Jeremy and Francis Huxley (eds), 2001. *Shamans Through Time: 500 Years on the Path to Knowledge*. New York: Tarcher.

Neher, Andrew, 1962. "A Physiological Explanation of Unusual Behavior in Ceremonies Involving Drums." *Human Biology* 34:151-160.

Neisser, Ulric, 2006. "The Self Perceived." in Ulric Neisser (ed), *The Perceived Self: Ecological and Interpersonal Sources of Self Knowledge*. New York: Cambridge University Press, pp. 3-21.

Neumann, Erich, 1969. *The Origins and History of Consciousness*. Princeton, NJ: Princeton University Press.

Neumann, Erich, 1974. *The Great Mother*. Princeton, NJ: Princeton University Press.

Newberg, Andrew and Eugene G. D'Aquili, 1994. "The Near Death Experience as Archetype: A Model for "Prepared" Neurocognitive Processes." Anthropology of Consciousness 5(4):1-15.

Newberg, Andrew, Eugene G. D'Aquili and Vince Rause, 2002. *Why God Won't Go Away: Brain Science and the Biology of Belief*. New York: Ballantine.

Nielsen, Tore A, 1991. "Reality Dreams and Their Effects on Spiritual Belief: A Revision of Animism Theory." in Jayne Gackenbach and Anees A. Sheikh (eds), *Dream Images: A Call to Mental Arms*. Amityville, NY: Baywood, pp. 233-264.

Nielsen, Tore A, 1999. "Mentation During Sleep: The NREM/REM Distinction." in Ralph Lydic and Helen A. Baghdoyan (eds), *Handbook of Behavioral State Control*. Boca Raton: CRC Press, pp 101-128.

Nielsen, Tore A, 2011a. "Ultradian, Circadian, and Sleep Dependent Features of Dreaming." in M.H. Kryger, T. Roth and W.C. Dement (eds), *Principles and Practice of Sleep Medicine*, 4th edition. Philadelphia: Elsevier, pp. 576-584.

Nielsen, Tore A, 2011b. "Dream Analysis and Classification: The Reality Simulation Perspective." in M.H. Kryger, T. Roth and W.C. Dement (eds), *Principles and Practice of Sleep Medicine*, 4th edition. Philadelphia: Elsevier, pp. 595-603.

Noll, richard, 1983. "Shamanism and Schizophrenia: A State-Specific Approach to the 'Schizophrenia Metaphor' of Shamanic States." *american Ethnologist* 10(3):443-459.

Nunez, Paul L., 2010. *Brain, Mind, and the Structure of Reality*. Oxford: Oxford University Press.

Nuttall, Denise, 2007. "A Pathway to Knowledge: Embodiment, Dreaming, and Experience as a Basis for Understanding the Other." in Jean-Guy A. Goulet and Bruce Granville Miller (eds), *Extraordinary Anthropology*. Lincoln, NE: University of Nebraska Press, pp. 323-351.

Obeyesekere, Gananath, 1981. *Medusa's Hair: An Essay on Personal Symbols and Religious Experience*. University of Chicago Press.

Obeyesekere, Gananath, 1990. *The Work of Culture: Symbolic Transformation in Psychoanalysis and Anthropology*. Chicago, IL: University of Chicago Press.

O'Flaherty, Wendy Doniger, 1984. *Dreams, Illusions and Other Realities*. Chicago: University of Chicago Press.

Ogilvie, R.D., H.T. Hunt, C. Sawicki and K. McGowan, 1978. "Searching for Lucid Dreams." *Sleep Research* 7:165.

Ogilvie, R.D., H.T. Hunt, C. Sawicki and J. Samahalski, 1982. "Psychological Correlates of Spontaneous Middle Ear Muscle Activity During Sleep." *Sleep* 5:11-27.

O'Nell, C.W., 1976. *Dreams, Culture and the Individual*. San Francisco: Chandler and Sharp.

Ortiz, Alfonso 1972. "Ritual Drama and the Pueblo World View." in Alfonso Ortiz (ed), *New Perspectives on the Pueblos*. Albuquerque: University of New Mexico Press, pp. 135-161.

Othmer, E., M.P. Hayden and R. Segelbaum, 1969. "Encephalic Cycles During Sleep and Wakefulness in Humans: A 24-Hour Pattern." *Science* 164(878):447-9.

Otto, Rudolf, 1958 [1917]. *The Idea of the Holy*. Oxford: Oxford University Press.

Pace-Schott, Edward F., 2007. "The Frontal Lobes and Dreaming." in Deirdre Barrett and Patrick McNamara (eds), *Biological Aspects*, Volume 1 of The *New Science of Dreaming*. Westport CT: Praeger, pp. 115-154.

Pace-Schott, Edward F., 2011. "The Neurobiology of Dreaming." in M.H. Kryger, T. Roth and W.C. Dement (eds), *Principles and Practice of Sleep Medicine*, 4th edition. Philadelphia: Elsevier, pp. 563-575.

Pagel, J.F., 2008. *The Limits of Dream: A Scientific Exploration of the Mind/Brain Interface*. Amsterdam: Elsevier.

Pagels, Elaine, 1989. *The Gnostic Gospels*. New York: Vintage.

Palagini, Laura and Nicholas Rosenlicht, 2011. "Sleep, Dreaming, and Mental Health: A Review of Historical and Neurobiological Perspectives." *Sleep Medicine Reviews* 15:179-186.

Palmer, J.A., 1979. "Community Mail Survey of Psychic Experiences." *Journal of the American Society for Psychical research* 73:221-251.

Paluso, Daniela M., 2004. "'That Which I Dream Is True': Dream Narratives in an Amazonian Community." *Dreaming* 14(2-3):107-119.

Pandya, Vishvajit, 2004. "Forest Spells and Spider Webs: Ritualized Dream Interpretation Among Andaman Islanders." in Charles Stewart (ed), *Anthropological Approaches to Dreaming*, Special issue. *Dreaming* 14(2-3):136-150.

Park, Willard Z., 1934. "Paviotso Shamanism." *American Anthropologist* 36(1):98-113.

Parker, Sue Taylor and Michael L. McKinney, 1999. *Origins of Intelligence: The Evolution of Cognitive Development in Monkeys, Apes, and Humans*. Baltimore, MD: Johns Hopkins University Press.

Parker, Sue Taylor, Robert W. Mitchell and Maria L. Boccia (eds), 1994. *Self Awareness in Animals and Humans: Developmental Perspectives*. Cambridge: Cambridge University Press.

Parkin, David and Linda Stone (eds), 2004. *Kinship and Family: An Anthropological Reader*. London: Blackwell.

Parman, Susan, 1979. "An Evolutionary Theory of Dreaming and Play," in Edward Norbeck and Claire R. Farrer (eds), *Forms of Play of Native North Americans*. West Publishing Co., pp. 17-34.

Parman, Susan, 1991. *Dream and Culture: An Anthropological Study of the Western Intellectual Tradition*. Westport, CT: Praeger.

Parrinder, Geoffrey, 1962. *African Traditional Religion*. New York: Harper and Row.

Peluso, Daniela M., 2004. "'That Which I Dream Is True:' Dream Narratives in an Amazonian Community." in Charles Stewart (ed), *Anthropological Approaches to Dreaming*, Special issue. *Dreaming* 14(2-3):107-119.

Penrose, Roger, 1987. "Minds, Machines and Mathematics." in Colin Blakemore and Susan Greenfield (eds), *Mindwaves*. Oxford: Blackwell. pp. 259-276.

Penrose, Roger, 1989. *The Emperor's New Mind*. Oxford: Oxford University Press.

Persinger, Michael A. (ed), 1974. *ELF and VLF Electromagnetic Field Effects*. New York: Plenum.

Persinger, Michael A., 1980. *The Weather Matrix and Human Behavior*. New York: Praeger.

Persinger, Michael A., 1987. *Neuropsychological Bases of God Beliefs*. New York: Praeger.

Persinger, Michael A., 2001. "The Neuropsychiatry of Paranormal Experiences." *The Journal of Neuropsychiatry and Clinical Neurosciences* 13(4):515-524.

Persinger, Michael A. and Stanley Krippner, 1989. "Dream ESP Experiments and Geomagnetic Activity." *Journal of the American Society For Psychical Research* 83:101-115.

Peters, Larry G., 1983. "The Role of Dreams in the Life of a Mentally Retarded Individual." *Ethos* 11(1/2):49-65.

Peters, Larry G. and Douglas Price-Williams, 1980. "Towards an Experiential Analysis of Shamanism." *American Ethnologist* 7(3):397-418.

Piaget, Jean, 1941. "Le mechanisme du developpement mental et les lois du groupement des operation." *Archives de psychologic, Genevé* 28:215-285.

Piaget, Jean, 1962. *Play, Dreams and Imitation in Childhood*. New York: Norton.

Piaget, Jean, 1971. Biology and Knowledge. Chicago: University of Chicago Press.

Piaget, J., 1977. *The Development of Thought*. New York: The Viking Press.

Piaget, Jean, 1980. *Adaptation and Intelligence*. Chicago: University of Chicago Press.

Piaget, J., 1985. *The Equilibration of Cognitive Structures: The Central Problem of Intellectual Development*. Chicago: University of Chicago Press.

Pick, D. and L. Roper, 2004. "Introduction," in D. Pick and L. Roper (eds), *Dreams and History: The Interpretation of Dreams from Ancient Greece to Modern Psychoanalysis*. New York: Routledge.

Pietrini, Pietro, Eric Salmon and Paolo Nichelli, 2009. "Consciousness and Dementia: How the Brain Loses Its Self." in Steven Laureys and Giulio Tononi (eds), *The Neurology of Consciousness: Cognitive Neuroscience and Neuropathology*. New York: Academic Press, pp. 204-216.

Piller, Robert, 2009. "Cerebral Specialization During Lucid Dreaming: a Right Hemisphere Hypothesis." *Dreaming* 19(4):273-286.

Pinker, Steven, 1994. *The Language Instinct: How the Mind Creates Languages*. New York: William Morrow.

Pinker, Steven, 1995. "Facts About Human Language Relevant to Its Evolution." in Jean-Pierre Changeux and Jean Chavaillon (eds), *Origins of the Human Brain*. Oxford: Clarenden, pp. 262-285.

Pinker, Steven, 1997. *How the Mind Works*. New York: Norton.

Pinker, Steven, 2003. *The Blank Slate: The Modern Denial of Human Nature*. New York: Penguin.

Plomin, R. 1996. "Beyond Nature vs. Nurture." in L. L. Hall (ed), *Genetics and Mental Illness: Evolving Issues for Research and Society*. New York: Plenum Press, pp. 29–50.

Poirier, Sylvie, 2003. "This Is Good Country. We Are Good Dreamers." in Roger Ivar Lohmann (ed), *Dream Travelers: Sleep Experiences and Culture in the Western Pacific*.

New York: Palgrave, pp. 107-125.

Popp, Fritz-Albert, Q. Gu and K.H. Li, 1994. "Biophoton Emission: Experimental Background and Theoretical Approaches." *Modern Physics Letters* B8:1269-1296.

Popp, Fritz-Albert, W. Nagl, K.H. Li, W. Scholz, O. Weingartner and R. Wolf, 1984. "Biophoton Emission: New Evidence for Coherence and DNA as Source." *Cell Biophysics* 6:33-52.

Posey, T.B. and M.E. Losch, 1983-84. "Auditory Hallucinations of Hearing Voices in 375 Subjects." *Imagination, Cognition and Personality* 3:99-113.

Powers, William T., 2005. *Behavior: The Control of Perception* (second edition). Escondido, CA: Benchmark Publications.

Premack, David, 1976. *Intelligence in Ape and Man*. Hillsdale, NJ: Lawrence Erlbaum.

Pribram, Karl H., 1971. *Languages of the Brain: Experimental Paradoxes and Principles in Neuropsychology*. Englewood Cliffs, NJ: Prentice-Hall.

Pribram, Karl H., 1980. "Mind, Brain, and Consciousness: The Organization of Competence and Conduct." in J.M. Davidson and R.J. Davidson (eds), *The Psychobiology of Consciousness*. New York: Plenum.

Price, Robert F. and David B. Cohen, 1988. "Lucid Dream Induction: An Empirical Evaluation." in Jayne Gackenbach and Stephen LaBerge (eds), *Conscious Mind, Sleeping Brain*. New York: Plenum, pp. 105-134.

Price-Williams, Douglas, 1992. "The Waking Dream in Ethnographic Perspective." in Barbara Tedlock (ed), *Dreaming: Anthropological and Psychological Interpretations*. Cambridge: Cambridge University Press, pp. 246-262.

Price-Williams, Douglas, and Lydia Nakashima Degarrod, 1996. "Dreaming as Interaction." *Anthropology of Consciousness* 7(2):16-23.

Price-Williams, Douglas and Rosslyn Gaines, 1994. "The Dreamtime and Dreams of Northern Australian Aboriginal Artists." *Ethos* 22(3):373-388.

Prince, Raymond, 1961. "The Yoruba Image of the Witch." *Journal of Mental Science* 107: 795-805.

Purcell, Sheila, Alan Moffitt and Robert Hoffman, 1993. "Waking, Dreaming, and Self-Regulation." in Alan Moffitt, Milton Kramer and Robert Hoffman (eds), *The Functions of Dreaming*. Albany, NY: State University of New York Press, pp. 197-260.

Purcell, Sheila, J. Mullington, Allan Moffitt, Robert Hoffman and R. Pigeau, 1986. "Dream Self-Reflectiveness as a Learned Cognitive Skill." *Sleep* 9(3):423-437.

Purcell, Sheila, J. Mullington, R. Pigeau, Robert Hoffman and Alan Moffitt, 1985. "Dream Psychology: Operating in the Dark." *Association for the Study of Dreams Newsletter* 1(4):1–4.

Purves, Dale, 1990. *Body and Brain: A Trophic Theory of Neural Connections*. Cambridge, MA: Harvard University Press.

Purves, Dale, 2010. *Brains: How They Seem to Work*. Upper Saddle River, NJ: Pearson Education.

Puthoff, Harold E., Russell Targ and Edwin C. May, 1981. "Experimental Psi Research: Implication for Physics." in Robert G. Jahn (ed), *The Role of Consciousness in the Physical World*. Washington, D.C.: American Association for the Advancement of Science, pp. 37-86.

Quiatt, Duane and Junichiro Itani (eds), 1994. *Hominid Culture in Primate Perspective*. Niwot, CO: University Press of Colorado.

Radha, Swami Sivananda, 1994. *Realities of the Dreaming Mind*. Boulder, CO: Shambala.

Radin, Dean I., 1997a. *The Conscious Universe: The Scientific Truth of Psychic Phenomena*.

New York: Harper.

Radin, Dean I., 1997b. "Unconscious Perception of Future Emotions: An Experiment in Presentiment." *Journal of Scientific Exploration* 11(2):163-180.

Radin, Dean, 2006. *Entangled Minds: Extrasensory Experiences in a Quantum Reality*. New York: Paraview.

Radin, Paul, 1927. *Primitive Man as Philosopher*. New York: Dover.

Radin, Paul, 1936. "Ojibwa and Ottawa Puberty Dreams." in Robert H. Lowie (ed), *Essays in Anthropology: Presented to A.L. Kroeber*. Berkeley, CA: University of California Press, pp. 233-264.

Radin, Paul, 1958. "Introduction to the Torchbook Edition." in E.B. Tylor, *Religion in Primitive Culture* (Part 2 of *Primitive Culture*). New York: Harper and Brothers, pp. ix-xvii.

Raizen, David M. *et al.*, 2008. "Lethargus Is a Caenorhabditis Elegans Sleep-like State." *Nature* 451.

Rakic, P.A., 1995. "A Small Step for a Cell, a Giant Step for Mankind: A Hypothesis of Neocortical Expansion During Evolution. *Trends in Neuroscience* 18:383-388.

Ramachandran, V. S., 2004. *A Brief Tour of Human Consciousness: From Impostor Poodles to Purple Numbers*. Honolulu, HI: Pi Press.

Randal, Patte, Jim Geekie, Ingo Lambrecht and Melissa Taimu, 2008. "Dissociation, Psychosis and Spirituality: Whose Voices Are We Hearing?" in Andrew Moskoitz, Ingo Schäfer and Martin J. Dorahy (eds), *Spychosis, Trauma and Dissociation*. London: Wiley-Blackwell, pp. 333-345.

Rao, K. Ramakrishna (ed), 2001. *Basic Research in Parapsychology* (Second Edition). Jefferson, NC: McFarland.

Rappaport, Roy A., 1984. *Pigs for the Ancestors* (second edition). New Haven, CT: Yale University Press.

Rappaport, Roy A., 1999. *Ritual and Religion in the Making of Humanity*. Cambridge: Cambridge University Press.

Rattray, Robert Sutherland, 1927. *Religion and Art in Ashanti*. Oxford: Clarenden Press.

Reay, Marie, 1962. "The Sweet Witchcraft of Kuna Dream Experience." *Mankind: Official Journal of the Anthropological Societies of Australia* 5(11):459-463.

Reed, Henry, 1977. "Dream Incubation." in Joseph K. Long (ed), *Extrasensory Ecology: Parapsychology and Anthropology*. Metuchin, NJ: Scarecrow, pp. 155-192.

Rehfisch, Farnham, 1971. "Death, Dreams, and the Ancestors in Mambila Culture." in Mary Douglas and Phyllis M. Kaberry (eds), *Man in Africa*. Garden City, NY: Doubleday, pp. 306-314.

Reichard, Gladys A., 1950. *Navaho Religion: A Study of Symbolism*. Princeton: Princeton University Press.

Reichel-Dolmatoff, Gerardo, 1949-1950. *Los Kogi: Una Tribu de la Sierra Nevada de Santa Marta, Columbia* (Volume 1). Instituto Ethnologico Nacional, Revista 4:1-319.

Reichel-Dolmatoff, Gerardo, 1976. "Training for the Priesthood Among the Kogi of Columbia." in Johannes Wilbert (ed), *Enculturation in Latin America: An Anthology*. Los Angeles, CA: University of California Press, pp. 265-288.

Resch, Robert Paul, 1992. *Althusser and the Renewal of Marxist Social Theory*. Berkeley: University of California Press.

Revonsuo, Antti, 2000. "The Reinterpretation of Dreams: An Evolutionary Hypothesis of the Function of Dreaming." *Behavioral and Brain Sciences* 23:793-1121.

Revonsuo, Antti, 2006. *Inner Presence: Consciousness as a Biological Phenomenon.* Cambridge, MA: MIT Press.

Rhine, L.E., 1969. "Case Study Review." *Journal of Parapsychology* 33: 228–66

Richards, Graham, 1998. "Getting a Result: The Expeditions' Psychological Research 1898-1913." in Anita Herle and Sandra Rouse (eds), *Cambridge and the Torres Strait: Centenary Essays on the 1898 Anthropological Expedition.* Cambridge: Cambridge University Press, pp. 136-157.

Richards, Keith and James Fox, 2010. *Live.* New York: Little, Brown.

Riceour, Paul, 1962. "The Hermeneutics of Symbols and Philosophical Reflection." *International Philosophical Quarterly* 2 (2):191-218.

Ridington, Robin, 1971. "Beaver Dreaming and Singing." *Anthropologica* 13 (1/2):115-128.

Ridington, Robin, 1988a. "Knowledge, Power, and the Individual in Subarctic Hunting Societies." *American Anthropologist* 90(1):98-110.

Ridington, Robin, 1988b. *Trail To Heaven: Knowledge and Narrative in a Northern Native Community.* Iowa City, IA: University of Iowa Press.

Ridington, Robin and T. Ridington, 1970. "The Inner Eye of Shamanism and Totemism." *History of Religions* 10 (1): 49-61.

Rilling, J.K. and T.R. Insel, 1999. "The Primate Neocortex in Comparative Perspective Using Magnetic Resonance Imaging." *Journal of Human Evolution* 37:191-223.

Rinpoche, Namkhai Norbu, 1992. *Dream Yoga and the Practice of Natural Light.* Ithaca, NY: Snow Lion.

Rinpoche, Tenzin Wangyal, 1998. *The Tibetan Yogas of Dream and Sleep.* Ithaca, NY: Snow Lion.

Ritz, Thorsten, Roswitha Wiltschko, P.J. Hore, Christopher T. Rodgers, Katrin Stapput, Peter Thalau, Christiane R. Timmel and Wolfgang Wiltschko, 2009. "Magnetic Compass of Birds Is Based on a Molecule with Optimal Directional Sensitivity. *Biophysical Journal* 96(8):3451–3457.

Rivers, W.H.R, 1918. "Dreams and Primitive Culture." *The Bulletin of the John Rylands Library* 4(3-4):5-28.

Rivers, W.H.R, 1923. *Conflict and Dream.* New York: Harcourt Brace.

Robbins, Michael C. and Philip L. Kilbride, 1971. "Sex Differences in Dreams in Uganda." *Journal of Cross-Cultural Psychology* 2: 406-408.

Roberts, J.M., 1964. "The Self-Management of Cultures." in W.H. Goodenough (ed), *Explorations in Cultural Anthropology: Essays in Honor of George Peter Murdock.* New York: McGraw-Hill, pp. 433-454.

Rock, Adam J. and Stanley Krippner, 2007a. "Does the Concept of 'Altered States of Consciousness' Rest on a Mistake?" *International Journal of Transpersonal Studies* 26:33-40.

Rock, Adam J. and Stanley Krippner, 2007b. "Shamanism and the Confusion of Consciousness with Phenomenological Content." *North American Journal of Psychology* 9(3):485-500.

Rock, Adam J. and Stanley Krippner, n.d. *Demystifying Shamans and Their World.* (in press)

Rodd, Robin, 2006. "Piaroa Sorcery and the Navigation of Negative Affect: To Be Aware, To Turn Away." *Anthropology of Consciousness* 17(1):35-64.

Rogers, Lesley J., 2000. " Evolution of Hemispheric Specialization: Advantages and Disadvantages." *Brain and Language* 73(2):236–253.

Róheim, Géza, 1949. "Technique of Dream Analysis and Field Work in Anthropology."

*Psychanalytic Quarterly* 18:471-479.

Rosaldo, M.Z., 1984. "Toward and Anthropology of Self and Feeling," in R. Shweder and R. Levine (eds), *Culture Theory: Essays on Mind, Self, and Emotion*. Cambridge: Cambridge University Press, pp. 137-157.

Rosch, Eleanor, 1977. "Human Categorization." in N. Warren (ed), *Studies in Cross-Cultural Psychology*, Vol. 1. New York: Academic Press.

Rosch, Eleanor, C.B. Mervis, W.D. Gray, D.M. Johnson and P. Boyes-Braem, 1976. "Basic Objects in Natural Categories." *Cognitive Psychology* 8:382-439.

Ross, Colin Andrew, 2010. "Hypothesis: The Electrophysiological Basis of Evil Eye Belief." *Anthropology of Consciousness* 21(1):47-57.

Ruby, Robert H. and John A. Brown, 1989. *Dreamer-Prophets of the Columbia Plateau: Smohalla and Skolaskin*. Norman, OK: University of Oklahoma Press.

Rubinstein, Robert A. and Charles D. Laughlin, 1977. "Bridging Levels of Systemic Organization." *Current Anthropology* 18(3): 459-481.

Ryback, David, 1988. *Dreams That Came True: Their Psychic and Transforming Powers*. New York: Bantam Doubleday.

Rycroft, Charles, 1979. *The Innocence of Dreams*. New York: Pantheon.

Sacks, Oliver, 1996. "Neurological Dreams." in Deirdre Barrett (ed), *Trauma and Dreams*. Cambridge, MA: Harvard University Press, pp. 212-216.

Saler, Benson, 1993. *Conceptualizing Religion: Immanent Anthropologists, Transcendent Natives, and Unbounded Categories*. New York: Brill Academic.

Sandner, Donald, 1991. *Navajo Symbols of Healing: A Jungian Exploration of Ritual, Image, and Medicine*. Rochester, VT: Healing Arts Press.

Sanes, Dan H., Thomas A. Reh and William A. Harris, 2005. *Development of the Nervous System* (second edition). New York: Academic Press.

Saniotis, Arthur, 2010. "Making Connectivities: Neuroanthropology and Ecological Ethics." *NeuroQuantology* 8(2):200-205.

Saniotis, Arthur and Maciej Henneberg, 2011. "An Evolutionary Approach Toward Exploring Altered States of Consciousness, Mind–body Techniques, and Non-local Mind." *World Futures* 67:182–200.

Santomauro, Julia and Christopher C. French, 2009. "Terror in the Night." *The Psychologist* 22(8):672-675.

Santos-Guanero, Fernando, 2003. "Pedro Casanto's Nightmares: Lucid Dreaming in Amazonia and the New Age Movement." *Tipiti* 1(2):179-210.

Santos-Guanero, Fernando, 2004. "The Enemy Within: Child Sorcery, Revolution, and the Evils of Modernization in Eastern Peru." in Neil L. Whitehead and Robin Wright (eds), *In Darkness and Secrecy: The Anthropology of Assault Sorcery and Witchcraft in Amazonia*. Durham, NC: Duke University Press, pp. 172-305.

Savary, Louis M., Patricia H. Berne and Strephon Kaplan Williams, 1984. *Dreams and Spiritual Growth: A Judeo-Christian Way of Dreamwork*. Mahwah, NJ: Paulist Press.

Schäfer, Ingo, Colin A. Ross and John Read, 2008. "Childhood Trauma in Psychotic and Dissociative Disorders." in Andrew Moskoitz, Ingo Schäfer and Martin J. Dorahy (eds), *Spychosis, Trauma and Dissociation*. London: Wiley-Blackwell, pp. 137-150.

Schechner, Richard, 2006. *Performance Studies: An Introduction* (second edition). New York: Routledge.

Schechner, Richard and Victor Turner, 1985. *Between Theater and Anthropology*. Philadelphia: University of Pennsylvania Press.

Schoenemann, P.T., M.J. Sheehan and L.D. Glotzer, 2005. "Prefrontal White Matter Volume is Disproportionately Larger in Humans Than in Other Primates." *Nature Neuroscience* 8:242-252.

Schore, Allan N., 2003. *Affect Regulation and the Repair of the Self.* New York: Norton.

Schredl, M., 2003. "Continuity Between Waking and Dreaming: A Proposal for a Mathematical Model." *Sleep and Hypnosis* 5:38-52.

Schutz, Alfred, 1945. "On Multiple Realities." *Philosophical and Phenomenological Research* 5:533-576.

Scollon, R., and S.B.K. Scollon, 1979. *Linguistic Convergence: An Ethnography of Speaking at Fort Chipewyan, Alberta.* London: Academic Press.

Schoolcraft, Henry Rowe, 1844. *Oneóta or the Red Race of America.* New York: Bergess Stringer and Co.

Skov, Martin and Oshin Vartanian (eds), 2009. *Neuroaesthetics.* Amityville, NY: Baywood.

Seamon, David, 2005. "Goethe's Way of Science as a Phenomenology of Nature." *Janus Head* 8(1):86-101.

Seamon, David and Arthur Zajonc (eds), 1998. *Goethe's Way of Science: A Phenomenology of Nature.* Albany, NY: State University of New York Press.

Seeley, Thomas D., 2010. *Honeybee Democracy.* Princeton, NJ: Princeton University Press.

Seligman, Martin and J. Hager, 1972. *Biological Boundaries of Learning.* New York: Appleton-Century-Crofts.

Selin, Helaine, 2001. *Astronomy Across Cultures: The History of Non-Western Astronomy.* New York: Springer.

Selleri, Franco, 1988. *Quantum Mechanics Versus Local Realism: The Einstein-Podolsky-Rosen Paradox.* New York: Plenum Press.

Selye, Hans, 1974. *Stress Without Distress.* Toronto: McClelland and Stewart.

Servadio, Emilio, 1966. "The Dynamics of So-called Paranormal Dreams." in G.E. von Grunebaum and R. Caillois (eds), *The Dream and Human Societies.* Berkeley: University of California Press, pp. 109-118.

Seyfarth, R.M., D.L. Cheney and P. Marler, 1980. "Monkey Responses to Three Different Alarm Calls: Evidence of Predator Classification and Semantic Communication." *Science* 210:801-803.

Shamdasani, Sonu, 2003. *Jung and the Making of Modern Psychology.* Cambridge: Cambridge University Press.

Sheldrake, Rupert, 1981. *A New Science of Life: The Hypothesis of Formative Causation.* Los Angeles: J.P. Tarcher.

Shields, D., 1978. "A Cross-Cultural Study of Out-of-the-Body Experiences, Waking, and Sleeping." *Journal of the Society for Psychical Research* 49:697-741.

Shinbrot, Troy and Wise Young, 2008."Why Decussate? Topological Constraints on 3D Wiring." *The Anatomical Record: Advances in Integrative Anatomy and Evolutionary Biology* Volume 291(10):1278–1292.

Shore, Bradd, 1996. *Culture in Mind: Cognition, Culture, and the Problem of Meaning.* Oxford: Oxford University Press.

Shulman, David and Guy G. Stroumsa, (eds), 1999a. *Dream Cultures: Explorations in the Comparative History of Dreaming.* New York: Oxford University Press.

Shulman, David and Guy G. Stroumsa, 1999b. "Introduction." in David Shulman and Guy G. Stroumsa (eds), *Dream Cultures: Explorations in the Comparative History of Dreaming.* New York: Oxford University Press, pp. 3-13.

Siegel, Jerome M., 1999. "The Evolution of REM Sleep." in Ralph Lydic and Helen A. Baghdoyan (eds), *Handbook of Behavioral State Control*. Boca Raton: CRC Press, pp 87-100.

Siegel, Jerome M., 2003. "Why We Sleep." *Scientific American*, November issue, pp. 92-97.

Siegel Jerome M. 2005. REM Sleep." in M.H. Kryger, T. Roth and W.C. Dement (eds), *Principles and Practice of Sleep Medicine*, 4th edition. Philadelphia: Elsevier, pp. 120-35.

Silva, F.C., 2007. *G.H. Mead. A Critical Introduction*. Cambridge: Polity Press.

Singer, June, 1990. "A Jungian Approach to Dreamwork." in Stanley Krippner (ed), *Dreamtime and Dreamwork*. Los Angeles: Tarcher, pp. 59-68.

Skov, Martin and Oshin Vartanian (eds), 2009. *Neuroaesthetics*. Amityville, NY: Baywood.

Slocombe, Katie and Klaus Zuberbühler, 2010. "Vocal Communication in Chimpanzees." in Elizabeth V. Lonsdorf, Stephen R. Ross and Tetsuro Matsuzawa (eds), *The Mind of the Chimpanzee: Ecological and Experimental Perspectives*. Chicago, IL: University of Chicago Press, pp. 192-207.

Smith, G. Eliot, 1923. "Preface." in W.H.R. Rivers, *Conflict and Dream*. New York: Harcourt, Brace.

Smith, Robert C., 1990. "Traumatic Dreams as an Early Warning of Health Problems." in Stanley Krippner (ed), *Dreamtime and Dreamwork*. Los Angeles: Tarcher, pp. 224-232.

Smith, W. John, 1980. *The Behavior of Communicating: An Ethological Approach*. Cambridge, MA: Harvard University Press.

Smyers, Karen A., 2002. "Shaman/Scientist: Jungian Insights for the Anthropological Study of Religion." *Ethos* 29(4):475-490.

Snyder. Thomas J. and Jayne Gackenback, 1991. "Vestibular Involvement in the Neurocognition of Lucid Dreaming." in Jayne Gackenbach and Anees A. Sheikh (eds), *Dream Images: A Call to Mental Arms*. Amityville, NY: Baywood, pp. 55-78.

Solms, Mark, 2003. "Dreaming and REM Sleep are Controlled by Different Brain Mechanisms." in Edward F. Pace-Schott, Mark Sohms, Mark Blagrovde and Stevan Harnad (eds), *Sleep and Dreaming: Scientific Advances and Reconsiderations*. Cambridge: Cambridge University Press. Pp. 51-58.

Solms, Mark and Oliver Turnbull, 2002. *The Brain and the Inner World: An Introduction to the Neuroscience of Subjective Experience*. New York: Other Press.

Speck, Frank G., 1963 [1935]. *Naskapi: The Savage Hunters of the Labrador Peninsula*. Norman, OK: University of Oklahoma Press.

Spencer, Jonathan, 2001. "Ethnography After Postmodernism." in Paul Atkinson, Amanda Coffey, Sara Delamont, John Lofland and Lyn Lofland (eds), *Handbook of Ethnography*. New York: Sage, pp. 443-452.

Sperber, Dan, 1996. *Explaining Culture: A Naturalistic Approach*. Oxford: Blackwell.

Sperry, Roger W., 1974. "Lateral Specialization in Surgically Separated Hemispheres." in P.J. Vinken and G.W. Bruyn (eds), *The Neurosciences: Third Study Program*. Cambridge, MA: MIT Press.

Sperry, Roger W., 1982. "Some Effects of Disconnecting the Cerebral Hemispheres." *Science* 217:1223-1226.

Spier, Leslie, 1928. *Havasupai Ethnography*. Anthropological Papers of the American Museum of Natural History 29(3).

Spier, Leslie, 1970[1933]. *Yuman Tribes of the Gila River*. New York: Cooper Square.

Spiro, Melford, 1993. "The Western Concept of the Self 'Peculiar' in the Context of the World Cultures." *Ethos* 21:107-153.

Spiro, Melford, 1994. "Collective Representations and Mental Representations in Religious Symbol Systems." in B. Kilbourne and L.L. Langness (Eds), *Culture and Human Nature*. New Brunswick, NJ: Transactions Publishers, pp. 161-184.

Spiro, Melford, 1997. *Gender Ideology and Psychological Reality*. Princeton: Princeton University Press.

Sporns, Olaf, 2010. *Networks of the Brain*. Cambridge, MA: MIT Press.

Stapp, Henry P., 2003. *Mind, Matter, and Quantum Mechanics* (second edition). Berlin: Springer-Verlag.

Stapp, Henry P., 2007. "Quantum Approaches to Consciousness." in P. D. Zelazo, M. Moscovitch, & E. Thompson (eds), *Cambridge handbook of consciousness*. New York: Cambridge University Press, pp. 881-908.

Stea, David, James M. Blaut and Jennifer Stephens, 1996. "Mapping As a Cultural Universal." in J. Portugali (ed), *The Construction of Cognitive Maps*. Netherlands: Kluwer, pp. 345-360.

Stephen, Michele, 1979. "Dreams of Change: The Innovative Role of States of Consciousness in Traditional Melanesian Religion." *Oceania* 50(1):3-22.

Stephen, Michele, 1995. *A'aisa's Gifts*. Berkeley, CA: University of California Press.

Stephen, Michele, 1997. "Cargo Cults, Cultural Creativity, and Autonomous Imagination." *Ethos* 25(3):333-358.

Stevens. Anthony, 1982. *Archetypes: A Natural History of the Self*. New York: William Morrow.

Stewart, Charles, 1997. "Fields in Dreams: Anxiety, Experience and the Limits of Social Constructivism in Modern Greek Dream Narratives." *American Ethnologist* 24(4):877–894.

Stewart, Charles (ed), 2004a. *Anthropological Approaches to Dreaming*, Special issue. *Dreaming* 14(2-3).

Stewart, Charles, 2004b. "Introduction: Dreaming as an Object of Anthropological Analysis." in Charles Stewart (ed), *Anthropological Approaches to Dreaming*, Special issue. *Dreaming* 14(2-3):75-82.

Stewart, Pamela J. and Andrew J. Strathern, 2003. "Dreaming and Ghosts among the Hagen and Duna of the Southern Highlands, Papua New Guinea." in Roger Ivar Lohmann (ed), *Dream Travelers: Sleep Experiences and Culture in the Western Pacific*. New York: Palgrave, pp. 43-59.

Stickgold, Robert and Erin J. Wamsley, 2011. "Why We Dream." in M.H. Kryger, T. Roth and W.C. Dement (eds), *Principles and Practice of Sleep Medicine*, 4th edition. Philadelphia: Elsevier, pp. 628-637.

Stockard, Janice E., 2001. *Marriage in Culture: Practice And Meaning Across Diverse Societies*. Florence, KY: Wadsworth.

Stocking, George W. Jr. (ed), 1974. *A Franz Boas Reader: The Shaping of American Anthropology, 1883-1911*. Chicago: The University of Chicago Press.

Stoerig, Petra, 2007. "Hunting the Ghost: Toward a Neuroscience of Consciousness." in P. D. Zelazo, M. Moscovitch, & E. Thompson (eds), *Cambridge handbook of consciousness*. New York: Cambridge University Press, pp. 707-730.

Stroumsa, Guy G., 1999. "Dreams and Visions in Early Christian Discourse." in David Shulman and Guy G. Stroumsa (eds), *Dream Cultures: Explorations in the Comparative History of Dreaming*. New York: Oxford University Press, pp. 189-212.

Stuss, D.T. and D.F. Benson, 1986. *The Frontal Lobes*. New York: Raven.

Sumegi, Angela, 2008. *Dreamworlds of Shamanism and Tibetan Buddhism*. Albany: State University of New York Press.

Sundkler, Bengt G.M., 1948. *Bantu Prophets in South Africa*. London: Lutterworth.

Super, C.M.. S. Harkness, N. Van Tijen, E. Van der Vlugt, M. Fintelman and J. Dijkstra, 1996. "The Three R's of Dutch Childrearinig and the Socialization of Infant Arousal." in S. Harkness and C.M. Super (eds), *Parents' Cultural Belief Systems: Their Origins, Expressions, and Consequences*. New York: Guilford, pp. 447-465.

Suppe, F., 1989. *The Semantic Conception of Theories and Scientific Realism*. Urbana, IL: University of Illinois Press.

Sutich, A.J., 1968. "Transpersonal Psychology: An Emerging Force." *Journal of Humanistic Psychology* 8:77-79.

Sutton, Peter, 1997. *Dreamings: The Art of Aboriginal Australia*. New York: George Braziller.

Suzuki, S., 1970. *Zen Mind, Beginner's Mind*. New York: Weatherhill.

Sviri, Sara, 1999. "Dreaming Analyzed and Recorded: Dreams in the World of Medieval Islam." in David Shulman and Guy G. Stroumsa (eds), *Dream Cultures: Explorations in the Comparative History of Dreaming*. New York: Oxford University Press, pp. 252-273.

Tart, Charles, 1975. *States of Consciousness*. New York: Dutton.

Taylor, E., and J. Piedilato, 2002. "Shamanism and the American Psychotherapeutic Counter-culture." *Journal of Ritual Studies* 16:129-139.

Taylor, Eugene, 1983. *Dream Work: Techniques for Discovering the Creative Power in Dreams*. New York: Paulist Press.

Taylor, Eugene, 1994. *Radical Empiricism and the Conduct of Research*. In New Metaphysical Foundations of Modern Science. Sausalito, CA: Institute of Noetic Sciences.

Taylor, Jeremy, 1996. "Traversing the Living Labyrinth: Dreams and Dreamwork in the Psychospiritual Dilemma of the Postmodern World." in Kelly Bulkeley (ed), *Among All These Dreamers: Essays on Dreaming and Modern Society*. Albany: State University of New York Press, pp 139-156.

Taylor, Jeramy, 2009. *The Wisdom of Your Dreams: Using Dreams to Tap into Your Unconscious and Transform Your Life*. New York: Tarcher.

Tedlock, Barbara, 1981. "Quiché Maya Dream Interpretation." *Ethos* 9(4):313-330.

Tedlock, Barbara, 1991a. "The New Anthropology of Dreaming." *Dreaming* 1(2):161-178; Reprinted in Graham Harvey (ed), *Shamanism: A Reader* (2003). New York: Routledge, pp. 103-122.

Tedlock, Barbara, 1991b. "From Participant Observation to Observation of Participation." *Journal of Anthropological Research* 47:69-94.

Tedlock, Barbara (ed), 1992a. *Dreaming: Anthropological and Psychological Interpretations*. Cambridge: Cambridge University Press.

Tedlock, Barbara, 1992b. "Dreaming and Dream Research." in Barbara Tedlock (ed), *Dreaming: Anthropological and Psychological Interpretations*. Cambridge: Cambridge University Press, pp. 1-30.

Tedlock, Barbara, 1992c. "Zuni and Quiché Dream Sharing and Interpreting." in Barbara Tedlock (ed), *Dreaming: Anthropological and Psychological Interpretations*. Cambridge: Cambridge University Press, pp. 105-131.

Tedlock, Barbara, 1999. "Sharing and Interpreting Dreams in Amerindian Nations." in David Shulman and Guy G. Stroumsa (eds), *Dream Cultures: Explorations in the Comparative History of Dreaming*. New York: Oxford University Press, pp. 87-103.

Tedlock, Barbara, 2004a. "The Poetics and Spirituality of Dreaming: A Native American Enactment Theory." in Charles Stewart (ed), *Anthropological Approaches to Dreaming*, Special issue. *Dreaming* 14(2-3):183-189.

Tedlock, Barbara, 2004b. "Mayan Shamanism." in Mariko Namba Walters and Eva Jane

Neumann Fridman (eds), *Shamanism: An Encyclopedia of World Beliefs, Practices, and Cultures* (2 volumes). Santa Barbara, CA: ABC-CLIO, Volume 1, pp. 431-435.

Tedlock, Dennis, 1999. "Mythic Dreams and Double Voicing." in David Shulman and Guy G. Stroumsa (eds), *Dream Cultures: Explorations in the Comparative History of Dreaming*. New York: Oxford University Press, pp. 104-118.

TenHouten, Warren D., 1993. "Dual Symbolic Classification, the Primary Emotions, and Mandala Symbolism." *Anthropology of Consciousness* 4(4):10-16.

Terrace, Herbert S. and Janet Metcalfe, 2005. "Introduction: From Descartes to Darwin and Beyond." in Terrace, Herbert S. and Janet Metcalfe (eds), *The Missing Link in Cognition: Origins of Self-Reflective Consciousness*. Oxford: Oxford University Press, pp. xi-xx.

Tholey, Paul, 1983a. "Techniques for Inducing and Maintaining Lucid Dreams." *Perceptual and Motor Skills* 57:79-90.

Tholey, Paul, 1983b. "Relation Between Dream Content and Eye Movements Tested by Lucid Dreams." *Perceptual and Motor Skills* 56:875–878.

Thompson, Evan and Varela, Francisco J., 2001. "Radical Embodiment: Neural Dynamics and Consciousness." *Trends in Cognitive Sciences* 5(10): 418.

Thompson, Jo A. Myers, 1994. "Cultural Diversity in the Behavior of *Pan*." in Duane Quiatt and Junichiro Itani (eds), *Hominid Culture in Primate Perspective*. Niwot, CO: University Press of Colorado, pp. 95-115.

Throop, C. Jason, 2000. "Shifting From a Constructivist to an Experiential Approach to the Anthropology of Self and Emotion." *Journal of Consciousness Studies* 7(3):27-52.

Throop, C. Jason, 2002. "Experience, Coherence, and Culture: The Significance of Dilthey's 'Descriptive Psychology' for the Anthropology of Consciousness." *Anthropology of Consciousness*. 13(1), 2-26.

Throop, C. Jason, 2003. "On Crafting a Cultural Mind - A Comparative Assessment of Some Recent Theories of 'Internalization' in Psychological Anthropology." *Transcultural Psychiatry* 40(1), 109-139.

Throop, C. Jason and Charles D. Laughlin, 2002. "Ritual, Collective Effervescence and the Categories: Toward a Neo-Durkheimian Model of the Nature of Human Consciousness, Feeling and Understanding." *Journal of Ritual Studies* 16(1):40-63.

Throop, C. Jason and Charles D. Laughlin, 2007. "Anthropology of Consciousness." in P. D. Zelazo, M. Moscovitch, & E. Thompson (eds), *Cambridge handbook of consciousness*. New York: Cambridge University Press, pp. 631-669.

Tiberia, Vincenza Antionette, 1977. "The Feminine Component of the Masculine Psyche as Anima Projection." *International Journal of Symbology* 8(1):1-16.

Tiberia, Vincenza Antionette, 1981. *Jungian Archetypal Themes in Cross-cultural Dream Symbolism*. Unpublished Doctoral Dissertation, School of Human Behavior, United States International University. Ann Arbor, MI: University Microfilms International.

Tillich, Paul, 1957. *Dynamics of Faith*. New York: Harper & Row.

Tillich, Paul, 1963. *Systematic Theology*. Chicago: University of Chicago Press.

Tobias, P.V., 1987. "The Brain of *Homo habilis*: A New Level of Organization in Cerebral Evolution." *Journal of Human Evolution* 16:741-761.

Tobias, P.V., 1995. "The Brain of the First Hominids." in Jean-Pierre Changeux and Jean Chavaillon (eds), *Origins of the Human Brain*. Oxford: Clarenden, pp. 61-83.

Tolpin, Phillip V., 1983. "Self Psychology and the Interpretation of Dreams," in A. Goldberg (ed), *The Future of Psychoanalysis: Essays in Honor of Heinz Kohut*. New York: International Universities Press, pp. 255–271.

Tomasello, Michael, 2008. *Origins of Human Communication*. Cambridge, MA: MIT Press.

Tomer, R, A.S. Denes, K. Tessmar-Raible, and D. Arendt, 2010. "Profiling by Image Registration Reveals Common Origin of Annelid Mushroom Bodies and Vertebrate Pallium." *Cell* 142 (5):800–809.

Tonkinson, Robert, 1978. *The Mardudjara: Living the Drema in Australia's Desert*. New York: Holt, Rinehart and Winston.

Tonkinson, Robert, 2003. "Ambrymese Dreams and the Mardu Dreaming." in Roger Ivar Lohmann (ed), *Dream Travelers: Sleep Experiences and Culture in the Western Pacific*. New York: Palgrave, pp. 87-105.

Tooby, J. & Cosmides, L., 1995. "Mapping the Evolved Functional Organization of Mind and Brain." in M. S. Gazzaniga (ed), *The Cognitive Neurosciences*. Cambridge, MA: MIT Press.

Totton, Nick (ed), 2003. *Psychoanalysis and the Paranormal: Lands of Darkness*. New York: Karnac.

Townsend, Joan B., 1988. "Neo-Shamanism and the Modern Mystical Movement." in Gary Doore (ed), *Shaman's Path: Healing, Personal Growth and Empowerment*. Boston, MA: Shambhala, pp. 73-83.

Townsend, Joan B., 2004. "Core Shamanism and Neo-Shamanism." in Mariko Namba Walters and Eva Jane Neumann Fridman (eds), *Shamanism: An Encyclopedia of World Beliefs, Practices, and Cultures* (2 volumes). Santa Barbara, CA: ABC-CLIO, Volume 2, pp. 49-57.

Trakhtenberg, Ephraim C., 2008. "The Effects of Guided Imagery on the Immune System: A Critical Review." *International Journal of Neuroscience* 118(6):839-855.

Tschopik, H., 1951. *The Aymara of Chucuito, Peru: Magic*. New York: Anthropological Papers of the American Museum of Natural History 44(2):1137-308, plus plates.

Turner, Edith B., 1986. "Encounter with Neurobiology: The Response of Ritual Studies." *Zygon* 21(2):219-232.

Turner, Edith, 1992. *Experiencing Ritual: A New Interpretation of African Healing*. Philadelphia: University of Pennsylvania Press.

Turner, Edith, 1993. "The Reality of Spirits: A Tabooed or Permitted Field of Study?" *Anthropology of Consciousness* 4(1):9-12.

Turner, Edith, 1994. "A Visible Spirit form in Zambia." in David E. Young & Jean-Guy Goulet (eds), *Being Changed by Cross-Cultural Encounters*. Peterborough, Ontario: Broadview Press, pp. 71-95; reprinted in 2002 in Graham Harvey (ed), *Readings in Indigenous Religions*. New York: Continuum, pp. 149-172.

Turner, Edith, 1996. *The Hands Feel It: Healing and Spirit Presence among a Northern Alaskan People*. DeCalb, IL: Northern Illinois University Press.

Turner, Victor, 1967. *The Forest of Symbols*. Ithaca: Cornell University Press.

Turner, Victor, 1969. *The Ritual Process: Structure and Anti-Structure*. Chicago: Aldine.

Turner, Victor, 1974. *Dramas, Fields, and Metaphors: Symbolic Action in Human Society*. Ithaca: Cornell University Press.

Turner, Victor, 1982. *From Ritual to Theatre*. New York: Performing Arts Journal Publications.

Turner, Victor, 1983. "Body, Brain, and Culture." *Zygon* 18(3): 221-245.

Turner, Victor, 1985. *On the Edge of the Bush: Anthropology as Experience*. Tucson: University of Arizona Press.

Turner, Victor, 1992. *Blazing the Trail: Way Marks in the Exploration of Symbols*. Tucson, AZ: University of Arizona Press.

Turner, Victor and E.M. Bruner (eds), 1986. *The Anthropology of Experience*. Urbana:

University of Illinois Press.

Tuszynski, Jack A., 2006. *The Emerging Physics of Consciousness*. New York: Springer.

Tuzin, Donald F., 1975. "The Breath of a Ghost: Dreams and the Fear of the Dead." *Ethos* 3:555-578.

Tylor, Edward B., 1905. "Obituary: Adolf Bastian." *Man* 5:138-143.

Tylor, Edward B., 1920 [1871]. *Primitive Culture*. New York: J.P. Putnam's Sons.

Ullman, Montague, 1999. "The Experiential Dream Group." in Montague Ullman and Claire Limmer (eds), *The Varieties of Dream Experience*. Albany: State University of New York Press, pp. 3-29.

Ullman, Montague, 2003. "Dream Telepathy: Experimental and Clinical Findings." in Nick Totton (ed), *Psychoanalysis and the Paranormal*. New York: Karnac. Pp. 15-46.

Ullman, Montague, 2006[1996]. *Appreciating Dreams - A Group Approach*. New York: Cosimo Books.

Ullman, Montague, Stanley Krippner and Alan Vaughan, 2001. *Dream Telepathy: Experiments in Nocturnal Extrasensory Perception*. Charlottesville, VA: Hampton Roads.

Ullman, Montague and Claire Limmer (eds), 1999. *The Varieties of Dream Experience*. Albany: State University of New York Press.

Ullman, Montague and Nan Zimmerman, 1989[1979]. *Working with Dreams* (second edition). Detroit, MI: Aquarian Press.

Underhill, Ruth M., 1936. *The Autobiography of a Papago Woman*. Memoirs of the American Anthropological Association, 46. Menasha, WI.

Underhill, Ruth M., 1946. *Papago Indian Religion*. Columbia University Contributions to Anthropology, No. 33. New York: Columbia University Press.

Valentine, C.A., 1965. "The Lakalai of New Britain." in P. Lawrence and M.J. Meggitt (eds), *Gods Ghosts and Men in Melanesia*. Melbourne: Oxford University Press, pp. 162-197.

Valli, Katja and Antti Revonsuo, 2007. "Evolutionary Psychological Approaches to Dream Content." in Deirdre Barrett and Patrick McNamara (eds), *Cultural and Theoretical Perspectives*, Volume 3 of *The New Science of Dreaming*. Westport CT: Praeger, pp. 95-116.

Vallortigara, G., L.J. Rogers and A. Bisazza, 1999. "Possible Evolutionary Origins of Cognitive Brain Lateralization." *Brain Research Reviews* 30:164–175.

Van de Castle, Robert L., 1994. *Our Dreaming Mind*. New York: Ballantine.

Van der Hart, Onno, Ellert Nijenhuis and Kathy Steele, 2006. *The Haunted Self: Structural Dissociation and the Treatment of Chronic Traumatization*. New York: Norton.

Van Dongen, Hans, P.A., Greg Maislin, Janet M. Mullington, and David F. Dinges, 2003. "The Cumulative Cost of Additional Wakefulness: Dose-Response Effects on Neurobehavioral Functions and Sleep Physiology From Chronic Sleep Restriction and Total Sleep Deprivation." *Sleep* 26(2):117-126.

Van Eeden, Frederik, 1913. "A Study of Dreams." *Proceedings of the Society for Psychical Research* 26:431-461.

Van Gennep, A.L., 1960 [1909]. *The Rite of Passage*. Chicago: University of Chicago Press.

Varela, Francisco J., 1979. *Principles of Biological Autonomy*. New York: North Holland.

Varela, Francisco J., Evan Thompson and Eleanor Rosch, 1991. *The Embodied Mind: Cognitive Science and Human Experience*. Cambridge, MA: MIT Press.

Vaughan, Charles J., 1964. "Behavioral Evidence for Dreaming in Rhesus Monkeys." *The Physiologist* 7(3):275.

Vaughan-Lee, Llewellyn, 1994. *In the Company of Friends: Dreamwork within a Sufi Group*.

Inverness, CA: Golden Sufi Center.
Vitiello, Giuseppe, 1995. "Dissipation and Memory Capacity in the Quantum Brain Model." *International Journal of Modern Physics* B9:973.
Voget, Fred W., 1984. *The Shoshoni-Crow Sun Dance*. Norman, OK: University of Oklahoma Press.
Von Franz, Marie-Louise, 1997[1979]. *Alchemical Active Imagination* (revised edition). Boston: Shambhala.
Von Grunebaum, G.E., 1966. "Introduction: The Cultural Function of the Dream as Illustrated by Classical Islam." in G.E. von Grunebaum and R. Caillois (eds), *The Dream and Human Societies*. Berkeley: University of California Press, pp. 3-21.
Von Grunebaum, G.E. and R. Caillois (eds), 1966. *The Dream and Human Societies*. Berkeley: University of California Press.
Voss, Ursula, Romain Holzmann, Inka Tuin and J. Allan Hobson, 2009. "Dreaming: A State of Consciousness with Features of Both Waking and Non-Lucid Dreaming." *Sleep* 32(9): 1191–1200.
Waggoner, Robert, 2009. *Lucid Dreaming: Gateway to the Inner Self*. Needham, MA: Moment Point Press.
Wagner, Roy, 1972. *Habu: The Innovation of Meaning in Danbi Religion*. Chicago: University of Chicago Press.
Wagner, U., S. Gais, H. Heider, R. Verleger and J. Born, 2004. "Sleep Inspires Insight." *Nature* 427:352-355.
Walde, Christine. 1999. "Dream Interpretation in a Prosperous Age? Artemidorus, the Greek Interpreter of Dreams." in David Shulman and Guy G. Stroumsa (eds), *Dream Cultures: Explorations in the Comparative History of Dreaming*. New York: Oxford University Press, pp. 121-142.
Walker, Evan Harris, 1970. "The Nature of Consciousness." *Mathematical Biosciences* 7:131-178.
Walker, Evan Harris, 1973. "Application of the Quantum Theory of Consciousness to the Problem of Psi Phenomena." in W.G. Roll, R.L. Morris and J.D. Morris (eds), *Research in Parapsychology*. Metuchen, NJ: Scarecrow Press. pp. 51-53.
Walker, Evan Harris, 1975. "Foundations of Paraphysical and Parapsychological Phenomena." in Laura Oteri (ed), *Quantum Physics and Parapsychology*. New York: Parapsychology Foundation, pp. 1-53.
Walker, Evan Harris, 1977. "Quantum Mechanical Tunnelling in Synaptic and Ephaptic Transmission." *International Journal of Quantum Chemistry* 11:103-127.
Walker, Evan Harris, 2000. *The Physics of Consciousness: Quantum Minds and the Meaning of Life*. New York: Basic Books.
Wallace, Anthony F.C., 1951. "Cultural Determinants of Response to Hallucinatory Experience." *Archives of General Psychiatry* 1:58-69.
Wallace, Anthony F.C., 1956. "Revitalization Movements" *American Anthropologist* 58:264-81.
Wallace, Anthony F.C., 1958. "Dreams and Wishes of the Soul: A Type of Psychoanalytic Theory among the Seventeenth Century Iroquois." *American Anthropologist* 60(2 - Part 1):234-248.
Wallace, Anthony F.C., 1966. *Religion: An Anthropological View*. New York: Random House.
Wallace, Anthony F.C., 1970 [1961]. *Culture and Personality* (second edition). New York: Random House.
Wallace, B. Alan, 2007. *Contemplative Science*. New York: Columbia University Press.

Wallace, Ron, 1993a. "Cognitive Mapping and Algorithmic Complexity: Is there a Role for Quantum Processes in the Evolution of Human Consciousness?" *Behavioral and Brain Sciences* 16: 614-615.

Wallace, Ron, 1993b. "The Algorithmic Animal: Complexity, Quantum Mechanics, and the Evolution of Consciousness." *Social Neuroscience Bulletin* 6(2):25-26.

Walsh, Roger, 2007. *The World of Shamanism: New Views of an Ancient Tradition.* Woodbury, MN: Llewellyn.

Walsh, Roger and Frances Vaughan, 1980. *Beyond Ego: Transpersonal Dimensions in Psychology.* Los Angeles, CA: J.P. Tarcher.

Walters, Mariko Namba and Eva Jane Neumann Fridman (eds), 2004. *Shamanism: An Encyclopedia of World Beliefs, Practices, and Cultures* (2 volumes). Santa Barbara, CA: ABC-CLIO.

Walters, Myrna and Robert T. Dentan, 1985a. "Are Lucid Dreams Universal? Two Unequivocal Cases of Lucid Dreaming among Haw Chinese University Students in Beijing." *Lucidity Letter* 4(1):128.

Walters, Myrna and Robert T. Dentan, 1985b. "Dreams, Illusions, Bubbles, Shadows: Awareness of Unreality While Dreaming among Chinese College Students." *Lucidity Letter* 4(2):86.

Wasson, R. Gordon, Stella Kramrisch, Jonathan Ott and Carl A.P. Ruck, 1986. *Persephone's Quest: Entheogens and the Origins of Religion.* New Haven: Yale University Press.

Watkins, Mark Hanna, 1943. "The West African 'Bush' School." *The American Journal of Sociology* 48(6):666-675.

Watkins, Mary M., 1976. *Waking Dreams.* New York: Harper.

Watson, Lawrence C. and Maria-Barbara Watson-Franke, 1977. "Spirits, Dreams, and the Resolution of Conflict among Urban Guajiro Women." *Ethos* 5(4):388-408.

Wax, Murray L., 1998. *Western Rationality and the Angel of Dreams: Self, Psyche, Dreaming.* Lanham, MD: Rowman and Littlefield.

Wax, Murray L., 2004. "Dream Sharing as Social Practice." in Charles Stewart (ed), *Anthropological Approaches to Dreaming,* Special issue. *Dreaming* 14(2-3):83-93.

Webb, Wilse B., 1992. *Sleep: The Gentle Tyrant* (second edition). New York: Anker.

White, Robert F. (ed & trans), 1975. *The Interpretation of Dreams (Oneirocritica by Artemidorus).*Torrance, CA: Original Books.

Whitehead, Harry, 2000. "The Hunt for Quesalid: Tracking Lévi-Strauss' Shaman." *Anthropology & Medicine* 7(2):149-168.

White-Lewis, Jane, 1996. "Dreams and Social Responsibility: Teaching a Dream Course in the Inner-City." in Kelly Bulkeley (ed), *Among All These Dreamers: Essays on Dreaming and Modern Society.* Albany: State University of New York Press, pp 3-12.

White-Lewis, Jane, 2001. "Reflecting on a Dream in Jungian Analytic Practice." in Kelly Bulkeley (ed), *Dreams: A Reader on the Religious, Cultural, and Psychological Dimensions of Dreaming.* New York: Palgrave, pp. 189-193.

Whiteman, Joseph Hilary Michael, 1961. *The Mystical Life: An Outline of its Nature and Teachings from the Evidence of Direct Experience.* London: Faber and Faber.

Whitin, Andrew and C. Boesch, 2001. "The Cultures of Chimpanzees." *Scientific American* 284:48-55.

Wilber, Ken, 1983a. *A Sociable God: Toward a New Understanding of Religion.* Boulder, CO: Shambhala New Science Library.

Wilber, Ken, 1983b. *Up From Eden.* Boulder: Shambhala.

Williams, Nancy M., 1986. *The Yolngu and Their Land: A System of Land Tenure and the Fight for Its Recognition.* Canberra: Australian Institute of Aboriginal Studies.

Williamson, A.M. and Anne-Marie Feyer, 2000. "Moderate Sleep Deprivation Produces Impairments in Cognitive and Motor Performance Equivalent to Legally Prescribed Levels of Alcohol Intoxication." *Journal of Occupational and Environmental Medicine* 57:649-655.

Wilson, Edward O., 1975. *Sociobiology: The New Synthesis.* Cambridge, MA: Harvard University Press.

Wilson, Monica Hunter, 1951."Witch Beliefs and Social Structure." *The American Journal of Sociology* 56(4):307-313.

Wing, Yun-Kwok, Sharon Lee and Char-Nie Chen, 1994. "Sleep Paralysis in Chinese: Ghost Oppression Phenomenon in Hong Kong." *Sleep: Journal of Sleep Research and Sleep Medicine* 17(7):609-613.

Winkelman, Michael J., 1982. "Magic: A Theoretical Reassessment." *Current Anthropology* 23(1): 37-66.

Winkelman, Michael J., 1986. "Trance States: A Theoretical Model and Cross-Cultural Analysis." *Ethos* 14:174-203.

Winkelman, Michael J., 1990. "Shamans and Other "Magico-Religious" Healers: A Cross-Cultural Study of Their Origins, Nature, and Social Transformations." *Ethos* 18:308-352.

Winkelman, Michael J., 1992. "Shamans, Priests and Witches: A Cross-Cultural Study of Magico-Religious Practitioners." Tempe, AZ: Arizona State University, *Anthropological Research Papers* 44.

Winkelman, Michael J., 1996. "Shamanism and Consciousness: Metaphorical, Political and Neurophenomenological Perspectives." *Transcultural Psychiatric Research Review* 33:69-80.

Winkelman, Michael J., 2004. "Neuropsychology of Shamanism." in Mariko Namba Walters and Eva Jane Neumann Fridman (eds), *Shamanism: An Encyclopedia of World Beliefs, Practices, and Cultures* (2 volumes). Santa Barbara, CA: ABC-CLIO, Volume 1, pp. 187-195.

Winkelman, Michael J., 2010. *Shamanism: A Biopsychosocial Paradigm of Consciousness and Healing* (second edition). Santa Barbara, CA: Praeger.

Wintrob, Ronald M., 1973. "The Influence of Others: Witchcraft and Rootwork as Explanations of Behavior Disturbances." *Journal of Nervous and Mental Disease* 156(5):318-326.

Wiredu, Kwasi, 1996. *Cultural Universals and Particulars: An African Perspective.* Bloomington, IN: Indiana University Press.

Wisman, Jon D. and Kevin W. Capehart, 2010. "Creative Destruction, Economic Insecurity, Stress, and Epidemic Obesity." *American Journal of Economics and Sociology* 69(3):936-982.

Witherspoon, Gary, 1977. *Language and Art in the Navajo Universe.* Ann Arbor: University of Michigan Press.

Wolf, Arthur P. and William H. Durham, (eds), 2004. *Inbreeding, Incest, and the Incest Taboo: The State of Knowledge at the Turn of the Century.* Stanford, CA: Stanford University Press.

Woods, Ralph L. and Herbert B. Greenhouse (eds), 1974. *The New World of Dreams.* New York: MacMillan.

Yonker, Dolores M., 1982. "Dream As Validator in Traditional African Cultures." *Dreamworks: An Interdisciplinary Quarterly* 2(3): 242-250.

Young, David E., 1994. "Visitors in the Night: A Creative Energy Model of Spontaneous Visions." in David E. Young & Jean-Guy Goulet (eds), *Being Changed by Cross-Cultural Encounters*. Peterborough, Ontario: Broadview Press, pp. 166-194.

Young, David E. and Jean-Guy Goulet (eds), 1994. *Being Changed by Cross-Cultural Encounters*. Peterborough, Ontario: Broadview Press.

Young, Serinity, 1999. *Dreaming Lotus: Buddhist Dream Narrative, Imagery, and Practice*. Boston: Wisdom.

Young, Serinity, 2001. "Buddhist Dream Experience: The Role of Interpretation, Ritual, and Gender." in Kelly Bulkeley (ed), *Dreams: A Reader on the Religious, Cultural, and Psychological Dimensions of Dreaming*. New York: Palgrave, pp. 9-18.

Zelaso, Philip David, Helena Hong Gao and Rebecca Todd, 2007. "The Development of Consciousness." in P. D. Zelazo, M. Moscovitch, & E. Thompson (eds), *Cambridge Handbook of Consciousness*. New York: Cambridge University Press, pp. 405-432.

Zepelin, H., 1989. "Mammalian Sleep." in M.H. Kryger, T. Roth and W.C. Dement (eds), *Principles and Practice of Sleep Medicine*. Philadelphia: Saunders.

Zimmerman, J., J. Stoyva and D. Metcalf, 1971. "Distorted Visual Feedback and Augmented REM Sleep." *Psychophysiology* 7:298-303.

Zimmerman J.E. *et al.*, 2006. "Multiple Mechanisms Limit the Duration of Wakefulness in Drosophila Brain." *Physiological Genomics* 27:337–350.

# Index

Achuar of Ecuador 211
acid reflux 127
active imagination
   see Jung
adaptation 17
   among Paleolithic people 121
   and brain 121, 431
   and culture 39
   and dreaming 14, 26
   and energy 130
   and evolution 431
   as involving a "regnant" process 339
   equilibration 340
   exaptation 347, 434-435
   imitation as 84
   neural 106
   pre-adaptation 87
   reduced viability 62
   species typical 17
   technological 50
   to reality 35, 340-41, 470-471
      affordancy and obduracy 437-438
   two poles of 129-130, 470-471
   Western cultural 62
Adler, Alfred 15
African peoples 216, 241, 284
AIM model
   see Hobson
Ainu of Japan 324
alienation, sense of 286
alternative state of consciousness (ASC)
   see consciousness
Althusser, Louis 482
Alzheimer's Disease 237-238
Amin, Idi 259
Anch, Michael 100
anima, the
   see archetype
animal dreaming
   see dreaming
animism
   and dreaming 80-86, 117, 303, 452-453, 501
   defined 45
   Tylor and 45
anlage 17, 455
anthropomorphism 83
anthropological theories (of dreaming)
   diffusionism 50
   evolutionism 43-46, 60-61, 184
   functionalism 46-49, 77
   psychoanalytic 46-49, 52, 64, 86, 217
   structuralism 17, 53-55
anthropology
   American 18, 51
   and neuroscience 16-17, 27-28, 504
   as science 166, 503-504
   cultural conditioning of 504
   "culture and personality" school 51, 87
   of dreaming 15, 37-66 *passim*, 152-159, 166, 331, 340, 354-355
   future of 503-506
   of the self 332, 341, 354-355
   of the senses 50
   "psychic archaeology" 383
   psychological 51
   sub-disciplines of 36
   transpersonal 359
      need for 384
   universalist/constructivist debate 176
*Anthropology of Consciousness* 360
aphasia 238
Arapaho Indians 344
Arapesh of New Guinea 367
Arawak of Peru 300-301
archetype(s) 43, 111, 125, 171, 417
   Ancestor, the 324, 326-327
   and dreaming 319-321, 343-345
   and instinct 308, 316
   and neurognosis, 328, 454
   and numinosity 190
   and the ego 339
   and the unconscious 309-310
   anima/animus 73, 309, 324, 325
   Archetypal Feminine ("Great Mother," "Divine Mother," "Terrible Mother," "Devouring Mother") 309, 324-325

as *a priori* "meaning" 309
as intuition 308
as neural circuits 314, 317, 338
as "psychoid" process 301
as structures
    "structure" vs. "content" 308-311
"big" and "little" archetypes 309
Bulkeley's "root metaphor" 311
"coagulation" 314
cross-culturally 311
defined 307
development of 310, 312-314, 339-341
Dissolution 322-323
Divine Child 309
Divine Maiden (or Kore) 309
encounters by Westerners 320
evolution of the 308
experiencing the 309-310
feces for money 324 n.6
Goddess of the Hearth 325
hero 309
"imago" 307
in fetal and infant dreams 126
inheritance of 308
"inner teacher" or guru 139, 218, 344, 420-421, 486
"internal" marriage 310-311
King 128, 237
losing teeth ("falling teeth") 324, 324 n.6, 327-328
    related to death and soul 327-328
mandala 309, 337, 338, 338 n.3
Marriage, the 309-311, 324, 325-326, 489
    *conjunctio*, the 489
    related to death 326
*Mista'peo* ("Great Man,") 323
models of reality 453-454
morbidity 324 n.6
numinosity and 312
ontological status of 315-317
over-identification with 312
progressive nature of 339
self, the archetypal 71, 324, 326, 338-343
    holocultural study of 344-345
species typical experiences 308
Transcendent Integration 322-323
transformations of 309-312, 328, 337

Trickster 309
types of 309-310
Wise Old Man 309
*see also* Jung, Jungian theory
architectonics 17
*Argonauts of the Western Pacific* (Malinowski) 46
Arnold-Forster, Mary 134
arousal 105, 110
art and dreaming 100-101, 250, 263-265, 323
    and mental health 476
    and spirit 263
    and the cycle of meaning 201
    defined 263-264
    mobiliary and parietal 201
    surrealism 263
    Western 263
Asabano of New Guinea 209-210
Aserinsky, Eugene 133
Ashanti of West Africa 345
*Astral Projection* (Fox) 135
Asurini do Tocantins of Brazil 280
attention
    *see* consciousness
Aurora of the New Hebrides 298
Australian Aborigine(s) 42, 86, 264-265, 293, 378
    Warlpiri 214-215, 219
author's, the
    fieldwork 36, 165
    experiences 16, 397, 408-422 *passim*, 482
        of *dumo* 419, 478
        of hypnopompic mandalas 409-412
        of the anima 73 n.3, 489-490
    interviews with "alien abductees" 366 n.2
    synesthesia 400
    training in neuroscience 28, 112
awake, function of being 470
awareness
    *see* consciousness
Aymara of Bolivia 326-327
Azande of Sudan 256, 287-288

Baganda of Uganda 259
Bantu speaking people
    of South Africa 284
    of Uganda 59
Barok of New Ireland 379-383

Barrett, Deirdre 100
Barthes, Roland 53
basic rest-activity cycle (BRAC) 399
Basso, Ellen 219
Bastian, Adolf 38-43, 72, 112, 199, 321
  "cross-cultural social psychobiology" 43
  evolutionism 43
Bastide, Roger 15
Bedouins 344-345
*Being and Becoming Human* (Count) 17
belief(s) 366
  defined 173-174
  *see also* knowledge
Bellah, Robert N. 270
Benedict, Ruth 51
Bennett, Wendell 283
Bengali Hindu pilgrims 107
Bennington, Joel H. 98-99
Bharati, Agehananda 205
Bierman, D.J. 376
binary opposition(s) 53, 55
  and mandalas 411
  "antinomies" 411
biogenetic structuralism 17
*Biogenetic Structuralism* (Laughlin & d'Aquili) 448
biogram
  *see* Count, Earl W
Bird-David, Nurit 82
Bird Man glyph (Lascaux Cave) 275-276
Blackfoot Indians 282
Bleek, D.F. 277
*Blessing Way, The* (Hillerman) 296 n.3
Boas, Franz 18, 39, 49-53
  and Bastian 50
  and cultural relativism 49
  and the story of Quesalid 290-291
  "Boas' puzzle" 291
  diffusion 50
Bohm, David 116-117, 385
  "implicate order" 116
Bohr, Niels 385
*Book of Dreams and Ghosts, The* (Lang) 44
Bororo of Brazil 278, 302
Bourguignon, Erika 57, 422
bracketing
  *see* phenomenology
brain(s) 62, 70, 84, 331

and culture 428
and color sense 105
and dreaming
  *see* dreaming
and endocrine system 177
and experience 103-105, 111
and lucid dreaming 150
and meaning 74
and memory 99
and sense of self 458
and sleep 95-103
and symbolism 201
as "blank slate" (*tabula rasa*) 123, 338, 341
as "community of cells" 97
as "organ of exaptation" 347
as self-regulating system 97
as trophic system 97, 126
autonomic nervous system 108 n.5, 110, 177, 189
  "tuning" of 189
avian 449
basal ganglia 105
brain stem 104
cingulate gyrus 104
dopamine 106
endocast 440
evolution of 429-434, 440-443
  early 429
  encephalization 440
  Miocene apes 429, 440
hippocampus 177
"holistic imperative" 342
hypothalamus 104, 177
lateralization, evolution of 443-446
limbic system 104, 106, 176
neural model
  *see* model
parallel processing 115
plasticity 124, 428
pons 104-105
primate(s) 109, 442
processing faces 125
"quantum brain" 116-121
  *see also* quantum
regional blood flow 106
reticular activating system 105, 133
sensorium 113-115, 207, 294
speech areas 440-441

striatum 104
support cells 98
thalamus 177
"tunneling" 118
ultradian rhythm 398-399
vestibular system 110
*Brain, Symbol and Experience* (Laughlin, McManus & d'Aquili) 20
Broughton, Roger 399
Bruce, Robert D. 150, 157-158, 225-226, 374
Buddha, the 499
Buddhism 168, 191
   and dreaming 408
   Buddha's *Parinirvana* (painting) 389
   "lesser sainthood." 333
   Mahayana 408
   *satipatthana* 333
   Tantric techniques 408
   *see also* Tibetan Buddhism
Buka of the Solomon Islands 327
Bulkeley, Kelly 311, 395-396, 494
Bunzel, Ruth 283
Burmese 88
Burridge, Kenelm 54, 397
   and "myth-dreams" 397
Buryat of Siberia 277
Bushmen of the Kalahari 277, 311

Cahuilla Indians 401-402
Callaway, Hugh George (aka Oliver Fox) 135
capitalism
   and materialism 26, 65, 154, 199, 316, 356, 375, 472, 493
   and mental illness 474
   and monophasic culture 65, 465-496 *passim*
   "false consciousness" 475-476, 481, 493-495, 499
      "determination in the last instance" 482, 495
   sleep and dreaming 474-476
categories, categorization
   crisp 172
   fuzzy 172, 446
   "generic species" designation 172
   natural 21, 172, 208, 446, 453
   of self, evolution of 457

"type dreams" 172
causation
   according to science 285-286
   backwards 287, 374 n.3
   invisible (hidden), the 213-214, 252, 286, 450
   magical ("spooky") 215, 229, 286-290, 295, 377, 384
   mechanical 286-287, 384
   modeling of
      *see* model
   mystical foresight 289
   non-local 118
   randomness 288
   revealed in dreams 213-214
   scientific defined 286-287
   synchronicity ("a causality") 385
   Western views on 285
cerebral blood flow 97
Chang, Garma C.C. 413
Chapple, Eliot D. 17
Charsley, S.R. 241
Chinese 154, 367
   *fung sui* 86
Christianity 241, 322
   influence of 210, 351
Chuckchee of Siberia 274, 277, 328
co-dreaming
   *see* paranormal
cognitive maps
   honeybee 436-437
cognitive imperative 74, 469
cognitive science 21-22
Colby, Kenneth 59 n.7
collective representations 41, 47-48, 244
collective unconscious
   *see* unconscious
Comanche Indians 345
*Committee of Sleep, The* (Barrett) 100
*Communing with the Gods*
   intent of 22
   outline of 22-27
comparative method 40, 50, 165, 194, 286
complex psychology
   *see* Jungian theory
condensation
   *see* dream
*Conflict and Dream* (Rivers) 252
consciousness

# INDEX

"alien abduction" 366
alternative state(s) of (ASC) 13, 16, 35, 45, 63, 65, 84-85, 107, 143, 146, 153, 167, 185, 189, 203, 251
animals, non-human 22, 450, 458
attention 107, 110
"attention shifting" 110
awareness 111, 129, 139
   "searchlight" 152, 458-459
   common structures 104-105
   contents of 20
   core consciousness 104, 312
   evolution of 309, 430, 500
   "holistic imperative" 342
   language and 458
   mind 13, 40-41, 50-55, 60-62, 80-84, 111
      as function of brain 111
      "collective mind" 41
      mind's-eye 115, 168, 263
   "motivation to control" 469
   movie metaphor for 21, 113, 139, 416, 430-431, 433, 499
   neurobiology of 103-105
   of babies 22, 355
   of plants 430 n.1
   possession states 312
   self-awareness
      defined 456
      evolution of 456-459
      mirror image 456-457
   sensory particles 115, 416
   state(s) of (SOC) 20, 103, 235, 415
      warp(s) between 141, 144, 398
      warp control 143, 398
   time consciousness 115 n.11
   William James 113
Constantinides, Pamela 299
contemplation
   *see* meditation
conversion 251, 312
Corbin, Henry 207
cortex
   *see* neocortex
cosmos 116
   "plenum void" 116
cosmology 289, 454
   and the cycle of meaning 201, 214-215, 271
   and the self 342, 454

Corbin on 207
cosmogony 271
eschatology 271
Navajo 342
scientific 207, 286
spiritual 80
traditional 198-202, 214
Count, Earl W. 17-18
   anlage 455 n.10
   "biogram" 17, 454
   "brainmind" 18, 427
   on myth 272
Cove, John 200, 286
Cree Indians 69, 241, 370
Crocker, Jon Christopher 302
Crow Indians 226, 402
cultural constructivism 18, 49, 332, 340, 455-456
cultural relativism 18, 49
"cultural schemas" 393
cultural theories of dreaming 37-66 *passim*, 169, 173, 197, 209, 215, 223
   defined 197
   instantiated by dreams 204
   praxis 197, 226-228, 251
cultural universal(s) 18, 29, 71, 459-462
   aesthetic sense 263
   mandala 410
   self-Other distinction 355, 456-457
cultural variation 71
culture(s) 60
   4000-plus 199
   and dreams 152, 199
   and the brain 428
   animal, non-human 450-451
   as "complex system of symbols" 334
   as information pool 61, 200, 337 n.2
   change
      *see* dreaming
   "culture-bearers" 428
   defined 60-62
   evolution of 428
   "learned and shared" aspect 243-244
culture pattern ("Big") dreams 175, 190, 193, 208, 210, 214, 238, 249, 260, 312, 455, 503
   Jung on 319, 322
   numinosity and 193, 214
cycle of meaning 23, 143, 199-208

*passim*, 220, 243, 250, 260, 322, 395, 397, 421, 454
  and religion 271, 405
  and lived experience 207
  axis of instantiation 214-215
  axis of interpretation 236
  broken (disrupted) 205
  child's top model 204-206
  creativity and conservatism of 203, 206, 502
  defined 200-202
  dynamic system 202
  illustrated 201
  modern dreamwork and 482-487
  negative and positive feedback 202-203, 220, 262, 347
    feed-forward systems 431, 439-440
  revitalization of 205, 238, 250
  science and 286
Czeisler, Charles 475

Dakota Indians 285
Damasio, Antonio 104, 354
*Dancing with the Wheel: The Medicine Wheel Workbook* (Bear, Wind, Mulligan) 484 n.12
D'Andrade, Roy 56, 123
  on control of the supernatural 56
D'Aquili, Eugene G. 17, 74, 244 n.1, 274, 322, 342, 448, 469
  "holistic imperative" 342
  on tool retention 442
Daribi of New Guinea 264, 280
Darwin, Charles 44, 95, 430
  on earthworm "intelligence" 430
Deacon, Terrence 448-449
death and dying 52, 59 n.7, 89, 180, 185, 214, 326
  "call of the dead" 327
"deep structures" 54
demythologization 63-64, 64 n.9, 422
Dene Tha
  *see* Dunne-za
Dentan, Robert Knox 154, 324 n.6
Descola, Philippe 211
development
  as "in-forming" (Varela) 125
  as inner obduracy 454
  influenced by culture 125, 129

  of archetypes 310
  of neural models 125, 129-130, 150
  Piagetian 146-148
Devereux, George 47, 217
Devereux, Paul 84-86, 221, 275
  on "alien abduction" 366
diffusionism
  *see* anthropological theories
Dilthey, Wilhelm 112
disease
  *see* healing
Disney cartoon 238
Dissanayake, Ellen 263
diversity, loss of 493
divination (prophesy) 210-211, 221-222, 245, 249, 453, 501-502
  Tungu "dreamer-diviner" 257
  Kogi Mamas 404
Dobuans of Melanesia 181, 198
Dombeck, Mary-Theresen 369
Domhoff, William 57
Donald, Merlin 451
D'Onofrio, Vincent 14, 348
Dow, James 292, 295
dream(s)
  and meditation 65
  and mythology 181, 203
    *see also* myth
  and sorcery 198
    *see also* witchcraft
  and visions 65, 108, 323
  archetypal-titanic 190, 317-321
  as-dreamt 37, 114, 151, 170, 191, 236
    defined 151
  as holograms 74
  as narrative 453
  as real 153, 500-501
  as-remembered (or recalled) 37, 151, 237
    defined 151-152
  as social facts 166
  as-text 166, 236
  as-told 37, 151, 170, 236-237
    defined 152
  beliefs about
    *see* belief
  "big" and "little"
    *see* culture pattern
  bizarre 110, 169, 317
  condensation 73, 127

day residue 127, 244, 260, 328, 352, 398
"dream within a dream" 402
emotional 177
    defined 177
    *see also* dreaming
epiphany 192
everyday 339
flying 104, 137, 157, 256, 469
"free" (Malinowski) 47
groups 65
healing (curing)
    *see* healing
hunting 211-213, 218, 278
incubation
    *see* dream incubation
"official" (Malinowski) 47
oneirology 194, 243
"past lifetime" 419-420
pilgrimage 85, 223
precognitive
    *see* paranormal
professions 65
recall 106-110, 140, 191
selfscape
    *see* selfscape dreams
shaman's
    *see* shaman
sharing
    *see* dream sharing
surreal 110, 149, 156, 317
telepathic
    *see* paranormal
theophanic 221
"titanic"
    *see* culture pattern
"true" and "false" 211
types of
    *see* dream types
"waking"
    *see* waking dream
dream book
    *see* dream interpretation
dream content
    "manifest" vs. "latent" 47, 174
dream culture(s) 23, 41, 197-231 *passim*, 264, 328, 395
    evolution of 449-455
    influence of 428
    monophasic vs. polyphasic 82, 133, 453

    re-establishing a polyphasic 492
    recurrent patterns in 500-503
dream-ego 45, 150, 152, 339
    as soul 501
    travel to specific location 186
    wandering of 45, 185, 339
dream incubation 107, 140-145, 156, 203-204, 221-231, 261, 276
    author's own 412-413
    autosuggestion 140, 145, 228
    Dragon Project experiments 221
    MILD technique 143-144
    "reflection technique" 144
    relaxation technique 145
    Tibetan dream yoga 409
    Trophonius' incubatorium 222
dream intentionality 261, 397-398
dream interpretation 88-89, 171, 219-220, 237-239
    archetypes 320, 349
    "dream book" systems 243-248
    "interpretation" defined 237
    interpretive frame 205
    inversion (reversal) of meaning 55, 212, 242
    Jungian 489-490
    Lacandon system 246, 453
    Mae Enga system 247
    Mehinaku system 247
    Muria system 248
    oneirocritic 181, 205, 239, 249
    oneirocriticism 194, 237
    "pre-interpreted" dreams 422
    "psycho-cultural time lag" 258-260
        politico-economic development and 259
    social aspects of 209, 228, 235-239, 502
    standardization of 239, 242-248
        Greek system 245
    Western 238-239
*Dream Life, Wake Life* (Globus) 149, 168
Dream Network, the 480
dream research
    Maimonides experiments 368-369
    on archetypes 321
    on children 147, 254-255
    polysomnographic research 467
        defined 467 n.2
    three major breakthroughs 133

dream sharing 74, 226-229, 240-242, 452, 502
   as vicarious experience 449, 455
   evolution of 449-455
   first dream sharers 450
   social factors influencing 242, 262
   unique to humans 442-443
dream song(s) 203, 262
dream symbols 52, 71, 306
   as language 72
dream theories (local)
   see cultural theories of dreams
dream types
   epiphany dream 192
   traditional 148, 151, 153, 180, 208-213, 215, 221, 244-245, 284
   Western 208
dreamwork 26, 70, 77, 127, 129, 190, 348
   and the cycle of meaning 482-487
   compensatory symptom of an un-sane society 481
   "experiential" format 481
   Jungian 127, 138, 317, 487-491
   modern "personal" mythology 483-485
      four universal aspects of 484
   movement(s) 199, 476-482
      Jungian 491
   need for a guru? 482-483
   pastoral care 479
   psychotherapeutic orientation to 479
   safety of 478
   "study group" format 481
   Sufi 479-480
   Ullman's approach 477-479
dream yoga(s) 394-422 *passim*
   and lucidity 395
   author's own work with 408-422
   Cahuilla 401-402
   defined 394-395
   "disciplined dreaming" 394
   Hindu 406-407
   Kogi Mamas 404-406
   Sun Dance 402-403
   Tibetan Buddhism
      see Tibetan dream yoga
dreamer(s)
   anxiety in 53, 180
   as culture bearer 80
   gender and 58-59, 182 n.6
   left/right handed 111
   monophasic 74
   psyche of 26
   self of 77
   skill of 171
   social relations and ethos of 78
   training of 505-506
   Western 131, 137
dreaming
   and aggression 57-58
   and animism
      see animism
   and anxiety 56-57, 177
   and archetypes 317-321
   and art
      see art and dreaming
   and brain 95-130 *passim*
   and conflict 252-255, 502-503
   and creativity 100-102, 149-150, 215, 250-251, 399, 439-440, 502
   and culture change 250-251
   and dissociation 467
   and education 62, 495-496
   and emotion 106, 108, 110, 176-183, 502-503
   and ethnographic fieldwork 59-60, 152, 340, 480, 504
   and gender 58-59, 255, 258-260
   and healing 77, 290-302, 502
   and identity 65, 71-76, 240, 359, 365
   and mental health
      see mental health
   and mental illness 465-466
   and naming 218, 250
   and olfaction 226-229
      'odor of sanctity.' 228
   and pilgrimage 85, 143
   and play 121-122
   and power 282
      see also spiritual power
   and problem solving 107, 502
   and psychopathology 178 n.4, 466
   and self
      see self
   and spiritual path 491
   and trauma 76-77, 127
   animal(s) 14, 35, 103, 260, 429
      birds 434

mammals 434
as communication 64, 72, 139, 190, 217
as ethnographic skill 65, 87, 174
as experience 95, 103, 165
as initiation 85, 141, 143, 203, 277-280
as psychotic delusion 467-468
as reality 65, 82, 298
as social experience 236
as window into one's spiritual depths 506
bliss
   *see* psychic energy
brain experiencing itself 456
co-dreaming
   *see* paranormal
color 158
control of 469-470
Crowley, Aleister 483
cross-warp transference 144, 398
cultural theories of
   *see* cultural theories of dreaming
defined 18
"dreaming" vs. "dream" 19
ecstasy 188
   *see also* psychic energy
evolution of 428-455 *passim*
   origins of 430, 432-434
   origin hypothesis 433-444
fear of 177
function(s) of 14, 72, 78-79, 103, 126-127, 129
   rehearsal and simulation 260-262, 434
   "virtual reality" hypothesis 261
future orientation of 64, 81, 210- 211, 219, 245, 374
   *see also* divination
in Western societies 62-64, 70, 199, 478
infant (baby) 14, 22, 126
knowledge about
   *see* knowledge
life-world 149, 165-169 *passim*, 499
neuropsychology of 105-111
of aggression 235
of ancestors
   *see* spirits
of falling 185
of ghosts
   *see* spirits

of gods
   *see* spirits
of portals 185, 223, 467
of sex 48, 136-137, 182 n.6, 211-212, 214, 242
   repressed sexuality 188
of social interactions 236
of spirits
   *see* spirits
parental attitudes toward 495-496
phenomenological ingredients of 171-193
phenomenology of
   *see* phenomenology
precognitive
   *see* paranormal
primate 442
"pseudo-perceptual" imagery 434
psychology of
   *see* psychology
quantum dreaming 116-121
REM/NREM and 106
sex and 137
shaman's
   *see* shaman
signaling while 106, 134
"single-mindedness" 169
social quality of 109
   transcendental nature of 489
social utility of 173, 235-265 *passim*
   oneiromancy 194
"spiritual dreaming" 494
transpersonal
   *see* transpersonal
universal aspects 461, 500-503
waking-dreaming interaction 261-262, 503
Dreaming, The (Australian Aborigine ontology) 214, 218-219
*Dreams and the Means of Directing Them* (Saint Denys) 134
dreams (author's own)
   *anima* dreams 489-490
   author's dream yoga work 408-422
   Bear Totem dream 41-42
   Black Child dream 352
   Full Moon dream 115-116
   Goddess dream 418
   Jesus praying at Golgotha dream 238
   Marriage dream 325

"past lifetime" dreams 419-420
President Obama dream 128
Prostration dream 419
Read Ezekiel dream 191-192, 320-321, 362-363, 368
Saffron Rice dreams 138-139
Social Mandala dream 412 n.5
Stubbed Toe dream 177
Tangled Bodies dream 338 n.3
Two Ears dream 13-14, 348
drivers
  see ritual
drugs, psychotropic
  see entheogens
Dunne-za (Dene Tha, or "Beaver") Indians of British Columbia 158-159, 170, 173-175, 200, 218, 277-278, 373, 375
  way of knowing 173-174
  "Trail to Heaven" 159
Durkheim, Émile 39, 53, 208, 244, 272, 321-322
  and Jung 322
  categories of understanding, the 322
Dussert's, Françoise 214

Edinger, Edward 314
education, role of 495-496
  changing "false consciousness" 495
  courses on dreaming 496
Eggan, Dorothy 52, 129, 397
  critique of Freudian methods 52, 87
ego, the 129, 319
  inflation of 489
  "meta-ego" 422
  permanent/impermanent 333-334, 388
  polyphasic 65, 478, 492
Einstein, Albert 286, 385
*Elementargedanken* (elementary ideas) 40, 51, 321
Eliade, Mircea 39, 272
  on shamanism 275 n.1
Elkin, A.P. 293
emic and etic descriptions 86 n.5, 209 n.3, 349
emotion(s)
  and emotions 352
  and projection 337
  brain and 176-177

development of 176
numinosity as 192
universalist vs. constructivist perspectives 176
  see also dreaming
enculturation 61, 239
  "bush schools" 405
entelechy 82
entheogens (psychotropic drugs) 363, 394
  ayahuasca 147, 170
  *Amanita muscaria* 363
entoptic images 85
epoch(s), experiential
  see experience
epoché, the
  see phenomenology
Erlacher, Daniel 261
*Erlebnis* ("lived experience") 112
Ese Eja of Peru 218
*Essays in Radical Empiricism* (James) 113
ethnocentrism 55, 70, 106 n.4, 151, 154
ethnography
  Bastian's vision of 38
  "we can't get into the native's head" 167, 173, 364-365, 386
  of dreaming
    see anthropology of dreaming
  perspectivist method 171, 387-388
  variety of methods 59-60
ethnotourism industry 482 n.13
  "ayahuasca tourism" 482 n.13
ethology of communication 450-451
Evans-Pritchard, E. E. 256, 287-288
Evans-Wentz, W.Y. 413
evolution 25, 29, 95, 125
  "cognitive extension of prehension" 244 n.1, 447-448
  evolutionary Rubicon 18, 447
  of dreaming 97, 103
  of iconography 84-85
  of sleep 97, 103
  of ritual 17, 143, 220
  of the brain 22, 28, 78, 97, 104-105, 109, 121-122, 429-462 *passim*
  of the human brain 440-455 *passim*
evolutionary psychology 121, 454 n.9
evolutionism
  see anthropological theories
Ewing, Katherine 218

on Kohut 336
on the self 341-342
on Sufism 364-365
experience(s) 111
   apodicticity (existential certainty) 173-174
   as sensory particles 115
   concept and 333
   confirming worldview 208, 454
   defined 112-113
   direct personal 46, 87, 174, 253
   evolution of 429-432
   experiential epoch(s) 114-115, 447
      defined 114
      flickering of 115
      particles 115
   fantasy 115, 173, 190
   flow 237
      *see also* psychic energy
   hot/cold 400
   mandala, author's own 409-412
   near death experience (NDE)
      *see* near death experience
   "now moment" 114-115
   of causation 286
   of unicellular animals 429-430
   orgasm 189
   "peak" 143
   "perceptual epochs" 114 n.10
   "pure experience"
      see William James
   "seal" experiences 388, 419
   transpersonal
      *see* transpersonal
   vicarious
      communication of 447-448
      defined 447
      sharing of 446-449
   yin/yang 400
   *see also* brain
extramental reality
   *see* reality
*Extraordinary Dreams and How to Work with Them* (Krippner *et al.*) 365
Ezekiel, book of 191

faith 312
fantasy
   *see* experience
Feinstein, David 483

Fijians 65, 179
Filipinos 182
Foster, George 179
Foulkes, David 101, 147
Freud, Sigmund 15, 44, 46-49, 237, 320
   and Kohut 336
   "manifest" vs. "latent" content 47, 209, 364
   transference 364
   "wish fulfillment" 47, 209
Freudian methodology, critique of 47, 52, 55, 90, 135, 137, 149, 174, 197, 219, 252
Frohlich, Herbert 118
Fromm, Erich 471
functionalism
   *see* anthropological theories
fuzzy logic 21
   fuzzy boundaries 65, 148, 172, 332, 422, 453, 500

Gackenbach, Jayne 147
games 122
Gandhi, Mahatma 251
Gawa Island people (New Guinea) 298
Geary, David 469
Geerz, Clifford 270, 334
Gell, Alfred 228
Gellhorn, Ernst 108 n.5, 189
gender
   *see* dreaming
"genetic principle" (Bastian) 40
George, Marianne "Mimi" 379-283
*Gesellschaftsgedanken*
   *see* collective representations
Gibson, James J. 314, 438
*Gift, The* (Mauss) 223
Gillespie, George 166, 406, 487
Globus, Gordon 149-150, 165, 168, 186
Glock, Charles 270
Goethe, Johann Wolfgang von 40, 306 n.1
Goodenough, Ward 61-62
Gould, James L. 436
Gould, Stephen J. 347
Goulet, Jean-Guy 65, 170, 173-176, 200, 373, 375
Grady, Harvey 378-379
Graham, Laura 203, 262-263
Graven, Philip S. 472 n.4

Greek(s), ancient 107, 185, 249
  Artemidorus of Daldis 244
  Asclepios 222 n.4
  dream book 244-245
  dream incubation 221-222
Green, Celia 133
Grindal, Bruce 361
Gros Ventre Indians 327
Guajiro of South America 65, 241
Guenther, Herbert 413
Gusii of Africa 243, 255

Hagan of New Guinea 182
Haitians 181, 217
Hall, Calvin S. 57
Hallowell, Irving 71, 175, 235, 335-336
hallucination 106
Hamilton, Mary 222 n.4
Harner, Michael 483
Harris, William 192
Hartmann, Ernest 127
Havasupai Indians 327
Herdt, Gilbert 242
Herskovits, Melville 250
healing 290-302
  and dreams 224-225, 283, 293, 502
  and stress 295
  as natural process 476
  "Boas' puzzle" 291
  cross-culturally 294-302
  curing 223
  defined 291
  diagnosis by dreaming 283, 291, 294-299
  divination and 283
  guided visualization 292
  herbal 292, 296
  "hocus-pocus" 291
  immune system 292
  "neurological dreams" 293
  Parkinson's and Tourette's syndromes 293
  "placebo effect" 291
  pregnancy 293
  sickness 284
  sorcery 293
  soul-loss 39, 243
  "stair step model" 291-292
  "sucking doctor" 290, 293-294
  symbolic healing 291-294

  theater of mind healing 294
  TLC 291-292
  "transactional symbols" 292
  *see also* shamanism
Hearn, Tarchin 413 n.6
Hebb, Donald 125
Hebraic culture (ancient) 224
Heidegger, Martin 111 n.8
Henley, William Ernest 352
  "Invictus" 352
Herdt, Gilbert 279
Hertz, Robert 322
Hewitt, Daryl 188
Hillerman, Tony 296 n.3
Hillman, Deborah Jay 465, 480-481
Hillman, James 39
Hinde, Robert 459
Hindu(s) 107
  dream incubation 222-224
  types of consciousness 406
  *yogin* 407
Hobson, Allan 20
  AIM model 20
Hoffman, Robert 146
holistic imperative 72
Hollan, Douglas 76-77, 244, 294, 331, 335, 345, 366-367, 427
holocultural studies 55-59, 165, 211, 260, 223-228, 344
  "control of the supernatural" dreams 56
  need for 323
Holloway, Ralph 440
hominid(s)
  *see* hominin
hominin(s) 109
  *Australopithecus afarensis* 441, 448
  defined 109 n.7
  *Homo erectus* 441
  *Homo habilis* 303, 440, 446, 448
  *Homo heidelbergensis* 448
  *Homo sapiens sapiens* 429, 441
  tool retention 442
  tool use 440
Honegger, Barbara 275
Hopi Indians 52, 59, 129, 250, 394, 397
  *Kachina* ceremonies 214, 397
horizontal decalages 147
Hsu, Francis L.K. 56
Hudson, Liam 491

human nature 40
  social primate 235
Human Relations Area Files (HRAF) 55-56, 323
Hunt, George (Quesalid) 290
Hunt, Harry T. 148, 190, 491-492
hunter-gatherers 45
Hussain, Usted Zakir 218
Husserl, Edmund 23, 149, 166
  on time consciousness 115 n.11, 166
  "return to the things" 149, 333, 388
hypnagogic/hypnopompic 107, 180, 263, 409, 413
  mandala experience during 409

"I Can't Get No Satisfaction" 100
Icelanders 80
*Idea of the Holy, The* (Otto) 192
ideology 332, 361
  trapped by 489
illness
  *see* healing
image(s)
  healing and 292
  imaging 107, 110-111
*Imaginatio* 207
incubation
  *see* dream incubation
*Incubation: Or, the Cures of Disease in Pagan Temples and Christian Churches* (Hamilton) 222 n.4
incubus attack
  *see* nightmare
inferior parietal lobule
  *see* neocortex
information
  and culture 61, 198
  from dreams 24, 37, 41, 186, 190, 204, 212, 216
intentionality 109-110, 397
interdisciplinary research 15-16, 311
interoception 114 n.10
interpretation
  *see* dream interpretation
*Interpretation of Dreams, The* (Freud) 15, 87
"In the Temple" (author's painting) 101
intra-psyche communication 72, 129, 294, 339, 394
  selfscape dreams as 345-346

intuition 63, 81, 100 n.1, 117, 128-129
Iñupiat of Alaska 377
Iroquois Indians 197, 467
Islam 224-225

Jackson, Michael 333
Jakobson, Roman 53
James, William 14, 175, 335
  "instant field" 114
  "pure experience" 113
  "radical empiricism" 113, 168, 336
Johns, Jasper 101
Johnson, Kenneth E. 259
Jorgensen, Dan 393
Jorgensen, Joseph G. 77, 165
Juergens, Heinrich 145
Jung, Carl G. 24, 39, 44, 72, 312, 359, 494, 499
  active imagination 73, 127, 320, 397, 488
  *betrachten* 489
  and Freud 306
  and ethnology 306
  and the self 71-72, 271
  and universal patterns 306, 410
  collective unconscious
    defined 307
  "complex above complexes" 416
  dreams of 190, 317, 411
  on Eastern frames inappropriate for Westerners 490
  on handedness in dreams 325, 328
  on mandalas 410-412
  on precognitive dreaming 372-373
  on quantum physics 384
  on telepathic dreaming 370-371
  phenomenology of 307. 312, 317
  *see also* archetypes
Jungian dreamwork
  *see* dreamwork
Jungian theory 305-321 *passim*, 487-491
  alchemy 320, 489-490
    and *The Red* Book 490 n.16
  ambiguity about the self 340
  binary opposition 53 n. 5
  development 342
  empirical research 321
  individuation 313, 319, 323, 340, 348, 488, 492

"law of opposites" 242, 311, 338
mind-body dualism in 315
of dreaming 456, 487-491
of the self 337-338, 340-341
persona 334-335
synchronicity ("acausality") 385
unity of the self 336, 341
see also archetypes
*Jungians, The* (Kirsch) 491

Kagwahiv of Amazonia 88-90, 200
    Jovenil's Dream 88-89
Kalapalo of Brazil 219-220, 339-340
Kardiner, Abram 51
Kellogg, Edward W. 378-379
Kilborne, Benjamin 211, 249
Kilbride, Philip 259
Kirsch, Thomas 491
Kleitman, Nathaniel 133, 398-399
Kluger, H.Y. 321
knowledge
    and realization 305, 333
    apodicticity 173
    direct experience 174
    dreaming as a form of 215, 298
    "effort after meaning" 207, 244
    "effort after truth" 207, 454
        "truing-up" 454
    empirical 288
    ethnoepistemology 173, 200, 202
    ethno-ontology 212, 214, 218-219
    from dreaming 214, 219, 298
    ideology 486
    mystical truth 165, 215
    "people of action" 289
    *post hoc* reasoning 374, 374 n.3
    truth is "closer than my nose" 494
    truth-value 173, 200
    see also belief
Kogi Indians of Columbia 328, 404-406, 413
Kohl, Johann Georg 229
Kohut, Heinz 336
    on the self 341-343
    "self-state" dreams 346
Kracke, Waud 88-90, 215, 240
Kroeber, A.L. 23 n.3, 344, 469
    "reality culture" 469, 469 n.3
Krippner, Stanley 20, 340, 483

on "alteration" of consciousness 275 n.1
on transpersonal dreaming 365-366, 368
Kuma of New Guinea 180, 418
Kuper, Adam 54-55, 294, 483
    on myth 54-55
Kwakiutl of British Columbia 290
Kyaka of New Guinea 288

LaBerge, Stephen 134, 143, 146, 151
Lacandon Maya 150, 157-158, 225-226, 245-246, 374-375
Lakalai of New Britain 289
Lang, Andrew 44, 184, 360
language
    and dreams 237
    and self-awareness 458-459
    Brother John 451-452, 458
    *Cetacea* 449 n.8
    communication of vicarious experience 447-448
    conceptualization 445, 453
    filter of 239
    evolution of 444-449
    lateralization of function and 445
    "paroxysmal aphasia" 451
    "simple" languages 448
    tensing 446
Laughlin, Martha F. 482 n.14
Laughlin, Robert 186
*Law and Order: Criminal Intent* 348
Le Carré, John 465
Lederman, Carol 189
LeDoux, Joseph 28, 458
Lee, S.G. 258
Lévi-Strauss. Claude 17, 39, 53-54, 70, 272, 290, 312, 322
Levine, Julia 254
Levine, Robert A. 258-259
Levine, Sarah 255
Lévy-Bruhl, Lucien 39, 202 n2
Lewis-Williams, J.D. 29, 277
*L'Homme nu* (Lévi-Strauss) 54
libido
    see psychic energy
Lifton, Robert 342
Lincoln, Jackson Steward 22
Lohmann, Roger 209
Loughner, Jared Lee 465-466, 477, 492

lucid dreaming 134-160 *passim*, 188, 402
  and ayahuasca 147
  and dream yoga 395
  and mental illness 465-466
  and polyphasic culture 134
  and prefrontal cortex
    see neocortex
  and REM 134
  anthropology of 134, 152-160 *passim*
  cross-cultural research 154-159
  control exercised in 153, 469-470
  defined 134
  "discovery" of 133
  ethnographic indicators of 159-160
  examples of 135-138
  "finding your hands" 134
  in polyphasic cultures 151
  learning to lucid dream 134
  lucid/lucidity 105, 110, 169, 173, 228, 237, 243, 395, 407, 413
  phenomenology of 135
  "pre-lucid dreams" 153
  Purcell continuum 151
  "quasi-lucid dreams" 153
  science of 150
  self-awareness in 146
  theories of 145-150
    Foulkes 147
    Gackenbach 147-148
    Globus 149-150, 169
    Hunt 148-149
    LaBerge 146
    Piaget 147
    Purcell *et al.* 146
*Lucid Dreams* (Green) 133
Lumpkin, Tara 62, 492-493
Lyell, Sir Charles 44
Lyon, Margot 334

Mack, John E. 366
Mae Enga of New Guinea 175, 246-248, 288
Mageo, Jeannette Marie 72-76, 393, 397
  "dream play" 74
  on Jung 72-73
magic 256, 285-290
  among the Azande 287-288
  defined 285-286
  "luck" as 288

  olfaction and 229
  "sympathetic magic" 289
  *see also* causation
Magoun, Horace 133
Maimonides Medical Center 365
Mekeo of New Guinea 242-243, 289, 298-299, 332
Makerere University (Uganda) students 259-260
*Making of Religion, The* (Lang) 184
Malays 189
Malham, Rodney 353
Malinowski, Bronislaw 46
Mambila of Nigeria 300
mandala(s)
  *see* symbol(s)
*Mandala Symbolism* (Jung) 411
Manus of the Admiralty Islands 298
Maracopa Indians 297
Marx, Karl 45
mature contemplation 114 n.9
  *see also* meditation
Mauss, Marcel 223, 322
Maya (classical) 274
McManus, John 150, 274
Mead, George Herbert 71, 334
Mead, Margaret 51, 70
meditation (contemplation) 114, 137 n.1, 186, 361, 363, 410
  "access concentration" 404
  and dreaming 138
  "arising yoga" 417, 488-489
  choiceless awareness 407
  groups 199
  Hindu yoga 406
  introspection 312
  "mandala offering" 138, 421 n.10
  mantra yoga 407
  *samadhi* 415
  *satipatthana* 333
  signs 404 n.2, 413
  "star group" 137
  the "watcher" 407
  "tunneling" experience 413-414
  visualization 144, 407
Meggitt, M.J. 246
Mehinaku of Brazil 240, 246-247
Melanesian peoples 251, 398
memory 99, 238

short-term recall 115
working memory 109, 207
see also brain
mental health 466-468
   defined 471-472
   depression 473-474
   "health" defined 476 n.10
   in the United States 473
   obesity 474
   sane society 470-477
   sanity defined 470-471
   sleep and dream deprivation 475
      "sleep machismo" 475
   "socially patterned defect" 472
   stress
      defined 474
      distress/eustress 474
   "surrationalist" art as indicator 476
   "thirst" for the spiritual 476
   "un-sane" society
      and monophasic culture 472, 492
      attribution 472 n.4
      defined 472
Messiaen, Olivier 400
Menzel, Emil W. 78, 457
Mill, John Stewart 474-475
Miller, George 439
mind
   see consciousness
mind-body dualism 61, 82, 112, 187
*Mind of Primitive Man, The* (Boas) 50
mnemonic induction of lucid dreams (MILD) 143-144
model(s), neural, cognitive or mental 431
   adaptation to reality 437-438
   archetypal 453-454
   brain builds 123
   causation 447
   creative 439-440
   defined 123-124
   development of 436, 439-440
   inherited 122
   neurognostic
      see neurognosis
   plan(s), planning 109, 441-442
      "time-binding" 447, 462
   representation of reality 123
   "schema" 431, 431 n.2
   seek unity 340

testing in reality (T.O.T.E. process) 439-440
   feed-forward process 440
Modesto, Ruby 401-402
Moffitt, Allan 146
Mohave Indians 47, 200, 217
monophasic and polyphasic cultures 62-66, 74, 151
   dreams in 190, 215
   monophasic culture(s) 213
      defined 63
   polyphasic culture(s) 166, 211, 215, 274, 307, 349
      defined 65
      re-establishing a 492
   polyphasic ego 65, 147
Morgan, Lewis Henry 45
Moroccans 211, 249
Moruzzi, Giuseppe 133
"multilineal" evolutionism 43
*Multiplicity of Dreams, The* (Hunt) 148
Munn, Nancy 219, 298
Murdock, George Peter 55
Muria of India 215-216, 248, 324, 328
*Mysterium Coniunctionis* (Jung) 320
mystical participation 202
myth(s) 53-55
   and dreaming 215, 263
   and religion 271
   and subjectivity 203
   and the cycle of meaning 201
   archetypal origins of 310
   as product of dreaming 203
   "come alive" in dreams 214
   loss of 220
   modern "personal" mythology 483-485
   "myth-dreams" 398
   myth-ritual complex 207-208, 220
   mythology 181, 201
   mythopoea(ic) 199, 205, 238, 270, 292
   "world as problem" 272

naive culturological perspective 60
Naskapi Indians of Labrador 108, 323
natural categories
   see categories
nature/nurture 50
Navajo Indians (Diné) 52, 325
   cosmology 81-82, 117

*Diyin Diné'e* (Holy People) 82
  healing 296-297
  healing ceremony ("sing") 296
  *hózhó* and dreaming 80, 296, 342
  "Moth Frenzy" 297
  *nilch'i* (Holy Wind) 81, 117
  "skinwalker" (werewolf) 81
  view of the self 342
  "way of beauty" 296
near death experience (NDE) 322
"nearly-hairless ape" 95
neocortex 97
  Broca's area 448
  cross-over (decussation), evolution of 443-446
  electroencephalography (EEG) 105-106
  encephalization quotient (EQ) 441
  evolution of 122, 435-436
  frontal lobe(s) 97, 104, 106, 108
  fusiform and lingual gyri 104-106
  gyrus 97
  hemisphere(s) 98, 111, 443-446
  higher cortical functions 109, 147
  inferior parietal lobule 98, 108, 446, 446 n.6
  parietal lobe(s) 98, 104
  prefrontal cortex (PFC) 98, 104, 442, 461
    and emotion 177
    and dreaming 108-110, 129
    and higher cortical functions 109, 397
    and lucidity 109, 141-142, 154
    and out-of-body experiences 182
    evolution of 109, 439
    executive functions 109
    importance of 109
    intelligence 109
    social quality of dreams 109
  somatosensory cortex 98
  split-brain studies 444
  sulcus 97
  temporal lobe(s) 98, 177
  temporo-parietal junction 183
  visual cortex 98, 104, 107, 111
*neophilia* 447
Nepali of Nepal 281
Neumann, Erich 314
neural model

*see* model
neural network(s)
  circuits 17, 20, 22, 104, 118, 124, 237
    complexity of 431-432
    "cross-talking circuits" 347
    from interneurons 431
    "prepared" circuits 118
    quantum circuits 385
  componential structure of 103-105, 115, 237
  evolution of neural circuits and networks 429-430
neuron(s) 97
  afferent 430
  axon(s) 98, 120, 125 n.13
  communication between 97, 346
  dendrite(s) 98, 120, 125 n.13
  efferent 430
  interneurons (local circuit neurons) 430-431
  membrane 119, 120
  microtubules 119, 120
  neurotransmitter 98
  nucleus 120
  pathways between "part-selves" 347
  synapse(s) 98, 120, 125 n.13
  synaptic junction 99
  "synaptic plasticity" 98
  *see also* neural networks
neuroaesthetics 101, 263
neuroanthropology 16, 27-29, 78, 421
  account of dreaming 306
neurognosis (neurognostic models) 124-126, 454
  and development 347
  and dreaming 461
  as archetypes 125, 338
  defined 124
  evolution of 427
  not hardwired 339
  *see also* archetypes
neurophenomenology 16, 112
  of dreaming 111-116
neuroscience
  and anthropology 16
  of dreaming 14, 78
  of emotion 176-177
"New Age"
  groups 199, 483-484

"neoshamanism" 274, 483
twin pitfalls of 486
see also dreamwork
Ngaing of New Guinea, 349-351
Nigerian peoples 260
nightmare(s) 148, 157, 178-180, 256, 279
  and trauma 77, 178
  being chased 178, 256
  cross-culturally 179-183, 217
  incubus 182
  "Old Hag" 182
night terrors (*pavor nocturne*) 178, 433 n.3
  and NREM 179, 433
non-rapid eye movement (NREM)
  see sleep
North American Native peoples 213-215, 223
Northwest Coast Indians 200
numinosity 190-193
  and archetypes 312
  defined 192
  epiphany 192
  *mysterium tremendum/mysterium fascinans* 192
  religion 271
  sense of the divine 192
Nuttall, Denise 218
Nyakyusa of Tanzania 256
Nayar of India 311


Obeyesekere, Gananath 203
Oceania peoples 241, 298
*Of Wonders Wild and New* (Laughlin) 186
Ojibwa Indians 175, 229-231, 345, 371-372
oneirocritic
  see dream interpretation
*Oneirocritica* 244
O'Nell, Carl W. 35
Ongee of Little Andaman Island 226-228, 241, 377
Ortiz, Alfonso 202
Other, the 23, 37, 170, 456-457
Otomi of Mexico 295
Ottawa Indians 229
Otto, Rudolf 192
out-of-body experience (OBE, OOBE, "astral projection," "soul flight") 46, 135, 183-187
  and brain 183

Pakistanis 364
Paleolithic people 121
Pandya, Vishvajit 226
Papago Indians 83
paranormal
  as transpersonal 362
  co-dreaming ("shared dreaming," "mutual dreaming") 377-383
    defined 377
    Marianne George on 379-383
  dreaming 366-384, 453
    defined 362
  experiences 43, 361
  "ocular extramissions" 287
  precognitive dreaming 116, 372-377
    "wait-and-see" attitude toward 374
  "presentiment" 376-377
  research 373, 378-379
  telepathic dreaming 368-372
parapsychological research 120-121, 373, 375-376
  as controversial 376
  on the "presentiment" effect 376-377
  "spooky" phenomena 121
Parintintin of Brazil 240-241, 397
Parman, Susan 121, 197, 260-61, 439
participant observation 19, 37, 169, 362
  "observation of participation" 169, 505
Pauli, Wolfgang 384
Paviotso Indians 278
perception 107
  and dreaming 146
  behavior as control of 107, 143
  function(s) of 115
"perceptual diversity" 62, 493
performance
  and dreams 260-263
  and the cycle of meaning 201
  of dreams 122, 262-263
Persinger, Michael A. 43, 369
phenomenologist, trained 114
phenomenology 23
  bracketing 167, 174, 186
  culture as a barrier to 459
  defined 166
  "double epoché" 168

epoché, the phenomenological 167, 213, 334, 388
   Husserlian 166
   introspection 312
   Jungian 307
   natural attitude 167, 186
   of dreaming 149-150, 165-193 *passim*, 398
   of out-of-body experiences 184, 420, 422
   of sensorium 114
   of the life-world 149, 165
      life-world defined 150 n.3
   of the self 333-334
   "phenomenological descent into the self" 73
   phenomenological typewriter, problem of 23, 169-171
   phenomenological "remove" 55, 155
   transcendental epoché 388
   *see also* neurophenomenology
*Phenomenology of Internal Time-Consciousness, The* (Husserl) 166
Piaget, Jean 147, 148, 312
   adaptation 454 n.9
   assimilation/accommodation 436
   equilibration 340
   horizontal decalages 147
plans
   *see* model
play 121-122, 260, 439
   evolution of 439
Pleistocene 121
polyphasic culture
   *see* monophasic and polyphasic cultures
Popp, Fritz-Albert 117
post-modernism 18, 90-92, 341
post-structuralism 18, 90-92
post-traumatic stress disorder (PTSD) 178 n.4
   Rivers on 252-253
Potter, Harry 288
power
   *see* spiritual
precognitive dreams
   *see* paranormal
prefrontal cortex (PFC)
   *see* neocortex
*Primitive Culture* (Tylor) 45
"primitive" societies 45, 84, 173, 289

*The Principles of Psychology* (James) 175
problem solving
   *see* dreaming
projection, psychological process of 73, 337
   projecting the guru on teachers 486
prophesy
   *see* divination
prosopagnosia 238
psyche 72
   defined 72 n.2
   Jung and the 307
psychic energy 187-190
   Aguaruna 419
   autonomic nervous system, retuning of 189
   bliss 187, 409
   Bushmen 419
   *chakras* 419
   *dumo* 187
   ecstasy 188, 418
   flow experience 187-188
   *Kia* 189
   *kundalini* 187
   libido 312, 418-419
   loving-kindness 419
   Malayans 419
   *prana* 187
   Quiché Maya 419
   range of experiences 187
   sex 418-419
   transformation 187
   *tumo* practice 408 n.3
psychic unity of mankind 39-43
psychoanalysis 46-49, 110
*Psychological Anthropology* (Hsu) 56
psychological complex(es) 77
psychology
   of dreaming 14
psychotherapy(ies)
   Western 199
Purcell, Sheila 146
Purves, Dale 97, 124

quantum
   brain 116, 385
   communication 116
   computation 116, 120, 385
   dreaming
      *see* dreaming

entanglement 386
memory 116
morphogenetic field 331
quantum sea 117-121
    brain and 117-118
    defined 117
    "tunneling" 118
quantum energy 116, 385
    bioelectromagnetism 119 n.12
    biophotons 117
    "Bose-Einstein condensation" 119
    "coherence" 118-119
    electromagnetic fields 119
    "ether" 116
    "soliton wave" 119
    "super-radiance" 119
    "vacuum fluctuations" 116
    "zero point energy" 116
quantum physics 116, 286-287
    Copenhagen account 385
    Einstein, Podolsky, Rosen effect (EPR system) 386
    "hidden variables" 385
    *see also* brain, dreaming
Quesalid, story of (George Hunt) 290-291
Quiché Maya Indians 37, 189-190, 243, 249, 283

"radical empiricism"
    *see* William James
Radin, Dean 376
Radin, Paul 44, 229
    on Tylor 44
Rappaport, Roy 504
rapid eye movement (REM)
    *see* sleep
Raqmos, Maximo 182
Reay, Marie 180
realism 35 n.1, 437
reality
    affordancy 438
    and models
        *see* model
    and the cycle of meaning 201
    archetypes and 316
    as illusion 421
    experienced and extramental reality 65
    extramental 35

    myths as 202
    of dreaming 153, 168, 173-175, 186, 294, 415, 500-501
    range of experienced 421
    sense of 153
    transcendental 123
*Red Book, The* (Jung) 490 n.16
Reichel-Dolmatoff, Gerardo 402-404
religion 45
    and cycle of meaning 271
    and dreaming 269-273
    complexity of 272
    defined 270-273
    Hermetic Order of the Golden Dawn 483
    "matters of ultimate concern" 80, 270
    morality 271
    mythology 271
    neo-paganism (Wicca) 483
    obduracy 437-438
    polyphasic 269-271
    profane 270
    sacred (sublime) 270-271
    Thelema cult 483
    types of 272
    Western view 270
    *see also* shamanism
*Religion in Primitive Culture* (Tylor) 44
reversed visual field research 106
Revonsuo, Antti 121
Richards, Graham 61
Richards, Keith 100
Ricoeur, Paul 490
Ridington, Robin 158, 218
Rinpoche, Chogye Trichen 16 n.1, 415 n.8, 420
Rinpoche, Karma Tenzin Dorje Namgyal 16 n.1
ritual 107, 261
    among animals 142
    and dreams 122, 203
    and the cycle of meaning 201
    Catholic Mass 142
    ceremonies 142
    control of experience 140-143, 220-221, 399
    defined 142, 220
    drivers 65, 107-108, 143, 223, 226, 261, 394, 404, 408

incubation
　*see* dream
initiatory 143
play 122
"rite of passage" 221, 229, 394
ritualization 142
Rivers, William H.R. 122, 252-254, 269
Rock, Adam 20
Ross, Colin 287
*rule of minimal inclusion, the* 19, 337
*rule of multiple interpretations* 489
Ryback, David 376

Sacks, Oliver 293
sacred landscape 83-85, 218-219
　and the cycle of meaning 201
sacred stories
　*see* myth
Saint Denys, Marquis d'Hervey de 134
Saler, Benson 270
Sambia of New Guinea 242, 279-280
Samoans 74-76
Samye Ling monastery 400
*Sane Society, The* (Fromm) 471
Santos-Guereros, Fernando 142, 156
Saussure, Ferdinand de 53
Schenker, Heinrich 53
Schutz, Alfred 272
Schwartz, Gary 466
"scientific racism" 61
scientism 361-362
　skeptical scientists 384
self, the 71, 240
　and culture 334
　archetypal self 326, 323-343, 349, 470
　archetypal dialogue with 338
　as microcosm 332
　awareness of 146, 335, 456-459
　categorization of the embodied self 457
　"cognized self" 360
　*complexio oppositorum* 338
　concept(s) 331, 335, 457
　defined 72 n.1, 337-338
　"embodied metaphors" 337
　experiential approach to 335-336
　four approaches to defining 322
　impermanence of the 333
　intra-psyche communication 72
　Jung and the 71-72

　Jung's definition of 336-337
　little homunculus 457
　mandalas and 411-412
　Navajo view of 342
　neural pathways between "part-selves" 347
　neuroscience perspective on 354-355, 458
　permanence/impermanence of 333-334
　persona and 334-335
　"personhood" 332
　phenomenology of 333-334
　postmodernist take on 341
　presentation 342
　"protean man" 342
　*quadratura circuli* 338
　realization of *anatta* 334 n.1
　recognition 456-457
　reflection 146, 351
　self-ego communication 348
　self-experience 457
　self-reference 457
　sense of 452, 456, 458
　social construction of 332
　social identity 240
　sociocultural approach to 334-335
　the "me" and the "I" 71, 333
　theorists "talking past each other" about 337
　transformation of 361
　unconscious activities of 457
　unity of 337, 353-354
　universal properties of 341
　universalist-archetypal approach to 336-337
selfscape dreaming (Hollan) 76-77, 127, 129, 294, 332, 339, 345-354, 412 n.5
　as intra-psyche communication 339, 345-346
　as "movie" about the self 347
　cross-culturally 348-354, 468
　defined 76, 345
　cross-talking circuits 347
　Kohut's influence on Hollan 345-346, 345 n.6
Seligman, C.G. 172
Senoi dreamwork 483 n.11
sensorium
　*see* brain

sensory deprivation 122
*Sex and Repression in Savage Society* (Malinowski) 46
*Sexual Life of Savages, The* (Malinowski) 46
Shakespeare, William 393
shaman(s) 397
  Aborigine 293, 361
  and the cycle of meaning 202, 205
  and schizophrenia 468
  as healers 273, 276, 281
  as spiritual mediator 279
  Asurini do Tocantins 280
  ayahuasca 147
  Bantu 284
  Blackfoot 282
  Bird Man glyph (Lascaux Cave) 275
  Bororo 278
  Brazilian 147
  Buryat 277
  Cahuilla 401-402
  "call" (recruitment) of 276-283
  Chuckchee 274, 277
  Dakota 285
  Daribi 280
  dreaming 190, 275-285
  Dunne-za 159
  initiation of 190, 249, 277-278, 396, 402-403, 404-406
  Iroquois 282
  Kogi Mamas 404-406
  Koryak 276
  Kwakiutl 290
  Mayan (classical) 274
  Manus 198
  Mekeo 243
  Nepali 281
  Navajo 296-297
  Otami 295
  Paviotso 278
  Plains Indian 223
  power of 282
  Quiché 37, 283
  Sambia 279
  San Bushmen 277
  Siberian peoples 276
  Tarahumara 283-284
  Upper Paleolithic, of the 275
  Zinacantán 280-281
  Zulu 284
Shamanism 187
  as religion 272, 279
  "core shamanism" 483
  defined 273-274
  "neoshamanism" 274, 483
  rock art 277
  shamanic principle 274
  "soul flight" 187, 190
  transpersonal dimension 274
  *see also* religion
Shearer, Jon 146
Shoshone Indians 402
Siberian peoples 190
sickness
  *see* healing
simulacrum 83
Skafte, Peter 281
sleep 35, 95-103
  among animals 429-432
    *Cetacea* 433
    invertebrates 432
    mammals 433
  and growth 100
  as metabolic "down time" 432
  Carleton University 146
  deprivation 96
  evolution of 429-432
  functions of 96-103, 432
  lab research 106, 151, 154
  non-rapid eye movement (NREM) 96-98, 105-106
  onset 96, 107, 141
  "paradoxical sleep" 434, 468
  paralysis 95
  penile erection 276
  rapid eye movement (REM) 14, 96-98, 105-106
    in large and small animals 433
    discovery of 133
  "sleep inertia" 96
  vulnerable to predation 95, 122
sleeping 95-103
  and dreaming 13, 35, 103, 332
  arrangements 227, 240
So of Northeastern Uganda 36, 165, 216
  *Kenisan* 217
  magic 289 n.2
*Sociable God, A* (Wilber) 388

social conflict
    see dreaming
Society for Psychical Research 44, 360
Society for the Anthropology of Consciousness 359-360
sociology 71
    of dreaming 15
*Sociology of the Paranormal, The* (Greeley) 373
soul 45, 184-185, 350
    dream-ego as 501
    flight or wandering of 45, 185, 190, 210, 215, 219, 240
spatial orientation 110
Speck, Frank 108
*Spectrum of Ritual, The* (d'Aquili, Laughlin & McManus) 29
spirit(s) 25, 45, 278, 289, 490, 501
    ancestors 39, 41, 84, 159, 175, 181, 198, 203, 216, 453, 501-502
    angel(s) 210
    as mediators 69, 216
    as real 366
    as visitors in dreams and visions 69, 105, 198, 214, 219
    communication with 190, 210, 214, 418
    demon 183
    *djinn* 211
    ghosts 175, 181, 216, 367
    gods/goddesses 214, 216, 324
    haunting in dreams 181
    heroes 214, 218
    instantiation of 366
    Jesus 210
    nixies 324
    "other-than-human persons" 175-176, 285, 288, 387, 501
    radiant figures 324, 417
    reality of 386-387
    shape-shifters 181, 310, 418
    sirens 324
    succubae 324
    vampire 181
    werewolf 181
    zombie 181
    *see also* witchcraft
spiritual
    and the cycle of meaning 202, 455
    development 25

dimension of dreaming 80, 193, 213
essence 184
experiences 43
familiar 42
force 81
guidance 149
life 63
movements 64
path 81, 465-496 *passim*
poverty 64
power 214, 218, 277, 280, 282, 380, 502
practices 36, 70, 143, 189
realization 205
"spiritual dreaming" 494
Spiro, Melford 87, 334
Stark, Rodney 270
*Star Wars* 152
state of consciousness (SOC)
    *see* consciousness
Steinbeck, John 100
Stephen, Michelle 251, 289, 298-299, 332
    "autonomous imagination" 347, 399
Stevens, Anthony 460
Stevens, Wallace 359
Steward, Julian 43
Stewart, Charles 166
Stewart, Pamela 182
Strathern, Andrew 182
structuralism
    *see* anthropological theories
*Studies in Dreams* (Arnold-Forster) 134
subjectivity 150 n.3, 203
    of the Other 23
    sharing with the Other 450
    study of 167, 170
Sudanese 299
Sufism 218, 364-365, 395-396
Sun Dance religion 205, 226, 285
    Trehero, John (Rainbow) 402-403
supernatural 175, 202
Swinney, Fred (Graywolf) 363
symbol(s)
    archetypal 71
    "comes alive" 398, 488
    "embodied metaphors" 337
    innervated metaphors 128, 337
    intra-psyche library of 129-130, 394
    "invite thought" 490
    "lattice imagery" 409

like child's toy magnet 127, 292, 435
mandala 72 n.1. 107, 338, 408
mythopoeic
    see myth
polysemic 127
"pregnant with meaning" 127, 237
"spy vs. spy" 338
*tao* 338
"wilderness" 494-495
yin/yang 400
symbolic healing
    see healing
symbolic interactionism 71
symbolic penetration 74, 115, 139, 397
symbolic process (principle) 74, 435
    evolution of 434-436, 445
    interneurons 435
symbolic system 201
*Synaptic Self: How Our Brains Become Who We Are* 28
synesthesia 399-401

Tangu of New Guinea 54, 257
Tarahumara of Mexico 283
Tart, Charles 20
Taylor, Jeremy 472
Tedlock, Barbara 37, 142, 153-154, 169, 243, 249, 371-372, 480
Tedlock, Dennis 243
Telefolmin of New Guinea 393
telepathy
    see paranormal
theater of mind 21, 73, 113, 294, 331, 347-348, 459
    evolution of 437
theories of dreaming (local)
    see cultural theories of dreaming
*Theory on the Fringe* conference 17
Theravada Buddhists in Burma 334
"Three Flags" (Johns painting) 102
Tholey, Paul 144
Thomas, W.I
    theorem 376-377
Thompson, Richard 259
Thoreau, Henry David 133
thought experiments 386, 500
Throop, C. Jason 112, 336
Thurman, Robert 361
Tiberia, Vincenza 323-328, 344

*Tibetan Book of the Dead* (*Bardo Thodol*) 414
Tibetan Buddhism 36, 138, 408-422 *passim*
    Bön tradition
    *bardo* 414
    signs, interpretation of 405 n.2
    Six Yogas of Naropa 408
    "The Teaching" 421
    *tumo* 408 n.3, 419
    "whispered" teachings 421
    *yidam* 416
Tibetan Tantric dream yoga 107, 144, 319, 412-422 *passim*
    "arising yoga" 417, 488-489
    author's experiences practicing 414-422
        as a monk 16 n.1, 25, 334 n.1
        "Baby Denny" 417
        guru yoga 420-421
        Jungian interpretive bias 421
        lengthening the hypnagogic 414
        out-of-body experiences 420
        prostration dream
        "rebirthing" 416-417
        sleeping box experiment 414-415
        sleeping sitting up 414
        "tunneling" experience 413-414
        visualizing *Mahamaya* 416
    foundation practices 419
    *kasina* practice 488
    "pith instructions" (*mengakde*) 488
    *rigpa* (*samadhi*) 415, 421
        defined 415
    techniques 414-415
        prostrations 419
        visualization 414, 416
    transpersonal work 422
Tillich, Paul 272
time consciousness
    see consciousness
Timpaus Islanders of Indonesia 200
Tolkien, J.R.R.
    coined "mythopoeia" 199 n.1
Tonkinson, Robert 219
Toraja of Indonesia 200, 210, 244, 294, 349-350. 366-368, 372
Torres Straits Expedition 122
trance states 57, 183, 186, 215, 251, 275, 363, 402, 410, 422
    possession 312

transpersonal 312, 359-389 *passim*
  anthropology 359
  cognitive dissonance and 360, 365
  defined 359
  dimension 274, 355
  dreaming 262-289 *passim*, 408
    defined 362
    Sufi dream 364-365
  experiences 169-170
  paranormal dreaming
    *see* paranormal
  psychology 359
  self 336, 355
  symbolism 307
  *see also* experience
*Traum-Exerzitien* (Juergens) 145
*Trauma and Dreams* (Barrett) 178
Trobriand Islanders 46, 48
Trehero, John (Rainbow) 402-403
Tukolor of Senegal 264
Tungu of New Guinea 257-258
Turner, Edith 361, 377
  co-dream of 383
  taking informants seriously 386
Turner, Victor 28, 208
Tuzin, Donald 367
Tylor, Edward B. 38, 44-46, 49, 173, 184, 360
  criticisms of 45-46
  on Bastian 44
  on religion 45
  on animism 45, 452
Tzintzuntzan of Mexico 179

Ullman, Montague 477
Umeda of New Guinea 229
unconscious 53, 71, 127, 306
  collective 71, 305-321 *passim*, 411
    defined 307
  emotion 177
  in charge 128
  messengers from the 352
Underhill, Ruth 83
"unilineal" evolutionism 43-46
universals
  *see* cultural universals
un-sane society 492
  dreaming and 70
ur-phenomenon 40, 306 n.1

Van Eeden, Frederik Willems 133
Vaughan-Lee, Llewellyn 479
vicarious experience
  *see* experience
visions 105, 215, 226, 276, 323
Voget, Fred 226
*Volkergedanken* (folk ideas) 41

Waggoner, Robert 137, 145
"waking dream" 46, 347, 360, 373, 377, 410 n.4
*Waking Dream* (Watkins) 394
Walker, Evan Harris 118
Wallace, Anthony F.C. 51, 61, 197, 272, 282
  "wishes of the soul" 51, 197, 467
Walters, Myrna 154
Wangapeka Study and Retreat Center (New Zealand) 413 n.6
Watkins, Mary 394
Wax, Murray 70, 77-79, 96, 240, 332
*Way of the Shaman, The* (Harner) 485
Wellenkamp, Jane 367
Wells, Roger 146
Whissler, Clark 282
Whitehead, Alfred North
  "presiding occasion" 416
Whitehead, Harry 290
White-Lewis, Jane 496
Whiteman, J.H.M. 139-140
Wilbur, Ken 171, 388-389
  injunction method 171, 388
Wilson, Monica 256
Winkelman, Michael 28, 187, 273-274
witchcraft 180, 198, 256-258, 297, 301
  child sorcerer 301
  sorcery 198, 256
*Witchcraft, Oracles and Magic Among the Azande* (Evans-Pritchard) 256
*Working with Dreams* (Ullman and Zimmerman) 477
worldview 175, 454
  adaptation and 84
  American 179
  "entheophilic" vs "entheophobic" 63
  interpretation and 46
  "self-validating" 200
*vodun* 181

*see also* cosmology

Xavante of Central Brazil 74, 203, 262
Yanesha of Peru 156
Yir Yoront of Australia 59
yoga
    defined 271
Young, David 370, 284
Yuman Indians of Arizona 297

Zen 388, 482
    "beginner's mind" 167
Zinacantán Maya of Mexico 186-187, 246, 280-281
Zuni Indians 243
Zulus of Africa 129, 240, 242, 258, 284, 324, 327, 372, 394

www.ingramcontent.com/pod-product-compliance
Lightning Source LLC
Chambersburg PA
CBHW030102010526
44116CB00005B/59